Volume 5

_____

The Broadman Bible Commentary

EDITORIAL BOARD

BROADMAN PRESS • Nashville, Tennessee

The Broadman Bible Commentary

14228

Volume 5

Proverbs - Isaiah

ISBN: 0–8054–1105–4

4211–05

Dewey Decimal Classification: 220.7
Library of Congress catalog card number:
78–93918
Printed in the United States of America

Preface

THE BROADMAN BIBLE COMMENTARY presents current biblical study within the context of strong faith in the authority, adequacy, and reliability of the Bible as the Word of God. It seeks to offer help and guidance to the Christian who is willing to undertake Bible study as a serious, rewarding pursuit. The publisher thus has defined the scope and purpose of the COMMENTARY to produce a work suited to the Bible study needs of both ministers and laymen. The findings of biblical scholarship are presented so that readers without formal theological education can use them in their own Bible study. Footnotes and technical words are limited to essential information.

Writers have been carefully selected for their reverent Christian faith and their knowledge of Bible truth. Keeping in mind the needs of a general readership, the writers present special information about language and history where it helps to clarify the meaning of the text. They face Bible problems—not only in language but in doctrine and ethics—but avoid fine points that have little bearing on how we should understand and apply the Bible. They express their own views and convictions. At the same time, they present alternative views when such are advocated by other serious, well-informed students of the Bible. The views presented, therefore, cannot be regarded as the official position of the publisher.

This COMMENTARY is the result of many years' planning and preparation. Broadman Press began in 1958 to explore needs and possibilities for the present work. In this year and again in 1959, Christian leaders—particularly pastors and seminary professors—were brought together to consider whether a new commentary was needed and what shape it might take. Growing out of these deliberations in 1961, the board of trustees governing the Press authorized the publication of a multivolume commentary. Further planning led in 1966 to the selection of a general editor and an Advisory Board. This board of pastors, professors, and denominational leaders met in September, 1966, reviewing preliminary plans and making definite recommendations which have been carried out as the COMMENTARY has been developed.

Early in 1967, four consulting editors were selected, two for the Old Testament and two for the New. Under the leadership of the general editor, these men have worked with the Broadman Press personnel to plan the COMMENTARY in detail. They have participated fully in the selection of the writers and the evaluation of manuscripts. They have given generously of time and effort, earning the highest esteem and gratitude of Press employees who have worked with them.

The selection of the Revised Standard Version of the Bible text for the COMMENTARY was made in 1967 also. This grew out of careful consideration of possible alternatives, which were fully discussed in the meeting of the Advisory Board. The adoption of an English version as a standard text was recognized as desirable, meaning that only the King James, American Standard, and Revised Standard Versions were available for consideration.

The King James Version was recognized as holding first place in the hearts of many Christians but as suffering from inaccuracies in translation and obscurities in phrasing. The American Standard was seen as free from these two problems but deficient in an attractive English style and wide current use. The Revised Standard retains the accuracy and clarity of the American Standard and has a pleasing style and a growing use. It thus enjoys a strong advantage over each of the others, making it by far the most desirable choice.

Throughout the COMMENTARY the treatment of the biblical text aims at a balanced combination of exegesis and exposition, admittedly recognizing that the nature of the various books and the space assigned will properly modify the application of this approach.

The general articles appearing in Volumes 1, 8, and 12 are designed to provide background material to enrich one's understanding of the nature of the Bible and the distinctive aspects of each Testament. Those in Volume 12 focus on the implications of biblical teaching in the areas of worship, ethical duty, and the world mission of the church.

The COMMENTARY avoids current theological fads and changing theories. It concerns itself with the deep realities of God's dealings with men, his revelation in Christ, his eternal gospel, and his purpose for the redemption of the world. It seeks to relate the word of God in Scripture and in the living Word to the deep needs of persons and to mankind in God's world.

Through faithful interpretation of God's message in the Scriptures, therefore, the COMMENTARY seeks to reflect the inseparable relation of truth to life, of meaning to experience. Its aim is to breathe the atmosphere of life-relatedness. It seeks to express the dynamic relation between redemptive truth and living persons. May it serve as a means whereby God's children hear with greater clarity what God the Father is saying to them.

Abbreviations

ANET — *Ancient Near Eastern Texts*
ASV — American Standard Version
BASOR — *Bulletin of the American Schools of Oriental Research*
BBC — *Broadman Bible Commentary*
BDB — Brown, Driver, and Briggs: *Hebrew and English Lexicon*
BV — Berkeley Version of the Bible
CBQ — *Catholic Biblical Quarterly*
ERV — English Revised Version
fn. — footnote
GT — Gesenius-Tregelles: *Hebrew-English Lexicon*
Heb. — Hebrew
IDB — *The Interpreter's Dictionary of the Bible*

Int. — Introduction
JB — Jerusalem Bible
JBL — *Journal of Biblical Literature*
JNES — *Journal of Near Eastern Studies*
JQR — *Jewish Quarterly Review*
JTS — *Journal of Theological Studies*
KB — Koehler-Baumgartner: *Lexicon in Veteris Testamenti Libros*
KJV — King James Version
LXX — Septuagint
MT — Masoretic Text
NEB — New English Bible
RSV — Revised Standard Version
VT — *Vetus Testamentum*
ZAW — *Zeitschrift für die alttestamentliche Wissenschaft*

Contents

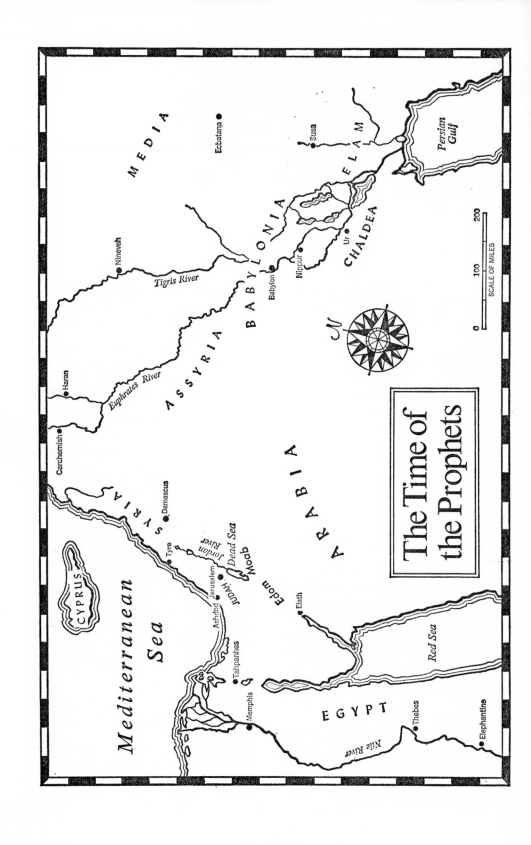

The Time of the Prophets

Proverbs

MARVIN E. TATE, JR.

Introduction

The book of Proverbs belongs to that part of the Old Testament which is commonly known as wisdom literature.[1] Generally, this literature contains teachings and writings of the Israelite wise men (*chᵃkamin*). They were more or less a particular group in Israel. In the time of Jeremiah, they could be ranked along with the priests and the prophets (Jer. 18:18).

The wise are linked with counsel, which leads us to look for them among those who filled the role of counselors in Israel. In fact, the association of wisdom and counsel is made explicit in more than one reference in the Old Testament. The "wise counselors of Pharaoh" are in parallel construction with "wise men" in Isaiah 19:11–12; while in Isaiah 29:14–15, the "wisdom of the wise" is evidently the same as the counsel hidden from Yahweh. Counsel and wisdom appear in Jeremiah 49:7. Daniel gave counsel to the Babylonian king as a wise man (cf. Dan. 1:4,17–20; 4:18,27).

The scribe had a role in ancient life very much like that of the counselor. Too much emphasis should not be placed on the scribe (*sopher*) as a writer, though he was that sometimes (as in Jer. 36:32; Ezek. 9:2; 1 Chron. 24:6; Esther 3:12). In Israel and in other countries as well, the scribe was frequently responsible for major operations of government and held positions which involved more than secretarial work in the common sense.[2] The functions of the scribes in Old Testament contexts correspond more closely to that of a secretary in our sense of Secretary of State, Secretary of the Treasury, or the like. The "secretary" of Ezra 4:8–9,17,23 was most likely a civil servant of considerable status and not an ordinary writing scribe.

The counselor and the scribe are related both to wisdom and to kingship. It seems clear that the wise men included officials of the royal court. The king himself was a wise man, and the Old Testament wisdom traditions are closely attached to Solomon and Hezekiah.[3]

---

1 The Israelite wisdom literature includes the books of Job, Proverbs, Ecclesiastes (Koheleth), and certain Psalms (e.g., 1; 19b; 37; 49; 73; 112) in the Masoretic canon. Ecclesiasticus (Sirach) and the Wisdom of Solomon are of major importance in the Apocrypha. See James Wood, *Wisdom Literature* (London: Gerald Duckworth) 1967, pp. 1–7; S. H. Blank, "Wisdom" *The Interpreter's Dictionary of the Bible* (Nashville: Abingdon, 1962), R–Z, 856. On the designation "wisdom literature," see Roland E. Murphy, "Assumptions and Problems in Old Testament Wisdom Research," CBQ, 29 (1967), 410; J. L. Crenshaw, "Method in Determining Wisdom Influence upon 'Historical' Literature," JBL, LXXXVIII (1969), 131–2; R. B. Y. Scott, "The Study of the Wisdom Literature," *Interpretation,* XXIV (1970), 28.

2 For a helpful discussion of the role of the scribe, see William McKane, *Prophets and Wise Men,* "Studies in Biblical Theology, No. 44" (Naperville, Ill.: Alec R. Allenson, Inc., 1965), pp. 23–47.

3 See 1 Kings 4:29–32; Prov. 1:1; 10:1; 25:1. For discussion see R. B. Y. Scott, "Solomon and the Beginnings of Wisdom in Israel," *Wisdom in Israel and in the Ancient Near East,* ed. M. Noth and D. Winton Thomas (Leiden: E. J. Brill, 1955), p. 262–79; Norman W. Porteous, "Royal Wisdom," Noth and Thomas, *op. cit.,* pp. 247–61. Note the references to wisdom and king in 2 Sam. 14:17,20; 16:23; Isa. 11:2; Prov. 8:14–16.

But we should not restrict the wise men to the roles of kings, counselors, and scribes and so assume that the wisdom literature is almost entirely a product of "men of affairs in high places of state." [4] The role of the teacher and the function of the school must be given serious consideration. Unfortunately, direct evidence for the institution of the school in Israelite history is very limited, particularly for the preexilic and earlier postexilic periods.[5] But there can be little doubt that schools did exist, especially in connection with the Temple and sanctuaries, and that they were sources of wisdom teaching and literature. Such schools were, in part, vocational schools designed to prepare young men for the professions and statecraft. But we should not think in terms of a technical curriculum exclusively. The wisdom teachers were interested in educating the kind of man who would be a clear thinker and balanced policy-maker in positions of leadership. They believed that professional effectiveness must be matched by worth of character.

But we cannot assume that we have taken into account all the wise men in the discussion of royal and school contexts. Parents and village wise men must also be included in the ranks of the sages. The "my son" type of address is common in the wisdom literature (e.g., Prov. 1:8; 2:1; 3:1), and it is reasonably certain that it should be treated as the address of a teacher to a student. However, it points back to a prior origin for such teaching by the father and/or mother in a family-clan context. The teacher superseded the father when the sons went to school; but the teacher's authority was exercised as that of the parent.

A further indication that folk and family circles were sources of wisdom in Israel is provided by the occurrence of short, folk-like sayings in various parts of the Old Testament (e.g., Judg. 8:21; 1 Sam. 10:11; 24:13; 1 Kings 20:11; Jer. 13:23; 23:28; 31:29; Ezek. 16:44; Hos. 4:9). It is reasonable to assume that such sayings originated and circulated among the ordinary people.

However, *few* of these popular sayings are found independently in the collections of the book of Proverbs. Some of the multiple part sayings may have been developed from the short popular proverbs: e.g., "A rich man's wealth is a strong city" (10:15a) appears again in 18:11, but it is followed by a different parallel statement in 18:11b than in 10:15b (see also 10:1 and 15:20; 16:2 and 21:2). But it is difficult to believe that very much of our extant wisdom literature was formed in either folk or family circles. R. B. Y. Scott, observes that the book of Proverbs is deliberately didactic and "reflects the schoolmaster, not the village wit" (p. 8).

Thus, the wise men and women of Israel were diverse in origin and function. The ranks of the sages included a wide range of people from kings to village peasants. And no mention has been made of the possibility that priests and prophets should be included also.[6] Nevertheless, the major centers of wisdom thought were located in the schools and in the upper levels of society, particularly in the multiple circles of the royal establishment. After the Exile, when the monarchy ceased to exist, the wise men must have continued but in closer relationship to the Temple and to the emerging institution of the synagogue.

I. The Wisdom Literature of the Ancient Near East

It is important to note that wisdom literature was not indigenous to Israel. The vast expansion of knowledge in the areas of ancient Near Eastern history, literature,

---

4 McKane, *op. cit.*, p. 44.

5 For discussion of the school in Israel see J. Kaster, "Education, OT," IDB, E-J, 27–34; McKane, *op. cit.*, pp. 36–40; and the comprehensive survey in Hans-Jürgen Hermisson, *Studien zur Israelitischen Spruchweisheit* (Neukirchen-Vluyn: Neukirchener Verlag, 1968), pp. 97–136.

6 The literature on wisdom and the prophets is now rather extensive. See McKane, *op. cit.*, and Scott, "The Study of the Wisdom Literature," *op. cit.*, pp. 36–39, for discussion and references.

culture, and religion has made us aware of large collections of wisdom literature from Egypt and Mesopotamia.[7] In fact, the non-Israelite wisdom literature is so great and of such antiquity that it justifies the conclusion that the wisdom literature of the Old Testament was the Israelite version of a cultural phenomenon common to the ancient world. There is hardly any basis for doubting that the Israelites adopted and adapted the styles and forms of such literature from the great cultural traditions of the world in which they lived. However, the Israelite sages were not mere copyists who borrowed materials indiscriminately from other people. They made the heritage of wisdom from the ancient cultures their own. When we read the wisdom literature of the Old Testament, we are reading literature which is Israelite, formed and preserved in the context of Yahwistic religion.

In addition to Egypt and Mesopotamia as the source of wisdom thought, mention should be made of the Canaanite culture of Palestine and "the people of the east."

At this time, the Canaanite wisdom is known to us only in fragments and from references in the Old Testament texts. But it is highly probable that Canaanite culture did foster extensive traditions of wisdom and that some of these may become known in the future.

Judges 5:28–29 provides information about professional wise women who were available to counsel the mother of a Canaanite leader. Ezekiel refers to the wisdom of the prince of Tyre (28:1–10,12–17), and the Tyrian wisdom was called upon by Solomon to provide needed skill for the construction of the Temple in Jerusalem (1 Kings 7:13–14; 5:1–18). Greek writers refer to Sanchuniathon of Tyre and Mochos of Sidon as Phoenician sages (R. B. Y. Scott, p. xli). At least two Canaanite proverbs are found in the Tell el-Amarna

letters.[8] It is probable that a considerable degree of Canaanite wisdom vocabulary and thought are still discernible in the book of Proverbs.[9]

The wisdom of Solomon is said to have surpassed "the wisdom of all the people of the east, and all the wisdom of Egypt" (1 Kings 4:30). It is probable that "the people of the east" means the people east of the Jordan and the Dead Sea. Job is pictured as a great skeikh and wise man among the "people of the east" (Job 1:1–5). (Scott, p. xli). The wisdom of Edom was famous and is referred to in the Old Testament (Jer. 49:7). Thus, the immediate historical context in which Israel came into being and lived contained considerable wisdom teaching and wisdom literature. Much of this wisdom was probably indigenous to Canaanite and other Palestinian cultures, though the Canaanites may have adopted much wisdom from the great cultures of Mesopotamia and Egypt.

II. The Composition of the Book of Proverbs

Having given some attention to the context of Proverbs in international wisdom, we must now consider the nature of the book itself. An outline is given at the end of this introduction and will not be repeated here. But a number of other subjects need attention.

1. The Text

The Hebrew text of Proverbs (the Masoretic Text) is often difficult to translate. This is due in large measure to the nature of the wisdom sayings and ex-

---

[7] See ANET, pp. 405–40; William McKane, Proverbs, "The Old Testament Library" (Philadelphia: Westminster Press, 1970), pp. 51–208; R. B. Y. Scott, pp. xl–lii.

[8] Scott, loc. cit.; Helmer Ringgren, "Sprüche," Das Alten Testament Deutsch (Göttingen: Vanderhoeck & Ruprecht, 1967), p. 7; B. Gemser, "Sprüche Salomos," Handbuch zum Alten Testament, 2nd ed. (Tübingen: J. C. B. Mohr, 1963), p. 2.

[9] See the studies by C. I. K. Story, "The Book of Proverbs and Northwest Semitic Literature," JBL, LXIV (1945), 319–37; W. F. Albright, "Canaanite-Phoenician Sources of Hebrew Wisdom," Wisdom in Israel and in the Ancient Near East, ed. M. Noth and D. Winton Thomas (Leiden: E. J. Brill, 1955), pp. 1–15.

pressions. These are frequently succinct and elliptical in nature, with few parallels of words and expressions elsewhere in the Old Testament. More than one translation is often possible with different nuances of meaning in each case. The reader will find some of these difficulties reflected in the commentary on the text. Recent translations incorporate many gains in Hebrew lexicography and are generally more accurate than older ones. Today's reader is fortunate to have readily available a number of translations.

The Greek text (LXX) of Proverbs often differs from the Hebrew text (for extensive discussion of the Greek text of Proverbs, see McKane, *Proverbs*, pp. 33–47). These readings can be of assistance in some cases. But caution must be used, because the changes in the Greek readings appear to have been the result, for the most part at least, of theological and stylistic considerations. It is doubtful that the Greek translator had a text very different from the Masoretic Text, and he often reflects the same difficulties which bother modern translators.

2. Authorship and Date

Five, and probably seven, titles in the book of Proverbs (1:1; 10:1; 22:17; 24:23; 25:1; 30:1; 31:1) seem to provide considerable information about authorship and date. Actually, their help is limited. Three titles (1:1; 10:1; 25:1) speak of the "proverbs of Solomon." But what does this mean? Proverbs written by Solomon? Collected by Solomon? Belonging to the Solomonic tradition? We have good reasons to link the wisdom movement in the history of Israel with Solomon. However, there is some difficulty with explicitly relating him to the book of Proverbs. Of the types of wisdom associated with Solomon, that of intellectual brilliance and encyclopedic knowledge of nature (as in 1 Kings 4:29–32) would seem to be most expected in Proverbs. However, the subject matter in those sections of Proverbs ascribed to Solomon deals largely with human be-

havior and social concerns.[10]

The wording of the title in 25:1 indicates some development after Solomon: "proverbs of Solomon which the men of Hezekiah king of Judah copied." The verb "copied" connotes more than mere transcribing of proverbs (see comment on 25:1). The titles in 30:1 ("the words of Agur") and 31:1 ("the words of Lemuel") point to other sources than Solomon; as do the probable titles in 22:17 and 24:23. The acrostic section in 31:10–31 seems to be independent.

More general considerations do not support Solomon's authorship. The widespread ascription of wisdom literature, in and out of the Old Testament, to Solomon in the post-exilic period indicates that the Hebrew pattern of collecting materials into one category and then assigning them to a dominant personality is true of Proverbs. The *torah* (Law) was ascribed to Moses, the psalms to David, and wisdom to Solomon.

Unfortunately, the date of the Instruction of Amenemope is uncertain. If the seventh-sixth century dating suggested by some scholars is correct, it would indicate that 22:17—24:22, which seems dependent on Amenemope, is later than Solomon. However, the dating of Amenemope is too uncertain to make a strong case. Arguments for date based on language, style, and theology are equally uncertain; though their cumulative weight is against Solomonic authorship (Toy, pp. xix-xxxi).

When all factors are considered, the best judgment is that which gives little probability to direct Solomonic authorship of any major part of the present book of Proverbs, but which gives high probability to the historical linkage of the wisdom traditions with the person and reign of Solomon. The personal identities of the authors of Proverbs remain unknown, though the kind of people they were and their major con-

[10] Scott, "The Study of the Wisdom Literature," p. 34, following A. Alt, "Die Weisheit Salomos," *Kleine Scheiften zur Geschichte des Volkes Israel*, II (1964), 90–99.

cerns can be determined to some degree.

The date of the book of Proverbs can be fixed only in broad outline. The limits are provided by the reign of Solomon in the tenth century B.C. (though some *content* may be pre-Solomonic) and the book of Sirach (Ecclesiasticus) at *ca.* 180 B.C. (Sirach 47:12–17 seems to allude to Prov. 1:6). These outer limits can be narrowed somewhat. The reference to Hezekiah in 25:1 makes it probable that the book was not written in its present form prior to *ca.* 700 B.C. The use of *torah* in Proverbs with the more general sense of teaching or instruction of the wise suggests strongly that the book was written before the work of Ezra, i.e., by *ca.* 400 B.C. It does not seem feasible to attempt more precise dating at the present time.

3. The Nature of the Literature

The Hebrew title of the book is translated as "The proverbs of Solomon, son of David, king of Israel." "Proverbs" is a translation of the Hebrew *mashal* in its plural form. Thus, the Hebrew designation for the literature of Proverbs is *meshalim*. The exact meaning of *mashal* is none too clear.[11] The root verbal form occurs in Hebrew with two basic ideas: to rule and to be like. Attempts have been made to link these ideas, but it is best to consider the primary meaning of *mashal* to be likeness or comparison. The usage of *mashal* in the Old Testament is varied. It may be used of short pithy sayings such as those in 1 Samuel 10:12; 24:14; Ezekiel 18:2, but also of prophetic oracles as in Isaiah 14:4; Micah 2:4 ("taunt song") and in poetry as in Psalms 49:4 and 78:2 ("parable"). Thus, the English word "proverb" is more restricted than the Hebrew *mashal,* and the reader must keep this in mind. It is probable that the *meshalim* of Proverbs 1:1 refers to the contents of the entire book. If *mashal* is de-

fined as a short, concise, popular proverb, it is an unsatisfactory characterization of the book as a whole. However, if *mashal* is understood in a more general sense as designating almost any type of wisdom literature the title becomes satisfactory. This is most probably the case.

But, satisfactory as *mashal* may be as a title, such generalized use does not help very much with attempts to be more specific about the nature of the literature in Proverbs. Comparative literary studies with the use of form critical methodologies have helped at this point. Two major types of literature may be discerned along with several minor types.

The first major type of literature is that of the Instruction genre, which is characterized by its father-to-son instruction format, along with the use of various types of imperatives plus conditional, motive, and consequential clauses. It dominates chapters 1–9; 22:17—24:22; 31:1–9, though considerable diminution of the genre is found in some passages: e.g., chapters 2; 3:13–20; 6:6–11; 7:6–23 (cf. McKane, p. 7).

An understanding of this genre of wisdom literature is important.[12] It is a type of literature which is characterized by the use of imperatives in various forms, positive and negative. The imperative may be preceded by conditional clauses ("If thou art one of those . . . ," etc.) and be followed by various types of motive clauses and consequential clauses which add elucidation and power to the imperatives. The imperatives themselves are mostly clear and simple statements with limited use of imaginative language. Basically, the imperative form of the Instruction is intended to give authoritative instruction in plain words without much explanation.

McKane says the function of the conditional clause is to define the situation in which the imperative(s) will apply (p. 76), while the function of the motive clause

---

11 The literature on *mashal* is rather extensive. Good discussions and references are found in A. R. Johnson, "Mashal," *Wisdom in Israel and in the Ancient Near East,* pp. 162–69; McKane, *Proverbs,* pp. 22–33.

12 For discussion of the forms of Instruction see McKane, *op. cit.,* pp. 75–82, 90–1, 99–102, 110–117; Christa Kayatz, *Studien zu Proverbien 1–9* (Neukirchen-Vluyn: Neukirchener Verlag, 1966), pp. 17–75.

is to show that the imperative(s) is reasonable and that of the consequential clause to show that the imperative(s) is effective (p. 78).

Thus, the Instruction has an authoritative tone. There is little invitation for critical evaluation of the imperative itself. The background of experience, tradition, and wisdom impose an obligation of receptivity and obedience on the recipient, who is typically addressed as "his son" or "my son." It seems probable that the original context of this language was the actual instruction of a son by his father. But in the course of time these forms of address became mere literary conventions and the Instructions show signs of general educational concern, especially for the type of young men being prepared for high positions, and probably for the public in general.

The second major type of literature is the Wisdom Sentence.[13] Wisdom Sentences of more than one kind are found in the Old Testament. They are the short, succinct statements (using indicative mood in contrast to the imperative of the Instruction) of the type which more closely conform to the meaning of the English word proverb (and probably to the most basic form of *mashal*): e.g., those in Genesis 10:9; 1 Samuel 24:14; 1 Kings 20:11; Ezekiel 16:44. But more artistic, literarily composed sayings constitute the largest segments of the book of Proverbs (10:1—22:16; 24:23–34; 25—29).

The Wisdom Sentence is composed with a considerable range of stylistic features. But when more than one line is involved, some form of parallelism is almost always used. The antithetical or contrast type, with a contrast in the second line, is very common in Proverbs 10:1—22:16 and 25—29 (e.g., 10:1; 14:11). However, the identical or synthetic parallelism is found as well. In this type, the same thing is said in different words on the second line, but the meaning of the first line may be ex-

tended or modified (e.g., 10:18; 18:16).

Different forms of style are used. One which is often found is the comparison by the use of "as (or 'like') . . . is a . . ."— e.g., 26:7–11, where a series of sentences with the same form are found. The comparison may be made by the use of "better than" as in 12:9; 15:16,17; 19:1; 21:9; 28:6.

For the most part the Wisdom Sentences have no immediate context. They are independent sentences which can stand alone as wise observations and judgments on particular subjects. They require no context. When collections of such sentences occur, the result is a very atomistic grouping with only a loose structure. The interpretation of each Sentence depends primarily upon the Sentence itself and not upon the immediate literary context. However, there are some secondary groupings of material in the book of Proverbs. Such groupings may be structured around catchwords, play on the sound of words, some common content, or similar secondary considerations.

It is possible that each of the major collections in Proverbs has a general motif or emphasis which gives them something of a thematic coherence. U. Skladny[14] has argued for such coherence in a recent study. He seeks to show that there are four collections, each with some thematic unity: A (10—15) is concerned with the antithesis between righteousness and wickedness; B (16:1—22:16) is especially concerned with the instruction of officers in royal service; C (25—27) is dominated by the concerns of agriculture and craftsmanship; D (28—29) is chiefly designed for the teaching of young men to become good members of the ruling class.

Skladny's study is helpful, but it is doubtful that there is as much coherence in the collections as he supposes. The collections are subordinate to the Sentences and cannot be used as a precise basis for interpretation.

If the assumption above is correct (viz.,

---

[13] Hermisson, *op. cit.*, pp. 141–71.

[14] *Die ältesten Spruchsammlungen in Israel* (Göttingen: Vandenhoeck & Ruprecht, 1962).

not the collections but the Sentences are basic in Proverbs 10—29), classification of the Sentences (independently of the collections) becomes of considerable interest and potential value. McKane (*op. cit.*, pp. 124–25,189,195,197,198,199) attempts to make a distinction between the "non-proverbial" and "proverbial" type of Wisdom Sentence. The Wisdom Sentence (or aphorism) of the non-proverbial type is a plain statement which is to be understood in a literal and limited way. They are prosaic communications which "set out to make observations in a straightforward and uncomplicated manner."

On the other hand, the proverbial Wisdom Sentence is less precise in its literal statements and is unsatisfactory if limited to being a simple observation or statement of fact. This type of Sentence has an openness to interpretation which is lacking in the non-proverbial type.

A close examination of the results of this approach reveals that it is highly subjective and dependent in many cases on the interpretive sensitivity of the reader. A statement may be a proverb to one interpreter and only a descriptive statement to another.

Nevertheless, some help is gained by an awareness of the distinction McKane makes. For example, in Proverbs there are a good number of statements which appear as observations, useful in daily life, but not intended to convey enduring ethical or theological values. Indeed, to attempt to extrapolate ethical principles or theological dictums from them could be very damaging. Examples of this type are the statements on bribery in 17:8; 18:16; 21:14 (cf. 15:27; 17:23); and wealth in 19:4,6,7.

Before giving attention to other types of literature in Proverbs, it is well to consider the question of the relationship between the Instruction and the Wisdom Sentence. It has been almost axiomatic in the study of the wisdom literature to conclude that the Instruction genre is a development of the Wisdom Sentence. The single line verse or statement (with an origin in popular or folk wisdom) has been considered most basic. Multi-line statements with poetic parallelism evolved only after a considerable process of development. By the same, or a very similar process, the multi-line statements grew into multi-verse instruction and into the larger units of wisdom literature (strophes, didactic poems, narratives). One result of this view of the relationship between Instruction and Wisdom Sentence has been the commonly held view that Proverbs 1—9 is later than chapters 10—29 because it lacks the, supposedly, older and shorter forms of the Sentence with the parallelism so common in the latter.

But this concept of the relationship of Wisdom Sentence to Instruction seems to be a hypothesis built on extremely little solid evidence. Various types of poetry and wisdom literature appear in all periods of Israel's literary history.[15] The assumption of an evolution from one genre to another is unnecessary. The imperative-admonitory genre of the Instruction need not be a development from the indicative-observatory genre of the Sentences. Both may be framed with didactic intent and be used in mixed and modified ways; but this does not demand an intrinsic developmental hypothesis. Both genres have their *own* histories of development—uncertain as the details of those histories may be.

A third type of literature which is found in the book of Proverbs is the Numerical Saying (e.g., 6:16–19; 30:7–9,15–31).[16] This type is composed of (1) a title-line which gives the subject and the number of items which have something in common with it and (2) a list which enumerates and describes the items. A good example appears in 30:24–28. Some scholars have

---

15 Roland E. Murphy, "The Interpretation of Old Testament Wisdom Literature," p. 300, finds little value in making a major distinction between a *Volksspruch* (folk saying) and a *Kunstspruch* (aphorism or artistic saying): "The fact of the matter is that Jotham can pronounce a well-turned fable (Judg. 9:8–15), the riddle of Samson (Judg. 14:14,18) is in neat couplets, and the cry against David's house (1 Kings 12:16) is in parallelism."

16 For an extensive study of the Numerical Sayings see W. M. W. Roth, *Numerical Sayings in the Old Testament*, "Supplements to Vetus Testamentum" (Leiden: E. J. Brill, 1965), XIII.

suggested that the Numerical Saying is related to the example-sequence (as in Amos 3:3–6) and to the riddle. Roth argues that there is little relationship in either case.[17] The example-sequence shares with the Numerical Sayings a series of things or cases which are related to a common subject. But the number is secondary and can be increased or decreased. This is not the case in the Numerical Saying because the number is fixed and basic for the subject. The riddle, like the numerical saying, supposes a question and seeks an answer. But the riddle is usually concerned with only one matter and is less directly didactic and comprehensive than the numerical saying.

Finally, a few sections of Proverbs do not seem to be either Instruction, Sentences, or Numerical Sayings. A kind of preaching genre is found in 1:20–33; 2:1–22; 6:6–11; 8:1–31; and 30:1–6.[18] Narrative is developed in 7:6–27; 9:1–6,13–18; 24:30–34; poetic sections appear in 3:13–20; 31:10–31 (an alphabetical poem).

III. Wisdom in the Book of Proverbs

One of the most striking features of the book of Proverbs is the appearance of wisdom as a person in chapters 1—9. Five passages are of special interest: 1:20–33; 3:19–20; 8:1–21; 8:22–31; 9:1–6.

The figure of Wisdom in these passages is highly personified and difficult to define. There are those who see only a poetic personification of an attribute of Yahweh.[19] Other definitions include the theory of a hypostasis[20] and a type of interpretation

termed "extension of divine personality."[21] None of these designations seems completely adequate. It is improbable that the passages involve only a literary metaphor with no theological reality. On the other hand, Wisdom does not appear as a separate deity, independent of Yahweh. It is best to think in terms of a basic personification of the wisdom of Yahweh to which has been added features drawn from various sources, including the mythologies of the ancient Near East. The result is a vivid personification which expresses a new theological conception of God.

1. Empirical Wisdom

For a fuller understanding of the significance of the figure of Wisdom it is necessary to know something of the use of the words "wisdom" (chokmah) and "wise" (chakam) in the Old Testament. The primary reference of "wise" or "wisdom" is to the skill and the ability to accomplish a task or to attain an objective. It is pragmatic and empirical. Thus, wisdom is associated with Bezalel and his associates in terms of their skill as craftsmen (Ex. 28:3; 35:31; 36:1–2). Weavers (Ex. 35:25), goldsmiths (Jer. 10:9), mourning women (Jer. 9:16), idol makers (Isa. 40:20), sailors (Ezek. 27:8), and judges (Deut. 16:19) are all referred to as wise. In the area of behavior, wisdom has to do with effectiveness of action regardless of ethical relevance (such actions may be described as shrewd or crafty). Thus, Jonadab is described as "an exceedingly wise man" in 2 Samuel 13:3 because his plan provided Ammon the opportunity to rape his half sister Tamar. Uses of "wise" in this sense of effective and successful action are also found in David's counsel to Solomon for

---

17 *Ibid.*, pp. 95–98.

18 Kayatz, *op. cit.*, pp. 119–134, analyzes 1:20–33 in terms of preaching.

19 E.g. H. W. Robinson, *Inspiration and Revelation in the Old Testament*, p. 260; W. A. Irwin, "Where Shall Wisdom Be Found?" JBL, LXXX (1961), 141; Scott, p. 71, "poetic only and not ontological."

20 The best study of wisdom as a hypostasis is that of Helmer Ringgren, *Word and Wisdom* (Lund: Håkan Ohlssons Boktryckeri, 1947). He defines a hypostasis, as a "quasi-personification of certain attributes proper to God, occupying an intermediate position between personalities and abstract beings" (p. 8). The origin of personal Wisdom is a hypostatization of a divine function (p. 149).

21 Proposed by the author in an unpublished dissertation, "A Study of the Wise Men of Israel in Relation to the Prophets" (Louisville: The Southern Baptist Theological Seminary Library, 1958), pp. 370–93; also, Edgar Jones, *Proverbs and Ecclesiastes*, "Torch Bible Commentaries" (New York: Macmillan Company, 1961), p. 43. The concept of "extension of divine personality" is from A. R. Johnson, *The One and the Many in the Israelite Conception of God* (Cardiff: University of Wales Press, 1942).

the execution of Joab and Shimei (see 1 Kings 2:6,9; see also Dan. 8:25, where the reference is to Antiochus Epiphanes). Such illustrations justify the definition of wisdom as the ability to bring a definite objective into focus and to discover the means for reaching it.

This kind of wisdom is found in animals as well as men. The ants, badgers, locusts, and lizards are "exceedingly wise" because, despite their smallness, they are very successful in their endeavors (30:24–28). Physical limitations may be overcome by wisdom (24:5–6).

But wisdom is not confined in meaning to a level of shrewd human action. Moral understanding and ethical behavior are included. Wisdom in the book of Proverbs is very much concerned with the art of good living; the techniques of the well-lived life. The expression in Proverbs 1:5 of the skill of "steering" (as of a ship) is instructive. The wise man knows how to pilot himself through the confusion of the experiences of life. On a broad basis of experience, tradition, and piety, he seeks to master life and live successfully. A part of such mastery is the ability to make the correct ethical decisions. This accounts, at least to a degree, for the great emphasis on the "righteous man" (especially in chs. 10—29).

The wisdom teachers wanted to teach their students this kind of wisdom. The "art of living" wisdom is found with major emphasis in the Instruction genre (e.g., 3:1–2; 4:10–12). The wisdom is that of experience, tradition, and the ability to learn. Little or no evidence for divine inspiration or revelation is found. This teaching does assume an order of existence which is basic for the good life and which can be grasped by the wise man—at least in part. Wisdom is the ability to gather the welter of life's threads into some sort of fabric. It assumes this as the intrinsic basis of human existence.

It is well to remember that wisdom was fundamentally noncultic (but not nonreligious). It did not have to do with rituals,

sacrifices, festivals, priests, and prophets. The wisdom teacher was concerned with the extensive areas of life which remained outside the direct regulation of the cult. In these areas, decisions of vital importance had to be made every day. The wisdom teacher did not approach this task with a collection of divine commandments or oracles. His was the way of counsel and persuasion which was derived from the canons of experience and tradition.[22]

2. Theological Wisdom

But wisdom is not always so humanistic in the Old Testament. A wisdom which we may call theological overshadows the merely pragmatic.[23] There are several aspects to this theological wisdom. First, it is not acquired fundamentally from the teaching of men. It is the gift of God to those whose wisdom has led them to fear him. This aspect of wisdom is illustrated in Proverbs 2. The first verse begins with the typical address of the Instruction "My son"; and continues with a protasis in the traditional language ("my words," "my commandments") of the wisdom teacher. But the apodosis in 2:5–8 is *not* traditional. Wisdom has become inseparably linked with the "fear of Yahweh" as in 1:7; 9:10; 15:33; etc. The fear of Yahweh is a phrase which expresses the totality of worship and obedience towards God. Thus, the practice of Yahwistic religion has become the primary basis for wisdom. The wisdom teacher blends the humanism of wisdom with theology, and wisdom is both learned and received.

Second, wisdom is present with God in

---

22 Rylaarsdam, *Revelation in Jewish Wisdom Literature,* p. 55, distinguishes between the religious outlook of the prophet as "vertical" while that of the sages was "horizontal."

23 Gerhard von Rad, *Old Testament Theology,* trans., D. M. C. Stalker (New York: Harper & Brothers, 1962), I, 440–1, notes that, at a date not precisely ascertainable, "wisdom teaching became the custodian of centralities of the faith and approached man's environment with the whole impact of the quest for salvation —it asked about the meaning of Creation. . . . Indeed, in odd inversion of its origin, it increasingly became the form *par excellence* in which all Israel's later theological thought moved."

creation. Proverbs 3:19 says that "The Lord by wisdom founded the earth . . ." In this regard the poem in Job 28 is of interest. It deals with the impotence of man to discover wisdom despite his great technological achievements. By his strength and skill man can accomplish what no bird or beast can do (28:7–8). He can penetrate the earth by mining and bring up great treasures. He can amass great wealth gathered from difficult and remote places of the world. But the ultimate secret—wisdom—lies beyond his power. Wisdom was established by God in the process of creation and, presumably, continues to have its "place" in the cosmos. But the location and way to wisdom's place is beyond the knowledge of man. God knows; man does not.

In Proverbs 8:22–31, Wisdom was created before the earth as "the first of his acts of old" and was present with God during the creation process (vv. 27–30). She rejoices in the world and delights in mankind (v. 31). There is a major difference between Wisdom in Job 28 and Wisdom in Proverbs 8. In the former, Wisdom can be known only in a secondary way through the "fear of Yahweh." But in the Proverbs passages, Wisdom goes out into public places and conspicuously entreats men to take her, promising rich rewards to those who receive her (8:34–35).

Thus, Wisdom is of divine origin but is found both in the created world of nature and in human society. It appears as far more than a humanistic weaving of the threads of life into an acceptable fabric. It has become the extension and expression of the will and presence of Yahweh in the world.[24]

It is important to note that the form of Wisdom found in Proverbs 1—9 does not come to man as an "it" (i.e., as a teaching, commandment, ritual or the like), but as a personal "I" who summons men to life. Wisdom is nothing less than the personal presence of Yahweh in the world and among men.[25]

Outline

I. Instruction (1:1—9:18)
  1. General introduction (1:1–7)
  2. Avoiding bad company and wisdom preaching (1:8–33)
    (1) Warning against the way of sinners (1:8–19)
    (2) Wisdom and her sermon (1:20–33)
  3. General advice to a pupil on the nature and value of wisdom (2:1–22)
  4. The rewards of a disciplined life (3:1–20)
    (1) Trusting in the Lord (3:1–12)
    (2) Praise of wisdom (3:13–20)
  5. Keeping sound wisdom (3:21–35)
    (1) The security of wisdom (3:21–26)
    (2) On being a good neighbor (3:27–35)
  6. A teacher's instruction in three parts (4:1–27)
    (1) Wisdom from generation to generation (4:1–9)
    (2) The ways of dawn and deep darkness (4:10–19)
    (3) On the discipline of the whole person (4:20–27)
  7. Instruction about sexual behavior (5:1–23)
    (1) Watch out for the strange woman (5:1–14)
    (2) Love your own wife (5:15–20)
    (3) Remember that God sees all (5:21–23)
  8. Lessons on economics and social behavior (6:1–19)
    (1) Against dealing with a money-lender (6:1–5)
    (2) The ant as a model (6:6–11)
    (3) The troublemaker (6:12–15)
    (4) Seven types of anti-social behavior (6:16–19)
  9. The folly of adultery (6:20–35)
  10. Instruction on the seductive power of the strange woman (7:1–27)
    (1) The preventive power of commandments and wisdom (7:1–5)
    (2) A young man snared by seduction (7:6–23)
    (3) The chambers of death (7:24–27)

---

[24] Kayatz, *op. cit.*, pp. 76–119, emphasizes the relationship of Wisdom to Yahweh in Prov. 8:22–31.

[25] James Wood, *Wisdom Literature, An Introduction,* "Studies in Theology" (London: Gerald Duckwood & Co., Ltd., 1967), p. 109.

Selected Bibliography

BARUCQ, ANDRE. *Le Livre des Proverbs.* ("Sources Bibliques.") Paris: J. Gabalda, 1964.

BOSTRÖM, GUSTAV. *Proverbiastudien, die Weisheit und das fremde Weib in Spr. 1–9.* ("Lund Universitets Arsskrift," N. F. Avd. 1 Bd 30. NR3.) Lund: C. W. K. Gleerup, 1935.

FICHTNER, JOHANNES. *Die Altorientaltische Weisheit irher israelitisch-jüdischen Ausprägung.* ("Beihefte zur Zeitschrift fur die alttestamentliche Weisheit," 62.) Giessen: Alfred Töpelmann, 1933.

FRITSCH, CHARLES T. "The Book of Proverbs," *The Interpreter's Bible,* Vol. IV. Ed. GEORGE ARTHUR BUTTRICK. Nashville: Abingdon Press, 1955.

GEMSER, BEREND. *Sprüche Salomos.* ("Handbuch zum alten Testament.") Vol. 16, 2d ed. Tubingen: J. C. B. Mohr (Paul Siebeck), 1963.

JONES, EDGAR. *Proverbs and Ecclesiastes.* ("Torch Bible Commentaries.") New York: Macmillan Company, 1961.

KIDNER, DEREK. *The Proverbs* ("The Tyndale Old Testament Commentaries.") Chicago: Inter-Varsity Press, 1964.

McKANE, WILLIAM. *Prophets and Wise Men.* ("Studies in Biblical Theology" No. 44.) Naperville, Ill.: Alec R. Allenson, Inc., 1965.

———. *Proverbs.* ("The Old Testament Library.") Philadelphia: The Westminster Press, 1970.

NOTH, M., and D. WINTON THOMAS, eds. *Wisdom in Israel and in the Ancient Near East.* ("Supplements to Vetus Testamentum," III.) Leiden: E. J. Brill, 1955.

OESTERLEY, W. O. E. *The Book of Proverbs.* ("Westminster Commentaries") London: Methuen and Company, Ltd., 1929.

RINGGREN, HELMER. *Sprüche,* ("Das alte Testament Deutsch.") Vol. 16, 2d ed. Göttingen: Vandenhoeck & Ruprecht, 1967.

RYLAARSDAM, J. COERT. *Revelation in Jewish Wisdom Literature.* Chicago: University of Chicago Press, 1946.

———. *Proverbs, Ecclesiastes, Song of Solomon.* ("The Layman's Bible Commentary.") Vol. 10. Richmond, Virginia: John Knox Press, 1964.

SCOTT, R. B. Y. *Proverbs, Ecclesiastes.* ("The Anchor Bible.") Vol. 18. Garden City, New York: Doubleday & Company, 1965.

SKLADNY, UDO. *Die ältesten Spruchsammlungen in Israel.* Göttingen: Vandenhoeck & Ruprecht, 1962.

TOY, CRAWFORD H. *A Critical and Exegetical Commentary on the Book of Proverbs.* ("The International Critical Commentary.") Edinburgh: T. & T. Clark, 1959 (reprint of 1899 edition).

WHYBRAY, R. N. *Wisdom in Proverbs.* ("Studies in Biblical Theology" No. 45.) Naperville, Ill.: Alec R. Allenson, Inc., 1965.

Commentary on the Text

I. Instruction (1:1—9:18)

1. General Introduction (1:1-7)

1 The proverbs of Solomon, son of David,
   king of Israel:
2 That men may know wisdom and instruction,
   understand words of insight,
3 receive instruction in wise dealing,
   righteousness, justice, and equity;
4 that prudence may be given to the simple,
   knowledge and discretion to the youth—
5 the wise man also may hear and increase in
   learning,
   and the man of understanding acquire
   skill,
6 to understand a proverb and a figure,
   the words of the wise and their riddles.
7 The fear of the LORD is the beginning of
   knowledge;
   fools despise wisdom and instruction.

These verses form a general introduction
not only to chapters 1—9 but also to the
entire book. Attention has been given to v.
1 in the Introduction. There are at least
two reasons to attribute the proverbs to
Solomon. (1) The historical relationship of
the wisdom movement in Israel with Solomon (1 Kings 4:29–34) tended to bring
all wisdom writing into the Solomonic
category. (2) The wisdom literature was
closely related to the royal establishment
(see Int.) and associated with the name of
a king or some other high official closely
associated with royalty.

The vocabulary of vv. 2–7 is extensive
and representative of the wisdom literature. *Wisdom* has been discussed in the
Introduction; the discussion need not be
repeated. *Instruction* is the translation of
musar, which may be translated "discipline" or even "chastisement" in some contexts (e.g., Deut. 4:36; 11:2). In Proverbs
it usually has a rather strong implication of
discipline, appearing in parallel with reproof in, e.g., 3:11,12; 6:23; 13:18,24;
and with rebuke in 13:1 (Gemser, p. 19).

It may be closely correlated with an
Egyptian word for instruction.

To *understand the words of insight* is a
basic objective of wisdom teaching. The
words of insight refer to rational discourse
(Toy, p. 5), the ability to make distinc-
tions and to organize thought into compre-
hensible expression. The capacity to decide upon right and wrong courses of action is involved (see 1 Kings 3:9 and
Solomon's prayer).

The *wise dealing* of v. 3 gives expression
to the practical, pragmatic bent of wisdom
teaching. David exhibited this aptitude in
his military competency and success in
missions assigned him by Saul (1 Sam.
18:5,14–15,30). The wise dealer is the
man of effective and successful actions.
However, the parallel line in v. 3 tends to
modify this connotation. For the words
righteousness, justice, and *equity* are more
closely connected with Yahwism and direct religious commitment than "wise dealing" as such. Thus, a moral and religious
check is placed on wise dealing. The basic
idea of *righteousness* is conformity to a
norm or a relationship—the relationship established in the Sinai covenant and in the
giving of the *torah*. *Justice* is fundamentally a term for a legal decision which
becomes a precedent for life. *Equity* carries the idea of straightness or levelness.
In conduct, it refers to straightforwardness
as opposed to crooked ways of behavior
(Toy, p. 7).[1]

The pragmatic language of wisdom returns in v. 4 with the words *prudence* and
discretion. Prudence is on occasion pejora-

---

[1] For a discussion of "righteousness" and "justice"
in general Old Testament usage see Edmond Jacob,
Theology of the Old Testament. Trans. A. W. Heath-
cate and Philip J. Allcock (New York: Harper &
Brothers, 1958), pp. 94–102; and Walther Eichrodt,
Theology of the Old Testament. Trans. J. A. Baker
(London: SCM Press, Ltd, 1961), pp. 239–49.

tive and means guile or shrewdness (e.g., it is used of the serpent in Gen. 3:1). But in a more general sense it indicates ability in incisive speaking and action. Discretion is also ethically neutral and may be pejorative (McKane, p. 265). Ideas of intrigue, resourcefulness, devising, and planning are conveyed by the term. It implies the ability to make a careful decision regarding a course of action and see it through to the desired end.

The *learning* of v. 5 (lit., that which is taken or received) points to the knowledge gained from tradition, the deposit of wisdom from the past. It is knowledge passed on from teacher to student. *Skill* is derived from the root for to bind and the noun rope. It conveys the idea of a sailor who steers a boat, i.e., nautical expertise. The discernment and skill needed to steer a good and successful course through life was the objective of the wise men.

The accomplishment of these objectives in wisdom teaching is dependent on the mastery of the forms of the literary art of the wise men (v. 6). *Proverb* has been discussed in the Introduction. The meaning of *figure* is not entirely certain (see McKane, p. 267); but it is probable that it refers to an expression or teaching which requires interpretation for proper understanding. *Riddle* originally referred to a puzzle put forward in contests of wits or games (Judg. 14:12–18; 2 Kings 10:1). However, the meaning in the context of Proverbs is likely to be more nearly that of "dark speech" (see Num. 12:6–8; cf. Hos. 2:10) or speech which is not readily understood without some commentary and explanation. The riddle like the proverb and the figure, must be penetrated by interpretation.

We may take note of the kinds of people with whom the wisdom teachers were concerned. The *men* of v. 2 is not in the Hebrew text (in vv. 2,3,4,6; the infinitive form of the verb is used without an expressed subject: to know or to understand, etc.). But a group of much concern to the wise men appears in v. 4, i.e., *the simple.*

"Simple" is not a happy translation, though it is difficult to find one that is. The simple were the inexperienced people, principally young (note the parallel with *youth*), male, and immature. The term does not bear the idea of a lack of intelligence. The simple were teachable, open to instruction, and in need of the guidance of a teacher.

However, the wisdom teaching is aimed at the *wise man* and the man of *understanding* as well. Two comments need to be made. (1) Verse 5 points to a general conclusion about knowledge and wisdom: no man ever reaches the limit (see 9:9; 19:25). There is always more to learn. (2) Verse 5 breaks the pattern of vv. 2–6 and has tempted some commentators to consider it as a parenthetical gloss (Toy, p. 8). It is parenthetical but should not be depreciated for this reason. Whether part of the original design of vv. 1–6 or not, it is an appropriate statement.

Verse 7 is somewhat independent, and it has been linked with vv. 9 f. rather than with vv. 1–6 (e.g., Gemser). But the verse does not relate as well to vv. 8–19 as to vv. 1–6. Verse 8 has no intrinsic connection with v. 7 (McKane, p. 265). Verse 7 is frequently called the motto or central motif of the book of Proverbs (it is repeated with variations in 9:10; Psalm 111:10; Job 28:28; Ecclus. 1:14). It blends the *fear of the Lord* with *knowledge, wisdom,* and *instruction*. The "fear" of God or Yahweh has a number of emphases in the Old Testament. It may refer to a standard of conduct which is considered to be generally accepted by decent people (cf. Gen. 20:11; Ex. 1:17,21). In connection with the worship of Yahweh, fear means reverence in worship and obedience (e.g., Deut. 4:10; Lev. 19:14,32; Psalm 34:11). As R. N. Whybray (p. 96) summarizes, "fearing Yahweh" most nearly expressed what we call Yahwism (or Judaism). Thus, Obadiah could say to Elijah, "I your servant have revered [feared] the Lord from my youth" (1 Kings 18:12).

Whybray (p. 97) also suggests that a real understanding of the term in the wisdom literature is dependent on observing the close connection between the fear of Yahweh and education. In some passages the fear of Yahweh is to be taught and learned (as in Psalm 34:11–14; Deut. 17: 18–20; 2 Kings 17:25–28). The repeated use of the expression in Deuteronomy and in Leviticus 17—26 adds further evidence of its relationship to instruction.

But this tension does not appear in Proverbs. The two systems of thought and education (wisdom and the fear of Yahweh) have been blended into one. The fear of Yahweh now colors the interpretation of all wisdom teaching. The context of wisdom is no longer (if it ever really existed completely as such) that of a severe educational discipline on a humanistic level, but one of piety *and* education (McKane, p. 264). But the source of authority is Yahweh (not the teacher), and there is no way to wisdom except via fear of him.

The beginning of knowledge. The word beginning probably carries both the idea of starting point and that of essence or ultimate purpose (Jones, p. 58). The *fools* are those who reject wisdom and instruction, which is equivalent to rejecting the effective presence of God (as in Psalm 14:1). The word for fools carries the ideas of dull, ignorant, and morally insensitive. This type of fool is not receptive to either wisdom of God or man; he spurns the instruction of both.

2. Avoiding Bad Company and Wisdom Preaching (1:8–33)

(1) Warning Against the Way of Sinners (1:8–19)

8 Hear, my son, your father's instruction,
   and reject not your mother's teaching;
9 for they are a fair garland for your head,
   and pendants for your neck.
10 My son, if sinners entice you,
   do not consent.
11 If they say, "Come with us, let us lie in wait for blood,
   let us wantonly ambush the innocent;
12 like Sheol let us swallow them alive
   and whole, like those who go down to the Pit;

13 we shall find all precious goods,
   we shall fill our houses with spoil;
14 throw in your lot among us,
   we will all have one purse"—
15 my son, do not walk in the way with them,
   hold back your foot from their paths;
16 for their feet run to evil,
   and they make haste to shed blood.
17 For in vain is a net spread
   in the sight of any bird;
18 but these men lie in wait for their own blood,
   they set an ambush for their own lives.
19 Such are the ways of all who get gain by violence;
   it takes away the life of its possessors.

The stylistic characteristics of Instruction marks these verses. The use of the imperative in the opening sentence and the address *my son* are basic. Motive clauses introduced by *for* provide support for the imperative mood in which the teaching is given. The extended conditional clauses in vv. 11–14 indicate the conditions which are especially applicable to the imperative.

Hear—the authoritative nature of the teaching is indicated by the imperative. Hearing, also in v. 5, points to the receptivity of the pupil to the instruction of a teacher. The instruction was usually given orally, and thus the ability and willingness to listen and receive was essential.

My son. This may be a general form of address for the pupil. It is rooted in the fact that the primary institution of education was the home. The first teachers were the parents of the child. The teachers in the schools took the place of the parents in subsequent training. They became "fathers" and "mothers" of the pupils. The inclusion of both parental terms is worthy of note. The mother's teaching is on a par with that of the father (for other references to the mother's influence see 6:20; 10:1; 15:20; 20:20; 30:17). Parental teachings do not produce shame or constitute a heavy burden; but they are *a fair garland* or crown for the head and pendants or jewels for the neck, reflecting both the great value of wisdom and the honor of obedience (Ringgren, p. 14).

The main topic of the teaching begins

in v. 10. It is a warning against the enticements of sinners. The young man is urged
to resist the persuasiveness of those who
want to participate in robbery and violence: *do not consent.* The propositions
confronted by the young man are set forth
in vv. 11–14.

The ways of violence (*let us lie in wait
for blood,* i.e., murder; *wantonly ambush
the innocent*) are offered as the way to
money and treasure (v. 13) as well as
participation in a communal fellowship (v.
14). The temptations of violence (v. 12
indicates an insatiable appetite for the
destruction of others), money, and acceptance in a fellowship of peers are very
powerful enticements.

But the young man is warned that the
consequences of accepting the invitation of
such sinners are not good (vv. 15–19).
For in vain is a net spread is none too clear
in meaning. Its most natural meaning
would be that a bird who watches the
preparation of a net designed to catch it
can easily avoid capture and, thus, makes
such preparation futile. The meaning in
the context would be that the consequences of crime are so obvious that they
should be easily avoided. However, v. 17
seems to be a metaphor for v. 18, which
expresses the conviction that the criminal
behavior described is self-defeating: *these
men lie in wait for their own blood.* Like a
boomerang their violence will come back
upon themselves (Jones, p. 61). If this is
the case, v. 17 should be understood in the
sense that even though the bird is aware
of the preparation of the net there is no
deterrent effect. The bait in the net distorts
judgment and self-control, and the bird
flies right into certain capture.

Verse 19 is a summary statement of the
Instruction. Dishonest gain gathered by
ways of violence and compulsive, destructive behavior produces death. A concept
of order lies under the teaching. The ways
of violence and destruction produce their
own retribution. There is a nexus between
act and consequence which is built into
the structure of reality.

(2) Wisdom and Her Sermon (1:20–33)

20 Wisdom cries aloud in the street;
      in the markets she raises her voice;
21 on the top of the walls she cries out;
      at the entrance of the city gates she
        speaks:
22 "How long, O simple ones, will you love be-
        ing simple?
    How long will scoffers delight in their scoff-
        ing
    and fools hate knowledge?
23 Give heed to my reproof;
    behold, I will pour out my thoughts to you;
    I will make my words known to you.
24 Because I have called and you refused to
        listen,
    have stretched out my hand and no one
        has heeded,
25 and you have ignored all my counsel
    and would have none of my reproof,
26 I also will laugh at your calamity;
    I will mock when panic strikes you,
27 when panic strikes you like a storm,
    and your calamity comes like a whirl-
        wind,
    when distress and anguish come upon
        you.
28 Then they will call upon me, but I will not
        answer;
    they will seek me diligently but will not
        find me.
29 Because they hated knowledge
    and did not choose the fear of the LORD,
30 would have none of my counsel,
    and despised all my reproof,
31 therefore they shall eat the fruit of their
        way
    and be sated with their own devices.
32 For the simple are killed by their turning
        away,
    and the complacence of fools destroys
        them;
33 but he who listens to me will dwell secure
    and will be at ease, without dread of
        evil."

Wisdom appears as a female person in
this section, as in chapters 8 and 9. The
peculiar plural form (Heb.) in v. 20
should be understood as a singular name.
The same form also appears in 9:1; 24:7.

Wisdom raises her voice in the streets
and gate areas of the city where people
gather and mingle. *On top of the walls* is
uncertain and may mean "in the places
where there is the most noise" because of
the busy activities of people. But the RSV
reading is not impossible (cf. McKane, p.

272). In any case, Wisdom gives her message in busy and conspicuous places in the city. We are reminded of the prophets who sometimes went into the streets and public places to preach their message to the people (see Isa. 20; Jer. 5:1; 7:2). However, it is most likely that the wise men, too, went into such places to do their teaching and seek out students (see the accounts of the wise woman in 2 Sam. 20:14–22; of Job in Job 29).

How long, O simple ones, will you love being simple? Wisdom addresses her message to the "simple ones" and the *scoffers* and *fools* (vv. 22,32). For the *simple* see the comment on 1:4. The *scoffers* may mean the scornful, mocking, insolent people as usually assumed. But the root verb may mean to talk freely; hence a babbler or free and careless talker may be the meaning. The Egyptian Instructions place much emphasis on careful speech, and the Israelite wisdom teachers were also concerned with this aspect of living (e.g., note the emphasis on the tongue and temperate speech in 10:19–20,31–32; 11:12–13; etc.). A lack of discipline in speech marks a person as immature (simple) and a fool. *Kesil* (v. 22c) denotes a brazen, insolent type of fool, hyperactive in mischief and pouring out foolish talk (see 10:23; 12:23).

Give heed to my reproof. Wisdom calls for a "turning" to her admonitions. She promises to pour out her spirit on those who do so—her spirit will flow or gush out on the recipient. There may be an echo of the prophetic promises of the pouring out of the Spirit (Isa. 44:3; Joel 2:28–29; Ringgren, p. 16). *I will make my words known to you* (v. 23b). Wisdom promises those who receive her a revelation of herself. Unlike the prophets, who were messengers with the word of Yahweh, Wisdom is herself the revelation in personal form.

In vv. 24–31 Wisdom harangues her audience with the vocabulary of a wisdom teacher and the stance of a prophet (McKane, p. 274). She speaks of *counsel* and *reproof* as a wisdom teacher, but her hand is stretched out with her preaching

like a prophet (Isa. 65:1–2). The language of vv. 26–27 is distinctly similar to that of the prophetic oracles of warning and threat. However, the prophetic oracles present Yahweh as the executor of judgment. That element does not appear here; but Wisdom herself, as a kind of surrogate for Yahweh, will laugh and mock when disaster comes to those who refuse her. The motifs of laughing, calling-out-but-not-hearing and seeking-but-not-finding are found of Yahweh in other contexts (see Psalm 2:4; Mic. 3:4; Isa. 1:15; Jer. 11:1; Hos. 5:6; Kayatz, pp. 124–5). Wisdom's offer of her message and herself is not unconditional and indefinite. She calls for a positive response without delay. A delayed response may be too late.

In v. 29 Wisdom links her teaching with *the fear of the Lord.* The authority of her message is not only that of her experience and skill. She has divine authority for her *counsel* and *reproof.*

The punishment for those who refuse Wisdom is in eating the *fruit* of their own *way* and *devices.* The joy they now find in their cleverness and independence will turn to a loathing and disgust, like that of the man who eats too much. But the choice is not simply between personal satisfaction and lack of it; it is the choice between death and secure life (vv. 32–33). *The complacence* [false sense of tranquility and well-being] *of fools destroys them.*

3. General Advice to a Pupil on the Nature and Value of Wisdom (2:1–22)

1 My son, if you receive my words
   and treasure up my commandments with you,
2 making your ear attentive to wisdom
   and inclining your heart to understanding;
3 yes, if you cry out for insight
   and raise your voice for understanding,
4 if you seek it like silver
   and search for it as for hidden treasures;
5 then you will understand the fear of the LORD
   and find the knowledge of God.
6 For the LORD gives wisdom;
   from his mouth come knowledge and understanding;

7 he stores up sound wisdom for the upright;
   he is a shield to those who walk in in-
     tegrity,
8 guarding the paths of justice
   and preserving the way of his saints.
9 Then you will understand righteousness and
     justice
   and equity, every good path;
10 for wisdom will come into your heart,
   and knowledge will be pleasant to your
     soul;
11 discretion will watch over you;
   understanding will guard you;
12 delivering you from the way of evil,
   from men of perverted speech,
13 who forsake the paths of uprightness
   to walk in the ways of darkness,
14 who rejoice in doing evil
   and delight in the perverseness of evil;
15 men whose paths are crooked,
   and who are devious in their ways.
16 You will be saved from the loose woman,
   from the adventuress with her smooth
     words,
17 who forsakes the companion of her youth
   and forgets the covenant of her God;
18 for her house sinks down to death,
   and her paths to the shades;
19 none who go to her come back
   nor do they regain the paths of life.
20 So you will walk in the way of good men
   and keep to the paths of the righteous.
21 For the upright will inhabit the land,
   and men of integrity will remain in it;
22 but the wicked will be cut off from the land,
   and the treacherous will be rooted out of
     it.

Chapter 2, like 1:20–23, has something of a preaching style. It is Instruction in the voluntative mood, not the imperative. The exhortation is in the form of an appeal to the hearer: "If you receive . . . then . . . Verses 1–4 contain a series of protases which form the prologue to the apodoses in vv. 5 and 9. The other verses provide explication, motivation, and consequences.

In vv. 1–4 the teacher appeals for the student to be receptive and zealous toward wisdom, which is equated with my commandments in v. 1. The verbs are strong and expressive: receive, treasure up, making your ear attentive, inclining your heart, etc. The student is urged to cry out for insight and raise your voice for understanding. These words can be understood

as (1) an appeal in the sense of calling for insight and understanding to come; or (2) receiving these qualities with shouts of acceptance and acclamation. The first is more probable and fits the intensity of the commitment to wisdom desired by the teacher. The student should seek and search for wisdom. Wisdom is not gained by passive effort.

Verses 5–8 contain the first apodosis, which assures the student that his intense desire and search for wisdom will not be disappointed: then you will understand. The quest for wisdom will end with understanding of the fear of Yahweh and the knowledge of God. As in 1:7, wisdom and the fear of Yahweh are merged. The confidence of v. 5 is guaranteed by the action of Yahweh in vv. 6–8. Wisdom is the gift of Yahweh, and he is the source of knowledge and understanding. Verses 7–8 provide commentary and explication of v. 6. The word sound wisdom (tushiyyah) in v. 7 is used chiefly in Proverbs and Job. It carries the idea of practical sense, power of action, help (3:21; 8:14; Job 6:14; 12:16). The quest for wisdom on the human level will be met by a favorable response from Yahweh, who is amply endowed and equipped to provide men with wisdom and its benefits. We are reminded of the teaching of Jesus in Matthew 7:7–12.

Verses 9–11 constitute the second apodosis. The quest in vv. 1–4 will result in moral understanding: Then you will understand righteousness and justice and equity, every good path. The reason for this result is the coming of wisdom into the mind and the welcome reception of knowledge into the soul. The recipient will be guarded by discretion and understanding. Discretion, which can mean intrigue or plot, is used in a positive sense: an alert and effective guard. Verses 12–15 explain the kind of behavior and person that wisdom and understanding protect against. A man needs all the discretion he can get when confronted by people like these!

The focus of attention shifts in vv. 16–

19 from the *men of perverted speech* to the danger of the *loose woman* (cf. marg., "strange"). She is the woman who is different, foreign or outside the usual circles of life, frequently related to fertility cults and posing a tempting danger for the men of the community (see ch. 7). She *forsakes the companion of her youth and forgets the covenant of her God* (v. 17). The "covenant of her God" has been interpreted as a reference to the covenant of marriage which is made with God as a witness (e.g., Toy, p. 47). It is much more probable that Boström is correct in interpreting it as a covenant with a foreign god and foreign religion. She is not an Israelite from the covenant with Yahweh.

Another interpretation (Ringgren's) holds that the woman in v. 17 is an Israelite who has forsaken the Yahweh covenant and become the devotee of an alien cult. The *companion of her youth* refers to Yahweh as in Jeremiah 3:4. The association of her *house* and her *paths* with death in vv. 18–19 is considered to strengthen this view, because the goddess of love (Ishtar-Astarte), who forms the model for the strange woman, is known in ancient Near Eastern literature both for giving life and destroying it.

The house of the woman is a dangerous place which inclines toward death (i.e., towards Sheol, the realm of the dead) and *her paths to the shades.* None come back from following her; they never *regain the paths of life.* The *shades* (*repha'im*) are the inhabitants of Sheol, the underworld of the dead. It is common to interpret *repha'im* as "shades" or "shadows" with the sense that the dead in their weakened and attenuated form of life exist as shadows of their former selves (e.g., Jones, p. 67). However, it is more probable that *repha'im* is related to the Ugaritic *rpūm* who appear as deities of the underworld.

The future of the man who quests for wisdom and receives it is set forth in vv. 20–22. The *upright* and the men of *integrity* will have the *land;* while the wicked will be cut off and removed from the land. The "land" is the land of Palestine (Gemser, p. 26), and the language is very Deuteronomic (see Deut. 4:10,26; 6:18; etc.). In the Deuteronomic theology the promised land is a basic component of Yahweh's great gift of salvation. But this gift is threatened by Israel's disobedience to the commandments of Yahweh. The promise of the land is no longer unconditional, but depends upon those who are faithful and obedient. Israel now exists in two groups: the *righteous* and the *wicked.* Ringgren (p. 19) remarks that "the promise to live in the land and to possess it is, therefore, not for the people as a whole; but only for those who obey the commandments of God, or who obey Wisdom, which is the same thing."

4. The Rewards of a Disciplined Life (3:1–20)

(1) Trusting in the Lord (3:1–12)

1 My son, do not forget my teaching,
    but let your heart keep my commandments;
2 for length of days and years of life
    and abundant welfare will they give you.
3 Let not loyalty and faithfulness forsake you;
    bind them about your neck,
    write them on the tablet of your heart.
4 So you will find favor and good repute
    in the sight of God and man.
5 Trust in the LORD with all your heart,
    and do not rely on your own insight.
6 In all your ways acknowledge him,
    and he will make straight your paths.
7 Be not wise in your own eyes;
    fear the LORD, and turn away from evil.
8 It will be healing to your flesh
    and refreshment to your bones.
9 Honor the LORD with your substance
    and with the first fruits of all your produce;
10 then your barns will be filled with plenty,
    and your vats will be bursting with wine.
11 My son, do not despise the LORD's discipline
    or be weary of his reproof,
12 for the LORD reproves him whom he loves,
    as a father the son in whom he delights.

McKane (p. 290) notes that this section opens with the conventional language of the Instructions: *My son, do not forget my teaching (torah).* But beginning with **v. 3** the content of the passage becomes very different from the usual Instruction: "its contents conduct us into the heartland of Yahwistic faith and practice." *Loyalty* is properly the designation of the unity and solidarity between the parties of a covenant relationship. *Faithfulness* refers to firmness, reliability, or trustworthiness. The words are used together of the relationship between father and son (Gen. 47:29); of God to men (Gen. 24:27; Deut. 7:6); of man and man (Hos. 4:1; Prov. 14:22). It is most probable that "loyalty and faithfulness" refer to the covenant solidarity of Israel's religion. The last parts of v. 3 are very similar to phraseology found in covenant and law contexts (e.g., Ex. 13:9,16; Deut. 11:18). Motivation for loyalty and faithfulness is found in v. 4.

Verses 5–12 are thoroughly religious and Yahwistic. These verses deal with four subjects (Gemser, p. 27). (a) *Trust in the Lord with all your heart.* Trust must be placed in Yahweh and not in *your own insight.* Yahweh will make the ways of life *straight,* i.e., remove obstacles and keep such a person from deviating into dangerous places.

(b) *Humility* is the way to health. (vv. 7–8). The man has little hope who evaluates himself more highly than he ought to do (cf. Isa. 5:21). A man's confidence cannot be placed in his own ability to think and act. The fear of Yahweh is the real basis of confidence. It produces invigorated health and vitality.

(c) *Honor the Lord with your substance. Honor* probably means to bring a gift, as in Isaiah 43:23 (Gemser, p. 28). The *first fruits* recalls Deuteronomy 18:4; 26:2; 1 Amos 6:6. The promise in v. 10 agrees with Deuteronomy 28:8 and Malachi 3:10–12.

(d) *My son, do not despise the Lord's discipline.* Submission and appreciation of the discipline of Yahweh is essential for the good life. Yahweh may administer severe punishment, but it is an expression of his love (v. 12). He acts as a father does towards a son who pleases him. Yahweh's correction of those who are under his discipline reveals his love for them.

(2) Praise of Wisdom (3:13–20)

13 Happy is the man who finds wisdom,
  and the man who gets understanding,
14 for the gain from it is better than gain from silver
  and its profit better than gold.
15 She is more precious than jewels,
  and nothing you desire can compare with her.
16 Long life is in her right hand;
  in her left hand are riches and honor.
17 Her ways are ways of pleasantness,
  and all her paths are peace.
18 She is a tree of life to those who lay hold of her;
  those who hold her fast are called happy.
19 The LORD by wisdom founded the earth;
  by understanding he established the heavens;
20 by his knowledge the deeps broke forth,
  and the clouds drop down the dew.

A hymnic style marks these verses. They have no personal address nor make any demands, though their objective is to instruct and recommend wisdom. They are much like the wisdom psalms (e.g., Psalms 37; 49; 73; 112). The man who enjoys the benefits of wisdom is praised in vv. 13–18. He is better off than the man who gains silver and gold (v. 14). A considerable degree of personification of wisdom appears in vv. 15–18. Three pictures of wisdom are framed to present her incomparable worth. (a) She is like a goddess who holds a symbol of life in one hand and a symbol of wealth and honor in the other (Kayatz, p. 105). (b) She is a good guide who leads those who follow her along pleasant and peaceful paths. (c) *She is a tree of life* for those who grasp her (cf. Gen. 2:9; Prov. 11:30; 13:12). The tree or vine is frequently a symbol of life (e.g., John 15:1–11).

The Lord by wisdom founded the earth. Again, wisdom is either personified or semi-personified. Vv. 19–20 presuppose some degree of independent existence of wisdom, an existence which antidates the universe.

5. Keeping Sound Wisdom (3:21–35)

(1) The Security of Wisdom (3:21–26)

21 My son, keep sound wisdom and discretion;
   let them not escape from your sight,
22 and they will be life for your soul
   and adornment for your neck.
23 Then you will walk on your way securely
   and your foot will not stumble.
24 If you sit down, you will not be afraid;
   when you lie down, your sleep will be sweet.
25 Do not be afraid of sudden panic,
   or of the ruin of the wicked, when it comes;
26 for the LORD will be your confidence
   and will keep your foot from being caught.

In vv. 21–24 the main thrust is the security which wisdom gives. *Sound wisdom* (cf. 2:7) and *discretion* (cf. 1:4) require constant attention. The disciple must keep them under constant guard. The verb for *escape* means to slip away or run away. These abilities must receive constant attention; but this attention results in life and security for the man who gives it. Verses 23–24 set forth the safety of such a man and are reminiscent of Psalm 91 and Job 7:13–15.

Verses 25–26 continue the theme of security in vv. 21–24 and ground it in confidence in Yahweh. Yahweh will keep the disciple from falling into dangerous places or snares. He need not fear the sudden terror and destruction which will overtake the wicked.

(2) On Being a Good Neighbor (3:27–35)

27 Do not withhold good from those to whom it is due,
   when it is in your power to do it.
28 Do not say to your neighbor, "Go, and come again,
   tomorrow I will give it"—when you have it with you.
29 Do not plan evil against your neighbor
   who dwells trustingly beside you.
30 Do not contend with a man for no reason,
   when he has done you no harm.
31 Do not envy a man of violence
   and do not choose any of his ways;
32 for the perverse man is an abomination to the LORD,
   but the upright are in his confidence.
33 The LORD's curse is on the house of the wicked,
   but he blesses the abode of the righteous.
34 Toward the scorners he is scornful,
   but to the humble he shows favor.
35 The wise will inherit honor,
   but fools get disgrace.

These verses have little or no direct relationship with vv. 21–26. Of course, they do illustrate one of the major ways in which sound wisdom and discretion are exercised; and the motivation clauses in vv. 33–35 are Yahwistic as in vv. 25–26. The character of a good neighbor is expressed in a series of commandments in vv. 27–31. The good neighbor meets his obligations, does not take advantage of an unsuspecting neighbor, does not stir up trouble with a man who has done him no harm, and does not envy the man who gets his own way by violent means.

The motivation for such behavior is not just an appeal to enlightened self-interest and human decency, but is based on Yahweh's attitude and action in vv. 32–35. The *perverse man* (crooked, devious, underhanded) is not acceptable to Yahweh. He is an *abomination to the Lord*. This expression is found several times in Proverbs in different contexts (6:16; 11:1,20; 12:22, etc.). However, besides its use in Proverbs, the expression is used in Deuteronomy (7:25–26; 14:3; 18:9, etc.) referring to exclusive cult devotion to Yahweh, i.e., as to purity and faithfulness in worship. In Proverbs it is related to ethical and social flaws in the conduct of men (McKane, p. 301).

The perverse man is an abomination to Yahweh, but the *upright are in his confidence*. The word translated "confidence" is ṣod, which carries connotations of fellowship, status, and unity. As Gemser remarks, "There is no greater honor for a man than to belong to the ṣod of Yahweh" (p. 32).

6. A Teacher's Instructions in Three Parts (4:1–27)

In contrast to chapter 3, chapter 4 has very little Yahwistic emphasis. It contains instruction in the pattern of general wisdom teaching. The authority is that of the discipline (*musar*) of the teacher.

(1) Wisdom from Generation to Generation (4:1–9)

¹ Hear, O sons, a father's instruction,
    and be attentive, that you may gain insight;
² for I give you good precepts:
    do not forsake my teaching.
³ When I was a son with my father,
    tender, the only one in the sight of my mother,
⁴ he taught me, and said to me,
"Let your heart hold fast my words;
    keep my commandments, and live;
⁵ do not forget, and do not turn away from the words of my mouth.
Get wisdom; get insight.
⁶ Do not forsake her, and she will keep you;
    love her, and she will guard you.
⁷ The beginning of wisdom is this: Get wisdom,
    and whatever you get, get insight.
⁸ Prize her highly, and she will exalt you;
    she will honor you if you embrace her.
⁹ She will place on your head a fair garland;
    she will bestow on you a beautiful crown."

The teacher addresses the students (sons) in vv. 1–5 and gives a fundamental basis for wisdom teaching. It is unlikely that we should think of a family context with a father addressing his sons—though this is not impossible. The plural *sons* indicates students. However, we should remember that the teacher-student relationship was modeled after the parent-child relationship. The teacher acted *in loco parentis*.

The basis for the teacher's authority in this context is the teaching he received from his father and mother (vv. 3–4). The teacher transits the teaching which he has earned from the past generation. He demands receptivity, attention, and obedience. He does not appeal to any authority beyond his own experience and the inherent quality of his teaching (v. 2). The teacher shows his personal involvement in

my teaching (*torah*). He has made what he received his own.

In vv. 5–9 the teacher exhorts his students to *get wisdom; get insight* (the lines should not be reversed as in RSV) and extols the rewards of wisdom. The emphasis in these verses falls on *get*. The verb in this context means acquire or bring into your possession—probably without regard for cost. The "get" is strengthened by *prize her highly* and *embrace her*. Some commentators (e.g., Ringgren) see the picture here as that of a bride or lover who should be embraced and kept (in contrast to the strange woman, cf. 2:16). The *fair garland* and *beautiful crown* are thought to refer to wedding customs, ornaments which the bride places on the bridegroom. But these adornments are more likely to belong to festival occasions (so Gemser, p. 33, who cites Isa. 28:1–6; 61:3,10; Ezek. 23:42; 16:12, Wisd. of Sol. 2:7–8); and McKane is probably correct in arguing that the picture is that of a lofty patron who cares for her protege and expects continual loyalty and admiration from him in return (p. 306).

(2) The Ways of Dawn and Deep Darkness (4:10–19)

¹⁰ Hear, my son, and accept my words,
    that the years of your life may be many.
¹¹ I have taught you the way of wisdom;
    I have led you in the paths of uprightness.
¹² When you walk, your step will not be hampered;
    and if you run, you will not stumble.
¹³ Keep hold of instruction, do not let go;
    guard her, for she is your life.
¹⁴ Do not enter the path of the wicked,
    and do not walk in the way of evil men.
¹⁵ Avoid it; do not go on it;
    turn away from it and pass on.
¹⁶ For they cannot sleep unless they have done wrong;
    they are robbed of sleep unless they have made some one stumble.
¹⁷ For they eat the bread of wickedness
    and drink the wine of violence.
¹⁸ But the path of the righteous is like the light of dawn,
    which shines brighter and brighter until full day.
¹⁹ The way of the wicked is like deep darkness;
    they do not know over what they stumble.

The key idea in this section is that of way: the *way of wisdom* and the *way of evil men* or parallel words like *path.* The two ways are contrasted in vv. 18–19. The path of the righteous becomes brighter and brighter, like the dawning day which continues to increase in light until noon (Psalm 97:11; Job 11:17; Isa. 58:8). But the way of the wicked is *like deep darkness* (the thick darkness which covered the Egyptians at the Exodus: Ex. 10:21–22; Deut. 28:28–29) in which they cannot avoid stumbling and falling. The *way* in this context refers to the way of life of the individual person, rather than to the way of Israel or the people of Yahweh (as in Deut. 8; see Scott, p. 51).

(3) On the Discipline of the Whole Person (4:20–27)

20 My son, be attentive to my words;
  incline your ear to my sayings.
21 Let them not escape from your sight;
  keep them within your heart.
22 For they are life to him who finds them,
  and healing to all his flesh.
23 Keep your heart with all vigilance;
  for from it flow the springs of life.
24 Put away from you crooked speech,
  and put devious talk far from you.
25 Let your eyes look directly forward,
  and your gaze be straight before you.
26 Take heed to the path of your feet,
  then all your ways will be sure.
27 Do not swerve to the right or to the left;
  turn your foot away from evil.

This discourse is put together around the idea of discipline of the heart, mouth, eyes, and feet. The *heart* is not primarily the symbol of emotion, though emotion is not excluded, but of thought, of the mind and will of the inner person. The heart must be guarded closely because it is the central source and controlling factor in life. The mouth must be disciplined in harmony with the heart. Likewise, the eyes and feet must be kept straight so that there is no deviation. The concern of the wise men for the whole person is made clear in these verses. The wisdom teachers were interested in educating a man to be the right kind of person to move "straight ahead" through life.

7. Instruction About Sexual Behavior (5:1–23)

The fifth chapter is concerned with a familiar theme in the wisdom literature, Israelite and international, namely, the danger of sexual affairs. The young man is warned in a "robust man-to-man" (McKane, p. 312) fashion of the bitter consequences of illicit relationships and encouraged by a graphic and enticing portrayal of the joys of sex at home with his own wife. Appeal is made directly to personal self-interest.

(1) Watch Out for the Strange Woman (5:1–14)

1 My son, be attentive to my wisdom,
  incline your ear to my understanding;
2 that you may keep discretion,
  and your lips may guard knowledge.
3 For the lips of a loose woman drip honey,
  and her speech is smoother than oil;
4 but in the end she is bitter as wormwood,
  sharp as a two-edged sword.
5 Her feet go down to death;
  her steps follow the path to Sheol;
6 she does not take heed to the path of life;
  her ways wander, and she does not know it.
7 And now, O sons, listen to me,
  and do not depart from the words of my mouth.
8 Keep your way far from her,
  and do not go near the door of her house;
9 lest you give your honor to others
  and your years to the merciless;
10 lest strangers take their fill of your strength,
  and your labors go to the house of an alien;
11 and at the end of your life you groan,
  when your flesh and body are consumed,
12 and you say, "How I hated discipline,
  and my heart despised reproof!
13 I did not listen to the voice of my teachers
  or incline my ear to my instructors.
14 I was at the point of utter ruin
  in the assembled congregation."

The danger of the *loose woman* (see 2:16, marg., "strange woman"; also see comment on 2:16–19) is described in vv. 1–6. She is extremely seductive, with lips that *drip honey* and utter seductively smooth speech. Her "strangeness" or "looseness" itself makes her exciting and tempting. She presents the young man—indeed, any man with a powerful sexual attraction.

But the warning is designed to dull her seductive appeal. The end result of yielding to her is *bitter as wormwood* and *sharp as a two-edged sword*. The sweetness of her lips turns into the terrible bitter taste of wormwood. The man who goes after her need expect no mercy. Her mouth, so soft and smooth in the seduction, becomes like the sharp edges of a sword. A man will find that she does not deal in mercy—and he deserves none if he is so foolish as to try to use her to satisfy his own sexual desires. She follows the way which leads to death; her wanderings ignore the road of life. The "strange woman" seems to offer a man the luxuries of sensual joy without the responsibility and commitments of marriage. But he will find that this is a snare. The irony of the matter is that her whole way of life, including the way she deals with men, is characterized by total irresponsibility (so v. 6b; cf. NEB, "her course turns this way and that, and what does she care?")

The method recommended for avoiding the seduction of the "strange woman" is found in vv. 7–8, viz., keep away from her. "Don't get near the door of her house!" The wise men knew that a man should never test his discipline by submitting it to unnecessary temptation!

The warnings in vv. 9–14 are generally clear, but there are some uncertain details. The "son" who gets too near the woman will suffer the loss of his *honor,* money, and hard-earned gains to strangers. When he is reduced to a miserable condition, he will recall with anguished remorse how he spurned the discipline of his teachers. The *strangers* probably refer to the woman and her associates, who are non-Israelites or at least alien to the normal circles of life in the community. The *merciless* is singular in the text (the cruel one) and probably refers to this woman, who is like the goddess Ishtar in her merciless treatment of her lovers. The *at the end of your life* is over-translated. The word is parallel

to *but in the end* of v. 4 and should be understood in the sense of "end result."

The *assembled congregation* can refer to a legal hearing by the community in which the penalty for adultery is about to be inflicted on the guilty party—apparently not here the death penalty as in Deuteronomy 22:22 and Leviticus 20:10 (but perhaps some form of physical punishment as in Prov. 6:33). Ex-communication, disgrace, and the confiscation of property may have been involved.

(2) Love Your Own Wife (5:15–20)

15 Drink water from your own cistern,
    flowing water from your own well.
16 Should your springs be scattered abroad,
    streams of water in the streets?
17 Let them be for yourself alone,
    and not for strangers with you.
18 Let your fountain be blessed,
    and rejoice in the wife of your youth,
19   a lively hind, a graceful doe.
    Let her affection fill you at all times with
        delight,
    be infatuated always with her love.
20 Why should you be infatuated, my son,
        with a loose woman
    and embrace the bosom of an adventuress?

The joys of sex at home with one's own wife are set in contrast with the bitter and disastrous results of loving a "strange woman." The meaning of v. 15 is that sexual intercourse should be had with one's own wife. The interpretation of the imagery in vv. 16–17 has been the subject of some debate. But assuredly they admonish against sexual intercourse with *strangers* (cf. Ecclus. 26:19–21). The sexual pleasures of a wife are commended in vv. 18–19. As Rylaarsdam (p. 33) notes "These verses eulogize the sensuous enjoyment of marriage in a wholesome and uninhibited manner . . ." The key word in vv. 19–20 is *infatuated.* There is an infatuation which is healthy and desirable; but such passionate attraction should not be given to a *loose woman.*

(3) Remember That God Sees All (5:21–23)

21 For a man's ways are before the eyes of the
        LORD,
    and he watches all his paths.

22 The iniquities of the wicked ensnare him,
　　and he is caught in the toils of his sin.
23 He dies for lack of discipline,
　　and because of his great folly he is lost.

An additional motivation is given for right behavior: Yahweh sees all. A man may think his sexual behavior is hidden; and it may be from human observation. But God sees all (15:3,11; 24:12), and he allows the wicked to be ensnared by their own iniquities. The wicked person becomes bound in the *toils* (ropes) of his sin. He will die because of a *lack of discipline*. He will be *lost* because of his folly. The verb for lost is the same as "infatuated" in vv. 19–20; but the parallelism seems to call for some such meaning as perish (Toy, p. 117) or carried away (Gemser, p. 36). McKane (p. 313), following G. R. Driver, thinks in terms of the wrapping of a corpse in a shroud—the shroud in this case is *his great folly*. This interpretation is reflected by the NEB translation: "wrapped in the shroud of his boundless folly."

8. Lessons on Economics and Social Behavior (6:1–19)

(1) Against Dealing with a Moneylender (6:1–5)

1 My son, if you have become surety for your neighbor,
　　have given your pledge for a stranger;
2 if you are snared in the utterance of your lips,
　　caught in the words of your mouth;
3 then do this, my son, and save yourself,
　　for you have come into your neighbor's power:
　　go, hasten, and importune your neighbor.
4 Give your eyes no sleep
　　and your eyelids no slumber;
5 save yourself like a gazelle from the hunter,
　　like a bird from the hand of the fowler.

The warning against becoming *surety* is repeated several times in Proverbs (11:15; 20:16; 22:26; 27:13), but the exact situation which the teacher has in mind in this context is difficult to ascertain. It seems unlikely that these strong admonitions are directed toward ordinary moneylending among members of the community—though that can be a major problem and may not be excluded entirely. The *stranger*

is an outsider, either Israelite or (probably) foreign. The *neighbor* may be a moneylender or broker whose business is that of working out financial deals of various sorts. Pledge giving and taking was common commercial practice in the ancient world (cf. Gen. 38:17–20; Ex. 22:26; Neh. 5:3).

In any case, it is clear that the complicated arrangements of finance and business must be treated with great caution and gotten out of as quickly as possible (vv. 2–5). If a man finds himself in such a relationship, he should make every effort to free himself, for he is as vulnerable as a gazelle is to a hunter and a bird to a fowler. This is no situation for allowing pride to interfere, and there must be no rest until freedom is gained. No legal means existed to free a man from a commitment sealed by an oath (cf. Num. 30:2). There were no bankruptcy laws to protect debtors. He could only *importune* (Scott's word is "pester," p. 56) his *neighbor* until a release was granted.

It should be remembered that the risks involved in the inability to meet financial obligations were great (Scott, p. 58). Terrible poverty and slavery could and did result from indebtedness (20:16; Gen. 44:32–33; 2 Kings 4:1). Financial involvements with foreigners increased the dangers, because such transactions were conducted with less personal concern than among Israelites (cf. Deut. 15:2–3).

(2) The Ant as a Model (6:6–11)

6 Go to the ant, O sluggard;
　　consider her ways, and be wise.
7 Without having any chief,
　　officer or ruler,
8 she prepares her food in summer,
　　and gathers her sustenance in harvest.
9 How long will you lie there, O sluggard?
　　When will you arise from your sleep?
10 A little sleep, a little slumber,
　　a little folding of the hands to rest,
11 and poverty will come upon you like a vagabond,
　　and want like an armed man.

In these verses the ant is presented as a model of self-discipline and industrious work. McKane (p. 323, quoting from

W. M. Thomson, *The Land and the Book,*
p. 509) notes that the sages chose to call
attention to the best side of the ant! They
did not note that it can retaliate with painful bites and be quite destructive. The ant
appears again only in 30:24–28. But it is
used in a Canaanite proverb from the
Amarna Letters.

The ant is the model for a wise man
because, first, she has foresight to plan at
harvest time for the winter months. One
of the prime virtues of a wise man was
alertness to the future and the ability to
anticipate. The fool is caught by surprise;
the wise man is prepared. Second, the
ant seems to work without the imposition
of a command by someone in authority.
She works by personal choice because it is
a part of her character. The wisdom
teachers wanted to develop the kind of
man who would do the right things without having to be told to do them. They
wanted to develop the attributes and habits in the student which would make him
the right kind of person—a wise man.

Verses 9–11 are aimed at the sluggard
who loves his sleep so well that he allows
poverty and want to overtake him, either
like a *vagabond* and an *armed man* as in
the RSV; or, more probably, like a va-
grant and a beggar who take advantage of
their victims without being restrained by
ethical considerations.

(3) The Troublemaker (6:12–15)

12 A worthless person, a wicked man,
　　goes about with crooked speech,
13 winks with his eyes, scrapes with his feet,
　　points with his finger,
14 with perverted heart devises evil,
　　continually sowing discord;
15 therefore calamity will come upon him
　　suddenly;
　　in a moment he will be broken beyond
　　healing.

These verses need little comment,
though some of the details of translation
are debatable. The person described is a
model of the kind of person the wisdom
teachers did not want to result from their
teaching: indirect, malicious, perverted, *a*

worthless person, a wicked man. He is the
wrong kind of man who constantly produces confusion and trouble in society.
He is headed for sudden disaster.

(4) Seven Types of Anti-social Behavior (6:16–19)

16 There are six things which the LORD hates,
　　seven which are an abomination to him:
17 haughty eyes, a lying tongue,
　　and hands that shed innocent blood,
18 a heart that devises wicked plans,
　　feet that make haste to run to evil,
19 a false witness who breathes out lies,
　　and a man who sows discord among
　　brothers.

These verses are an example of what is
called a "graded numerical saying." [2] The
picture is, as in vv. 12–15, that of an undesirable type of person who *sows discord
among brothers* and who gives evidence
of a "deepseated malevolence tantamount
to a total incapacity for neighborliness"
(McKane, p. 326). The bad personal
qualities of a man (note that five of the
sayings are concerned with parts of the
body, vv. 16–18) make him a false witness
(especially dangerous in legal proceedings) and a sower of dissension.

9. The Folly of Adultery (6:20–35)

20 My son, keep your father's commandment,
　　and forsake not your mother's teaching.
21 Bind them upon your heart always;
　　tie them about your neck.
22 When you walk, they will lead you;
　　when you lie down, they will watch over
　　you;
　　and when you awake, they will talk with
　　you.
23 For the commandment is a lamp and the
　　teaching a light,
　　and the reproofs of discipline are the way
　　of life,
24 to preserve you from the evil woman,
　　from the smooth tongue of the adven-
　　turess.
25 Do not desire her beauty in your heart,
　　and do not let her capture you with her
　　eyelashes;
26 for a harlot may be hired for a loaf of bread,
　　but an adulteress stalks a man's very life.
27 Can a man carry fire in his bosom

---

2 See W. M. W. Roth, *Numerical Sayings in the
Old Testament* "Supplements to Vetus Testamentum,"
Vol. XIII (Leiden: E. J. Brill, 1965), p. 86.

and his clothes not be burned?
28 Or can one walk upon hot coals
      and his feet not be scorched?
29 So is he who goes in to his neighbor's wife;
      none who touches her will go unpunished.
30 Do not men despise a thief if he steals
      to satisfy his appetite when he is hungry?
31 And if he is caught, he will pay sevenfold;
      he will give all the goods of his house.
32 He who commits adultery has no sense;
      he who does it destroys himself.
33 Wounds and dishonor will he get,
      and his disgrace will not be wiped away.
34 For jealousy makes a man furious,
      and he will not spare when he takes
      revenge.
35 He will accept no compensation,
      nor be appeased though you multiply
      gifts.

The opening verses of this section (vv. 20–22) read as if they have been adapted from Deuteronomy 11:19 and 6:7, and this is a feasible conclusion; though it is also possible that Deuteronomy borrowed from the wisdom teaching. However, the context of parental instruction in Deuteronomy is most likely continued only in the formal language of v. 20. The instruction of the wise men is a repetition and development of the teaching of the parents (see 1:8; 4:1). The *commandment* and *teaching* should be highly treasured by the student. He should wear them over his heart like an expensive locket or signet ring which hangs from a necklace (cf. 4:9; 7:3). They will be for him like a loyal companion who is always with him, guiding him as he walks, guarding him as he sleeps, and conversing with him when he wakes in the morning. The functions of the commandment and teaching are those of the Mosaic *torah* in Deuteronomy 6:6–9 (cf. Gemser, p. 4).

Teaching so closely and constantly kept will guard a man *from the evil woman* and *from the smooth tongue of the adventuress.* By a small vowel change (in the Heb.) the reading will agree with the LXX: "another's wife" or a "neighbor's wife" rather than "evil woman." Verse 25 is a warning against her seductive and sexually exciting appearance and mannerisms.

Verse 26 continues the warning by citing the consequences of yielding to her—though the exact meaning of this verse is difficult to fix. The RSV represents the interpretation that sexual intercourse with an adulteress is far more dangerous and expensive than with a harlot, who is content with a price while the adulteress *stalks a man's very life*—perhaps meaning that she can make such costly demands upon him that he will come to extreme poverty and disgrace. But it is equally likely that v. 26b should read "but an adulteress stalks a man of means," i.e., a man who has money and who will be able to provide the things she wants (See McKane, pp. 329–30). A young man from the upper strata of social and economic life (as most of the wisdom students must have been) would be prime prey for such a woman.

A man can no more expect to escape the consequences of sexual intercourse with a married woman than he can carry fire in his clothes without being burned or walk on hot coals without scorching his feet (vv. 27–29). Adultery is like playing with fire. It is more dangerous and costly than burglary. If the thief is caught, regardless of his motivation, he will have to pay a heavy penalty (*sevenfold* goes beyond the requirements in Ex. 22:1–7) even if it requires *all the goods of his house.* The man who commits adultery *has no sense* ("is a senseless fool," NEB), because he destroys himself and has no hope of getting out of the penalty by the payment of money (vv. 32–35). The adulterer will have to deal with an angry husband (and probably an angry community; v. 33 may refer to public scourging) who cannot be bought off because of his jealous rage. A loss by theft may be settled by the restitution of property, but adultery involves an irreparable loss. A man cannot buy his way out of such a situation.

The sexual ethic of the wise men may be disappointing to some. There are no appeals to high idealism and lofty standards of behavior. These teachers are pragmatic and realistic. Their admonitions are aimed directly at self-interest and personal welfare. Ethical idealism has its proper place in dealing with sexual behavior; but as a practical matter it is far more likely that the thought of painful confrontation with a powerful husband (the "man" in v. 34 is *geber*, a word which denotes strength and power) is a more effective deterrent to adultery than a treatise on marriage! Few motivations are more powerful than self-interest. It must be added, however, that we should look at the pragmatic sexual ethic of Proverbs in the light of the Christian gospel, which requires self-control under the lordship of Christ and through the strength of Christ.

10. Instruction on the Seductive Power of the Strange Woman (7:1–27)

(1) The Preventive Power of Commandments and Wisdom (7:1–5)

1 My son, keep my words
　　and treasure up my commandments with you;
2 keep my commandments and live,
　　keep my teachings as the apple of your eye;
3 bind them on your fingers,
　　write them on the tablet of your heart.
4 Say to wisdom, "You are my sister,"
　　and call insight your intimate friend;
5 to preserve you from the loose woman,
　　from the adventuress with her smooth words.

The wisdom teacher asserts his authority with his *words, commandments,* and *teachings* (*torah*). These are the terms used to designate the authoritative, and even mandatory, nature of the wisdom teaching. They are words shared by the wisdom literature with the Pentateuch, Prophets, and Psalms. The verbs in vv. 1–3 are strong and active, asking for concentration and retention on the part of the student (McKane, p. 332). A vivid expression is found in *keep my teachings as the apple of your eye* (lit., "as the little man of your eye," i.e., the pupil). The pupil is the light of the eye and very precious. If it is damaged, one must live in darkness. Likewise the teaching of the wise

man as the light of the eye keeps a person from living in darkness. Both the outer and inner aspects of wisdom teaching are emphasized in v. 3.

Bind them on your fingers (cf. Deut. 6:4–8) is a way of saying that the commandments and teachings should be always in sight—perhaps, like a signet ring or an amulet ring against evil influences. At the same time the commandments and teachings are to be written *on the tablet of your heart.* The wisdom teaching is not designed, basically, as a deposit of external, arbitrary traditions and counsels to which appeal can be made in a mechanical kind of way. The wise man is the one who has assimilated the traditions and teachings until they have become a component of his inner being, his "heart." Their presence on his finger is a symbol and reminder of their presence in his heart.

Wisdom is personified and offered as an alternative to the *loose woman* in vv. 4–5. The student is exhorted to say to Wisdom: *You are my sister.* This is almost certainly a form of address which means bride or wife (see Song of Sol. 4:9–12; 5:1–2; Ecclus. 15:2). However, *intimate friend* appears to mean relative or kinsman (as in Ruth 2:1; 3:2). The "relative" was the male kinsman on whom members of a family group could depend for protection. Rylaarsdam (p. 38) is probably correct when he says that the parallelism of the verse is not that of "sister" and "intimate friend" but that of "wisdom" and "insight." Wisdom is like a good wife, and insight is like a strong relative *to preserve* (protect) a man from the "loose woman."

(2) A Young Man Snared by Seduction (7:6–23)

6 For at the window of my house
　　I have looked out through my lattice,
7 and I have seen among the simple,
　　I have perceived among the youths,
　　a young man without sense,
8 passing along the street near her corner,
　　taking the road to her house
9 in the twilight, in the evening,
　　at the time of night and darkness.
10 And lo, a woman meets him,

dressed as a harlot, wily of heart.
11 She is loud and wayward,
    her feet do not stay at home;
12 now in the street, now in the market,
    and at every corner she lies in wait.
13 She seizes him and kisses him,
    and with impudent face she says to him:
14 "I had to offer sacrifices,
    and today I have paid my vows;
15 so now I have come out to meet you,
    to seek you eagerly, and I have found
    you.
16 I have decked my couch with coverings,
    colored spreads of Egyptian linen;
17 I have perfumed my bed with myrrh,
    aloes, and cinnamon.
18 Come, let us take our fill of love till morn-
    ing;
    let us delight ourselves with love.
19 For my husband is not at home;
    he has gone on a long journey;
20 he took a bag of money with him;
    at full moon he will come home."
21 With much seductive speech she persuades
    him;
    with her smooth talk she compels him.
22 All at once he follows her,
    as an ox goes to the slaughter,
    or as a stag is caught fast
23 till an arrow pierces its entrails;
    as a bird rushes into a snare;
    he does not know that it will cost him
    his life.

This section is more nearly narrative than Instruction proper. The imperatives and conditional clauses are absent. But the passage is didactic in a descriptive way and is an extensive example of the model (in this case negative) used to add color and vividness to the normally straightforward language of the Instruction genre (note the models in 6:6–19). It is put in the form of a testimony of a dramatic experience. The wisdom teacher draws a verbal scene for his students which they will not forget. This is truly "audiovisual" teaching!

Little explication of this section is needed beyond a good translation, except at a few points. One such matter is the fact that the Masoretic Text makes the speaker to be the wisdom teacher (or possibly Wisdom personified). The LXX rendering of v. 6a makes the woman, not the wisdom teacher, the one who looks out

of the window. Some scholarly opinion to the contrary, there is no major reason for changing the reading of the text. The wisdom teacher, a trained observer of human life, tells how he glanced out of the window of his house and saw the scene which he describes.

A young, immature man, one of *the simple*, encounters a woman who uses all her sexual skills to seduce him (vv. 9–20). She is a woman who lives "at fever temperature" (McKane, p. 336). She is bold in action and invitation. She has prepared her bed for a night of love-making, and she promises security from interference by her husband because he is away from home.

The attempt to determine the exact meaning of vv. 14–15 produces division of opinions among commentators. Boström thinks that the portrayal is that of a devotee to a fertility cult whose cultic obligations include a vow to have sexual intercourse to supplement her sacrifices (translating v. 14b in the present tense, "Today I am to fulfil my vows"). The need to keep her sexual vow becomes the reason for her seeking out the man.

Boström's interpretation may provide the correct background for vv. 14–15. However, McKane (pp. 338–340) is wise in refusing to accept Boström's entire case. Verses 16–20 suggest that the woman is the wife of a well-to-do merchant, probably a foreigner, who travels away from home for long periods on business. Thus, she is a foreign woman, or at least not a native of the town where she lives, probably a devotee of an Astarte cult, passionate, lonely, restless, and careless with her reputation. The wisdom teachers were concerned with the threat of this kind of woman for two reasons. (1) She was a religious threat because of her connections and practice with fertility cults. (2) She was the most dangerous sexual threat a young man could encounter. She was not the ordinary prostitute whose services could be bought with a modest price (as in 6:26), for she had little need for money (note the expensive and foreign furnishings in vv. 16–17). The combination of sexual passion and religion with freedom of action makes her the paradigm of the seductive and promiscuous woman.

The young man yields to her seduction (vv. 21–22) and goes with her. But he goes like an ox to the slaughter; like an animal tied to a stake to be killed; like a bird hopelessly caught in a trap: *he does not know that it will cost him his life.* Rylaarsdam (p. 41) comments aptly that this can mean that the husband will return and kill the offenders (man and woman), or have others, who are legally appointed to do so, to kill them. But this is not the only way that the capitulation to such a woman will cost his life. The real strength and true quality of a man's character will be lost. He will be a man who has given the vital actions of his life over to forces beyond his control, over to wickedness that corrupts and ruins.

(3) The Chambers of Death (7:24–27)

24 And now, O sons, listen to me,
       and be attentive to the words of my
       mouth.
25 Let not your heart turn aside to her ways,
       do not stray into her paths;
26 for many a victim has she laid low;
       yea, all her slain are a mighty host.
27 Her house is the way to Sheol,
       going down to the chambers of death.

This is a short exhortation and warning which concludes the discourse and refers back to the woman in vv. 6–23. The student is admonished: *Let not your heart turn aside to her ways.* The wisdom teachers were much concerned with the "heart" (mind or will) because the basic decisions which control a man's actions are made here (note that heart occurs in 1:1,3,5; 4:4,21,23; 6:14,18,21; 7:3,23). Their optimism is revealed in their confidence that a man *can* make the decisions required and must be held responsible for them— or for the lack of them.

The house of the woman is not a place of festal joy and love-making (as she describes it in vv. 14–20), but a place of death where *many a victim has she laid low.* Her house is the point of convergence for the roads that lead to Sheol and the halls of death (see 5:5; 9:18; Ezek. 32:27; Isa. 14:15–16). A man cannot hope to return from that place.

11. The Preaching of Wisdom (8:1–36)

The nature and significance of the figure of Wisdom has been discussed in the Introduction and the relevant sections should be consulted with the study of this chapter.

(1) The Call of Wisdom (8:1–5)

1 Does not wisdom call,
       does not understanding raise her voice?
2 On the heights beside the way,
       in the paths she takes her stand;
3 beside the gates in front of the town,
       at the entrance of the portals she cries
       aloud:
4 "To you, O men, I call,
       and my cry is to the sons of men.
5 O simple ones, learn prudence;
       O foolish men, pay attention.

The locus of Wisdom's preaching and the people to whom she addresses her message are the subjects of these verses. Unlike the woman in 7:6–23, Wisdom does not speak in a seductive voice under the cover of twilight (Gemser, p. 47). She speaks clearly and freely in public places where she can be heard by all who will listen. And she does not reserve her message for a select audience of the learned and faithful. She works at the intersections and gate areas of the town, where the people are engaged in business, legal proceedings, and social life. Like a street preacher she seeks to gather around her an audience to hear her message—*she takes her stand.* Wisdom goes into the midst of the teeming activity of urban life to give her message.

The audience she seeks is both broad and narrow (vv. 4–5). On the one hand, she appeals to men in general; but, on the other hand, she particularly addresses the *simple ones* and *foolish men.* These are the young men who lack the maturity and the ability to make wise decisions.

They are untutored; but they are potential wise men, who may be lost forever if they do not hear and heed the message of Wisdom before their ways of life have been warped and ruined by the world.

(2) The Worth of Wisdom (8:6–11)

6 Hear, for I will speak noble things,
  and from my lips will come what is right;
7 for my mouth will utter truth;
  wickedness is an abomination to my lips.
8 All the words of my mouth are righteous;
  there is nothing twisted or crooked in them.
9 They are all straight to him who understands
  and right to those who find knowledge.
10 Take my instruction instead of silver,
  and knowledge rather than choice gold;
11 for wisdom is better than jewels,
  and all that you may desire cannot compare with her.

Wisdom proposes to speak words to those who will listen, words which are more valuable than *silver* and *gold* or *costly jewels.* The emphasis in vv. 6–9 is on the straightness and rightness of Wisdom's speaking. Her words do not twist and turn. The hearer need not fear ambiguity, lack of integrity, and hyper subtlety. *They are all straight to him who understands.* Toy (p. 163), followed by Gemser (p. 47), argues that v. 9 is an appeal to the moral consciousness of men and a recognition of the insight of conscience (an appeal which is rare in the Old Testament; cf. Ezek. 18:25; it comes into clear expression in later writings: Ecclus. 14:1–2; 37:13–14; Wisd. of Sol. 17). The principle is affirmed that those who receive Wisdom will be able to comprehend her (cf. John 3:21; 7:17; 8:31–32). Involvement is necessary for understanding.

(3) The Power of Wisdom (8:12–16)

12 I, wisdom, dwell in prudence,
  and I find knowledge and discretion.
13 The fear of the LORD is hatred of evil.
  Pride and arrogance and the way of evil and perverted speech I hate.
14 I have counsel and sound wisdom,
  I have insight, I have strength.
15 By me kings reign,
  and rulers decree what is just;

16 by me princes rule,
  and nobles govern the earth.

Wisdom depicts herself as having great power in human affairs. She knows her way about in the world, for she dwells *in prudence* (v. 12, better: "I am Wisdom: I dwell with prudence") and finds *knowledge* and *discretion.* These expressions connote adroitness, shrewdness, and knowledge in worldly matters. Wisdom knows how to get things done in the affairs of men. She is a fully prepared counselor, who is competent to guide men in the art of living. The abilities of Wisdom are those of a competent statesman, who can formulate policies and implement them effectively.

Verse 13 seems to fit the context badly and some commentators have considered it an insertion. It adds a Yahwistic interpretation to Wisdom which is missing in vv. 1–12. The *fear of the Lord* is put in juxtaposition with Wisdom. The verse brings an ethical element to the passage which is lacking in the preceding verses. Further, it is one of the two verses in this chapter in which Wisdom directly links those who follow her to Yahweh (vv. 13, 35). The verse, and its vocabulary (which is very much like that of the prophets), points to Yahwistic reinterpretation of the older wisdom, which was more secular and less directly concerned with the religious aspects of life (McKane, p. 349). Verse 13 blends education and religion together.

Wisdom claims that it is by her power that kings and rulers govern (vv. 14–16). These verses recall the description of the ideal king in Isaiah 11:2 (and of God in Job 12:13; Gemser, p. 47). But the dynamics of the two contexts differ significantly. The Isaiah passage thinks of a king who is endowed with the gifts of the Spirit of Yahweh, while vv. 14–16 think in terms of the less religiously oriented counsel of Wisdom herself.

(4) The Rewards of Wisdom (8:17–21)

17 I love those who love me,
  and those who seek me diligently find me.

¹⁸ Riches and honor are with me,
   enduring wealth and prosperity.
¹⁹ My fruit is better than gold, even fine gold,
   and my yield than choice silver.
²⁰ I walk in the way of righteousness,
   in the paths of justice,
²¹ endowing with wealth those who love me,
   and filling their treasuries.

Wisdom guarantees that she will respond to those who love her. She will not hide herself from those who seek her (those who seek eagerly, like those who look for the dawn). The language is very similar to that found in Deuteronomy 4:29 and Jeremiah 29:12–14, which is used of Yahweh and his presence. Wisdom promises to do for her followers what Yahweh does for his people. Her rewards are exceedingly great and rich. The blessings which she bestows on her adherents are material. But they also include *honor,* righteousness (the RSV translates this *prosperity* in v. 18, but "righteousness" is better), and *justice.* Wisdom offers more than wealth. She offers a well-provided-for and satisfying way of life. She walks *in the way of righteousness, in the paths of justice.* Her greatest reward is a way of life which is right and properly balanced. Rylaarsdam (p. 44) comments that what Wisdom really offers is herself, for she is the embodiment of the presence and action of God. "This is the divine Wisdom; in her, God offers himself to man" (*ibid.*).

(5) The Person of Wisdom (8:22–31)

²² The Lord created me at the beginning of
   his work,
   the first of his acts of old.
²³ Ages ago I was set up,
   at the first, before the beginning of the
   earth.
²⁴ When there were no depths I was brought
   forth,
   when there were no springs abounding
   with water.
²⁵ Before the mountains had been shaped,
   before the hills, I was brought forth;
²⁶ before he had made the earth with its fields,
   or the first of the dust of the world.
²⁷ When he established the heavens, I was
   there,
   when he drew a circle on the face of the
   deep,

²⁸ when he made firm the skies above,
   when he established the fountains of the
   deep,
²⁹ when he assigned to the sea its limit,
   so that the waters might not transgress his
   command,
   when he marked out the foundations of the
   earth,
³⁰ then I was beside him, like a master
   workman;
   and I was daily his delight,
   rejoicing before him always,
³¹ rejoicing in his inhabited world
   and delighting in the sons of men.

Wisdom testifies of her cosmic credentials in this passage. The locus is not the world as in vv. 1–21. It is the cosmos and Wisdom's place in it. The objective in vv. 22–31 is the same as in vv. 1–21, i.e., to commend Wisdom to men and to emphasize her authority and power. But the apologetic presuppositions are different. The basic presupposition of vv. 1–21 is that Wisdom offers men a rewarding, successful, and satisfying way of life in the world. She seeks to summon them from their multiple distractions to a discipleship which offers more than they can achieve in any other way. The basic presupposition of vv. 22–31 is that of the primeval antiquity of Wisdom and of her relationship to Yahweh.

It is unlikely that 8:1–31 is a simple unity. Verses 22–31 represent a further (and probably later) interpretation of Wisdom than that found in 1:20–33 and 8:1–21. This passage (vv. 22–31) is not designed to contradict or correct the earlier passages, but to supplement them with the cosmological aspects of Wisdom.

There are several emphases in the passage. (a) The ancient age of Wisdom is stressed. She has priority in time before anything or anyone in creation except Yahweh. Wisdom was created as *the first of his acts of old.* She was set up *ages ago* and *before the beginning of the earth.* She has temporal priority in existence over the *depths* and the *mountains.* Before the earth and the heavens were made and established, Wisdom was with Yahweh (vv. 26–30). The authority and power of

Wisdom are grounded in antiquity and temporal priority (cf. Ecclus. 1:4; 24:9; Wisd. of Sol. 9:9).

(b) Wisdom is a child of Yahweh. This aspect of Wisdom is present in two regards. First, there is the origin of Wisdom in vv. 22–26. The verb translated *created me* (from the verb *qanah*) in v. 22 has been the subject of considerable discussion. Its most basic meaning seems to be to acquire or to get. It can mean to possess in a general sense without the idea of to create or to make. But the use of the verb in Psalms 139:13 seems meaningless unless some idea of creating or making is understood. The same is true of Ezekiel 8:3, and probably true of Deuteronomy 32:6 (it is harder to demonstrate in Gen. 14:19,22). With this usage and the context in vv. 22–31, it can hardly be doubted that the meaning is either create or beget. The higher probability lies with beget or brought into existence (cf. viewpoint and discussion by Whybray, p. 101). The parallel verbs in vv. 23,24,25 can all be interpreted with reference to giving birth, and none of these verbs is used of the creation otherwise in this passage. The *I was set up* (*nissakti*) of v. 23 has been understood in the sense of installed or enthroned (cf. Psalm 2:6) as of a king. Whybray (*ibid.*) argues that it is more probable that the verb is derived from a root meaning to weave and is used metaphorically of the conception process (as in Psalm 139:13). This meaning goes well with *I was brought forth* of vv. 24–25, which has the connotation of "brought forth in the labor of birth" (as in Deut. 32:18). When this evidence is combined with the use of *qanah* in Genesis 4:1 and the Ugaritic evidence for the use of the verb *gny* to mean procreate,[3] there seems to be good reason for concluding that Wisdom is presented in this passage as a being procreated by Yahweh. It is most probable that ancient Near Eastern mythological concepts—especially the ideas of a "child of a god"

3 G. R. Driver, *Canaanite Myths and Legends*, p. 144; Scott, p. 71.

and the Egyptian *maat* mythology—have colored the language. The status and authority of Wisdom is enhanced by relationship to Yahweh by procreation.

The second aspect of Wisdom as a child of Yahweh is found in vv. 30–31 and the much debated word translated *master workman* (*'amon*). The RSV marginal reading is "little child." The translation "master workman" is linked with the word *'amman* in the Song of Solomon 7:1 (v. 2 in Heb.) and with the Akkadian *ummanu*, "craftsman." The translation "child" supposes the word *'amun* (one who is supported, a protege, ward, etc.). Lamentations 4:5 is appealed to for support. The idea of a child fits well with the context, which describes Wisdom as *rejoicing* (or playing) before Yahweh and *in his inhabited world*. The NEB translation (v. 30) reflects this approach: "Then I was at his side each day, / his darling and delight, / playing in his presence continually, / playing on the earth, . . ."

Other theories link the *'amon* with an original *'omen* which means binding or uniting. This is the view of Scott (p. 72), who thinks that Wisdom is viewed as the principle of coherence and order in the world, the binding link between the Creator and his creation (he cites Ecclus. 43:26; Wisd. of Sol. 1:7; Col. 1:17; Heb. 1:3).

Though scholarly opinion varies, it is best to read the *'amon* as "child" or "ward." Wisdom plays beside Yahweh, and in the world, as his child. She is the playmate of God and man, whose status is unparalleled in the whole creation. Her message to men is grounded in a unique relationship with Yahweh. She represents the joyful presence of Yahweh in the world.

(c) Wisdom is a witness of creation. It is important to note that Wisdom takes no active part in the creation of the world. Repeatedly, we are told that creation was the work of Yahweh. There is no real indication that Wisdom was the agent or the principle by which Yahweh created the earth, contrary to 3:19. A key expression of Wisdom's role in creation is found in v. 27: *I was there*. Wisdom's authority is grounded in her role as a witness to primeval events. The wise men valued personal experience and the ability to give testimony of it to others. Experiential knowledge is one of the hallmarks of Wisdom in and out of Israel. We have seen this emphasis in 4:1–5. It is stressed in the wisdom psalms (e.g., see Psalm 37:25,35–36) and in the speech of Eliphaz (Job 4:7–17). Wisdom is the witness of God par excellence. To the question which Yahweh puts to Job (Job 38:4), Wisdom can answer: *I was there!*

(6) The Admonition of Wisdom (8:32–36)

32 And now, my sons, listen to me:
   happy are those who keep my ways.
33 Hear instruction and be wise,
   and do not neglect it.
34 Happy is the man who listens to me,
   watching daily at my gates,
   waiting beside my doors.
35 For he who finds me finds life
   and obtains favor from the LORD;
36 but he who misses me injures himself;
   all who hate me love death."

In the concluding exhortation Wisdom urges her pupils to heed her message and to keep her ways. A continual vigil outside her doors is encouraged, for whoever finds her finds life *and obtains favor from the Lord*. Wisdom's will and ways are those of Yahweh. The picture in v. 34 is that of a wisdom teacher whose students gather about the doorway of his residence for instruction cf. Ecclus. 14:20–27). Those who miss Wisdom inflict death upon themselves.

12. The Invitations of Wisdom and Folly (9:1–18)

The contrasting invitations of Wisdom and "a foolish woman" (v. 13) constitute the main subject matter of this chapter. The section in vv. 7–12 seems to have no direct connection with the context (Gemser, p. 51). It may be that these verses are intended to emphasize, in indirect manner, the role of Wisdom as a teacher (McKane, p. 360). The simple function of providing

a buffer section between Wisdom and folly should not be ruled out.

(1) The Invitation of Wisdom (9:1–6)

1 Wisdom has built her house,
   she has set up her seven pillars.
2 She has slaughtered her beasts, she has
   mixed her wine,
   she has also set her table.
3 She has sent out her maids to call
   from the highest places in the town,
4 "Whoever is simple, let him turn in here!"
   To him who is without sense she says,
5 "Come, eat of my bread
   and drink of the wine I have mixed.
6 Leave simpleness, and live,
   and walk in the way of insight."

The portrayal of Wisdom is constructed on the model of the woman in 7:6–23, and the women devotees of a goddess of love are in the background (McKane, following Boström, p. 360; see comment on 2:16–19 and ch. 7). However, Wisdom offers life, not death (cf. 7:26–27).

The *seven pillars* of Wisdom's house have given rise to numerous interpretations (Toy, p. 185, lists eleven or more and the number has increased; see also the discussions by Gemser, p. 51; McKane, pp. 364–365; and Albright[4]). In spite of a possible faint reflection here of a temple or shrine and of devotees of the fertility cults, Wisdom is not really a substitute for a goddess, she is the Presence of Yahweh among men, who offers life and the *way of insight* to those who will accept her invitation. Hers is a way of life which gives satisfaction in understanding and effectiveness and which does not degenerate or, by blunder, end in disaster.

(2) The Uselessness of Correcting a Scoffer (9:7–12)

7 He who corrects a scoffer gets himself
   abuse,
   and he who reproves a wicked man in-
   curs injury.
8 Do not reprove a scoffer, or he will hate
   you;
   reprove a wise man, and he will love
   you.

4 "Canaanite-Phoenician Source of Hebrew Wisdom," *Wisdom in Israel and in the Ancient Near East*, pp. 8–9.

9 Give instruction to a wise man, and he will
   be still wiser;
   teach a righteous man and he will increase in learning.
10 The fear of the Lord is the beginning of
   wisdom,
   and the knowledge of the Holy One is
   insight.
11 For by me your days will be multiplied,
   and years will be added to your life.
12 If you are wise, you are wise for yourself;
   if you scoff, you alone will bear it.

Commentators have observed a degree
of pessimism in these verses, and it may be
that their location in this context was determined in part by the desire to tone down
the optimism of vv. 1–6.

In any case, these verses recognize that
there is an incorrigibility in some men. The
wisdom teacher should not waste his time
and energy on those who are unwilling to
receive instruction (see 13:1; 23:9; 27:22;
Ecclus. 22:9–12). There are two classes of
people: the wise man, who is a fearer of
Yahweh, and the scoffer, who is the arrogant and cynical opposite of the wise
man. The wise man can be taught. This is a
basic and desirable characteristic (1:5;
19:25).

Verse 10 (cf. 1:7) emphasizes the Yahwistic element of *wisdom* and *insight*. Religious discipline is needed as well as the
educational discipline of wisdom proper.
The word for *beginning* is different from
that than in 1:7. The word there indicates
more nearly the idea of principal part or
main constituent component. The *t°chillah*
in v. 10 indicates a necessary prerequisite
or qualification—though no absolute distinction can be drawn in the use of the two
words. Wisdom is the speaker in v. 11.
Personal responsibility is stressed in v. 12.
Toy (p. 195) remarks that "the writer has
in mind, however, not a selfish isolation
. . . but the impossibility of vicariousness
in the moral life." Each man experiences
personally the consequences of the conduct
of his life.

(3) The Invitation of Folly (9:13–18)

13 A foolish woman is noisy;
   she is wanton and knows no shame.
14 She sits at the door of her house,
   she takes a seat on the high places of
   the town,
15 calling to those who pass by,
   who are going straight on their way,
16 "Whoever is simple, let him turn in here!"
   And to him who is without sense she
   says,
17 "Stolen water is sweet,
   and bread eaten in secret is pleasant."
18 But he does not know that the dead are
   there,
   that her guests are in the depths of
   Sheol.

In contrast to Wisdom the foolish
woman is presented. Like Wisdom, she has
a *house* (probably the idea of a temple or
shrine is in the background) and gives an
invitation to the *simple* and to the immature who go by her door. She sits at the
door like a sexually passionate and seductive woman and tempts the men who pass
with the pleasures of sexual intercourse
(v. 17; cf. 5:15; 7:18; 30:20). Some contrast between the expensive meal of Wisdom in 9:1–6 and the bread and water of
v. 17 may be intended; but the primary
emphasis is on the nature of the invitation.
Wisdom invites men as a teacher while the
foolish woman invites them as a lover who
wants to use their bodies for her pleasure.
The result is death for those who accept
the invitation (v. 18). Her house is not
only a vestibule of Sheol (see 2:18–19;
7:27), but the realm of death itself; for
the dead are there, and her meal is a death
meal to be eaten with her guests in Sheol
(Gemser, p. 52).

II. The Solomonic Proverb Collections (10:1—22:16)

The collections in this part of the book
are composed largely of wisdom sentences
which have few immediate contexts. Many
of them must be interpreted independently.
However, the atomistic character is dimin-
ished in some sections by various types of
contextual groupings. Such groupings may
be based on content, word play, word association, and mnemonic considerations.
But the groupings are secondary, and the
main burden of exegesis must be borne by
the individual sentences.

1. Collection A (10:1—15:33)

(1) The Wise and the Foolish (10:1-14)

The proverbs of Solomon.

1 A wise son makes a glad father,
   but a foolish son is a sorrow to his mother.
2 Treasures gained by wickedness do not profit,
   but righteousness delivers from death.
3 The LORD does not let the righteous go hungry,
   but he thwarts the craving of the wicked.
4 A slack hand causes poverty,
   but the hand of the diligent makes rich.
5 A son who gathers in summer is prudent,
   but a son who sleeps in harvest brings shame.
6 Blessings are on the head of the righteous,
   but the mouth of the wicked conceals violence.
7 The memory of the righteous is a blessing,
   but the name of the wicked will rot.
8 The wise of heart will heed commandments,
   but a prating fool will come to ruin.
9 He who walks in integrity walks securely,
   but he who perverts his ways will be found out.
10 He who winks the eye causes trouble,
   but he who boldly reproves makes peace.
11 The mouth of the righteous is a fountain of life,
   but the mouth of the wicked conceals violence.
12 Hatred stirs up strife,
   but love covers all offenses.
13 On the lips of him who has understanding wisdom is found,
   but a rod is for the back of him who lacks sense.
14 Wise men lay up knowledge,
   but the babbling of a fool brings ruin near.

Wisdom is necessary for the good life, which parents desire for their children. The awareness that a son is willing to be taught and learn wisdom brings pleasure. A son who rejects discipline and acts like a fool brings sorrow to his parents. For further references to this theme see 15:20; 17:21, 25; 23:24-25; 28:7; 29:3.

Verses 2-3 reflect Yahwistic theology and think in terms of Yahweh enforcing a moral order in relation to the behavior of individuals. Here the will and action of God are primary, while wisdom statements of the ordinary type simply assume that there is an order inherent in existence with which the wise cooperate—perhaps even manipulate to some degree—and which the fool either fails to discern or disregards. The emphasis in sentences of this type is upon the person and his basic approach to life. Few specific actions are mentioned, but a great many generalized statements are made. However, v. 2 is specific to the degree that it passes a judgment on riches gained wrongly. There is no real security in wealth gotten wickedly. It matters how a man acquires his money and property, for they do not properly belong to a man of defective character who cannot match his *treasures* with his *righteousness*. Yahweh will not tolerate such imbalance in a man's life (v. 3). He *thwarts the craving of the wicked*. The wicked lives with unfulfilled ambition; frustrated desires which cannot be brought to fruition.

The wise men seem to have been rather constantly concerned with laziness (see 10:26; 11:16, 29; 12:11, 24, 27; 13:4; 14:23; 26:13-16; etc.). Disciplined and thoughtful application of one's energies was considered very necessary. Poverty is the product of indifferent work. Verse 5 reflects the agricultural harvest time when the entire family was needed in the field or vineyard. A son shows his true quality (or lack of it) in such times. There is a time for sound sleep, but harvest time is not it. The wise man knows his "times" (see Eccl. 3:1-8); the fool is prone to confuse his "times" and sleep when he should be working!

Verses 6-7 contrast the righteous and the wicked, while vv. 8-9 contrast the ways of the wise and the fool. The juxtaposition is probably not accidental. The righteous man is *wise of heart* and *walks in integrity*. He will *heed commandments;* better: "he will receive (or accept) commandments." The "commandment" in this context can be that of the wisdom teacher and/or that of Yahweh. The righteous-wise man receives blessings (v. 6), and he leaves a good reputation behind him when he dies (v. 7). His *memory* will be a blessing to those who come after him. McKane (p. 423) notes that such a man creates something permanent which enriches ongoing life. He moves through life securely without crippling anxiety (v. 9). Verse 6*b* (also in 11*b*, cf. v. 18) is somewhat uncertain in this context, but the meaning seems to be that destructive hostility is hidden behind the speech of the wicked. They are motivated by an aggressiveness which is harmful to others and to themselves.

A contrast is made between the kind of person who causes trouble in the community and the one who contributes to its welfare (vv. 10–14). The man whose speech cannot be taken at face value, because of some manner of secret sign giving, such as winking, is a source of trouble (lit., pain) in society (see 6:12–15; Ecclus. 27: 22–23). Verse 10*b* in the RSV follows the Greek text and makes a better parallel than the Masoretic Text, which repeats v. 8*b*. Frank and honest confrontation makes for *peace* among people. "Peace" is the quality of wholeness and well-being. The speech of a righteous man is healthy for the community; it is a source of "life" which flows forth like the water of a fountain. The parallel in v. 11*b* is better than in v. 6*b*. *Love* conceals acts of transgression in such a way that they do not produce the strife made by *hatred* (cf. 1 Pet. 4:8). The person who loves does not agitate strife and discord. Verses 13 and 14 emphasize the significance of speech. The quality of speech is evident in the results which ensue for the speaker. The speech of a fool gets himself and others into trouble.

(2) The Rich and the Righteous (10:15–22)

15 A rich man's wealth is his strong city;
  the poverty of the poor is their ruin.
16 The wage of the righteous leads to life,
  the gain of the wicked to sin.
17 He who heeds instruction is on the path to life,
  but he who rejects reproof goes astray.
18 He who conceals hatred has lying lips,
  and he who utters slander is a fool.
19 When words are many, transgression is not lacking,

but he who restrains his lips is prudent.
20 The tongue of the righteous is choice silver;
  the mind of the wicked is of little worth.
21 The lips of the righteous feed many,
  but fools die for lack of sense.
22 The blessing of the LORD makes rich,
  and he adds no sorrow with it.

The wise men did not underestimate the power of wealth. A rich man finds protection in his wealth, while the poor are constantly in danger of ruin because of their vulnerability (cf. 19:1–7). Verse 16 has an antithesis between *life* as the *wage* of the righteous and the *gain* of the wicked as *sin*. In its present position, the verse serves to qualify indirectly the statements in v. 15. The *gain* of the wicked man will result in sin, which is equivalent to death, regardless of his wealth. No man—wealthy or poor—can beat this fact of life.

An element of self-discipline is present in each of the sentences in vv. 17–19. Verse 17 is a familiar expression of the importance of *instruction,* i.e., the educational discipline of the wisdom teachers. The RSV involves slight emendation. The Hebrew text translates more naturally: "He who heeds instruction is a path to life [to others], but he who ignores reproof causes to stray [i.e. others]." The self-discipline of v. 18*a* is, however, an undesirable discipline which conceals the deceit and malevolence of a man who is faking his real intentions. The undisciplined slanderer is a *fool.* The teaching of v. 19 is aimed at excessive and careless talk. Scott translates 19*a,* "In too much talk there is sure to be some error." This is good, but the "error" is that of saying something which offends or damages others.

Concern for speech and its power is a frequent occurrence in all wisdom literature. The RSV is clear in vv. 20–21, except that it is possible that *feed* in v. 21*a* (which could be nourish or sustain) could be shepherd, guide or teach (NEB has teach following the Greek reading).

The question in v. 22 is that of the nature of *makes rich.* The RSV reads as if the *blessing* is the wealth which Yahweh gives, i.e., spiritual enrichment. This is possible, but I am inclined to agree with McKane (p. 422), and translate it with the NEB: "The blessing of the Lord brings riches and he sends no sorrow with them." The verse should be linked with 10:2 and interpreted with the idea that the way wealth is gotten is important. If a man wants wealth without sorrow, he must get it by being the kind of man who can receive the blessing of Yahweh. Wealth, in itself, is not a sure index of a man's character or an indication that he is due the respect of his neighbors. The character of the acquisition is fundamental—a truth often forgotten in the present generation.

(3) The Righteous and the Wicked (10: 23–32)

23 It is like sport to a fool to do wrong,
   but wise conduct is pleasure to a man of understanding.
24 What the wicked dreads will come upon him,
   but the desire of the righteous will be granted.
25 When the tempest passes, the wicked is no more,
   but the righteous is established for ever.
26 Like vinegar to the teeth, and smoke to the eyes,
   so is the sluggard to those who send him.
27 The fear of the LORD prolongs life,
   but the years of the wicked will be short.
28 The hope of the righteous ends in gladness,
   but the expectation of the wicked comes to nought.
29 The LORD is a stronghold to him whose way is upright,
   but destruction to evildoers.
30 The righteous will never be removed,
   but the wicked will not dwell in the land.
31 The mouth of the righteous brings forth wisdom,
   but the perverse tongue will be cut off.
32 The lips of the righteous know what is acceptable,
   but the mouth of the wicked, what is perverse.

These sentences are dominated by the contrast between the righteous and the wicked. Extended comment is not required, and the translation is reasonably clear. The NEB reads better than the RSV. *To do wrong* appears to refer to the clever, devious, disrupting behavior of the *fool,* who

finds this kind of conduct easy (because of his character). It is "like laughing" for him. But to the *man of understanding* wisdom is equally easy. He finds pleasure in wisdom because it is compatible with his way of life. Verse 26 is different because of its double simile construction ("like vinegar . . . like smoke . . .") and deals with the subject of the irritation and unpleasantness caused by the lazy performance of one sent on a mission. Verse 30 reflects the Deuteronomic theology of the land (see 2:21–22), i.e., the fulfillment of Yahweh's promise of the land is conditional and dependent upon how the Israelites respond to the Law. Israel becomes two nations: the wicked who will be taken out of the land and the righteous who will dwell in the land.

(4) The Value of Righteousness (11:1–11)

1 A false balance is an abomination to the LORD,
   but a just weight is his delight.
2 When pride comes, then comes disgrace;
   but with the humble is wisdom.
3 The integrity of the upright guides them,
   but the crookedness of the treacherous destroys them.
4 Riches do not profit in the day of wrath,
   but righteousness delivers from death.
5 The righteousness of the blameless keeps his way straight,
   but the wicked falls by his own wickedness.
6 The righteousness of the upright delivers them,
   but the treacherous are taken captive by their lust.
7 When the wicked dies, his hope perishes,
   and the expectation of the godless comes to nought.
8 The righteous is delivered from trouble,
   and the wicked gets into it instead.
9 With his mouth the godless man would destroy his neighbor,
   but by knowledge the righteous are delivered.
10 When it goes well with the righteous, the city rejoices;
   and when the wicked perish there are shouts of gladness.
11 By the blessing of the upright a city is exalted,

but it is overthrown by the mouth of the wicked.

Verse 1 expresses a fundamental requirement of integrity in business. Scales which are accurate and true are pleasing to Yahweh (See Deut. 25:15; Lev. 19:35–36; etc.). The direct relationship of business practices to religious ethics is characteristic of the Old Testament. The dynamic for honesty and the concern for correctness comes from God. It is *his delight.*

Verses 2–11 are all concerned with righteousness, the righteous or the upright, except vv. 2 and 7. Verse 7 has a missing contrast (supplied by the LXX: "When a righteous man dies his hope does not perish, but the boast of the wicked perishes"). *Disgrace* of v. 2 is literally lightness in contrast to the heaviness of honor. The arrogant man of undisciplined egotism reveals himself as a "lightweight." The first line of this sentence is probably a colloquial saying which has been expanded by the addition of the less alliterative second line. The *humble* (cf. Mic. 6:8) is the mark of a reasonable man of self-control and restraint of emotion. This quality does not connote a timidity which stems out of fear or a lack of strength. The NEB translates it "sagacity" which, perhaps, is in the root meaning of the word (also, Gemser, p. 112). The inner guidance of good character is stressed in vv. 3,5. *Integrity* provides safe guidance for the *upright.* The verb *guides* is a word used of a shepherd guiding his sheep. God is often the one who guides (see Gen. 24:27; Ex. 13:17; Psalm 23:3). *Treacherous* (i.e., twisted or perverse) men are destroyed by their own *crookedness.* The *righteousness* of the *blameless* man (the mature, sincere, good man) keeps him on a straight, safe way, while the wicked stumbles and falls because of his wickedness. The course of a man's life is set by the intrinsic nature of his inner self. What he is will determine the nature of what happens to him.

The deliverance of the righteous is the repeated subject in vv. 4,6,8,9. The deliverance from *death* in v. 4 probably should be thought of as being saved from a premature or dishonorable death (note 10:27). However, the *day of wrath* can be a reference to the eschatological judgment of God (such as the day of Yahweh in Zeph. 1:15,18) and in that case "death" could refer to the judgment which will come on the world. McKane quite properly notes that deliverance in vv. 6,8 is not to be understood as complete immunity from danger and trouble. The righteous man does not live behind a shield which guarantees him a serene progress to success and fulfillment. It is better not to put limits on the concept of death in a sentence like this. The thrust of the statement is that the righteous man can be delivered from anything.

Verses 10–11 deal with the effect of the righteous and the wicked on a city. The wise men were always concerned with individual persons, but they were not unaware of corporate relatedness. The complex social unit which is the city is dependent on the character and behavior of its citizens. Every city has occasion to rejoice when *it goes well with the righteous,* because its own well-being is tied up with them. What's good for the righteous is good for the city!

(5) A Collage of Characters (11:12–17)

¹² He who belittles his neighbor lacks sense,
  but a man of understanding remains silent.
¹³ He who goes about as a talebearer reveals secrets,
  but he who is trustworthy in spirit keeps a thing hidden.
¹⁴ Where there is no guidance, a people falls;
  but in an abundance of counselors there is safety.
¹⁵ He who gives surety for a stranger will smart for it,
  but he who hates suretyship is secure.
¹⁶ A gracious woman gets honor,
  and violent men get riches.
¹⁷ A man who is kind benefits himself,
  but a cruel man hurts himself.

The subject of vv. 12–13 is the man who exercises restraint in his speech regarding his neighbors and respects confidence. If a man *belittles his neighbor,* or shows his contempt, he lacks the good sense of a wise man. The discriminating man, *man of understanding*, controls the temptation to express himself about his neighbor (Scott, p. 84, "keeps his opinions to himself"). The *trustworthy* man (v. 13) does not gossip and he does not talk about confidential matters. He is dependable in a relationship and does not treat matters of personal concern to others as suitable for ordinary conversation.

Verse 14, like vv. 10–11, has a corporate note. *Guidance,* the art of steering, is essential for the welfare of a nation. Safety is found in a group of *counselors* (cf. 15:22; 24:6). The group has strength greater than any one member. In matters of state, decisions based on a wide consensus are more likely to be successful in their outcome. The NEB translates this as applying to military affairs, as in 24:6.

A prudent man stays out of bargains and business deals, especially with strangers (v. 15, see 6:1). The man who hates deals is secure. An unusual contrast between women and men is found in v. 16, though the exact meaning is debatable. The RSV supposes a contrast between *gracious woman* and *violent men.* But "violent men" can be understood as energetic or strong, hence: "A gracious woman obtains honor, but energetic men obtain wealth" (assuming a contrast between "honor" and "wealth," which the text may not intend). The contrast may be only between two ways to success. The *kind* man of v. 17 more probably should be understood as the "loyal man" (so NEB). The Hebrew is *chesed*, which refers to the dependability and loyalty which are necessary to keep a relationship (such as a covenant) intact. A loyal man is kind in the sense that he cares for others. The cruel man is self-centered and ruthless.

(6) The Upright and the Wicked (11: 18–23)

18 A wicked man earns deceptive wages,
   but one who sows righteousness gets a
      sure reward.

19 He who is steadfast in righteousness will
      live,
   but he who pursues evil will die.
20 Men of perverse mind are an abomination
      to the LORD,
   but those of blameless ways are his delight.
21 Be assured, an evil man will not go unpunished,
   but those who are righteous will be delivered.
22 Like a gold ring in a swine's snout
   is a beautiful woman without discretion.
23 The desire of the righteous ends only in
      good;
   the expectation of the wicked in wrath.

The contrast between upright and wicked or evil men is the subject of these sentences except for v. 22. This verse sets forth two incongruities, that of a gold ring in the nose of a hog and that of a beautiful woman without *discretion* (lit., taste). The *gold ring* was a nose-ring which was worn as an ornament by women. "Discretion" represents good taste in moral and intellectual discrimination. *Be assured* in v. 21 is a translation of the Hebrew "hand to hand" which is similar to the English saying, "Here's my hand on it!" The same expression is found in 16:5 (see 6:1; 11:15). There may be a background of legal proceedings in v. 21. The *evil* man will not receive a verdict which frees him from guilt. The righteous will be set free in the sense that their innocence is established (see McKane, p. 437). The desire of the righteous is satisfied, but the wicked can expect only frustration and anger. Their anticipation will be thwarted, and their hopes of achievement will end in disappointed rage.

(7) Some Anomalies (11:24–31)

24 One man gives freely, yet grows all the
      richer;
   another withholds what he should give,
      and only suffers want.
25 A liberal man will be enriched,
   and one who waters will himself be
      watered.
26 The people curse him who holds back grain,
   but a blessing is on the head of him who
      sells it.
27 He who diligently seeks good seeks favor,

but evil comes to him who searches for it.
28 He who trusts in his riches will wither,
but the righteous will flourish like a green leaf.
29 He who troubles his household will inherit wind,
and the fool will be servant to the wise.
30 The fruit of the righteous is a tree of life,
but lawlessness takes away lives.
31 If the righteous is requited on earth,
how much more the wicked and the sinner!

Most of these sentences express results of human actions which are not those anticipated in common expectations. The reverse order is normally expected in v. 24, i.e., the man who spends freely should be in trouble, while the man who holds on to his money should be safe. But the verse is an observation on the economic facts of life. Money which is invested earns money, while the money hoarder finds himself headed for poverty. Perhaps, this verse reflects experience with an inflationary economy! Verse 26 expresses the attitude of the community towards a man who will not sell his grain, though normally it is wise to keep a reserve of grain. However, when grain is needed, the people bless the man who sells it—regardless of the consequences. Another anomaly is found in v. 28.

Favor in v. 27a can be the favor or approval of God with the meaning being that he who strives after good finds God's approval. But it probably means the favor and goodwill of other people, i.e., he receives the esteem of his neighbors. The negative side is in v. 27b. Verse 29a expresses the result of family mismanagement which destroys prosperity and leaves nothing (*wind*) to inherit. Verse 29b refers to the fool who manages his business affairs so badly that he becomes the slave of a wise man, i.e., the man who knows how to manage his affairs properly.

The interpretation of v. 30 is problematic. The RSV uses an emendation. A somewhat different translation is better, assuming the same emendation: "The fruit of a righteous man is a tree of life, but that (the fruit) of him who takes life is vi-

olence." Some commentators take the Hebrew for *takes away lives* as positive rather than negative. For example, Ringgren (p. 49) translates this, "the wise man wins men for himself." The KJV reads, "he that winneth souls (is) wise." Dahood suggests another interpretation.[5]

Verse 31 means that reward works both ways; for the righteous man and the sinner. They both get what they deserve. The Greek text of this verse is reproduced almost exactly in 1 Peter 4:18.

(8) Contrast of Goodness and Evil (12:1–7)

1 Whoever loves discipline loves knowledge,
but he who hates reproof is stupid.
2 A good man obtains favor from the LORD,
but a man of evil devices he condemns.
3 A man is not established by wickedness,
but the root of the righteous will never be moved.
4 A good wife is the crown of her husband,
but she who brings shame is like rottenness in his bones.
5 The thoughts of the righteous are just;
the counsels of the wicked are treacherous.
6 The words of the wicked lie in wait for blood,
but the mouth of the upright delivers men.
7 The wicked are overthrown and are no more,
but the house of the righteous will stand.

Verse 1 emphasizes the need for discipline if knowledge is to be attained. *Knowledge* is the power to live life with proper discrimination and effectiveness. It points to the authority of the wisdom teacher and his *discipline.* The one who rejects the *reproof,* correction and guidance, of the teacher is *stupid* or animal-like. The stupid man lacks the rational ability of a man and acts by instinct (cf. Psalms 73:22; 92:6;

5 In *Proverbs and Northwest Semantic Philology,* (Rome: Pontificum Institutum Biblicum, 1963), pp. 24–25, he wants to interpret *nephashoth* as "eternal life": "The fruit of the virtuous is the tree of life, and the wise man attains eternal life." This is improbable, though he does cite a Ugaritic illustration of the verb *lkch* as attain or get. However, the Old Testament usages of this expression in connection with *npsh* mean to take away life (see 1:19; Psalm 31:13; 1 Kings 19:4; Jonah 4:3; also, on the "tree of life" see 3:18; 13:12; 15:4).

49:10).

The contrast expressed in vv. 2–3 is a familiar one. The *evil devices* (*m'zzimmoth*) of v. 2 is used here in a pejorative sense, while in other contexts (e.g., 1:4; 8:12) it is commendable. Where the criterion is simply effectiveness, the capacity for *m'zzimmah* is good. But this word in v. 2 implies a contrast between the man who receives the favor of Yahweh and the man who tries to live by his own schemes. The *good man* is not defined, but the position of the verse after v. 1 may indicate some relation to the "discipline" and "knowledge" of that verse. By implication these become attached to Yahweh. It is by the divine *musar* that a man receives *favor from the Lord*.

The *good wife* is one of strong character, who complements a man and enables him to realize status and success (see the discussion of the "good wife" in 31:10–30). But the wife who brings a man *shame* is like a cancer which saps his body and constantly keeps him from doing his best. The Hebrew word for "shame" is a general one which could include any embarrassing, incompetent, or immoral behavior which damages the respect and reputation of a man before the world (see 18:22; 19:13).

As in v. 2, a word which is good in other contexts is used in a bad sense in v. 5. The *counsels* (cf. 1:5) are here those of the *wicked*. The art of "steering" is not sufficient in itself, but it must be exercised by the right sort of person. The steering must be controlled by the *thoughts* (plans or policies) of the righteous. The words of the wicked can destroy life, but the *mouth* of the *upright* delivers those who would be trapped in the ambush of the wicked. Verse 7 contrasts the security of the righteous with the insecurity of the wicked (cf. Matt. 7:24–27).

(9) The Fallacy of Facades (12:8–28)

8 A man is commended according to his good sense,
   but one of perverse mind is despised.
9 Better is a man of humble standing who works for himself

than one who plays the great man but lacks bread.
10 A righteous man has regard for the life of his beast,
   but the mercy of the wicked is cruel.
11 He who tills his land will have plenty of bread,
   but he who follows worthless pursuits has no sense.
12 The strong tower of the wicked comes to ruin,
   but the root of the righteous stands firm.
13 An evil man is ensnared by the transgression of his lips,
   but the righteous escapes from trouble.
14 From the fruit of his words a man is satisfied with good,
   and the work of a man's hand comes back to him.
15 The way of a fool is right in his own eyes,
   but a wise man listens to advice.
16 The vexation of a fool is known at once,
   but the prudent man ignores an insult.
17 He who speaks the truth gives honest evidence,
   but a false witness utters deceit.
18 There is one whose rash words are like sword thrusts,
   but the tongue of the wise brings healing.
19 Truthful lips endure for ever,
   but a lying tongue is but for a moment.
20 Deceit is in the heart of those who devise evil,
   but those who plan good have joy.
21 No ill befalls the righteous,
   but the wicked are filled with trouble.
22 Lying lips are an abomination to the LORD,
   but those who act faithfully are his delight.
23 A prudent man conceals his knowledge,
   but fools proclaim their folly.
24 The hand of the diligent will rule,
   while the slothful will be put to forced labor.
25 Anxiety in a man's heart weighs him down,
   but a good word makes him glad.
26 A righteous man turns away from evil,
   but the way of the wicked leads them astray.
27 A slothful man will not catch his prey,
   but the diligent man will get precious wealth.
28 In the path of righteousness is life,
   but the way of error leads to death.

The outline of the text at this point is artificial to a considerable degree, but several of the sentences contrast outward appearance with reality. Verse 9 commends the man who is willing to content himself with small success rather than overextend himself in order to play the part of the *great man.* The man who enjoys modest, but solid, prosperity is better off than the man who puts up a front of affluence but in reality lacks bread, i.e., he suffers painful privations in areas of life which are essential for good living.

The same kind of contrast is found in v. 11, a verse which is repeated with some change in 28:19. The man who *tills his land* is better off than the man who *follows worthless pursuits.* The "worthless pursuits" are not defined, but it is safe to assume that dubious, speculative mercantile and financial dealings are in mind. There is a kind of agricultural ideal in Proverbs, which regards the care of land and animals as the best way of making a living (see 27:23–27).

The fool deceives himself (v. 15) into thinking that the way on which he is going is right. His reliance on his own opinions makes him deaf to the *advice* (counsel) that a wise man heeds (cf. 15:22). In v. 23 the restraint of the *prudent man* making known his knowledge is commended. The wise man does not try to live behind a facade of omniscience—that is the fool's way. The prudent man does not talk too much and seeks to speak effectively, which is impossible to do if one talks all the time. Verse 27 is difficult, but it may be translated:

> "A lazy man does not roast his game,
> but the worth of a man is valuable diligence."

The verb translated *catch* in the RSV is used only here in the Old Testament. The meaning "roast" is derived from its use in later Hebrew. The meaning of v. 27a seems to be that which McKane (p. 445) gives it, i.e., there is a kind of man who makes a show of doing things, but he never sees them through to a full conclusion (he does not cook his game after he catches it). He lacks the keenness of the diligent man, who may seem less successful but really has greater worth.

Various subjects are dealt with in other verses. Verse 10 reflects a concern for animals. Verse 12 is uncertain, but it is better to translate it:

> "The wicked covet the power of evil men,
> but the roots of the righteous are lasting."

The *m⁰tsod* (*strong tower* in RSV) can mean net, or may be a form of *m⁰tsudah* (fortress or stronghold). The translation "power" is free, but it expresses the idea. The parallelism which results is poor, unless it is understood that the coveting of the wicked is futile and doomed to failure. The importance of speech is stressed in vv. 13,14,18,19,22,25. The power of words is very great. Notice should be taken of the healing power of speech in vv. 18,25. The wise man knows the therapeutic value of words. A pastoral concern, which appears from time to time in the wisdom teachings, is probably found in v. 26, which is another verse with some difficulties. McKane's translation (p. 229) is preferable: "A righteous man shows his friend the way, / but the way of wicked men leads (others) astray." Verse 16 is closely related to speech. The fool reacts to an affront or irritating situation without taking time to bring his feelings under control and allow time for an appraisal of the situation. But the prudent man keeps his emotions under cover and responds calmly and deliberately.

Verse 28 is of some interest because of its statement relating to death. Scott (p. 91) translates it: "On the road of righteousness there is life, / And the treading of its path (reading *n⁰tibato* for MT *n⁰tibah*) is deathlessness." [6] It is doubtful that the text of the verse is as corrupt as it is often argued to be. Translate: "On the path of righteousness there is life, / And on the way of its path there is no death." However, Dahood assumes too much when he translates "immortality." The verse says that the way of righteousness is life and not

---

6 Scott indicates his agreement with M. Dahood in *Biblica,* 41 (1960), 176–81; *Proverbs and North-west Semitic Philology,* p. 28, that *life* and *deathless-ness* (lit., "no-death") constitute a synonymous parallel. Note the different view of McKane, p. 451.

death without further definition. It leaves the interpretation open, and the translation should not go too far beyond the text.

(10) A Father's Teaching (13:1–13)

1 A wise son hears his father's instruction,
   but a scoffer does not listen to rebuke.
2 From the fruit of his mouth a good man eats good,
   but the desire of the treacherous is for violence.
3 He who guards his mouth preserves his life;
   he who opens wide his lips comes to ruin.
4 The soul of the sluggard craves, and gets nothing,
   while the soul of the diligent is richly supplied.
5 A righteous man hates falsehood,
   but a wicked man acts shamefully and disgracefully.
6 Righteousness guards him whose way is upright,
   but sin overthrows the wicked.
7 One man pretends to be rich, yet has nothing;
   another pretends to be poor, yet has great wealth.
8 The ransom of a man's life is his wealth,
   but a poor man has no means of redemption.
9 The light of the righteous rejoices,
   but the lamp of the wicked will be put out.
10 By insolence the heedless make strife,
   but with those who take advice is wisdom.
11 Wealth hastily gotten will dwindle,
   but he who gathers little by little will increase it.
12 Hope deferred makes the heart sick,
   but a desire fulfilled is a tree of life.
13 He who despises the word brings destruction on himself,
   but he who respects the commandment will be rewarded.

The outline reflects more coherence than these verses actually have. But the sentences do contain the kind of teaching that a teacher or "father" might give a pupil or "son," and there is an element of the Instruction genre in v. 13. Verses 1,10,13 deal with acceptance and rejection of teaching and correction. Unlike a *wise son*, a *scoffer* will not listen to a rebuke or accept educational discipline. The scoffer lacks the abilities of concentration and receptivity. The wise student knows how to accept the

corrections of his teacher. The RSV translates v. 1 freely. The cryptic Masoretic Text has no verb in v. 1a and *hears* is adopted from v. 1b (and the LXX). If any change is made, it is better to read the *musar* (*instruction*) as a verb form and translate: "A wise son is one who allows himself to be disciplined by his father" (note NEB).

In v. 10 arrogance is contrasted with *those who take advice*. The RSV emends the Masoretic Text of v. 10a. The change (*rek* for *rak*) is acceptable and may improve the meaning with a translation like that of McKane (p. 230): "An empty-head produces strife by his arrogance . . ." However, the Masoretic Text can be retained and translated with Toy (p. 267), "Pride causes only strife . . ." The arrogant and contentious man generates quarrels and hurt feelings, while those who are willing to confer and receive counsel have the characteristics of wisdom. Wisdom emerges from the dialogue which is involved in counseling together. The "loner" is not usually wise.

In v. 13 it is better to interpret the *word* and the *commandment* as the authoritative instructions of the wisdom teachers (McKane, p. 454). The man who disregards the guidance of his teachers will ruin himself, while the man who respects their teaching will be *rewarded* (or, if a slight change in the verb is made: "secure," "in good condition").

The familiar theme of the control and proper use of speech is found in vv. 2–3. A good man's speech is fruitful and he gains benefits from it along with others (cf. 12: 14), while the *treacherous* have an appetite for violence and trouble. Verse 3 deals with indiscreet and impulsive speech. The man who says the first thing that comes into his mind with little or no care for its expression can expect trouble (cf. 10:14b). Verse 4 is linked with vv. 2–3 by its use of the term *nephesh* (*soul*, which may mean life or throat or appetite). The meaning is that the lazy man always wants food and good things, but he does not have them. The desire of the diligent is satisfied because he works to provide himself with that which he wants.

Somewhat related to v. 4 are vv. 7–8,11 where the subject is wealth and poverty. The ostentatious person who *pretends to be rich* is compared with the wealthy person who *pretends to be poor*—both extremes are bad and symbolize a pretence which brings about distortion in society. As Toy remarks (p. 264), "The moral is that men should be simply honest and unpretentious." The RSV translation of v. 8*b* uses an emendation which makes the parallelism easier but which is unnecessary. Retain the Masoretic Text: "but a poor man does not hear rebuke." The meaning is that the rich man is always liable (and able) to pay a *ransom* in order to protect himself from threats and blackmail. The poor man does not hear the kind of rebuke directed at the rich man. There is no reason to blackmail or sue the poor man; he has no money. Verse 11 condemns the acquisition of wealth by speculative, dubious financial dealing—the probable meaning, rather than getting it *hastily.* The proper way to get wealth is *little by little* as it develops from honest effort which is geared to a stable and sound character. The wise men had no approval for the money grabber who wheels and deals (usually with other people's money) in order to gain money and property unmerited by his real ability and worth.

Three sentences contrast the righteous and the wicked: vv. 5,6,9. The righteous man hates falsehood which causes so much misunderstanding and is so productive of credibility gaps in society. But the *wicked man* stirs up slander (lit., causes a bad smell) and discord. Translate v. 5*b* with McKane: "but a wicked man spreads the smell of scandal" (p. 230). The RSV has emended "he causes to stink" to "he acts shamefully." Verse 6 is clear. It is better to translate the *light of the righteous rejoices* in v. 9*a* as "the light of the righteous will burn brightly."

Verse 12 expresses the debilitating results

of expectation which repeatedly fails to attain fulfillment. As McKane (p. 459) notes, the translation of desire into reality is "an exhilarating achievement." Desire realized is a *tree of life* (see 3:18) which energizes effort and activates confidence in one's ability to live with a sense of satisfaction.

(11) The Teaching of the Wise (13:14–25)

14 The teaching of the wise is a fountain of
     life,
       that one may avoid the snares of death.
15 Good sense wins favor,
       but the way of the faithless is their ruin.
16 In everything a prudent man acts with
     knowledge,
       but a fool flaunts his folly.
17 A bad messenger plunges men into trouble,
       but a faithful envoy brings healing.
18 Poverty and disgrace come to him who ig-
     nores instruction,
       but he who heeds reproof is honored.
19 A desire fulfilled is sweet to the soul;
       but to turn away from evil is an abomina-
     tion to fools.
20 He who walks with wise men becomes wise,
       but the companion of fools will suffer
     harm.
21 Misfortune pursues sinners,
       but prosperity rewards the righteous.
22 A good man leaves an inheritance to his
     children's children,
       but the sinner's wealth is laid up for the
     righteous.
23 The fallow ground of the poor yields much
     food,
       but it is swept away through injustice.
24 He who spares the rod hates his son,
       but he who loves him is diligent to disci-
     pline him.
25 The righteous has enough to satisfy his ap-
     petite,
       but the belly of the wicked suffers want.

The outline reflects v. 14 and is a generalization for the diverse sentences in vv. 14–25. Most of the verses deal with familiar themes and need little explanation if the general contours of this type of wisdom teaching are kept in mind. Verse 16 contrasts the careful action of the *prudent man* with that of a fool who *flaunts his folly,* i.e., "he spreads out folly" like a salesman setting out his display before a potential customer. The acts of a fool expose his lack of acumen to the world. The character and intellectual ability of a man is demonstrated in what he does.

Verse 19a has the same thought as v. 12. Verse 19b seems to have no direct connection with the first line, but it is similar to 29:27b. Some opinion to the contrary, it seems better to treat the two parts as separate statements without any direct relationship.

The influence of associates is emphasized by v. 20 (cf. 1:8–19). The man who wants to become wise will keep company with wise men. This is a cardinal principal of education. Wise men stimulate the development of their own kind. Unfortunately, the converse proposition is true also: fools beget fools—and there are more fools than wise men!

Verse 23 has baffled commentators in the past and remains uncertain. The RSV translation yields the picture of a poor man who cultivates new ground until it becomes productive only to lose it because of a lack of justice. But it is doubtful that this is the correct understanding of the verse. It is better to read the *poor* (*ra'shim*) as "head men" or "chiefs." They are not the poor, but those who own land and belong to the upper strata of the economy. They produce much food, but despite their productivity they will find that they will be deprived of the use of it because of their lack of justice. The verse is pointed toward the gain of wealth by improper methods and by the wrong kind of people (cf. 13:11).

Verse 24 advocates corporal punishment as a proper form of parental discipline (see 22:15; 23:13; 29:17). The *diligent* of the RSV is unnecessary. Translate either "but one who loves him keeps him in order" (NEB) or "but he who loves him begins discipline early" (McKane, p. 457).

(12) Wisdom and Folly; Sadness and Joy (14:1–13)

1 Wisdom builds her house,
   but folly with her own hands tears it down.
2 He who walks in uprightness fears the Lord,
   but he who is devious in his ways despises him.
3 The talk of a fool is a rod for his back,
   but the lips of the wise will preserve them.
4 Where there are no oxen, there is no grain;
   but abundant crops come by the strength of the ox.
5 A faithful witness does not lie,
   but a false witness breathes out lies.
6 A scoffer seeks wisdom in vain,
   but knowledge is easy for a man of understanding.
7 Leave the presence of a fool,
   for there you do not meet words of knowledge.
8 The wisdom of a prudent man is to discern his way,
   but the folly of fools is deceiving.
9 God scorns the wicked,
   but the upright enjoy his favor.
10 The heart knows its own bitterness,
   and no stranger shares its joy.
11 The house of the wicked will be destroyed,
   but the tent of the upright will flourish.
12 There is a way which seems right to a man,
   but its end is the way to death.
13 Even in laughter the heart is sad,
   and the end of joy is grief.

As the RSV margin indicates, the translation omits a word in v. 1 and understands *Wisdom* as singular in meaning, treating it as personified (see 9:1). The problem of the "women" in the verse is left unresolved. The NEB is preferable: "The wisest of women build up their homes; / the foolish pull them down with their own hands." In any case, the contrast is between the constructive nature of wisdom and the destructive nature of *folly*.

The fear of Yahweh is the subject of v. 2 (as also of 14:26,27). The straight way is the way of the one who *fears the Lord*. The man of twisted, double-dealing ways despises Yahweh. The other side of this contrast is found in v. 9 according to the RSV. But this verse is very uncertain, and the RSV must be read as a possibility only.

Verses 3,6,7,8 feature the fool-wise man antithesis. The fool is characterized by arrogant and careless speech. A fool's talk gets him into trouble (v. 3), and it is a waste of time to remain in his presence because he will not say anything worthwhile (v. 7). Knowledge is easily learned by a *man of understanding*, i.e., a man who has the capacity to make careful judgments. The *scoffer* cannot find wisdom. The two are incompatible. The *prudent man* uses his wisdom to make his way through life with precise judgment, while the fool is deceived and misdirected by his own folly. The character of a fool is self-deceiving.

Verse 4*a* in the RSV uses a changed text and, in this case, is improbable. I prefer to read either, "Where there are no oxen, there is an empty crib" (see NEB); or (with McKane, pp. 231,471), "Where there are no oxen, there is a crib of grain." In either case, the emphasis is on the value of oxen for the farmer's production of crops.

Verse 5 contrasts the faithful with the false witness (see 12:25).

Verses 10,12, and 13 temper the optimism of the wise men. As Rylaarsdam (p. 58) has expressed it, we catch the wise man "when he is off duty, alone, and looking at himself in a 'low' moment." There is an inner self which knows its own *bitterness* and *joy* beyond the comprehension of anyone else. "There is a sense in which a man's life is 'a long loneliness,' so that he cannot communicate what is most real about himself, but can only talk to himself" (Rylaarsdam, p. 58). Joy and sorrow are never completely separated. *The end of joy is grief* expresses the view that the satisfactions of life are transient and that joy moves on to sorrow. Verse 12 has something of the same sentiment. A way which seems straight and clear to a man may end in death (also 16:25). Life has its inexplicable aspects.

Verse 11 expresses a familiar contrast between the fate of bad men and good men. It is possible that *tent* in v. 11*b* should be understood as "family."

(13) *Varieties of Human Character* (14: 14–25)

14 A perverse man will be filled with the fruit of his ways,
   and a good man with the fruit of his deeds.
15 The simple believes everything,
   but the prudent looks where he is going.
16 A wise man is cautious and turns away from evil,

but a fool throws off restraint and is careless.
17 A man of quick temper acts foolishly,
   but a man of discretion is patient.
18 The simple acquire folly,
   but the prudent are crowned with knowledge.
19 The evil bow down before the good,
   the wicked at the gates of the righteous.
20 The poor is disliked even by his neighbor,
   but the rich has many friends.
21 He who despises his neighbor is a sinner,
   but happy is he who is kind to the poor.
22 Do they not err that devise evil?
   Those who devise good meet loyalty and faithfulness.
23 In all toil there is profit,
   but mere talk tends only to want.
24 The crown of the wise is their wisdom,
   but folly is the garland of fools.
25 A truthful witness saves lives,
   but one who utters lies is a betrayer.

These verses vary in their subject matter, but all of them highlight some feature of human character. The text of v. 14 is difficult, but it seems clear that a contrast is made between results experienced by a *perverse man* and a *good man*.

Verses 15,16,17 are differentiated by their use of active verbs. The subjects behave in different ways with different results. The simple man believes too easily what he hears. He lacks the caution and analytical abilities of the prudent man (v. 15). The fool is careless and acts impulsively (v. 16). He fails to control his temper (v. 17). The wise man is deliberate, careful, and patient (v. 17*b*) in his acts. The fool lacks moderation (v. 16). He becomes overconfident about his own ability and strength.

Verses 18,19,20,22,24 give examples of the kind of things which happen to people of differing character and status. For example, the poor man is *disliked* (better, "hated") by his own neighbor, but a rich man has many *friends* (lit., many lovers). This is an observation of a reality of life. It is not necessarily the way it *ought* to be; but it is just the way life in human society *is*. *Acquire* in v. 18 is unlikely to be correct: the *simple* are the immature, untutored people, who already have *folly* as a part of their nature. It is better to translate this:

"The simple ones have folly as their portion." But the parallelism with v. 18*b* is poor, and a small change of vowels in the verb produces a good parallel: "The simple ones wear (or adorn themselves with) folly, . . ." (see NEB). Verse 24 is frequently emended (as, e.g., in RSV), and something like the RSV is desirable in v. 24*b*. But it is better to follow the Masoretic Text in v. 24*a* and translate, "The crown of the wise is their wealth." The prosperity and well-being of the wise man is his crown. The *fools* have no *garland* but their own folly (see McKane, p. 466).

Verse 23 sets forth a basic maxim of life: work produces more than talk does. The wise men believed in work. A man can talk himself into poverty.

Verse 25 expresses the same idea as 14:5.

(14) The Fear of the Lord (14:26–28)

²⁶ In the fear of the LORD one has strong confidence,
　　and his children will have a refuge.
²⁷ The fear of the LORD is a fountain of life,
　　that one may avoid the snares of death.
²⁸ In a multitude of people is the glory of a king,
　　but without people a prince is ruined.

Verses 26–27 are linked by their use of the concept of *the fear of the Lord* (see 1:7). Reverent obedience towards Yahweh is a source of confident security and life. Verse 27 is very similar to 13:14, but "the fear of the Lord" has been substituted for "the teaching of the wise." Verse 26 may convey a picture of the home of a pious man, surrounded by the protective care of Yahweh (McKane, p. 474). It is unlikely that the *snares of death* in v. 27*b* refers to life after death. The fear of Yahweh will keep a man from fatal pitfalls, disaster, and premature death along the road of life.

An argument has been made for "big battalions" instead of *multitude of people* in v. 28 (Jones, p. 138). A king's power is related to the size of the population he rules. Without people in large enough numbers, a prince has no future. Verse 28*b* may mean simply a reduction in population, i.e., an insufficiency of people. But a hint of

a more drastic state of affairs may be found in the verse. The word *ruined* seems out of place for a king whose only problem is a small population. It may be that the idea of defection or withdrawal of allegiance and support by groups of people is in the background (McKane, p. 469).

(15) Contexts of Wisdom and Folly (14: 29–35)

²⁹ He who is slow to anger has great understanding,
　　but he who has a hasty temper exalts folly.
³⁰ A tranquil mind gives life to the flesh,
　　but passion makes the bones rot.
³¹ He who oppresses a poor man insults his Maker,
　　but he who is kind to the needy honors him.
³² The wicked is overthrown through his evildoing,
　　but the righteous finds refuge through his integrity.
³³ Wisdom abides in the mind of a man of understanding,
　　but it is not known in the heart of fools.
³⁴ Righteousness exalts a nation,
　　but sin is a reproach to any people.
³⁵ A servant who deals wisely has the king's favor,
　　but his wrath falls on one who acts shamefully.

The man of *understanding* (i.e., discrimination and keen judgment) controls his temper. He knows that anger cripples a man's ability to make good decisions. The quick-tempered man increases folly. A connection between tranquillity of mind and bodily health is made in v. 30. The wise men were aware of psychosomatic factors in life.

Verse 31 deals with the treatment of the poor, whose oppression is contrary to the will of God (see 17:5; 19:17). The care of the needy is a way of honoring God (cf. Matt. 25:31–46).

The RSV in v. 32*b* follows the Greek text in using *integrity*, a change which is widely accepted and may be correct. But it is well to note that the Masoretic Text reads "in his death"; and the statement makes good sense read as, "And the righteous man has a security even at his death" (Barucq,

p. 130).

The text in v. 33b has an uncertainty also. The RSV has adopted a solution which adds a negative. Wisdom finds a place in the mind of a man who has the ability to understand, but it has no suitable place in the life of a fool. This is acceptable and is certainly not far from the meaning of the verse.

Verse 34 is a frequently quoted verse in American life. It applies the common formula for successful individual life to the nation. *Righteousness* should not be thought of exclusively in moralistic and ethical terms. It is doing the "right thing" in any given set of circumstances both in relationship to one's self and others. Thus, it includes social responsibility as well as personal ethics. A "righteous" nation is one which orders its affairs with wisdom and keeps "right" in the needs and relationships of its people. Often, too much attention is given to personal sins. The *sin* of v. 34b is the failure of a nation to attain its proper objective and to remain on its true course. The word used for sin is the familiar one of "missing the mark." The *reproach* or "disgrace" of a people is the failure to live in "rightness." Their energies are misdirected and their purpose is warped out of true alignment.

Verse 35 is an observation on the quality of service which kings favor and reward. The wise men believed in looking at life realistically. Skilled and competent men are needed for the intricate affairs of government.

(16) The Discipline of Temper and Tongue (15:1–7)

1 A soft answer turns away wrath,
     but a harsh word stirs up anger.
2 The tongue of the wise dispenses knowledge,
     but the mouths of fools pour out folly.
3 The eyes of the LORD are in every place,
     keeping watch on the evil and the good.
4 A gentle tongue is a tree of life,
     but perverseness in it breaks the spirit.
5 A fool despises his father's instruction,
     but he who heeds admonition is prudent.
6 In the house of the righteous there is much treasure,
     but trouble befalls the income of the wicked.
7 The lips of the wise spread knowledge;
     not so the minds of fools.

Verses 1,2,4,7 all deal with speech in one form or another. Verse 1 states a truism of life. Irritating, sharp, harsh words stir up anger in those who hear them. A wise man avoids the hot retort. The conciliatory response lessens tension and makes for reasonableness and dialogue. Polemical speech is inflammatory and devisive. The speech of the wise man "makes knowledge good" (v. 2), i.e., commends or adorns knowledge. Style and skill in presentation marks the knowledge of the wise man. But the *mouths of fools pour out folly* like water coming from a flowing spring.

The *gentle tongue* of v. 4a should be understood as "healing speech" (see McKane, p. 483) as in 12:18; 13:17. Therapeutic speech is *a tree of life* (see 3:18), but twisted, perverse speech *breaks the spirit* of the speaker. Such a speaker causes a fragmentation of his own personality.

Verse 7, also, refers to the dissemination of knowledge through the speech of the wise. Verse 7b has been the subject of various proposed text changes, but it is better to leave it as it is in the RSV (cf. Psalm 1:4).

The omnipresence of God is the subject of v. 3. He is *keeping watch on the evil and the good* (cf. 2 Kings 9:17; Isa. 52:8; etc.). Nothing escapes his scrutiny. Even Sheol and Abaddon (cf. 15:11) are open before him. These words refer to the realm of the dead. "Abaddon" is a synonym for Sheol or the grave (cf. Job 26:6; 28:22; 31:12; Psalm 88:11) and means something like "destruction."

Familiar contrasts are found in vv. 5 (cf. 13:1,18) and 6. The translations of v. 6 vary among commentators, but the RSV is acceptable. It is a generalization from (a) the fact that virtues and vices often have visible consequences (cf. 10:4,22; 11:18) and (b) that wisdom and righteous living point men toward life while wickedness and folly point them toward death (cf. 3:18; 10:16; 12:28).

(17) The Fear of the Lord and Wisdom (15:8–33)

8 The sacrifice of the wicked is an abomination to the Lord,
   but the prayer of the upright is his delight.
9 The way of the wicked is an abomination to the Lord,
   but he loves him who pursues righteousness.
10 There is severe discipline for him who forsakes the way;
   he who hates reproof will die.
11 Sheol and Abaddon lie open before the Lord,
   how much more the hearts of men!
12 A scoffer does not like to be reproved;
   he will not go to the wise.
13 A glad heart makes a cheerful countenance,
   but by sorrow of heart the spirit is broken.
14 The mind of him who has understanding seeks knowledge,
   but the mouths of fools feed on folly.
15 All the days of the afflicted are evil,
   but a cheerful heart has a continual feast.
16 Better is a little with the fear of the Lord
   than great treasure and trouble with it.
17 Better is a dinner of herbs where love is
   than a fatted ox and hatred with it.
18 A hot-tempered man stirs up strife,
   but he who is slow to anger quiets contention.
19 The way of a sluggard is overgrown with thorns,
   but the path of the upright is a level highway.
20 A wise son makes a glad father,
   but a foolish man despises his mother.
21 Folly is a joy to him who has no sense,
   but a man of understanding walks aright.
22 Without counsel plans go wrong,
   but with many advisers they succeed.
23 To make an apt answer is a joy to a man,
   and a word in season, how good it is!
24 The wise man's path leads upward to life,
   that he may avoid Sheol beneath.
25 The Lord tears down the house of the proud,
   but maintains the widow's boundaries.
26 The thoughts of the wicked are an abomination to the Lord,
   the words of the pure are pleasing to him.
27 He who is greedy for unjust gain makes trouble for his household,
   but he who hates bribes will live.
28 The mind of the righteous ponders how to answer,
   but the mouth of the wicked pours out evil things.
29 The Lord is far from the wicked,
   but he hears the prayer of the righteous.
30 The light of the eyes rejoices the heart,
   and good news refreshes the bones.
31 He whose ear heeds wholesome admonition
   will abide among the wise.
32 He who ignores instruction despises himself,
   but he who heeds admonition gains understanding.
33 The fear of the Lord is instruction in wisdom,
   and humility goes before honor.

Verse 8 is one of the few sentences in Proverbs which deal directly with worship. Yahweh approves the prayer of the upright man, but the *sacrifice of the wicked* is abominable to him. The expression *abomination to the Lord* is found only in Proverbs and Deuteronomy (e.g., Deut. 7:25,26; 18:12). "Abomination" (*to'ebah*) is found in other contexts, especially, Leviticus 18 (and the use of the plural in Ezek. e.g., 5:9, 11; 6:9,11; etc.). As McKane notes (p. 486), this verse is similar to the preaching of Isaiah (1:10–17) and Amos (5:21–24). The word abomination denotes something which is abhorrent, repulsive and to be rejected. That which is abominable to Yahweh is inconsonant with his will and subject to his repudiation. The prayer which Yahweh hears is that of the righteous (v. 29), but he makes himself remote from the wicked.

Verse 9 is linked with v. 8 by the expression *abomination to the Lord,* in this case, the *way of the wicked.* Yahweh approves of the man who *pursues righteousness,* i.e., the man who behaves in a manner acceptable to the will of Yahweh. Verse 26 also makes use of the expression *abomination of the Lord.* The *thoughts* means the schemes or plans of the wicked. This verse indicates something of God's concern for the motivations and intentions in a man's life.

Verse 10 is linked to v. 9 by the use of *way,* though two different Hebrew words are used (the word is "path" in v. 10; cf.

12:28). The "path" in this context is the pursuit of righteousness as set forth in v. 9. But it is likely that the verse originally referred to the teachings of the wise men, the educational discipline necessary for the living of a good life. The man who wants to live must be willing to learn and accept the corrections necessary in the learning process. V. 12 says much the same thing. The incorrigibility of the *scoffer* keeps him from accepting discipline and from finding the company of wise men who could teach him if he were willing to learn. The opposite of such a man is described in v. 31, a rare example of synthetic parallelism in this collection. The attentive person ("an ear which listens to the teaching of life") will live and find congenial lodging among the wise.

The man described in v. 32 is like the one in v. 10. The person who rejects discipline harms himself most of all; he "holds himself cheap" (Scott, p. 102). The one who *heeds admonition* is the one "who creates a mind" for himself, i.e., he gets the ability to think and act well. This is the kind of man who can follow the *wise man's path* (v. 24), which is a path upward and away from the world of the dead (*Sheol*) which lies below. It is the path which turns him away from death towards life. In its present form the verse can be interpreted in the sense of a prolongation of life for the wise man in antithesis with the way of death. It supposes a doctrine of immortality (see the discussion in McKane, pp. 479–80).

A commendation of the even-tempered man is found in v. 18. He is the man who keeps his emotions under restraint and is not prone to quarreling. The vocabulary of the verse suggests that excessive litigation and legal action is the major concern. The man who is quick to say "I'll sue you" is a troublemaker in any community (cf. 1 Cor. 6:1–8).

Verse 19 is one of numerous warnings by the wise men about laziness (cf. 6:6–11; 10:26; 11:29; 19:15,24; 26:13–16; etc.); with v. 19a, cf. Hos. 2:6; with v. 19b, cf.

Isa. 57:14).

Verse 20 repeats 10:1 with minor changes.

Verse 22 picks up the theme of 11:14 and 13:10. Consultation aids the success of plans, by the individual or the community. Collective wisdom is better and stronger than individual wisdom.

Verses 16,17,25, and 27 share some common concern in the relationship of property to life. The *house of the proud* will not endure because Yahweh will pull it down (v. 25). He is the champion of those who need protection and care—such as the widow, whose property is likely to be taken by men of power who do not hesitate to use their ability to rob people who cannot defend themselves.

Verses 16–17 advocate the philosophy that piety and love are better than wealth and luxury (cf. Mark 10:23–27; Matt. 19:23–26; Luke 18:24–27). The *fatted ox* of v. 17b is a symbol of lavish banqueting. The simplest dish of greens when shared with love is better than a gourmet's fare shared with hostility. Verse 27 focuses on the greed of a man for unjust profit and power which destroys "his house," i.e., his family and those associated with him. The word translated *unjust gain* carries the idea to cut off; thus the literal meaning of the expression is "the one who cuts off a big cut." Verse 27b represents a different attitude towards bribery than that found in 17:8; 19:6; 21:14.

Psychological observations are found in vv. 13,14,15,21,23,30. The word *heart* (properly translated as *mind* in v. 14) appears in all these verses except v. 23 (in v. 21 a "lack of heart" is translated as *no sense*). The attitudes of the heart or mind are very significant in determining the way life is lived. The inner condition of a man shows in his outward appearance (v. 13). But when there is pain and hurt in the mind, the inner being, the *spirit is broken,* i.e., the vigor and power of life is lacking.

The mind determines the course a man will take (v. 14). The mind of the one *who has understanding* thrusts him towards knowledge, while the fool is content to be satisfied with folly. Indeed, *folly is a joy* to the man with a deficient heart (*no sense,* in v. 21). But the wise man knows how "to make his going straight" (v. 21*b*) and finds joy in an appropriate answer and a fitting word (v. 23). A well-timed word, which is helpful and acceptable to others, brings a glow of satisfaction to the speaker. Of course, the other side of this joy is the sadness and hurt of an ill-timed and hurtful word. The right use of speech is an art requiring exquisite skill.

Verse 30, in a way, reverses the process of v. 13*a*. There the gladness comes from within, while in v. 30 it comes from without. The meaning of the expression *light of the eyes* is somewhat obscure. It could mean the brightness of the eyes of a messenger who brings good news (Toy, p. 317); or the shining eyes of a person who is friendly toward another. The Greek text translates the phrase, "An eye which sees beautiful things," and could indicate that relatively minor changes should be made in the Masoretic Text so that the lines can read as "something seen with pleasure gives joy to the mind" (see McKane, p. 481). Good news is always a tonic for the body and the soul.

Verse 33 closes not only chapter 15 but the entire collection which began with 10:1. It is a fitting conclusion which expresses the reinterpretation into theological terms of wisdom what was originally more secular in nature. *The fear of the Lord* is laid down as the proper nature of the discipline of wisdom (see 1:7; 9:10). The *humility* of v. 33*b* is no longer submission to the authority of the wisdom teacher but rather submission to the will of Yahweh; though that will may be expressed through the wisdom teacher.

2. Collection B (16:1—22:16)

(1) God's Guidance of Human Life (16: 1-9)

¹ The plans of the mind belong to man,
      but the **answer of the tongue** is from
      the Lord.

² All the ways of a man are pure in his own
      eyes,
      but the Lord weighs the spirit.
³ Commit your work to the Lord,
      and your plans will be established.
⁴ The Lord has made everything for its purpose,
      even the wicked for the day of trouble.
⁵ Every one who is arrogant is an abomination to the Lord;
      be assured, he will not go unpunished.
⁶ By loyalty and faithfulness iniquity is atoned
      for,
      and by the fear of the Lord a man avoids
      evil.
⁷ When a man's ways please the Lord,
      he makes even his enemies to be at peace
      with him.
⁸ Better is a little with righteousness
      than great revenues with injustice.
⁹ A man's mind plans his way,
      but the Lord directs his steps.

The limitation of a man's ability to plan his life is the subject of vv. 1,2,9. Yahweh's will is normative and determinative. The ways of a man may be judged *pure in his own eyes,* but his judgment has to be subjected to the decision of God. Yahweh weighs the motives of men in *this* life. The determinative factor of the will of Yahweh is expressed in v. 9. A man may make his plans, but their implementation depends upon the divine will (see James 4:13–17) (see 19:21). This proverb is often compared to the English saying, "Man proposes, but God disposes."

The interpretation of v. 1 depends upon the meaning of v. 1*b*. One interpretation takes the expression to mean that man has to do his own thinking but that Yahweh has to be depended upon to give him the appropriate words for the expression of his thoughts. Hard thinking comes to nothing unless God gives the ability for effective verbalization. Another approach is that which considers *the answer of the tongue* as from Yahweh, and thus, equal to "decision." In terms of this view, the verse would mean that man may think out his plans, but they must match the divine "decision" for his life if there is to be any expectation of success (see McKane, p. 496). The first interpretation is preferable.

God's control of human life is also the theme of vv. 4,5,6,7. We should not read a moral dilemma into v. 4 in the form of the idea that God has made the wicked for judgment (Jones, p. 148). The sentence declares simply and directly that God controls the world, and all its systems work. Scott's translation of the verse helps to bring out the meaning (p. 104): "The Lord has made everything with its counterpart, / So the wicked will have his day of doom." The wicked man is headed for an evil day —but his destiny is not fixed irrevocably, because he need not remain a wicked man. Iniquity may be atoned for, and a man may be saved from *evil* by Yahweh. But the atonement in v. 6 is based on loyalty and faithfulness paralleled with the *fear of the Lord*. Commitment to Yahweh and loyalty to him will save a man from the evil of the punishment which is certain for every man who arrogantly assumes the right to choose his own ways (v. 5; cf. 11:20a,21a).

Yahweh makes even the enemies to be at peace with the man whose ways are pleasing to the divine will (v. 7, though the man may be the subject in v. 7b, not Yahweh; in which case, the verse does not speak of direct action by Yahweh but of the result of ways that please Yahweh). Thus, a man should commit himself to Yahweh (v. 3) with the assurance that his "plans will be established." Even if this means that one must be content with a *little* (v. 8) it is best (see 15:16; 16:19).

(2) Royal Responsibilities (16:10–15)

10 Inspired decisions are on the lips of a king;
   his mouth does not sin in judgment.
11 A just balance and scales are the LORD's;
   all the weights in the bag are his work.
12 It is an abomination to kings to do evil,
   for the throne is established by righteousness.
13 Righteous lips are the delight of a king,
   and he loves him who speaks what is right.
14 A king's wrath is a messenger of death,
   and a wise man will appease it.
15 In the light of a king's face there is life,
   and his favor is like the clouds that bring the spring rain.

Kingship and preparation for service in the royal establishment are major motifs of this collection (16:1—22:16). The Israelites views on kingship have much in common with those of the ancient world. The king is an exalted figure with a sacral personality, who is the representative (even the "son of") of Yahweh among the people (see 1 Sam. 29:9; 2 Sam. 7:1–17; Psalms 2; 72; 89). Chapter 16:10–15 reflects this concept of kingship.

Verse 10 contains the word translated *inspired decisions,* which elsewhere in the Old Testament means divination and is used in a bad sense (e.g., Deut. 18:10; 1 Sam. 15:23; 2 Kings 17:17). But it is used in a good sense in this verse and may refer to oracles given by the king (JB translates, "The lips of the king utter oracles"). The king has divine wisdom and speaks as an inspired man (see 8:14–16; Isa. 11:2). But the parallel in v. 10b may indicate that we should understand the "decisions" of v. 10a as legal decisions, analogous to that found in 2 Sam. 14:17,20. The *sin* of v. 10b should be understood as: "his mouth does not err in judgment"; i.e., he does not make foolish or fraudulent mistakes in his decisions.

For v. 11 see 11:1. The position of the verse in the present context serves to qualify the exalted status of the king. Scales and weights used in commerce are the king's business (cf. Toy, p. 324). But the verse is a reminder that such matters are ultimately Yahweh's business. The king is responsible for conducting his reign with justice (cf. Psalms 72:1–4; 89:30–33), and his responsibility is to Yahweh.

Commentators are divided on the reading of v. 12a. Some read the *abomination to kings* as meaning that the wrongdoing of others is undesirable to kings (e.g. Scott, JB), while others assume that the "abomination to kings" should be understood by analogy with the "abomination of kings" (also the "delight of kings" in v. 13a). In any case, these verses do set forward high ideals for kingship—either directly or indirectly.

Regardless of the reading of v. 13, the point is that honest, candid speech is good for the king and his people. Verse 14 stresses the power of a king's wrath. But a wise man will know how to deal with kings in such a way that temper and passion are not allowed to get out of hand. Verse 15 is a further statement of the power and status of kings. He literally and figuratively has the power of life and death.

(3) The Worth of Wisdom (16:16–25)

16 To get wisdom is better than gold;
   to get understanding is to be chosen
      rather than silver.
17 The highway of the upright turns aside
      from evil;
   he who guards his way preserves his life.
18 Pride goes before destruction,
   and a haughty spirit before a fall.
19 It is better to be of a lowly spirit with the
      poor
   than to divide the spoil with the proud.
20 He who gives heed to the word will prosper,
   and happy is he who trusts in the Lord.
21 The wise of heart is called a man of dis-
      cernment,
   and pleasant speech increases persuasive-
      ness.
22 Wisdom is a fountain of life to him who
      has it,
   but folly is the chastisement of fools.
23 The mind of the wise makes his speech
      judicious,
   and adds persuasiveness to his lips.
24 Pleasant words are like a honeycomb,
   sweetness to the soul and health to the
      body.
25 There is a way which seems right to a man,
   but its end is the way to death.

Verse 16, along with vv. 8,19,32, belongs to the "Better than . . ." form of sentence. *Wisdom* and *understanding* are better than gold and silver. Unlike 15:16; 16:8, there is no idea here of equating true religion with poverty and wealth with a lack of piety. The comparison is between a greater and a lesser good (McKane, p. 489). But this is not the case with v. 19 where the *poor* are those who have the right kind of spirit as opposed to the proud. The *word* of v. 20a can refer to the word of Yahweh. But I think it better to interpret the two lines of the verse as either complementary or anti-

thetic. If they are complementary, v. 20a refers to the word of the wisdom teacher, which enables the one hearing it to find prosperity. But this is supplemented by the happiness of trusting in Yahweh. On the other hand the lines may be antithetic, and the benefit which comes from close atten-tion to learning is not as good as the bless-edness which Yahweh gives.

Verses 17 and 18 contrast the ways of life of the upright and the proud. The upright man moves along a highway that *turns aside from evil*, i.e., it is safe and suitable for good progress. He preserves his life and keeps it moving forward in a satisfactory manner (v. 17b). But no such smooth prog-ress is in store for the person who allows *pride* and a *haughty spirit* to control him. He can expect to stumble and be broken.

The intellectual qualities of a wise man are described in vv. 21,22,23. The man who is *wise of heart* (i.e., who has a mature and sagacious mind) will gain a reputation for *discernment* or "intelligence" (Scott, p. 105). The RSV of v. 21b follows most re-cent commentaries and interprets the line as referring to the persuasiveness of pleas-ant speech. But it is better to follow McKane (p. 489) and read the *leqach* as "teaching." Courteous and pleasant speech enhances the effectiveness of a teacher. This is probably the meaning of the uncer-tain v. 23b also. The man who can make his meaning clear (Scott, p. 105) is able to increase learning. Verse 22 expresses a familiar wisdom theme (cf. 10:11; 13:14; etc.). Verse 24 may be added to these verses because of its emphasis on pleasant speech. Like honey, kindly, courteous words have a therapeutic value. Verse 25 repeats 14:12, and serves as a kind of com-mentary on the behavior depicted in vv. 26–30. Basically it is a comment on the fini-tude of man, who may choose a way which *seems right* only to find that it ends in the "ways of death."

(4) The Agitators (16:26–30)

26 A worker's appetite works for him;
   his mouth urges him on.

27 A worthless man plots evil,
   and his speech is like a scorching fire.
28 A perverse man spreads strife,
   and a whisperer separates close friends.
29 A man of violence entices his neighbor
   and leads him in a way that is not good.
30 He who winks his eyes plans perverse things,
   he who compresses his lips brings evil to
   pass.

Verse 26 appears to have little connection with the context. It states a self-evident truth: men work (the "work" here is hard toil) because they have to in order to meet their needs. However, if McKane (p. 491) is correct in seeing here a genuine "proverbial" sentence, there is a possibility of a relationship to vv. 27–30. The incentive for violent and deceptive behavior in society is that which stems out of personal motivation. Hence, man may be pushed on by the need to satisfy his inner desires (personal revenge, release from boredom, etc.).

The descriptions of the agitators in vv. 27–30 need little comment. The RSV is acceptable, though there are differences among commentators and translations. Verse 30 assumes that there is a relationship between mannerisms and character. Read v. 30b with *The Jerusalem Bible,* "he who purses his lips has already done wrong."

(5) Proverbs About Life and Conduct (16:31—17:10)

31 A hoary head is a crown of glory;
   it is gained in a righteous life.
32 He who is slow to anger is better than the
   mighty,
   and he who rules his spirit than he who
   takes a city.
33 The lot is cast into the lap,
   but the decision is wholly from the LORD.

1 Better is a dry morsel with quiet
   than a house full of feasting with strife.
2 A slave who deals wisely will rule over a
   son who acts shamefully,
   and will share the inheritance as one of
   the brothers.
3 The crucible is for silver, and the furnace is
   for gold,
   and the LORD tries hearts.
4 An evildoer listens to wicked lips;
   and a liar gives heed to a mischievous
   tongue.
5 He who mocks the poor insults his Maker;

he who is glad at calamity will not go
   unpunished.
6 Grandchildren are the crown of the aged,
   and the glory of sons is their fathers.
7 Fine speech is not becoming to a fool;
   still less is false speech to a prince.
8 A bribe is like a magic stone in the eyes of
   him who gives it;
   wherever he turns he prospers.
9 He who forgives an offense seeks love,
   but he who repeats a matter alienates a
   friend.
10 A rebuke goes deeper into a man of understanding
   than a hundred blows into a fool.

Verse 31 views old age in a positive way. It reflects "a society where the status of greybeards was assured . . . where wisdom was correlated with a long experience of life and the elders had weight in counsel and power in affairs" (McKane, p. 501). It hardly reflects the contemporary mania for life under thirty!—which is more in keeping with Isaiah 3:4–6.

Verse 32 places the emphasis on self-discipline. *Spirit* here means disposition and temperament (cf. 14:29). The wise man is quick to learn, but slow to anger. Verse 32 refers to the casting of lots, which was a means of obtaining an oracle for finding out God's will (see, e.g., 1 Sam. 14:41–42; Jonah 1:7; Acts 1:26). The *lap* is an allusion to the pocket in the priestly garment where the lots (probably the Urim and Thummim) were kept (see Ex. 28:30; Lev. 8:8). The sentence declares that Yahweh's will is made known through this seemingly chancy process. As Jones comments, "The principle is that what men do not control God does" (p. 153).

The thought of 17:1 is that of 15:17. It is better to have a very simple meal with quiet concord than to have feasting (lit., sacrifices of discord) with contention and a lack of friendship. It is probable that the "sacrifices" is derived from the eating of meals in connection with sacrifices (cf. Deut. 12:7; 1 Sam. 9:12–13; Isa. 34:6).

Verse 2 declares that a faithful servant may take the place of an unworthy son and *share the inheritance as one of the brothers.* A man who learns how to *deal wisely,* i.e., with skill and success, can overcome the disadvantages of a poor status in society (for further comment, see Scott, p. 110).

Men possess the abilities to test silver and gold, but Yahweh is the assayer of the real character of men (v. 5, cf. 15:11; 16:2; etc.) Gossip is a problem in every group and community (v. 4). There is never a lack of those who "bend over" to hear the talk of malicious lips. These are the people who are dedicated to the production of discord and strife among others. For v. 5 see the comment on 14:31.

The cohesion of the family unit is a major feature of the Old Testament (Jones, p. 154). It was considered to be very good that a family chain could be kept intact. There are no "generation gaps" in v. 6! Unfortunately, the picture of family life projected here is too rare today. The *crown* and the *glory* go both ways in v. 6—from parents to children and from children to parents.

Two incongruities are set up in v. 7 (cf. 11:22). *Fine speech* is out of place with a fool, just as *false speech* is with a *prince* or, better, "a man of honor," to whom truthful speech is natural (cf. Isa. 32:5–8). The particular word for *fool* (*nabal*) in this verse is used very little in Proverbs (17:21; 30:22). It denotes a contemptuous, gross, non-religious type of person (Fritsch, p. 880).

Verse 8 is an observation on the powerful effectiveness of a bribe. Judiciously used, it can bring success to the user wherever he turns. The bribe is *like a magic stone*, a talisman or amulet with magical qualities. Verse 8a can be translated with a sense which makes the bribe the possession of the one who receives it (so Scott, p. 108); but the sense is better with the RSV (see McKane, p. 502). The realism of the wise men reminds us of the unfortunate truth that bribery has been and still is a standard feature of governments and businesses all over the world. It would be a mistake to assume that the wise men thought that the procedures of bribery were righteous (see vv. 15,23,26). But they

did face the facts of living in a very imperfect world. A righteous man might not make use of the powers of bribery, but he may have them used against him. Only a fool would ignore the reality of the power of a bribe.

Verses 9 and 10 deal with tolerance and sensitivity. There are two lines of approach to the understanding of v. 9. (1) One may think in terms of a personal affront to a person, who *seeks love* and *forgives.* The wronged man covers or overlooks the fault in contrast to the man who *repeats* or harps on such an injury until he breaks the friendship. (2) A third person(s) may be thought of, and thus the point becomes that of the "overlooking" of another's weaknesses and transgressions in order not to break up friendships by gossip (McKane, p. 508). Either approach is acceptable, but the second gives a better contrast (see 16:28).

The person who "seeks love" keeps in close confidence words and information which could be damaging to friendships. In order to do this, he needs the kind of sensitivity expressed in v. 10a. *A man of understanding* requires little reproof, because he is willing and able to react positively. A fool rejects discipline and retains his incorrigibility. Thus, there is no direct relationship between vv. 9 and 10, but the alert, intelligent man of v. 10 is the man who knows how to keep unnecessary information from destroying friendships.

(6) Varied Teachings (17:11–28)

11 An evil man seeks only rebellion,
    and a cruel messenger will be sent against
    him.
12 Let a man meet a she-bear robbed of her
    cubs,
    rather than a fool in his folly.
13 If a man returns evil for good,
    evil will not depart from his house.
14 The beginning of strife is like letting out
    water;
    so quit before the quarrel breaks out.
15 He who justifies the wicked and he who
    condemns the righteous
    are both alike an abomination to the
    LORD.

16 Why should a fool have a price in his hand
        to buy wisdom,
    when he has no mind?
17 A friend loves at all times,
    and a brother is born for adversity.
18 A man without sense gives a pledge,
    and becomes surety in the presence of
        his neighbor.
19 He who loves transgression loves strife;
    he who makes his door high seeks destruc-
        tion.
20 A man of crooked mind does not prosper,
    and one with a perverse tongue falls into
        calamity.
21 A stupid son is a grief to a father;
    and the father of a fool has no joy.
22 A cheerful heart is a good medicine,
    but a downcast spirit dries up the bones.
23 A wicked man accepts a bribe from the
        bosom
    to pervert the ways of justice.
24 A man of understanding sets his face toward
        wisdom,
    but the eyes of a fool are on the ends of
        the earth.
25 A foolish son is a grief to his father
    and bitterness to her who bore him.
26 To impose a fine on a righteous man is not
        good;
    to flog noble men is wrong.
27 He who restrains his words has knowledge,
    and he who has a cool spirit is a man of
        understanding.
28 Even a fool who keeps silent is considered
        wise;
    when he closes his lips, he is deemed
        intelligent.

In terms of contemporary idiom, v. 11 may be understood as a "law and order" verse. The rebellious man who seeks "evil" (trouble and disorder) will be dealt with severely by the community. He will be punished by a *cruel messenger* (cf. 16: 14a) of society, who will not fail to get his man. The RSV translation of v. 11a is a common one, but a preferable translation is: "The wicked man thinks of nothing but rebellion" (JB).

Verse 12 is a forceful comment on the danger of *a fool in his folly* (cf. 2 Sam. 17:8; Hos. 13:8; Amos 5:19). Verse 13 expresses an idea of retribution which is common in the wisdom literature. You reap what you sow (cf. 25:21–22).

Verse 14 provides good advice for avoiding serious quarrels: stop before they be-gin. The picture is that of a leak in a dam which begins as only a trickle, but, unless stopped, it may soon produce a break in the dam and a flood. The way to prevent a fight is to stop it before it gets started!

The background of v. 15 is that of legal proceedings. Either deviation mentioned is repulsive to Yahweh. He wants justice for innocent and guilty alike. It is better to think of school fees in v. 16 rather than just of a generalized statement that money cannot buy wisdom—true as that is (see Job 28:15–19). A student cannot buy wisdom by paying tuition to a teacher if he lacks the capacity and discipline for learning.

There are two ways of understanding v. 17—both true. If *friend* and *brother* are taken as synonymous, the verse means that real friendship is a strong and enduring relationship, which has its best qualities in times of crisis. If "friend" and "brother" are not synonymous, the verse distinguishes between friendship and blood relationship. As McKane (p. 506) notes, friends are usually chosen because they are congenial company. Brothers may not be as congenial as friends, but there is a bond of kinship which creates obligations, particularly in times of trouble (cf. 18:24; 27:10).

For v. 18 see the comment on 6:1 and 11:15.

The thrust of vv. 19–20 is that a contentious person seeks trouble and finds it. *He who makes his door high* in v. 19b is obscure, but it probably refers to arrogant speech.

Verses 6 and 21 give the two sides of parenthood: joy and sorrow (see 10:1; 15:20). The therapeutic results of good inner conditions were well known to the wise men (v. 22; cf. 14:30; 15:13). Verse 23 is another observation on bribery (see 17:8; 15:27). For *bosom* see the comment on 16:33, where the same Hebrew word was translated "lap." Bribery is viewed as the action of a corrupt man in this verse.

The fool is characteristically unable to concentrate his attention and energy in thought and action (v. 24). His eyes are *on the ends of the earth*—roving about and skipping from thing to thing. The perceptive *man of understanding* always keeps wisdom in sight.

Verses 27–28 give expression to a major theme of wisdom teaching: self-control. The man who has a *cool spirit* (cool is used of water in 25:25) is composed and able to think clearly about hot issues. The wise men knew that thinking and acting on the basis of "hot blood" has been a devastating human trait.

Verse 28 has a twist of ironic humor in it. Even a fool may gain a reputation for intelligence if he does not give himself away by talking! It is difficult to overestimate the wisdom of keeping your mouth shut unless you have something to say that is healthy and needs to be said.

(7) Foolish Ways (18:1–8)

1 He who is estranged seeks pretexts
   to break out against all sound judgment.
2 A fool takes no pleasure in understanding,
   but only in expressing his opinion.
3 When wickedness comes, contempt comes also;
   and with dishonor comes disgrace.
4 The words of a man's mouth are deep waters;
   the fountain of wisdom is a gushing stream.
5 It is not good to be partial to a wicked man,
   or to deprive a righteous man of justice.
6 A fool's lips bring strife,
   and his mouth invites a flogging.
7 A fool's mouth is his ruin,
   and his lips are a snare to himself.
8 The words of a whisperer are like delicious morsels;
   they go down into the inner parts of the body.

Verse 1 is an observation on the behavioral patterns of an alienated person. Such a person is always ready for a quarrel ("to bare his teeth"); contentious about sound policies and competent people. There is some difficulty in the translation of this verse (compare RSV, NEB, JB, BV). I prefer Scott: "An unsociable man cares only about his selfish concerns, / He rails against every sound enterprise."

The fool loves to pour out his opinions, but he *takes no pleasure* in trying to grasp

real understanding (v. 2). The hard work of thinking through the issues is of little interest for such a man. He prefers "to display his wit" (NEB).

Verse 3 is an observation on the results of *wickedness* and *dishonor*. *Disgrace* is better understood as reproach or insult. *Dishonor* indicates lightness, a lack of social status and respect.

Several sentences in this chapter are concerned with speech (vv. 4,6–8,13,20, 21). As it stands, v. 4 seems to give a generalized endorsement of human speech which is not in keeping with the usual teaching of the wise men. Thus it is not surprising that some commentators argue that we should read the opening phrase, "The words of the wise . . . " (e.g., Jones, p. 160). The wise man has a perennial source of words and wisdom. A less probable approach to the interpretation of the sentence is to assume antithetic parallelism and read a contrast between v. 4a and v. 4b; i.e., the speech of an ordinary man is difficult to understand (like drawing water from a deep well), while that of a wise man flows out like water from a spring.

For the thought of v. 5, see 17:15,26. This maxim is concerned with judicial procedures, as is 18:17. The expression *to be partial to* is literally "to lift up the face." It is, probably, derived from the practice of raising the face of a prostrate suppliant when his plea has been granted and the case decided in his favor.

Verses 6–7 are observations on the speech of a fool. A fool's talk constantly gets him in trouble (cf. 17:14,19; 20:3). He attracts hostility and retaliation. Verse 8 is an assessment of the human desire for gossip. It is swallowed greedily, like good-tasting bits of food; and it is swallowed thoroughly, *into the inner parts*. We may forget the good things we hear about people, but we recall easily the bad things and "whisper" them to others who devour them eagerly.

(8) On Avoiding Destruction (18:9–15)

9 He who is slack in his work
   is a brother to him who destroys.

10 The name of the LORD is a strong tower;
    the righteous man runs into it and is
    safe.
11 A rich man's wealth is his strong city,
    and like a high wall protecting him.
12 Before destruction a man's heart is haughty,
    but humility goes before honor.
13 If one gives answer before he hears,
    it is his folly and shame.
14 A man's spirit will endure sickness;
    but a broken spirit who can bear?
15 An intelligent mind acquires knowledge,
    and the ear of the wise seeks knowledge.

The slack worker is a *brother* to one who *destroys* or a "master of destruction." "Brother" in this context has the sense of belonging to the same class and sharing the same nature. The phrase *the name of the LORD* is used only here in Proverbs (cf. 30:9). The "name" represents Yahweh himself (cf. Ps. 20:7). It is his presence and power. The *righteous man* who runs to it will find security like that provided by a fortified tower, which is inaccessible from the dangers below. On the security of the righteous man, see 10:2,9,24,25,29, 30; 11:4,6,8,21; etc.

Verse 11, also, describes strength and security, but quite differently than in v. 10. In v. 11, it is the wealth of a rich man which is like a strong city (see 10:15a).

For v. 12a, compare 16:18a and for v. 12b, compare 15:33b. Before the shattering reality of life comes, a man may be proud and think that he can bend the world to suit his ideas. Afterwards, he learns that humility is a prerequisite to greatness.

Verse 13 speaks for itself: don't answer until you hear the whole statement and know what is involved (cf. Eccles. 11:8). It pays to listen before talking. The RSV could be clearer in v. 14. The sentence says that it is a man's spirit which permits him to cope with sickness. Physical weakness can be counterbalanced by determination of the spirit, i.e., the mind and will. If the spirit is crushed, a man's sickness is fatal because the inner source of resistance and control is gone.

Verse 15 presents a picture of a mind which is the opposite of that in 18:2. Unlike the "fool" in v. 2, a man of understanding is continually getting knowledge, because he has an ear that is continually seeking knowledge, i.e., listening to teachers and learning from the experiences of others. It is this kind of mind which powers a man to a strong, able, and successful life.

(9) Teachings and Precepts (18:16–24)

16 A man's gift makes room for him
    and brings him before great men.
17 He who states his case first seems right,
    until the other comes and examines him.
18 The lot puts an end to disputes
    and decides between powerful contenders.
19 A brother helped is like a strong city,
    but quarreling is like the bars of a castle.
20 From the fruit of his mouth a man is
    satisfied;
    he is satisfied by the yield of his lips.
21 Death and life are in the power of the
    tongue,
    and those who love it will eat its fruits.
22 He who finds a wife finds a good thing,
    and obtains favor from the LORD.
23 The poor use entreaties,
    but the rich answer roughly.
24 There are friends who pretend to be friends,
    but there is a friend who sticks closer
    than a brother.

Verse 16 is another comment on the use of bribery as in 17:8 (which see). Money, properly used, can gain a man entrance into the circles of high society and great influence. The *gift* widens the path to success and brings the giver into the presence of those people who can promote his interests.

The value of cross-examination is the point of v. 17. The translation speaks for itself. Verse 18 also has reference to legal cases, particularly those where litigation is protracted and indecisive. In such situations, a settlement by the use of casting the lot is commendable. We should probably think of the lot as a divine decision (see 16:33), which can settle what men cannot decide, or will not decide, by normal legal procedures.

Verse 19 is obscure, but it is doubtful that the antithetic parallelism assumed in the RSV (from the versions) is correct. Scott's (p. 113) rendering is preferable: "A brother offended is harder [to be won] than a strong city, / And his antagonism is

like the bar of a castle." In this case, the
meaning would be that the quarrels and
antagonisms which divide men are as hard
to break down as the walls and gate bars of
a fortified city. If the *brother* is intended to
indicate kinship, rather than the neighbor
or the community "brother," the deep animosity which emerges from family quarrels
is in mind.

The sentences in vv. 20–21 express some
of the consequences of speech (see 12:14;
13:2). The tongue has the power of *death
and life.* It is imperative to use it properly.
Verse 20 should be understood more literally. The NEB translates it: "A man may
live by the fruit of his tongue, / his lips
may earn him a livelihood."

A good wife is a blessing from Yahweh
(*obtains favor from the Lord* is used of
Wisdom in 8:35). The wisdom teachers
believed in marriage, despite its obvious
hazards (e.g., see 21:9). It is safe to assume that a "good wife" (as in 31:10) is
intended, though the text does not say so
explicitly.

Verse 23 is an observation on a reality of
life—undesirable, but true. The poor man
has to ask for things, hoping for some help
for his impoverished situation. The rich
man does not have to worry about the tone
of his voice. He has the power to give and
get without much regard for what others
think.

There are linguistic and textual difficulties in v. 24; but the RSV may be accepted
as a reasonable attempt to reconstruct the
verse. The point seems clear in v. 24*b*:
there is a friendship which endures more
strongly and loyally than kinship. There
are genuine friends; but there are also
superficial friends who are easily lost.

**(10) Proverbs on Various Subjects (19:
1–18)**

¹ Better is a poor man who walks in his integrity
   than a man who is perverse in speech,
   and is a fool.
² It is not good for a man to be without
knowledge,
   and he who makes haste with his feet

misses his way.
³ When a man's folly brings his way to ruin,
   his heart rages against the Lord.
⁴ Wealth brings many new friends,
   but a poor man is deserted by his friend.
⁵ A false witness will not go unpunished,
   and he who utters lies will not escape.
⁶ Many seek the favor of a generous man,
   and everyone is a friend to a man who
   gives gifts.
⁷ All a poor man's brothers hate him;
   how much more do his friends go far
   from him!
   He pursues them with words, but does not
   have them.
⁸ He who gets wisdom loves himself;
   he who keeps understanding will prosper.
⁹ A false witness will not go unpunished,
   and he who utters lies will perish.
¹⁰ It is not fitting for a fool to live in luxury,
   much less for a slave to rule over princes.
¹¹ Good sense makes a man slow to anger,
   and it is his glory to overlook an offense.
¹² A king's wrath is like the growling of a
   lion,
   but his favor is like dew upon the grass.
¹³ A foolish son is ruin to his father,
   and a wife's quarreling is a continual
   dripping of rain.
¹⁴ House and wealth are inherited from fathers,
   but a prudent wife is from the Lord.
¹⁵ Slothfulness casts into a deep sleep,
   and an idle person will suffer hunger.
¹⁶ He who keeps the commandment keeps his
   life;
   he who despises the word will die.
¹⁷ He who is kind to the poor lends to the
   Lord,
   and he will repay him for his deed.
¹⁸ Discipline your son while there is hope;
   do not set your heart on his destruction.

Because v. 1*a* appears in 28:6 with a
parallel which contrasts the *poor man* of
integrity with a rich man of perverse character, some commentators want to alter the
text here to "poor" or understand the fool
as a "rich fool." However, neither is necessary. We may have an example of one line
of a sentence being used in different contexts. There is nothing wrong with saying
that it is better to be poor with integrity
than to be a fool—though the implication
is strong that the *fool* in v. 1*b*, is intended
to be the type of person who tries to con
his way into wealth by speech which takes
advantage of others. He uses twisted, misleading speech.

Verse 3 comments on the man whose way is "twisted" (though a different word is used than in v. 1), and this *folly* brings him to ruin. But he is bitter towards Yahweh for his failure. This is properly a proverb which says: Take responsibility for your own failures. You cannot blame God for *your* foolishness.

Verse 2 is an observation on impulsive action, which is not a good thing and causes the impulsive person to miss his objectives. *Misses his way* is a major Hebrew word for sin, i.e., missing the mark (cf. 8:36; Job 5:24). The verse draws a parallel between two bad lines of action. It is best to translate v. 2*a* as, "Enthusiasm (or zeal) without knowledge is not good." *Nephesh* in this context means energy, drive, vitality or the like.

For the thought of v. 4 see 14:20. The wise men were realistic about wealth. A poor man can expect to find himself deserted by his neighbors. This is not the way it ought to be; but it is the way it very frequently is. Even the kin by blood relationship may have no use for a poor man (v. 7), though the obligations of family life may force them to give him some support. Verse 7 has an extra line (perhaps, a marginal comment which has been added to the text, or a fragment of a separate proverb) which probably should be understood as saying that though a poor man pursues kinsmen and friends with pleas for help they will desert him.

Verse 6 is closely related in thought and observes that there are plenty of people to praise those of high rank and those who are generous givers. McKane (p. 526) may be correct when he suggests that this verse points to the dubious character of a rich man's friends and to the difficulty which such a man has in sorting out those who are true friends from those who want to use him and his wealth for their own ends.

The NEB is more accurate than the RSV in v. 8*a*: "To learn sense is true self-love." I like the sense of Scott's rather free translation (p. 115): "He who develops his mind is his own best friend." Note that v. 9

repeats the thought of v. 5.

Verse 10 is an expression of the wise men's belief that there should be a correspondence between the social order and the moral order. Both statements in v. 10 set forth incongruities which are improper (cf. 17:7). The NEB of v. 10*a* follows a suggestion (for discussion see McKane, p. 528) that the word translated *to live in luxury* really means administration or management —Thus, "A fool at the helm is out of place." This makes sense, but it is uncertain.

There is a kind of thinking which believes it best to be quick to fight for your rights and to refuse to allow a personal offense to go unanswered. But this is not the approach of v. 11. A man shows his *good sense* and his glory when he is forbearing and ready to overlook the faults of others. These qualities are those of a real toughness of intellect and temperament.

Verse 12 is an observation on the moods and power of kings (cf. 16:14–15; 20:2).

Verse 13 is another contrast to the happy family life of 17:6. Jones (p. 166) notes that there is an Arabic proverb which lists three things making a house unbearable: *tak*, a leak of rainwater; *nak*, a wife's nagging; and *bak*, bugs!

A *prudent wife* is not come by as are other possessions, some of which may be inherited (v. 14) (see 18:22). As Rylaarsdam (p. 67) notes, the wise men recognized that there was a considerable element of uncertainty in the choice of a wife. Thus, a good wife was ascribed to the favor of Yahweh. No demanding personal decision may be involved in acquiring *house and wealth* (of course, such decisions may be required in other circumstances), but one takes his chances when he chooses a wife.

Verse 15 is an indictment of sloth (cf. 6: 9–10; 20:13; 24:33–34). It is possible that *deep sleep* means "sleeping place" (so Scott, p. 117, following Dahood) and that v. 15*a* means "slothfulness causes the sleeping place to fall" (cf. NEB). If this change is not made, v. 15*a* refers to the lethargic, apathetic condition.

The problem in v. 16*a* is the meaning of

the commandment (lit., a commandment). The term may be a technical term which equals *torah* or law. This is quite possible in the present context. But it is equally as probable that the "commandment" had an original reference to the authoritative instruction of a wisdom teacher (cf. 13:13). The RSV emends "his ways" in v. 16*b* to *the word.* But this change is not required, and it is doubtful that it should be made. "His ways" in this context refers to the "ways" of Yahweh (note NEB); but the original reference was probably to the "ways" (i.e., instructions and examples) of the wisdom teacher.

Verse 17 stresses the obligation to care for the poor. In a striking way, such action is said to be equivalent to lending to God, who takes the cause of the poor and needy for his own and repays their debts. Yahweh is ready to go in debt for the poor.

Verse 18*a* emphasizes the value of disciplinary action while there is still time for it to influence the life of a child. But it is equally possible to translate "for there is hope," i.e., as a motive clause which reassures the parent that parental discipline will produce results if sustained (see JB; McKane, p. 524). Verse 18*b* may set a limit to discipline. Thus, the NEB translates: "but be careful not to flog him to death."

(11) Character: Good and Bad (19:19–24)

¹⁹ A man of great wrath will pay the penalty;
    for if you deliver him, you will only have
        to do it again.
²⁰ Listen to advice and accept instruction,
    that you may gain wisdom for the future.
²¹ Many are the plans in the mind of a man,
    but it is the purpose of the LORD that
        will be established.
²² What is desired in a man is loyalty,
    and a poor man is better than a liar.
²³ The fear of the LORD leads to life;
    and he who has it rests satisfied;
        he will not be visited by harm.
²⁴ The sluggard buries his hand in the dish,
    and will not even bring it back to his
        mouth.

Verse 19 is a very difficult verse to translate, and the translations usually given are largely based on tradition. What we have may be accepted as a reasonable conjecture. The question of meaning remains. Apparently, the point is that there can be an incorrigibility about a man which is best left alone. If one tries to help him (or pay his fine, which may be the idea in v. 19*a*), the result may be encouragement for him to continue his intemperate ways. It may be better to translate: "Let a man of bad temper (or unacceptable behavior) bear his punishment, / for if you help him out, you will have to do it again and again."

Verse 20 is a bit of instruction which is standard for the wisdom teachers. The student is admonished to listen and receive teaching in order that the end result will be the development of a wise man. The teachers considered themselves to be imparting authoritative instruction, proven by experience and guaranteed to bring results.

Verse 21 is another expression of the idea that God's purpose is worked out regardless of the plans and purposes of men (see 16:1; Isa. 46:10; Psalms 33:11; Job 23:13; Gen. 50:20).

The meaning of v. 22*a* uncertain. I prefer either the NEB: "Greed is a disgrace to a man; better be a poor man than a liar"; or, McKane (p. 532), who with dependence upon the Greek text derives the meaning: "A man's productivity is his loyalty (reading *chsd* with this meaning, not as in 14:34; 25:10) and a poor man is better than a false one." The sentence seems to say that the real measure of a man is his character, not his profit and property.

Verse 23 is a variation of the concept found in 14:27. The picture of satisfied and secure rest or lodging is an attractive one. Verse 24 is a *reductio ad absurdum* of laziness (Jones, p. 168). There is an element of humor in the picture of a person too lazy to eat the food which has been provided for him (see 26:15).

(12) Sundry Observations (19:25–29)

²⁵ Strike a scoffer, and the simple will learn
        prudence;
    reprove a man of understanding, and he

will gain knowledge.
26 He who does violence to his father and
chases away his mother
is a son who causes shame and brings
reproach.
27 Cease, my son, to hear instruction
only to stray from the words of knowledge.
28 A worthless witness mocks at justice,
and the mouth of the wicked devours
iniquity.
29 Condemnation is ready for scoffers,
and flogging for the backs of fools.

Verse 25 seems to mean that the punishment given to a scoffer may provide *the
simple* with the opportunity to learn from
it. The simple person is a man who is immature and untutored but open to instruction. On the other hand, the mature *man of
understanding* needs no such process of
learning as seeing the punishment of others.
He can accept and utilize correction directly.

Verse 26 describes the unacceptable behavior of a son who treats his parents in
cruel and callous ways. The rejection of
responsibility for parents, even out-right
eviction, is a contemporary problem; but it
is not new.

Verse 27 appears to be a sentence of the
Instruction genre, but really it is different. The imperative is in a kind of rhetorical construction which is intended to
show the bad consequences of straying
away from knowledge learned (McKane, p.
525). The sentence is ironic.

Verse 28 is another observation on the
evil of perjury (see vv. 5,9; 6:12). The
parallelism is clearer if v. 28*b* is translated
with either "pours out" or "communicates"
rather than *devours* (see McKane, p. 529).
An assortment of punishments are available, (and will be used) for the scoffers and
fools (v. 29).

**(13) *Drunkenness and Other Matters* (20:
1–11)**

1 Wine is a mocker, strong drink a brawler;
and whoever is led astray by it is not
wise.
2 The dread wrath of a king is like the
growling of a lion;
he who provokes him to anger forfeits

his life.
3 It is an honor for a man to keep aloof from
strife;
but every fool will be quarreling.
4 The sluggard does not plow in the autumn;
he will seek at harvest and have nothing.
5 The purpose in a man's mind is like deep
water,
but a man of understanding will draw
it out.
6 Many a man proclaims his own loyalty,
but a faithful man who can find?
7 A righteous man who walks in his integrity—
blessed are his sons after him!
8 A king who sits on the throne of judgment
winnows all evil with his eyes.
9 Who can say, "I have made my heart
clean;
I am pure from my sin"?
10 Diverse weights and diverse measures
are both alike an abomination to the
LORD.
11 Even a child makes himself known by his
acts,
whether what he does is pure and right.

Drunkenness is a symptom of a lack of
self-discipline and overindulgence. The wisdom teachers were aware of its dangers and
did not fail to warn their students (see 23:
19–21,29–35; 31:4–5; cf. 31:6–7). The
normal use of wine on festal occasions was
accepted (3:10; 9:2,5; Eccl. 9:7; Psalm
104:15; Job 1:13; Ecclus. 31:27–28). But
the wise men, like the prophets, attacked
the excessive use of intoxicating beverages
(e.g., Amos 6:6; Hos. 7:5; Isa. 5:11–12,22;
Jer. 23:9). Jones (p. 170) is correct in
noting that the RSV *led astray* is "too gen-
teel." The meaning is "to stagger drunk-
enly" (cf. Isa. 28:7; Jer. 25:27). Also, it is
probably better to translate the *is not wise*
as "can not act wisely." The person who is
under the influence of alcohol cannot act
with precision and good judgment.

A king's anger can be as frightening as
the roar of a lion—and as dangerous (v. 2;
cf. 16:14; 19:12). Whoever provokes a
king, puts his life in danger. It is an honorable thing to do to avoid disputes and
fights (v. 3). The fool is always "baring his
teeth" in an angry quarrel (see 17:14;
18:1).

It is a characteristic of the sluggard that he does not work when he is supposed to do so (v. 4; *autumn* was the time for plowing in Palestine; see 6:6–11; 10:5). But he looks for a crop nevertheless. He knows what he wants, but he lacks the energy and planning ahead in order to obtain it.

Verse 5 says that the counsel or *purpose* in a man's mind is like water in a deep well or spring. It is not easily drawn out, though a man with *understanding* will have the skill to do it. Wisdom is not found on the surface of life—either of oneself or another —it must be "educated," drawn out by instruction, clarification, and experience. Bringing about the process in another is a skilled operation—roughly analogous to drawing a bucket of water from a deep well (those who have tried this tricky process will understand the analogy).

True friendship is rare (v. 6)—a realistic comment. There are many "superficial professors" in this area of life! It is the dependable, truthful, *faithful* man who is really loyal. The corporate nature of family life appears in v. 7. The children of a *righteous man* of *integrity* receive the benefits of his character (cf. Ex. 20:6).

Verse 8 is another presentation of the exalted and powerful role of the king (see 16:10,13). He sifts out the evidence of legal cases before him in order to make the right judgment. Perhaps, we should think of this verse as setting forth more of the ideal than the reality relative to the way kings make their decisions (see 20:26).

The universality of human imperfection —a matter which kings needed to remember—is the subject of v. 9 (cf. Job 4:17–19; Psalm 51:5; 130:3; Eccl. 7:20). Verse 10 is a variation of 11:1; 20:23 (see also 16:11; Deut. 25:13–16; Amos 8:5). Verse 10*a* refers to the weights and measures used in buying and selling. Either way, they should be accurate. Character is made known in conduct (v. 11). Verbal professions and external appearances are not decisive; performance is essential. This is a verse which could well be taken to heart by both young

ant old in today's world (cf. Matt. 7:20; James 2:14–26).

(14) Things Better Than Gold (20:12–18)

12 The hearing ear and the seeing eye,
    the Lord has made them both.
13 Love not sleep, lest you come to poverty;
    open your eyes, and you will have plenty
        of bread.
14 "It is bad, it is bad," says the buyer;
    but when he goes away, then he boasts.
15 There is gold, and abundance of costly
        stones;
    but the lips of knowledge are a precious
        jewel.
16 Take a man's garment when he has given
        surety for a stranger,
    and hold him in pledge when he gives
        surety for foreigners.
17 Bread gained by deceit is sweet to a man,
    but afterward his mouth will be full of
        gravel.
18 Plans are established by counsel;
    by wise guidance wage war.

The juxtaposition of vv. 12 and 13 (probably on the basis of the catchword "eye") is fortunate. The divine endowment of human life with the essential faculties for life and work (v. 12) should be used to avoid poverty and obtain food (v. 13; cf. 6:9–11; 19:15). Apparently, the wisdom teachers were early risers and considerably concerned about sleeping too much.

Verse 14 is an observation of the methods used in commercial deals. No judgment is expressed as to the merit or lack of merit in such processes; but there is some evidence to suggest that the wisdom teachers were wary of these techniques (cf. 6:1–5; 11:15; 17:18). The verse should be read with an appreciation of the humor in it, and of the bargaining rituals of the Near East—still common today.

Wisdom is worth more than any wealth (v. 15; cf. 3:14–15; 16:16; 22:1).

The practice of becoming financial surety for another is the subject of v. 16 (repeated in 27:13; cf. 6:1–5; 11:15; 17:18). The exact situation envisioned in this sentence is difficult to bring into focus. Scott (pp. 121–3) assumes that the lender is advised to be more strict with foreigners than with Israelites (cf. Ex. 22:26–27: Deut. 15:1–3). McKane (p. 543) takes the verse somewhat more generally as meaning that if you are dealing with a person who is a bad credit risk, particularly if he is liable for the debts of foreigners, then get security for yourself ("take his garment") at once.

The satisfaction of dishonesty may be sweet for awhile; but it does not last (v. 17; cf. Lam. 3:16). Verse 18 should be compared with 12:15; 15:22. However, the subject here is war. No one man should try to direct a military campaign by himself. He needs the counsel and guidance of others. Let kings, prime ministers, presidents, and generals take notice.

(15) About Life and Conduct (20:19—21:5)

19 He who goes about gossiping reveals secrets;
   therefore do not associate with one who speaks foolishly.
20 If one curses his father or his mother,
   his lamp will be put out in utter darkness.
21 An inheritance gotten hastily in the beginning
   will in the end not be blessed.
22 Do not say, "I will repay evil";
   wait for the LORD, and he will help you.
23 Diverse weights are an abomination to the LORD,
   and false scales are not good.
24 A man's steps are ordered by the LORD;
   how then can man understand his way?
25 It is a snare for a man to say rashly, "It is holy,"
   and to reflect only after making his vows.
26 A wise king winnows the wicked,
   and drives the wheel over them.
27 The spirit of man is the lamp of the LORD,
   searching all his innermost parts.
28 Loyalty and faithfulness preserve the king,
   and his throne is upheld by righteousness.
29 The glory of young men is their strength,
   but the beauty of old men is their gray hair.
30 Blows that wound cleanse away evil;
   strokes make clean the innermost parts.

1 The king's heart is a stream of water in the hand of the LORD;
   he turns it wherever he will.
2 Every way of a man is right in his own eyes,
   but the LORD weighs the heart.
3 To do righteousness and justice
   is more acceptable to the LORD than sacrifice.
4 Haughty eyes and a proud heart,
   the lamp of the wicked, are sin.
5 The plans of the diligent lead surely to abundance,
   but every one who is hasty comes only to want.

For v. 19 see 11:13; 18:8. The talebearer will not keep confidences, so do not associate with him.

The law collections of the Pentateuch contain stipulations against the cursing of parents by children (see Ex. 21:17; Lev. 20:9; Deut. 27:16). Verse 20b refers to death, probably the darkness of Sheol. Commentators have noted that v. 20 seems to say nothing about legal punishment. The curse uttered by the offender will bring an appropriate punishment upon himself.

The sense of v. 21 is similar to v. 17. Gains gotten improperly do not end in blessing. The thrust of the verse is directed against the "get rich quick" syndrome (see 13:11; 15:27) which subordinates means to ends in a ruthless fashion. However, the means in this case appears to be a premature grabbing of the family estate. vv. 20 and 21 (McKane, p. 539).

The divine control of the issues of life is expressed in one way or another in vv. 22, 24,27; 21:1,2. The principle of personal retaliation is rejected in v. 22 in favor of waiting upon the help of Yahweh. Victory will come through dependence on the action of God (see 24:29; cf. Rom. 12:17; 1 Thess. 5:15; 1 Peter 3:9). The wording of v. 24a is also found in Psalm 37:23 (cf. Jer. 10:23), but the contexts are different. This sentence is an affirmation of God's ultimate control of human living. There is no understanding which a man can gain by education and discipline to substitute for dependence on God. However, it is a mistake to read a rigid theological determinism into the verse. Man's freedom of action is not denied, but a basic limitation of that freedom is affirmed.

Verse 27 is a statement of the action of God in the inner being of man. The *spirit of a man* (the word for "spirit" is used for the breath of life in Gen. 2:7) becomes the *lamp of the Lord* which searches out the inner parts of the human personality. The exact meaning of the verse is debatable. It can be an expression of the equivalency of the image of God, i.e., man functions with faculties which are like those of the divine existence. On the other hand, the verse may mean no more than that nothing is hidden from the divine scrutiny—'there are no secrets hidden from God.' Some commentators may have read too much into this verse.

In chapter 21, vv. 1 and 2 continue the idea of God's control of life. The king is no exception. His mind is *in the hand of the Lord* like a stream of irrigation water which may be turned into any canal by the one controlling it. Of course, this cuts two ways; i.e., it can mean that the actions and decisions of a king have divine qualities. The king does the will of God and represents him in his reign. For the thought of v. 2, see 16:2; though there is some difference in wording. No man ever has the capacity to know all about himself.

For v. 23 see 21:10 and 16:11.

Verse 25 is directed toward the error of making rash religious vows (cf. Eccl. 5:1–6; Lev. 27). One should count the cost before he commits himself or his property to that which is holy, i.e., belongs to God (cf. Luke 14:25–33). The point is caution, not evasion or misuse of vows as in Matthew 15:4–6; Mark 7:10–13 (McKane, p. 538).

Verses 26 and 28 deal with kingship. Verse 26 is closely related to 20:8. There is some uncertainty about the meaning of *drives the wheel over them.* It can be a figurative phrase for punishment, reflecting the practice of driving chariots over prostrate enemies by a victorious king (Scott, p. 122); or, the wheel may be understood as that of a threshing cart or winnowing machine which helps to separate the grain and

straw when it is driven over the unthreshed wheat or barley.

The importance of *loyalty and faithfulness* in the reign of a king is emphasized by v. 28. A king is supported (or protected) by loyalty and faithfulness on the part of his people. There is, probably, an intended allusion to Yahweh's loyalty and faithfulness which sustained the Davidic king (see 2 Sam. 7:15–16; Psalm 89:34; McKane, p. 546). There may be some idea of a personification of loyalty and faithfulness as guardian angels of the king (so Gemser, p. 79; note Psalm 61:7). It is better to translate v. 28b as, "and he sustains his throne with loyalty (i.e., his own)." The king must manifest in his administration the same qualities which are so essential for his coming to and continuing in power at all.

Verse 29 is an observation on life (see 16:31). The *beauty of old* age is, unfortunately, a lost element in much of life today—when we have more of it than ever before—though we recognize much inspiring evidence to the contrary.

Verse 30 says that corporal punishment is good for the character and moral life. But the text is difficult and commentators struggle with it. Compare the translations.

Verse 3 of chapter 21 strikes a very prophetic note (see 1 Sam. 15:22; Amos 5:22–24; Hos. 6:6; Isa. 1:11–14; Mic. 6:6–8; cf. Prov. 3:9–10; 15:8; 21:27). Sacrifices are subordinated to those qualities which are more essential. Verse 4 is an illustration of the kind of behavior which make sacrifices unacceptable, though the Hebrew of this verse is difficult to read. *Lamp* follows the ancient versions for the Masoretic Text's "plowed ground." This phrase may be kept if it is understood that the "tillage" of the wicked produces sin (so McKane, p. 559).

The *diligent* of v. 5 has the idea of sharpness or incisiveness (Scott, p. 123, translates "the keen man"). This is the kind of person who can cut through the issues and options with plans that work out successfully. The contrast in v. 5b is that of hasty action, not well thought through, which ends in failure.

(16) The Ways of the Wicked (21:6–13)

6 The getting of treasures by a lying tongue
   is a fleeting vapor and a snare of death.
7 The violence of the wicked will sweep
   them away,
   because they refuse to do what is just.
8 The way of the guilty is crooked,
   but the conduct of the pure is right.
9 It is better to live in a corner of the housetop
   than in a house shared with a contentious woman.
10 The soul of the wicked desires evil;
   his neighbor finds no mercy in his eyes.
11 When a scoffer is punished, the simple becomes wise;
   when a wise man is instructed, he gains
   knowledge.
12 The righteous observes the house of the
   wicked;
   the wicked are cast down to ruin.
13 He who closes his ear to the cry of the poor
   will himself cry out and not be heard.

Various ways of undesirable or unacceptable behavior are described in these
verses (with the exception of v. 11). The
sentences need little comment beyond translation. Verse 9 (very similar to 21:19 and
repeated in 25:24) returns to the theme of
the nagging wife (see 19:13) and has stimulated quite a bit of discussion regarding
the precise meaning of *a corner of the
housetop* (see McKane, pp. 553–4). It
probably refers to a small room, sometimes
used for guests, built on the flat roof of a
house near a corner (possibly to be near a
stairway or ladder). We should not think
of a well-equipped guest room, but of
makeshift accommodations less comfortable
than the normal living space below. For the
sense of v. 11 see 19:25. Compare v. 13
with James 2:13.

**(17) Bribery and Other Subjects (21:14–
31)**

14 A gift in secret averts anger;
   and a bribe in the bosom, strong wrath.
15 When justice is done, it is a joy to the
   righteous,
   but dismay to evildoers.
16 A man who wanders from the way of understanding
   will rest in the assembly of the dead.
17 He who loves pleasure will be a poor man;
   he who loves wine and oil will not be
   rich.
18 The wicked is a ransom for the righteous,
   and the faithless for the upright.
19 It is better to live in a desert land
   than with a contentious and fretful
   woman.
20 Precious treasure remains in a wise man's
   dwelling,
   but a foolish man devours it.
21 He who pursues righteousness and kindness
   will find life and honor.
22 A wise man scales the city of the mighty
   and brings down the stronghold in which
   they trust.
23 He who keeps his mouth and his tongue
   keeps himself out of trouble.
24 "Scoffer" is the name of the proud, haughty
   man
   who acts with arrogant pride.
25 The desire of the sluggard kills him
   for his hands refuse to labor.
26 All day long the wicked covets,
   but the righteous gives and does not hold
   back.
27 The sacrifice of the wicked is an abomination;
   how much more when he brings it with
   evil intent.
28 A false witness will perish,
   but the word of a man who hears will
   endure.
29 A wicked man puts on a bold face,
   but an upright man considers his ways.
30 No wisdom, no understanding, no counsel,
   can avail against the Lord.
31 The horse is made ready for the day of
   battle,
   but the victory belongs to the Lord.

The subject of bribery appears again in
v. 14, with the same idea as in 17:23. As
Jones (p. 179) says, we have "social report-
ing" again rather than a recommended practice; though the wisdom teachers knew that
it was virtually impossible to get along in
the world without some use of this technique.

Verse 15 is clear. Verse 16 implies a contrast between the two ways of life and
death (McKane, p. 553). Whoever wanders
away from the path of understanding laid
down by his teachers and the knowledge
gained from them begins to move toward
the *assembly of the dead.*

The translation of v. 17 speaks for itself.
Verse 18 is a parallel to 11:8. But the trans-

lation does not convey an easy meaning. The *ransom* (*kopher*) refers, in a free sort of way at least, to the sum of money which was paid when a legal penalty was removed (e.g., Ex. 21:30). This suggests that the verse means that the wicked is the *kopher* for the righteous—an improbable interpretation in the general context of Old Testament thought. Thus, it seems better to follow either McKane (p. 561), who thinks that it is a "novel way" of making an emphasis on reward and retribution ("The righteous man's meat is the wicked man's poison"), or else the idea that the wicked person gets into the trouble he has planned for the righteous (see Scott, p. 126).

Verse 19 is a variation of 21:9 (which see).

The wise man knows how to possess and preserve wealth (v. 20), while the fool will squander it. The verb *pursues* in v. 21 is a strong one (used in Psalm 23:6) and carries the idea of energetic and urgent action (cf. Matt. 5:6).

The strength of wisdom is affirmed with vigorous language in v. 22 (cf. 24:5). Intelligent action is stronger than military fortifications (cf. Eccl. 9:13–16). The importance of disciplined speech is the subject of v. 23 (cf. 12:13; 13:3; 15:23). A strongly worded definition of a *scoffer* or scorner is found in v. 24. He is a man of overweening pride.

Verse 25 returns to the subject of the lazy person, whose sloth leads, eventually, to death (cf. 19:15,24; 24:34). This kind of person has tremendous desire for achievement, but he lacks the character to work in the real world to attain his ambitions. It is his *desire* which brings death to him. Death begins when dreams become impotent.

The contrast in v. 26 is between the constant covetousness of the wicked man and the generous readiness of the righteous man to give to others. The translation, *the wicked covets,* is based on the Greek text. This is acceptable, but the position of v. 26 with v. 25 may indicate that the subject is the sluggard of v. 25, who is unable to be a benefactor, despite his desire for things and status.

The *sacrifice of the wicked* is repeated in 15:8*a* (cf. Amos 5:21–24; Isa. 1:11–17; Prov. 21:3). Verse 28 is another comment on the consequences of bearing false witness (see 19:5,9). A good listener is a good witness. The wicked man is capable of very confident and bold behavior because he has to be (v. 29). Unlike the honest man, he does not choose his ways carefully (or, if the alternate reading is preferred, "he does not establish his ways"; i.e., he does not make his ways firm and sure). The wicked man must try to bluff his way through with a "business-like" appearance which hides his real lack of strength.

As Ringgren (p. 86) notes, chapter 21 begins and ends with two sentences on the omnipotence of God. Yahweh holds supremacy over all human wisdom (v. 30). Men need not try to set their *wisdom, understanding,* and *counsel* against his will (cf. Job 5:12–13; Jer. 9:23). The *horse* (v. 31) was a symbol of military power (cf. Isa. 31:3). It is highly probable that these verses were aimed at the political and military confidence of wise men in positions of leadership, who were prone to think that strategy, tactics, and programs ("operations" in the current jargon) were sufficient.

(18) Sundry Observations (22:1–16)

1 A good name is to be chosen rather than
       great riches,
    and favor is better than silver or gold.
2 The rich and the poor meet together;
       the Lord is the maker of them all.
3 A prudent man sees danger and hides him-
       self;
    but the simple go on, and suffer for it.
4 The reward for humility and fear of the
       Lord
    is riches and honor and life.
5 Thorns and snares are in the way of the
       perverse;
    he who guards himself will keep far from
       them.
6 Train up a child in the way he should go,
    and when he is old he will not depart
       from it.
7 The rich rules over the poor,
    and the borrower is the slave of the
       lender.

⁸ He who sows injustice will reap calamity,
  and the rod of his fury will fail.
⁹ He who has a bountiful eye will be blessed,
  for he shares his bread with the poor.
¹⁰ Drive out a scoffer, and strife will go out,
  and quarreling and abuse will cease.
¹¹ He who loves purity of heart,
  and whose speech is gracious, will have
  the king as his friend.
¹² The eyes of the Lord keep watch over
  knowledge,
  but he overthrows the words of the faithless.
¹³ The sluggard says, "There is a lion outside!
  I shall be slain in the streets!"
¹⁴ The mouth of a loose woman is a deep pit;
  he with whom the Lord is angry will fall
  into it.
¹⁵ Folly is bound up in the heart of a child,
  but the rod of discipline drives it far from
  him.
¹⁶ He who oppresses the poor to increase his
  own wealth,
  or gives to the rich, will only come to
  want.

The Masoretic Text has no word for *good,* but the idea is that of a reputation which is preferable to riches and so, "good." *Favor* is the favorable impression of others, or popularity (cf. 3:4; 13:15). Verse 1 reflects the wisdom teachers' conviction that wealth alone is not enough. Only as wealth and character complement each other is there a satisfactory condition.

In terms of the personal and social contexts of life, the rich and the poor share little in common (v. 2). But they do have the same creator, and thus, they share a common humanity. Verse 2 may also mean that God has given them their stations in life—which, of course, is a reminder at the same time that he can reverse them! It is better to translate the *meet together* as "have this in common" (NEB) or "live side by side" (McKane, p. 244).

The *prudent man* (which is the word used of the serpent in Gen. 3:1; see 1:4) is the shrewd man who looks ahead and anticipates difficulties before they come (v. 3, repeated with only slight change in 27:12). The *simple* are not prepared to live in a dangerous and complex world. Such persons need teaching and experience before they know how to take the "necessary

evasive action" (McKane, p. 563) to steer a successful course through life.

The consequences of true piety and *humility* are set forth in v. 4. Humility is the absence of pride and the willingness to accept discipline and teaching. Gemser (p. 82) notes that the *reward* should be understood more nearly as consequence or result. The life described in v. 5 contrasts with that in v. 4. The obstinate, crooked, perverse person can expect tough going. The person who takes life seriously (translate *himself* as "his life" in v. 5b) stays away from the *thorns and snares* that plague the way of the "twisted man."

The *way he should go* of v. 6 is not defined specifically, but in the context there can be little doubt that it includes the way reflected in the positive elements of vv. 1,3,4,5, i.e., pious and properly prepared for life. However, this may well include vocational training as well. The training needed for life should be given in the early years, when habits and patterns of behavior and work are set.

Verse 7 is a realistic observation. This is the way it is; let the wise be alert. The poor man is constantly in the slavery of debt. The future of the borrower is not bright.

The sower of injustice can expect no success in his future either (v. 8). He will *reap calamity,* and his power will not last (v. 8b, though this line is frequently emended to get a wording which means that the rod smites the sower of injustice; see Scott, McKane, NEB). The future of the generous man, on the other hand, is one that will be blessed (v. 9). The *bountiful eye* is literally "good of eye," i.e., well disposed and opposite to the "evil of eye" in 23:6; 28:22. The eye is an index of character (cf. Matt. 6:22–23).

Community discipline will not allow the continued presence of the *scoffer* who is ever stirring up trouble. He should be expelled for the sake of the welfare of the whole group (v. 10). The word translated *quarreling* carries the idea of judgment or legal dispute, but it probably has the broader idea of contention or strife in this context (see Toy, p. 417).

The Masoretic Text of v. 11 is uncertain, and the RSV represents an emendation (see Toy, p. 417). The verse seems to say that the king will approve of reliable character and good speech. These are qualities which will win his favor (cf. 16:13) and gain promotion for the young official of his court.

Despite the protests of some commentators (e.g., Toy, p. 418), the rendering of v. 12a should be retained. The vigilance of Yahweh is infallible; he watches over *knowledge* (cf. 15:3) and *overthrows* the words of deceitful men.

Verse 13 is a humorous and satirical comment on laziness (cf. 19:24; 26:13). The reason for not going to work is absurd; but most of the excuses of lazy people belong in the same category! *There is a lion outside!* —one tall tale is as good as another.

For the *loose woman* or "strange woman" see 2:16; 5:3; 7:5 (outside of chs. 1—9, the term appears only here and in 23:27). As noted in the discussion of the earlier passages, the woman is probably a foreigner whose sexually promiscuous behavior is greater because of her foreignness. Her seductive speech (*mouth*, v. 14) is very potent. But the man who yields to her will suffer irretrievable punishment.

Verse 15 returns to the subject of the discipline of the young (cf. 13:24; 22:6; 29:15,21), in this case to the use of corporal punishment. *Folly* is very much *bound up* with the mind of a boy. The *rod of discipline* is needed to get rid of the folly. The educator should remember that he has a difficult task in dealing with "folly." His student comes to him with a deeply ingrained foolishness which will not be removed without considerable pain and effort.

The translation and meaning of v. 16 are not certain. Verse 16a can be read to mean that oppression of the poor man will be for his benefit, presumably, by making him work harder. But as Jones (p. 186) remarks, this may not be a strain on the Hebrew, but it is on credulity! It is better to read v. 16a with the RSV or other translations which give the idea that oppression of the poor may bring gain to the oppressor. There is

also ambiguity in v. 16b (Who comes to want? The rich? Or, the one giving to the rich?); but, again, the RSV may be accepted. Even so, the meaning remains obscure. Yahweh "makes nonsense of men's intentions" and achieves what the divine purpose intends (also, Ringgren, p. 87).

III. Instruction in Thirty Sayings (22:17— 24:22)

The general type of this section of Proverbs is the same as that of chapters 1—9. It is Instruction, which is characterized by the extensive use of the imperative mood in direct address (note the use of "my son" in 23:15,19,26; 24:13,21; also note the frequency of second person "you" or "your" in comparison with the Sentences in 10:1— 22:16; see Int. for discussion of Instruction and Sentences types of wisdom literature). Another feature is the use of motive clauses to support the Instruction proper. These clauses are often recognizable by the translation beginning "for . . ." or "because . . ." (e.g., 22:22—23, from the Hebrew *ki*), though this is not always the case (for the motivation may appear in varied ways, see McKane, p. 370, and the commentary which follows).

The division of this section into a prologue and thirty sayings is based in part on the natural outline of the material. But the key to it is found in the "thirty sayings" of 22:20. This is almost certainly the correct reading of a word which was long an uncertainty in the interpretation of Proverbs. Traditionally, the Masoretic Text *shilshom* was translated "formerly" or "three days ago"; or with the marginal note of the Hebrew as "nobles" and thus "excellent things" (as in KJV). But very small changes (reading *sheloshim*) produce "thirty" and thus "thirty sayings."

This change of the text was stimulated by the publication of the Egyptian Instruction of Amenemope which has thirty chapters.[7]

---

[7] For discussion, translations, and references see ANET, pp. 421–24; *Documents From Old Testament Times*, ed. D. Winton Thomas (New York: Harper & Brothers, Torchbooks, 1958), pp. 172–186. For references and summaries of more recent discussions see McKane, *Proverbs*, pp. 371–74; Kidner, pp. 23–24.

In addition to the sameness of the number of sayings, close parallels were discovered between the content of the chapters in the Egyptian writing and 22:17—23:11 (and, perhaps, 24:10–12).

Though scholars have different theories of explanation, it is reasonable and highly probable to assume a relationship between Proverbs and Amenemope. But the Israelite editor or writer must be allowed a great deal of freedom. The Israelite work is far from a copy of the Egyptian material. It has its own characteristics and theology. The evidence points toward the Israelite use of the Egyptian work as a model and as a limited source of material. However, the possibility that both works have a common source, probably Canaanite, must not be ruled out.

1. The Prologue (22:17–21)

17 Incline your ear, and hear the words of the wise,
   and apply your mind to my knowledge;
18 for it will be pleasant if you keep them within you,
   if all of them are ready on your lips.
19 That your trust may be in the LORD,
   I have made them known to you today,
   even to you.
20 Have I not written for you thirty sayings
   of admonition and knowledge,
21 to show you what is right and true,
   that you may give a true answer to those who sent you?

The prologue opens with a demand for attention and the discipline of learning. The expression *the words of the wise* is most probably the title of this section which has been accidentally assimilated into the text. The original was likely "Incline your ear, and hear my words."

Verse 18 supplies motivation by pointing to the pleasant consequences of taking the teaching seriously. The *within you* is a translation of the literal "in your belly" (which is the reading in Amenemope also; see McKane, p. 374). The teacher's words must be retained within, along with the ability and readiness to articulate them in proper fashion at the right time.

Verse 19 modifies the wisdom teacher's authority by pointing to trust in Yahweh as

the objective of the teaching. There is a strong element of direct address for emphasis in v. 19*b*. Compare this verse with 3:21–24.

For v. 20 see the comments in the introduction to this section. The *thirty sayings* of the teacher are full of "counsels and knowledge."

The Instructions were intended, typically (but not exclusively), for the guidance of young men who were being prepared for high office in government or other very responsible positions. One of the qualifications for such positions was reliability and accuracy in the role of a messenger or negotiator. This seems to be the point of v. 21. The messenger and/or negotiator must know how to sort out the truth and keep it true. If he cannot be depended upon for accuracy and honesty, he is useless in such a job. There are similar words in Amenemope, which set forth as one purpose of that work as "to know how to return an answer to him who said it, and to direct a report to one who has sent him . . ." (ANET, p. 421).

2. The Sayings (22:22—24:22)

(1) Robbing the Weak and the Danger of Anger (22:22–25)

22 Do not rob the poor, because he is poor,
   or crush the afflicted at the gate;
23 for the LORD will plead their cause
   and despoil of life those who despoil them.
24 Make no friendship with a man given to anger,
   nor go with a wrathful man,
25 lest you learn his ways
   and entangle yourself in a snare.

The inability of the poor to defend themselves seems to be the point of v. 22*a*. The *gate* was the place in the town where legal proceedings and business were conducted (cf. Amos. 5:10–15). The defender of the poor is Yahweh (v. 23; cf. 23:11; Ex. 22:21–24; Deut. 10:17–19).

Chapter 9 of Amenemope has these lines which are somewhat similar to v. 24: "Do not associate to thyself the heated man; / Nor visit him for conversation" (ANET, p. 423). The point is clear: watch the company you keep! If you *learn* (a verb which

conveys the idea of learning by association)
the ways of a bad-tempered man, your way
of life will become dangerous and incapable
of being properly controlled.

(2) Avoid Surety; Cultivate Skill (22:26–29)

26 Be not one of those who give pledges,
    who become surety for debts.
27 If you have nothing with which to pay,
    why should your bed be taken from under
        you?
28 Remove not the ancient landmark
    which your fathers have set.
29 Do you see a man skilful in his work?
    he will stand before kings;
    he will not stand before obscure men.

For a discussion of the danger of involvement in uncertain financial dealings (vv.
26–27), see the comment on 6:1; also, see
11:15; 17:18; 20:16.

The saying in verse 28 is very similar to
23:10 and corresponds closely with Deuteronomy 19:14 (cf. Deut. 27:17; Hos. 5:
10; Amenemope, ch. 6, ANET, p. 422b).
The *landmark* refers to boundary stones
marking property lines. They were relatively easy to move; and if a man was poor,
it was difficult for him to make an adequate
defense in the gate. There is marked emphasis on the age of the boundary lines in
this passage. They were not recent develop-
ments, which might have been a less serious
matter (see Toy, p. 427).

Verse 29 recalls the use of models in
Instructions (cf. 6:6–15). The word translated skillful is literally "quick" or "ready"
and is used of the work of a scribe (see
Psalm 45:1; Ezra 7:6). The reference is to
the acumen and ability in statecraft which
earns a scribe promotion to a high office.
Of course, the meaning can be extended in
proverbial fashion to all kinds of work and
professions. The person who is *skillful in
his work* will gain success in any endeavor.

(3) Table Manners and Other Subjects (23:1–11)

1 When you sit down to eat with a ruler,
    observe carefully what is before you;
2 and put a knife to your throat
    if you are a man given to appetite.
3 Do not desire his delicacies,

for they are deceptive food.
4 Do not toil to acquire wealth;
    be wise enough to desist.
5 When your eyes light upon it, it is gone;
    for suddenly it takes to itself wings,
    flying like an eagle toward heaven.
6 Do not eat the bread of a man who is
        stingy;
    do not desire his delicacies;
7 for he is like one who is inwardly reckon-
        ing.
    "Eat and drink!" he says to you;
    but his heart is not with you.
8 You will vomit up the morsels which you
        have eaten,
    and waste your pleasant words.
9 Do not speak in the hearing of a fool,
    for he will despise the wisdom of your
        words.
10 Do not remove an ancient landmark
    or enter the fields of the fatherless;
11 for their Redeemer is strong;
    he will plead their cause against you.

McKane (p. 381) notes that vv. 1–3 are
intended to direct the prospective statesman not only to a well-proportioned style of
life, which exercises self-control even in
table manners, but also erflects the conviction that "something of the essential man is
revealed in how he eats, that there will be
a correspondence between his habits of eating his habits of diplomacy." Our own day
is characterized by bad manners, table and
otherwise. Our manners are indicative of
the sickness of our society, and of the great
dichotomies between "form and function"
which plague contemporary life. Good
manners and good living go together. Part
of the reason for the lack of good manners
today is the awareness, particularly by the
young, that manners have not been soundly
linked with character and quality of life.

It is better to retain the "who is before
you" (marg.) in v. 1b (Toy, p. 428). The
guest should keep his host in mind and observe him closely. He can learn a great deal
from this kind of observation. Verse 2 refers
to curbing appetite (not "use a knife to eat
with," so Scott, p. 139). The delicious food
and titbits of a ruler's table must not allow
one to take his mind off his business and
fall into public gluttony. The *deceptive
food* of v. 3b can refer to hospitality offered
with an ulterior motive. On the other hand,

the expression may have in mind the danger of gluttony posed to a young man by the rich fare of his host.

There is much similarity between the saying in vv. 4–5 and Amenemope (ch. 7; ANET, pp. 422–3), though the latter is much longer and more complex. The force of the Hebrew text is clear: do not wear yourself out in the struggle for wealth, for wealth is very transient and elusive. Like an eagle, it may suddenly soar away out of reach towards the heavens.

Verses 6–8 paint a picture of a stingy host who carefully and critically calculates the cost of his entertainment. He entertains because he has to and he hopes to gain for himself thereby. Such a man should be avoided. His food may be good, but the consequences of sharing his company are most unpleasant. The words of v. 8 are metaphorical—though real nausea may result when one is forced to eat with this kind of duplicity. The Hebrew text of v. 7 is uncertain. McKane (p. 246) chooses to build on the LXX and translates "for he is like a hair in the throat" in v. 7a. But the RSV reading fits the context well.

The fool is incapable of appreciating wisdom (v. 9). He will scorn the real intelligence of words spoken to him and will reject good sense when he hears it.

The saying in vv. 10–11 is very similar to 22:28 (see also 15:25). However, the emphasis is on the role of Yahweh as the *Redeemer* (*go'el*) of the *fatherless*, i.e., orphans or other people who are unable to defend themselves against having their property swindled away by dishonest neighbors. The *go'el* was a kinsman who was willing to assume the responsibility for the land and family of his relatives (see Lev. 25:25; Ruth 4:1–8). The language is legal in character in v. 11. Yahweh is the powerful advocate or champion of the rights of those who cannot help themselves. There is an interesting parallel in Amenemope (ch. 6; ANET, p. 422).

(4) Discipline a Necessity (23:12–16)

12 Apply your mind to instruction
    and your ear to words of knowledge.

13 Do not withhold discipline from a child;
    if you beat him with a rod, he will not die.
14 If you beat him with the rod
    you will save his life from Sheol.
15 My son, if your heart is wise,
    my heart too will be glad.
16 My soul will rejoice
    when your lips speak what is right.

Verse 12 is sometimes considered to be a secondary introduction to 23:13—24:22 (e.g., Scott, pp. 140, 143). But v. 13 is addressed to a father or teacher, while v. 12 is addressed to the student directly (McKane, p. 585). Compare v. 12 with 1:2 and 22:17.

Verses 13–14 emphasize the need for discipline, including physical punishment (see 13:24; 19:18; 22:15 for similar statements). The seriousness of discipline is stressed. The issues are life and death. *He will not die*—from the rod—but he will if he fails to receive the right direction in life. "He will not die" may be an idiomatic expression which means "he will not be harmed very much" (see McKane, p. 386). The NEB translates v. 13b as "take the stick to him, and save him from death"— which is better.

The student is told that if he is wise, the teacher will rejoice (vv. 15–16). When the *heart* (mind) of the teacher can correspond with the *heart* of the pupil there is a happy relationship. The *soul* of v. 16 is a translation of the word for kidneys ("reins" in older translations), which were considered to be a source of emotion (cf. Job 19:27; Psalm 16:7). The "heart" is the more intellectual word, while "my kidneys" indicates emotional satisfaction.

(5) Sundry Teachings (23:17–35)

17 Let not your heart envy sinners,
    but continue in the fear of the LORD all the day.
18 Surely there is a future,
    and your hope will not be cut off.
19 Hear, my son, and be wise,
    and direct your mind in the way.
20 Be not among winebibbers,
    or among gluttonous eaters of meat;
21 for the drunkard and the glutton will come to poverty,
    and drowsiness will clothe a man with

rags.
22 Hearken to your father who begot you,
   and do not despise your mother when
   she is old.
23 Buy truth, and do not sell it;
   buy wisdom, instruction, and understanding.
24 The father of the righteous will greatly rejoice;
   he who begets a wise son will be glad in
   him.
25 Let your father and mother be glad,
   let her who bore you rejoice.
26 My son, give me your heart,
   and let your eyes observe my ways.
27 For a harlot is a deep pit;
   an adventuress is a narrow well.
28 She lies in wait like a robber
   and increases the faithless among men.
29 Who has woe? Who has sorrow?
   Who has strife? Who has complaining?
   Who has wounds without cause?
   Who has redness of eyes?
30 Those who tarry long over wine,
   those who go to try mixed wine.
31 Do not look at wine when it is red,
   when it sparkles in the cup
   and goes down smoothly.
32 At the last it bites like a serpent,
   and stings like an adder.
33 Your eyes will see strange things,
   and your mind utter perverse things.
34 You will be like one who lies down in the
   midst of the sea,
   like one who lies on the top of a mast.
35 "They struck me," you will say, "but I was
   not hurt;
   they beat me, but I did not feel it.
   When shall I awake?
   I will seek another drink."

The temptation to envy sinners for their
worldly success is a perennial one (cf.
Psalms 37:1; 73:3). There is a need for
continual concentration on the *fear of the
Lord,* which will keep the reality of the
situation in focus (v. 17). The text of v.
17*b* has no verb (*continue* is added), and
it is quite possible that the verb of v. 17*a*
controls the action in v. 17*b*. In this case
the meaning is shifted slightly to say that
sinners should not be envied, but that the
fear of Yahweh should be the object of
constant desire (see McKane, p. 387, who
translates: "Do not let sinners excite your
envy, but let the fear of Yahweh do it at
all times," p. 247). Verse 18 gives the

reason for the exhortation in v. 17. Keep
your eye on the "end" for it is the source
of hope. The advantages of sinners may be
very exciting and desirable when viewed
without the perspective of ultimate result
(see Psalm 73:17–20).

The *son* or pupil is admonished to *be
wise* by learning the instruction of the
teacher and by keeping his mind on *the
way,* i.e., the way of wisdom (vv. 19–21).
The idea of *direct* is to be straight: thus
"get your mind straight about your way
of life." It is probable that vv. 20–21 are
simply examples of the kind of people who
are not characterized by "straight thinking." But McKane (p. 388) suggests, on
the basis of Deuteronomy 21:20, that the
description is a paradigm of the recalcitrant
and incorrigible youth. For v. 21 see 6:9–
11; 19:15; 20:13.

The theme of vv. 22–25 is that of the
Fifth Commandment: "Honor your father
and your mother" (Ex. 20:12). The "generation gap" must not be allowed to break
the relationship between parent and child.
Wisdom can be learned from those whose
years have given them experience and maturity. The joy of parents in wise and successful children is expressed in vv. 24,25.

Verse 23 fits poorly in this context and
is not in the Greek text. It is possibly a
secondary verse or misplaced. It would fit
well after v. 19 (Jones, p. 194). The worth
of the "commodities" of the wisdom teacher
is great. Buy *truth, wisdom, instruction,*
and *understanding*—and do not sell them!
There are some things which should not
be sold for any price.

The teacher (or parent) asks for the son
or student's attention in v. 26, and offers
himself as a model for behavior. It is not
"do as I say," but "do as I do." However,
this is the interpretation of the marginal
reading of the Hebrew text. The written
text says "and let your eyes approve of my
ways"; i.e., do not oppose my teaching or
try to think for yourself independently of
instruction (cf. NEB). Either interpretation
is acceptable.

The warning which follows in vv. 27–

29 has to do with the *harlot* and *adventuress* (see 2:16; 5:20; 6:24; 7:5). Such women are like a *deep pit* or a *narrow well*—both dangerous and extremely difficult to get out of if fallen into. Indeed, they are symbols of a state of death. But the situation is not just a passive one into which a man may blunder. This kind of woman will ambush him like a *robber* (v. 28). In the discussions related to 2:16; 5:20; 7:5, considerable emphasis was given to the foreign status of the woman described as an "adventuress" (in parallel with the *zarah*. the "loose" or "strange" woman). However, in this passage the parallel is with "harlot" (*zonah*), which is the general word for a prostitute or promiscuous woman. But there is, probably, little difference in meaning (see the discussion in McKane, pp. 390-1). The picture is that of a foreign woman whose sexual mores are free and aggressive, thus a dangerous threat to men.

The consequences of drunkenness are graphically described in vv. 29–35, which really form a brief didactic essay (Jones, p. 195). The use of the repeated question also suggests the riddle technique of teaching. The translation needs little commentary, though there are a few details which are troublesome or uncertain. Dahood [8] translates v. 30b as "who come to plumb the mixing bowl," i.e., they come to the bowl looking for more wine (also Scott, p. 143). The word *mimsak* is also used in Isaiah 65:11, and mixing bowl is a suitable translation in that context. But "blended wine" makes sense in both contexts, and the uncertainty remains. The blended wine is wine mixed with water, honey, and spices (McKane, p. 393; note 9:2 also).

The sparkling wine in the cup (v. 31) has an end result which is like being bitten by a poisonous snake (v. 32). The *adder* should probably be identified with the *Daboia Xanthina*, a highly venomous viper and the largest snake of Palestine. It has been described as the most dreaded serpent

mentioned in the Old Testament. *Stings* is uncertain, but it probably means to bite, to puncture, or to secrete (venom). The hangover from drunkenness includes hallucinations and befuddled speech (v. 33). The literal meaning of v. 33b is "and your mind will speak things which are upside down."

The general condition described in v. 34 is clear, though commentators differ on the precise interpretation. Everything is moving around a drunkard. It is like lying down in the midst of the sea! When the drunk tries to sleep he heaves and tosses like a sailor trying to sleep on the deck of a ship in very rough weather.

Verse 35 is a sad picture of the condition of the alcoholic. He is insensitive to mistreatment and pain because of his intoxication. But when he awakens, he is back to drinking. Scott (p. 142) translates: "As soon as I can wake up I shall want another drink!" The terrible cycle goes on and on. Before one hangover is finished, the alcoholic is anticipating drinking again.

(6) Avoid Bad Men; Seek Wisdom (24: 1–10)

1 Be not envious of evil men,
  nor desire to be with them;
2 for their minds devise violence,
  and their lips talk of mischief.
3 By wisdom a house is built,
  and by understanding it is established;
4 by knowledge the rooms are filled
  with all precious and pleasant riches.
5 A wise man is mightier than a strong man,
  and a man of knowledge than he who has strength;
6 for by wise guidance you can wage your war,
  and in abundance of counselors there is victory.
7 Wisdom is too high for a fool;
  in the gate he does not open his mouth.
8 He who plans to do evil
  will be called a mischief-maker.
9 The devising of folly is sin,
  and the scoffer is an abomination to men.
10 If you faint in the day of adversity,
  your strength is small.

Young people (and sometimes older people too) are frequently fascinated by the kind of glamour and aura of success and power which is characteristic of the *evil men* described in vv. 1–2. But the real nature of their lives should be remembered. Their minds are concentrated on causing trouble for others. Their selfish, destructive motives dominate them (see 24:19–20).

Verses 3–4 have the characteristics of Sentences rather than those of Instruction (McKane, p. 396). However, they may be treated as a kind of teaching by the use of a model (see 6:6–15). A *house* is built by the use of wise, knowledgeable action. The picture is that of a successful man who has built a house which is well furnished and prepared for expensive and pleasant living. The force of the teaching is "Go and do likewise."

The RSV follows the Greek text in v. 5, which results in comparisons in both lines of the verse. This is acceptable, but it is not really required in v. 5*b* where the Masoretic Text may be retained: "And a man of knowledge strengthens (or, assures) power." Verse 6 is an illustration of a situation which has special need for *wise guidance* (for v. 6*a* see 20:18, and for v. 6*b* see 11:14). Brawn needs to be directed by careful thinking if it is to be used well.

Wisdom and *a fool* are simply not compatible (v. 7). The competent understanding of wisdom is beyond the grasp of a fool. Thus, he is not prepared or able to hold his own in the conversations and proceedings conducted in the *gate*. The gate area was the town meeting place where many matters of great importance were decided. It was also a place for social life and everyday conversation. The fool lacks the ability to participate effectively in any of this.

The emphasis of vv. 8–9 is on the *plans* and *devising* of the fool. This type of fool is not a dullard who cannot think. Rather, he is characterized by his intense scheming and planning of ways to accomplish his evil objectives. He earns the epithet *mischief-maker* (lit. master of schemes). He is repulsive to men (v. 9). The intriguer is an undesirable kind of thinker.

The Hebrew text is cryptic in v. 10 and has a play on the words for *adversity* (*tsarah*) and *small* (*tsar*). The meaning seems to be simply an admonition to remember that the test of strength occurs in times of crisis. Weakness shows up under pressure. On a more positive note, real strength is demonstrated in adverse circumstances. The word for "small" carries the idea of narrowness or constriction. Stamina is tested and revealed in the tight places of life.

(7) Contrasting Sayings (24:11–22)

11 Rescue those who are being taken away to death;
   hold back those who are stumbling to the slaughter.
12 If you say, "Behold, we did not know this,"
   does not he who weighs the heart perceive it?
 Does not he who keeps watch over your soul know it,
   and will he not requite man according to his work?
13 My son, eat honey, for it is good,
   and the drippings of the honeycomb are sweet to your taste.
14 Know that wisdom is such to your soul;
   and if you find it, there will be a future, and your hope will not be cut off.
15 Lie not in wait as a wicked man against the dwelling of the righteous;
   do not violence to his home;
16 for a righteous man falls seven times, and rises again;
   but the wicked are overthrown by calamity.
17 Do not rejoice when your enemy falls,
   and let not your heart be glad when he stumbles;
18 lest the LORD see it, and be displeased,
   and turn away his anger from him.
19 Fret not yourself because of evildoers,
   and be not envious of the wicked;
20 for the evil man has no future;
   the lamp of the wicked will be put out.
21 My son, fear the LORD and the king,
   and do not disobey either of them;
22 for disaster from them will rise suddenly,
   and who knows the ruin that will come from them both?

Some commentators want to link v. 10 with vv. 11–12 (e.g., Gemser, p. 89). This interpretation would identify the "day of adversity" in v. 10 with the testing situation in vv. 11–12; i.e., it is the day of a neighbor's adversity. This is unlikely, but the juxtaposition of the verses is not unhappy. Verses 11–12 do present a situation which tests a man's real strength. The obligation to rescue a man being dragged away to be killed is forcefully put in these verses. The circumstances in v. 11 are not spelled out, but there can be little doubt (though not all commentators agree) that the situation in mind is that of oppression and violence. Any attempt to avoid the duty of deliverance in such circumstances is unacceptable (v. 12). It is easy for a group (note the plural in v. 12) to say, "But we don't know this man, it is none of our business" and refuse to become involved in a difficult and dangerous matter. But God takes note (*he who weighs the heart;* cf. 16:2), and he will *requite man according to his work*—not, "according to his excuses." Noninvolvement is a policy which may be permitted by men, but God holds all men responsible for their care of neighbors (cf. Luke 10:25–37).

Honey is pleasant to the taste and wholesome for the body (v. 13; cf. 1 Sam. 14:27, 29 for the energizing effect of honey). Wisdom, too, is pleasant and life-giving (v. 14). A teacher exhorts his student to remember that if wisdom is found there is prospect for a favorable future. He can avoid having his hope cut short (cf. 2:10; 16:24). Verse 14c is also found in 23:18.

The moral of vv. 15–16 seems to be, "Be careful with whom you start a fight!" A *righteous man* is hard to keep down. He has resilience and durability which the wicked lack. The words for *dwelling* and *home* have rural, agricultural connotations, and the warning may be addressed to urban dwellers who think they can take easy advantage of those who live in farming villages (Cohen, p. 162; see NEB translation.

As Jones (p. 199) remarks, vv. 17–18 should be understood against the background of vendettas in the ancient world. The ferocity of hatred in the contemporary Middle East is evidence of the continuing practice of gloating over the misfortune of an enemy. The motivation in v. 18 is

earthy in its opportunism; though it is possible that Toy (p. 448) is correct when he argues that *turn his anger from him* does not mean that God will stop punishing a wicked man because another man rejoices over the punishment; but, rather, means that God will "turn from him to thee." The punishment intended for the wicked will be turned back on the gloater. But this is probably reading too much into the verse.

The admonition in vv. 19–20 is directed toward the perennial problem of envy of the seeming well-being of the wicked (cf. Psalm 73). *Fret not yourself* is literally "Don't get yourself heated up" (v. 19 is identical with Psalm 37:1). The *evil man has no future;* it is a mistake to get too disturbed and envious about him, for he can only look forward to a future which ends in the darkness of death when his *lamp* is put out (cf. 13:9). This saying is a variation of 23:17–18.

As the margin indicates, the accepted reading follows the Greek text of v. 21 rather than the Hebrew (though the change in the Hebrew is very small). But the Masoretic Text may be retained and understood either as "men of revolutionary tendencies" (Cohen, p. 163) or "men of high rank" (Ringgren, p. 97; NEB translates "men of rank"). If this is done, the verse carries a warning about becoming involved with court conspiracies and plots. McKane (p. 406) translates "noblemen" and argues that such men are prone to play dangerous games of intrigue because of their greed for power. A young man who hopes to have a future in the royal establishment should respect and obey both Yahweh and king and avoid involvement with the power plays of court officials. The high position of noblemen offers no real security.

IV. A Collection of the Wise Men (24: 23–34)

This short collection of miscellaneous material has been added as an appendix to 22:17—24:22. Verse 23a is a title which seems to be linked to 22:17. The material is varied, but it is not basically Instruction in genre (though vv. 27–29 do appear to have this form).

1. Sundry Observations (24:23–29)

23 These also are sayings of the wise.
Partiality in judging is not good,
24 He who says to the wicked, "You are innocent,"
will be cursed by peoples, abhorred by nations;
25 but those who rebuke the wicked will have delight,
and a good blessing will be upon them.
26 He who gives a right answer
kisses the lips.
27 Prepare your work outside,
get everything ready for you in the field;
and after that build your house.
28 Be not a witness against your neighbor without cause,
and do not deceive with your lips.
29 Do not say, "I will do to him as he has done to me;
I will pay the man back for what he has done."

The RSV joins v. 23b with vv. 24–25. The subject is that of impartiality and integrity in judgment. It is possible that a line similar to 18:5b or 28:21b has been lost from the text in the verse (so Gemser, p. 89). The contrast between those who favor the wicked and those who rebuke the wicked in legal proceedings is made in vv. 24–25.

The expression in v. 26 is unusual. The kissing practices normally referred to are to kiss the hand, foot or knee. One interpretation sees the verse as an expression of true friendship. A kiss given with a dishonest answer is a betrayal like that of Judas. Another interpretation views the verse as saying that the pleasure of a kiss and that of honest words are comparable (Ringgren, p. 99).

The point in v. 27 seems to be something like "count the cost" or "get ready before you try to do a big job" (Scott, p. 149, cf. Luke 14:28–32). The verse has been understood as an admonition for financial preparation for marriage (Cohen, p. 164), but it may have wider meaning. McKane (p. 576) notes that a correct sequence of action is

inculcated. Fields and outside operations should be put in order before a house is built because they provide the income for the house and household (both ideas are probably in the word *house*). The wrong sequence of operations can be disastrous—as many a suburbanite paying too much for a house can verify!

Verses 28 and 29 are directed toward giving false witness and retaliation. Perhaps, we should understand the *without cause* of v. 28 as "for spite" (so Scott, p. 148). This would connect the verse well with v. 28. However, the idea in v. 27 may be that of the informer who because of spite, pay, or just meddlesomeness bears false witness.

Verse 29 is a kind of "negative form of the 'Golden Rule'" (Scott, p. 149; cf. 20:22; Matt. 5:38–48). The legal principle set forth in Exodus 21:23–25 (cf. Deut. 19:19–21; Lev. 24:19–20) is denied to the individual man (Gemser, p. 90); though the principle here is similar to that in Leviticus 19:18. An attitude of retaliation should not be allowed to rule a man's conduct. The passion to get even is enervating for both the individual and the community.

2. On Idleness (24:30–34)

30 I passed by the field of a sluggard,
by the vineyard of a man without sense;
31 and lo, it was all overgrown with thorns;
the ground was covered with nettles,
and its stone wall was broken down.
32 Then I saw and considered it;
I looked and received instruction.
33 A little sleep, a little slumber,
a little folding of the hands to rest,
34 and poverty will come upon you like a robber,
and want like an armed man.

This is a brief didactic essay which uses the experience of the wisdom teacher as the basis for a warning against indolence (cf. 6:6–11). The teacher drew a lesson from what he saw (v. 32). The sluggard is usually an ordinary type of person who makes too many excuses, puts off too many jobs that need doing until serious trouble suddenly overwhelms him (Kidner, p. 43).

V. Wisdom Collection of the Men of Hezekiah (25:1—29:27)

According to 25:1, the material in these chapters belongs to the "proverbs of Solomon which the men of Hezekiah king of Judah copied." It is unlikely that "copied" (from the root 'tk) means only copied from another writing or transcribed as in the late Hebraic sense. The verb has the idea of moving or proceeding (note its use in Gen. 12:8; Job 9:5). Thus the meaning is "the proverbs of Solomon which the men of Hezekiah . . . moved on." We can not restrict the work of these scribes to dealing only with written traditions, but we must also think in terms of their retrieving teachings from oral traditions as well as composing and editing on their own in terms of the Solomonic legacy.[9] Also, it is probable that the collecting and editing of the wisdom of the past was part of the process of teaching. It was not merely intended to preserve ancient lore (Rylaarsdam, p. 82).

1. Collection A (25:1—27:27)

(1) On Kingship (25:1-7a)

¹ These also are proverbs of Solomon which the men of Hezekiah king of Judah copied.
² It is the glory of God to conceal things,
but the glory of kings is to search things out.
³ As the heavens for height, and the earth for depth,
so the mind of kings is unsearchable.
⁴ Take away the dross from the silver,
and the smith has material for a vessel;
⁵ take away the wicked from the presence of the king,
and his throne will be established in righteousness.
⁶ Do not put yourself forward in the king's presence
or stand in the place of the great;
⁷ for it is better to be told, "Come up here," than to be put lower in the presence of the prince.

These verses set forth the nature of kingship and behavior appropriate for deal-

ing with kings. The view of the king gives him great status, as the "philosopher-king ideal" is praised (Rylaarsdam, p. 83). The glory of a king is his ability to search things out, sift them thoroughly, and clarify issues for himself and his people. As Cohen remarks, "It is not to his credit if his ordinances and policies are unintelligible to the people" (p. 164). Wisdom is a quality expected of kings (2 Sam. 14:17; 1 Kings 3:9; Isa. 11:3). On the other hand, the glory of God is the hiddenness of his ways and purposes (cf. 30:4; Deut. 29:28; Psalms 77:14; 97:2; Isa. 45:15; Job 11:7–10; 26:14; Eccl. 3:11).

In v. 3 the king is himself more or less like God. The mind of kings is almost as incomprehensible to ordinary men as that of God. The attempt to understand a king has the dimensions of understanding creation. We should allow for an (1) element of hyperbole in these verses, and (2) the setting forth of an ideal of kingship hardly realizable in the real world. A mind and will so resourceful, mobile, and "splendidly inscrutable" (McKane, p. 579) is the ideal for a king. Unfortunately, it only rarely appears in men who hold high office. We should read these verses as the picture of what an executive should be as well as representative of high respect for kingship.

Verses 4–5 set forth the need for the king to have trustworthy, proven servants and advisors. We may think of the teacher holding these standards before young men aspiring to service in the royal establishment. For v. 5 see 16:12; 20:28.

Proper demeanor before kings is the subject of vv. 6–7a. The translation speaks for itself (cf. Ecclus. 7:4–5; Luke 14:8–11).

(2) Gossip and Personal Confrontation (25:7b-10)

What your eyes have seen
⁸ do not hastily bring into court;
for what will you do in the end,
when your neighbor puts you to shame?
⁹ Argue your case with your neighbor himself,
and do not disclose another's secret;
¹⁰ lest he who hears you bring shame upon you,
and your ill repute have no end.

[9] See the discussion in R. B. Y. Scott, "Solomon and the Beginnings of Wisdom in Israel" in Wisdom in Israel and in the Ancient Near East, pp. 272–3; also, Gemser, p. 91.

The RSV joins v. 7c with v. 8, which makes good sense and follows the ancient versions. There is a question, however, about the main line of meaning in these verses. One interpretation considers them as directed against hasty litigation. One should not go to court with every little thing that he sees (Ringgren, p. 102). Every effort should be made to settle matters with a neighbor outside of court (cf. Matt. 5: 25–26; 18:15).

Another line of interpretation, considers the main point to be a warning against indiscreet and hurtful gossip (see Toy, pp. 460–1). This involves a change in the vowels of the Masoretic Text for *do not hastily bring into court* so that it reads (with Symmachus), "do not bring out to the multitude hastily" (or, perhaps, "do not be in a hurry to broadcast"; so McKane, p. 581). This approach is better if vv. 7c–10 are thought of in conection with vv. 6–7b. The young court official is warned not to talk too freely about what he sees and hears in court circles. The stigma of disloyalty and the inability to keep confidential information is a matter which cannot be overcome quickly or easily (v. 10). Despite the Hebrew text change required, I prefer this interpretation.

(3) Counsel for a Good Life (25:11–28)

11 A word fitly spoken
   is like apples of gold in a setting of silver.
12 Like a gold ring or an ornament of gold
   is a wise reprover to a listening ear.
13 Like the cold of snow in the time of harvest
   is a faithful messenger to those who send him,
   he refreshes the spirit of his masters.
14 Like clouds and wind without rain
   is a man who boasts of a gift he does not give.
15 With patience a ruler may be persuaded,
   and a soft tongue will break a bone.
16 If you have found honey, eat only enough for you,
   lest you be sated with it and vomit it.
17 Let your foot be seldom in your neighbor's house,
   lest he become weary of you and hate you.
18 A man who bears false witness against his neighbor
   is like a war club, or a sword, or a sharp arrow.
19 Trust in a faithless man in time of trouble
   is like a bad tooth or a foot that slips.
20 He who sings songs to a heavy heart
   is like one who takes off a garment on a cold day,
   and like vinegar on a wound.
21 If your enemy is hungry, give him bread to eat;
   and if he is thirsty, give him water to drink;
22 for you will heap coals of fire on his head,
   and the LORD will reward you.
23 The north wind brings forth rain;
   and a backbiting tongue, angry looks.
24 It is better to live in a corner of the housetop
   than in a house shared with a contentious woman.
25 Like cold water to a thirsty soul,
   so is good news from a far country.
26 Like a muddied spring or a polluted fountain
   is a righteous man who gives way before the wicked.
27 It is not good to eat much honey,
   so be sparing of complimentary words.
28 A man without self-control
   is like a city broken into and left without walls.

The meaning of v. 11 is basically that of 15:23. The Hebrew for *fitly* remains obscure. But the RSV may be accepted as reasonably accurate.

The *wise reprover* of v. 12 is the wisdom teacher. A teacher and a student with a *listening ear* complement one another like pieces of jewelry which are enhanced by being worn together.

A reliable messenger is as refreshing as unexpected coolness during the heat of harvest time (v. 13; cf. the unreliable messenger in 10:26; also 13:17). The *cold* of snow (note 26:1) is probably a hyperbole for unseasonably cool weather (note Scott, p. 155), though commentators have speculated that the reference is to drinks cooled by snow brought from the mountains (Toy, p. 464). McKane (p. 585) thinks in terms of cold water from springs fed from underground sources.

Verse 14 is a vivid portrayal of the frustration produced by a man who excites anticipation of gifts, which he does not produce. Of course, the force of the picture is increased by the dry climate of Palestine.

Verse 15 counsels *patience* and a *soft tongue* in dealing with a high official (prince or judge). Resistance can be broken down by soft, but persuasive, negotiation. The power of the tongue is also the subject of v. 23. Since the winds which bring rain in Palestine usually come from the west, "northwest" may be the meaning here. Some commentators have suggested an Egyptian context for this sentence, because there the *north wind* would seem to fit better (see Gemser, pp. 92, 113). If the Egyptian context is correct, the interpretation may differ in regard to the meaning of the rain. In Palestine the rain was a blessing, but in Egypt it could be destructive because the regular flooding of Nile was the source of water; thus both v. 23*a* and 23*b* would be negative. But I prefer Ringgren's (p. 103) simple explanation (regardless of the direction of the wind): just as rain clouds darken the sky (and it is possible to translate the *north wind* as a "dark wind"— though it is doubtful that this should be done), so a slandering tongue darkens the face.

Two verses deal with the eating of honey (vv. 16,27). Verse 16 advises moderation. Too much of a good thing will make anyone sick. Overindulgence should be avoided. Honey is a wholesome and pleasant food when eaten properly. In regard to moderation, v. 17 is closely related to v. 16, though the subject matter is different. It is good to visit a neighbor—but do not overdo it! Overfamiliarity breeds contempt; and welcomes can be worn out.

Verse 27*a* is clear, but v. 27*b* is totally uncertain. One possibility is that the second line should read something like the RSV. However the NEB may represent a better conjecture: "and the quest for honour is burdensome." Presumably, the meaning in NEB is that seeking for too much honor or worrying too much about it is like eating too much honey. Both actions are good when properly done. However, the interpretation remains conjectural.

Two unpleasant and undesirable types of people are described in vv. 18,19. The *false witness* is extremely dangerous—his weapons are like an arsenal of war used against his neighbor. A *faithless man* cannot be trusted. He is like a *bad tooth* or a *weak foot* ("limping" or "palsied" is better than *slips*); either one of which can cause painful failure when badly needed for their normal functions.

The precise meaning of the Hebrew text in v. 20 is extremely difficult to determine (compare the translations), but the general meaning is probably that of appropriateness. There is a time to hear the singing of "gay songs" (Scott, p. 154), but that time is not when the heart is heavy with sorrow and in no mood for it. Such singing can be as painful as taking off your coat on a cold day or pouring *vinegar on a wound*. However, it is possible that we should understand the *heavy heart* as that of the singer rather than of another ("he who sings songs on a heavy heart"). The meaning is then focused on the painfulness of trying to sing (perhaps, joyful songs for others; cf. Psalm 137) with a sad and heavy heart. I prefer this interpretation.

Verses 21–22 set a high ethical standard for dealing with enemies (cf. 12:16; 20:22; 24:17–18,29). The mood is quite different from that reflected in Psalms 58; 59; 109; 137. However, it should be noted that the motivation here is not exactly that of Christian love (cf. Matt. 5:44; 6:4,6; Rom. 12:19–21). The emphasis is, partially at least, pragmatic; i.e., this is simply the most practical way to deal with an enemy. If you fight him, he fights you, and then you respond, etc. Vengeance escalates at a rapid rate and swiftly moves beyond the control of the participants. Kings and presidents have demonstrated over and over that it is easy to start or prolong a war with "retaliatory strikes" but that it soon becomes beyond their power to stop what they start. The enemy is frequently far more vulnerable to generosity and kindness than to threats and violence, against which he has set himself with determination. Kindness to an enemy may inflict on him the punishment of remorse, and out of that may come a new and sound relationship. Needless to say, the discipline required for this type of behavior towards a foe must be as strong as steel.

Verse 24 is almost the same as 21:9, which see, also the comment on it.

Water is the common subject of vv. 25, 26; though used in different ways. Verse 25 is a graphic expression of the refreshing results of good news. The meaning is clear to anyone who has longed for and gotten a drink of cold water during the heat and fatigue of a hot day. The spring in v. 26 is one which has been "trampled" in by men or animals so that the water becomes undrinkable. Thus, that which could have been an asset—and a valuable one in dry Palestine—is lost. This is the way it is when a *righteous man gives way before the wicked,* though the precise meaning of this expression is a matter of question. The sense may be that of moral failure (as in Psalm 17:5); i.e., the righteous man yields to the temptations of the wicked and loses his purity and usefulness (see Toy, p. 470). Another approach is to understand the expression as a loss of social standing and power. Thus, a righteous man who cannot stand up to a wicked man is "as perplexing a phenomenon as a wasted spring" (McKane, p. 593). The man who is looked to as a source of unfailing strength and as a model of prosperity becomes a disappointment like a polluted spring or fountain.

Verse 28 is somewhat related in thought context to v. 26. A man without himself under control is as helpless as a city with its walls broken down and invaded. A disciplined man can take care of himself.

(4) Caricatures of Folly and Laziness (26: 1-16)

1 Like snow in summer or rain in harvest,
    so honor is not fitting for a fool.
2 Like a sparrow in its flitting, like a swallow
    in its flying,
    a curse that is causeless does not alight.
3 A whip for the horse, a bridle for the ass,
    and a rod for the back of fools.
4 Answer not a fool according to his folly,
    lest you be like him yourself.
5 Answer a fool according to his folly,
    lest he be wise in his own eyes.
6 He who sends a message by the hand of a
    fool
    cuts off his own feet and drinks violence.
7 Like a lame man's legs, which hang useless,
    is a proverb in the mouth of fools.
8 Like one who binds the stone in the sling
    is he who gives honor to a fool.
9 Like a thorn that goes up into the hand of a
    drunkard
    is a proverb in the mouth of fools.
10 Like an archer who wounds everybody
    is he who hires a passing fool or drunkard.
11 Like a dog that returns to his vomit
    is a fool that repeats his folly.
12 Do you see a man who is wise in his own
    eyes?
    There is more hope for a fool than for
    him.
13 The sluggard says, "There is a lion in the
    road!
    There is a lion in the streets!"
14 As a door turns on its hinges,
    so does a sluggard on his bed.
15 The sluggard buries his hand in the dish;
    it wears him out to bring it back to his
    mouth.
16 The sluggard is wiser in his own eyes
    than seven men who can answer discreetly.

Verses 1–12 except v. 2 describe one aspect or another of a fool. There is a richness and exaggeration of imagery which approaches caricature.

Verses 1 and 8 share the same expression: "honor to a fool." The comparison is clear in v. 1; honor is as appropriate for the fool as the weather conditions specified. Unfortunately, v. 8 is not so clear. The *one who binds a stone in the sling* seems illogical as a comparison, since, presumably, that is the normal thing to do with a stone and a sling! Perhaps, the translators thought in terms of binding a stone in a sling so that it could not be thrown (Fritsch, p. 929) and thus be likely to come back to hit the thrower (JB), which would provide a comparison.

Behind v. 2 lies the belief that there is a dynamic and continuing power in the spoken word either in the form of a curse or of a blessing (cf. Gen. 27:33–38; Judg. 17:1–2; Isa. 55:10–11; Zech. 5:1–4). The point in this verse is that a *causeless* curse will not hit its intended target because an innocent person is being attacked. It will flit about like a sparrow or swallow but will miss its goal (or come back to the one who sent it out if the marginal reading of MT is adopted).

The fool, like the horse and the ass, requires compulsive discipline (v. 3; cf. 10: 13; 19:29). Therefore, the exercise of caution in dealing with a fool is in order (vv. 4–5). These two verses seem to be contradictory and worried the Jewish rabbinic interpreters considerably. They resolved the matter by deciding that v. 4 dealt with secular matters and v. 5 dealt with religious matters. More recent interpreters consider the verses as complementary with the application of each proverb dependent on the circumstances. There are times when a fool should not be answered, and there are times when a fool should be answered (see Mc-Kane, p. 596); cf. Gal. 6:2,5; also Job 12: 12–13; Eccl. 9:16,18).

The function of a messenger lies behind the imagery of v. 6. The messenger took the place of the one sending him. He was the feet, hands, and voice of the sender. Thus, to send a message by a fool, who is unreliable and likely to communicate in a damaging way, is like cutting off your own feet and inviting trouble (though the MT of v. 6a remains difficult).

A proverb (*māshāl*) is as useless to a fool as the legs of a lame man (v. 7). Verse 7b is repeated in v. 9b, but the meaning shifts. Here the meaning may be that the *mashal* is not dangling and ineffective, but is as sharp and painful as a thorn in the hand of a drunkard, who gets hurt in ways which he avoids when sober. This is a possible interpretation, but it is more probable that the meaning is that of a thornstick or thorn-branch in the hand of a drunk reveller who attempts to use it as a weapon in some absurd way (so McKane, with references, p. 599).

The translation of v. 10 is very uncertain. If the RSV is right, the meaning seems to be that hiring a passing fool is in the same category with the man who decides to shoot arrows at everyone in sight—both are crazy! Note the NEB translation.

The fool never learns, and like a dog returning to his vomit the fool keeps on trying to do the things that will not work (v. 11). The fool has great difficulty learning from experience. But there is more hope for a fool than for an ignoramus who thinks he is wise (v. 12)! He is the worst of all.

Verses 13–16 deal with a frequent theme in wisdom teaching; that of the lazy person who lacks the will to do his work (see 6: 6–11; 10:26; 11:16; 13:4; 15:19; 18:9; 19:15, 24; 20:4,13; 21:25; 22:13; 24:30– 34; 31:27). Verse 13 is very similar to 22: 13 and v. 15 to 19:24 (see these verses). Verse 14 means that both a door and a fool move, but neither goes anywhere. The sluggard turns in his bed, but he fails to get up and go to work. These verses should be read with appreciation for their humor. Despite his laziness, the sluggard considers himself to be very wise. He considers himself wiser than *seven* (a whole team!) of competent men who have undergone intensive training in answering difficult problems. One need not wonder that he likes to stay in bed, for there he will not find out how ignorant he really is.

(5) Interference and Malicious Actions (26:17–28)

¹⁷ He who meddles in a quarrel not his own
   is like one who take a passing dog by the
      ears.
¹⁸ Like a madman who throws firebrands, arrows, and death,
¹⁹ is the man who deceives his neighbor
   and says, "I am only joking!"
²⁰ For lack of wood the fire goes out;
   and where there is no whisperer, quarreling ceases.
²¹ As charcoal to hot embers and wood to fire,
   so is a quarrelsome man for kindling strife.
²² The words of a whisperer are like delicious morsels;
   they go down into the inner parts of the body.
²³ Like the glaze covering an earthen vessel
   are smooth lips with an evil heart.
²⁴ He who hates, dissembles with his lips

and harbors deceit in his heart;
25 when he speaks graciously, believe him not,
    for there are seven abominations in his
    heart;
26 though his hatred be covered with guile,
    his wickedness will be exposed in the
    assembly.
27 He who digs a pit will fall into it,
    and a stone will come back upon him who
    starts it rolling.
28 A lying tongue hates its victims,
    and a flattering mouth works ruin.

Verse 17 speaks for itself. It is well to remember that dogs were not domestic pets in Palestine and "to grab" the *ears* (the Greek text has "tail") of a dog was a rather sure way to get bitten. The man who thinks that he can deceive or trip his neighbor and then pass it off as a joke is in the same class with a *madman* who hurls firebrands and arrows about without concern for their deadly consequences. The word for "madman" is somewhat uncertain. It is possible that it may mean something like a "practical joker" (McKane, p. 602).

A variety of undesirable actions are described in vv. 20–28. All of the verses except vv. 26–27 deal in one way or another with slanderous or false speaking. The *whisperer* is the subject of vv. 20,22 (which is the same as 18:8; see discussion there). The "whisperer" keeps the fires of contention going with his slanderous gossip (cf. 16:28). The *quarrelsome man* also provides fuel for burning controversy. These are the people who constantly undermine human relationships and keep the community hot with dissension and fear. *Smooth lips* (see marg.; "burning lips" in the sense of ardent or fervent) may cover an *evil heart* like glaze covers the rough earthenware of a piece of pottery. The pleasing surface covers the real nature of the interior.

The theme of deeply malicious inner attitudes cloaked with outer charm of speech and manner is also found in vv. 24–26. There is the kind of man who disguises his hate and deceit by gracious speaking. He should not be trusted. The *seven abominations* is a round number which means any

number of repulsive motivations and acts. Verse 26 expresses the confidence that the *wickedness* of such a man will be exposed *in the assembly*. The community will see through his disguise and reveal his real nature.

Verse 27 has been defined as describing "the boomerang effect of evil" (Jones, p. 215). The trouble which a man prepares for others most probably will come back to him (cf. Psalms 7:15–16; 9:15–16). Verse 28 is an observation on the nature of false speech. The result is always trouble. The translation of this verse is beset with difficulties. It seems better to translate v. 28*a* with *The Jerusalem Bible* (relying on the Greek text): "the lying tongue hates the truth"; or with McKane (p. 253, see the discussion on pp. 605–06): "a lying tongue hates to see innocence established."

(6) Lessons for Life (27:1–27)

1 Do not boast about tomorrow,
    for you do not know what a day may
    bring forth.
2 Let another praise you, and not your own
    mouth;
    a stranger, and not your own lips.
3 A stone is heavy, and sand is weighty,
    but a fool's provocation is heavier than
    both.
4 Wrath is cruel, anger is overwhelming;
    but who can stand before jealousy?
5 Better is open rebuke
    than hidden love.
6 Faithful are the wounds of a friend;
    profuse are the kisses of an enemy.
7 He who is sated loathes honey,
    but to one who is hungry everything bitter
    is sweet.
8 Like a bird that strays from its nest,
    is a man who strays from his home.
9 Oil and perfume make the heart glad,
    but the soul is torn by trouble.
10 Your friend, and your father's friend, do not
    forsake;
    and do not go to your brother's house in
    the day of your calamity.
Better is a neighbor who is near
    than a brother who is far away.
11 Be wise, my son, and make my heart glad,
    that I may answer him who reproaches
    me.
12 A prudent man sees danger and hides him-
    self;
    but the simple go on, and suffer for it.

13 Take a man's garment when he has given
surety for a stranger,
and hold him in pledge when he gives
surety for foreigners.
14 He who blesses his neighbor with a loud
voice,
rising early in the morning,
will be counted as cursing.
15 A continual dripping on a rainy day
and a contentious woman are alike;
16 to restrain her is to restrain the wind
or to grasp oil in his right hand.
17 Iron sharpens iron,
and one man sharpens another.
18 He who tends a fig tree will eat its fruit,
and he who guards his master will be
honored.
19 As in water face answers to face,
so the mind of man reflects the man.
20 Sheol and Abaddon are never satisfied,
and never satisfied are the eyes of man.
21 The crucible is for silver, and the furnace is
for gold,
and a man is judged by his praise.
22 Crush a fool in a mortar with a pestle
along with crushed grain,
yet his folly will not depart from him.
23 Know well the condition of your flocks,
and give attention to your herds;
24 for riches do not last for ever;
and does a crown endure to all generations?
25 When the grass is gone, and the new
growth appears,
and the herbage of the mountains is
gathered,
26 the lambs will provide your clothing,
and the goats the price of a field;
27 there will be enough goats' milk for your
food,
for the food of your household
and maintenance for your maidens.

Verses 1–9 are characterized by pene-
trating observations and a tough, realistic
concept of counsel for life. Though religious
language is minimal, the sentences represent some of the best of the teachings of
the wise men. They "tell it like it is."

Verse 1 is an admonition not to "praise
yourself" regarding the future. We cannot
control what will come forth in a day,
though this does not exclude a positive
acceptance of that which does come nor
does it mean that there should be no planning for the future. The verse is a reminder
of the limitations of human finitude. *Praise*
should come from others. The wise man
does not try to build his reputation by
praising himself. Verses 3 and 4 are observations on anger and jealousy. Nothing
is harder to bear than the uncontrolled and
misguided anger of a fool. Anger is very
destructive and cruel, but jealousy is worse.
The answer expected to the question in
v. 4 is "no one."

Verses 5 and 6 are related because they
deal with proper forms of rebuke. *Open
rebuke* is better than approval which remains mute and ineffective. It is better to
have a friend whose honest confrontations
leave their *wounds* than profuse kisses from
one who hates you. Real friendship cannot
be what it should be if the friends must
constantly be timid and restrained with one
another.

Verse 7 is a proverbial observation on
one aspect of life. It could have a number
of applications along the line of meaning
that need creates desire for things otherwise rejected, while an abundance may
lead to the rejection of that which is wholesome and good (as honey for example; cf.
24:13; 25:16).

Verse 8 is an observation on the strain
and stress of moving. Moving away from a
home context where things and people are
known and familiar can be traumatic. In the
highly mobile culture of the contemporary
world, there are millions who are like a
bird that strays from its nest. The causes of
moving about are, of course, numerous. The
living dead include those who know that
they can never go home again.

The Hebrew text in v. 9 is extremely
difficult. The RSV in v. 9*b* follows the
Greek text to produce a comparison with v.
9*a*. Perhaps a better approach is a statement
which complements v. 9*a*, something like
"but the sweetness of his friend is better
than scented wood" (Ringgren, p. 9). *Oil
and perfume* bring joy to life, but friendship is better.

Verses 10–13 comprise a kind of Instruction, though some features of that
genre are lacking. Verse 10 is troublesome
because it seems to disagree with 17:17

(e.g., Toy, p. 486). But the verse should be allowed to stand. Kinship can be stronger than friendship, but it is also true that a family friend (note *your father's friend*) can sometimes do more in time of trouble than a relative (cf. 18:24).

Verse 11 is a teacher's (or father's) exhortation to a pupil. It is somewhat different in that good consequences for the teacher rather than for the pupil are emphasized. A teacher can answer his critics by pointing to the successful accomplishments of his students. Verse 12 is a comment on the behavior of a *prudent* (or crafty) *man* in contrast to the *simple* (or ignorant). Perhaps, it was considered appropriate as a preliminary comment to the admonition in v. 13 (repeated from 20:16, which see).

Verse 14 is aimed at insincerity in greeting concealed by a loud but hypocritical voice. *Blesses* may mean simply greets in a show of friendship. *Rising early* immediately brings to mind the picture of the hardy early-riser who loudly greets his friends while they are still groggy with sleep. There is little wonder that it seems like a curse (note Scott's translation, p. 162). But these words are probably only an idiomatic way of expressing the idea of persistent or zealous action (Toy, p. 487; cf. Gen. 20:8; 22:3; Jer. 7:13; 25:3–4). Verse 14*b* is ambiguous in the sense that it can mean (1) let the greeting be counted as a curse to the one receiving it, or (2) it can be reckoned as a curse on the one who gives the greeting. I prefer the first interpretation.

Verses 15–16 compose an extended variation of 19:13 (which see). The RSV of v. 16 is a paraphrase of an obscure text which links it to v. 15; but it very probably has the correct meaning (cf. NEB).

Human relationship is the subject of vv. 17,19. The wisdom teachers considered the intercourse of human personalities and minds to be very important. Thus a man's choice of company was a critical factor (cf. 13:20; 22:24–25). We become dull without the sharpening of mind and personhood in study and work with others. Verse 19 seems to say that we get to know ourselves in relationships. However, interpretations of this verse vary, and it is unwise to be dogmatic. It should be recognized that there is no verb in v. 19*a*, though *answers* (or reflects) is a reasonable assumption.

Verse 20 is an observation on the nature of man's desire. He never has enough of anything he really wants. *Sheol* and *Abaddon* are terms for the underworld of death (cf. 15:11). The *eyes of man* are constantly looking for something else to see, just as the death world is never satisfied.

An ambiguity is also present in v. 21*b*. The RSV interprets the line as meaning that a man's character is evaluated by the praise he receives from others. But it is equally possible to understand the line as saying that a man is judged by what he praises. The *is judged* is added by the RSV to the literal "and a man according to his praise." It is difficult to form a judgment regarding the two meanings. Perhaps, both are possible.

The imagery of v. 22 is troublesome, but the meaning is clear: it is a very tough business to get folly out of a fool. Even if he is pulverized with a pestle like mortar in a pounding bowl there is no guarantee that his folly will leave him. The most drastic discipline may not work.

Verses 23–27 give directions for successful living in a rural setting. Sound animal husbandry is better than possessions and status gained from business deals (v. 24). The stable life of the land, based on a pastoral economy, was preferable to a more luxurious life in the city. The RSV translation is acceptable and reasonably clear. The *crown* in v. 24 seems to fit the text badly, unless it is understood in the sense of status and honor (Cohen, p. 184). Some commentators make the changes necessary to read "treasure" or "riches" (Gemser, p. 97). The main thrust of the psssage is along the line that a way of life linked with the proper care of flocks and herds is a secure and fruitful one. Money made in commerce may go as quickly as it comes.

2. Collection B (28:1—29:27)

There are several reasons for classifying chapters 28—29 as a separate collection. Perhaps, the most obvious is the strong return of antithetic parallelism versus the relatively little use of it in chapters 25—27. In those chapters the simile is very prominent, but it occurs only a few times in chapters 28—29 (e.g., 28:3,15). There are very few sentences which are connected into groups in 28—29 while grouping is a major feature of 25—27 (e.g., 26:1–12,13–16,20–28; 27:23–27). The rich imagery of 25—27 fades somewhat in 28—29. There is also a shift in content. It is notable that God (or Yahweh) is mentioned only twice in 25—27 (25:2,22), and that section has very little directly religious content. On the other hand, the religious coloring, either directly or indirectly, is strong in 28—29.[10]

(1) Observations and Teachings (28:1–14)

1 The wicked flee when no one pursues,
    but the righteous are bold as a lion.
2 When a land transgresses
    it has many rulers;
  but with men of understanding and knowledge
    its stability will long continue.
3 A poor man who oppresses the poor
    is a beating rain that leaves no food.
4 Those who forsake the law praise the wicked,
    but those who keep the law strive against them.
5 Evil men do not understand justice,
    but those who seek the LORD understand it completely.
6 Better is a poor man who walks in his integrity
    than a rich man who is perverse in his ways.
7 He who keeps the law is a wise son,
    but a companion of gluttons shames his father.
8 He who augments his wealth by interest
  and increase
    gathers it for him who is kind to the poor.
9 If one turns away his ear from hearing the law,
    even his prayer is an abomination.
10 He who misleads the upright into an evil way
    will fall into his own pit;
  but the blameless will have a goodly inheritance.
11 A rich man is wise in his own eyes,
    but a poor man who has understanding will find him out.
12 When the righteous triumph, there is great glory;
    but when the wicked rise, men hide themselves.
13 He who conceals his transgressions will not prosper,
    but he who confesses and forsakes them will obtain mercy.
14 Blessed is the man who fears the LORD always;
    but he who hardens his heart will fall into calamity.

The wicked man flees when there is no reason for such flight because he has to think like a fugitive. The righteous man can be *bold* because he knows that his reserves of strength are great. The text of v. 2 is obscure, and the meaning remains uncertain. The meaning seems to be that a country gets the rulers it deserves (McKane, p. 631). A corrupt and rebellious society will get a succession of rulers who will fail to bring stability. The point seems to be "Like people, like rulers."

The *poor man* of v. 3 troubles commentators, and the suggestions to emend to "wicked" or "rich" (the Hebrew text changes are relatively minor) are frequent. The Masoretic Text supports the RSV. It is bad enough to be oppressed by wealthy and powerful men, but when poor men gain power it is worse (cf. Isa. 3:1–5). The consequences of a *beating rain* in Palestine can be devastating, especially at harvest time.

The critical point in v. 4 is the meaning of *law* (*torah*). It probably does not refer to the instruction of the wisdom teachers (as in 3:1; 4:2; 7:2) but to the law of Yahweh in a religious and formal sense. The same meaning is probable in vv. 7–9,

---

10 An indication of this is found in McKane's classifications in chs. 25–29 (dubious as these may be in individual cases, they are a good overall guide). In chs. 25–27, he classifies only *one* verse to be definitely in his class C (religious). Whereas, in chs. 28–29, he classifies 30 verses as C. See McKane, *op. cit.*, pp. 579, 594, 607; also, Gemser, *op. cit.*, p. 101.

though it is possible that the *torah* in v. 7 refers to the instruction of parents. But it is more likely that, in this context, the verse extols a pious son rather than one who is obedient to parental teaching (McKane, p. 603). The religious meaning of *torah* (as "law of Yahweh") is almost certainly the case in v. 9 (cf. Isa. 1:15; Jer. 7:8–20; 15:1).

The religious note is sounded strongly in v. 5. Yahweh is the real source of understanding, not only of *justice*, but of everything (which is an alternative translation of the RSV *completely*; see JB).

Verse 6 is a variant of 19:1 (see the comment on that verse).

There are several sentences in this chapter which are related to wealth and poverty (vv. 3,6,8,15,19,20,21,22,25,27). Verse 8 observes that wealth gained by *interest and increase* will not be kept permanently. Eventually, it will go to the man who helps the *poor*—a very optimistic view of things to say the least. Interest on loans between Israelites is forbidden in the Old Testament law collections (see Ex. 22:25; Lev. 25:35–37; Deut. 23:19–20), but foreigners may be charged. In any case, the wise men considered it improper to gain wealth by ruthless and greedy means, and high interest rates were classified as such. The words translated *interest and increase* are technical terms for different types of interest on money. The "interest" may refer to what we would call discounting; i.e., if the borrower is borrowing $100 he will actually receive $90, while he pays back $100. However, a more usurious system may be in mind in which the borrower receives the $100 and pays it back plus $10 "increase" *plus* interest (see Gemser, p. 114; McKane, p. 626).

For v. 9 see the comment above on v. 4.

The thought of v. 10 is found in 26:27, though v. 10 is expanded to include an illustration of the anti-social behavior involved, i.e., misleading the upright. There is also a bit of motivation added in v. 10c. Poor men know what rich men really are (v. 11)! The rich may fool themselves

into believing that they are wise and good, but the poor see through the masks to their true worth. Toy's translation (p. 500) of v. 11b gets the force of the text: "But an intelligent poor man will probe him thoroughly."

The RSV of v. 12 has adopted an emendation in the *men hide themselves* for the literal "men are sought out (or searched)." This is a reasonable change in view of 28:28, which is very similar. Also, it is probable that the force of the unchanged verb in v. 12b conotes the idea of getting out of the way (note Scott's translation, p. 165) because wicked men are in power and search out people in order to punish those who oppose them. When they are in positions of authority, men must hide themselves from the exploitation of the wicked.

Unconfessed guilt is a barrier which prevents success (cf. Psalm 32:1–5). But confession cleans away guilt and, when accompanied by a positive leaving behind of transgressions, opens the way to mercy (v. 13). It has been observed that this is the only sentence in the book of Proverbs which speaks directly of the confession of sin and the mercy of God (Gemser, p. 99).

Verse 14 is read in the RSV as if the *fears* refers to God (Heb. has no object after the verb). The verb for "fears" is not the normal one used in the "fear of Yahweh." The root idea of the verb is to shake or tremble in apprehension or dread, and it is more likely to refer to sin. The one who *hardens his heart* against this fear will experience serious trouble. The fear of sin, when not pushed to an unhealthy and crippling degree, can be a help in the process of self-discipline.

(2) A Wicked Ruler and Other Subjects (28:15–22)

15 Like a roaring lion or a charging bear
　　is a wicked ruler over a poor people.
16 A ruler who lacks understanding is a cruel
　　oppressor;
　　but he who hates unjust gain will prolong
　　his days.
17 If a man is burdened with the blood of
　　another,

let him be a fugitive until death;
let no one help him.

¹⁸ He who walks in integrity will be delivered,
but he who is perverse in his ways will
fall into a pit.

¹⁹ He who tills his land will have plenty of
bread,
but he who follows worthless pursuits will
have plenty of poverty.

²⁰ A faithful man will abound with blessings,
but he who hastens to be rich will not go
unpunished.

²¹ To show partiality is not good;
but for a piece of bread a man will do
wrong.

²² A miserly man hastens after wealth,
and does not know that want will come
upon him.

The oppression of a *wicked ruler over a
poor people* is compared to the fierce attacks of powerful wild animals (v. 15).
There is no curbing of their appetite. The
verb translated *charging* is used of locusts
in Joel 2:9. Jones remarks that "the oppression of the rich needs the language of
the jungle to describe its essential cruelty"
(p. 225). The general meaning of v. 16 is
clear, but there are problems in the translation of v. 16a. One of the most attractive
interpretations involves a slight change in
the word translated *cruel* (or great) to
form a verb (*wrb* into *yrb*) which means
"makes great (or many) oppressions" (note
Toy, p. 503): "A ruler who lacks understanding causes much oppression." Such a
ruler will not be tolerated very long (v.
16b).

There is difficulty in understanding v.
17. The verse appears to be prose rather
than poetry, but that does not automatically
exclude it from Proverbs. McKane is probably correct when he interprets the verse as
expressing the theological conviction that
a man who is guilty of murder is under an
inexorable death sentence by God and no
one should try to retard its execution (p.
625).

The RSV correction in v. 18 (*into a pit;*
see marg., "in one") is acceptable; however, there are other ways of understanding
the matter. For example, "in one" could
refer to the *ways* and mean that such a man
is destroyed by his own perverse behavior,

i.e., the "boomerang" result of evil as in
28:10b; 26:27.

Generally, v. 19 says that steady work in
one job is better than trying to do too many
different things at once. Beyond this, it
reflects the stable rural way of life seen in
27:23–27. The verse is a variant of 12:11.
The *worthless pursuits* are not defined, but
they are probably to be understood as
speculative ventures in business and finance.

The *faithful man* in v. 20 is the man who
is dependable and honest in his transactions. He is not a man who is in such a
hurry to get rich that he loses his trustworthiness in the process. The punishment
referred to is probably to be thought of as
from God, but a sense of general guilt is a
factor also: "he will not be declared innocent." Verse 21 is an observation on the
propensity of men to pervert justice for
small prices. An effective bribe does not
have to be expensive (cf. 18:5; 24:23–25).
The *miserly man* (i.e., "a man of evil eye";
also in 23:6; cf. 22:9) makes a serious mistake when he fails to calculate the cost of
his pursuit of riches (v. 22). The "evil eye"
should be understood to mean greedy,
grasping, or selfish.

(3) Matters of Conduct and Life (28:23–28)

²³ He who rebukes a man will afterward find
more favor
than he who flatters with his tongue.

²⁴ He who robs his father or his mother
and says, "That is no transgression,"
is the companion of a man who destroys.

²⁵ A greedy man stirs up strife,
but he who trusts in the Lᴏʀᴅ will be enriched.

²⁶ He who trusts in his own mind is a fool;
but he who walks in wisdom will be delivered.

²⁷ He who gives to the poor will not want,
but he who hides his eyes will get many
a curse.

²⁸ When the wicked rise, men hide themselves,
but when they perish, the righteous increase.

Flattery will not be received as well in
the long run as honest outspokenness (v.
23); cf. 25:12; 26:28; 27:5; 29:5. Verse

24 is aimed at attempts of children to get the property of their parents by dishonest means while maintaining that there is really *no transgression* since they are entitled to the inheritance. There may be no technical violation of the law, but there is grave irresponsibility, and in reality such a person belongs in the company of brigands (cf. JB) or murderers (cf. McKane, p. 632; (cf. Mark 7:9–13; 1 Tim. 5:4,8).

The most fruitful source of trust is Yahweh (v. 25). The *greedy man* stirs up trouble for himself and others; and he does not enjoy the abundant life of those who trust in God (cf. Matt. 6:19–34). In contrast to the proper source of trust, an improper trust in his own ability is characteristic of a fool (v. 26). The wise man can be confident about his way of life, because of his own disciplined and controlled ability and his trust in Yahweh.

Positive concern for the poor is a reoccurring theme in the wisdom teachings (v. 27; cf. 11:24–25; 14:21,31; 19:17; 22: 9,16,22–23). For v. 28, see the comment on 28:12.

(4) Varieties of Men (29:1–11)

1 He who is often reproved, yet stiffens his neck
   will suddenly be broken beyond healing.
2 When the righteous are in authority, the people rejoice;
   but when the wicked rule, the people groan.
3 He who loves wisdom makes his father glad,
   but one who keeps company with harlots squanders his substance.
4 By justice a king gives stability to the land,
   but one who exacts gifts ruins it.
5 A man who flatters his neighbor
   spreads a net for his feet.
6 An evil man is ensnared in his transgression,
   but a righteous man sings and rejoices.
7 A righteous man knows the rights of the poor;
   a wicked man does not understand such knowledge.
8 Scoffers set a city aflame,
   but wise men turn away wrath.
9 If a wise man has an argument with a fool,
   the fool only rages and laughs, and there is no quiet.
10 Bloodthirsty men hate one who is blameless,
   and the wicked seek his life.
11 A fool gives full vent to his anger,
   but a wise man quietly holds it back.

The idiom of the "stiff neck" (v. 1) is found in descriptions of a stiff-necked people (cf. Ex. 32:9; 33:3,5; Deut. 9:6; etc.). The meaning is that of a stubborn will which refuses to bend in obedience. The outcome of this condition will be a sudden and irretrievable breaking (cf. 6:15). The thought of v. 2 is found in 28:12,28. When the righteous "increase" (the RSV has either interpreted this as *authority* or changed MT slightly to read "rule" and thus "authority"; see Fritsch, p. 942; Gemser, p. 100), there is occasion for rejoicing. A father rejoices when he has a son who *loves wisdom* (v. 3; cf. 10:1; 23:15,24). Of course, a parent is pained if a son wastes his money and energy with prostitutes. Sexual promiscuity is a type of behavior which is very debilitating and dangerous.

A king brings *stability* to his people by the practice of justice in his administration (v. 4). But a king who is "a man of exactions" brings ruin. The word for exactions is normally used for parts of sacrifices given to the priests, but it is used here for gifts or revenue obtained from the people.

The interpretation of v. 5b depends on the antecedent of *his feet*. It could be understood as the man who flatters. Equally probable is the idea that the victim of flattery may be so thrown off guard that he will not notice that his feet are caught in a net spread by the flatterer.

A small text change supported by at least one Hebrew text in v. 6b gives a reading like that of Scott: "But the good man runs away, happy to escape." However, this is not absolutely necessary, and the RSV may be left intact. A change of a Hebrew vowel in *sings* could give "shouts for joy" or "exults" and be put together with *rejoices* to equal "extremely happy." *Transgression* has an inherent snare in it. There can be no escape.

The *righteous man* knows and cares about the cause of the poor (v. 7; cf. 28:

27 and the references there). There is an active concern in the verb *knows*. He "knows" and gets involved in doing something about the situation of the poor. *Set a city aflame* in v. 8 is metaphorical; i.e., scorners arouse the people into a "blaze" of disorder and anger. However, as we know, the internal ferment provoked by such people may result in actual burnings.

The argument of v. 9 may refer to a case in court or legal proceedings but can mean an argument in general. The RSV reads v. 9*b* with the fool as the subject. This is more natural, but actually the subject is ambiguous and could be the wise man (as in JB) or the fool. The fool will not treat the case seriously and goes on and on with his sneering and ranting.

The problem in v. 10*b* is that *seek his life* usually means to plot someone's death, thus the difficulty of the "upright" in the Masoretic Text. But this need not always be the meaning of the expression; and if it is read here in the sense of "seek his well-being," no change of "upright" need be made. Another solution is that of the ASV: "And as for the upright [man], they seek his life."

(5) Miscellaneous Sentences (29:12–27)

12 If a ruler listens to falsehood,
    all his officials will be wicked.
13 The poor man and the oppressor meet together;
    the Lord gives light to the eyes of both.
14 If a king judges the poor with equity
    his throne will be established for ever.
15 The rod and reproof gives wisdom,
    but a child left to himself brings shame to his mother.
16 When the wicked are in authority, transgression increases;
    but the righteous will look upon their downfall.
17 Discipline your son, and he will give you rest;
    he will give delight to your heart.
18 Where there is no prophecy the people cast off restraint,
    but blessed is he who keeps the law.
19 By mere words a servant is not disciplined,
    for though he understands, he will not give heed.
20 Do you see a man who is hasty in his words?
    There is more hope for a fool than for him.
21 He who pampers his servant from childhood,
    will in the end find him his heir.
22 A man of wrath stirs up strife,
    and a man given to anger causes much transgression.
23 A man's pride will bring him low,
    but he who is lowly in spirit will obtain honor.
24 The partner of a thief hates his own life;
    he hears the curse, but discloses nothing.
25 The fear of man lays a snare,
    but he who trusts in the Lord is safe.
26 Many seek the favor of a ruler,
    but from the Lord a man gets justice.
27 An unjust man is an abomination to the righteous,
    but he whose way is straight is an abomination to the wicked.

The point of v. 12 is "like ruler, like officials." The servants of a ruler tend to accommodate themselves to the practices of the ruler and become like him. Verse 13 is a variant of 22:2. Yahweh gives life to all men—poor, rich, oppressor, upright, etc. Incongruities are found in the created order. Perhaps the verse implies a faith that, though the meaning of all this "togetherness" is often obscure, there is a divine purpose in it.

The problem of the poor is one which plagues the administration of any government (v. 14). A king who deals with the poor faithfully and justly (often not the case) will establish his throne securely (cf. 29:4; 16:12; Psalms 45:6–7; 72:1–4). The *for ever* means for extended duration or for a long time.

All of vv. 15–21 deal directly with discipline of one type or another except vv. 16,20. For v. 16, see 29:2 and the references there. The difference in this verse is the conviction that the righteous will have the satisfaction of seeing the downfall of the wicked. Verse 20 is a variant of 26: 12, but the emphasis in v. 20 is on rash, ill-considered speech (cf. Ecclus. 9:18).

Verses 15,17 set forth ways and motivations for disciplining a son. Verses 19,21 give advice on the discipline of a slave. More than *mere words* is required. The slave may understand the words, but his response will be dependent on some form of force (cf. Ecclus. 33:24–28). There is danger in pampering a slave (v. 21), though there is some obscurity in the verse. *Heir* does not occur elsewhere in the Old Testament and has been the subject of considerable study (see McKane, p. 634).

The meaning of v. 18 is tied up with the understanding of *prophecy* (vision) and *law*. "Vision" (*chazon*) is a word normally used of the prophetic vision (e.g., Hos. 12:11; Isa. 1:1; 29:7). It is safe to say that the meaning here is not that of vision or dreams in general. Definite revelation(s) from God is (are) considered to be a necessary element in keeping a people from casting off *restraint* (lit., let loose as of the hair of the head in Lev. 10:6 or run wild as in Ex. 32:25). Happiness (*blessed*) comes with keeping the *law*.

There are several options open in understanding v. 18. The major ones are as follows. (1) The verse may be taken as an endorsement by the wise men of the "vision" of the prophets and the "law" (*torah*) or instruction of the priests. The nation cannot be really blessed until these two things are taken seriously. (2) The "vision" and "law" may apply to the wise men themselves, who are adopting the terminology and the authority of the prophets for their own instruction. The sages are claiming an inspiration and authority equal to that of the prophets and priests (Scott, p. 170, who cites Ecclus. 24:32–33, cf. 11:14; 1 Sam. 3:1). (3) It is possible that the "vision" (*chazon*) is a misunderstanding of a word which means superintendent or magistrate; i.e., referring to a person who oversees the keeping of the law (as in the Greek text, see Gemser, pp. 101, 114, citing the suggestions of G. R. Driver). (4) The view of McKane (p. 640) is very attractive. He notes that the disorder of the people because of a lack of "vision" (which he interprets as prophecy) is set in antithesis to the blessedness of the individual who keeps the "law." This suggests that the age of prophecy to the nation (or people)

is past and, as a consequence, the people are open to a lack of discipline. The remedy for this situation lies in the *individual* keeping of the *torah* (which he understands as law). But no absolutely final decision regarding these interpretations seems possible.

For v. 22, see 15:18 (the first line is almost identical) and 14:17,29; 22:24. For v. 23, see 11:2; 16:18,19. Pride *brings him low* because it seals a man off from learning and motivates him to accommodate himself to second rate behavior in order to try to gain the *honor* which he craves. The modest man, who is *lowly in spirit*, is not blocked out from honor by an arrogant will.

The background of v. 24 appears to be like that in Leviticus 5:1. A curse is pronounced on an unknown thief, which is heard by one of his associates. However, the associate does not reveal what he knows and so he bears the full brunt of the curse as well as does the thief. Such a man *hates his own life*. The crime is bad enough, but the failure to confess is suicidal.

The *fear of man* is not analogous to the fear of Yahweh. It is man's fear or human fear which sets a snare for a man in various ways (e.g., in telling the truth as in v. 24). Safety is found in trusting Yahweh (Scott, p. 169). Another interpretation is that of the RSV; i.e., cringing before men (especially, evil and powerful men) will be a snare which causes a man's ruin. Trust God and fear no man. I prefer the first interpretation.

Verse 26*a* is an observation of the way life is: there are many who seek a ruler's goodwill. Verse 26*b* is a reminder that ultimate judgment comes from no ruler but from Yahweh. The verse would be particularly apt for those who seek high office. Let such a man remember that because many seek his favor, he should not conclude that God has abdicated his concern for justice. On the other hand, let the ordinary man remember that he will gain nothing really worthy by asking for privileged treatment by a ruler. Let him wait in trust for Yahweh to give him a favorable judgment (McKane,

p. 639).

The *unjust man* (or devious man) and the *wicked* man are mutually repulsive to the *righteous* man and to the man whose *way is straight.*The parallelism goes "righteous-man" // "wicked man"; "crooked-man" // "straight-man."

VI. The Words of Agur (30:1–33)

1. The Skepticism of Agur (30:1–4)

¹ The words of Agur son of Jakeh of Massa.
  The man says to Ithiel,
    to Ithiel and Ucal:
² Surely I am too stupid to be a man.
    I have not the understanding of a man.
³ I have not learned wisdom,
    nor have I knowledge of the Holy One.
⁴ Who has ascended to heaven and come down?
  Who has gathered the wind in his fists?
  Who has wrapped up the waters in a garment?
  Who has established all the ends of the earth?
  What is his name, and what is his son's name?
    Surely you know!

My use of the title "The words of Agur" for all of chapter 30 should not be understood as a judgment that all the material in this chapter belongs to Agur, though that is not impossible. I am only using it as a general title as in the RSV. There are many uncertainties about vv. 1–9. The identity of Agur himself is one of these. The names *Agur* and *Jakeh* (I am assuming that they are personal names and not appellations, see Toy, p. 518) are not found elsewhere in the Old Testament. But with no evidence to the contrary, we may assume that Agur was a wise man of some reputation of an unknown date. The Jewish and Christian traditional assumption that the name is a *nom-de-plume* for Solomon is unnecessary and almost certainly wrong (see Toy, p. 518; Kidner, p. 178).

A further problem arises with the term *hammassa'* which the RSV emends slightly and takes as a territorial or tribal designation: *Massa*. The RSV margin indicates that the translation is properly "the oracle" (lit. the burden), a term used of prophetic utterance as in Isaiah 13:1; Jeremiah 23:33–40. But "the oracle" seems to fit poorly in the context, and the more definite (but not certain) use of "Massa" in 31:1 as a place or clan name seems to me to point towards such a meaning here. A "Massa" appears as a clan name among the sons of Ishmael (located in northern Arabia); cf. Gen. 25:14; 1 Chron. 1:30).

A third problem arises with the translation of v. 1*b,c. Ithiel* and *Ucal* appear as proper names. "Ithiel" does appear as a proper name in Nehemiah 11:7, but Ucal is otherwise unknown. The Greek and Latin texts do not recognize proper names here, and it seems that the context makes more sense if they are not read as such. The Hebrew consonants can be revocalized to read: "I have wearied myself, O God, I have wearied myself, O God, and I am exhausted (or at my wit's end)." If an Aramaic text is assumed and vocalized, the reading is "There is no God! There is no God! and I am exhausted" (Scott, pp. 175–6, in part; McKane, p. 645). It is difficult to say which translation is superior (and there are other possibilities). I am more confident that the *surely* of v. 2 should be read as "for" (the *ki* introduces a motive clause). Verses 2–3 express the reasons for the skepticism and/or fatigue of Agur in v. 1.

Agur maintains, probably with some irony, that his understanding of wisdom and the *Holy One* (lit. holies which could be holy things or holy place as in Psalm 73:17, but probably "Holy One") is so plagued by human finitude that it is really at a sub-human level: he feels *too stupid to be a man* (cf. Psalm 73:22). God and his ways are a great mystery to him, though others claim to know all about the divine. Note the ironical *I have not learned wisdom* of v. 3 (cf. Job 12:2).

While some commentators (e.g., Barucq, p. 219) assume that v. 4 is God's reply to Agur's words in vv. 1–3, I prefer to side with those who think that Agur is still speaking in v. 4. It is an ironical commentary on the transcendence and hiddenness of God. The verse ends with a taunting question. Agur wants to know God's *name*, or the name of his *son* (perhaps, someone taught by him), if anyone really knows.

2. Counsel and Prayer (30:5–9)

5 Every word of God proves true;
>   he is a shield to those who take refuge in
>   him.
6 Do not add to his words,
>   lest he rebuke you, and you be found a
>   liar.
7 Two things I ask of thee;
>   deny them not to me before I die:
8 Remove far from me falsehood and lying;
>   give me neither poverty nor riches;
>   feed me with the food that is needful
>   for me,
9 lest I be full, and deny thee,
>   and say, "Who is the LORD?"
>   or lest I be poor, and steal,
>   and profane the name of my God.

The skepticism of Agur in vv. 1–4 is answered by an orthodox wise man in vv. 5–6.[11] The thrust of vv. 5–6 is that absolute trust must be put in the words of God, in opposition to the "words of Agur" in v. 1. Everything God (the name used is Eloah, common in Job) has said *proves true* (i.e., smelted or refined); it has stood the test of time and faith (cf. Psalms 12:6; 18–30). The words of God do not need to be added to (v. 6), but trusted as a *shield* (v. 5*b*). These verses may indicate that an authoritative canon of scripture was taking shape and may belong to a later stage of wisdom history.

A prayer in vv. 7–9 is appended to vv. 1–6. It is probable that the major connecting link is the use of *liar* and *falsehood* in vv. 6 and 8. Nevertheless, the verses do serve as suitable prayer for the orthodox speaker in vv. 5–6 (as Scott argues, p. 176). The form is that of the Numerical Saying (see Int.). The *two things* which are requested are (1) freedom from false and lying speech and (2) a balance in life be-

tween *poverty* and *riches*. If life becomes too affluent, one may be so self-satisfied that he will say *Who is the Lord?* But if one becomes too poor, he may be led to *steal* and violate the commandment of the Law.

3. Further Counsel (30:10–14)

10 Do not slander a servant to his master,
>   lest he curse you, and you be held guilty.
11 There are those who curse their fathers
>   and do not bless their mothers.
12 There are those who are pure in their own
>   eyes
>   but are not cleansed of their filth.
13 There are those—how lofty are their eyes,
>   how high their eyelids lift!
14 There are those whose teeth are swords,
>   whose teeth are knives,
>   to devour the poor from off the earth,
>   the needy from among men.

Verse 10 is quite independent and seems to be placed here because of word association with v. 11 (common use of the word *curse*). The *slander* is better translated "inform on" or "denounce." The verse does convey a message of fairness and concern for the underprivileged (Kidner, p. 179).

Four categories of evildoers are described in vv. 11–14. These verses are very much like the numerical sayings with a missing title line, and this is assumed to be the case by W. M. W. Roth [12] and others. However, this may be only a series associated together because of the common use of the word "generation" (*there are those;* cf. "there is a breed of man" in JB). McKane (p. 651) thinks that a strong prophetic element colors this section, though the preaching is put in the form of observations. The meanings are apparent in the translation.

4. Warning Against Evil Ways (30:15–17)

15 The leech has two daughters;
>   "Give, give," they cry.
>   Three things are never satisfied;
>   four never say, "Enough":
16 Sheol, the barren womb,
>   the earth ever thirsty for water,
>   and the fire which never says, "Enough."
17 The eye that mocks a father
>   and scorns to obey a mother

---

[11] I find it difficult to follow the cogency of Mc-Kane's protest that vv. 1–9 are not "formally a dialogue" and that there is no "original artistic unity between vv. 1–4 and 5–6," pp. 643. Granted that there is no such unity and that vv. 5–9 are a "subsequent corrective comment", a kind of formal dialogue —not unlike that in Job—does result. See Scott, pp. 175–6.

[12] *Numerical Sayings in the Old Testament*, pp. 38–9.

will be picked out by the ravens of the valley and eaten by the vultures.

There is a question regarding the relation of v. 15a to what follows. A link with vv. 15b–16 should be rejected both on the basis of form (vv. 15b–16 constitute a normal numerical saying) and content (see the discussion in McKane, pp. 652–3). Scott interprets v. 15a as a retort to the person who is always asking for favors. However, it may be a more general comment on the innate nature of human greed (so McKane, p. 654). The *leech* is better understood as a reference to the bloodsucking horseleech which was common in Palestine (Cohen, p. 204).

The numerical saying in vv. 15b–16 is clear. *Enough* of v. 16c can mean either the uncontrolled burning of fire or the endless task of providing a supply of fuel.

There is a strong note of irony in v. 17, which is quite independent of the context but is somewhat similar to v. 11. The language conveys a sneering, scornful looking toward parents. Verse 17c,d indicate that such a son will be denied burial and his body left for the birds of carrion. There is some uncertainty about the word translated *obey* in v. 17b. Perhaps it should be read as "aged", i.e., "and scorns an aged mother."

5. Four Incomprehensible Wonders (30: 18–20)

18 Three things are too wonderful for me;
   four I do not understand:
19 the way of an eagle in the sky,
   the way of a serpent on a rock,
 the way of a ship on the high seas,
   and the way of a man with a maiden.
20 This is the way of an adulteress:
   she eats, and wipes her mouth,
   and says, "I have done no wrong."

The question of interpretation in vv. 18–19 is whether the point of these *wonderful* things is their mystery or the fact that there is no clear trace of their movement. Certainly, there is fascination and mystery about the flight of a bird, a serpent's movement without benefit of legs, a ship's ability to stay afloat, and the process of courtship. But it seems better to emphasize the repeated use of the word *way*. It is the "way" of each of these things which cannot be recovered; thus, they reach their objectives but leave no evident trace behind.[13] We need to remember that courtship was not carried on so long and openly in ancient cultures as in our own. Even so, the culmination of a love affair often comes quite unexpectedly for us and we ask "How did that happen?" The reader may note that the word translated *maiden* is the *'almah* of Isaiah 7:14: "young woman."

Verse 20 is attached to vv. 18–19 by the catch-word principle (the use of *way*), but it also serves as an interpretation of those verses applied to a particular case.[14] The behavior of an adulteress is characterized by her own nonchalant actions and protestation of innocence. She treats her sexual intercourse as casually as eating a meal, outwardly, at least, unconcerned and unrevealing about her conduct.

6. Four Unbearable Kinds of People (30:21–23)

21 Under three things the earth trembles;
   under four it cannot bear up:
22 a slave when he becomes king,
   and a fool when he is filled with food;
23 an unloved woman when she gets a husband,
   and a maid when she succeeds her mistress.

It is probable that v. 21 should be read as satirical and hyperbolic, rather than as a serious sociological observation. Nevertheless, the thrust of the entire saying is directed towards the imbalances which do occur in society with intolerable consequences. There is some uncertainty about the expression *unloved woman* (lit. hated). Roth[15] argues that it is a legal term (as in Deut. 21:15–17; Gen. 29:31,33) for a hated wife who remained in her husband's household but was relegated to a status similar to a female slave and practically barred forever from having a full marital status. It is also

---

13 See the discussion by Roland E. Murphy, "The Interpretation of Old Testament Wisdom Literature," *Interpretation*, XXIII (1969), 295–6.
14 (Murphy, *op. cit.*, p. 296).
15 *Op. cit.*, p. 36.

possible that here the word means "divorcee" (G. R. Driver, in Gemser, p. 106; cf. Deut. 24:1–4; Jer. 3:1). But it is more probable that the meaning in v. 23 is unpopular and/or unattractive; possibly, rejected or jilted (JB).

7. Four Small but Wise Creatures (30:24-28)

24 Four things on earth are small,
  but they are exceedingly wise:
25 the ants are a people not strong,
  yet they provide their food in the summer;
26 The badgers are a people not mighty,
  yet they make their homes in the rocks;
27 the locusts have no king,
  yet all of them march in rank;
28 the lizard you can take in your hands,
  yet it is in kings' palaces.

These four small animals are characterized as *exceedingly wise*. They provide models for human wisdom (cf. 6:6–11) and cannot be taken as "simply descriptive of the habits of animals, a bit of natural history." [16] The saying is aimed at human life and intends to convey teaching about wisdom by means of the model form. Of course, this does not rule out careful observation of the natural habits of interesting creatures, but the primary focus is not scientific.

Prime qualities of wisdom are exhibited by each creature. The ant is a model of foresight, planning ahead to meet future needs. The badger (apparently the hyrax, a rock-dwelling mammal) [17] is a model of the use of skill and resourcefulness to gain a high degree of security (cf. Psalm 104:18). The locusts are models of organization and discipline. Like the ant in 6:7, they are not dependent on external compulsion but have a discipline which has become an inherent part of their lives. The lizard in the palaces of kings is a model of the use of the resources of the mind to overcome severe physical limitations.

[16] Toy, p. 534; approved by Roth, *op. cit.*, p. 21.
[17] For an identification of the badger with the "whistle pig" of the American Rockies and an exposition of v. 26, see Clyde T. Francisco, "The Conies," *Professor in the Pulpit*, ed. W. Morgan Patterson and Raymond Bryan Brown (Nashville, Tennessee: Broadman Press, 1963), pp. 119–22.

8. Four Beings with Stately Stride (30: 29-31)

29 Three things are stately in their tread;
  four are stately in their stride:
30 the lion, which is mightiest among beasts
  and does not turn back before any;
31 the strutting cock, the he-goat,
  and a king striding before his people.

This numerical saying is more nearly a codification of observations in the natural order than the preceding verses. The theme is leadership and dignity of personal bearing. It is difficult to decide whether the saying is satirical or intended as another series of models to be studied in a positive way. Part of the problem lies in the difficulties of the text. Various translations are possible, but the RSV represents reasonable conjectures. Despite the uncertainties, I prefer to take the passage as setting forth positive examples of leadership, though this is not sustained very well by the tone of the RSV translation.

9. Self-Control (30:32-33)

32 If you have been foolish, exalting yourself,
  or if you have been devising evil,
  put your hand on your mouth.
33 For pressing milk produces curds,
  pressing the nose produces blood,
  and pressing anger produces strife.

Chapter 30 closes with a bit of instruction for the person who either has or is about to allow himself to get out of hand in pride and over self-confidence. The repeated use of *pressing* (or wringing) in v. 33 is very effective. Butter was produced by wringing a skin-bottle of whole milk suspended from a tripod until curds (or butter) were produced. If a nose is twisted, it bleeds, and twisted wrath *produces strife* (there is a close connection between the Heb. for "nose" and "wrath"). The point is simple: do not provoke others too far because the end result will be serious trouble (cf. James 1:15; 4:1–3).

VII. The Instruction of Lemuel (31:1-9)

1. Title and Address (31:1-2)

1 The words of Lemuel, king of Massa, which his mother taught him:

2 What, my son? What, son of my womb?
      What, son of my vows?

As was the case with 30:1, several decisions have to be sorted out in dealing with the opening of this section. First, it is better not to follow the Greek text in refusing to read **Lemuel** as a proper name (as does Scott, p. 184), despite the fact that nothing is known elsewhere of such a king. The meaning of the name is uncertain, but it probably has the idea of belonging to God or dedicated to God (see Gemser, p. 108; McKane, p. 408). A second decision involves the understanding of **Massa** (cf. 30:1). The RSV reads it as a place or tribal name, which involves disregarding an accent in the Masoretic Text. The alternative is to read the word as "oracle." But this seems to fit badly with the subject matter, and it is better to take it with the RSV as a proper name, probably of a tribe of Ishmaelites in northern Arabia (Gen. 25:14; 1 Chron. 1:30). The Aramaisms in the passage may also point to a non-Israelite context for its origin.

The genre of the material appears to be that of Instruction (see Int.), which is frequently directed to a king, a prospective king, or a high official (McKane, p. 407). While such Instructions in the form of a father-to-son relationship are well known, an Instruction in the "mother-to-son" relationship is, apparently, unique (Gemser, p. 107; Ringgren, p. 119).

Verse 2 seems somewhat enigmatic (Toy, p. 539). McKane proposes that the *what* be read with the Arabic sense of "listen," "take heed." In any case, the verse is a direct address which earnestly directs Lemuel's attention to what is said.

2. Warning Against Women (31:3)

3 Give not your strength to women,
      your ways to those who destroy kings.

The king is warned against the exhaustion of his strength with women which would diminish his effectiveness in carrying out his duties. The thought in mind here is probably that of a large and expensive harem,

which was a standard fixture of kingship in the ancient world (cf. 2 Sam. 16:20–23; 1 Kings 11:1–3). The *strength* involved was both physical and financial (and, in the case of Solomon, spiritual). The *ways* of v. 3*b* may be changed to "thighs" or "loins" (as in Scott, JB, etc.) by the alteration of one consonant and would then refer to sexual intercourse.

3. The Proper Use of Wine and Justice for the Poor (31:4–9)

4 It is not for kings, O Lemuel,
      it is not for kings to drink wine,
      or for rulers to desire strong drink;
5 lest they drink and forget what has been
         decreed,
      and pervert the rights of all the afflicted.
6 Give strong drink to him who is perishing,
      and wine to those in bitter distress;
7 let them drink and forget their poverty,
      and remember their misery no more.
8 Open your mouth for the dumb,
      for the rights of all who are left desolate.
9 Open your mouth, judge righteously,
      maintain the rights of the poor and
         needy.

Kings should not drink wine or *strong drink* (stronger than wine and made from the fermentation of fruit juices), it may leave them befuddled and forgetful in matters of state, particularly regarding the *rights of all the afflicted* (i.e., those who are especially needful). No one knows the appalling toll which alcoholic beverages have taken and do take from good government.

On the other hand, it is the responsibility of the king to supply alcohol and wine to those who are dying (or in a desperate condition; note NEB) and to those in *bitter distress*. Alcohol is considered to have its proper use, not as an intoxicating drink (see 23:29–35) but for medicinal and restorative purposes (cf. 1 Tim. 5:23). But a king who is drunken will not know how to make this carefully controlled used of alcohol, nor will he be able to see that justice is done, particularly with the *poor and needy*. There are some technical problems in the translation of vv. 8–9 (see McKane, pp. 410–12 and the translations), but the RSV is sufficient to convey the force of the demand for justice and precision of administration on the part of the king.

VIII. A Paradigm for a Wife (31:10–31)

10 A good wife who can find?
   She is far more precious than jewels.
11 The heart of her husband trusts in her,
   and he will have no lack of gain.
12 She does him good, and not harm,
   all the days of her life.
13 She seeks wool and flax,
   and works with willing hands.
14 She is like the ships of the merchant,
   she brings her food from afar.
15 She rises while it is yet night
   and provides food for her household
   and tasks for her maidens.
16 She considers a field and buys it;
   with the fruit of her hands she plants a
   vineyard.
17 She girds her loins with strength
   and makes her arms strong.
18 She perceives that her merchandise is profitable.
   Her lamp does not go out at night.
19 She puts her hands to the distaff,
   and her hands hold the spindle.
20 She opens her hand to the poor,
   and reaches out her hands to the needy.
21 She is not afraid of snow for her household,
   for all her household are clothed in scarlet.
22 She makes herself coverings;
   her clothing is fine linen and purple.
23 Her husband is known in the gates,
   when he sits among the elders of the
   land.
24 She makes linen garments and sells them;
   she delivers girdles to the merchant.
25 Strength and dignity are her clothing,
   and she laughs at the time to come.
26 She opens her mouth with wisdom,
   and the teaching of kindness is on her
   tongue.
27 She looks well to the ways of her household,
   and does not eat the bread of idleness.
28 Her children rise up and call her blessed;
   her husband also, and he praises her:
29 "Many women have done excellently,
   but you surpass them all."
30 Charm is deceitful, and beauty is vain,
   but a woman who fears the LORD is to
   be praised.
31 Give her of the fruit of her hands,
   and let her works praise her in the gates.

The book of Proverbs closes with an acrostic poem in which the initial letters of 22 couplets follow the order of the Hebrew alphabet. This accounts for the length and somewhat contrived structure of the poem. A number of psalms are composed by the use, in greater or lesser degree, of this principle (e.g., Psalms 9–10; 25; 37; 119; cf. also Lam. 1—4; Nahum 1:2–10). The only guiding principles in the arrangement of the subject matter appears to have been the acrostic and the general theme of the able wife. The poem can be another example of the model technique which was used by the wisdom teachers in Instruction (see 6:6–11). In this case a very extended and diverse model is presented.

The RSV translation is reasonably clear and needs little elucidation. *Good wife* of v. 10 is better translated as the "capable wife." The expression carries the idea of strength and worth. Gemser (p. 108) is right in arguing that no pessimistic presentation is intended here, but the verse does make it clear that such wives are rare (cf. 18:22). Indeed, it is a mistake to assume that all the virtues in this section are likely to be embodied in any one woman.

One of the outstanding characteristics of the wifely paradigm is the assistance rendered to the husband (vv. 11–12,23,28–29). She merits the full confidence of her husband, and she more than justifies his trust. He joins with her children in praise of her (vv. 28–29). The *excellently* of v. 29 is the same word translated *good* in v. 10 (cf. NEB, "Many a woman shows how capable she is; but you excel them all"). She enhances the status of her husband in the *gate*, which was the center of commercial, legal, and social activity. Cohen (p. 213) suggests that this is because of the excellence of the clothes she makes for him—she makes him a good dresser! But the meaning is more general. She undergirds and sustains the reputation of her husband. One of the best reputations which any man can attain is to become known as the husband of a good wife.

Another striking feature of the poem is that of the commercial activity of the woman (vv. 14,16,18,24). She likes to work

(v. 13) and apparently extends her activities beyond those ordinarily associated with a housewife. *Like the ships of the merchant* in v. 14 is probably idiomatic for the outreach of her work beyond the immediate domestic context (McKane, p. 667). There may be, also, an element of venturesomeness intended. She has the nerve to try things which her husband fears to tackle.

Her eye is sharp for business opportunities, especially in real estate (v. 16). When she knows that her merchandise is good and selling well, she keeps her light burning at night in order to attain maximum production (v. 18); though there are other interpretations of v. 18*b*, notably, that the light burned all night is a sign of life and prosperity (Toy, p. 545; Gemser, p. 110). She knows how to deal with the *merchant* (v. 24, lit. the Canaanite, a term for a trader) in the sale of her goods.

The capable wife is noted for the way she looks after her household (vv. 13,19,21,22, 27,28). Her activities outside the domestic context do not prevent her from caring for needs at home. She provides her family and herself with adequate clothes of quality (vv. 21–22). A good number of commentators make the small change necessary to read *scarlet* as "double" (as in NEB, which has "two cloaks"). However, this is not necessary and doubtful. The "scarlet" may be retained as an idiom for quality (McKane, p.

668–9). She is alert to the needs of her family (v. 27) and energetic in meeting them. She supervises carefully. She has full confidence in her ability and resources to meet the challenges of the future (v. 25). Perhaps, this is her most enviable characteristic.

She does not forget the *poor* and *needy* who are not members of her household (v. 20). She is generous in her care of the unfortunate. The wisdom teachers repeatedly emphasized the responsibility of those with the means to do so to help the needy (e.g., 19:17; 28:27). Indeed, she *is* a wisdom teacher (v. 26), who speaks of wisdom and *kindness* (better "loyalty"; the word is *chesed*). She is well worth listening to when she talks.

A deeply religious note is found in v. 30. Charm and beauty are deceitful (in the sense that they do not reveal the real person) and fleeting (lit. a breath). The real worth of a woman is her devotion to God. Such a woman, endowed with the virtues set forth in the poem, deserves the praise she receives (v. 31). She is no slave of a master husband, but a person in her own right who takes a full and honored place in the life of the home and community (Gemser, p. 109, who cites Gen. 2:18). May her number increase and the praise that belongs to her be heard in *gates* all over the world.

Ecclesiastes

WAYNE H. PETERSON

Introduction

Ecclesiastes is not frequently read. Its neglect is due partly to its character. Unlike the Psalms or the Gospel of John, it is not a book for general use, but rather a book for a special need. When that need is present it demonstrates its value. B. H. Carroll testified that in the days of his infidelity Ecclesiastes and Job exerted an "unearthly power" on him, expressing the emptiness of his life and pointing him to God.[1] Many who are under the spell of secularism, materialism, skepticism, and unbelief will also find in this book an unearthly power.

Name

The name Ecclesiastes comes from the Greek title of the book in the Septuagint but follows the Latin spelling of the Vulgate. The Greek word *ekklēsiastēs* means a member or speaker of an assembly. It translates the Hebrew title *koheleth*, which is a feminine participle from the verb *kahal* (to assemble) and is related to the noun *kahal* (assembly). It has been variously explained as (1) a name given to the author as a personification of wisdom, (2) one who collects or gathers, in the sense that the author collected proverbs (cf. 12:9–10), or (3) one who addresses an assembly, that is, a speaker or teacher. The critique of wisdom contained in 1:16–18 and 7:23–24 argues against the assumption that the title is the personification of wisdom. Since the verb never means to gather things, Koheleth cannot mean a collector of proverbs. While it can mean a convener of an assembly, the interpretation teacher is more likely, since 12:9 states that Koheleth[2] "taught the people knowledge." Since Jerome, the word has frequently been rendered "Preacher" (Luther, KJV, ARV, RSV), but "Teacher" is more appropriate to the pedagogic nature of the book.

The feminine gender of the Hebrew participle *koheleth* agrees with Hebrew usage. Such names must first have been used to designate an office and then became personal names, such as our names Smith and Baker. Two names of this kind are Hassophereth for "Scribe" (Ezra 2:55) and Pochereth-hazzebaim for "Gazelle Hunter" (Ezra 2:57).

Koheleth—or Ecclesiastes, from the Greek—is certainly not the personal name of the author. In most passages it is used without an article as a name would be used (1:1–2; 12:9–10). In 1:12, "I Koheleth have been king over Israel," as well as in the other passages just mentioned, the word is clearly used as a name. However, in 7:27[3] and 12:8 where it is used with the definite article, i.e., "the Koheleth" or "the teacher," it refers to an

---

[1] B. H. Carroll, *Jesus the Christ* (Nashville: Broadman Press, 1937), p. 19.

[2] The name Koheleth will be used in this commentary for the writer and Ecclesiastes for the book.

[3] In 7:27 the article should be read with Koheleth as in the Septuagint.

100

office. Thus it is an epithet like teacher or pastor which passes easily from title to name and back again.

Authorship

The author of Ecclesiastes does not give his name anywhere in the book. He simply designates himself as Koheleth or Teacher. In 1:1 he is called "son of David, king in Jerusalem." In 1:12 he says, "I the Preacher have been king over Israel in Jerusalem." He loves proverbs and has included many in his book (12:9). He says that he is wealthy and has many concubines (2:8). These were all characteristics of Solomon, and on the basis of this information Solomon has traditionally been considered the author.

The earliest traditions concerning the authorship of Ecclesiastes come from the rabbis. They believed the book was written by Solomon. Nevertheless, they showed a certain hesitation in this view, since they went to great lengths to explain problems caused by the opinion. The statement, "I the Preacher have been king over Israel in Jerusalem" (1:12), implies that he wrote at a time when he was no longer king. Yet both Kings and Chronicles present Solomon as king until his death. One rabbinic story explained this by saying that in his old age Solomon was forced to yield his throne to an angel who assumed his likeness and to go about begging and saying, "I, Koheleth, have been king over Israel in Jerusalem." [4]

Another problem lies in the vast differences in the three books attributed to Solomon. This the rabbis solved by ascribing the three books to different periods of the king's life. An early rabbinic commentary says that Solomon wrote the Song of Solomon on love while he was young, Proverbs on the practical affairs of life in middle age, and Ecclesiastes on the vanities of life in old age. [5]

For various reasons Bible students began to reevaluate the traditional view of the book's authorship. Martin Luther, in the sixteenth century, was the first to assert the non-Solomonic authorship. Hugo Grotius, almost a century later, argued that Solomon could not have written it. Since about 1850, when ancient customs of writing and the development of the Hebrew language had come to be better understood, most scholars have argued that Ecclesiastes was written by someone other than Solomon.

There are several statements in the book which Solomon could not have made. Solomon was king until his death. Yet Koheleth says, "I the Preacher have been king over Israel in Jerusalem," which in Hebrew implies that he is no longer king. He shows a fearful respect of the king's authority (8:2–9; 10:20) and a lack of confidence in the nation's leaders from the king on down (5:8; 10:5–7). He also feels helpless before the injustices practiced in his own nation (4:1–3) and the dishonesty throughout the governmental bureaucracy (5:8). Had he been king he surely would have used his authority to overcome such practices.

The description of Koheleth in 12:9–10 calls him a wise man and a teacher but does not hint that he was a ruler. In fact, the identification of Koheleth with Solomon is found only in the title 1:1 and in 1:12—2:12, and even there the identification is not made with complete consistency (1:12,16; 2:9). The book is not a pseudepigraph. If it were, the author would have called himself by the name of Solomon. G. S. Hendry says:

The author does not really claim to be Solomon but places his words in Solomon's mouth. We may compare the practice of ascribing written works to famous historical personages which was a familiar literary device in antiquity. It was intended to indicate the type, or genus, of literature to which a work belonged. It was not intended to deceive anyone, and none of its original readers would in fact have been deceived. [6]

4 *Palestinian Talmud. Sanhedrin* II. 6.
5 *Midrash Rabba. The Song of Songs* I.I, 10.

6 F. Davidson, A. M. Stibbs, and E. T. Kevan, *The New Bible Commentary* (Grand Rapids: Wm. B. Eerdmans Publishing Co., 1967), p. 539.

Thus the Solomonic identification is purely a literary guise assumed in chapter 1 and 2 for the purpose of showing the limitations of wisdom and pleasure as life goals. One may conclude that the book was written by an inspired Jewish wisdom teacher who lived much later than Solomon (see Date).

While scholars are not in full agreement as to the unity of Ecclesiastes, any lack in this respect would seem to arise from Koheleth's use of proverbs containing views against which he wishes to argue (see commentary on 4:5–6) and to the tentative nature of some conclusions he reaches (3:21; 6:3; cf. 9:4) while searching for meaning in life.

All that is known about the author is what is stated in 12:9–10 and what can be inferred from allusions in the book.

He is identified as a wisdom teacher (12:9–10). His knowledge of the Old Testament is shown by references to the Torah (Gen. 3:19 in Eccl. 12:7; Deut. 23:21–23 in Eccl. 5:4–6) and probable allusions to the books of Samuel, Kings, and Proverbs. He may have been living in Jerusalem (5:1; 8:10) when he wrote this book. The Aramaic and Phoenician influence on his Hebrew suggests, however, that he was originally from northern Palestine. Like most wise men, he was probably from the upper class and a man of means. He was evidently cultured, educated, and widely traveled (1:14; 4:1; 12:9). He may have been married (9:9) but apparently had no children to inherit his estate (2:18–21). He talks as if his productive years are behind him, and so he must be an elderly man (11:9–12:8).

He was certainly a sensitive man with a deep but reserved faith. He was shocked by injustice (4:1–2; 5:17; 7:15; 10:6–7) and sought to learn what was valuable in life (1:3) and to know what God has done (3:11) and what the future holds (7:14). Because he could not fathom God's plans or know the future or change life to fit his ideal, he has a note of cynicism and pessimism in all that he writes; but he realizes

that God knows these things even if he does not, and consequently, he tries to be content with life's limitations.

Date

The book of Ecclesiastes contains no explicit indication of the date of its origin. Fortunately, its language and thought content give unmistakable indications of the general period when it was written.

The language of Ecclesiastes shows unmistakably a late date. The presence of two Persian words requires a date after the rise of the Persian empire in the sixth century.[7] Greek linguistic influence is possible but difficult to prove with certainty (Rankin, pp. 12–13).

The Hebrew of Ecclesiastes is from a time much later than Solomon. Franz Delitzsch (p. 190) says: "If the Book of Koheleth were of old Solomonic origin, then there is no history of the Hebrew language." The language is different from that of other Old Testament books. One reason for this is the strong Phoenician influence on the Hebrew.[8] Such influence points to a date between the seventh and third centuries B.C.[8a] For a long time marked Aramaic characteristics have also been recognized, indicating a postexilic date.[9] Scott (p. 192) calls the Hebrew of Ecclesiastes "a dialect developed in certain circles . . . shortly before the Christian era." Thus the language of Ecclesiastes indicates that it was written in the late postexilic period.

Another indication of the date is the position the book holds in the development of Old Testament thought. God's revelation in both Testaments shows a progression from an elementary to an advanced form.

---

[7] *Pardesim,* park (2:5) and *Pitgam,* sentence (8:11).

[8] This has been recently demonstrated by Mitchell J. Dahood. See *Biblica* 47 (1966), 264–82 and the articles cited there.

[8a] William F. Albright, *From the Stone Age to Christianity* (Anchor Edition; Garden City, N. Y.: Doubleday and Co., 1957), p. 318.

[9] Some scholars have asserted that Ecclesiastes is a Hebrew translation from an Aramaic original. However, the poetic nature of parts of the book argues against this view.

As one can observe in the book of Proverbs and the majority of the wisdom psalms, the wisdom movement in Israel placed great emphasis on the competence of wisdom and the unfailing success of the righteous (see Psalms 1, 37, 112). In the postexilic period a skepticism developed toward both of these teachings of the wisdom movement. Ecclesiastes shows this skepticism. Moreover, it presupposes a time in Jewish life when monotheism was no longer seriously threatened. Thus the thought content of Ecclesiastes also indicates an origin late in the postexilic period.

On the other hand, Ecclesiastes was written before the wisdom of Jesus ben Sirach (190 B.C.) and the Wisdom of Solomon (100 B.C.). The former shows abundant influence from Ecclesiastes. The latter quotes the book in order to argue against its teachings (Barton, pp. 53–58). Additional evidence for the *terminus ad quem* comes from fragments of a manuscript of Ecclesiastes found in cave 4 at Qumran, which James Muilenburg dates at about 150 B.C.[10] Thus the book had to be written early enough to achieve general circulation by about 200 B.C.

The evidence cited above indicates a date in the late Persian or early Greek period of Jewish history, that is, in the third or fourth century B.C.

Canonicity

All evidence indicates that Ecclesiastes was among the last books to be accepted into the canon. In the Hebrew Bible and the Talmudic list of Old Testament books it occurs in the third division called the "Writings" or "Hagiographa." The earliest evidence that this third division was recognized as Scripture is the prologue to the Wisdom of Jesus ben Sirach (Ecclesiasticus) about 117 B.C.[11] But since the writer

of this prologue did not enumerate the books in this division, it is not certain that Ecclesiastes was included. About 100 B.C. the writer of the Wisdom of Solomon attempted to disprove statements contained in Ecclesiastes, indicating that he, at least, did not accept its canonicity (Wis. of Sol. 2:1–9). It may have been a part of the canon of the Qumran community in 150 B.C., but this is not certain.[12] The first clear evidence of the inclusion of Ecclesiastes in the canon (Barton, p. 6) comes from the rabbinical discussions at Jamnia (ca. A.D. 90), 2 Esdras (ca A.D. 100) [13] and Josephus (ca. A.D. 100).[14] The conviction that Ecclesiastes was properly a part of the canon must, of course, have existed for some years before it was given official recognition. For some time the rabbis of the school of Shammai argued against the acceptance of Ecclesiastes, but the school of Hillel, which favored its inclusion, prevailed. The New Testament does not clearly refer to the book, but it was accepted by Christians at least as early as the second century.

Contents

Koheleth struggles with the question: How can life best be lived? He discovers the answer only after he has walked hopefully down many blind alleys of human experience only to discover that each ends in a blank wall of frustration on which is written: "Vanity of vanities! All is vanity." That inscription becomes the constantly recurring theme of his disheartening search. Little by little he finds clues pointing to a passageway through life, but even when he follows that passageway fulfillment is tempered with vanity.

His essay begins with the theme of the vanity of life (1:2). He illustrates this

10 "A Qoheleth Scroll from Qumran," *Bulletin of the American Schools of Oriental Research* 135 (October, 1954), pp. 20–28.

11 The allusions to Ecclesiastes in the Wisdom of Jesus ben Sirach (190 B.C.) itself do not indicate canonicity, since Jesus ben Sirach does not recognize the Hagiographa as Scripture.

12 On the basis of four fragments of Ecclesiastes found near Qumran at the Dead Sea, James Muilenburg concludes that "we must reckon with the possibility that Qoh [i.e. Ecclesiastes] had attained canonical status, or something approaching it, in the Essene community." *Bulletin of the American Schools of Oriental Research,* 135 (October, 1954), p. 27.

13 2 *Esdras* 14:44.

14 *Against Apion* I, 8.

vanity first by the endless repetitions of society and nature (1:3–11).

Koheleth then assumes the guise of the wise Solomon (1:12). With his wisdom he examines all man's activities only to discover that all is meaningless (1:13–15). Even wisdom fails as a life goal, for it brings vexation (1:16–18). Next he turns to wisdom's opposite—folly. He tries pleasure, buildings and gardens, slaves, abundant wealth, singers, and sensuality. This too is without lasting profit (2:1–11). Dropping the Solomonic guise, he observes that death spoils everything (2:12–23). Because of the limits of life, the best way of living is the simple enjoyment of food, drink, and work, as God gives a man the ability to enjoy these (2:24–26).

God is sovereign in man's affairs. Every human activity has its time which is fixed by God. But man does not know these times. Man must accept these limitations and learn to enjoy the simple activities of life as God's gift to man (3:1–15).

Koheleth now turns to observe society. Man's injustice and his fate at death show that he is really no better than an animal (3:16–22). Oppression is so bad that it is better to be dead than living, and better yet not to be born (4:1–3). Man's toil and development of skill come from envy and greed (4:4–8) and are therefore vain. Better than greed is the work of two persons in helping each other (4:9–12). Better also is poverty with wisdom (4:13–16).

In a parenthetical passage Koheleth counsels reverence and sincerity in worship (5:1–7). He then returns to the frustrations of life. Corruption in political life is due to corrupt officials on all levels (5:8–9). Wealth is also disappointing; the love of money brings no satisfaction (5:10–17). On the other hand, wealth considered as a gift from God and the acceptance of one's share of life do bring joy (5:18–20). But if a man has wealth without the ability to enjoy life he might as well not have lived (6:1–6). It is better to learn to be satisfied with what one has than to strive after an unattainable dream (6:7–9), since

all things are determined by God and man does not know what is best for himself (6:10–12).

Life must be tempered by the awareness of its limitations. For man there is no absolute good. He must simply choose the best way open to him. Koheleth inserts a series of proverbs illustrating this better way (7:1–14). Since life is so circumscribed, Koheleth counsels moderation, wisdom, and a forgiving attitude (7:15–22). But he admits that in the ultimate sense wisdom is unattainable. Few men and no women have it (7:23–29).

The wise governmental official will carry out the royal commands, even if they are unreasonable. He will use his wisdom to discover the best time and manner to execute them (8:1–9). Koheleth knows that God will judge; yet in times of such an oppressive government the good people often suffer misfortune, while the wicked thrive (8:10–17).

Koheleth returns to the theme of man's helplessness. The good and the bad suffer the same fate—death (9:1–6). In view of this limitation one should make the most of life (9:7–10). Success is not assured by strength, wisdom, intelligence, or skill (9:11–12). Even when a poor wise man delivered a city he was soon forgotten (9:13–16). Nevertheless, wisdom has its advantages (9:17–18). Koheleth then inserts a series of loosely connected sayings on wise men, fools, and the risks of life (10:1—11:6).

In his final exhortation Koheleth advises the young to rejoice in their youth, to live cheerful, serene, and godly lives now. Because the light of youth will soon be dimmed by the dusk of old age and the darkness of death (11:7—12:8).

The book ends with an epilogue of praise for Koheleth and wisdom in general (12:9–12) together with a final exhortation to a godly life (12:13–14).

Thought

The book of Ecclesiastes is a product of the wisdom movement in Israel. In order of development, it like Job stands after Proverbs in that it is skeptical of the value of wisdom and the teaching that the righteous always prosper.

Koheleth finds life puzzling in the extreme. The anomalies of life baffle him. The wicked experience what the righteous deserve and the righteous suffer the fate of the wicked (7:15; 8:12,14). Nor does superior ability insure success (9:11). Princes live like slaves, and slaves like princes (10:6). Moreover, in spite of God's judgment, injustice and oppression abound (3:16; 4:1; 5:8). People who seem to have everything they need to be happy are not satisfied (5:10–12; 6:1–9). Even wisdom does not do what the wise men have promised (1:18; 8:16–17) and true wisdom seems impossible to obtain (7:23–24).

Life has an order, established by God, but man cannot know it (3:1–15; 6:10–12). Death is the final enemy; it negates all achievements of wisdom (2:12–23; 9:2–3). Because of these anomalies Koheleth finds all life meaningless.

Unlike many who face the anomalies of life, Koheleth never loses his faith in God. For him God is the transcendent, all-powerful creator (7:13,29; 11:5). He judges the righteous and the wicked (3:17–18; 5:6; 11:9). Man can have communion with him, although it is a distant communion (5:1–7).

The real problem for Koheleth is that when he sees "everything that is done under the sun," he cannot accept the traditional view of life and God. Because of life's anomalies, it is vanity. The communion he has with God is limited. God is not so much Lord as he is the Sovereign (7:13; 9:1), or even a distant providence (1:13; 3:10–11,14; 7:14). He has determined man's environment and destiny so that they are unchangeable (3:14; 7:13). He encompasses the life of man (9:1), and yet he is unknowable and so is man's destiny which he has determined (3:11; 8:17; 9:12). Therefore, man must submit and accept what comes in his life (11:6,8).

Koheleth uses wisdom in his search for value in life (1:13; 2:3; 8:16). Wisdom, he concedes, is good. It is God's gift (2:26). It aids a man in his daily life (2:14; 7:11–12,19), in accomplishing difficult tasks (8:5), but it does not insure one's daily bread (9:11). It fails as a life goal (1:16–18), and it is powerless to fathom God (8:16–17).

In Ecclesiastes men are viewed as individuals, rather than as a nation. Some are wise, others fools. But all are engaged in the common task of living. Koheleth is grieved that he sees so little happiness and success among men. Their best efforts are frustrated by the anomalies of life. They have no hope beyond death (3:19–21; 9:4–6,10). Faced with this melancholy situation Koheleth asks: How should a man live in order to be happy and find lasting value? Unable to interpret life in terms of God's deliverance and leadership of Israel, or a future life, he arrives at a this-worldly solution of finding enjoyment in food, drink, toil, a cheerful demeanor, companionship with one's wife, and reverence for God.

The Abiding Value of Ecclesiastes

Our age is often described as one of secularism, change, and despair. Secularism has, for many, undermined the certainties which were grounded in religion. Old ways of thinking and living are being rejected and new ones attempted. When values are in doubt, decisions are hard to make and the resulting uncertainty leads to despair. In such a time men are forced to ask the fundamental questions of life: Why am I here? What is the meaning of life? What is the best way to live? Modern man finds himself thinking along with the writer of Ecclesiastes, and from him he can learn some lessons. He can learn that:

1. Life must be appraised realistically. Koheleth set out to see "all that is done under heaven." He found much frustration, hypocrisy, injustice, and oppression. Yet he did not seek to shield himself from the hard realities of his time by spouting the platitudes of a simplistic faith. Instead of painting everything with optimistic colors, he acknowledged the inequities of life and fashioned a world view which was adequate for confronting both the vanities and values of life as he knew it.

2. The unchangeable must be accepted. When Koheleth saw the vanity of life he "hated life" (2:17). Yet he did not give up in despair. Since the best way was closed to him, he followed the better way (2:24; 6:9; 9:16–18). He learned to seize the opportunity for rejoicing whenever it presented itself (7:14), to take the middle way (7:16–17,21), and to submit to authority even when submission was difficult (8:2–9).

3. Secularism is unsatisfactory. Koheleth says that at times he has made certain secular pursuits his goal in life—wisdom and knowledge (1:16–18), pleasure, material greatness, and possessions (2:1–11). All of these he declares to be vanity. On the other hand, he affirms that wisdom, enjoyment, and wealth have certain advantages (2:24; 7:11,14) and, therefore, have a place in life not as its goal but as resources for living.

He saw that human efforts at autonomy are vain, man's knowledge inadequate (11:5–6), his life short (6:12) and unpredictable (7:15), and his freedom limited (9:3). He also recognized that God is the ultimate ruler and admonished his readers to venerate God (12:1).

4. There is an acute need for Christ and the New Testament revelation. Ecclesiastes, more than any other book, demonstrates the provisional and inadequate nature of Old Testament revelation. If the writer by some prophetic insight could have known the fullness of the revelation in Christ, his constant cry of vanity would have been replaced by shouts of rejoicing.

Koheleth shows the need for a clear conviction of life after death, the reward of the righteous, and individual redemption. Christians have the assurance of those things about which Koheleth had grave doubts.

Outline

Bibliography

ALLEMAN, HERBERT C. "Ecclesiastes," *Old Testament Commentary*. Philadelphia: The Muhlenberg Press, 1954. Pp. 626–35.

BARTON, GEORGE AARON. *The Book of Ecclesiastes*. ("International Critical Commentary.") Edinburgh: T. & T. Clark, 1959.

DELITZSCH, FRANZ. *Commentary on the Song of Songs and Ecclesiastes*, Grand Rapids: Wm. B. Eerdmans Publishing Company, n. d.

GORDIS, ROBERT. *Koheleth—The Man and His World*. 2nd ed. New York: Block Publishing Company, 1962.

HENDRY, G. S. "Ecclesiastes," *The New Bible Commentary*. 2nd ed. Grand Rapids: Wm. B. Eerdmans Publishing Co., 1967. Pp. 538–46.

HERTZBERG, HANS WILHELM. "Der Prediger," *Kommentar zum Alten Testament*. XVII, pt. 4. Gütersloh: Gütersloher Verlagshaus Gerd Mohn, 1963.

JONES, EDGAR. *Proverbs and Ecclesiastes*. ("Torch Bible Commentaries.") London: SCM Press, 1961.

PODECHARD, E.: *L'Ecclésiaste*. ("Études Biblique.") Paris: Librairie Victor Lecoffre, 1912.

RANKIN, O. S. "The Book of Ecclesiastes," *The Interpreter's Bible*. V. Ed. GEORGE ARTHUR BUTTRICK. Nashville: Abingdon Press, 1956.

RYDER, E. T. "Ecclesiastes," *Peake's Commentary on the Bible*. London: Nelson, 1962. Pp. 458–467.

RYLAARSDAM, J. C. *The Proverbs, Ecclesiastes, The Song of Solomon*. ("The Layman's Bible Commentary.") London: SCM Press, 1964.

SCOTT, R. B. Y. *Proverbs, Ecclesiastes*. ("The Anchor Bible.") Garden City: Doubleday and Co., Inc., 1965.

WILLIAMS, A. LUKYN. *Ecclesiastes*. ("Cambridge Bible for Schools and Colleges.") Cambridge: University Press, 1922.

Commentary on the Text

I. Introduction (1:1–11)

1. Title (1:1)

1 The words of the Preacher, the son of David, king in Jerusalem.

The Preacher is a translation of the Hebrew word *koheleth*, used here without the article, as a proper name. A better translation is "Teacher." (On the meaning of Koheleth and its identification with Solomon, see "Name" and "Authorship" in the Int.)

2. Theme: Vanity of Life (1:2)

2 Vanity of vanities, says the Preacher, vanity of vanities! All is vanity.

The theme of Ecclesiastes stands at the beginning (1:2) and end (12:8) of Koheleth's arguments. This verse is like an overture which states the motif and constantly recurring themes of an opera. The principal theme of Ecclesiastes is the futility of life. The subtheme is how one should live in view of this futility of life.[15]

Vanity translates a Hebrew word meaning breath or vapor and then, in a figurative sense, (1) futility, meaninglessness, emptiness, the quality of not being worthwhile, and (2) transitoriness. In Ecclesiastes the word has both meanings. Life is both futile and brief. It has no enduring significance. The word vanity occurs in the

book with phrases which have a similar meaning, such as "unhappy business," "striving after wind," "What use is it?" "nothing to be gained," "despair," "great evil," "pain," and "vexation." On the other hand, the benefits which Koheleth seeks in life are: permanent gain from his toil, the power to change life, enduring remembrance, joy, freedom from pain, the continuance of the pleasant life of youth, and an understanding of God and of the future. Because life is full of the former and withholds the latter, it is vanity.

The twice repeated **vanity of vanities** is a superlative in Hebrew, like holy of holies or king of kings. Thus it means greatest vanity or utter vanity. It is probably intended as an exclamation, an outcry of profound despair—Oh, utter vanity, all is vanity! *All* refers not to the universe, but is limited by the subject of the book, i.e., life "under the sun," the activities of the "sons of men." It asserts that the totality of the human enterprise is utter vanity.

3. Prologue: Monotonous Cycle of Life (1:3–11)

3 What does man gain by all the toil
   at which he toils under the sun?
4 A generation goes, and a generation comes,
   but the earth remains for ever.
5 The sun rises and the sun goes down,
   and hastens to the place where it rises.
6 The wind blows to the south,
   and goes round to the north;
   round and round goes the wind,
   and on its circuits the wind returns.

---

[15] The subtheme is stated in 2:24–26; 3:12–13,22; 5:19–20; 6:12—7:18,20; 8:2–9,15; 9:7–10; 11:7—12:8.

7 All streams run to the sea,
    but the sea is not full;
    to the place where the streams flow,
    there they flow again.
8 All things are full of weariness;
    a man cannot utter it;
    the eye is not satisfied with seeing,
    nor the ear filled with hearing.
9 What has been is what will be,
    and what has been done is what will be
    done;
    and there is nothing new under the sun.
10 Is there a thing of which it is said,
    "See, this is new"?
    It has been already,
    in the ages before us.
11 There is no remembrance of former things,
    nor will there be any remembrance
of later things yet to happen
    among those who come after.

All is vanity because man has no gain for all his labor (v. 3). The same holds true of the endless processes of nature (vv. 5–7) and the repetition of human generations (vv. 4,8–11). These are all without progress or profit and so are vain.

What does man gain by all the toil? The question implies a negative answer. For Koheleth life is vain because it requires painful labor but does not return a profit. *Gain* translates a word used to express the profit accruing from a business deal. Profit is a cardinal concept for Koheleth. By it he does not mean simply material wealth, although that is included (5:10–16). He means enjoyment of life and toil (3:12–13), knowledge of or even control over the future as it affects his own destiny (6:12; 8:7–8), and enduring benefit from his toil (2:18–23). Toil refers to the common activities by which one sustains life and attempts to lay up a surplus for future comfort and satisfaction. One may find enjoyment in his toil, and it may sustain life, but it offers no permanent satisfaction (2:11; 5:14–15; 6:7). The phrase *under the sun* is the equivalent of "under heaven" (1:13; 2:3) "on earth" (8:14,16), and "those who see the sun" (7:11). These all indicate Koheleth's sphere of vision—man's life on earth.

In vv. 4–11 he underlines his assertion in v. 3. Generation follows generation, but the earth remains constant. The sun continually rises and sets. The wind blows this way and that. The streams flow ceaselessly into the sea, yet it is never full. Nature communicates this weary motion to man who in his endless talking, seeing, and hearing shares in this unprofitable activity. What seems to be new has long existed. Not only does this constant motion accomplish nothing, but—and here is the final blow—man's noble efforts will not be remembered. Verse 11 should be translated, "Past generations have been forgotten, and so will future generations be forgotten by those that follow them."

Since life is only *toil* and no *gain*, it is all *vanity*.

II. Two Experiments (1:12—2:26)

1. Search for Satisfaction (1:12–15)

12 I the Preacher have been king over Israel in Jerusalem. 13 And I applied my mind to seek and to search out by wisdom all that is done under heaven; it is an unhappy business that God has given to the sons of men to be busy with. 14 I have seen everything that is done under the sun; and behold, all is vanity and a striving after wind.
15 What is crooked cannot be made straight,
    and what is lacking cannot be numbered.

In 1:12—2:12 Koheleth assumes the identity of Solomon (see "Authorship" in Int.) for the purpose of presenting two experiments which prove his theme that all is vanity. Solomon was renowned for wisdom, wealth, building, and women. He had abundant opportunity to discover whether these luxuries really brought lasting pleasure and satisfaction.

The statement "I was king" is difficult to explain, since Solomon was king until he died, and the statement implies that he is speaking at a time when he has ceased to reign. Delitzsch (p. 226) suggests that the author thinks of Solomon as resuscitated and reflecting on his past life as king.

In vv. 13–15 Koheleth tells how, in general, he knows that all is vanity. He has investigated and searched out all human activities and found them to yield disappointing results. These verses introduce the two experiments narrated in 1:16–18 and 2:1–11. In a general sense, they also introduce the entire discussion, since the conclusions stated in the later chapters are the results of his search. The object of his search is *all that is done under heaven.* By this he means all the deeds by which people try to produce a profit, that is, make life productive and satisfying (see comment on 1:3).

Koheleth uses *wisdom* as a tool by which to search out and evaluate the works of men. Although he rejects wisdom as a life goal (1:16–18) and as a means of knowing God's purpose in governing the world (3:10–11; 8:16–17), he does affirm the value of wisdom as a guide in one's daily affairs (7:19,23; 8:5; 10:12).

The result of careful investigation is the conclusion that life is an *unhappy business. Vanity and a striving after wind* (v. 14) [16] expresses man's toil or business as a constant exertion which produces nothing that is lasting. It is the pursuit of a phantom, and therefore vanity.

As a wise man Koheleth knew many proverbs and used them to clarify his point. Verse 15 is an example. In this context *what is crooked* and *what is lacking* characterize the *unhappy business* which God has given to man.[17] Man can do nothing to change the unpleasant circumstances under which he has to live his life.

2. Failure of Wisdom (1:16–18)

[16] I said to myself, "I have acquired great wisdom, surpassing all who were over Jerusalem before me; and my mind has had great experience of wisdom and knowledge." [17] And I applied my mind to know wisdom and to know madness and folly. I perceived that this also is but a striving after wind.

[18] For in much wisdom is much vexation,
and he who increases knowledge increases sorrow.

[16] The translation "striving after wind" is better than "vexation of spirit" (KJV).

[17] In 7:13 Koheleth says that it is God who is responsible for the crookedness. This fits Koheleth's general view of providence.

The first experiment was with wisdom. Assuming the character of Solomon, Koheleth speaks of attaining *great wisdom* and *knowledge.* These he found to be futile, merely a *striving after wind.* Surpassing all *who were over Jerusalem before me* betrays the fact that the use of the name Solomon is only a literary guise, since there was only one Israelite king who reigned over Jerusalem before Solomon. Some commentators understand this statement to mean the Jebusite kings who ruled over Jerusalem. But they were not known among the Israelites as having wisdom, and it is not likely that they would be classed in a group with David.

Verse 17 is better translated, "I applied my mind to know wisdom and knowledge, madness and folly." The Hebrew text supports this translation just as well as that of the RSV, and it agrees better with the use of *knowledge* as a noun in vv. 16 and 18. The reason for knowing *madness* and *folly* is to know *wisdom* and *knowledge* better by knowing their opposites.

Even wisdom and knowledge proved themselves to be a *striving after wind.* The proverb which Koheleth quotes in v. 18 tells why. Wisdom and knowledge increase a person's awareness of the inequities of life without giving him the ability to remedy them. This inability to fulfill desires causes frustration.

In v. 13 and elsewhere Koheleth speaks of wisdom as useful. In these verses he speaks of it as a liability. There he is speaking of wisdom as an aid to living. Here he is thinking of wisdom as the goal of one's life.

3. Failure of Pleasure and Possessions (2:1–11)

[1] I said to myself, "Come now, I will make a test of pleasure; enjoy yourself." But behold, this also was vanity. [2] I said of laughter, "It is mad," and of pleasure, "What use is it?" [3] I searched with my mind how to cheer my body with wine—my mind still guiding me with wisdom—and how to lay hold on folly, till I might see what was good for the sons of men

to do under heaven during the few days of their life. 4 I made great works; I built houses and planted vineyards for myself; 5 I made myself gardens and parks, and planted in them all kinds of fruit trees. 6 I made myself pools from which to water the forest of growing trees. 7 I bought male and female slaves, and had slaves who were born in my house; I had also great possessions of herds and flocks, more than any who had been before me in Jerusalem. 8 I also gathered for myself silver and gold and the treasure of kings and provinces; I got singers, both men and women, and many concubines, man's delight.

9 So I became great and surpassed all who were before me in Jerusalem; also my wisdom remained with me. 10 And whatever my eyes desired I did not keep from them; I kept my heart from no pleasure, for my heart found pleasure in all my toil, and this was my reward for all my toil. 11 Then I considered all that my hands had done and the toil I had spent in doing it, and behold, all was vanity and a striving after wind, and there was nothing to be gained under the sun.

The experiment with wisdom as an end in itself proved wisdom's inadequacy (1:16–18). Now Koheleth turns to the sensate pleasures. Again he uses King Solomon as an example, since he had the opportunity to pursue pleasure to an extent which staggered the imagination of ancient man.

Koheleth first summarizes the second experiment and its results (vv. 1–2). He gave himself over to unrestrained pleasures. The experiment issued in the conclusion that *laughter* is folly and *pleasure* accomplishes nothing.

In vv. 3–10 Koheleth describes his second experiment in detail. He *searched with* his *mind* guided by *wisdom.* He did not merely give himself over to debauchery. Rather he pursued a purposeful plan for discovering a meaningful life. His wisdom guided him. He sought to know *what was good for the sons of men to do under heaven during the few days of their life. Sons of men* and *under heaven* (like "under the sun" in 1:3 *et passim*) indicate that Koheleth was seeking a solution for all men everywhere. *Good* is equivalent to "profit" in 1:3. By *few days* he reminds the reader again that life is a disappointment.

In this second experiment he tried to find profit in wine, women, song, and possessions. These he refers to as folly, the opposite of the wisdom he tried in the earlier experiment (cf. 2:12–13; 7:25; 10:1,13).

Besides the stimulation of wine he tried the excitement of building. Among his *great works* were houses, vineyards, gardens, parks, and pools. The *parks*, which contained *all kind of fruit trees,* may be thought of as orchards, containing such fruits as olives, figs, apricots, dates, and pomegranates. The *pools* would be either cisterns made to hold the water from rain throughout the dry summer or reservoirs built to receive the water from natural springs. Since in Palestine there is no rainfall from May to October, these reservoirs would be necessary for the irrigation of the gardens and parks.

In addition to his house-born slaves he acquired other *male and female slaves.* Slaves would be needed for his building projects, for the planting and upkeep of his gardens and parks, and for the care of his large herds and flocks. He also possessed great pecuniary wealth and persons for entertainment and sensual pleasure.

These pleasures he pursued to their limits (vv. 9–10). He tasted the glory of greatness and the joys of unrestrained pleasures. He received pleasure from these activities, but that was all he received. The good he found was only a relative good. When he carefully considered this relative good in the light of the profit he desired it was inadequate. He could only conclude *that all was vanity, a striving after wind,* and *nothing to be gained.*

Note the self-centeredness of Koheleth's way of living in this experiment. His building operations, slaves, singers, concubines, and wealth were all for his personal pleasure. The New Testament also rejects this way of living on the grounds that it gives no lasting profit for this life and none at all for the next (Luke 12:13–21). Such practice contradicts the teachings of love for one's neighbor basic to both Testaments (Lev. 19:18; Matt. 22:39; 1 Cor. 10:24).

4. Death, the Destroyer of Satisfaction (2:12–23)

12 So I turned to consider wisdom and madness and folly; for what can the man do who comes after the king? Only what he has already done. 13 Then I saw that wisdom excels folly as light excels darkness. 14 The wise man has his eyes in his head, but the fool walks in darkness; and yet I perceived that one fate comes to all of them. 15 Then I said to myself, "What befalls the fool will befall me also; why then have I been so very wise?" And I said to myself that this also is vanity. 16 For of the wise man as of the fool there is no enduring remembrance, seeing that in the days to come all will have been long forgotten. How the wise man dies just like the fool! 17 So I hated life, because what is done under the sun was grievous to me; for all is vanity and a striving after wind.

18 I hated all my toil in which I had toiled under the sun, seeing that I must leave it to the man who will come after me; 19 and who knows whether he will be a wise man or a fool? Yet he will be master of all for which I toiled and used my wisdom under the sun. This also is vanity. 20 So I turned about and gave my heart up to despair over all the toil of my labors under the sun, 21 because sometimes a man who has toiled with wisdom and knowledge and skill must leave all to be enjoyed by a man who did not toil for it. This also is vanity and a great evil. 22 What has a man from all the toil and strain with which he toils beneath ths sun? 23 For all his days are full of pain, and his work is a vexation; even in the night his mind does not rest. This also is vanity.

Koheleth considers *wisdom* and its opposites, *madness and folly*. He *concludes* that wisdom has a decided advantage over folly. The wise man understands life whereas the fool does not. However, the advantage which wisdom has over folly fades when he considers two things: (1) Death comes to both the wise man and to the fool (v. 16). Therefore, he hates life. (2) He must leave the product of his toil to someone after he dies, and he does not know whether that man will be wise or foolish; in any case, the latter will not have toiled for it (v. 21). Therefore, he despairs (v. 20). He again concludes that all is vanity. He knows he will receive no permanent profit for his painful toil.

For what can the man do who comes after the king? Only what he has already done. This is a difficult passage. It has been transferred, on purely subjective grounds, after 2:11 or after v. 18. Some commentators understand the question to refer to men in general, while others take it to refer to Solomon's successor, Rehoboam (cf. v. 18). The statement following the question is also susceptible to different interpretations. The KJV translates "that which hath already been done," i.e., people of later generations will simply repeat the deeds which they have previously done. The RSV translates "Only what he has already done," i.e., Solomon's successor will simply repeat his vain deeds. In view of v. 18 the latter interpretation is probably correct for both parts of the verse.

Gordis is probably right in suggesting that Koheleth in vv. 13 and 14 quotes proverbs which state the conventional attitude toward wisdom among the sages. *One fate* refers to death and oblivion (v. 16). Since Koheleth has no belief in life after death in the Christian sense, death is for him the negation of all values. *What is done under the sun* is the hard and tedious work which wisdom demands for a worthwhile life. Since death makes it not worthwhile at all, Koheleth hates life. It is *vanity and a striving after wind*. The thought of death also raises the question of who will inherit all for which Koheleth has worked. Koheleth is afraid his heir will be a *fool* (v. 19). In any case, he will not have *toiled for* the inheritance, and Koheleth will no longer enjoy the gain of his hard toil (vv. 22–23). Accordingly he gives his heart up to despair (v. 20) and pronounces all vanity (v. 21).

5. Solution: Enjoyment of the Simple Life (2:24–26)

24 There is nothing better for a man than that he should eat and drink, and find enjoyment in his toil. This also, I saw, is from the hand of God; 25 for apart from him who can eat or who can have enjoyment? 26 For to the man who pleases him God gives wisdom and knowledge and joy; but to the sinner he gives the work of gathering and heaping, only to

give to one who pleases God. This also is vanity and a striving after wind.

This is the first of the passages in which Koheleth gives a partial solution to the problem of living in this world where life is vanity (3:12–13,22; 5:18–20; 6:12—7: 18; 8:15; 9:7–10; 11:9—12:1). In view of the ambiguities of life he can only point to a better way, not the best or a completely satisfying way of living. This better way of living he sums up in v. 24, *eat and drink, and find enjoyment in toil.*

By *eat and drink* he apparently means the common activities of daily life, eating and drinking being merely two representative activities. Even though Koheleth thinks of toil as painful and exhausting (2:22), he nevertheless finds pleasure in it (2:10). He is not advocating a life of sensate pleasures and hedonistic excesses. He has examined that life and found it unsatisfactory (2:1–11). He does not mean pleasure as the goal of life. Rather, because he fails to find an absolute solution, he has learned to pursue the simple life, enjoying the ordinary routines of living. This way of living is *from the hand of God*, i.e., God-ordained. It is God himself who gives the *wisdom* and *knowledge* to gain wealth and the ability to find *joy* in it. These he gives only to those who *please him* (v. 26). The *sinner* labors only to see his produce given finally to the *one who pleases God*. His labor is *vanity and a striving after wind*.

III. Life's Limitations (3:1—11:6)

1. God's Sovereignty (3:1–15)

¹ For everything there is a season, and a time for every matter under heaven:
² a time to be born, and a time to die;
   a time to plant, and a time to pluck up what is planted;
³ a time to kill, and a time to heal;
   a time to break down, and a time to build up;
⁴ a time to weep, and a time to laugh;
   a time to mourn, and a time to dance;
⁵ a time to cast away stones, and a time to gather stones together;
   a time to embrace, and a time to refrain from embracing;
⁶ a time to seek, and a time to lose;

   a time to keep, and a time to cast away;
⁷ a time to rend, and a time to sew;
   a time to keep silence, and a time to speak;
⁸ a time to love, and a time to hate;
   a time for war, and a time for peace.
⁹ What gain has the worker from his toil?
¹⁰ I have seen the business that God has given to the sons of men to be busy with. ¹¹ He has made everything beautiful in its time; also he has put eternity into man's mind, yet so that he cannot find out what God has done from the beginning to the end. ¹² I know that there is nothing better for them than to be happy and enjoy themselves as long as they live; ¹³ also that it is God's gift to man that every one should eat and drink and take pleasure in all his toil. ¹⁴ I know that whatever God does endures for ever; nothing can be added to it, nor anything taken from it; God has made it so, in order that men should fear before him. ¹⁵ That which is, already has been; that which is to be, already has been; and God seeks what has been driven away.

In his search for life's meaning, Koheleth has observed "everything that is done under the sun" (1:11). He concludes that every human activity has its own appropriate time (vv. 1–8), which is ordained by God and which recurs endlessly (v. 15). Man cannot determine these events (vv. 10–11), but his life is determined by them. Therefore he receives no satisfying gain from life (v. 9) and must be satisfied with the enjoyment of the limited activities of his daily routine (vv. 12–13). The limitations which God imposes on man's life drive him to fear God (v. 14).

A season and a time refers not to duration of time, but to the period of time when an action must take place. The thought is elaborated in a brief poem of great beauty. It contains seven couplets, each line of which expresses two opposite actions. These include the most characteristic activities of an individual's life.

Be born . . . die express the limits of earthly life. *To pluck up* should probably be translated "to harvest," [18] making a better parallel with *plant*. *Weep . . . laugh . . . mourn . . . dance*, express the sorrows and joys of life. *Dance* refers to

---

[18] Dahood, *op. cit.*, p. 270.

jumping for joy (Job 21:11). The phrase *cast away . . . and gather stones* has been interpreted in various ways: (1) Throwing stones in a field to make it uncultivable and removing stones from a field to make it cultivable. (2) The marriage act and abstinence from it. (3) Scattering stones from the ruins of an old building and gathering stones to build a new one. The second interpretation is accepted by many commentators (Levy, Gordis, Williams, Jones, Ryder, and Rankin) and makes a good parallel with v. 5b if the latter refers to romantic embraces. However, no other line is metaphorical; and since v. 7 is not parallel it is not certain that v. 5 is. The last interpretation is more likely correct, in that it understands the words in the same literal sense as the other words of the poem. However, stones were gathered to build many things in ancient Israel—walls, buildings, altars, monuments—and it is probable that the reference is to the gathering of stones for any purpose.

The reference to embracing (v. 5b) is often taken to be a romantic embrace. However, it is probably best, as in v. 5a, to take it in a more general sense. The embrace was a common way of greeting friends as is the handshake today. Either physical absence or anger would cause a person to abstain from embracing.

Seek . . . lose may refer to acquisition and loss in business. *Keep . . . cast away* probably allude to guarding possessions and to throwing away what is no longer usable. It was customary to *rend* one's garment as a sign of mourning or deep disgust (2 Sam. 1:11; 2 Kings 5:7; 22: 19). Later the garment would be sewed up again.

All this Koheleth states in the poem of 14 terse lines (vv. 2–8). In vv. 9–15 he interprets the poem in terms of his own experience. The poem shows no progress but only an endless round of activities. It expresses well Koheleth's opinion that man's labor brings him no *gain* which is substantial and satisfying (v. 9). The *business* which God gives to man merely keeps him busy and that is all. It is simply busy-ness (v. 10).

The meaning of v. 11 is well expressed by the NEB. "He has made everything to suit its time; moreover he has given men a sense of time past and future, but no comprehension of God's work from beginning to end." The phrase, "He has put eternity into man's mind," is one of the hardest parts of the entire book to interpret. It has been understood to mean: (1) God has put knowledge in man, but not the knowledge of his deeds. (2) God has put a love of the world in man but withheld from him knowledge of his work. (3) God has put ignorance in man so that he cannot understand God's deeds. Most probably it means (4) that God has put eternity (or the desire to understand the past and future) in man but has withheld from him the knowledge he desires, especially the knowledge of God's deeds. Man cannot discover how God has fixed the seasons, much less how he controls them, and if there is a satisfying meaning in their endless repetition he does not know it. In this way Koheleth underscores again the distance between man and God and the limitations imposed on man's life.

Given these limitations, man must accept them and find his happiness (vv. 12–13) on the level of those activities for which God provides the season (vv. 2–8), as already stated in 2:24. This is *God's gift to man*. Man cannot change God's deeds, including the times which God in his sovereignty has determined for human activities. Therefore, man fears God (v. 14). These activities are constantly repeated (v. 15; cf. 1:1–11). *God seeks what has been driven away* means that God brings each activity back into the endless cycle of events (cf. 1:4–8).

2. Man's Injustice (3:16—4:3)

16 Moreover I saw under the sun that in the place of justice, even there was wickedness, and in the place of righteousness, even there was wickedness. 17 I said in my heart, God will judge the righteous and the wicked, for he has appointed a time for every matter, and

for every work. [18] I said in my heart with regard to the sons of men that God is testing them to show them that they are but beasts. [19] For the fate of the sons of men and the fate of beasts is the same; as one dies, so dies the other. They all have the same breath, and man has no advantage over the beasts; for all is vanity. [20] All go to one place; all are from the dust, and all turn to dust again. [21] Who knows whether the spirit of man goes upward and the spirit of the beast goes down to the earth? [22] So I saw that there is nothing better than that a man should enjoy his work, for that is his lot; who can bring him to see what will be after him?

[1] Again I saw all the oppressions that are practiced under the sun. And behold, the tears of the oppressed, and they had no one to comfort them! On the side of their oppressors there was power, and there was no one to comfort them. [2] And I thought the dead who are already dead more fortunate than the living who are still alive; [3] but better than both is he who has not yet been, and has not seen the evil deeds that are done under the sun.

Koheleth now turns to a different argument for the vanity of everything. He seeks to show that man is no higher than animals (v. 18) because (1) he practices an animal-like ethic in the law court (vv. 16–17) and (2) he dies on animal-like death (vv. 19–21).

Place of justice . . . and *place of righteousness* both refer to the law court. The latter does not refer, as Barton (p. 108) suggests, to the "place of piety." Righteousness is here (as often in the Old Testament, e.g., Lev. 19:15; Isa. 11:4) the standard by which justice is dispensed. The denial of justice in the halls of justice prompts Koheleth to remind the reader that *God will judge the righteous and the wicked* at some time in the future. He allows men to continue their abuse of justice in the present *to show them that they are but beasts.*

Koheleth then turns to his second reason for concluding that man is on a level with animals—they are both frail creatures and die alike. Here he seems clearly to have Genesis 2 and 3 in mind. As a creature man, he says, is similar to animals in three respects: (1) they share the same

fate—death (v. 19a, cf. Psalm 49:16–20). In 2:14–15 he used the same reason for saying that the wise man has no advantage over the fool. Now he reduces man to the level of beasts. (2) They share the same breath (rûach) (v. 19b). (3) They both return to the same place at death, i.e., to the dust (cf. Gen. 3:19). The question in v. 21 implies a negative answer. It cannot be proved, he says, that man's spirit (rûach, the word translated "breath" in v. 19) goes up at death and that an animal's spirit goes down. However, in 12:7 he affirms that it does. By *spirit* (rûach) he means "breath" as in v. 19b, not soul.

It seems clear that Koheleth has no belief in life after death, except a very shadowy existence in Sheol (9:10).

Because of man's animal-like status, Koheleth reaffirms his thesis that all is vanity (v. 19) and that man's best alternative to despair is to learn to *enjoy his work* (v. 22), for he will not *see what will be after him.*

In 4:1–3 Koheleth further supports his thesis by pointing to the oppression in the world. The oppressor is deeply entrenched in the power structure and the oppressed have *no one to comfort them.* Therefore, it is better to be dead than alive and better still not to have been born at all (cf. 6:3–6; 7:1; Job 3:3–19). That this bleak judgment is not Koheleth's final appraisal of life is clear from 9:7–10 and 11:7–10.

3. Futility of Striving (4:4–16)

[4] Then I saw that all toil and all skill in work come from a man's envy of his neighbor. This also is vanity and a striving after wind. [5] The fool folds his hands, and eats his own flesh. [6] Better is a handful of quietness than two hands full of toil and a striving after wind. [7] Again, I saw vanity under the sun: [8] a person who has no one, either son or brother, yet there is no end to all his toil, and his eyes are never satisfied with riches, so that he never asks, "For whom am I toiling and depriving myself of pleasure?" This also is vanity and an unhappy business. [9] Two are better than one, because they have a good reward for their toil. [10] For if

they fall, one will lift up his fellow; but woe to him who is alone when he falls and has not another to lift him up. 11 Again, if two lie together, they are warm; but how can one be warm alone? 12 And though a man might prevail against one who is alone, two will withstand him. A threefold cord is not quickly broken.

13 Better is a poor and wise youth than an old and foolish king, who will no longer take advice, 14 even though he had gone from prison to the throne or in his own kingdom had been born poor. 15 I saw all the living who move about under the sun, as well as that youth, who was to stand in his place; 16 there was no end of all the people; he was over all of them. Yet those who come later will not rejoice in him. Surely this also is vanity and a striving after wind.

From his observation of mankind Koheleth cites instances of human striving which do not produce lasting satisfaction. These instances support his thesis that all is vanity. In this passage he makes frequent use of proverbs to illustrate his subject.

Both *toil* and *skill* in their totality come from the unworthy motive of *envy* or rivalry. The KJV takes this to mean that the neighbor so envies the one who toils that the satisfaction of his toil is ruined. The RSV understands the Hebrew text to say that a man's envy of his neighbor, i.e., status seeking, motivates him to work hard.

In vv. 5 and 6 Koheleth introduces, for the sake of comparison, two contradictory proverbs which show how the wise men differed on the subject of cessation from toil. Some of them viewed it as self-destroyed laziness (v. 5). Others taught that the wise man ceases from toil after he has gained a *handful*, i.e., enough to provide the necessities of life. More would be an empty striving after wind (v. 6). Koheleth, who clearly agrees with the second proverb sees it in contrast to the excessive toil of the envious (v. 4) and the miser (v. 8–9). It agrees with his counsel of moderation (2:24–26; 7:1–22).

The miser is addicted to work. He does not cease from his endless toil long enough to ask for whom he is hoarding such an excess and *depriving* himself *of pleasure.* The miser and the envious man work alone,

each in selfish competition with his neighbor. To work in cooperation with another person brings a better *reward*. This reward is illustrated by three examples drawn from common experiences in the Near East: (1) If two fall, *one will lift up his fellow* (v. 10). (2) If two sleep together during the cold night, they will be warmer than if one sleeps alone (v. 11). (3) *One* might be overcome by a robber, but *two* can *withstand him* (v. 12a). Verse 12b is clearly a proverb used to underscore the illustrations in vv. 10–12a.

Finally Koheleth cites an example of a wise young man who replaces a foolish king. The youth has achieved a great status and is better off than the old king he replaced. Nevertheless his wisdom and accomplishments are vain, because future generations will *not rejoice* in him (cf. 1:11, 9:13–16).

Koheleth is deeply aware of the transitory nature of today's triumphs and glory. His perspective is needed whenever men become overawed with their own achievements.

4. Sincerity in Worship (5:1–7)

1 Guard your steps when you go to the house of God; to draw near to listen is better than to offer the sacrifice of fools; for they do not know that they are doing evil. 2 Be not rash with your mouth, nor let your heart be hasty to utter a word before God, for God is in heaven, and you upon earth; therefore let your words be few.
3 For a dream comes with much business, and a fool's voice with many words.
4 When you vow a vow to God, do not delay paying it; for he has no pleasure in fools. Pay what you vow. 5 It is better that you should not vow than that you should vow and not pay. 6 Let not your mouth lead you into sin, and do not say before the messenger that it was a mistake; why should God be angry at your voice, and destroy the work of your hands?
7 For when dreams increase, empty words grow many: but do you fear God.

This section about the need for reverence and honesty in worship expresses another of life's limitations—the necessity for man to be cautious and sincere in worshiping God.

Guard your steps expresses the need for discretion and care, both in general conduct and in performing the acts of worship. This verse is no more a rejection of sacrifice than is 1 Samuel 15:22. In fact a vow (v. 4) frequently entailed the offering of a sacrifice (Num. 15:3). *House of God* designates the Temple (as commonly in later Old Testament books, e.g., 2 Chron. 4:11; 5:1; Dan. 1:2) rather than the synagogue.

To listen means to hear, understand, and obey. Some commentators have introduced a false antithesis by defining the word "to listen" as meaning either to hear or else to obey, to the exclusion of the other idea. The word often means to obey (e.g., Jer. 7:23; 17:24; Deut. 17:12) but always in a context which involves hearing. The *fool* may offer his *sacrifice* with mechanical apathy, but the wise man will be receptive and responsive toward the anthems and prayers of the temple service and the teaching of the priests. This advice is similar to the teaching of the prophets and other wise men that obedience, loyalty, and justice are more important than the rituals performed in worship (1 Sam. 15:22; Hos. 6:6; Prov. 15:8; 21:3; cf. Jesus in Matt. 5:23–24).

Utter a word probably refers to prayer (cf. 1 Kings 8:59 and Matt. 6:7). Just as one exercises the utmost care when speaking before another man who has an exalted position in society, so one has to be even more careful in the presence of the exalted God. Verse 3 contains a proverb used to underscore the teaching of the previous verse. *Business* does not refer to the labor which brings restful sleep (5:12) but is associated with vexation and worry (1:13; 2:23,26; 5:14). The proverb can best be translated: "As worry brings on fitful dreams, so a multitude of words indicates a fool."

A wise man must watch his words, especially in making vows (vv. 4–6). Koheleth refers here to Deuteronomy 23:21–23. The identity of the messenger before whom the delinquent worshiper makes excuses is not clear. He has been identified as: (1) God, (2) an angel, (3) a priest who supervises the vows, or (4) a temple servant whose duty it is to oversee the payment of vows. The evidence for each of these interpretations is inconclusive. Most likely *messenger* refers either to a priest (cf. Mal. 2:7) or to a temple servant. The excuse given to the messenger is that the failure to fulfill the vow was only a *mistake*, i.e., a minor error. Far from being a negligible error, this failure to fulfill a sacred promise is a sin which will bring God's judgment (cf. Deut. 23:21).

The first part of v. 7 is very difficult to interpret. It seems to be a warning against a religion which consists in a multitude of futile dreams and words (cf. RSV marg.). Rather than practice such a religion, the wise man should sincerely reverence God.

5. Futility of Wealth (5:8—6:12)

8 If you see in a province the poor oppressed and justice and right violently taken away, do not be amazed at the matter; for the high official is watched by a higher, and there are yet higher ones over them. But in all, a king is an advantage to a land with cultivated fields.
10 He who loves money will not be satisfied with money; nor he who loves wealth, with gain: this also is vanity.
11 When goods increase, they increase who eat them; and what gain has their owner but to see them with his eyes?
12 Sweet is the sleep of a laborer, whether he eats little or much; but the surfeit of the rich will not let him sleep.
13 There is a grievous evil which I have seen under the sun: riches were kept by their owner to his hurt, 14 and those riches were lost in a bad venture; and he is father of a son, but he has nothing in his hand. 15 As he came from his mother's womb he shall go again, naked as he came, and shall take nothing for his toil, which he may carry away in his hand. 16 This also is a grievous evil: just as he came, so shall he go; and what gain has he that he toiled for the wind, 17 and spent all his days in darkness and grief, in much vexation and sickness and resentment?
18 Behold, what I have seen to be good and to be fitting is to eat and drink and find enjoyment in all the toil with which one toils under the sun the few days of his life which God has given him, for this is his lot. 19 Every

man also to whom God has given wealth and possessions and power to enjoy them, and to accept his lot and find enjoyment in his toil—this is the gift of God. 20 For he will not much remember the days of his life because God keeps him occupied with joy in his heart.

1 There is an evil which I have seen under the sun, and it lies heavy upon men: 2 a man to whom God gives wealth, possessions, and honor, so that he lacks nothing of all that he desires, yet God does not give him power to enjoy them, but a stranger enjoys them; this is vanity; it is a sore affliction. 3 If a man begets a hundred children, and lives many years, so that the days of his years are many, but he does not enjoy life's good things, and also has no burial, I say that an untimely birth is better off than he. 4 For it comes into vanity and goes into darkness, and in darkness its name is covered; 5 moreover it has not seen the sun or known anything; yet it finds rest rather than he. 6 Even though he should live a thousand years twice told, yet enjoy no good—do not all go to the one place?

7 All the toil of man is for his mouth, yet his appetite is not satisfied. 8 For what advantage has the wise man over the fool? And what does the poor man have who knows how to conduct himself before the living? 9 Better is the sight of the eyes than the wandering of desire; this also is vanity and a striving after wind.

10 Whatever has come to be has already been named, and it is known what man is, and that he is not able to dispute with one stronger than he. 11 The more words, the more vanity, and what is man the better? 12 For who knows what is good for man while he lives the few days of his vain life, which he passes like a shadow? For who can tell man what will be after him under the sun?

Koheleth returns to the subject of the greedy accumulation of material possessions (cf. 4:4–8). He gives a series of reasons why the accumulation of wealth as a goal in life is vain (5:8–17; 6:1–9) and again commends the simple life (5:18–20).

Koheleth gives six reasons why the possession of wealth is futile. First, oppression of the poor is caused by the avarice of government officials. The situation is hopeless because above each official there is a higher official who watches him for an opportunity to extort money from him and so on up the bureaucratic pyramid to the very top (5:8). Nevertheless, in spite of this oppressive and top-heavy government, a monarchy is best for a country which is predominantly agricultural (5:9). Second, the tragic flaw of the greedy is that they are never satisfied with the money they seek (5:10). Third, wealth will always attract parasites. Since the wealthy man can only consume a small amount of his riches himself, Koheleth says ironically that his only *gain* is to see them consumed by a growing group of spongers (5:11). Fourth, although his laborers enjoy a restful sleep, his own satiety will not permit him to sleep (5:12). Fifth, such possessions cause their possessor sorrow (5:13–17). They may be lost through a *bad* business *venture* so that the formerly wealthy man has nothing to give to his son (5:14). Besides that he cannot take his wealth with him when he dies (5:15–16), and he will spend many years in miserly self-denial to amass his wealth (5:17).

In contrast to the greedy person and his disappointing life, Koheleth recommends once more the enjoyment of the simple necessities of life. One should, he says, *eat and drink and find enjoyment in all the toil with which one toils under the sun the few days of his life which God has given him* (cf. 2:24–26). In vv. 19–20 he applies this kind of life to the wealthy who have gained their wealth, not through greed or oppression, but honestly as a gift of God. They should learn to enjoy the simple staples of life too as God gives them the ability. It is clear from these verses that Koheleth does not condemn wealth, as such, but rather he condemns a life lived for the sake of wealth.

The sixth reason is that the possession of wealth does not guarantee its enjoyment (6:1–12). He describes a man who has everything one would think necessary for happiness. God, he says, has given him *wealth, possessions, and honor, so that he lacks nothing of all that he desires. Wealth, possession, and honor* were highly desirable assets in the ancient world, as they are today (cf. 2 Chron. 1:11). Yet this man lacked the ability to enjoy his wealth, but a *stranger* who did not work for the fortune enjoyed it. Apparently in v. 2 Koheleth is thinking of a man who has no natural heirs and, perhaps, also dies young. The only people who can enjoy his wealth are people outside his family who by some legal process receive his wealth. In the ancient world to die without sons who would inherit one's property was considered a great tragedy. Consequently for this man to work hard to attain wealth and honor and never enjoy it was *vanity . . . and a sore affliction.*

In vv. 3–6 Koheleth makes the point of his argument stronger by introducing a hypothetical situation. In this case the man has *children*—a *hundred* of them—and *lives many years,* but *he does not enjoy life's good things, and also as no burial.* In v. 6 the illustration is strengthened still more by the supposition that the man lived a *thousand years twice told,* i.e., two thousand years. Both long life (Prov. 3:16; 4:10) and many children (Psalms 127:3–5; 128:3–4; Prov. 17:6) were considered great blessings. Proper burial was very important, and to be denied it was a great curse (Jer. 16:4; 1 Kings 14:11). This man has wealth, children, and long life, yet he has no enjoyment while he lives and no honor when he dies. Koheleth says that *an untimely birth is better off than he.* Since enjoyment of life is the one ameliorating element in this vain existence, this man is worse off than a child born before its time and dead at birth (vv. 3–5). Since all go to one place, i.e., Sheol (v. 6; cf. 9:10), the untimely birth is better off. The one untimely born arrives there by a more direct course and without the sufferings of this life.

In v. 7 Koheleth cites a proverb which teaches that people exhaust themselves trying to accumulate enough to satisfy an appetite which in the end proves itself insatiable. The two questions of v. 8 are intended to draw the obvious conclusions from the proverb in v. 7. They both imply a negative answer. The toil expended to become wise and to *conduct* oneself well

before the living does not bring the *advantage* of satisfied desires (cf. v. 7). The only solution is to live in *the sight of the eyes,* i.e., the enjoyment of whatever one has. The *wandering of desire* is the desire for more and more possessions or greater and greater achievements. It is the insatiable appetite of v. 7. This curbing of the appetite belongs to the simple life which is advocated first in 2:24–26.

In vv. 10–12 Koheleth appeals again to God's sovereignty as the rationale for the life he advocates. *Whatever has come to be* refers to the entirety of creation. *Has already been named* is a Hebrew way of expressing not only the existence of something but also its subordination to the one who named it (cf. Isa. 40:26; Psalm 147:4). Thus, Koheleth says, all—both people and the material creation—are subject to God. *It is known what man is,* i.e., man is what God called him long ago. Since man is God's creature and therefore his subject, man *is not able to dispute* with God—the *one stronger than he. The more words* refers to man's efforts to argue with God. The questions in v. 12 imply a negative answer. Man does not know what is *good* for his life, because he does not know the future. Therefore, he must not dispute with God; it will only increase the vanity of his already vain existence.

6. Reflections on Wisdom (7:1–22)

1 A good name is better than precious ointment;
   and the day of death, than the day of birth.
2 It is better to go to the house of mourning
   than to go to the house of feasting;
   for this is the end of all men,
   and the living will lay it to heart.
3 Sorrow is better than laughter,
   for by sadness of countenance the heart is made glad.
4 The heart of the wise is in the house of mourning;
   but the heart of fools is in the house of mirth.
5 It is better for a man to hear the rebuke of the wise
   than to hear the song of fools.
6 For as the crackling of thorns under a pot,

so is the laughter of the fools;
this also is vanity.
7 Surely oppression makes the wise man foolish,
and a bribe corrupts the mind.
8 Better is the end of a thing than its beginning;
and the patient in spirit is better than the proud in spirit.
9 Be not quick to anger,
for anger lodges in the bosom of fools.
10 Say not, "Why were the former days better than these?"
For it is not from wisdom that you ask this.
11 Wisdom is good with an inheritance,
an advantage to those who see the sun.
12 For the protection of wisdom is like the protection of money;
and the advantage of knowledge is that wisdom preserves the life of him who has it.
13 Consider the work of God;
who can make straight what he has made crooked?
14 In the day of prosperity be joyful, and in the day of adversity consider; God has made the one as well as the other, so that man may not find out anything that will be after him.
15 In my vain life I have seen everything; there is a righteous man who perishes in his righteousness, and there is a wicked man who prolongs his life in his evil-doing. 16 Be not righteous overmuch, and do not make yourself overwise; why should you destroy yourself? 17 Be not wicked overmuch, neither be a fool; why should you die before your time? 18 It is good that you should take hold of this, and from that withhold not your hand; for he who fears God shall come forth from them all.
19 Wisdom gives strength to the wise man more than ten rulers that are in a city.
20 Surely there is not a righteous man on earth who does good and never sins.
21 Do not give heed to all the things that men say, lest you hear your servant cursing you; 22 your heart knows that many times you have yourself cursed others.

This section is a collection of proverbs (7:1–14,19–22) plus a personal experience (7:15–18). The subject matter is varied. In general this chapter teaches that in this world the good has not absolute but relative value. Consequently one must live by moderation.

In vv. 1–6 Koheleth expresses the life orientation which he commends to the wise. He teaches this orientation by means of a series of proverbial paradoxes which can only be explained as hyperbolic maxims arising out of his sense of the tragic nature of life. True understanding, he says, comes not from the carefree mirth of the fool, but from a sober-minded contemplation of the end of one's earthly existence. This realistic assessment of life in view of its shortness should lead to its responsible use.

Verse 1 contains a proverb in two parts. The first part, which contains a play on words (shem—*name;* shemen—*ointment*), states the obvious truth that a good reputation is of greater value than *precious ointment.* The latter was the perfumed oil used to anoint the body (Esther 2:12; Song of Sol. 1:3). The second half of the verse, in an abrupt contrast, pronounces the day of death better than the day of birth (cf. 6:3–6). Koheleth follows this with similar proverbs stating the superior value of giving sympathy to the bereaved in the *house of mourning* (a private home where there has been a death, vv. 2,4), of experiencing sorrow (v. 3), and of listening to the *rebuke of the wise* (v. 5; cf. Prov. 27:6). These experiences are better than spending one's time where there is feasting (doubtless with the common excesses of gluttony and drunkenness) and listening to the *song* and *laughter of fools* (v. 6).

The *house of mourning* is in the end better than the *house of mirth,* because in the former the living will learn the meaning of life (cf. 12:1–7; Psalm 90:12) and, as an outcome, the heart will be *made glad.* The meaning of this phrase seems to be that the discipline of sorrow leads to a realistic appraisal of life which brings happiness, while the excesses of mirth lead to unhappiness. In v. 6 the *laughter of fools* is compared to thorns used in an attempt to heat a pot. Instead of the quiet steady heat of the usual charcoal, they burn quickly with a crackling sound and give little heat. Thus the laughter of a fool gives little real satisfaction.

Koheleth also includes proverbs on other subjects. *Oppression,* i.e., the granting of wrong legal decisions in return for bribes, corrupts even the *wise man* (v. 7). Since a true appraisal of an enterprise can only be made from the standpoint of its completion, the *end* is, he says, better than the *beginning* (cf. vv. 1–4). But the end is often slow to arrive, and a wise man must be *patient* rather than *proud* and *quick to anger* (vv. 8–9). Some are impatient, not for the end but for an idealized beginning—the good old days. Koheleth warns that this failure to live in the present is not the way of wisdom (v. 10). In vv. 11–12 he states that it is desirable to have both *wisdom* and wealth. Each gives *protection* of its own kind (cf. Prov. 2:9–19; 18:11). In addition, *wisdom preserves* the life, giving longevity (cf. Prov. 3:16–18). God is all-powerful, and man cannot change what God has willed (v. 13; cf. 1:15); therefore, man must learn to make the most of the good and bad experiences of life, conscious of his own limitations (v. 14).

In vv. 15–22 Koheleth observes that the neat formula of long life for the righteous and a short, troubled life for the wicked is not always true to human experience. He then counsels moderation, for no one is perfect. The need for moderation is illustrated by the example of the servant who reviles his master.

A righteous man who perishes in his righteousness means, of course, a godly man who, in contrast to the usual expectation, dies young. The *wicked man who prolongs his life* was also a contradiction to the usual teachings of the wise men (Prov. 2:21–22; 11:19; Psalm 37:25–29). Koheleth mentions this same anomaly in 8:14 to show the vanity of life. Here he uses it to introduce his warning against the excesses of righteousness and wickedness in vv. 16 and 17.

The interpretation of vv. 16 and 17 is difficult. Does Koheleth mean that one should not be very good or very bad morally and thus that he should do some righteousness and some wickedness (Barton)? Or, does he mean that one should

avoid being overscrupulous in keeping the law and guard himself against discarding the law altogether (most commentators)? It is possible to argue for either alternative from Ecclesiastes. But what if one argues for the first alternative? What kind of evil does Ecclesiastes advise a person to indulge in? Elsewhere he rejects drunkenness (2:3), sensuality (2:8), oppression (3:16–17; 4:1), irreverence (5:1–2), untruthfulness (5:4–6), avarice (5:11–12), uncontrolled anger (7:9), and hypocrisy (8:10). He warns explicitly against sin in general (8:12–13). In those passages where he gives his advice about how to live he does not counsel wickedness (e.g., 2:14–16; 9:7–9; 12:1).

Therefore, it is best to conclude that he intends here to warn against an overpious attitude, on the one hand, and its opposite, an antinomian disdain of the law, on the other. This excessive scrupulosity in matters of righteous living according to the law, along with an overzealous cultivation of wisdom may lead to self-destruction (v. 16). On the other extreme, antinomianism, debauchery, drunkenness—the life of a fool—may lead to an early death (v. 17). *Take hold of this, and from that withhold not your hand* advises the reader to heed the two teachings of vv. 16 and 17. The one who *fears God* will escape both extremes.

In spite of the limitations which Koheleth places on wisdom, he does recognize its value. In v. 19 read, "Wisdom comes to the aid of the wise man, more than ten rulers that are in a city."[19] *Ten rulers* refers to the committee of ten prominent citizens who ruled many of the Hellenistic cities. Since Koheleth associates righteousness and wisdom he may have placed this statement here to underline his warning against excessive wickedness. The statement that no one is perfectly *good and never sins* (cf. 1 Kings 8:46) may be intended to strengthen his advice in v. 16 not to be too wise. A corollary both to the

---

[19] The phrase "comes to the aid of" follows the Septuagint and the Qumran manuscript of Ecclesiastes.

proscription of excessive righteousness in v. 16 and the theological denial of sinlessness in v. 20 is the instruction to avoid a faultfinding attitude toward others (v. 21). One must modestly remember that he is a sinner too (v. 22).

7. Limits of Wisdom (7:23–29)

23 All this I have tested by wisdom; I said, "I will be wise"; but it was far from me. 24 That which is, is far off, and deep, very deep; who can find it out? 25 I turned my mind to know and to search out and to seek wisdom and the sum of things, and to know the wickedness of folly and the foolishness which is madness. 26 And I found more bitter than death the woman whose heart is snares and nets, and whose hands are fetters; he who pleases God escapes her, but the sinner is taken by her. 27 Behold, this is what I found, says the Preacher, adding one thing to another to find the sum, 28 which my mind has sought repeatedly, but I have not found. One man among a thousand I found, but a woman among all these I have not found. 29 Behold, this alone I found, that God made man upright, but they have sought out many devices.

Koheleth states the results of his inquiry. *All this* refers to the preceding discussion in 7:15–22 and in a larger sense to all he has said since 1:13. He has conducted his test, or rather his search (v. 25), *by wisdom* as in 1:13 and 2:3. He means that he used practical *wisdom* (v. 23) as an instrument to search for absolute *wisdom* (v. 25), i.e., the ability to live without vexation, to solve the mysteries which limit mankind, and to reshape life's contradictions (see comment on 1:13–15,16–18). His search resulted in failure. Absolute wisdom was too remote and too profound for him.

Koheleth had sought to examine *wisdom* and its opposite *wickedness* (v. 25; cf. 1:17). He had learned little about wisdom. About *wickedness* he had learned that it is *folly*. As an example he singles out the bad woman whose attraction is *more bitter* ["stronger" 20] *than death. He who pleases God,* i.e., he "who seeks happiness wisely" (Gordis), will escape her wiles. Koheleth

20 Translate "stronger," rather than "more bitter," with NEB and Dahood, *Biblica* 39, pp. 308–309.

has found few men and no women who correspond to his ideal of wisdom (vv. 27–28). Man's poor record is, however, his own fault, not God's (v. 29).

8. Necessity of Submission (8:1–9)

1 Who is like the wise man? And who knows the interpretation of a thing?
A man's wisdom makes his face shine,
and the hardness of his countenance is changed.
2 Keep the king's command, and because of your sacred oath be not dismayed; 3 go from his presence, do not delay when the matter is unpleasant, for he does whatever he pleases. 4 For the word of the king is supreme, and who may say to him, "What are you doing?" 5 He who obeys a command will meet no harm, and the mind of a wise man will know the time and way. 6 For every matter has its time and way, although man's trouble lies heavy upon him. 7 For he does not know what is to be, for who can tell him how it will be? 8 No man has power to retain the spirit, or authority over the day of death; there is no discharge from war, nor will wickedness deliver those who are given to it. 9 All this I observed while applying my mind to all that is done under the sun, while man lords it over man to his hurt.

These verses teach how the wise courtier will serve a despotic king. He recognizes that the king must be obeyed, but exercises his wisdom to choose the time and way to carry out the King's commands in such a way that his government service will not conflict too greatly with his conscience.

Koheleth begins with a pair of proverbial statements which praise wisdom for giving insight and charm (v. 1). Because of his oath of allegiance (v. 2) and the king's authority (vv. 4,5), the wise man who is in government service will obey the king's commands. He will show this obedience even when the command is personally distasteful to him. His wisdom will enable him to choose the best *time* and *way* to accomplish the task (vv. 5,6a). But even the wise man faces limitations which make these choices difficult. Verses 6b–7 should be translated: "although man is greatly troubled by ignorance of the future; who can tell him what it will bring?" (NEB). The wise man must remember that there are many situations over which he has no power. He cannot control the wind, or the time of *death,* nor can he obtain a discharge from the army while a war is being fought. Translate *to retain the spirit* as "restrain the wind" (NEB). *Wickedness* should be translated "riches." [21] Thus v. 8*b* means that even great wealth will not enable the wealthy to defy these limitations. The wise man must live by wisdom and submission in a time when *man lords it over man to his hurt.*

9. Success of the Wicked (8:10-15)

[10] Then I saw the wicked buried; they used to go in and out of the holy place, and were praised in the city where they had done such things. This also is vanity. [11] Because sentence against an evil deed is not executed speedily, the heart of the sons of men is fully set to do evil. [12] Though a sinner does evil a hundred times and prolongs his life, yet I know that it will be well with those who fear God, because they fear before him; [13] but it will not be well with the wicked, neither will he prolong his days like a shadow, because he does not fear before God.

[14] There is a vanity which takes place on earth, that there are righteous men to whom it happens according to the deeds of the wicked, and there are wicked men to whom it happens according to the deeds of the righteous. I said that this also is vanity. [15] And I commend enjoyment, for man has no good thing under the sun but to eat, and drink, and enjoy himself, for this will go with him in his toil through the days of life which God gives him under the sun.

Koheleth returns to his main theme that all is vanity. His evidence is that the wicked sometimes fare better in life and death than do the righteous. He then reiterates his advice for living in a vain world (v. 15).

The Hebrew text of v. 10 is difficult to read and probably corrupt. This difficulty has led to several different interpretations. All of them, however, agree that Koheleth complains that the wicked were treated as though they were righteous. They frequented the *holy place* or Temple and *were praised* as though they had not oppressed people. The delay of justice en-

21 NEB and Dahood, *Biblica,* 47, pp. 227-228.

couraged them in their iniquity. Koheleth knows the general rule that those who fear God will fare well and live long and that those who do not fear God will not (vv. 12-13). However, he also knows cases which do not conform to this general rule (vv. 12*a*,14). For that reason he pronounces all to be vanity and again recommends the life of simple earthly pleasures —the only good which one can count on (see 2:24-26).

10. Man's Helplessness (8:16—9:6)

[16] When I applied my mind to know wisdom, and to see the business that is done on earth, how neither day nor night one's eyes see sleep; [17] then I saw all the work of God, that man cannot find out the work that is done under the sun. However much man may toil in seeking, he will not find it out; even though a wise man claims to know, he cannot find it out.

[1] But all this I laid to heart, examining it all, how the righteous and the wise and their deeds are in the hand of God; whether it is love or hate man does not know. Everything before them is vanity, [2] since one fate comes to all, to the righteous and the wicked, to the good and the evil, to the clean and the unclean, to him who sacrifices and him who does not sacrifice. As is the good man, so is the sinner; and he who swears is as he who shuns an oath. [3] This is an evil in all that is done under the sun, that one fate comes to all; also the hearts of men are full of evil, and madness is in their hearts while they live, and after that they go to the dead. [4] But he who is joined with all the living has hope, for a living dog is better than a dead lion. [5] For the living know that they will die, but the dead know nothing, and they have no more reward; but the memory of them is lost. [6] Their love and their hate and their envy have already perished, and they have no more for ever any share in all that is done under the sun.

In his search for the meaning of man's existence, Koheleth concludes that this meaning is undiscoverable (8:16-17). Men cannot determine their own fate (9:1). Rather the lives of all men end the same (9:2-3). Even so, it is better to be alive than dead (9:4-6).

Koheleth calls attention once more to the search he announced in 1:13. He has observed *the business that is done on earth*

(v. 16a) where there is ceaseless activity (v. 16b). He found this *business* impossible to understand, because man's activity is under God's control (*in the hand of God,* 9:1) and God's *work* is inscrutable (cf. Rom. 11:33). Neither diligent searching nor great wisdom can enable man to penetrate the mystery of God's providential work (8:17). *Whether it is love or hate,* i.e., since God's ways are opaque one cannot know whether God's providential actions toward him will be favorable or unfavorable (9:1).

This inscrutability of human life spoken of in 8:16—9:1 affects the individual person at the point of his inability to find meaning in his own life. A man cannot choose his own fate by being *righteous* or *wicked*. *One fate comes to all* alike, and that fate is death (9:2–3; cf. 8:14; 2:14–16). Because men believe that the righteous have no advantage over the wicked, they turn away from goodness and wisdom and fill their hearts with *evil and madness.*

From this dismal picture of death as the equalizer of all the unequal, Koheleth turns to life as man's hope. It is better to be alive than dead (contrast 4:2–3). The one who is alive still has hope that he will get some enjoyment out of life (9:7–10). Even the lowly dog is better off than a dead lion. Koheleth gives his appraisal of life an ironic twist when he defines the advantage of life to consist in the knowledge that death will come (9:5). In this way he underscores his evaluation of the whole of existence as vanity.

11. Solution: Enjoyment of Earthly Life (9:7-10)

⁷ Go, eat your bread with enjoyment, and drink your wine with a merry heart; for God has already approved what you do. ⁸ Let your garments be always white; let not oil be lacking on your head. ⁹ Enjoy life with the wife whom you love, all the days of your vain life which he has given you under the sun, because that is your portion in life and in your toil at which you toil under the sun. ¹⁰ Whatever your hand finds to do, do it with your might; for there is

no work or thought or knowledge or wisdom in Sheol, to which you are going.

Since man's deeds are in God's hands (9:1) and death is certain (9:2–3), Koheleth teaches the enjoyment of life while it lasts. This is a penultimate solution to the problem of life's vanity (see 2:24–26). He adopts it because all his attempts to go beyond this solution to an ultimate one have been frustrated (see "Contests" in Int.).

Rather than languish in the knowledge of the limitations of his earthly existence, Koheleth chose to savor the circumscribed joys of life. He has previously given admonitions to enjoy life's daily activities (v. 7) and work (v. 10, see comment on 2:24–26). To these he adds the command to wear white garments and anoint the head with fragrant spiced oil—symbols of festivity and joy (cf. Esther 8:15; Psalm 45:7). He recommends further the companionship of a loving wife to make this disappointing existence livable (v. 9; cf. Prov. 5:18–19).

The reference to Sheol in v. 10 shows that Koheleth had no understanding of a future life in God's presence, such as is taught in a few places in the Old Testament (Psalms 49:15; 73:23–25; Dan. 12:2–3) and throughout the New Testament (1 Thess. 4:13–18). In common with the majority of the people of his time he still thought of life after death as a peaceful but pleasureless existence in the underworld. Because this earthly life alone offered the possibility of pleasure, he taught the duty of full enjoyment of these pleasures while life on earth lasted.

12. Limitations and Advantages of Wisdom (9:11-18)

¹¹ Again I saw that under the sun the race is not to the swift, nor the battle to the strong, nor bread to the wise, nor riches to the intelligent, nor favor to the men of skill; but time and chance happen to them all. ¹² For man does not know his time. Like fish which are taken in an evil net, and like birds which are caught in a snare, so the sons of men are snared at an evil time, when it suddenly falls upon them.

13 I have also seen this example of wisdom under the sun, and it seemed great to me. 14 There was a little city with few men in it; and a great king came against it and besieged it, building great siegeworks against it. 15 But there was found in it a poor wise man, and he by his wisdom delivered the city. Yet no one remembered that poor man. 16 But I say that wisdom is better than might, though the poor man's wisdom is despised, and his words are not heeded. 17 The words of the wise heard in quiet are better than the shouting of a ruler among fools. 18 Wisdom is better than weapons of war, but one sinner destroys much good.

After expounding briefly on the one way to find enjoyment in this vain life, Koheleth pursues again his main subject of the vanity of life. He asserts that success does not depend on effort (vv. 11–12) and backs up his assertion with an illustration (vv. 13–16). Finally he admits again that wisdom does have a limited advantage (vv. 17–18).

Neither strength nor wisdom brings assured results (v. 11). *Time and chance,* i.e., evil time and calamity, come on all kinds of men alike. The reference to (evil) *time* (v. 11) leads to the statement that man is also ignorant of the time of his own death, but is taken by it abruptly and unawares like a fish or animal caught in a trap (v. 12).

Verses 13–16 illustrate the failure of wisdom to bring lasting personal advantage to a wise man. The poor wise man who saved a small city from a powerful army was not honored for his deed. Indeed, there was no lasting remembrance of him (cf. comment on 1:11), nor did his advice continue to be heeded.

Wisdom does, to be sure, have its advantages as the two proverbs of vv. 17–18 indicate. Nevertheless its accomplishments are so fragile that they may be destroyed by one sinner. For Koheleth there is little difference between the sinner and the fool.

13. A Collection of Proverbs (10:1—11:6)

1 Dead flies make the perfumer's ointment
  give off an evil odor;
  so a little folly outweighs wisdom and
   honor.
2 A wise man's heart inclines him toward
  the right,

but a fool's heart toward the left.
3 Even when the fool walks on the road, he
  lacks sense,
  and he says to every one that he is a fool.
4 If the anger of the ruler rises against you,
  do not leave your place,
  for deference will make amends for great
   offences.
5 There is an evil which I have seen under the sun, as it were an error proceeding from the ruler: 6 folly is set in many high places, and the rich sit in a low place. 7 I have seen slaves on horses, and princes walking on foot like slaves.
8 He who digs a pit will fall into it;
  and a serpent will bite him who breaks
   through a wall.
9 He who quarries stones is hurt by them;
  and he who splits logs is endangered by
   them.
10 If the iron is blunt, and one does not whet
  the edge,
  he must put forth more strength;
  but wisdom helps one to succeed.
11 If the serpent bites before it is charmed,
  there is no advantage in a charmer.
12 The words of a wise man's mouth win him
  favor,
  but the lips of a fool consume him.
13 The beginning of the words of his mouth is
  foolishness,
  and the end of his talk is wicked madness.
14 A fool multiplies words,
  though no man knows what is to be,
  and who can tell him what will be after
   him?
15 The toil of a fool wearies him,
  so that he does not know the way to the
   city.
16 Woe to you, O land, when your king is a
  child,
  and your princes feast in the morning!
17 Happy are you, O land, when your king is
  the son of free men,
  and your princes feast at the proper time,
  for strength, and not for drunkenness!
18 Through sloth the roof sinks in,
  and through indolence the house leaks.
19 Bread is made for laughter,
  and wine gladdens life,
  and money answers everything.
20 Even in your thought, do not curse the king,
  nor in your bedchamber curse the rich;
  for a bird of the air will carry your voice,
  or some winged creature tell the matter.

1 Cast your bread upon the waters,
  for you will find it after many days.
2 Give a portion to seven, or even to eight,
  for you know not what evil may happen
   on earth.
3 If the clouds are full of rain,

they empty themselves on the earth;
and if a tree falls to the south or to the
  north,
    in the place where the tree falls, there it
    will lie.
4 He who observes the wind will not sow;
    and he who regards the clouds will not
    reap.
5 As you do not know how the spirit comes
to the bones in the womb of a woman with
child, so you do not know the work of God
who makes everything.
6 In the morning sow your seed, and at
evening withhold not your hand; for you do
not know which will prosper, this or that, or
whether both alike will be good.

This collection of proverbs on various
subjects probably represents the variety of
emphases which Koheleth made in his
teaching. Most of them agree with the
traditional wisdom found in the book of
Proverbs. Some of them are so clear that
they will not require comment.
Right and *left* (10:2) symbolize good
and evil (cf. Matt. 25:33). Even in the
simple act of walking, the fool reveals his
true self (v. 3). When an officer of the
kings court becomes an object of the king's
anger, he may either *leave* his *place,* i.e.,
resign his office, or appease the king's anger by courteous respect for the king's
wishes. Koheleth counsels the latter
(10:4). In times of weak leadership, the
unworthy may gain power and prestige
(cf. Prov. 30:21–22; Isa. 3:4–5). This is
an *evil* which the author himself has witnessed (10:5–7). It is not only in the
king's employment that occupational hazards threaten one's safety. Such hazards
exist in other types of work as well (10:8–
9). *Will fall* is better translated "May fall"
and so the other verbs in these two verses.
Verses 10–11 teach the advantages of
preparation. A man who sharpens his mind
with *wisdom* will more readily achieve
success. If a snake has already bitten, there
is no need to call a *charmer.* One might
compare the modern proverb about the
folly of closing the gate after the horse has
escaped.
Verses 12–15 contain proverbs about the
fool. Both wise men and fools are known
by their speech. The speech of the wise

man charms, while that of a fool consumes
or destroys him (10:12). It progresses
from *foolishness* to *wicked madness* (10:
13) and is abundantly profuse, in spite of
man's limited knowledge (10:14). What
would be an easy task for a wise person
is exhausting labor to a fool with his foolish
ways of doing a job, "for" (not *so that* as
in RSV) he is so stupid he can not follow
a plainly marked road (10:15).
The nation ruled by an immature king
(cf. Isa. 3:4) and decadent princes is
unfortunate. *Feast in the morning* suggests
frivolous leaders who spend all their time
in revelry. *Son of free men* means one born
a noble and educated for leadership (10:
16–17).
Koheleth has emphasized many times
that no one knows the future and therefore must make the most of the present.
One is not to conclude from this that he
is against planning for the future or taking
risks where the chances for success are
good. In 11:1 he advises the undertaking
of business ventures. *Cast your bread upon
the waters* likely refers to sea trade. At
the same time he advises caution. One
must diversify his investments, lest *evil,*
i.e., calamity, strike and destroy one's entire business. The principle may be applied
to other phases of life in which one must
make commitments to live a full life. These
two verses are sometimes interpreted as
teaching generosity to other people. This
interpretation, however, disregards the
meaning of the verb translated *cast.* It
means "to send" rather than "to throw" as
the KJV and RSV erroneously suggest.
The NEB has correctly translated, "Send
your grain across the seas, and in time
you will get a return. Divide your merchandise among seven ventures, eight
maybe, since you do not know what disasters may occur on earth."
Continuing in the vein of caution, v. 3
adds that causes inevitably produce effects. Perhaps Koheleth means that the
"disaster" spoken about in v. 2 will inevitably come and one must prepare for it.
Nevertheless, one must not be overly cautious (11:4). He must not wait until he

understands all causes (11:5) but must go about his work trusting that his risk will be rewarded (11:6).

The teaching of prudent venturesomeness may be applied to every area of life to business, to social life, and to spiritual matters. Those who work in faith will receive the reward.

IV. Conclusion (11:7—12:14)

1. Serene and Godly Life (11:7—12:8)

⁷ Light is sweet, and it is pleasant for the eyes to behold the sun.
⁸ For if a man lives many years, let him rejoice in them all; but let him remember that the days of darkness will be many. All that comes is vanity.
⁹ Rejoice, O young man, in your youth, and let your heart cheer you in the days of your youth; walk in the ways of your heart and the sight of your eyes. But know that for all these things God will bring you into judgment.
¹⁰ Remove vexation from your mind, and put away pain from your body; for youth and the dawn of life are vanity.

¹ Remember also your Creator in the days of your youth, before the evil days come, and the years draw nigh, when you will say, "I have no pleasure in them"; ² before the sun and the light and the moon and the stars are darkened and the clouds return after the rain; ³ in the day when the keepers of the house tremble, and the strong men are bent, and the grinders cease because they are few, and those that look through the windows are dimmed, ⁴ and the doors on the street are shut; when the sound of the grinding is low, and one rises up at the voice of a bird, and all the daughters of song are brought low; ⁵ they are afraid also of what is high, and terrors are in the way; the almond tree blossoms, the grasshopper drags itself along and desire fails; because man goes to his eternal home, and the mourners go about the streets; ⁶ before the silver cord is snapped, or the golden bowl is broken, or the pitcher is broken at the fountain, or the wheel broken at the cistern, ⁷ and the dust returns to the earth as it was, and the spirit returns to God who gave it. ⁸ Vanity of vanities, says the Preacher; all is vanity.

In this section Koheleth reaches the conclusion of his whole argument. He has spoken eloquently of the vanity of life on earth and advised the enjoyment of the common activities of life. Here he teaches the necessity of enjoying life before old age (11:7-10) and adds the admonition to remember God (12:1). This admonition he follows with a beautiful allegory of old age by which he seeks to add force to his exhortations (12:2-8).

Verse 7 functions as an introduction to the admonitions of vv. 8-10. *Light* and *sun* stand for life in its fullness, here described as *sweet* and *pleasant*. There follows a series of four admonitions, each accompanied by a reason. The first three are admonitions to enjoy life. One should *rejoice* during the *many years* of his life, for *the days of darkness will be many. Days of darkness* may mean existence in sheol (cf. 9:10; Job 10:20-22), or, more probably, the period of senility (cf. 12:1-2).

In the second admonition, Koheleth says that one should *rejoice* while he still has his *youth*. He admonishes the young man *to walk in the ways of* his *heart and* [in] *the sight* of his *eyes*. By this he means the enjoyment of the normal and sensible pleasures of life. Some commentators have concluded that he meant unrestrained sensual enjoyment and have pronounced v. 9b an addition by a moralist. This interpretation, however, is excluded by Koheleth's rejection of such excesses in 2:1-11. The phrase *God will bring you unto judgment* reminds the *young man* that he is to exercise responsibility in seeking pleasure (cf. 3:17).

The final admonition is to remember God, the Creator. God often remembers people to bless them (1 Sam. 1:11; Psalm 20:3-4; Neh. 13:31). Here man is to remember God to reverence and worship him. This is "a plea for a strong religious faith to be founded in youth as a safeguard in old age." (Jones)

Verses 2-7 have been called an "Allegory of Old Age." They contain a poignant description of senility, partly metaphorical and partly literal. They give a reason for the teaching to remember God and enjoy life, namely, that the opportunity will all-too-soon be irrevocably passed. They also give moving support to the general theme —the vanity of life (1:2; 12:8).

In old age life takes on the characteristics of a dark, cold winter in Palestine when storm after storm hides the luminaries (v. 2). The metaphor changes to that of a house with undependable domestic help. *The keepers of the house* describes the trembling arms of the aged. The *strong men* represent the *bent* and tottery legs. The grinders (i.e., women grinding grain) are the *few* teeth which are still in place. *Those that look through the windows* (i.e., women who look anxiously out of the house) are the eyes. The *doors* which are *shut* probably represent the deafness which cuts the elderly person off from society. The *sound of the grinding* may refer to the voice which becomes *low*. *One rises up at the voice of a bird* suggests the light sleep of the aged which is disturbed by the singing of a bird so that he raises himself with a start. *Daughters of song* may mean the sounds which seem faint to the hard-of-hearing.

Old people are afraid of high places and of the dangers of a journey. The white blossoms of the *almond tree* probably refer to white hair. The old man drags himself along like a *grasshopper* trying to walk. Sexual *desire fails*. Finally he goes to his grave or *eternal home,* and the paid, professional *mourners* mill about outside waiting to do their job at his funeral.

Verse 6 contains two figures—the lamp, which provides light, and the well, which provides water. The *silver cord* held the *golden bowl* or lamp. When the *cord* broke the lamp fell, putting out the light. *Broken,* in reference to the lamp, must be understood as hyperbole. When the *wheel* and *pitcher* at the well are *broken,* no more water can be drawn. Light and water are common biblical symbols of life. Man's body then molders into *dust,* and the *spirit* or breath of life returns to God who originally gave it (Job 34:14–15; Gen. 2:7).

The arguments of Ecclesiastes end with a reassertion of its thesis: *all is vanity* (see comment on 1:2).

2. Epilogue (12:9–14)

⁹ Besides being wise, the Preacher also taught the people knowledge, weighing and studying and arranging proverbs with great care. ¹⁰ The Preacher sought to find pleasing words, and uprightly he wrote words of truth. ¹¹ The sayings of the wise are like goads, and like nails firmly fixed are the collected sayings which are given by one Shepherd. ¹² My son, beware of anything beyond these. Of making many books there is no end, and much study is a weariness of the flesh. ¹³ The end of the matter; all has been heard. Fear God, and keep his commandments; for this is the whole duty of man. ¹⁴ For God will bring every deed into judgment, with every secret thing, whether good or evil.

The concluding section praises Koheleth and the teachings of the wise men, in general (vv. 9–11), warns against excessive study (v. 12), and exhorts the reader to be loyal to God (vv. 13–14).

Since Koheleth speaks in the first person and would hardly give such a tribute to himself, most commentators believe that these verses were written by someone else. Scott says that they were written by another wise man, who added the title and the words "says the Preacher" at 1:2; 7:27, and 12:8.

Koheleth is here identified as a wise man who taught the *people* through *proverbs* which he carefully prepared. He was concerned that they be both beautiful and true. As *goads* and *nails firmly fixed* the proverbs of the wise men have the power to motivate and to stick in the mind and heart. They are from God, *the one Shepherd,* who is the source of wisdom (Job 28:20–28; cf. James 3:17). Shepherd is a frequent designation of God in the Old Testament (Gen. 49:24; Psalms 23:1; 80:1; 95:7).

My son is a favorite term of the wise men for addressing a disciple (cf Prov. 1:8,10,15). It is never used by Koheleth himself. Perhaps the warning against too much study is intended to discourage the reader from reading the pagan literature which was becoming more and more available in Palestine at the time Koheleth was written.

The epilogue ends by pointing the reader to God as Koheleth himself has done (5:1–7; 7:18; 8:12–13; 12:1).

Song of Solomon

JOHN T. BUNN

Introduction

I. History of Interpretation

Probably no book of the Old Testament has received more varied attempts at interpretation than the Song of Solomon. This process has been little more than a series of attempts to justify its presence in the canon. The book reveals no prophetic or priestly religious acts. It mentions neither temple nor sacred precinct, and contains no religious legislation. The muteness of the book on matters of Israelite religious tradition is quite striking.

Historically, five interpretive approaches have emerged.

1. Allegorical. Allegorical interpretation is a way of treating biblical narratives in a nonliteral manner. One ignores the literal meaning of the words and derives new and hidden meanings for the terms in the narratives.

Rabbinical.—The Midrash, Targum, and medieval Jewish commentators interpreted the book allegorically. Scholars from Philo of Alexander, a contemporary of Jesus, to Samuel ibn Tibban (*ca.* A.D. 1230) saw the shepherd lover and maiden as representative of God and Israel. Therefore, the book allegorically related the union between God and Israel as a result of the Sinai covenant and the subsequent historical events of this alliance. Such a concept, inferred from the ancient marriage metaphor (Hos. 2:4; 21; Isa. 62:5; Jer. 2:2; Ezek. 16:8), likely had its origin in cultic sacred marriage.

Christian.—The early church fathers slightly adjusted rabbinical allegorical interpretation viewing the lover and beloved as symbols for God and the church. Even though Origen (third century A.D.) interpreted the book as a wedding song or poem performed at the marriage of Solomon to an Egyptian princess and though Jerome highly praised the work of Origen, its interpretive result remained allegorical.

The Council of Constantinople (A.D. 553) reaffirmed allegorical interpretation as the official church position. This position was embraced by the reformers, especially Martin Luther. The lingering influence of allegorical interpretation is evidenced by editorial captions in the KJV.

2. Literal. The term "literal" is here applied to that type of interpretation which looks upon the book as a collection of conventional love songs or poems. Such a view appears to be as old, if not older, than allegorical interpretation. The threatened exclusion of the book at the Council of Jamnia (A.D. 90–110), the injunction of Rabbi Akiba against those who would use parts of the book as bawdy songs in wineshops, and the statement in Sanhedrin 101*a*, "He who recites any of the verses as a wine song at a feast brings evil into the world," attest to a widespread literal interpretation.

Theodore of Mopsuestia (*ca.* A.D. 360–429) interpreted the book in a non-sacred vein, and his views were banned by the Council of Constantinople. The father of

128

Samuel ibn Tibban (*ca.* A.D. 1200) accepted the book as a pure love poem. Sebastian Castellio (*ca.* 1545) became the object of John Calvin's indignation when he took the position that the theme of the Song of Solomon was sexual love, and Luis de Leon (*ca.* 1567) was delivered into the hands of the Inquisition for holding to a similar view. One of the most ardent exponents of literal interpretation was Goethe, who in 1776 translated the Song of Solomon and lavished praise upon its free poetic love imagery.

3. Wedding Cycle. Herder (1778) reshaped literal interpretation. He suggested that the love poems were utilized in wedding celebrations. Renan (1860) pointed to the similarity between certain passages in the Song of Solomon and Syrian wedding songs. Wetzstein (1873) equated the passages 4:1–7; 5:10–16; 6:4–7; 7:1*b*–9 to Syrian *wasfs* (i.e., descriptive songs used to praise the physical charms of a couple during wedding celebrations). It was, however, K. Budde (1894) who systematized and popularized the wedding celebration theory.

4. Drama. Due to the effectiveness of higher critical studies the fortunes of allegorical interpretation waned, and a new interpretative approach arose, the pastoral drama. H. Ewald (*ca.* 1826) championed a three-character drama with the participants being Solomon, the maiden, and the shepherd lover. F. Delitzsch (1877) proposed a two-character drama (Solomon and maiden). The two-character approach maximized the bliss of marital love between Solomon and the maiden, while the three-character approach emphasized the faithfulness of the maiden to her shepherd in spite of Solomon's inducements.

Adherents of the drama theory have been divided as to how the drama was executed. Some considered it a dramatic reading, while others conceived it to be a staged production. One of the most thoroughgoing presentations of the drama theory is that of Patterson, who views the work as a lyrical drama to be staged as a Greek play.[1]

5. Cultic. T. J. Meek, following Erbt's previous suggestions, pointed out striking similarities between the Song of Solomon and the myth and ritual of the Adonis-Tammuz cult.[2]

In the cultic approach the book is considered to have as its primitive background the cult of renewal personified by the shepherd and maiden who would typify such mythical pairs as Baal and Anath or Tammuz and Ishtar. Its adherents affirm that the cultic significance of the poetic units became lost when the work is humanized (i.e., looked upon as expressions of human love). Although such an approach is little more than cultic allegorical interpretation, its influence is evidenced in the Oxford Annotated edition of RSV.

II. Canonization

Canonization of the Song of Solomon was hotly contested. While the Palestinian rabbinical school of Shammai opposed its canonization, the liberal Babylonian school of Hillel championed its cause.[3]

Rabbi Akiba's defense of the book led to its retention in the canon following the Jamnia conferences, A.D. 90–110.

III. Date, Authorship, and Composition

From late New Testament times until the flowering of higher criticism in the nineteenth century, little effort was exerted to determine date and authorship for the Song of Solomon. Internal references to Solomon (1:1, 5; 3:7–9, 11; 8:11–12), together with the statement in 1 Kings 4:32, were deemed authoritative enough to ascribe the work to him. A question did arise, however, as to when Solomon com-

---

1 John L. Patterson, *The Song of Songs.*
2 Meek, "Canticles and the Tammuz Cult," *American Journal of Semitic Languages,* XXXIX (1922–23), 1–14; "Commentary on the Song of Songs," *The Interpreter's Bible,* V (New York: Abingdon Press, 1956), 91–148.
3 Mishnah, Yedaim 3. 5; Tosephta Yedaim 2. 14; Aboth of Rabbi Nathan I, Tosephta Sanhedrin 12. 10; Babylonian Talmud, Sanhedrin 101a. Cf. Herbert E. Ryle, *The Canon of the Old Testament* (New York: Macmillan and Company, 1895), pp. 209 ff.

posed the book. Rabbinical rationalization resolved the question by assuming that Solomon wrote the book during his youth "for it is the way of the world that when a man is young he composes songs of love."[4] Thus the date of writing would have been shortly before 961 B.C.

Once it was reasonably established that the title, "The Song of Songs, which is Solomon's," was a potentially late editorial insertion and could have disparate meaning, the entire question of authorship was keenly debated.

The Song of Solomon appears to be a collection of diverse poetic units centralized about a major theme. Recurrence of phrases and numerous isolated fragments point to an editorial collation (cf. 2–7, 15, 17; 3:5; 4:6; 5:1; 6:11–12; 8:4–5). Some 20 to 30 units were likely combined to produce the book.

Although many of the poetic fragments predated by hundreds of years the time of editing, the presence within the book of Aramaic, Persian, and Greek language influences indicates a late date for its finalized form.[5] Generally a date within the span of the third century B.C. is assigned to the composition as it now stands.[6]

IV. Setting

Since the book is unique in biblical literature in composition, character, content, style, and vocabulary, any attempt to draw from the poetic units the immediate setting and from this to develop an orderly account is at the best hypothetical.

Geographical references are predominantly north Palestinian and Syrian (3:9; 4:1, 4:8; 6:4; 7:5), yet sites in the Negev and Transjordan are included (1:14; 7:4).

It is, however, the immediate setting which so vitally influences interpretation. The following reconstruction is but one of many viable options.

The author selects the harem of Solomon as the immediate background, with the maiden telling the women of the harem her story of love unrequited. Events unfold in the following manner.

The maiden was reared in a village household with several brothers (2:9; 1:6; 6:9). As she rapidly approached puberty she, as well as her brothers, protected her chastity (8:9). But when she achieved womanly maturity, she fell in love with a shepherd and gave herself to him (8:10; 7:2–12). Despite her brothers' anger and community disapproval, she continued the relationship (1:6; 8:1). Clandestine meetings were effected (1:16, 17; 3:2–4; 5:2–7) despite efforts at separation.

The exceeding beauty of the maiden came to the attention of Solomon, who desired her for his harem (cf. comment on 6:13). An agreement was reached, one most profitable to the family, and the maiden went into the harem of Solomon (1:4; 3:6–11). Discounting lavish court inducements she scorned the position of harem favorite (8:11–12) and continued to have furtive meetings with her lover (1:12; 8:13). She longed for her shepherd lover knowing that she possessed an impossible love, one which could never be truly fulfilled (8:6–7). The maiden's pitiful laments rend the heart (1:7; 2:6, 7; 3:1,5; 5:6a, 8; 8:1, 3–4). Her longing, despair, and destructive jealousy make this book a hauntingly tragic work.

V. Theme

With consummate skill the author centralized Israel's traditional folk love poetry about a moving theme of love unrequited. This was a love doomed because it dared breach established and acceptable socioreligious boundaries. As the motif develops with its earthy and sensuous poetic imagery little is left to the imagination.

This, however, should be anticipated.

---

[4] S. M. Lehrman, "The Song of Songs, Introduction and Commentary," *The Five Megilloth*, ed. A. Cohen. (Hindhead: Soncino Press, 1946), p. x.

[5] In 1:12 and 2:7 an Aramaic form is used; 3:9 contains the Greek or Sanskrit word *appiryon* (palanquin); 4:12 has the Persian word *pardes* (garden); 4:13 uses the Persian word *nerd* (nard) and the late Hebrew word *shelach* (shoots).

[6] Otto Eissfeldt, *The Old Testament, An Introduction*, Trans. Peter R. Ackroyd (New York: Harper and Row, 1965), p. 490.

The frankness of the Near Eastern mind in appraising the way of man and woman should not be reckoned as gross sensuality. The mores of that day readily accepted the realistic discussion of human passion. In the Old Testament physical relationships between the sexes are related in an open manner, but not in a way to indicate sanction or approval of offensive acts.[7]

Emphasis upon the physical attractiveness of the maiden (4:1–7; 7:1b–9), the shepherd's entreaty to the maiden to join him in secretive trysts (1:15–17; 2:8–13), and references to the maiden's body as a fruitful garden (4:12–15; 5:1; 6:2–3) may be offensive to Western sensitivities. But the lovers' thoughts honestly translated into poetic language are neither coarse nor vulgar. Only when such imagery is refabricated by a gross mind-set does the content become uncouth.

The primary thrust of the book resolutely affirms that love regardless of mutual commitment and trust is destined to failure unless it is practiced within the acceptable religious morality of the society. In a series of laments (2:7; 3:5; 5:8; 8:3) the maiden acknowledges this fact. Forcefully she asserts that it is most imprudent to arouse physical and psychological cravings for love and to anticipate meaningful and lasting gratification in an illicit affair.

It may be for this reason that Rabbi Akiba, while considering the other books of the Old Testament as holy, described the Song of Solomon as the "holy of holies"[8] and added that "the whole world attained its supreme value only on the day when the Song of Songs was given to Israel."[9]

Only when love embraced Israelite morality did it become acceptable. And within this context the sexual relationship produced a sacred physical and psychological

experience. That a book which speaks so openly and frankly of this particular human experience and its futility when illicitly practiced should find its way into the canon is most proper.

Outline

I. Title statement (1:1)
II. The first declaration of regret (1:2—2:7)
1. The absentee lover (1:2–4)
2. The comely maiden's inquiry (1:5–8)
3. The memory of words and acts of love (1:9—2:5)
(1) The meeting in a wooded glen (1:9–17)
(2) The meeting in a vineyard (2:1–5)
4. The lament (2:6–7)
III. The second declaration of regret (2:8—3:5)
1. The lover summons the maiden (2:8–17)
2. The maiden seeks her lover (3:1–4)
3. The declaration (3:5)
IV. The third declaration of regret (3:6—5:8)
1. The procession of the king (3:6–11)
2. A description of the maiden's charms (4:1–15)
3. The eloquent plea of the shepherd elicits an affirmative response (4:16—5:1)
4. The maiden seeks her lover (5:2–7)
5. The declaration (5:8)
V. The fourth declaration of regret (5:9—8:4)
1. The maiden's defense of her lover (5:9—6:3)
(1) The lover's charms are described (5:9–16)
(2) The assertion of mutual faithfulness (6:1–3)
2. The second description of the maiden's charms (6:4–10)
3. The impulsive maiden (6:11–13)
4. The third description of the maiden's charms (7:1–9)
5. The invitation to love (7:10—8:2)
6. The declaration (8:3–4)
VI. The unique powers of love (8:5–14)
1. The awakening of physical love is recalled by the maiden (8:5)
2. The cost of the maiden's love (8:6–7)
3. The worth of the maiden's love (8:8–10)
4. The intent of the maiden (8:11–12)
5. The maiden awaits her lover (8:13–14)

Bibliography

GORDIS, ROBERT. Song of Songs: a study, modern translation and commentary. New York: Jewish Theological Seminary of America, 1954.

---

[7] Abraham and Jacob had children born of wives and handmaidens (Gen. 16:1–4; Gen. 29:1—30:24). Polygamy was a normal practice (2 Sam. 5:13–16; 1 Kings 11:1,3; Esther 2:3,14). The prostitute was accepted in society (Gen. 38; Josh. 2:4–16). Situations involving perversion, incest, and rape were publicly related (cf. Gen. 19:1–11,30–38; 34).

[8] Megillah 7a.

[9] Yadaim, iii. 5.

HARPER, A. *Song of Songs.* ("Cambridge Bible.") New York: Macmillan Company, 1902.

KNIGHT, E. *Song of Songs.* ("Torch Bible Commentaries.") New York: Macmillan Company, 1955.

MARGOLIS, MONTGOMERY, Hyde, Edgerton, Meek, Schaff. *The Song of Songs: A Symposium.* Philadelphia: Commercial Museum, 1924.

MEEK, T. J. "The Song of Songs," *The Interpreter's Bible,* Vol. V. Ed. GEORGE ARTHUR

BUTTRICK. Nashville: Abingdon Press, 1956.

ROWLEY, H. H. "The Interpretation of the Song of Songs," *The Servant of the Lord and Other Essays on the Old Testament.* London: Lutterworth Press, 1965, pp. 195–245.

RYLAARSDAM, J. C. *Proverbs, Ecclesiastes, Song of Solomon* ("Layman's Bible Commentary.") Richmond: John Knox Press, 1964.

SEGAL, M. H. "The Song of Songs," *Vetus Testamentum,* XII (1962), 470–490.

Commentary on the Text

I. Title Statement (1:1)

¹ The Song of Songs, which is Solomon's.

The doubling of the noun in the title statement expresses the superlative degree in Hebrew. Another example of the device is found in Exodus 29:37. The title therefore contends that this is the best of all songs.

The Vulgate, RDV, and *The Jerusalem Bible* entitle the book "Canticles" from the Latin *canticum canticorum* ("canticle of canticles"), while others entitle it "The Song of Solomon" (RSV, ASV).

Ascription of the book to Solomon was probably the work of a late compiler or editor. The phrase *which is Solomon's* contains a preposition which may be translated "to," "for," "about," or "concerning." Thus the title should not categorically be pressed to indicate Solomonic authorship.

II. The First Declaration of Regret (1:2—2:7)

The maiden, in the harem of Solomon, begins her story of ungovernable love. She pensively speaks of desire for the shepherd from whom she is separated. She wishes to know where he is. As she talks, the haunting memory of words and acts of love which have been indelibly etched upon her emotions rise to the surface. The emotional stress of recall and the possibility of nonfulfillment bring forth a pitiable lament.

1. The Absentee Lover (1:2–4)

² O that you would kiss me with the kisses of your mouth!
For your love is better than wine,
³   your anointing oils are fragrant,
your name is oil poured out;
**   therefore the maidens love you.**
⁴ Draw me after you, let us make haste.
**   The king has brought me into his chambers.**
**   We will exult and rejoice in you;**
**   we will extol your love more than wine;**
**   rightly do they love you.**

The shepherd's love is considered to be better than *wine.* The noun *love* has special connotation. It means the acts of love such as kisses or caresses (cf. v. 4; 4:10; Ezek. 16:8; 23:17). It implies that the expressions of the shepherd's love were headier—more intoxicating, stimulating, and provocative—than wine.

The noun *almah* in Hebrew (here *maidens*) signifies a maiden of marriageable age who may or may not be a virgin. Both the ERV and the KJV translate "virgins." In this verse, however, the reference is either to the "daughters of Jerusalem" (2:7; 3:5; 5:8) or women of the harem (6:8). This militates against translating "virgins."

A different Hebrew word for love is used in v. 3. It conveys the idea of desire, to breathe after, or to long for. The maiden infers that other women desire her lover but only she possesses his love.

The *king* may be interpreted figuratively

as signifying bridegroom, and is so construed by exponents of the drama and cultic-myth theory. If "king" is interpreted as bridegroom, it has meaning only if one accepts the Syrian wedding song or fertility cult approach. In the latter, the king assumed the role of the bridegroom in order to participate in a fertility rite. In the former the bridegroom was considered a king. It would be better to interpret king in the literal sense as referring to Solomon.

We is corporate identification meaning all the company or specifically all the women. There is justifiable reason for the maiden's desire, the exceeding handsomeness of the shepherd.

2. The Comely Maiden's Inquiry (1:5–8)

5 I am very dark, but comely,
      O daughters of Jerusalem,
   like the tents of Kedar,
      like the curtains of Solomon.
6 Do not gaze at me because I am swarthy,
      because the sun has scorched me.
   My mother's sons were angry with me,
      they made me keeper of the vineyards;
   but, my own vineyard I have not kept!
7 Tell me, you whom my soul loves,
      where you pasture your flock,
      where you make it lie down at noon;
   for why should I be like one who wanders
      beside the flocks of your companions?
8 If you do not know,
      O fairest among women,
   follow in the tracks of the flock,
      and pasture your kids
      beside the shepherds' tents.

The maiden tells the women of the harem why she is so dark. *Very dark* literally implies swarthiness. The impression is that her complexion excessively blackened from exposure to sun and wind while watching over the vineyards.

One cannot help but admire the spirit of the maiden who simply states without haughtiness that she may be dark, exceedingly so, but still lovely. She accepts the fact that her fairness does not equal that of the *daughters of Jerusalem,* who were sheltered from the elements.

She compares her complexion to *tents of Kedar* and *curtains of Solomon.* The Kedarites were a nomadic desert tribe linked to the Ishmaelites (cf. Gen. 25:12–

18; Isa. 42:11; 60:7; Jer. 49:29–32). They were noted for their tents woven from the hair of the black goat. Thus the simile is most apparent. Second Chronicles 2:3–16 contains a description of the rich hued fabrics to be used in the Temple and 3:14 particularizes the finished curtain. Noticeably the colors are dark. It would be well to take the first of the parallel phrases, "tents of Kedar," as a reference to facial color and the second, "curtains of Solomon," as an allusion to flesh texture.

Even in her misfortune the maiden does not wish to be looked upon by the women of the harem with solicitude (v. 6). Her brothers were justifiably *angry* and had banished her to the vineyards because she did not keep her *own vineyard.* This becomes a key verse in understanding the Song of Solomon. Wrath, on the part of the brothers, was incurred because she had not protected her chastity. She had given herself to the shepherd lover.

By this errant act she had brought disrepute upon herself, damaged the family image, broken the ethic of Israel and severely impeded the possibilities of a lucrative marriage contract. Little wonder the brothers were angered!

The wording of vv. 7–8 might be taken to imply that all was not well with the lovers and that the maiden related a lovers' quarrel. Of basic difficulty in comprehending these verses is the phrase *like one who wanders.* Although the Septuagint, Syriac, Vulgate, and RSV read alike, the word in Hebrew literally means "as one covered or veiled." Veiling, in certain instances, is related to the practice of prostitution (cf. Gen. 38:14–19).

There is evidence that the maiden's family endeavored to keep the lovers apart and that only clandestine meetings could be arranged. If she inquired from one shepherd group to another for the location of her beloved she would not only draw unwanted attention but risk being branded by gossip as "one covered or veiled," i.e., a prostitute. The lover solves the problem by telling her to pose as a shepherdess (v. 8). He instructs her to follow the tracks of the flocks to the shepherd encampment and there she will find him. If she brings a flock with her, then she will innocently appear to all eyes as a simple shepherdess.

3. The Memory of Words and Acts of Love (1:9—2:5)

The maiden recalls two specific meetings with her lover: one in a wooded glen, the other in a vineyard.

(1) The Meeting in a Wooded Glen (1:9–17)

9 I compare you, my love,
  to a mare of Pharaoh's chariots.
10 Your cheeks are comely with ornaments,
  your neck with strings of jewels.
11 We will make you ornaments of gold,
  studded with silver.
12 While the king was on his couch,
  my nard gave forth its fragrance.
13 My beloved is to me a bag of myrrh,
  that lies between my breasts.
14 My beloved is to me a cluster of henna blossoms
  in the vineyards of Engedi.
15 Behold, you are beautiful, my love;
  behold, you are beautiful;
  your eyes are doves.
16 Behold, you are beautiful, my beloved,
  truly lovely.
  Our couch is green;
17   the beams of our house are cedar,
  our rafters are pine.

The term *my love* is used only once outside the Song of Solomon (Judg. 11:37), where it is translated "my companions." It literally means "my friend." The comparison is not between the woman and the mare. It is between the ornate trappings of the embellished harness of a king's chariot-horse and the adornments of the maiden.

The maiden describes her lover when they meet in a secluded retreat (vv. 12–14). The significance of these verses is largely dependent upon the interpretation given to the initial phrase *while the king was on his couch.* As noted previously (cf. 1:4), "king" may be looked upon as a synonym for the shepherd or as a literal reference to Solomon. The last seems to be the more appropriate and may infer

the maiden somehow effected secret meetings with her lover after entering the harem.

The *couch* is a dining couch upon which one reclined while eating. It may suggest that while the monarch lounged upon the dining couch she was with one whose company was preferred to that of the monarch.

In comparative terms the lover is described (vv. 13–14). The term *beloved* may be traced in its usage to an early appelation of endearment for the fertility god.[10] In striking a metaphor the closeness of the lover to the beloved is revealed (v. 13). He was as close to her as a sachet of myrrh nestling in her bosom. *Myrrh* was a gum resin bled from certain Indian and Arabian shrubs (cf. Gen. 37:25; Psalm 45:8; Prov. 7:17). Women would wrap a bit of the pungent resin in a piece of cloth, attach a cord, place it about the neck, and drop the sachet into the bodice of their garment.

A second comparison is to *henna blossoms.* An extremely fragrant white to pastel yellow flower with clusters of blossoms is produced by the henna plant. It is quite common in the Near East and is cultivated in gardens on the Coastal Plain and in the Jordan Valley.

En-gedi (spring of the kid) is a lush oasis below a plateau overlooking the Dead Sea north of Masada. Its beauty and vegetation is the gift of a mountain spring of phenomenal flow.

In vv. 15–16 the lover responds and speaks of the maiden's beauty. Although the Hebrew word *rayati,* translated *my love,* may be rendered "wife" or "mate" it is not expedient to do so in this context. The root meaning of the word is to associate with, and a preferable translation might well be "my companion."

Equally striking to the metaphor of v. 13 is that of v. 15 where the maiden's eyes are likened to *doves.* The implication could be a pair of doves signifying perfectly

[10] T. J. Meek, "Canticles and the Tammuz Cult," *American Journal of Semitic Languages and Literature,* XXXIX (1922–23), 4–6.

matched eyes. An alternative would be to interpret the analogy as alluding to the soft delicate shading and luster of the eyes which radiated tenderness (cf. 4:1).

Next described is the meeting place of the lovers (vv. 16–17). In symbolic language a wooded sanctuary is detailed. Their couch of green was a carpet of grass. The cedar beams and rafters of pine were the spreading and protective trunks and limbs of cedar and fir trees which enclosed them as the roof and walls of a house.

(2) The Meeting in a Vineyard (2:1–5)

1 I am a rose of Sharon,
    a lily of the valleys.
2 As a lily among brambles,
    so is my love among maidens.
3 As an apple tree among the trees of the wood
    so is my beloved among young men.
    With great delight I sat in his shadow,
    and his fruit was sweet to my taste.
4 He brought me to the banqueting house,
    and his banner over me was love.
5 Sustain me with raisins,
    refresh me with apples;
    for I am sick with love.

The maiden recalls another meeting with her lover but in more intimate words. Without false modesty she describes herself as a *rose of Sharon*, a *lily of the valleys*. This evaluation should be taken in contrast to the following description of her beloved (2:3). I am but a wild flower the maiden is saying; on the other hand my lover is truly magnificent.

The *rose* is the wild crocus which blooms either in spring or autumn dependent upon the specie. On the Plain of Sharon, which extends from Joppa to south of Mount Carmel, the crocus blooms profusely. The elevated areas of the plain are crowned with oaks and the tableland lush with vegetation. *Lily of the valleys* may refer to any species of the wild flower which has the appearance of a lily.[11]

The shepherd responds to the maiden's evaluation of herself (v. 2). His beloved's beauty is incomparable, and only the most marked of contrasts are sufficient to describe her appearance. He will not permit her to demean herself by underestimating her loveliness for, compared to other women, she is a lovely blossom among drab and thorny brambles.

The maiden responds by speaking of her lover's superiority over other men and the joy of being loved by him (vv. 3–4). As he has likened her to a lily among thorns, she likens him to an apple tree set in a wooded area (2:3). There is some question about *apple* (Heb., *tappuach*). It may allude to the apple-like apricot or quince fruit (cf. Joel 1:12; Prov. 25:11). If it is the true apple, then the simile would be less than striking. This tree was all but absent in ancient biblical times and produced extremely poor fruit.[12] In the Old Testament, especially in the Song of Solomon, the apple tree is characterized as one which gives shade, produces sweet and nourishing fruit, provides freshness to the breath, and bears fruit which is gold in color (cf. 7:8; Prov. 25:11).

The maiden thus sees her lover as a lush, fruitful tree set among the lackluster trees (i.e., men) of the forest. The difference is apparent! The maiden asserts that her greatest delight is to be under the protective embrace of the shepherd and to partake of the fruit of his love.

Their meeting place was a *banqueting house*, better translated "wine house." It does not necessarily imply a place of public feasting and revelry. It could be the place of the wine press and vats, the wine house of the vineyards, where the two shared the intimacies of lovers.

The translation of *digelu (banner)* is most difficult. It would be well to follow the suggestion of Gordis and translate this word as "glance" or "look," thus reading "and his glance over me was loving."[13]

---

11 The Heb. *shoshanath*, translated "lily," could be an Egyptian loan word derived from *sssn* meaning "lotus."

12 A. L. and H. N. Moldenke, *Plants of the Bible* (New York: Stechert-Hafner, 1952), pp. 184–188.

13 Cf. Robert Gordis, "The Root d-g-l in the Song of Songs," *Journal of Biblical Literature*, LXXXVIII (June: 1969), 203, 204.

The recall and relating of these events was too taxing for the maiden. Memory had brought to acute climax the emotional strain of separation. She appeals to the women of the harem to bring food (v. 5). Evidently the love-sick maiden, during the period of separation, had not properly eaten. Once she retraced the steps of love's journey, she was drained of all energy and languished.

Important to the staple diet were *raisins* and frequent references are found to this food (cf. 1 Sam. 25:18; 30:12; 2 Sam. 6:19; Hos. 3:1). The ASV translates this as "cakes of raisins," which conveys a more literal meaning. Raisins were dried and pressed into patties and then sun dried.

The two verbs *sustain* and *refresh* share a common basic meaning which is to support, to prop up, or to shore. Thus the maiden implores the women to bring her food because the emotional trauma has drained all her bodily reserves.

4. The Lament (2:6-7)

6 O that his left hand were under my head,
    and that his right hand embraced me!
7 I adjure you, O daughters of Jerusalem,
    by the gazelles or the hinds of the field,
    that you stir not up nor awaken love
    until it please.

From the emotional depths of the maiden there wells forth a disconsolate lament. The voicing of regret is touching (2:6). This plea of the maiden is cast in strong imagery. The phrase *under my head* might better be rendered "cradle my head" for the word in Hebrew literally means encircle.

The declaration of regret (v. 7) is the first of four times the identical refrain is voiced by the maiden (cf. 3:5; 5:8; 8:3). With each use there is a definitive break in mood and movement. It twice follows the phrase *O that his left hand were under my head, and that his right hand embraced me!* (2:7; 8:3). In each instance the previous context deals with strong physical desire and inordinate emotional distress due to separation.

What then does the advice of the maiden to the *daughters of Jerusalem* imply? Is she asserting one should not force love which can only be rewarding in due season? Is she insinuating love has come prematurely? Or does she mean that illicit love is self-destructive, preconditioned to failure?

At this point the ethical issue of the book is enjoined. Love, regardless of its inherent simplicity, purity, fidelity, and singular commitment is doomed when practiced outside of acceptable social and religious boundaries. It becomes an affront to admissable norms, and pressures from established institutions will ultimately turn its dreams to dust. Sage advice is being offered to the daughters of Jerusalem. It is folly to arouse the slumbering deeps of physical and psychological cravings for love and to hope for meaningful gratification until these can be brought within the confines of acceptable ethical standards.

The Hebrew noun for *love* (*ahab*) basically means human love to human object (v. 7). It may or may not have the connotation of physical love. Contextually this passage, like that of Proverbs 7:10-20, calls for an interpretation of *ahab* in the sense of sexual love.

III. The Second Declaration of Regret (2:8—3:5)

The maiden continues the story of her love affair. She speaks of the lover seeking her in the spring of the year and of her search for him by night.

1. The Lover Summons the Maiden (2:8-17)

8 The voice of my beloved!
    Behold, he comes,
    leaping upon the mountains,
    bounding over the hills.
9 My beloved is like a gazelle,
    or a young stag.
    Behold, there he stands
    behind our wall,
    gazing in at the windows,
    looking through the lattice.
10 My beloved speaks and says to me:
    "Arise, my love, my fair one,
    and come away;

11 for lo, the winter is past,
  the rain is over and gone.
12 The flowers appear on the earth,
  the time of singing has come,
and the voice of the turtledove
  is heard in our land.
13 The fig tree puts forth its figs,
  and the vines are in blossom;
they give forth fragrance.
Arise, my love, my fair one,
  and come away.
14 O my dove, in the clefts of the rock,
  in the covert of the cliff,
let me see your face,
  let me hear your voice,
for your voice is sweet,
  and your face is comely.
15 Catch us the foxes,
  the little foxes,
that spoil the vineyards,
  for our vineyards are in blossom."
16 My beloved is mine and I am his,
  he pastures his flock among the lilies.
17 Until the day breathes
  and the shadows flee,
turn, my beloved, be like a gazelle,
  or a young stag upon rugged mountains.

With the passing of inclement weather, spring provided the lovers an escape from public scrutiny. Harsh weather and prohibitive family injunctions has separated them. The wording indicates the maiden had been restricted to the home (v. 14). The shepherd longed to see her face and hear her voice. Thus he coaxes her to secretively join him in the fields.

Intensified awareness causes the maiden to sense the approach of her lover (vv. 8–9). She describes his movements as those of a gazelle or young stag, surefooted, covering torturous terrain. No obstacle thwarted his coming.

Verse 9 describes the stealth and feeding habits of the gazelle. In early morning or late evening during spring, these animals are irresistibly drawn to the tender shoots of the farmers' crops. Barriers about fields and gardens are leaped by the gazelles so they may forage. Thus the lover like a young stag or gazelle with agility, swiftness, and stealth has approached the house seeking his beloved.

The shepherd implores the maiden to join him in the fields. The precise season is detailed (v. 11). Winter rains in Palestine end in March and the growing season begins. Between April and October the land is bathed in brilliant sunshine and canopied with blue, virtually cloudless skies.

Radical changes occur in the landscape (v. 12). Hillsides and valleys erupt into dazzling displays of color. Wild flowers such as crocus, yellow marigold, poppy, moon-daisies, phlox, and lilies carpet the moist earth. Oleander and henna burst into bloom along streams and beside springs. While flowers give color and fragrance, the stillness is broken by calls of song birds. The dove (v. 12) was a harbinger of spring (Jer. 8:7), and its song is referred to in Scripture (cf. Lev. 12:6; Isa. 38:14; 59:11; Ezek. 7:16; Nah. 2:7). *Turtledove* is from a verb which means to go about, round, seek out, spy, or explore. This is particularly descriptive of the erratic, darting, circular flight of the migratory dove which arrives in Palestine in April.

With emphasis the lover entreats the maiden to come away with him (v. 13). *Fig* is the green fig which grows from the branches prior to leafing out. *Puts forth,* in early Hebrew, meant to make spicey or to embalm. Although embalm may seem a strange translation, the implication is clear when it is understood that to embalm is to make the corpse spicey. A better translation may be, "The fig tree makes its figs spicey ripe."

The maiden, cloistered in the house, was as unapproachable as a pigeon perched among rocky cliffs. The *dove* (v. 14) is the rock pigeon whose nesting place was among gaunt cliffs along precipitous mountain valleys (cf. Jer. 48:28; Ezek. 7:16).

There is no more enigmatic passage in the Song of Solomon than v. 15. It appears to be totally out of context. Judges 15:4; Ezra 13:4; and Nehemiah 4:3 do, however, refer to the damaging action of animals, either fox or jackal, in the vineyards.[14] Gordis takes it to mean a reference to the

14 Cf. Leo W. Schwarz, "On Translating the 'Song of Songs,'" *Judaism,* XIII (1964), 64–76.

maiden as a vineyard and the foxes as the young men who pursue her. Meek, on the other hand sees the passage as a remnant of a primitive fertility rite. If one equated the tender grapes of the vine to the love of the pair and the destructive foxes to the enemies of their love, then v. 15 may imply that the lovers must resist those forces which would be destructive to their love.

The maiden reaffirms the mutuality of love and wishes the presence of her lover (vv. 16–17).

At points in the account it is plain the harem companions were disparaging the maiden's love and her lover, subtly insinuating that he would not be faithful in separation (cf. 5:9; 6:1). The maiden asserts, however, that such is not the case. She claims he is pasturing his sheep (i.e., minding his business and being faithful).

The words *Until the day breathes and the shadows flee* have pointed inference. In Palestine the evening breeze dispels the heat of day. Thus the evening was the time when the day breathed (cf. Gen. 3:8). It also created lengthening shadows, literally causing them to be elongated or to flee. This was the accustomed meeting time for the lovers, and she longed for another such meeting.

2. The Maiden Seeks Her Lover (3:1–4)

¹ Upon my bed by night
   I sought him whom my soul loves;
  I sought him, but found him not;
   I called him, but he gave no answer.
² "I will rise now and go about the city,
   in the streets and in the squares;
  I will seek him whom my soul loves."
  I sought him, but found him not.
³ The watchmen found me,
   as they went about in the city.
  "Have you seen him whom my soul loves?"
⁴ Scarcely had I passed them,
   when I found him whom my soul loves.
  I held him, and would not let him go
   until I had brought him into my mother's
    house,
   and into the chamber of her that conceived me.

The maiden continues her account relating how she searched at night for her lover. It is here that one senses the in-

ordinate compulsion of the maiden in her love affair. This passage and 5:2–7 are generally interpreted as dream sequences. Although 3:1 does refer to nightly dreams borne of an obsession for the shepherd lover, they turn out to be nightmares. She seeks and calls her lover but cannot find him! The dreams intensify a most dreaded fear, loss of her lover. Irresistibly driven by uncurbed emotions she seeks to dispell fear by finding her lover. Suspicion that the repetitious dream was a portent of reality drove the maiden into the night.

The quest led her into the *streets* and *squares*. The squares were broad ways or open spaces by city gates or at street intersections. These served as gathering places for talk or transaction of business.

She inquired of the *watchmen* if they had seen her beloved. Watchmen were of two categories, wall sentries and gatekeepers (cf. 1 Sam. 14:16; 2 Sam. 18:24; 2 Kings 9:7; Jer. 51:12). Since *squares* and *watchmen* are related, it may indicate that the maiden went to the gateway areas inquiring if her lover had left the city. The query of the maiden to the watchmen *Have you seen him whom my soul loves?* presupposes their knowledge of the love affair. Such an affair could not escape public notice!

Once the lover was found the distraught maiden would not let him go (v. 4). She leads him to her home and into her mother's bedchamber.

3. The Declaration (3:5)

⁵ I adjure you, O daughters of Jerusalem,
   by the gazelles or the hinds of the field,
  that you stir not up nor awaken love
   until it please.

Again the tragic lament is voiced. Repetition of the same words augment their force. Her immoderation and license in love have created an erosive emotional trauma.

IV. The Third Declaration of Regret (3:6—5:8)

With swift change of pace the account of the maiden's meeting with Solomon and her subsequent removal to the harem is related.

1. The Procession of the King (3:6–11)

6 What is that coming up from the wilderness,
    like a column of smoke,
   perfumed with myrrh and frankincense,
    with all the fragrant powders of the merchant?
7 Behold, it is the litter of Solomon!
   About it are sixty mighty men
    of the mighty men of Israel,
8 all girt with swords
    and expert in war,
   each with his sword at his thigh,
    against alarms by night.
9 King Solomon made himself a palanquin
    from the wood of Lebanon.
10 He made its posts of silver,
    its back of gold, its seat of purple;
   it was lovingly wrought within
    by the daughters of Jerusalem.
11 Go forth, O daughters of Zion,
    and behold King Solomon,
   with the crown with which his mother crowned him
    on the day of his wedding,
    on the day of the gladness of his heart.

The description of the cortege moving through the *wilderness, like a column of smoke* is most apt. Areas designated as *wilderness* are specified as open country which may or may not contain water and pasture. The *column of smoke* doubtless was a swirling dust cloud rising from the dry road bed, as the retinue moved along.

In preparation the king had sprinkled himself with perfumes. Both liquid and powder balms were used. *Myrrh* and *frankincense* were imported from South Arabia. These were applied either as a liquid, when mixed with oil, or as a powder.

The royal conveyance is described in detail (vv. 7–10). It was richly embellished and elaborately wrought. This traveling *litter* was in the form of a mobile reclining couch.[15]

A description of the materials used in fabricating the litters follows (vv. 9–10).[16]

15 "Litter" (Heb., *mittato*) is from the verb *natan* meaning to stretch out, spread out, extend, or recline.
16 In v. 9 "palanquin" (Heb., *appiryon*) appears to be a loan word from Persian or Sanskrit. The

Interior decorations such as curtains, cushions, and coverlets were designed and executed by the women of the royal court, more specifically the women of the harem.[17]

2. A Description of the Maiden's Charms (4:1–15)

1 Behold, you are beautiful, my love,
    behold, you are beautiful!
   Your eyes are doves
    behind your veil.
   Your hair is like a flock of goats,
    moving down the slopes of Gilead.
2 Your teeth are like a flock of shorn ewes
    that have come up from the washing,
   all of which bear twins,
    and not one among them is bereaved.
3 Your lips are like a scarlet thread,
    and your mouth is lovely.
   Your cheeks are like halves of a pomegranate
    behind your veil.
4 Your neck is like the tower of David,
    built for an arsenal,
   whereon hang a thousand bucklers,
    all of them shields of warriors.
5 Your two breasts are like two fawns,
    twins of a gazelle,
    that feed among the lilies.
6 Until the day breathes
    and the shadows flee,
   I will hie me to the mountain of myrrh
    and the hill of frankincense.
7 You are all fair, my love;
    there is no flaw in you.
8 Come with me from Lebanon, my bride;
    come with me from Lebanon.
   Depart from the peak of Amana,
    from the peak of Senir and Hermon,
   from the dens of lions,
    from the mountains of leopards.
9 You have ravished my heart, my sister, my bride,
    you have ravished my heart with a glance of your eyes,
   with one jewel of your necklace.
10 How sweet is your love, my sister, my bride!
    how much better is your love than wine,

Septuagint translates *phoreion* and the Vulgate *ferculum*. Both words share a common ancestry, *phero*, "to bear." In Sanskrit *paryana*, "saddle," means "that which bears" such as a saddle or litter. If the Hebrew does derive from Persian, it forcefully argues for a late date (*ca.* third century B.C.) for the Song of Solomon.
17 Cf. G. R. Driver, "Supposed Arabisms in the Old Testament," *Journal of Biblical Literature,* LV (1936), 111.

and the fragrance of your oils than any
spice!
11 Your lips distil nectar, my bride;
honey and milk are under your tongue;
the scent of your garments is like the
scent of Lebanon.
12 A garden locked is my sister, my bride,
a garden locked, a fountain sealed.
13 Your shoots are an orchard of pomegranates
with all choicest fruits,
henna with nard,
14 nard and saffron, calamus and cinnamon,
with all trees of frankincense,
myrrh and aloes,
with all chief spices—
15 a garden fountain, a well of living water,
and flowing streams from Lebanon.

Veiled from view was the exquisite
beauty of the maiden's face (vv. 1–3). The
lustrous eyes are compared to *doves* and
the flowing tresses to *flocks of goats* moving
in rippling formation down the slopes of
Gilead.[18]

The snow-white teeth of the maiden enhanced her beauty. They are likened to
ewes freshly washed before shearing.[19] Ad-
ditionally, they are perfectly matched, each
is the exact duplicate of the other being a
twin, and none are missing, i.e., *bereaved.*

Attention is given to the *lips* of the
damsel. The first half of v. 3 is quite clear,
while the second half is rather confusing.
*Your cheeks . . . like halves of a pome-
granate* may be made clearer by a different
translation. "Cheek" has a basic meaning
of cleavage, split, or slice from *palach* (to
cleave). The word meaning and poetic
parallelism in this verse would permit an
alternate translation, "Your cleavage (i.e.,
lips) are like halves of a pomegranate."
The pomegranate fruit has an inner reddish

pulp filled with bright red seeds. Thus the
lips were not only *like a scarlet thread* but
like a "pomegranate split."

The maiden's neck is described as a
citadel tower. Since *tower of David* is regarded in the Masoretic Text and the
Septuagint as a proper name, it may indicate a well-known landmark. The exact
meaning is lost to modern scholarship. The
tower embellished with *a thousand . . .
shields* is an accurate simile denoting the
necklace of metal discs which adorned the
maiden's stately neck (cf. 1 Kings 10:16,17).

The breasts of the maiden were perfectly
proportioned (v. 5) and given symbolical
names (v. 6). Their comparison to myrrh
and frankincense, the two most priceless
unguents of the day, is understandable.

The import of the entire section is that
the lover expects to achieve union with the
maiden (i.e., *I will hie me to . . .*). As the
passage ends the shepherd affirms that his
beloved has no blemish; she is the epitome
of physical perfection (v. 7).

Again the shepherd urges the maiden to
join him (v. 8). This verse may be interpreted from the standpoint of poetic
symbolism and imagery. The allusion is not
to literal *Lebanon, Amana, Senir,* or
Hermon. These but symbolize seclusion.
The maiden was cut off from him, re-
manded either to home or harem. When
the lover previously called the maiden
(2:10 ff.) he spoke of her as one inaccessible (2:14). *Lions* and *leopards* may
thus refer to human predators or destroyers,
those who would separate them. The implication could thus be that the court of
Solomon or the maiden's family were
beasts of prey![20]

With renewed zeal the shepherd pleads
his case to the maiden (vv. 9–15). She
has totally captivated him with a single
glance (v. 9). The intensive mood of the

---

18 "Moving down" (Heb., *shegaleshu,* from *galash,*
to sit, sit up, recline) has been variously translated
"come down," "run down," or "hang down from."
Its Arabic cognate means to sit up. Regardless of the
translation, the meaning is awkward. It could mean
the raven hair fell from her head and flowed over
her shoulders.
19 In Heb. the passive participle is expressive of
action yet to be completed. It makes no sense to
compare "teeth" to "ewes" after shearing for their
bodies would bear the bloody marks of the shearers'
knives. Therefore a different rendering, "Your teeth
are like a flock of ewes to be shorn," might be considered.

20 The Heb. noun *kallah* is variously translated
"bride, daughter-in-law, spouse." The word, however, does not necessarily indicate marital status, as
implied by translation (vv. 9–10). *Kallah* defines a
woman before marriage (Isa. 49:18; 61:10; 62:5;
Jer. 2:32) as well as after marriage (Hos. 4:13–14).

phrase *ravished my heart* is significant. Since heart in Hebrew means inner man, mind, or will, this could imply that by a glance the maiden had deprived him of reason. She had dispossessed him of mind or will!

A storehouse of sweetness is the maiden to the lover (vv. 10–11). Again the physical love of the girl is compared to wine (cf. comment on 1:2) and likened to precious ointments. Her kisses were sweetest honey dripping from the comb, and her garments emitted the fragrance of cedar, cyprus, and wild herbs (v. 11).

The maiden's body is depicted as a delightfully fruitful yet staunchly defended garden; *a garden locked, . . . a fountain sealed.* Gardens were plots of ground protected by hedges or walls. Such enclosures were used for cultivating vegetables, or as pleasant retreats where flowers, shrubs, trees, and vines grew. Frequently they contained a pool for bathing (cf. Deut. 11:10; Neh. 3:15; Esther 7:7–8; Jer. 39:4).

The sealed fountain imagery is taken from an ancient custom, that of covering a water source to prevent intruders from using or despoiling its content (cf. 2 Kings 20:20). The implication is clear. The maiden gave herself only to her lover. Her garden (i.e., her body) was barred to all others who might attempt encroachment.

Praises are lavished upon the maiden who as a delectable garden produces every exquisite fruit, exotic herb, and choice spice (vv. 13,14).[21] Finally the maiden is epitomized as a garden of limitless fertility saturated with water, *well of living water* and *flowing streams.* These are the choicest of words to convey the meaning of endless fertility like the "streams of water" of Psalm 1.[22]

[21] For alternate interpretation cf. Paul Haupt, "The Book of Canticles," *The American Journal of Semitic Languages,* XVIII ((July, 1902) No. 4, p. 238.

[22] Two late words "orchard" and "nard" are probably of Persian origin. Nard (Heb., *nerd*) could be of Sanskrit origin with Persian as the intermediate to Hebrew.

3. The Eloquent Plea of the Shepherd Elicits an Affirmative Response (4:16—5:1)

16   Awake, O north wind,
     and come, O south wind!
  Blow upon my garden,
     let its fragrance be wafted abroad.
  Let my beloved come to his garden,
     and eat its choicest fruits.

1   I come to my garden, my sister, my bride,
     I gather my myrrh with my spice,
     I eat my honeycomb with my honey,
     I drink my wine with my milk.
  Eat, O friends, and drink:
     drink deeply, O lovers!

The preceding passage represented the girl as a choice spice garden. This theme is picked up by the maiden who hopes the sweetness of her spices will be wafted to her lover. She desires him to be enticed to come and enjoy the fruits of his garden (v. 15). The shepherd reacts by visiting the garden where he gathers its sweetest fruits (v. 16). This invitation and response relates yet another clandestine meeting between the lovers.

4. The Maiden Seeks Her Lover (5:2–7)

2   I slept, but my heart was awake.
  Hark! my beloved is knocking.
  "Open to me, my sister, my love,
     my dove, my perfect one;
  for my head is wet with dew,
     my locks with the drops of the night."

3   I had put off my garment,
     how could I put it on?
  I had bathed my feet,
     how could I soil them?

4   My beloved put his hand to the latch,
     and my heart was thrilled within me.

5   I arose to open to my beloved,
     and my hands dripped with myrrh,
  my fingers with liquid myrrh,
     upon the handles of the bolt.

6   I opened to my beloved,
     but my beloved had turned and gone.
  My soul failed me when he spoke.
  I sought him, but found him not;
     I called him, but he gave no answer.

7   The watchmen found me,
     as they went about in the city;
  they beat me, they wounded me,
     they took away my mantle,
     those watchmen of the walls.

As on a previous occasion (3:1–4) the maiden sought her lover by night. Vainly she attempted sleep. Due to thoughts of love she drifted in and out of consciousness.

The maiden, in describing this episode, said, *I slept, but my heart was awake.* Asleep but not asleep! (5:2). Therefore this was no dream state, rather a drifting back and forth across the borderline of full awareness.

When the lover arrived at her door, his hair was *wet with dew . . . drops of the night.* Heavy summer dews occur during the last half of the night in Palestine. Frequently such early morning mists are of sufficient volume to be accumulated in catch-basins and used for crop irrigation. The inference is that the lover came in the wee hours of the morning.

When the lover arrived the maiden had already *put off her garment.* Literally the maiden had prepared for bed (cf. Gen. 9:23; Ex. 22:26; Deut. 24:13; Job 22:6). One may surmise that during the hot season one slept unclothed using a garment worn by day as a coverlet. The garment implies a light linen shift.

Her beloved attempted to open the door —*put his hand to the latch.* Doors had an aperture through which the hand was inserted from the outside to release the catch. Special devices in the form of pins or bars were slipped into the latches at night to prevent intrusion. Thus entrance could be gained only with the occupant's help.

When this happened the maiden's *heart was thrilled.* Heart (*meyeh*) denotes inward parts or abdominal viscera such as stomach, intestines, liver, and kidneys. These were considered the seat of emotions. *Thrilled* means be in commotion, to stir, to be in tumult. These words reveal the tumultuous emotions of the maiden when she realized her lover had come.

The absence of her lover, when she opened the door to admit him, impelled the maiden to rush out into the streets. On the previous occasion the watchmen had taken no action against her (3:3). This time, however, she was abused by the guards (v. 7). Such treatment may have been occasioned by the disturbance resulting from the maiden wandering through the streets calling her lover. On the other hand, the watchmen may have acted on the basis of family or palace edict. Whatever the cause, the episode was tragic. To this sad state the maiden has been brought by her unrestrained love.

5. The Declaration (5:8)

8 I adjure you, O daughters of Jerusalem,
  if you find my beloved,
 that you tell him
  I am sick with love.

The maiden, after relating the abortive attempt to find her lover, pleads with her companions for assistance. Should they find him, he is to be told that she is *sick with love.* *Sick* denotes in this case an intense condition. Basically the word means to be weak or sick. The force of the word here is important in understanding the maiden's condition. She languishes as one who has lost strength, vitality, and will due to bereavement or acute illness. Again the maiden's inability to control her emotional involvement is forcefully attested.

V. The Fourth Declaration of Regret (5:9—8:4)

1. The Maiden's Defense of Her Lover (5:9—6:3)

When the companions begin to frame satirical questions, deriding not only the shepherd but the maiden, she defends her lover (v. 9). She builds one image upon another and concludes her apology with a classic summation (vv. 10–16).

(1) The Lover's Charms Are Described (5:9–16)

9 What is your beloved more than another beloved,
   O fairest among women?
  What is your beloved more than another beloved,
   that you thus adjure us?
10 My beloved is all radiant and ruddy,
   distinguished among ten thousand.

11 His head is the finest gold;
     his locks are wavy,
     black as a raven.
12 His eyes are like doves
     beside springs of water,
     bathed in milk,
     fitly set.
13 His cheeks are like beds of spices,
     yielding fragrance.
     His lips are lilies,
     distilling liquid myrrh.
14 His arms are rounded gold,
     set with jewels.
     His body is ivory work,
     encrusted with sapphires.
15 His legs are alabaster columns,
     set upon bases of gold.
     His appearance is like Lebanon,
     choice as the cedars.
16 His speech is most sweet,
     and he is altogether desirable.
     This is my beloved and this is my friend,
     O daughters of Jerusalem.

In v. 10 she gives an all-encompassing appraisal describing the shepherd as both *radiant and ruddy,* one who would be immediately set apart by his looks if he were *among ten thousand.* The term *radiant* means dazzling, glowing, or clear. It is used as descriptive of heat (Isa. 18:4) and of wind (Jer. 4:11). Certainly this does not apply to a physical characteristic. It rather implies an exceedingly striking, literally radiant personality. Some assistance may be gained from Lamentations 4:7, which uses similar imagery. In both instances the references may be to character.

His head is described as *finest gold,* the golden sheen of the neck and facial tissue, and his eyes with irises surrounded by clear white were perfectly spaced. His mouth is pictured as a dispenser of spices and myrrh (cf. comment on 3:3). The comparison of lips to lilies refers not to color but to the open lily blossom which dispenses its nectar to bees. The entire verse has reference to the sweetness of the shepherd's kisses.

The descriptive imagery used to detail the arms, body, and legs of the shepherd is rarely surpassed in biblical literature. To the maiden he is so commanding and majestic, she likens him to Mount Hermon,

the most prominent and arresting mountain of the Palestinian coastline (v. 15). Not only was her lover the epitome of character and of striking physique, but he wielded the language of love with eloquent sweetness (v. 16). Thus the maiden informs the women that he is utterly desirable.

(2) The Assertion of Mutual Faithfulness (6:1–3)

1 Whither has your beloved gone,
     O fairest among women?
     Whither has your beloved turned,
     that we may seek him with you?
2 My beloved has gone down to his garden,
     to the beds of spices,
     to pasture his flock in the gardens,
     and to gather lilies.
3 I am my beloved's and my beloved is mine;
     he pastures his flock among the lilies.

Cuttingly the women of the harem taunt the lovesick maiden. With mock sincerity they infer that since they now know of the shepherd's extraordinary handsomeness they will personally assist the maiden in finding him (v. 1). The maiden's retort is an affirmation of trust. She is as certain of her lover's faithfulness to her as she is to him (v. 3a). In effect she is saying to the maidens it will do you no good if you do find him: He is mine, and I am his.

The two phrases *pasture his flock in the gardens* and *gather lilies* (vv. 2b,3b) are quite meaningless unless taken with the phrase *gone down to his garden.* Once they are so understood, it is apparent that the images imply sexual gratification (cf. comment on 4:12–15).

2. The Second Description of the Maiden's Charms (6:4–10)

4 You are beautiful as Tirzah, my love,
     comely as Jerusalem,
     terrible as an army with banners.
5 Turn away your eyes from me,
     for they disturb me—
     Your hair is like a flock of goats,
     moving down the slopes of Gilead.
6 Your teeth are like a flock of ewes,
     that have come up from the washing,
     all of them bear twins,
     not one among them is bereaved.
7 Your cheeks are like halves of a pomegranate

behind your veil.
8 There are sixty queens and eighty concu-
    bines,
    and maidens without number.
9 My dove, my perfect one, is only one,
    the darling of her mother,
    flawless to her that bore her.
    The maidens saw her and called her happy;
    the queens and concubines also, and they
    praised her.
10 "Who is this that looks forth like the dawn,
    fair as the moon, bright as the sun,
    terrible as an army with banners?"

Since the maiden is uniquely lovely to
the shepherd, he compares her to Tirzah
and Jerusalem (v. 4). The proper name
Tirzah means delight or pleasant (cf. 1
Kings 15:21; 16:6,8–9,15,17,23). Jerusalem, according to Lamentations 2:15,
was looked upon by ancient Israel as the
epitome of beauty. Thus the maiden is
compared in beauty with the loveliest of
cities. The last phrase *terrible as an army
with banners* becomes at once more in-
telligible if translated "awe inspiring as
these great sights" (Gordis, *loc. cit.*).

The remainder of the passage is a repeat
of 4:1–3.

The aggregate beauty of the entire
harem is eclipsed by that of the dusky
maiden (vv. 8–10). Three harem classifications are indicated: *queens, concubines,*
and *maidens.* Queens were those allied to
the thrones through royal marriages generally as a result of political, military, or economic alliances. Concubines were female
slaves purchased, traded, taken as captives
of war, or in certain cases counted as
chattel in payment of debts. Certain concubines achieved high station especially if
they bore male children to their masters
(Gen. 21:10; Ex. 23:12). Maidens were
personal attendants of queens who were
brought to the harem by their mistresses.
These too were the domain of the king.

Although the king possessed an unlimited harem, the only *perfect one, . . .
flawless* was the beloved of the shepherd
(v. 9). She was truly unique and from
the womb of her mother without blemish.
Even the women of the palace conceded
her preeminence in loveliness. Her beauty

was as awe inspiring as the *dawn,* the
moon, the *sun* (cf. comment on 6:4 for
meaning and translation of the last phrase
of v. 10).

3. The Impulsive Maiden (6:11–13)

11 I went down to the nut orchard,
    to look at the blossoms of the valley,
    to see whether the vines had budded,
    whether the pomegranates were in bloom.
12 Before I was aware, my fancy set me
    in a chariot beside my prince.
13 Return, return, O Shulammite,
    return, return, that we may look upon
        you.
    Why should you look upon the Shulammite,
    as upon a dance before two armies?

The interpretation of vv. 11–13 is fraught
with extreme difficulty. It seems that the
maiden in the spring of the year visited the
fields and while there joined company with
others. The plea *Return, return, O Shulammite* may indicate that she departed (v.
12) leaving behind those whom she had
originally intended to be with. One can
only speculate as to the meaning. Verse 12
may imply that the maiden impulsively
joined with the king and his retinue leaving
her shepherd lover and his companions.
Thus it would be the shepherd group who
implore her to return.

The designation *Shulammite* may indicate the maiden was from Shulem (i.e., a
variant of Shunem), a village in the Plain
of Esdraelon. This was the home of Abi-
shag, the loveliest woman of her day (cf.
1 Kings 1:1–4,15; 2:17–22). There are
additional references in 2 Kings 4:11,25–
26 to a wealthy Shunammite woman.[23]

The phrase *a dance before two armies* is
translated as a proper name, "Mahanaim,"
in the KJV and ERV. The Septuagint reads
"she comes dancing like the camps," while
the Vulgate renders it "dances of camps."
If indeed it is a place name, then it likely
refers to the Transjordanian town where
David sought refuge (2 Sam. 17:24).
Genesis 32:2, however, provides a basis for

---

23 Cf. H. H. Rowley, "The Meaning of 'The Shulammite,'" (*American Journal of Semitic Languages,*
LVI (1939), 84–91.

interpreting the word to mean *two armies*.[24] If Mahanaim is interpreted as "armies" or "double-camp," then the meaning may be as follows. The shepherd and his companions plead for the return of the maiden. Why should she dance and be looked upon by the monarch's company like a camp follower who danced before the lascivious eyes of the troops?

4. The Third Description of the Maiden's Charms (7:1–9)

1 How graceful are your feet in sandals,
   O queenly maiden!
   Your rounded thighs are like jewels,
   the work of a master hand.
2 Your navel is a rounded bowl
   that never lacks mixed wine.
   Your belly is a heap of wheat,
   encircled with lilies.
3 Your two breasts are like two fawns,
   twins of a gazelle.
4 Your neck is like an ivory tower.
   Your eyes are pools in Heshbon,
   by the gate of Bathrabbim.
   Your nose is like a tower of Lebanon,
   overlooking Damascus.
5 Your head crowns you like Carmel,
   and your flowing locks are like purple;
   a king is held captive in the tresses.
6 How fair and pleasant you are,
   O loved one, delectable maiden!
7 You are stately as a palm tree,
   and your breasts are like its clusters.
8 I say I will climb the palm tree
   and lay hold of its branches.
   Oh, may your breasts be like clusters of the vine,
   and the scent of your breath like apples,
9 and your kisses like the best wine
   that goes down smoothly,
   gliding over lips and teeth.

There is first a description of the maiden's feet and thighs. She walks with gracefully arched feet in sandals. The thighs are described as *rounded* (from the verb *chamah*, to turn, to turn to and fro, to rotate, to swivel, to undulate). The meaning here is curving thighs. Literally her thighs were like metal ornaments (not *jewels*, which is misleading) curvaceously molded by the hands of a master craftsman.

A depiction of the *belly* is striking (v. 2). *Navel* may denote the lower abdomen, and in Arabic the word came to mean "secret part." There are alternative interpretations of *mixed wine*. Wines were blended to achieve subtle changes in taste. Also wine was laced with herbs to increase potency. Another possible explanation is found in the Talmud. It gives an exact formula for cutting the strength of wine with water: two parts water, one part wine. A choice between the first two possibilities seems best. To the shepherd his private garden possessed unlimited nuances of delight.

The *belly* is described as a *heap of wheat, encircled with lilies*.[25] The simile "heap of wheat" could denote skin color (i.e., the amber of harvested wheat) or physical appearance, (i.e., a protruding mound). Either aspect, contour or color, would be to the ancient Near Eastern mind the epitome of feminine attractiveness. As to the encircling with lilies this implies the covering of the mons veneris.

Again the breasts are likened to twin fawns (cf. comment on 4:5), and the shepherd continues with a description of the neck, face, and head of the maiden (vv. 4–5). The neck is likened to an *ivory tower*. This may refer to specific structures embellished with ivory inlay (cf. Psalm 45:9; 1 Kings 22:39; Amos 3:15). It could well be similar imagery to that in 4:4 and infer that her neck was adorned with precious jewelry as a tower was decorated with exquisite ivory.

Her eyes were like *pools in Hesbon, by the gate of Bath-rabbim*. Hesbon was a Transjordanian town west of Amman which played a fairly prominent role in early Israelite history.[26]

---

24 Cf. S. Cohen, "Mahanaim," *The Interpreter's Dictionary of the Bible*, III (New York: Abingdon Press, 1962), 226.

25 "Belly" (Heb., *beten*) is quite uncertain in exact meaning and is variously translated. When applied to a woman it, at times, has the connotation of womb. Cf. Brown, Driver, and Briggs, *A Hebrew and English Lexicon of the Old Testament* (London: Oxford University Press, 1959), pp. 105b, 106a.

26 Siegfried H. Horn, "The 1968 Heshbon Expedition," *The Biblical Archaeologist*, XXXII (May, 1969) No. 2, pp. 26–41.

The gate name *Bath-rabbim* literally means "daughter of multitudes," which may indicate that this was the primary city gate through which throngs passed. Names for city gates generally were connected with the purpose for which the gate was used (cf. 2 Kings 14:13; 2 Chron. 9:18; 2 Chron. 23:5; Neh. 2:13–15; Jer. 19:2). It may well have been that the ancient city of Heshbon had two lovely pools by the gate Bath-rabbim, pools of unusual beauty.

The description of the nose as *a tower of Lebanon* appears somewhat ludicrous, but the metaphor implies little more than the fact that she possessed a prominent nose looked upon by Semites as truly beautiful.

The maiden's head was as finely set as majestic Mount Carmel, which crowned the coastline of Palestine (cf. Isa. 35:2; Jer. 46:18), while her flowing hair of deep sheen was of sufficient beauty to captivate a king (v. 5).

Comparison of the hair to *purple* is not an allusion to color. This appears to be a reference to Tyrian purple cloth produced by treating fabric with a dye extracted from the murex shellfish of the coastal waters. Material treated with this agent was costly, much in demand, and looked upon as the epitome of sumptuousness. Thus her flowing hair was as striking and lovely as Tyrian purple cloth.

The Hebrew word translated *tresses* is uncertain in meaning. In Genesis 30:38,41; Exodus 2:16 it is used in a literal sense and translated "troughs." It may infer that the hair hung in flowing but deep waves like troughs.

Contained in 7:6–8 is a description of the maiden's stature. She was like a *palm tree* (Heb., *tamar*). This distinguishes between the different species of palms for the word means date palm. Tamar was a common name for women in the Old Testament (cf. Gen. 38:6; 2 Samuel 13:1 ff.). It implies the figure of the maiden was stately like the date palm.

As the shepherd thus describes his beloved he suddenly speaks in symbolical language of anticipated love (7:8–9). He boldly asserts his intentions and anticipations.

5. The Invitation to Love (7:10—8:2)

¹⁰ I am my beloved's,
   and his desire is for me.
¹¹ Come, my beloved,
   let us go forth into the fields,
   and lodge in the villages;
¹² let us go out early to the vineyards,
   and see whether the vines have budded,
   whether the grape blossoms have opened
   and the pomegranates are in bloom.
   There I will give you my love.
¹³ The mandrakes give forth fragrance,
   and over our doors are all choice fruits,
   new as well as old,
      which I have laid up for you, O my beloved.
¹ O that you were like a brother to me,
   that nursed at my mother's breast!
   If I met you outside, I would kiss you,
   and none would despise me.
² I would lead you and bring you
   into the house of my mother,
   and into the chamber of her that conceived me.
   I would give you spiced wine to drink,
   the juice of my pomegranates.

The maiden now invites her lover to receive her love (7:10–13). She acknowledges that she belongs to her lover and believes that his desire is only for her. Recurrent affirmations tend to indicate the maiden had doubts as to her lover's fidelity (cf. 2:16; 6:3). She invites him to a tryst in the fields where they may share mutual fulfillment in love.

Desire means physical attraction, impelling of desire, or longing in the relationship between sexes. Here it implies such a desire by the shepherd for the maiden (v. 10). She invites him to *lodge* (lit., to pass the night) with her in the fields. The noun *villages* could equally as well be translated "henna blossoms" from *koper* (henna). Hebrew poetic parallelism might be better served by translating the phrase, "and pass the night among henna blossoms."

She promises fulfillment to him if he will join her and speaks of the delights which will be his (vv. 12–13). The *new* and *old* fruits may imply she has reserved for her lover not only all of the delights previously shared but new delights borne by desire for him.

Included in this passage on fulfillment is a reference to *mandrakes*. At only one other place in the Old Testament is this plant alluded to (Gen. 30:14 ff.). The ancients considered it to be a potent aphrodisiac which stimulated sexual desire and increased fertility.

The import of the proposal weighed heavily upon the maiden. She decries the overwhelming impossibility of the situation wishing it was not necessary to exercise such love outside acceptable boundaries. She longs for the removal of all obstacles to their relationship (8:1–2).

Social, religious, and family convention, as well as public opinion, were in opposition to their love affair. She wishes that her lover was like a *brother* so they could escape condemnation. If he were a brother, then she could publicly embrace him and take him into her own home. These verses again affirm the ethical moment of the book: an illicit love affair brings only inordinate stress and lack of total fulfillment.

6. The Declaration (8:3–4)

3   O that his left hand were under my head,
       and that his right hand embraced me!
4   I adjure you, O daughters of Jerusalem,
       that you stir not up nor awaken love
       until it please.

In spite of opposition the maiden longs for her lover and covets the expressions of his love (v. 3). Once again there is the haunting refrain *stir not up nor awaken love until it please.*

VI. The Unique Powers of Love (8:5–14)

In this, the climax of the book, the full force of its ethical implications become clear. The author delicately but forcefully shows the destructive nature of love which circumvents the dimension of acceptable Israelite religious morality.

1. The Awakening of Physical Love Is Recalled by the Maiden (8:5)

5   Who is that coming up from the wilderness,
       leaning upon her beloved?

Under the apple tree I awakened you.
There your mother was in travail with you,
   there she who bore you was in travail.

The events of 8:5 appear to be flashbacks to the time when the lovers had their initial experience in the wilderness solitude. This was the advent of physical love for the maiden.

2. The Cost of the Maiden's Love (8:6–7)

6   Set me as a seal upon your heart,
       as a seal upon your arm;
    for love is strong as death,
       jealousy is cruel as the grave.
    Its flashes are flashes of fire,
       a most vehement flame.
7   Many waters cannot quench love,
       neither can floods drown it.
    If a man offered for love
       all the wealth of his house,
       it would be utterly scorned.

The inordinate power of love, when it totally dominates the emotions and becomes an obsession, wreaks havoc in a life. This knowledge is passed from the maiden to her companions.

Utter faithfulness from the shepherd is desperately argued for by the maiden (v. 6). In giving herself to him she had compromised personal and family reputation. She feels the excruciating torment of jealousy and succumbs to a fear of being abandoned. She had been enticed and lured by her own desire, and an inextricable trap of love had enslaved her. There was no escape! She pleads that her lover set her as . . . *a seal upon . . . heart . . . upon . . . arm.* . . . These figures apply to the seal worn about the neck on a cord or upon the finger in the form of a ring (cf. Gen. 38:18,25; Jer. 22:24 ff.).

This simile has forceful import. The maiden desires the shepherd indelibly to impress love for her, in a binding way, upon his heart. As the imprint of a seal becomes a part of the vessel, brick, or document, so she desires to become in the life of her lover.

Such a love as she possesses, the maiden affirms, is as *strong as death.* As death is an inflexible point of no return, so is her love for the shepherd. It is sealed! She cannot escape! She has been caught up in an overwhelming finality in love.

This theme is intensified by the words *jealousy . . . cruel as the grave.* The basic meaning of the verb in Hebrew from which jealousy is derived is "to be red with flame." The inflamed jealousy of the maiden is as consuming as the *grave* (i.e., Sheol), and the *flashes* of jealousy like jagged searing streaks of lightning (cf. Deut. 32:24; Job 5:7; Psalm 78:48).

As she continues the pleas for faithfulness, the maiden indicates that such a love cannot be quenched and is beyond price, surpassing all one's wealth (v. 7).

3. The Worth of the Maiden's Love (8:8–10)

8 We have a little sister,
     and she has no breasts.
   What shall we do for our sister,
     on the day when she is spoken for?
9 If she is a wall,
       we will build upon her a battlement of
         silver;
     but if she is a door,
       we will enclose her with boards of cedar.
10 I was a wall,
     and my breasts were like towers;
   then I was in his eyes
     as one who brings peace.

The maiden shares with the women of the harem her new understanding as to why her brothers had so carefully guarded her. They had sought to protect her from precisely what had occurred. The opportunity for an acceptable and profitable marital arrangement was predicated upon the intactness of the sister's reputation and virtue since she possessed the other indispensable quality, beauty.[27]

[27] For the role of brothers in such negotiations cf. Gen. 24 (the case of Rebekah) and Gen. 34 (the case of Dinah).

The brothers were determined to protect her until she married provided she exercised self-control (vv. 8–9). And the maiden affirms that she did exercise self-restraint, she was *a wall.* She did for a while keep her virtue intact, but when she reached ripe maturity, with *breasts . . . like towers,* then she became to the shepherd *as one who brings peace.* Which is to say, she surrendered herself to him.

4. The Intent of the Maiden (8:11–12)

11 Solomon had a vineyard at Baalhamon;
     he let out the vineyard to keepers;
       each one was to bring for its fruit a thou-
         sand pieces of silver.
12 My vineyard, my very own, is for myself;
     you, O Solomon, may have the thousand,
     and the keepers of the fruit two hundred.

Despite suspicions, doubts, fears, and all social and religious standards, the maiden reaffirms her intent to continue the affair.

The harem of Solomon is likened to a large vineyard with many *keepers,* i.e., the eunuchs who kept order among the women of the harem. Although Solomon has his harem (i.e., *vineyard*) and its profits, her *vineyard* (i.e., her body) was for her lover alone.

5. The Maiden Awaits Her Lover (8:13–14)

13 O you who dwell in the gardens,
     my companions are listening for your
       voice;
     let me hear it.
14 Make haste, my beloved,
     and be like a gazelle
   or a young stag
     upon the mountains of spices.

The account ends as it began, with the call of the lover to the maiden (v. 13) and the maiden's response (v. 14), a forceful and dramatic conclusion.

Isaiah

PAGE H. KELLEY

Introduction

In the book of Isaiah one encounters the word of God that "will stand for ever" (40:8). Across the centuries God has spoken through it both to admonish and to comfort his people. The genius of Isaiah —as of the other Hebrew prophets—lay in his ability to look realistically at his nation's sin and rebellion without, however, despairing of its future. Even as he pronounced judgment upon Israel, therefore, he remained firm in his conviction that God would yet raise up a righteous remnant through whom his purposes would be fulfilled. The prophet's message of judgment and redemption is as relevant today as it was in the eighth century B.C.

I. Isaiah and the Canon

The book of Isaiah stands as the first of the prophetic books in the Hebrew Bible, otherwise known as the Masoretic Text. It is followed by Jeremiah, Ezekiel, and the twelve "minor prophets." The Greek version of the Old Testament, customarily referred to as the Septuagint, follows the same order as the Masoretic Text, except that it places the book of Lamentations between Jeremiah and Ezekiel. This accounts for the present arrangement of these books in English versions of the Bible.

It is by no means certain that the prophetic books have always stood in this same sequence. Evidence to the contrary is found in the writings of the ancient Jewish Talmud. In the section known as Baba Bathra 14b, it is reported: "Our rabbis taught: The order of the Prophets is Joshua, Judges, Samuel, Kings, Jeremiah, Ezekiel, Isaiah, and the Twelve."

The explanation which the Talmud gave for this arrangement was theological rather than chronological. It placed Isaiah after Jeremiah and Ezekiel because the message of consolation in Isaiah 40—66 formed an appropriate sequel to the prophecies of judgment and destruction in these two books. The ancient rabbis customarily arranged prophetic materials in such a manner that oracles of judgment were followed by oracles of redemption. This explanation however hardly justifies the adoption of the order of the Talmud in preference to that of the Masoretic Text or the Septuagint. The Masoretic Text has the distinct advantage of presenting the "major prophets" in their chronological order and is, therefore, to be preferred.

II. The Personal Life of the Prophet

The book bears the name of the prophet Isaiah. This name appears both as *y⁰sha-ʻyahu* and, in a slightly abbreviated form, as *y⁰shaʻyah*. In both cases the meaning is the same: "The Lord is salvation." It is similar in origin and meaning to other Hebrew names such as Joshua, Jesus, and Hosea. Other persons besides the prophet Isaiah were named *y⁰shaʻyahu* or *y⁰shaʻyah*, but this fact has been obscured by English translators. Since the appearance of the King James Version only the eighth-century prophet has been called Isaiah. All other individuals bearing this name have been designated as Jeshaiah (cf. 1 Chron. 3:21; 25:3,15; 26:25).

Very little is known about the personal life of Isaiah. According to 1:1, he prophesied concerning Judah and Jerusalem during the days of Uzziah (783–742 B.C.), Jotham (742–735), Ahaz (735–715), and Hezekiah (715–687).[1] Isaiah thus shared the stage with three other well-known prophets of the eighth century, Amos and Hosea in the Northern Kingdom of Israel and Micah in Judah.

Isaiah's father was named Amoz. He must not be confused with the prophet Amos, however, for although their names bear a striking similarity in English translation they are written quite differently in Hebrew. The Babylonian Talmud lists Amoz as the brother of King Amaziah (cf. 2 Kings 14:1 ff.). This tradition seems to have no basis other than the fact that both Amoz and Amaziah are derived from the same verbal root.

It is assumed that Isaiah was born in Jerusalem between 770 and 760 B.C. If this assumption is correct, he would have been between 20 and 30 years of age when he began his prophetic ministry. This of course is based upon the further assumption that the vision described in chapter 6 as having occurred in the year that King Uzziah died was indeed the inaugural vision of Isaiah. The views of those who disagree with this latter assumption will be discussed in the commentary.

Isaiah was married, and his wife is referred to as "the prophetess" (8:3). The office of prophetess was not uncommon in the Old Testament, and others who bore this title included Miriam (Ex. 15:20), Deborah (Judg. 4:4), Huldah (2 Kings 22:14), and Noadiah (Neh. 6:14). Most scholars believe that Isaiah's wife was called a prophetess merely because she

was married to a prophet. It is not impossible, however, that she could have been a prophetess in her own right, exercising a ministry independent of that of her husband. This would seem to be the most natural interpretation of the title given to her in 8:3.

Isaiah had two sons to whom he, like Hosea, gave symbolic names. The first was named Shearjashub, meaning "a remnant shall return" (7:3). The second was named Maher-shalal-hash-baz, translated "the spoil speeds, the prey hastes" (8:3). Because of their symbolic names these two sons of the prophet served as signs to Ahaz and the people of Judah during the Syro-Ephraimitic crisis of 735–734 B.C.

Isaiah's ministry spanned a period of at least 40 years. His last dated prophecies come from the reign of Hezekiah. Manasseh, who succeeded Hezekiah as king of Judah in 687 B.C., was strongly pro-Assyrian in his foreign policy. From a religious standpoint, his reign was characterized as the worst period of apostasy in the history of Judah (2 Kings 21). According to a tradition preserved in early Jewish and Christian writings, Isaiah was sawn asunder during the religious persecutions that occurred during the reign of this wicked king.[2]

After Ahaz rejected Isaiah's counsel and concluded an alliance with Assyria in the crisis of 735–734 B.C., the prophet announced his withdrawal from public life. It is impossible to point with certainty to any public utterance made by him between this date and the death of Ahaz in 715. In the interval Isaiah seems to have gathered a group of disciples about him and devoted himself to their instruction (8:16–20). We are indebted to these disciples for collecting, editing, and preserving the prophet's messages.

---

[1] Cf. John Bright, *A History of Israel* (Philadelphia: The Westminster Press, 1959), p. 468. All subsequent dates cited in this commentary will be based upon Bright's chronology, unless otherwise indicated.

[2] This tradition is preserved in chs. 1—3 and 5 of the Ascension of Isaiah, an apocalyptic work compiled by a Christian editor from three separate sources, namely, the Martyrdom of Isaiah, a Jewish document, the Testament of Hezekiah, and the Vision of Isaiah, the latter two of Christian origin. Isaiah is said to have been cut in two with a wood-cutting saw while hiding inside a hollow tree (cf. Heb. 11:37).

III. The Historical Background

1. The Assyrian Crisis

No prophet was more closely related to the historical events of his time than Isaiah. He served as spiritual adviser to the kings of Judah during the latter half of the eighth century B.C. Perhaps more than any other prophet he deserves to be called "God's politician." The book of Isaiah can be properly understood only when it is interpreted in the light of events that transpired from the mid-eighth century to the end of the sixth century.

Isaiah was born during the reign of Uzziah (783–742 B.C.). The long and prosperous reign of this king in Judah coincided with that of Jeroboam II (786–746) in Israel. By the beginning of the eighth century Israel and Judah had forgotten their earlier rivalries and were willing to work together for their mutual welfare and prosperity. A temporary power vacuum in the great kingdoms north and south of them relieved them of the threat of outside interference. The result was an era of prosperity and splendor unparalleled in the history of Israel, except perhaps during the reign of Solomon.

The accomplishments of Uzziah are described in 2 Chronicles 26:1–23. He is credited with the modernization of his army and with the conquest of the Philistines, the Arabians, and the Ammonites. These conquests gave him control over the main trade routes between Africa and Asia and enabled him to tax the caravans that used these routes. He rebuilt the ancient city of Elath, a center for the manufacture of copper and iron. He also developed the agricultural resources of his country, for he "loved the soil."

It seems axiomatic that when a nation enjoys material prosperity it falls into moral and spiritual decay. Judah was no exception. A half century of peace and economic well-being lulled the people into a false sense of security. They were laboring under four false assumptions: (1) that God's covenant with Israel was indissoluble; (2) that Israel was fully discharging her covenant obligations by observing the ritual of cult and sacrifice; (3) that the day of the Lord would be a day of triumph for God and for Israel; (4) that, no matter how difficult matters might become, God would never allow Jerusalem to be captured or destroyed. There was—so they thought—a magic circle around the city, and its inhabitants led charmed lives.

Isaiah took issue with these assumptions. He launched a vigorous attack against the social and moral evils which he encountered, speaking out against the leaders' oppression of the poor, their miscarriage of justice, their insatiable desire for wealth and power, and their total indifference to the moral and ethical demands of God. Isaiah knew that a society such as Judah had spawned already carried within it the seeds of its own destruction.

The last half of the eighth century was one of the most decisive periods in biblical history. It witnessed the rise of the Assyrian Empire and the speedy downfall of the Northern Kingdom of Israel.

The rise of Assyria began in earnest when Tiglath-pileser III (745–727 B.C.), also known as Pulu or Pul, seized the throne. He soon proved himself to be an exceedingly vigorous and able ruler. First he subdued the neighboring kingdoms of Babylon and Urartu, and then turned his attention to the west. Perhaps as early as 743,[3] and certainly by 738, he made a successful expedition against several western states, including Syria, Israel, Tyre, and Judah. From their rulers he demanded submission and a heavy annual tribute. Reference to this expedition is found in the annals of Tiglath-pileser, and also in 2 Kings 15:19–20: "Pul the king of Assyria came against the land; and Menahem gave Pul a thousand talents of silver, that he might help him to confirm his hold of the royal power. . . . So the king of Assyria turned back, and did not stay there in the

---

[3] Cf. F. F. Bruce, *Israel and the Nations* (Grand Rapids: Wm. B. Eerdmans Publishing Co., 1963), pp. 60 f.

land."

Under Tiglath-pileser the Assyrian army developed into a formidable striking force. Its speed and efficiency are vividly described in 5:27-29: "None is weary, none stumbles, / none slumbers or sleeps, / not a waistcloth is loose, / not a sandal-thong broken; / their arrows are sharp, / all their bows bent, / their horses' hoofs seem like flint, / and their wheels like the whirlwind. / Their roaring is like a lion, / like young lions they roar; / they growl and seize their prey, / they carry it off, and none can rescue."

Unlike previous world rulers who had invaded Palestine, Tiglath-pileser was not content with merely collecting tribute and departing. He was instead intent upon keeping these lands under his control. The heavy tribute which he exacted from them provided the funds necessary for maintaining his army and operating his government. Those who voluntarily submitted to him received relatively mild treatment, though they were heavily taxed. Those who resisted were ruthlessly crushed. The worst fate of all was reserved for those who first swore allegiance and later broke their oath and rebelled. They were destroyed with a fury that beggars description as a warning to others who were contemplating rebellion.

Menahem (745-738 B.C.) continued to pay tribute throughout his reign over Israel. His son and successor, Pekahiah (738-737), followed his example but met with increasing opposition from his subjects. They wished to be free from the burdensome responsibility of raising the annual tribute. Rebellion soon broke out, led by Pekah the son of Remaliah, an army officer who promptly assassinated Pekahiah.

Once on the throne, Pekah organized an anti-Assyrian alliance in coalition with Rezin king of Syria. At that moment Tiglath-pileser was engaged in a campaign against the kingdom of Urartu. Therefore the time seemed to be ripe for throwing off the Assyrian yoke. Pekah and Rezin immediately attempted to draw Judah into their alliance. They apparently made overtures toward Jotham (742-735 B.C.), the son and successor of Uzziah, but their overtures were rejected. Jotham preferred to follow an independent course. This resulted in an invasion of his territory, for the record of his reign states that "in those days the Lord began to send Rezin the king of Syria and Pekah the son of Remaliah against Judah" (2 Kings 15:37).

At this point Jotham died and was succeeded by his 20-year-old son Ahaz (735-715 B.C.). Ahaz thus came to the throne at a very crucial moment in Judah's history. Pekah and Rezin had determined to invade the country, depose Ahaz, and replace him with "the son of Tabeel" (7:6). In the meantime Edom had taken advantage of Judah's predicament to launch an attack in the south, driving Ahaz's troops from Elath (2 Kings 16:6). According to the Chronicler, Ahaz was also being attacked on the west by the Philistines (2 Chron. 28:18).

It is small wonder that the threat of an attack from all sides caused panic to seize the king and his people (cf. 7:2). It was perhaps at this time that Ahaz resorted to the extreme measure of offering his own son as a burnt offering (2 Kings 16:3), thereby hoping to secure God's favor and protection.

Isaiah refused to be unduly alarmed by the threat of invasion. He saw the folly of the course of action taken by Pekah and Rezin. He counseled Ahaz to have no fear of these two "smoldering stumps of firebrands" (7:4). God would deal with both of them in due season. In the meantime, he warned, Ahaz should avoid all foreign entanglements and trust steadfastly in God. Otherwise his throne would not be established (7:9).

Ahaz was unable, or at least unwilling, to follow Isaiah's advice. Instead, he resolved to appeal directly to Tiglath-pileser to come to his aid (2 Kings 16:7-9). Isaiah viewed this as foolish and unnecessary. Tiglath-pileser would punish the rebels as soon as he was free to do so, even without Ahaz's intervention. The move contemplated by Ahaz would only insure that Judah also would come under the political and religious domination of Assyria. Subsequent events proved Isaiah to be right. Tiglath-pileser quickly destroyed the coalition, as both the Bible and his own inscriptions indicate. Damascus was destroyed in 732 B.C., and Samaria would likely have suffered a similar fate had not her people risen up in revolt against Pekah, who was slain and replaced by Hoshea (732–724; cf. 2 Kings 15:29–30). After the destruction of Damascus, Tiglath-pileser summoned Ahaz to meet him and to work out the terms of their agreement. Though the biblical record of their encounter is far from complete, it nevertheless indicates that the Assyrian king made sweeping demands (cf. 2 Kings 16:10–18). For all practical purposes, Judah had become a full vassal of Assyria.

Isaiah reacted to Ahaz's stubborn refusal to follow his counsel by withdrawing from public ministry during the remainder of the king's reign (8:16–18). The next dated oracle to appear among his prophecies is assigned to the year that Ahaz died (14:28 ff.). In the meantime Isaiah and his two sons served as living signs of the messages he had already proclaimed (cf. 8:18).

In the kingdom of Israel, meanwhile, Hoshea continued as a faithful subject of Assyria until the death of Tiglath-pileser in 727 B.C. Tiglath-pileser was succeeded by Shalmaneser V (727–722). Thinking that the opportune moment had arrived and that he could count on Egyptian support, Hoshea decided to revolt. This was his fatal mistake. Torn by internal strife, Egypt was unable to defend herself, much less to provide support for Judah. Shalmaneser dealt with the rebellion as decisively as his father would have done. In 724 he launched his attack against Israel. Hoshea was brought before him and thrown into prison, and the entire land of Israel, except for the city of Samaria, soon fell into his hands. Samaria's defenses were so strongly built that they withstood the onslaught of the Assyrian army for almost three years.

Near the end of the siege there was a change of rulers in Assyria, and Shalmaneser was displaced by Sargon II (722–705 B.C.).

The new king completed the conquest of the city in 721 B.C. His own account of its capitulation reads as follows: "I besieged and conquered Samaria (Sa-me-ri-na), led away as booty 27,290 inhabitants of it. I formed from among them a contingent of 50 chariots and made remaining (inhabitants) assume their (social) positions. I installed over them an officer of mine and imposed upon them the tribute of the former king." [4]

Isaiah was vitally interested in the events related to the fall of Samaria. The oracle in 9:1–7 was probably occasioned by Tiglath-pileser's conquest of Zebulun and Naphtali in 734–732 B.C. Isaiah seems to have expected an early defeat of the Assyrians and the reunion of the kingdoms of Israel and Judah under a Davidic prince.[5] Later he earnestly warned of the disastrous end awaiting the Northern Kingdom (9:8—10:4; 5:25–30). When news of that end came, he surely was among those who received it with mourning.

Ahaz died in 715 B.C. His reign was remembered by later generations as one of the worst periods of apostasy Judah had ever known. He was condemned not only for his political blunders but also for filling his land with idolatrous practices (2 Chron. 28:1–4,22–25). Both Isaiah and Micah spoke out against the social injustices that accompanied the religious apostasy of his reign (cf. 1:21–23; 5:20–23; Mic. 3:1–4, 9–11).

Ahaz was succeeded by his son Hezekiah (715–687 B.C.), whose accession to the throne touched off a wave of messianic expectation throughout the land. Hopes ran high that God had at last visited his people and raised up an ideal prince of

---

4 James B. Pritchard, ed., *Ancient Near Eastern Texts* (Princeton: University Press, 1955), pp. 284 f.

5 Cf. Marvin E. Tate, "King and Messiah in Isaiah of Jerusalem," *Review and Expositor*, LXV (1968), pp. 416 ff.

the line of David, one who would be anointed with God's Spirit and whose reign of justice and peace would extend to the ends of the earth (cf. 9:1–7; 11:1–9; Mic. 5:2–6). Hezekiah completely reversed the political and religious policies of his father. He attempted to throw off the Assyrian yoke and to purge religion of its pagan elements. In his religious reforms he was influenced by Isaiah and Micah (cf. Jer. 26:17–19). These passages are written in hymnic form, and it is possible that they were first written to be sung at the coronation ceremonies of Hezekiah or some Judean king.

The religious reforms were made possible by a change in the political situation. When Sargon came to the throne in Assyria, Merodach-baladan revolted and had himself installed as king of Babylon on the Babylonian New Year's Day in 721 B.C. Thus Sargon lost control of Babylonia and did not regain it until approximately a dozen years later. Sometime during this interval Merodach-baladan dispatched an embassy to Jerusalem, presumably to congratulate Hezekiah upon his recovery from a serious illness, but more likely to secure his commitment to an alliance against Assyria (cf. Isa. 39:1–8). Sargon's position was so precarious that he was unable to mount a major military campaign against Palestine after 721.

Egypt meanwhile had a change of dynasties, and was able to regain part of her former power and prestige. The new dynasty (the 25th) was of Ethiopian origin and lasted from 715 until 663 B.C. Once established in control of all Egypt, its pharaohs set about inciting the border states to the north to revolt against their Assyrian overlords. Though these states were promised aid in case of attack, the promises were seldom kept. Egypt was merely using them as pawns in the game of power politics.

The first revolt of any consequence took place in the tiny kingdom of Ashdod. It began when Ashdod's king withheld tribute from the Assyrians, at the same time dispatching messengers to the neighboring kingdoms urging them to join the revolt.

Since the rebellion, which lasted for three years, was crushed in 711 B.C., it must have begun at least as early as 713. Hezekiah was among those who were urged to rebel against Assyria. Information to this effect is found not only in the Bible but also in the records of Sargon (ANET, pp. 286 f.). The people of Judah were sharply divided over the issue. A strong pro-Egyptian party urged the king to seize the opportunity to throw off Assyrian rule. Isaiah, on the other hand, counseled against this course of action. He believed the revolt was doomed to failure. He therefore argued against any involvement with Egypt. In order to dramatize his message, he walked about Jerusalem disrobed and barefoot for a period of three years (20:1–6). This was his way of saying that both Ashdod and Egypt would be conquered and their people led away in the garb of prisoners of war. His warning seems to have been heeded, for Judah escaped harm when Sargon crushed the revolt in 711.

Hezekiah's neutrality during the Ashdod rebellion left him free to carry out his religious reforms. One such action involved the destruction of various cult objects associated with the worship of God, including a bronze serpent called Nehushtan (2 Kings 18:4). After he had purified worship in Judah, the king invited the inhabitants of the former territory of Israel to join in celebrating the Passover at Jerusalem (2 Chron. 30:1–12). This move had political as well as religious significance, for he apparently hoped to forge a political and religious reunion of the two territories, as in the days of David. Perhaps this hope had been inspired by prophetic oracles such as 9:1–7. His plan did not succeed, however, for according to 2 Chronicles 30:10, his couriers were laughed to scorn as they passed throughout the territory of Israel.

Sargon died in 705 B.C., and was succeeded by his son Sennacherib (705–681). This change of kings was the signal for widespread revolt throughout the Assyrian Empire. The subject states foolishly imagined that Sennacherib would not be able to control his vast empire. Before the turn of the century, however, they learned how badly they had underestimated his strength and determination.

Prodded by the pro-Egyptian party, Hezekiah decided to make a bid for freedom. Anticipating retaliation from Assyria, he took steps to strengthen the defenses of Jerusalem. A tunnel was cut through 1,700 feet of solid rock in order to bring the waters of the Gihon spring into the upper pool of Siloam in the southeast quarter of the city (2 Kings 20:20; 2 Chron. 32:3–4), assuring the city of a protected water supply in the event of a siege.

Isaiah was relentless in criticizing this course of action. He ridiculed those who advocated reliance upon Egypt (30:1–7; 31:1–3). His attitude toward foreign alliances had not changed since the Syro-Ephraimitic crisis of 735–734 B.C.; he regarded dependence on foreign powers as abandonment of the covenant with God. His counsel to Hezekiah is summed up in these words: " 'In returning and rest you shall be saved; in quietness and in trust shall be your strength' " (30:15).

Sennacherib lost no time in moving against the rebels. He first defeated Merodach-baladan, who had temporarily regained control of Babylon, and then marched into Palestine. His route of conquest took him through Phoenicia and down into Philistia. An Egyptian army marching to the relief of Ekron was intercepted and soundly defeated at Eltekeh in the Judaean foothills.

Another division of Sennacherib's army moved across Samaria and approached Jerusalem from the north. It is possible that 10:27c–34 describes the rapid advance of this army. In his account of the campaign, Sennacherib claimed to have destroyed 46 of the fortified cities of Judah and to have shut Hezekiah up in his royal city "like a bird in a cage" (ANET, p. 288). He required of Hezekiah an increased annual tribute, which Hezekiah's envoys subsequently delivered to him (2 Kings 18:14–16). The whole land of Judah

was devastated, and Jerusalem was left "like a booth in a vineyard, like a lodge in a cucumber field, like a besieged city" (1:8).

Not content with having exacted tribute from Hezekiah, the Assyrians demanded in addition the complete capitulation and surrender of Jerusalem (2 Kings 18:17 ff.). Hezekiah refused to yield to these demands. He was supported in his resistance by the prophet Isaiah (cf. 29:1–8; 30: 27–33; 31:4–9; 37:33–35). The history of these happenings and of the unexpected turn of events is found in 2 Kings 18—19 and in the parallel account in Isaiah 36—37. The Assyrians left as suddenly as they had come. The Bible states that 185,000 of their troops perished in one night (2 Kings 19:35). This account is supported by a statement in Herodotus, repeated by Josephus, that Sennacherib's army was overrun by a plague of rats at the border of Egypt. It may well be that the army fell victim to an attack of the bubonic plague. Whatever the means devised, God intervened to deliver his people.

Jerusalem had escaped destruction, but her victory was a hollow one. The situation led Isaiah to say, "If the Lord of hosts had not left us a few survivors, we should have been like Sodom, and become like Gomorrah" (1:9). Isaiah 22:1–14 may have come from this same period. If so, it gives us a description of the victory celebration that followed the lifting of the siege of Jerusalem. Amidst all the shouting Isaiah stood alone weeping bitter tears, as he said, "for the destruction of the daughter of my people." [6]

Chapter 10 of Isaiah also belongs to the period of the Assyrian invasion. In it the

---

[6] The reconstruction of these events outlined above has been along traditional lines. Not all scholars would accept this reconstruction. John Bright, for example, argues that there were two invasions of Judah by Sennacherib, the first in 701 B.C. and the second about 688. They only appear to be one because the redactor of Kings has telescoped the two accounts. For a full discussion of this problem, see John Bright, op. cit., pp. 282–287; and Brevard S. Childs, Isaiah and the Assyrian Crisis, "Studies in Biblical Theology," Second Series, No. 3 (Naperville: Alec R. Allenson, Inc., 1967).

prophet wrestles with the enigma of history in a world allegedly ruled over by God. In so doing he gives classic expression to the proposition that God is directing all history in accordance with his purpose of establishing his rule on earth. Though the Assyrians seem to be invincible, they are still under the scrutiny of the Almighty. God is but using them as a rod to chasten his wayward people. Once this work has been accomplished, the rod will be broken and cast aside. Isaiah knew that history was not governed by caprice or by the nation that possessed the largest battalions. Rather it was firmly under God's control with the final outcome never in doubt. Over against the kingdoms of this world stood the kingdom of God, and it alone was invincible. It was largely this interpretation of history that enabled the people of Judah to survive the catastrophes of 701 and 587 B.C.

We have no evidence that Isaiah continued to prophesy after 701. There is some indication that the persistent stubbornness of his people caused him to make a second and final withdrawal from public ministry (cf. 30:8–11). If so, he probably devoted his final years to the instruction of his disciples. Some would assign his messages of hope to this final period of his life. In poems of immortal beauty he spoke to his disciples of the golden age to come when an ideal king would rule the land in righteousness and justice, when wars would cease, and when the knowledge of the Lord would cover the earth as the waters cover the sea (cf. 2:1–4; 9:1–7; 11:1–9; 32:1–8,15–18,20).

2. The Babylonian Crisis

The historical background we have traced thus far covers only those events that are related to chapters 1—39 of Isaiah. Chapters 40—66 are set against the background of the late exilic and early postexilic period. It remains for us to examine the events bearing upon these latter chapters in Isaiah. In so doing we shall avoid entering into a discussion of the unity and authorship of the book, since these problems will be dealt with in a later section of the introduction. Even those who subscribe to the view that Isaiah wrote the entire prophecy recognize that chapters 40—66 must be interpreted against the background of the Babylonian exile.

The death of Josiah in 609 B.C. marked the beginning of the end for Judah. Even though the last years of his reign witnessed the downfall of the mighty Assyrian Empire, Judah was not able to achieve peace and freedom. Instead she simply changed taskmasters, for the Babylonians quickly assumed the role formerly played by the Assyrians. In the end Judah learned that the new yoke was even heavier than the old.

Josiah was slain by the Egyptians at Megiddo when he apparently tried to prevent their marching northward to aid in the Assyrians' fight against the combined force of the Medes and Babylonians. His son Jehoahaz succeeded him but was removed from the throne and exiled to Egypt after a reign of only three months. A second son, Eliakim, was placed upon the throne as Pharaoh Neco's vassal, and his name was changed to Jehoiakim (609–598 B.C.). In 605 the Babylonians decisively defeated the Egyptians at Carchemish, thus ending Egypt's bid to control Palestine. Shortly thereafter Jehoiakim was forced to transfer his allegiance to Nebuchadnezzar and to become his vassal (cf. 2 Kings 24:1). In 601 B.C. Nebuchadnezzar was unsuccessful in his attempt to invade Egypt, and many of his vassals took advantage of his temporary setback to withhold their payment of tribute. Against the advice of the prophet Jeremiah, Jehoiakim joined the revolt. This was his fatal mistake, for the Babylonians launched a counterattack in 598 under the direction of Nebuchadnezzar himself. Jehoiakim died during the ensuing battle and was replaced by his son Jehoiachin. Within three months the city of Jerusalem had surrendered, and 3,000 of its citizens, including the king, the queen mother, and the city's leading officials, had been deported to Babylon. This was the first captivity.

Nebuchadnezzar left Zedekiah (597–587 B.C.) to rule over Judah. He immediately fell under the influence of a strong pro-Egyptian party that urged rebellion against Babylon on the strength of promised aid from Egypt. Jeremiah recognized the suicidal nature of this course of action and made a valiant but unsuccessful effort to stop it. The first captivity had deprived the land of its ablest statesmen, and Zedekiah was too weak to withstand the seductions of Egypt. The flag of revolt was raised in 589 when he withheld the annual tribute demanded by Babylon.

Retaliation came swiftly. The Babylonian army arrived early in 588 and quickly overran the land of Judah and laid seige to Jerusalem. Egypt's one attempt to aid the beseiged city was unsuccessful. After suffering unspeakable privation and hardship, the city was finally captured and destroyed in the fall of 587. Thousands more of her leading citizens were exiled to Babylon, where they joined the ranks of those of the first captivity.

Having captured Zedekiah, Nebuchadnezzar appointed Gedaliah to serve as governor of Judah. Gedaliah was a Jew of noble birth. His father Ahikam had once saved Jeremiah's life (Jer. 26:24), and his grandfather Shaphan was closely associated with the reforms of Josiah (2 Kings 22:3). The appointment of Gedaliah failed to bring peace to the land, however, for he was soon assassinated by a radical element that refused to accept defeat. After describing this futile and senseless assassination, the record breaks off, and we know virtually nothing of what happened in Judah during the next 50 years. A third deportation of Jews in 582 B.C. is reported in Jeremiah 52:30. This may have been in reprisal for the murder of Gedaliah, or it may have resulted from some further disorder.

Nebuchadnezzar ruled over the Babylonian Empire from 605 to 562 B.C. His death marked the beginning of the decline and fall of Babylon. His son and successor, Amel-marduk (562–560), known in the Old Testament as Evil-merodach, is remembered for having released Jehoiachin from prison (2 Kings 25:27–30). Amel-marduk was assassinated in a palace revolt, and his brother-in-law, Nergal-shar-usur, sometimes identified with the Babylonian officer Nergal-sharezer mentioned in Jeremiah 39:3,13, seized the throne. Nergal-shar-usur died four years later, leaving only a minor son, Labashi-marduk, to rule in his stead.

Nabonidus (556–539 B.C.) immediately took advantage of this situation and seized the throne. He was not a native of Babylon but came from Haran in northwest Mesopotamia, where his mother had been a priestess of the moon-god Sin. He is first mentioned in Babylonian records as an officer under Nebuchadnezzar in 585. For reasons that are not entirely clear, Nabonidus seized the oasis of Teima in the Arabian desert southeast of Edom and made it virtually his second capital. He retired to this desert fortress in 552 and remained there for some eight years, leaving affairs in Babylon in the hands of his son Bel-shar-usur, otherwise known in the Old Testament as Belshazzar (Dan. 5:1).

The prolonged absence of Nabonidus from Babylon caused deep resentment there, especially among the priests of Marduk, the patron god of the land. The king of Babylon was expected to "take the hands of Marduk" in the Babylonian New Year Festival, the annual rite celebrating Marduk's victory over the chaotic waters and acclaiming the renewal of his kingship. Nabonidus' absence from the city, therefore, was attributed to his deliberate neglect of Marduk in favor of the moon-god Sin. It was felt that if he could have had his way, he would have established Sin as the chief god in the Babylonian pantheon.

There is evidence that Nabonidus had alienated himself also from the Jews throughout his empire.[7] It appears that the

---

7 Cf. F. F. Bruce, *op. cit.,* p. 96.

fortunes of the Jewish exiles, who had hitherto enjoyed a large measure of freedom and prosperity, suffered a severe reversal during the latter part of his reign. His downfall, therefore, was hailed with equal joy by the Jews who wished to return to their homeland and by those who chose to remain in Babylon.

Early in his reign Nabonidus, fearful of the might of the Medes, had allied himself with the tiny kingdom of Anshan, also known as Persia. Until this time the Persians had been subject to the Medes, but now their ambitious young ruler, Cyrus II (558–530 B.C.), decided to revolt against his Median overlords. It was at this juncture that Nabonidus lent him his support. The revolt was so successful that by 550 Cyrus had not only defeated Astyages the king of Media but had also annexed the territory of the vast Median Empire. In so doing he laid the foundations of a new empire, the empire of the Medes and the Persians, which was to endure until the conquests of Alexander the Great.

The alliance between Cyrus and Nabonidus was dissolved as soon as Media ceased to be their common enemy. Nabonidus, now more fearful of Cyrus than he had been of the Medes, allied himself instead with Lydia and Egypt. Cyrus responded to this challenge by launching an attack against Lydia. Crossing the Halys in the winter of 546 B.C., he caught Croesus, the king of Lydia, completely by surprise, captured the capital at Sardis, and incorporated Lydia into his realm.

The news of Cyrus' victories electrified the subject peoples of the Babylonian Empire. His apparently irresistible progress raised the hope that he would conquer Babylon also and release them from their bondage. This hope was especially strong among the Jewish exiles, as evidenced in Isaiah 40—55, where Cyrus is hailed as one who "tramples kings under foot; he makes them like dust with his sword, like driven stubble with his bow" (41:2). He was called not only the Lord's shepherd (44:

28) but also his anointed (45:1), and his appointed mission was to restore Israel to its former glory. Emboldened by the previous conquests of Cyrus, the prophet confidently predicted that he would conquer Babylon also (48:14–15) and set Israel free (48:20).

All that the prophet foretold came to pass. Cyrus soon marshaled his forces for a final confrontation with Babylon. His task was made considerably easier by the internal dissent within the Babylonian Empire itself. Many Babylonians were, in fact, sympathetic with his cause, and the kingdom fell into his hands like a piece of overripe fruit. He was looked upon more nearly as a liberator than a conqueror.

Cyrus captured Babylon by a very clever piece of strategy. The Euphrates River flowed under the heavily fortified walls of the city. With the counsel and assistance of Gobryas, an officer of the Babylonian army who had deserted Nabonidus, Cyrus reduced the flow of the river above the city, thus enabling his troops to enter the city by way of the riverbed. His army completed the conquest of the city on October 13, 539 B.C.

It was the policy of Cyrus to treat conquered peoples with benevolent concern. Therefore, having conquered Babylon, he immediately restored to the other cities of the Babylonian Empire their gods, whom Nabonidus had brought to the capital. In addition, he appeased the priests of Babylon by "taking the hand of Marduk" in the Babylonian New Year Festival, a ceremony which also officially proclaimed him as the new king of Babylon.

Cyrus' victory over Babylon gave him title to the lands formerly ruled over by the Babylonians, which included Palestine. In 538 B.C., therefore, he issued his famous decree permitting Jewish exiles to return to their homeland and to rebuild their Temple (Ezra 1:1–11; 6:3–5). This act was in keeping with his policy of giving conquered peoples a large measure of local autonomy and religious freedom while retaining control over their political affairs. In the light of his humanitarian policies, it is easy to understand the glowing terms in which the author of Isaiah 40—55 speaks of him.

It would be a mistake for us to imagine that all of the Jews were eager to leave Babylon and return to Jerusalem. Many of the original captives had died and had been buried in the land of their exile, and a new generation had arisen which had no memory of the hill-country of their fathers. Furthermore, many of them had become relatively prosperous during the latter years of their exile and were not eager to give up their security for an uncertain future in the war-shattered land of Judah. They were willing to settle for easy success rather than risk great failure. This may explain why Isaiah 40—55 contains many urgent appeals to the exiles to forsake Babylon, coupled with an overoptimistic description of what the return to Jerusalem would be like (cf. 41:17-20; 48:20-21; 52:7-12; 55:1-13). We will never fully understand the author of these chapters unless we see him somewhat as a recruiting sergeant in the army of the Lord. His task was to persuade his fellow exiles to undertake the difficult but glorious journey back to Zion.

The Bible reports that Cyrus entrusted the task of rebuilding the Temple in Jerusalem to "Sheshbazzar the prince of Judah" (Ezra 1:7-11), whom many identify with Shenazzar the son of King Jehoiachin (or Jeconiah), mentioned in 1 Chronicles 3:18. This initial return probably took place in 537 B.C.

Sheshbazzar soon disappears from the account in Ezra, and his place is taken by Zerubbabel. Considerable confusion surrounds the relationship and identity of these two men. Both are given the title of governor (Ezra 5:14; Hag. 1:1), and both are credited with having initiated the work of rebuilding the Temple (Ezra 3:2-3, 8-11; 5:14-16).

The difficulty of correlating the activities of Sheshbazzar and Zerubbabel has led some historians to conclude that they are but two names for the same person. Another solution to the problem, that proposed by Bright,[8] is to suppose that the biblical historian has simply telescoped the careers of two different men so that they appear to be one. According to this interpretation, Sheshbazzar led a small group of exiles back to Jerusalem in 537 B.C., where, after an unsuccessful attempt to rebuild the Temple, he died. In the meantime Zerubbabel, the nephew of Sheshbazzar (cf. 1 Chron. 3:17-19; Hag. 1:1), arrived in Jerusalem with a larger contingent of exiles, perhaps in time to participate in the initial attempt to lay the foundations of the Temple. When Sheshbazzar died, he was succeeded as governor of the land by Zerubbabel. The work of rebuilding the Temple, having been delayed for approximately 18 years, was finally brought to completion under Zerubbabel's leadership in 515.

Many Old Testament scholars believe that the bulk of the material in Isaiah 56—66 is set against the background of the early postexilic period, i.e., between the first return under Sheshbazzar (537 B.C.) and the completion of the temple (515). Familiarity with the major events and movements outlined above will therefore enable us to interpret these chapters with greater understanding.

IV. Unity and Authorship

In attempting to examine the problem of the unity and authorship of Isaiah we are in no way calling into question the inspiration of any part of the book. Nor are we suggesting that the sections judged to be later than Isaiah contain less of the revealed truth of God. As a matter of fact, it is precisely in those chapters the authorship of which is most widely debated that we are led into the very heart of the Old Testament. Whoever the human author, or authors, may have been, this book, both in its entirety and in its various parts, belongs

8 John Bright, *op. cit.*, pp. 344-349.

to the enduring word of God (40:8).

When one turns from chapter 39 to chapter 40 of Isaiah he covers a time span of a century and a half. It is almost as if he had closed one book and opened another. He is ushered from the end of the eighth century into the middle of the sixth century B.C., and is transported from Jerusalem to Babylon.

One searches in vain for any further references to Isaiah in chapters 40—66. Catastrophic changes had taken place since he walked the streets of Jerusalem. The center of world power had shifted from Assyria to Babylon, and the exile which he predicted (39:5-8) had come to pass (40:2; 42:24-25; 47:6). Jerusalem now lay in ruins (44:26,28; 49:19; 51:17-20; 52:9; 60:10), and its Temple had been burned by fire (63:18; 64:10-11).

The dark night of exile was about to end, however, for God had raised up a new world conqueror who would soon break the power of Babylon and release the Jews from captivity. That man was Cyrus, hailed both as the Lord's shepherd (44:28) and his anointed (45:1). When Babylon had fallen, the liberated captives would march across the desert in a second great exodus (41:17-20; 43:1-7,14-21; 48:20-21; 45: 8-13; 55:12-13). The ransomed of the Lord would return to Zion with everlasting joy upon their heads, and sorrow and sighing would flee away (51:11). The watchmen on Jerusalem's walls would greet their return with shouts of joy, and waste places of the city would break forth into singing (52:8-9).

It has been suggested that a good rule of thumb for dating a biblical passage is to regard it as later than that which it presupposes but earlier than that which it predicts. Nowhere in chapters 40—66 is the Babylonian exile predicted; it is presupposed, and only the release from exile is predicted. Many therefore have concluded that chapters 40—66 were written much later than the eighth century and that they should be assigned to the disciples of Isaiah. The assigning of the chapters to the

prophet's disciples would account for the fact that although they are placed in an entirely different historical setting from that of the earlier chapters, they are, nevertheless, thoroughly Isaianic in spirit and character.

The distinction between Isaiah 1—39 and 40—66 is based not only upon arguments from history but also upon differences in language and style and in theological outlook. These differences were first noted in A.D. 1167, in a commentary by Rabbi Ibn Ezra which denied the Isaianic authorship of chapters 40—66. Over 600 years later a similar position was taken by two German scholars, Eichhorn in 1783, and Döderlein in 1789. They designated the unknown author of chapters 40—66 as "Deutero-Isaiah," or "Second Isaiah." The distinction between First Isaiah (chs. 1—39) and Second Isaiah (chs. 40—66) is almost universally accepted today.

In an epoch-making commentary published in 1892, Bernhard Duhm suggested that chapters 56—66 belonged to the last half of the fifth century B.C., and that they were written by a second anonymous author, whom he designated as Trito-Isaiah, or Third Isaiah. The weightiest argument against the unity of chapters 40—66 is the difference in historical setting between chapters 40—55 and 56—66. In the earlier section the Jews are in exile in Babylon; in the later section they are back in Jerusalem, struggling with the problems of the postexilic era.

The question here is how much of Isaiah 40—66 one can confidently assign to Second Isaiah. Since chapters 56—66 do not show the same internal unity as chapters 40—55, most scholars have abandoned the view that they were written by one author, whether Second Isaiah or Third Isaiah. The prevailing view at present is that chapters 56—66 should be dated in the early postexilic period—no earlier than 537 B.C. and no later than 445—and that they should be attributed to the disciples of Second Isaiah.

This position has not gone unchallenged.

Torrey [9] developed an elaborate theory of the unity of chapters 40—66, together with chapters 34—35, all of which he assigned to the late Persian period, although this involved deleting from the text all references to Cyrus and to Babylon.

Torrey's theory has been recently revived, although in a somewhat modified form, by James D. Smart.[10] Smart's position is that chapters 35 and 40—66 constitute a unity, that their author lived and worked in Palestine between 587 and 538 B.C., that he was concerned not simply with the release of a few Babylonian captives but with the ingathering of scattered Jews from all corners of the earth, and that all references to Cyrus and Babylon were later additions to his work.

Others also have argued for the unity of chapters 40—66, but without resorting to the extreme measures of Torrey and Smart. After carefully weighing the arguments based upon history, style, and theology, Francisco stated his position thus: "After a study of chs. 40—66 the writer of this thesis concluded that they were written by Deutero-Isaiah, chs. 40—56 in Babylonia and chs. 57—66 in Palestine after the return under Zerubbabel. . . . The necessity for a Trito-Isaiah is groundless, and all the allusions that Duhm said were applicable to the age of Nehemiah refer more consistently to the years 536–520 B.C. . . . Therefore, the writer takes the stand that Deutero-Isaiah wrote chs. 57—66 after he had returned with the exiles from Babylon and before the rebuilding of the Temple." [11]

More recently, Bright has expressed a similar view. Concerning chapters 56—66, he wrote: "The bulk of this material is best dated in the decades just after 538, with little of it much after ca. 515. . . . I feel that the chapters contain words of Second Isaiah spoken after the return, supplemented by utterances of disciples. The great prophet would surely have made the return—had he been able so much as to crawl!" [12]

Further doubts regarding the unity of chapters 40—55 have arisen as a result of the work of form critics. The prevailing form critical view for the past 50 years has been that these chapters consist of 50 or more originally independent oracles and poems which were first delivered orally and only later committed to writing. These small units, or pericopes, are said to stand in no perceptible logical relationship to one another. According to Sigmund Mowinckel,[13] one of the strongest proponents of this view, the only principle evident in the arrangement of these separate units is the catchword principle.

Recently there has been a reaction against reducing Second Isaiah to a series of isolated fragments. Both Muilenburg and McKenzie have argued that a basic unity underlies these chapters. McKenzie [14] maintains that there is a basic unity in Second Isaiah that makes it even more difficult to isolate separate sayings in it than in the earlier prophetic books. The individual oracles have been arranged "so that one flows into another." Muilenburg [15] believes that in its structure Second Isaiah gives evidence of "a fusion of literary types, a combination of several forms to make a whole." He has suggested that the units are often more extensive than has been generally supposed, and that what are construed to be independent poems are in reality strophes or subordinate units in longer poems.

To question the conclusions of form critics is not to deny the validity of their search for the literary types and forms in

[9] C. C. Torrey, The Second Isaiah (Edinburgh: T. & T. Clark, 1928).

[10] History and Theology in Second Isaiah (Philadelphia: The Westminster Press, 1965), pp. 10, 18 f., 30 ff., 102 ff., 115 ff.

[11] Clyde T. Francisco, "The Authorship and Unity of Isaiah 40—66," (Th.D. thesis, Southern Baptist Theological Seminary, 1944), p 192.

[12] John Bright, op. cit., p. 349 n.

[13] "Die Komposition des deuterojesajanischen Buches," Zeitschrift für die Alttestamentliche Wissenschaft, 49 (1931), pp. 87–112, 242–60.

[14] John L. McKenzie, Second Isaiah ("The Anchor Bible"), (Garden City: Doubleday & Company, 1968), pp. xxxi–xxxvii.

[15] James Muilenburg, The Interpreter's Bible, V, 384–386.

Second Isaiah. Some would reject the view that these chapters consist of many small units assembled by the later disciples of Second Isaiah in favor of the view that they constitute one carefully constructed poem arranged by the prophet himself in substantially the form in which we now have it. The true understanding of the literary form and structure of these chapters probably lies somewhere between these two extreme views.

While some scholars continue to debate the question of the unity and authorship of chapters 40—66, a small but outspoken minority would still defend the Isaianic authorship of all 66 chapters. The leading American spokesmen for this group of scholars have been Edward J. Young and Oswald T. Allis. Young has expressed his basic position in these words: "The prophet Isaiah himself was the author of the entire book; he himself committed it all to writing, and he was responsible for collecting his messages and placing them in the present book which bears his name." [16]

In support of this position, Young has pointed out that the entire book was ascribed to Isaiah at least as early as 180 B.C., as evidenced by the testimony of Ben Sirach in Ecclesiasticus 48:17-25. This has recently been confirmed by the discovery among the Dead Sea Scrolls of a complete manuscript of Isaiah which has been assigned to the second or first century B.C. This manuscript shows no evidence of a division between chapters 1—39 and 40—66.

In response to Young, others have noted that there is an apparent break in the Dead Sea Scroll of Isaiah between chapters 33 and 34. At the bottom of the leather sheet containing chapter 33 are three empty ruled lines, a phenomenon that occurs nowhere else in the Isaiah scroll.[17] Scholars have long contended that, in view of their marked similarity in style and content to chapters 40—66, chapters 34 and 35 should also be assigned to Second Isaiah. Furthermore, everyone recognizes that chapters 36—39 constitute a block of material borrowed and adapted from 2 Kings. It is more feasible, therefore, to expect a break after chapter 33 than after chapter 39. That is apparently what one encounters in the Isaiah scroll.

A second argument used in support of the theory of Isaianic authorship is the witness of the New Testament. Nine passages from Isaiah 40—66 are cited in the New Testament and attributed to the prophet Isaiah. This proves that the disciples of Jesus simply assumed that Isaiah was the author of the entire prophecy. Further evidence to substantiate this is found in John 12:38-41, which quotes from Isaiah 53:1, and Isaiah 6:10, and attributes both to the prophet Isaiah. There are devout scholars who sincerely believe that the testimony of the New Testament writers settles the question of authorship once and for all. They, therefore, view the suggestion that someone else wrote chapters 40—66 as an attack upon the inerrancy of the Bible.

It may be said in response to this argument, however, that it was never intended that the New Testament should become a primer of biblical criticism. Even if Jesus had believed in a "Second Isaiah," it is doubtful that he would have attempted to enlighten his disciples on this subject. He revealed to them all that was necessary for their spiritual growth, but he did not make them omniscient. It was natural that they should regard Isaiah as the author of the entire prophecy, for this was the view shared by all of their contemporaries. As Francisco [18] has noted, the discovery of a Deutero-Isaiah awaited a later date. The New Testament references to Isaiah, therefore, should not be used as evidence either for or against Isaianic authorship.

A further argument used to support the view that Isaiah wrote the entire prophecy is the remarkable similarity in vocabulary

16 Edward J. Young, The Book of Isaiah ("The New International Commentary on the Old Testament," Vol. I, [Grand Rapids: Wm. B. Eerdmans Publishing Co., 1965]), p. 8; idem, Who Wrote Isaiah? (Grand Rapids: Wm. B. Eerdmans Publishing Co., 1958).

17 Cf. Millar Burrows, ed., The Dead Sea Scrolls of St. Mark's Monastery, I (New Haven: American School of Oriental Research, 1950), plate XXVII.

18 Clyde T. Francisco, op. cit., p. 84.

between chapters 1—39 and 40—66. For example, God is called "the Holy One of Israel" 12 times in the first section and 14 times in the second, though the title appears only five or six times in the rest of the Bible. Another example is the use of Rahab as a designation for Egypt, which occurs both in 30:7 and in 51:9. There are other examples that could be cited.

Those responding to this argument readily admit that there are similarities between the vocabulary of chapters 1—39 and 40—66. They hasten to add, however, that there are also impressive differences between the style and vocabulary of the two sections. The theory of Isaianic authorship could account for the similarities but not for the differences. Only the theory that there was a Second Isaiah, a later disciple of Isaiah who was thoroughly familiar with his master's style and vocabulary, could account for both the differences and the similarities.

A final argument used in favor of Isaianic authorship of chapters 40—66 is that it seems highly improbable that the author of such a great work should have remained unknown. This argument is not so formidable as it might seem, however, for there are many reasons why a prophet of the Exile might have wished to conceal his identity. Since he prophesied the downfall of Babylon and the release of the Jewish captives, he may have feared to make himself known to the Babylonian officials. He also spoke of his fellow exiles as being blind and deaf (42:18–20), so he may have suffered persecution from his own people. Or it may be that he simply did not want to identify himself, preferring instead to remain "a voice crying in the wilderness."

Green, who prefers to speak of the book of Isaiah as an anthology, makes this significant observation: "The thing that really matters about any book in the Bible is not who wrote it but whether the voice of God is heard in it. Authorship and date are significant but not central. Is it the word of the living God? This is paramount. As far as I am concerned, there is no doubt concerning the answer with regard to the inspired prophecy of Isaiah." [19]

In summary, let it be noted that there is evidence that suggests that the book of Isaiah was composed of a collection of materials ranging from the eighth to the sixth century B.C. The formation of the book began with Isaiah of Jerusalem and was continued by his disciples, of whom the greatest was Second Isaiah. As later disciples collected, edited, and expanded Isaiah's materials, they were confident that they were speaking not only in his name but also in his spirit. It was this living stream of tradition that gave the book its inner unity and cohesion.

V. The Servant of the Lord in Isaiah 40—55

The full expression "the servant of the Lord" occurs only once in Isaiah 40—55, namely in 42:19, where it unquestionably refers to Israel. Elsewhere in the Old Testament it occurs a total of 19 times, not counting two references to David as the servant of the Lord in the titles to Psalms 18 and 36. Of the 19 occurrences, 17 refer to Moses and two to Joshua. Moses is referred to also as "the servant of God" in four Old Testament passages.

The shorter expressions "my servant" and "his servant" are found with much greater frequency throughout the Old Testament. Like the expression, "the servant of the Lord," they also describe those who in some special sense are God's servants. In all cases except one, the reference to Nebuchadnezzar king of Babylon (Jer. 25:9; 27:6; 43:10), these expressions are applied only to Israelites.

The term "my servant" appears 14 times in Isaiah 40—55 (41:8,9; 42:1,19; 43:10; 44:1,2,21 [twice]; 45:4; 49:3,6; 52:13; 53:11), while "his servant" is found four times (44:26; 48:20; 49:5; 50:10). The only occurrence of either of these terms in chapters 56—66 is in 63:11, where Moses is mentioned as "his servant." On the other hand, chapters 56—66 frequently employ the plural form "servants" to designate the

19 James Leo Green, God Reigns (Nashville: Broadman Press, 1968), p. 10.

people of God (56:6; 63:17; 65:9,13,14, 15; 66:14). The sole occurrence of this form in chapters 40—55 is in 54:17.

An examination of all of the Old Testament references will reveal that the individuals most frequently designated as the Lord's servants are Abraham, Jacob, Moses, and David. This fact alone should warn us against interpreting this term in a servile sense only. In Old Testament times one of the highest officials in the land was one known as "the servant of the king." He was a trusted friend appointed by the king to administer his affairs and to serve as his personal representative. In like manner, for one to be called "the servant of the Lord" meant that he had been elevated to a place of honor and responsibility. For the nation Israel to be so designated meant that God had chosen Israel from among all nations to be his own special possession (cf. 41:8-10).

One of the most influential though controversial commentaries on Isaiah is that written by Bernhard Duhm and published in 1892.[20] Besides dividing chapters 40—66 into a Deutero- and a Trito-Isaiah, Duhm also isolated four poems from the rest of Isaiah 40—55, and labeled them "Servant Songs." They are 42:1-4; 49:1-6; 50:4-9; and 52:13—53:12. Duhm noted a marked contrast between the character and mission of the individual servant depicted in the songs and that of the servant Israel as depicted elsewhere in chapters 40—55. From this he concluded that the songs were written by someone other than Second Isaiah, and only later incorporated into the text of Second Isaiah. They were seen somewhat as freestanding columns, unrelated to the contexts in which they stood. Duhm identified the servant of the four songs as a leprous Jewish rabbi who became the agent of God's redemption through suffering and death.

Duhm's work paved the way for an avalanche of literature on this subject. The existence of the four Servant Songs has come to be accepted as one of the proven results of biblical criticism. Scholarly opinion differs widely, however, on such matters as authorship of the songs, the extent of the songs in the text, the relationship of the songs to their context and to one another, the identity of the servant, and the nature of his mission.

Was Second Isaiah the author of these songs, or were they written by someone else? Those who attribute them to another author do so on the grounds that they are unrelated to the context and that the concept of the servant which they embody contrasts sharply with that of the servant outside the songs. Many scholars feel that the differences in vocabulary, style, and theology between the Servant Songs and the remainder of Second Isaiah demand a theory of dual authorship.

A careful examination of these arguments has been made by North.[21] He examines Gressmann's view that Second Isaiah consists of a series of independent short oracles, a view now widely accepted by Old Testament scholars, and concludes that the acceptance of such a view diminishes the force of the argument that the songs are unrelated to their context. If there is no basic unity in chapters 40—66, then the songs are no more an interruption of the context in which they stand than are the many other independent oracles that make up Second Isaiah. They represent but one of the many recurring themes that characterize the work of this prophet.

Regarding the alleged differences in style and vocabulary between the songs and the remainder of Second Isaiah, North concludes that these are outweighed by the close similarities. After a detailed exami-

[20] Concerning the influence of Duhm's work, one scholar has written: "Duhm is still important after seventy years because of the fact that his theories have dominated the interpretation of Second Isaiah for three quarters of a century, most existing commentaries in English and German being largely variations upon Duhm." James D. Smart, op. cit., p. 10.

[21] Christopher R. North, The Suffering Servant in Deutero-Isaiah (London: Oxford University Press, 1948), pp. 156-191. Cf. Hugo Gressmann, "Die literarische Analyze Deuterojesajas," Zeitschrift für die Alttestamentliche Wissenschaft, 34 (1914), pp. 254-297.

nation of the language, style, and metrical forms of the songs, he affirms that these "are not only consistent with, but actually point to, common authorship with the main body of Deutero-Isaiah." [22]

Of far greater significance is the sharp contrast between the portrait of the servant of the Lord in the songs and the portrait of the servant Israel outside the songs. It is difficult to avoid the conclusion that the servant within the songs is described as an individual, whereas the servant passages outside the songs refer to Jacob/Israel. Furthermore, the servant of the Lord and the servant Israel are basically different in their character and in the nature of their mission. The servant Israel is despondent and fainthearted and must be admonished again and again to trust in God (40:27–31; 41:8–10,14–16; 42:18–19; etc.); the servant of the Lord, on the other hand, trusts implicitly in the God of his salvation (50:7–9). The servant Israel is sinful and has been severely punished for his sins (40:1–2; 42:22–25; 43:22–28; 47:6; 50:1; 54:4–8); the servant of the Lord, while innocent of any guilt of his own, has had to suffer for the sins of others (50:5–6; 53:4–6,9,11–12). The servant of the Lord suffers patiently (53:7); the servant Israel bitterly complains against the discomforts of the exile (40:27; 49:14; 50:1–2). Finally, the servant of the Lord performs a ministry not only on behalf of the nations but also on behalf of Israel (49:5–6); the servant Israel is most aptly described not as one who ministers but as one who is ministered unto.

Recognition of the differences between the two portraits of the servant does not necessarily imply acceptance of the theory of dual authorship. The same author could conceivably have written about two servants, thus pursuing in the four Servant Songs a religious insight differing in scope and character from anything else found in chapters 40—55. The differences between the songs and their context may perhaps

be an indication that they were written later than the rest of the prophecy. The progression of thought within the songs themselves, coming to a climax in the fourth song (52:13—53:12), suggests that the prophet may have only gradually apprehended the truth with which he was confronted and may have written the songs over a considerable period of time.

There is also the possibility that the songs are more closely related to the context than most scholars have been willing to concede. Muilenburg, in particular, has argued that the songs are an integral part of the whole sweep of Deutero-Isaiah. They fit naturally into the framework of the surrounding chapters, and their removal would create more problems than it would solve. Even McKenzie,[23] who adopts the position that the songs are not related to the context, has to recognize that there is a close relationship between the first three and the responses which follow them (42:5–9; 49:7–13; 50:10–11). Of course, he would attribute not only the songs but also the responses to someone other than Second Isaiah. This seems to be begging the question, however, and even he is frank to admit that his opinion is "ultimately a critical judgment based on subjective taste."

It is safe to say that no other problem related to Old Testament study has been so widely discussed as that of the servant's identity. The discussions, however, have not led to any consensus among scholars. The field may be divided roughly between those who hold to an individual interpretation and those who advocate a collective interpretation.

Those who belong to the first group insist that the figure of the servant as presented in the four Servant Songs is so highly individualized that a collective interpretation is out of the question. Attention is called to the sharp contrast between the servant and Israel in Isaiah 49:5–6, where the servant ministers to the nation but is distinct from it. Further support for this

---

[22] Ibid., p. 178.

[23] John L. McKenzie, op. cit., pp xxxix–xlii.

interpretation is furnished by the fourth song (52:13—53:12), where the treatment is entirely individualistic.

The individual interpretation has recently gained unexpected support from Jewish scholars. Morgenstern [24] sees the servant as an individual of Davidic descent—perhaps a son of Zerubbabel—who suffered martyrdom in an unsuccessful revolt against the Persians about 486 B.C. In spite of the fact that the name Israel is once applied to the servant (49:3), this scholar rejects the notion that the servant of the Lord is to be identified with the people Israel.

In a more recent work, Orlinsky [25] has stated that "Israel cannot be the central personage in Isaiah 53." He reviews the evidence that the central figure in this chapter is rather an individual who did not complain even though he had to endure suffering and humiliation. Then he points out that all of this came upon the servant through no guilt or transgression of his own. Orlinsky concludes that the affirmation of the sufferer's innocence alone excludes the people Israel from further consideration. He quotes with approval the observation of Smart: "Would any prophet of Israel worthy of the name make the statement that Israel 'had done no violence, nor was any deceit in his mouth?' . . . The writer of Isa. 40—66 was under no such delusions about his people. He reminds them of sins of the past, and assails them for sins of the present . . ." Orlinsky's conclusion is that the servant is not to be identified as the people of Israel nor as King Cyrus, but as Second Isaiah himself.

As our discussion has already shown, those who hold to the individual interpretation are still faced with the thorny problem of deciding which individual the

[24] Julian Morgenstern, "The Suffering Servant—A New Solution," Vetus Testamentum, XI (1961), 425–431.

[25] Harry M. Orlinsky, "The So-Called 'Servant of the Lord' and 'Suffering Servant' in Second Isaiah," Studies on the Second Part of the Book of Isaiah, Supplements to Vetus Testamentum, XIV (Leiden: E. J. Brill, 1967), 17–51.

prophet had in mind when he wrote those songs. "About whom, pray, does the prophet say this, about himself or about some one else?" The question of the Ethiopian eunuch, addressed to Philip and recorded in Acts 8:34, expresses the perplexity that many readers have felt when confronted with this problem.

Before the beginning of modern biblical criticism, Christian writers were almost unanimous in interpreting the Servant Songs, especially Isaiah 53, as messianic prophecies. In the pre-Christian era, as Muilenburg has noted, the rabbis also identified the servant with the Messiah, though in so doing they eliminated all references to his suffering. Controversy with the early Christians caused them to abandon this interpretation and to adopt the view that the servant was the nation Israel.

If by "Messiah" is meant a descendant of David who would reestablish the Davidic kingdom and dynasty as the concrete realization of God's rule on earth (cf. 9:1–6; 11:1–9; Jer. 23:5–6; Mic. 5:2–4), then one must ask if the songs are indeed messianic. In other words, is the servant of the songs presented as a royal figure, or is the model for his life and ministry derived from another source?

There are some scholars who would seek support for the messianic interpretation by drawing an analogy between the Suffering Servant and the part played by the Babylonian king in the annual New Year festival. They see in the servant the features of the divine king as he appears in the royal psalms and elsewhere in the Old Testament. On the basis of such passages as Psalms 2; 18; 89; and 118:5 ff., Aubrey R. Johnson concludes: "The Davidic king is the Servant of Jahweh; but . . . at the New Year Festival he is the suffering Servant. He is the Messiah of Jahweh; but on this occasion he is the humiliated Messiah. The fact is that we are here dealing with a ritual humiliation of the Davidic king which in principle is not unlike that suffered by the Babylonian king in the analogous New Year

Festival." [26] The celebration of the Babylonian New Year Festival centered around the ritual recital and reenactment of the death and resurrection of the god of vegetation, and involved the ritual humiliation of the ruling king, who played the role of the dying and rising god.

Johnson's analogy seems to be based on the most tenuous kind of evidence. Since the author of Isaiah 40—55 was so hostile to Babylonian religion, it is highly unlikely that he would borrow a theme directly from the Babylonian New Year Festival. Furthermore, there is no conclusive proof that such a festival was ever celebrated in Israel. If this is the only basis for the argument that the servant is a royal figure, then it appears to be a rather nebulous argument.

Rowley seems to be much nearer the truth when he states that there is no serious evidence that the concepts of the Suffering Servant and the Davidic Messiah were merged before the Christian era. On the contrary, there is tangible and positive evidence in the New Testament which refutes such a view. Concerning this evidence he writes: "The Gospels tell us that the disciples were always confused and bewildered when Jesus spoke of His mission in terms of suffering. They were thinking in terms of the Davidic Messiah, and it is clear that they did not bring the idea of suffering and death into relation with that concept. . . . It is equally clear that the disciples knew nothing of any equation of the terms Son of Man and Suffering Servant, since though Jesus is said to have spoken of Himself as Son of Man from the outset of His ministry, at its end they were completely unprepared for the idea of His suffering." [27]

The conclusion which the evidence seems to dictate is that the Suffering Servant and the Davidic Messiah were two entirely separate concepts within the Old Testament

itself, and that they were first brought together in the teachings of Jesus as he expressed his own self-understanding. We must not identify the servant with the Messiah, unless we are prepared to define the latter in a sense that is alien to the rest of the Old Testament. The only other alternative would be to delete from the portrait of the servant all references to his suffering and humiliation, which is what ancient Judaism chose to do. From the Jewish point of view, a suffering Messiah was a contradiction in terms, so that the preaching of Christ (Messiah) crucified became to the Jews "a stumbling block" (1 Cor. 1:23).

The question we are seeking to answer is whether or not the prophet and those who first listened to him understood the servant to be a royal or messianic figure. To answer this question in the negative is not to deny that the early Christian community identified Jesus as both servant and Messiah, or that this identification went back to Jesus himself. Mowinckel has expressed the view that the Servant Songs, like so many other Old Testament prophecies, are only indirectly Christological. Concerning the manner in which the church has always seen their true fulfillment in Jesus Christ, he writes: "In Jesus Christ they are fulfilled in a way beyond anything the prophet ever imagined. It is a *new* fulfillment that comes to pass. God creates something new, a new reality, which fulfills the prophecy in a higher sense than that of which the prophets and their contemporaries were aware. God, who inspired their thought and expression, saw farther than they did; but this can be realized only when the higher fulfillment has come. In its light we can then see that God's thoughts were higher than those of the prophets." [28]

In addition to those who favor a messianic interpretation, there are other individualists who would identify the servant with some historical figure of the past. Al-

[26] Aubrey R. Johnson, "The Role of the King in the Jerusalem Cultus," *The Labyrinth*, ed. S. H. Hooke (London: S.P.C.K., 1935), p. 100.

[27] H. H. Rowley, *The Servant of the Lord*, 2nd ed., rev. (Oxford: Basil Blackwell, 1965), pp. 84—85.

[28] S. Mowinckel, *He That Cometh*, trans. G. W. Anderson (Nashville: Abingdon Press, 1954), p. 247.

most every conceivable candidate had been nominated for this honor at one time or another. One scholar, Ernst Sellin, changed his mind no less than four times, advocating in succession Zerubbabel (1898), Jehoiachin (1901), Moses (1922), and finally Second Isaiah himself (1930). Other names suggested include Hezekiah, Uzziah, Jeremiah, Cyrus, Eleazar, Ezekiel, Meshullam the son of Zerubbabel, and an anonymous martyr from the time of the Maccabees.

It can be said that these attempts to identify the servant have only resulted in greater chaos and confusion. North has aptly observed that most of these theories have either been abandoned by, or have died with, their authors. They are "curiosities in the museum of exegesis," rather than permanent contributions to the solution of the problem. Furthermore, nothing is gained by suggesting, as some have done, that the servant is to be variously identified in the different songs, that he is one person in one song and another in another. No single individual can be found, prior to Christ, who fits the description of the servant in any of the Servant Songs.

Most Old Testament scholars, Christian as well as Jewish, have rejected the individual approach to the identity of the servant. They favor the view that the servant is a collective entity and is to be identified with Israel. This theory, too, has taken many different forms, the servant being identified as real Israel, ideal Israel, a faithful core within Israel, the company of the prophets, or a combination of these various elements.

The collective interpretation is based primarily upon the fact that in the larger context of chapters 40—55 Israel is repeatedly referred to as the servant of the Lord. The servant is also identified as Israel in one of the Servant Songs (49:3), and there is no reason to doubt the genuineness of this reading. As a rule, therefore, those who support the collective interpretation insist upon the unity of the Servant Songs with the larger context in which they stand.

One of those who protests most strongly

against the isolation of the Servant Songs from the rest of Deutero-Isaiah is N. H. Snaith. He writes: "There are no Servant songs in any exclusive sense. . . . If there are no distinct and separate Servant-songs, then the Servant of the so-called Songs is the Servant of the rest of the book. Who then is the Servant of the LORD? . . . Our proposition is therefore: The Servant of the LORD is primarily the 597 exiles, but gradually it tends to widen in conception to include all the Babylonian exiles." [29]

Muilenburg also defends the collective interpretation of the servant in his commentary on Isaiah 40—66. He lists the points of similarity between the Servant Songs and the rest of Second Isaiah and concludes by saying that "if the servant songs are the work of Second Isaiah and an integral part of his poetic compositions, then the servant of the Lord is certainly Israel." [30] In response to those who say that the characterization of the servant is so personal and concrete that reference to a community is unlikely, Muilenburg affirms that Orientals do not speak about a community as we do, as the Old Testament itself bears witness. Thus in Second Isaiah, Israel is constantly addressed by the second person singular pronoun, "you." One also encounters heightened individualization outside the Servant Songs in such passages as 44:1–4; 46:3–4; 47:1–3,5,7,8; and 54:1–8.

It is further claimed that the mission of Israel and the servant is one and the same; both have been called to be a light to the nations and to proclaim the law, or revelation, of God to the ends of the earth. Both must suffer in the accomplishment of their mission. Temporary discouragement overtakes both, but in the end both are crowned with victory and everlasting joy. Even if the collective interpretation is applied to the fourth song (52:13—53:12), the death and resurrection of Israel may be explained in

---

[29] N. H. Snaith, "Isaiah 40—66, A Study of the Teaching of the Second Isaiah and its Consequences," *Studies on the Second Part of the Book of Isaiah, Supplements to Vetus Testamentum*, XIV (Leiden: E. J. Brill, 1967), 169–170, 175.

[30] James Muilenburg, *op. cit.*, p. 408.

the light of Ezekiel's vision of the valley of dry bones (Ezek. 37:1–14).

However there are some rather formidable objections to the collective view. In the first place, the servant of the songs is described in highly individualistic terms: he is anointed with the Spirit of God (42:1); he is called from the womb of his mother (49:1); he gives his back to the smiters and his cheeks to those who pull out the beard (50:6); his grave is with the wicked (53:9). Even those scholars who identify the servant with Israel are forced to admit that the servant is presented as if he were an individual. Thus Lindblom writes: "The servant of the Songs is thought of as an individual (I belong decidedly to 'the individualists' among the students of this problem, not to 'the collectivists'), but he symbolizes allegorically a community, namely Israel." [31]

Another serious objection to the collective view is the contrast that is drawn between the servant and Israel in 49:5–6. If the servant is Israel, then we are presented with the strange prospect of Israel being sent on a mission to Israel. Even Muilenburg, who favors the collective interpretation, has to admit that this passage constitutes "the strongest argument for the individualistic interpretation."

A final objection to the collective view is one that has already been alluded to, namely, that Second Isaiah does not view the sufferings of Israel as due to the sins of others but rather as the result of God's righteous judgment upon her own rebellion and apostasy. How could the same author have written Isaiah 42:24–25 and Isaiah 53:7–9, if they are both to be interpreted as referring to Israel? Those who would deny that Second Isaiah wrote the Servant Songs are simply attempting to evade the issue. The contrast between the servant within the poems and outside the poems cannot be ignored, however, and in reality it constitutes the Achilles' heel of the collective interpretation.

[31] Joh. Lindblom, *The Servant Songs in Deutero-Isaiah* (Lund: C. W. K. Gleerup, 1951), p. 103.

In recent years another theory which tends to ease the tension between the individual and collective interpretations has been put forward. Its origin and development are associated primarily with Pedersen, Eissfeldt, Wheeler Robinson, and Rowley. It is based upon the concept of "corporate personality," according to which a group, viewed as a continuing entity, might function as a single individual through any representative member of the group. Thus the servant may be viewed both as an individual representing the nation and as the nation whose proper mission is actually being fulfilled only through the servant. Because of their inclusive nature, these theories are described by Rowley as "fluid theories."

In the light of this approach, we are free to recognize that there are some features in the Servant Songs which clearly suggest that the servant stands for the nation Israel, while there are other features which just as clearly indicate that he is an individual. The "corporate personality" theory is an attempt to harmonize these seemingly contradictory features. Thus it has been said of Wheeler Robinson that while up to a point he is to be classed with the collective theorists, he is also to be classed with the individualists.

Although such a theory may tend to relieve the tension between the collective and individual interpretations, it does not alter the fact that the preponderance of the evidence seems to be on the side of the individual interpretation. This is the position that will be advocated in this commentary.

Who, then, is the servant of the Servant Songs, if he is neither Second Isaiah, nor the Messiah of Jewish expectation, nor a historical individual from the past, nor a personification of Israel? The very fact that he shares some traits with all of these makes it even more difficult to identify him. For example, he, like Second Isaiah, is a prophetic figure, and the model for his life and ministry is that of prophet rather than king. However, like the Messiah, he is an eschatological figure whose appearing signals the consummation of the ages. Moreover, like Israel he is called and chosen to be a light to the nations and to mediate the knowledge of God to the ends of the earth. But while he resembles all of these, he is not to be equated with any one of them.

In the final analysis the servant must be viewed as one who is *sui generis,* and thus unlike any other figure portrayed elsewhere in the Old Testament. In his vision of the servant, Second Isaiah saw what no one before him had ever seen. The figure he envisioned was far more than merely the extension and culmination of a concept already present in the Old Testament, whether it be that of Israel, or of the messianic king, or of the prophets. By means of the servant figure an entirely new dimension was added to the eschatological outlook of the Old Testament. From this time forward Israel could look for the appearing of a radically different kind of leader, one whose mission would be soteriological rather than political.

The pattern of the servant was admirably suited to the life and ministry of Jesus, for he consistently described his messiahship in soteriological rather than political terms. He steadfastly refused to be the kind of Messiah that Israel wanted him to be. Instead he chose the concept of the servant as the appropriate model for what he had come to be and to do. In him, therefore, two Old Testament streams flowed together and became one. If Israel had only had eyes to see, she would have beheld one who was both Messiah and Suffering Servant. It was surely no accident that he was proclaimed king upon a cross. He not only saw his way by the light that these songs shed upon his path, but in him also the intention of the Author of all Scripture reached its ultimate fulfillment.

Referring to the prophet's initial vision of the servant, Smart has written: "He did not know how perfectly his words would one day describe the crucial event of all history when another and greater Servant would make himself an offering for sin and by his obedience break the power of evil over mankind, establishing God's rule on earth and bringing God's forgiveness, peace, and healing to the door of every man." [32]

VI. The Message of the Book of Isaiah

If there is any validity to the claim that the book of Isaiah consists of three separate but related units of material written over a time span of approximately two centuries, then it becomes necessary to examine the message of each of these units separately. We will, therefore, review in order the teachings of chapters 1—39, of 40—55, and of 56—66.

1. The Message of Chapters 1—39

It is in these chapters that we encounter the words of Isaiah the son of Amoz. He was a prophet of such challenge and stern demand that one commentator has written of him: "If you hear him you grow confused because he upsets your notions, if you go with him you run into trouble because you are pushing against the crowd, if you deny him you feel guilty because you know he is right." [33]

Isaiah made many important contributions to the religion of Israel. In a remarkable way most of the emphases of his theology are already present in an abbreviated form in the account of his call. Chapter 6, therefore, has been appropriately referred to as his "most revealing page." Through this experience he came to a new understanding of the concepts of holiness, sin, judgment, repentance, forgiveness, faith, and the remnant. This does not mean, of course, that one may expect to find here or elsewhere in Isaiah a treatise on systematic theology. The prophets were not systematic theologians, nor even systematic thinkers. They were rather proclaimers of a divine word that was sent to them as the situation demanded.

Through this first episode in his long prophetic career Isaiah came to a new

[32] James D. Smart, *op. cit.,* p. 206.
[33] Sheldon H. Blank, *Prophetic Faith in Isaiah* (New York: Harper & Brothers, 1958), p. 1.

understanding of the holiness of God. It is no exaggeration to say that as a result of this experience a new dimension was added to the Old Testament concept of holiness. Prior to this men had thought of God's holiness in terms of his "otherness,"—that is, his transcendent exaltation above all things created. The root meaning of holiness is separation, and to say that God was holy meant first of all that he was God and not man (cf. Hos. 11:9). Isaiah saw a new vision of the holiness of God as it was proclaimed in the cry of the winged seraphim (6:1–3). As he stood in the awesome presence of the thrice-holy God, he was not so much aware of his creatureliness as of his defilement. He was terrified not because he was a man, but because he was a *sinful* man. "Woe is me," he cried, "for I am a man of unclean lips." Here holiness had acquired a moral significance that it had not had before. God's holiness was thus understood to be his perfect moral purity, in combination with his transcendent exaltation. Henceforth, Isaiah's favorite designation for God would be "the Holy One of Israel," a title which appears some thirty times throughout the book.

New insight into the meaning of holiness brought new insight also into the meaning of sin and judgment. No prophet spoke out more fearlessly than Isaiah against the pride of Judah, her selfish indulgence, and her callous injustice toward the poor. He was convinced that her hour of judgment had come. Her reliance upon sacrifices and the externals of religion did not remedy the situation but only made matters worse. Isaiah believed that judgment was close at hand and that it would come in the form of an invasion by the armies of Assyria.

This brings us to another important aspect of the prophet's teaching: the belief that God was directing all history in accordance with his purpose of establishing his rule on earth. The classic statement of this belief is in chapter 10, which belongs to the time of the invasion of Palestine in 701 B.C., when the Assyrians had reached the zenith of their power and seemed to be invincible. They were possessed of an attitude of arrogant self-sufficiency which Kilpatrick has described as "the atheism of force." Out of the Assyrian crisis Isaiah developed the rudiments of a philosophy of history, for he came to see that one and the same nation could be both an instrument of God's purpose and a rebel against God. Assyria, therefore, was but the rod with which Israel was being chastened, and when the chastening was over, the pride of Assyria would also be punished. Here then was the key to the inner meaning of history: it was not governed by caprice or by the nation with the largest battalions but was firmly under the control of the Holy One of Israel, with the final outcome never in doubt.

Isaiah was the first of the Hebrew prophets to present faith in God as a central religious demand. One writer has even ventured to suggest that it was he who coined the biblical concept of faith.[34] In every crisis in the political life of his people he counseled faith in God as the only alternative to frustration and defeat. He strongly opposed reliance upon military might, or diplomacy, or political alliances. This explains why he reacted as he did to the crises of 735 and 701 B.C. His advice to Ahaz and later to Hezekiah was that neither the strengthening of their defenses nor the forging of military alliances would afford national security. This could be achieved only through a resolute faith in God alone (cf. 7:4, 9; 28:16; 30:15). Isaiah believed that such a faith would make it possible for the Lord to intervene on behalf of his distressed people. The prophet, therefore, was not opposed to human effort as such, but rather to the attitude in which human effort was being undertaken. Feverish activity and anxiety over the defenses of Jerusalem, together with the endless appeals to foreign powers for help, indicated an attitude of arrogant unbelief. Judah's kings were guilty of setting

---

34 Cf. Claus Westermann, *A Thousand Years and a Day*, trans. Stanley Rudman (Philadelphia: Fortress Press, 1962), pp. 222 f.

the power of man above the power of God.

Another salient point in the message of Isaiah is his doctrine of the remnant. This doctrine must have taken shape early in his ministry, perhaps as early as his call, although the last clause in Isaiah 6:13—"The holy seed is its stump"—is not present in the Septuagint. Certainly by the time of the birth of his first son he had formulated the rudiments of this doctrine, for he named his son Shear-jashub, meaning "a remnant will return." At first his name seems to have had a sinister import, suggestive of the fact that *only* a remnant would survive the coming judgment (cf. 6:13; 10:22–23). Later, however, it became the vehicle whereby the prophet expressed his confidence that the nation would never be utterly destroyed or the divine promises withdrawn. A remnant, cleansed in the fires of judgment, would inherit the ancient promises. (cf. 10:20–21; 11:11,16). Isaiah's doctrine of the remnant gave a basic optimism to his ministry, without compromising his message of inevitable judgment against wickedness. The doctrine was of tremendous significance in the subsequent history both of Judaism and of Christianity.

A final emphasis in the preaching of Isaiah remains to be considered: his contribution to the development of the messianic hope of the Old Testament. He was one of the first of the prophets to proclaim the coming of a personal Messiah [35] and the advent of an ideal age of righteousness and peace. Bewer would assign the messianic passages in Isaiah to the latter part of the prophet's ministry, that is, to the final period of semi-retirement after 701 B.C., when the aged prophet "increasingly looked with longing to the future. In poems of immortal appeal he told his disciples of the time when wars would be no more and

the ideal age would begin, with an ideal king and true officials in a world of righteousness and universal peace (9:1–7; 11:1–9; 32:1–8,15–18,20; 2:1–4)." [36]

Isaiah's messianic expectation was born largely of his intense anguish of soul when Ahaz (cf. 7:10–13; 8:5–8) and, to a lesser extent, Hezekiah (cf. ch. 39) proved to be faithless rulers. In the familiar trilogy of prophecies found in chapters 1—12, Isaiah speaks of Messiah's birth (7:14), his accession to the throne (9:2–7), and his righteous rule (11:1–9). The overriding impression which emerges from a study of these passages is that the prophet fully expected these things to come to pass in his own day and age. He had no way of knowing that their fulfillment would be postponed for another seven centuries. When in the fullness of time the Messiah did come, the glories of his kingdom far exceeded even the fondest expectations of the prophet.

In summarizing the contributions of Isaiah to the religion of Israel, Fleming James has written these memorable words: "To the modern Christian Isaiah makes a unique appeal. The majestic impetuosity and piercing beauty of his diction, his brilliant, ever-changing word pictures, his trumpet-peal of faith, his ringing challenges, his inexorable demands, his white-hot purity, his scorn of all base things, his championing of the poor, his tender assurances, his clear vision of the Messianic age to be, are to be found in their clustered brightness nowhere else in the Bible." [37]

2. The Message of Chapters 40—55

The author of chapters 40—55 was the poet laureate of the Old Testament. His poetic oracles have been described as "the distilled essence of language" . . . "the noblest literary monument bequeathed to us from Semitic antiquity" . . . "the heart

---

[35] Messiah is here understood to mean a descendant of David who would reestablish the Davidic kingdom and dynasty as the concrete realization of God's rule on earth. While it is true that the term Messiah, or Anointed One, is never used in the Old Testament to designate such a king, the concept is nevertheless present in a number of passages (cf. 7:14; 9:1–6; 11:1–9; Jer. 23:5–6; Mic. 5:2–4).

[36] Julius A. Bewer, *The Prophets* (New York: Harper & Brothers Publishers, 1955), p. 12.

[37] Fleming James, *Personalities of the Old Testament* (New York: Charles Scribner's Sons, 1939), pp. 268–269.

of the Old Testament." He, more than any other prophet, addressed himself to the emotions of men and was able to stir and move their hearts. If any note predominated in his preaching, it was the note of victory. He was so filled with confidence in the ultimate victory of God that he could scarcely contain himself. Time after time he broke into hymns of glad and joyous praise. He employed the hymnic form not because it had aesthetic appeal but because it was the only form adequate for the expression of his message. It is no wonder that Handel drew so heavily upon these chapters when he wrote *The Messiah*. This prophet helped to make the religion of the Old Testament a singing religion.

Muilenburg has described Isaiah 40—55 as "an eschatological drama in which creation, history, and redemption constitute the central themes," and in which "God is the central figure from beginning to end." [38] The two basic points in this description that call for further clarification are the centrality and uniqueness of Israel's God and the eschatological outlook of the exilic Isaiah.

Chapters 40—55 contain the clearest and most passionate expressions of the incomparable nature of Israel's God to be found anywhere in the Old Testament. The historical background out of which these expressions arose makes them even more significant. The crushing defeat of Jerusalem at the hand of the Babylonians in 587 B.C. had led many Israelites to conclude that the Babylonian god Marduk had triumphed over Yahweh. Some even declared that they would have fared better if they had worshiped and burned incense to the gods of their conquerors (cf. Jer. 44:15–19). The prolonged years of exile had only accentuated the problem, for it appeared to the captives that Yahweh was as incapable of delivering them from bondage as he had been of preventing their downfall.

It was against this background of hopelessness and despair that these oracles were uttered. The prophet was well aware that Israel's being in exile seemed to indicate that her God had not been able to withstand the gods of Babylon. He did not hesitate to affirm, however, that this interpretation of events was wrong. The exile did not signal the defeat of Israel's God, but was rather the expression of his judgment upon her sins.

The passage which most clearly expresses the prophet's philosophy of history is 42:24–25: "Who gave up Jacob to the spoiler, / and Israel to the robbers? / Was it not the Lord, against whom we have sinned, / in whose ways they would not walk, / and whose law they would not obey? / So he poured upon him the heat of his anger / and the might of battle; / it set him on fire round about, but he did not understand; / it burned him, but he did not take it to heart."

In a related passage the prophet pictures Babylon as being merely the agent of God's judgment against his people. This is brought out in the charge that God made against Babylon: "I was angry with my people, I profaned my heritage; I gave them into your hand, you showed them no mercy; on the aged you made your yoke exceedingly heavy" (47:6). There is, incidentally, a marked similarity between the thought of this passage and that of 10:5–19, where in an earlier setting Assyria is described as the agent of God's judgment.

The prophet believed that when Israel's chastisement has been accomplished, Babylon, like Assyria before her, would herself experience the judgment of God. This belief is expressed in the form of a promise delivered to the downtrodden people of Israel: "Behold, I have taken from your hand / the cup of staggering; / the bowl of my wrath / you shall drink no more; / and I will put it into the hand of your tormentors, / who have said to you, / 'Bow down, that we may pass over'" (51:22–23).

One of the controlling purposes of the

---

[38] James Muilenburg, *op. cit.*, p. 387.

prophet was to demonstrate the superiority of Yahweh over idols. Classic expression is given to this theme in 41:21–29. Here the prophet issues a challenge to the idols to prove their divinity by three tests. Can they give a meaningful interpretation of past history? Can they forecast the future? Can they intervene in history, either for good or for evil? When they fail all of these tests, the prophet contemptuously declares, "Behold, you are nothing, and your work is nought; an abomination is he who chooses you" (v. 24).

The prophet goes on to show that what the idols could not do Yahweh has abundantly accomplished. He has provided the proofs of his sovereignty by raising up Cyrus to deliver his people from their bondage. His purposes are being announced beforehand by one who has been sent to be a herald of good tidings to Jerusalem. No idol is able to match such feats.

Apart from the polemics against idol gods, there are positive statements regarding Israel's incomparable God. He is the only God, beside whom there is no other (44:6–8; 45:5,6,21). Related to this is the repeated use of the statement "I am he," which is tantamount to saying "I am the only true God" (41:4; 46:4; 48:12). Yahweh is "the first and the last" (41:4; 44:6; 48:12), which is to be interpreted not as an expression of the eternity of God but as an affirmation of his lordship over history. His activity preceded the beginning of history and will extend beyond history.

More than any other prophet, Second Isaiah magnified Yahweh as Creator. The verb "to create" appears 16 times in chapters 40—55 (cf. 40:26,28; 43:1; 45:18). Significantly, this verb occurs only once in Isaiah 1—39 (4:5), and only 11 times in all of Genesis. Wherever it occurs, God is always its subject. It thus describes a unique creative act which he alone can perform.

Because they originated during the latter part of the Babylonian exile, the references to God as Creator are important for two reasons. In the first place, the Babylonians possessed an elaborate creation myth

in which the creation was attributed to Marduk. The Jewish exiles had been exposed to this myth during their long years of captivity. The prophet refuted the claims of this myth as he repeatedly asserted that Yahweh alone created the heavens and the earth. In the second place, these references are important because they furnished proof to the exiles that their God was a God of power and therefore able to deliver them from their enemies. This was a word of assurance which the exiles needed to hear.

The second point emphasized by Muilenburg has to do with the eschatological outlook of the exilic Isaiah. "Eschatology" as used here has reference to the decisive end of the age, which the prophet believed was near at hand. Throughout these chapters there is an intense eschatological longing and expectation. It was felt that the time of Israel's captivity had come to an end. The night of captivity was passing away and a new day was about to dawn. At any moment God would appear in power and glory to restore his people to their homeland and to establish his universal rule of righteousness and peace.

It is possible to reconstruct the order of events that was to lead to the eschatological age. The first was to be the great day of God's appearing, when his glory would be revealed and all flesh would see it together. This was to be followed by the ingathering of Israelites from all the nations where they had been dispersed. The restoration would be not only physical but also spiritual. The sins of the past would be forgiven, and God would reestablish his covenant with Israel. The twofold promise of land and descendants given in previous covenants would now be fulfilled. The eschatological age would reach its climax in the extension of God's covenant to include both Israel and all nations of mankind. Israel, restored and forgiven, would thus become a light to the nations and a witness to the uniqueness of her God.

The eschatological hope of the prophet raises a serious question. Since no transformation such as he expected ever took place, how are we to interpret these chapters? While it is true that Cyrus' conquest of Babylon permitted the Jews to return to Jerusalem, they nevertheless returned not as a free people but as the subjects of Cyrus. They had merely exchanged one overlord for another. Once they had arrived in Jerusalem, they waited for Yahweh to fulfill the promises made by Second Isaiah, but the years grew into decades and nothing happened. One has only to read the book of Malachi to see the disillusionment that resulted. Expectations long deferred made the hearts of the people grow sick. Instead of seeing Zion become a crown of beauty and a royal diadem, they saw themselves utterly ignored in the maelstrom of militarism that surged around them.

Any attempt at solving this problem must take into account the fact that one encounters the same problem, to a lesser or greater degree, in all biblical eschatology. The promises regarding the future served a vital purpose in the religious experience of Israel, even though they were not fulfilled as soon as the prophet had expected or in the manner in which he had predicted. The Jews who lived in anticipation of the fulfillment of the promises constituted a waiting community, which through its very waiting experienced the transforming power of God to change its weakness into strength. It thus learned that faith itself is the victory, and not merely the instrument whereby the victory is achieved.

Christians believe that the eschatological age foretold by the prophet was initiated when Jesus Christ was born and will be consummated at the end of the age. It is highly significant that the words of 40:3 were on the lips of John the Baptist as he began his public ministry and proclaimed the coming of the kingdom of God (Matt. 3:3; Mark 1:3; Luke 3:4–6; John 1:23). A careful study suggests that both John the Baptist and Jesus were strongly influenced in their eschatological views by Second Isaiah.

A direct corollary of the prophet's faith in the essential uniqueness of Israel's God was his missionary concern. Since there was only one God, then his purpose included all mankind. This truth implied a new role and a new mission for Israel. The clearest statement of Israel's responsibility is given in 43:10–13, where the nation is designated as a witness to the oneness of God. Muilenburg has noted the significance of this passage in these words: "He—he alone—is God, and Israel is his witness. Here the missionary motif, so strong a feature of other poems, becomes almost incandescent in its intensity." [39]

The prophet envisioned the day when every knee would bow before God and every tongue swear allegiance to him (45:22–24). This would be accomplished not only through the ministry of Israel but also through that of the servant of the Lord. The first of the Servant Songs depicts the servant bringing forth justice to the nations and establishing justice in the earth, while the coastlands wait for his law (42:1,4). Justice has often been interpreted in this context as signifying true religion.

The second Servant Song reaches its climax in a divine affirmation regarding the enlarged mission of the servant: "It is too light a thing that you should be my servant to raise up the tribes of Jacob and to restore the preserved of Israel; I will give you as a light to the nations, that my salvation may reach to the end of the earth" (49:6). In the fourth and last Servant Song it is stated that many nations will be startled and kings will shut their mouths because of what they see and hear regarding the servant (52:15). This clearly implies that the effects of his ministry will be felt beyond the borders of Israel.[40]

The listing of Second Isaiah's contributions to the religion of Israel would be incomplete without further reference to his

[39] *Ibid.*, p. 405.
[40] Not all scholars are agreed that there is a missionary message in Second Isaiah, at least not in the usual sense of the term. Among those who take the opposite view are Robert Martin-Achard, *A Light to the Nations*, trans. John Penney Smith (Edinburgh: Oliver and Boyd, 1962); Harry M. Orlinsky, *op. cit.*; and Norman H. Snaith, *op. cit.* These scholars interpret the promises of salvation in Second Isaiah as applying to Israel alone.

concept of the servant of the Lord. Since the Servant Songs have already been discussed in some detail, it will not be necessary to repeat the discussion here. It should, nevertheless, be pointed out that the concept of the Servant of the Lord helped to shape the theology not only of Israel but also of the early Christian community. By formulating the concept the prophet made an invaluable contribution to Israel's understanding of her mission, to the disciples' understanding of the person and mission of Jesus, to the church's understanding of its mission to be the servant-people of God, and to the solution of the problem of suffering.

This last point has been stressed by John Paterson.[41] He has pointed out three stages in the development of the understanding of suffering during the time of the Old Testament. The first stage was characterized by the view that *all sufferers were sinners,* a view given classical expression in the speeches of the friends of Job. The second stage was reached when men began to understand that *some sufferers were saints.* This provided a more adequate explanation for the suffering of men such as Job and Jeremiah, whose suffering could not be attributed to their sin. The third and highest stage in the understanding of suffering was reached in the Servant Songs of Deutero-Isaiah, especially in the fourth song (52:13—53:12). Here for the first time it was clearly revealed that *some sufferers were saviors.* The view that suffering can be vicarious, that the innocent can suffer on behalf of the guilty, is nowhere so clearly stated as here.

Because of this prophet's clear statement on the idea of vicarious suffering, his teaching concerning the universal purpose of God and his idea of the love and compassion of God, he has been called the Evangelist of the Old Testament. The appropriateness of this title can also be demonstrated linguistically, for he frequently employed the verb *basar,* meaning "to bear

41 John Paterson, *The Book That Is Alive* (New York: Charles Scribner's Sons, 1954), pp. 89–91.

tidings, to preach or proclaim good tidings" (cf. 40:9; 41:27; 52:7; 60:6; 61:1). This verb, through the medium of the Septuagint, was the basis of the New Testament *euangelizein,* "to proclaim the gospel (good news)." The gospel, both in Second Isaiah and in the New Testament, was the good news that God had come to his people in their sin and distress, had forgiven them through the sacrifice of his Servant, and had initiated his rule over the nations, a rule that would be consummated in the creation of new heavens and a new earth.

3. The Message of Chapters 56—66

As we indicated above, these chapters reflect a Palestinian setting and are to be dated in the period immediately following the Jews' return from the Babylonian exile. They were probably written either by Second Isaiah or by one or more of his disciples. In any event, they reflect a later stage in the theological development of the book of Isaiah. They furnish invaluable insight into the religious life of Israel in the decades following 538 B.C.

One of the first things one notes in these chapters is a renewed interest in the worship life of the Jewish community. Idolatry is condemned in language reminiscent of the preexilic prophets (cf. 57: 3–13; 65:1–12; 66:17). The people are enjoined to keep the sabbath (56:1–2; 58: 13–14), and great stress is placed upon the efficacy of prayer (56:6–7; 64:1–12).

This does not imply, however, that the author endorsed ritual for ritual's sake. On the contrary, nowhere in the Old Testament is there a more forceful condemnation of ritual divorced from righteous living than that found here. In keeping with the finest traditions of the preexilic prophets, he condemns fasting that has become a substitute for social justice (58:1–12). His reflections upon the Temple and its services are among the most remarkable in the Old Testament. He insists that the eunuch and the alien are not to be excluded from participating in its worship (56:6–8), and, according to one interpretation, even proposes that foreigners should be chosen to serve as priests and Levites (66:18–21).

These chapters strongly emphasize the pastoral nature of the prophetic ministry. The passage that expresses this most clearly is 61:1–3: "The Spirit of the Lord God is upon me, because the Lord has anointed me to bring good tidings to the afflicted; he has sent me to bind up the brokenhearted, to proclaim liberty to the captives, and the opening of the prison to those who are bound; . . ." The prophet not only shows concern for the oppressed of his own people (58:6–7) but also speaks out in defense of the rights of foreigners (56: 6–8). He often prays for Israel, and a remarkable prayer of intercession has been preserved in 63:15—64:12.

Sin and judgment, themes that hardly occur at all in chapters 40—55, receive prominent attention in these chapters. Judgment is usually described in apocalyptic terms. It is final, and issues in the creation of new heavens and a new earth (65:17–25). As it applies to Israel, it is a selective judgment: the faithful will be spared but the wicked will be punished (65:13–25); 66:22–24). The final scene in the book is set in Jerusalem and depicts the assembled worshipers going forth to view the dead bodies of the damned, forever eaten by worms, but never devoured, and burned by eternal fires, but never consumed (66:24). It is understandable that the ancient rabbis customarily repeated v. 23 after v. 24, in order that the book might not end on such a pessimistic note.

VII. The Text of the Book of Isaiah

Isaiah is remarkably free of textual problems. The Masoretic Text as a whole is extremely well-preserved and is closely supported by the Qumran texts. Thus far, two manuscripts of Isaiah have been discovered among the Dead Sea Scrolls. The first of these (IQIsᵃ) is complete, and its differences from the Masoretic Text consist mainly of variations in orthography. The translators of the RSV adopted only 13 of

its readings in preference to those of the Masoretic Text, and even these did not substantially change the interpretation.

The other scroll (IQIsᵇ) is fragmentary, but where it has survived it follows the Masoretic Text almost word for word. This means that the Hebrew text of the book of Isaiah was virtually fixed in its present form at least as early as the beginning of the Christian era. Few scholars would have dared make this statement prior to the discovery of the Qumran texts.

Outline

Part One: Chapters 1—39

I. Oracles concerning Judah and Israel (1:1 —12:6)
  1. God's case against his people (1:1–31)
    (1) Favor without gratitude (1:1–3)
    (2) Punishment without repentance (1:4–9)
    (3) Religion without ethics (1:10–17)
    (4) A call to decision (1:18–20)
    (5) The moral decay of Jerusalem (1: 21–23)
    (6) God's purifying judgment (1:24–26)
    (7) The righteous and the wicked (1: 27–31)
  2. Jerusalem, present and future (2:1—4:6)
    (1) A vision of universal peace (2:1–5)
    (2) The day of the Lord (2:6–22)
    (3) The disintegration of Judean society (3:1–15)
    (4) The haughty women of Jerusalem (3:16—4:1)
    (5) The restoration of Jerusalem (4: 2–6)
  3. Sin and judgment (5:1–30)
    (1) The parable of the vineyard (5: 1–7)
    (2) Six woes against the wicked (5: 8–25)
    (3) The invader from afar (5:26–30)
  4. The call of Isaiah (6:1–13)
    (1) Vision and response (6:1–5)
    (2) Purification and commission (6: 6–13)
  5. A national crisis (7:1—9:7)
    (1) The sign of Immanuel (7:1–17)
    (2) The consequences of unbelief (7: 18–25)
    (3) The sign of Maher-shalal-hashbaz (8:1–4)
    (4) The oracle of the two rivers (8:

5-8)
(5) Fearing God and not man (8:9–15)
(6) A time of withdrawal (8:16–22)
(7) The messianic king (9:1–7)
6. The outstretched hand of God (9:8—10:4)
    (1) God's fruitless chastisement of Israel (9:8–17)
    (2) The fire of God's wrath (9:18–21)
    (3) Legalized robbery (10:1–4)
7. Oracles against Assyria (10:5–34)
    (1) Assyria the rod of God's anger (10:5–11)
    (2) Punishment of the pride of Assyria (10:12–19)
    (3) Encouragement of the remnant of Israel (10:20–27b)
    (4) The Assyrian invasion (10:27c–34)
8. The messianic age (11:1–16)
    (1) The messianic king (11:1–9)
    (2) Reunion in the messianic kingdom (11:10–16)
9. Two songs of praise (12:1–6)
    (1) A song of deliverance (12:1–2)
    (2) A song of thanksgiving (12:3–6)
II. Oracles addressed to foreign nations (13:1—23:18)
1. The doom of Babylon (13:1—14:23)
    (1) The day of the Lord against Babylon (13:1–22)
    (2) The return of the exiles (14:1–2)
    (3) A taunt song against the king of Babylon (14:3–21)
    (4) God's broom of destruction (14:22–23)
2. The destruction of Assyria (14:24–27)
3. Warning to Philistia (14:28–32)
4. The doom of Moab (15:1—16:14)
    (1) Distress in Moab (15:1–9)
    (2) A request for refuge (16:1–5)
    (3) Denial of the request (16:6–7)
    (4) Lamentation over Moab's misfortune (16:8–14)
5. Oracles of threat and promise (17:1–14)
    (1) The doom of Damascus and Ephraim (17:1–6)
    (2) The restoration of true worship (17:7–8)
    (3) The futility of idolatry (17:9–11)
    (4) The raging of the nations (17:12–14)
6. Oracles concerning Ethiopia and Egypt (18:1—20:6)
    (1) Oracle addressed to the envoys of Ethiopia (18:1–7)
    (2) The doom of Egypt (19:1–15)

    (3) The conversion of Egypt and Assyria (19:16–25)
    (4) A sign against Egypt and Ethiopia (20:1–6)
7. The fall of Babylon (21:1–10)
8. Edom's uncertain future (21:11–12)
9. The doom of Dedan and Kedar (21:13–17)
10. Revelry on the eve of disaster (22:1–14)
    (1) A tumultuous city (22:1–4)
    (2) A besieged city (22:5–11)
    (3) An unheeded call to repentance (22:12–14)
11. Denunciation of an ambitious politician (22:15–25)
12. Oracles concerning Tyre and Sidon (23:1–18)
    (1) The downfall of Tyre and Sidon (23:1–12)
    (2) Tyre's future restoration (23:13–18)
III. Prophecies of judgment and redemption (24:1—27:13)
1. An announcement of judgment (24:1–20)
    (1) The impending doom (24:1–3)
    (2) The broken covenant (24:4–13)
    (3) Premature rejoicing (24:14–16)
    (4) Inescapable judgment (24:17–20)
2. A liturgy of praise and promise (24:21—27:1)
    (1) The Lord's enthronement on Mount Zion (24:21–23)
    (2) A song of thanksgiving (25:1–5)
    (3) The Lord's enthronement feast (25:6–9)
    (4) The doom of Moab (25:10–12)
    (5) The security of the righteous (26:1–6)
    (6) A prayer for vindication (26:7–19)
    (7) The sword of the Lord (26:20—27:1)
3. The Lord's plans for his people (27:2–13)
    (1) The new song of the vineyard (27:2–6)
    (2) A people without discernment (27:7–11)
    (3) The ingathering of Israel (27:12–13)
IV. Divine wisdom and human folly (28:1—32:20)
1. Oracles concerning Ephraim and Judah (28:1–29)
    (1) Drunken leaders of the Lord's people (28:1–13)
    (2) True and false security (28:14–22)
    (3) The parable of the farmer (28:23–

(1) The coming of the Gentiles to the light (60:1–14)
(2) The reversal of Zion's humiliation (60:15–22)
2. Tidings of great joy (61:1–11)
(1) The anointed herald of salvation (61:1–4)
(2) A people blessed of the Lord (61: 5–9)
(3) A hymn of rejoicing (61:10–11)
3. Pleading the promises of God (62:1– 12)
(1) Beulah land (62:1–5)
(2) The prayer vigil of Zion's watchmen (62:6–9)
(3) The highway of the redeemed (62: 10–12)
4. The divine avenger (63:1–6)
5. A psalm of intercession (63:7—64:12)
(1) Remembrance of past mercies (63: 7–14)
(2) A plea for present help (63:15— 64:12)
6. Prophecies of judgment and salvation (65:1—66:24)
(1) God's warning to an apostate people (65:1–16)
(2) New heavens and a new earth (65:17–25)
(3) God's disapproval of corrupt worship (66:1–4)
(4) The voice of judgment (66:5–6)
(5) The rebirth of Zion (66:7–14)
(6) The judgment of the nations (66: 15–16)
(7) Condemnation of pagan worship (66:17)
(8) The gathering of the nations on Mount Zion (66:18–23)
(9) The everlasting punishment of the rebels (66:24)

Selected Bibliography

DUHM, BERNHARD. "Das Buch Jesaia," *Göttenger Handkommentar zum alten Testament.* Göttengen: Vandenhoeck & Ruprecht, 4th edition, 1922.

GRAY, GEORGE BUCHANAN. *The Book of Isaiah, I–XXXIX.* ("The International Critical Commentary.") Edinburgh: T. and T. Clark, 1912.

GREEN, JAMES LEO. *God Reigns.* Nashville: Broadman Press, 1968.

JONES, DOUGLAS RAWLINSON. *Isaiah 56—66 and Joel.* ("Torch Bible Commentaries.") London: SCM Press, Ltd., 1964.

KISSANE, EDWARD J. *The Book of Isaiah,* Vol. II. Dublin: Brown & Nolan, 1943.

KNIGHT, GEORGE A. F. *Deutero-Isaiah.* Nashville: Abingdon Press, 1965.

LESLIE, ELMER A. *Isaiah.* Nashville: Abingdon Press, 1963.

MAUCHLINE, JOHN. *Isaiah 1—39.* ("Torch Bible Commentaries.") London: SCM Press, Ltd., 1962.

McKENZIE, JOHN L. *Second Isaiah.* ("The Anchor Bible.") Garden City: Doubleday & Company, Inc., 1968.

McNAMARA, M. "The Book of Isaiah, Chapters 1—39," *Old Testament Reading Guide.* Collegeville, Minnesota: The Liturgical Press, 1966.

MUCKLE, J. YEOMAN. *Isaiah, Chapters 1—39.* ("Epworth Preacher's Commentaries.") London: The Epworth Press, 1960.

MUILENBURG, JAMES. "The Book of Isaiah, Chapters 40—66," *The Interpreter's Bible,* Vol. V. Ed. GEORGE ARTHUR BUTTRICK. Nashville: Abingdon Press, 1956.

NORTH, CHRISTOPHER R. *The Second Isaiah.* Oxford: The Clarendon Press, 1964.

———. *The Suffering Servant in Deutero-Isaiah.* London: Oxford University Press, 1948.

ORLINSKY, HARRY M. and SNAITH, NORMAN H. "Studies on the Second Part of the Book of Isaiah," *Supplements to Vetus Testamentum,* Vol. XIV. Leiden: E. J. Brill, 1967.

PRITCHARD, JAMES B., ed. *Ancient Near Eastern Texts Relating to the Old Testament.* Princeton: University Press, 1950.

SCOTT, R. B. Y. "The Book of Isaiah, Chapters 1—39," *The Interpreter's Bible,* Vol. V. Nashville: Abingdon Press, 1956.

SKINNER, JOHN. "The Book of the Prophet Isaiah," *Cambridge Bible.* Cambridge: University Press, 1915.

SMART, JAMES D. *History and Theology in Second Isaiah.* Philadelphia: The Westminster Press, 1965.

STUHLMUELLER, CARROLL. "The Book of Isaiah, Chapters 40—66," *Old Testament Reading Guide.* Collegeville, Minnesota: The Liturgical Press, 1965.

THEXTON, S. CLIVE. *Isaiah, Chapters 40—66.* ("Epworth Preacher's Commentaries.") London: The Epworth Press, 1959.

WARD, JAMES M. *Amos and Isaiah.* Nashville: Abingdon Press, 1969.

WESTERMANN, CLAUS. "Isaiah 40—66," trans. David M. G. Stalker, *The Old Testament Library.* Philadelphia: The Westminster Press, 1969.

WRIGHT, G. ERNEST. *The Book of Isaiah.* ("The Layman's Bible Commentary," Vol. 11.) Richmond: John Knox Press, 1964.

YOUNG, EDWARD J. *The Book of Isaiah,* Vols. I, II, and III. Grand Rapids: Wm. B. Eerdmans Publishing Company, 1965.

Commentary on the Text

Part One: Chapters 1—39

The reasons for treating chapters 1—39 as a separate unit were given in the Introduction. This part of Isaiah is sometimes designated as the preexilic section, since it contains all of the extant oracles of the eighth-century Isaiah. It falls naturally into the following divisions: the early oracles concerning Judah and Israel (1:1—12:6); oracles against foreign nations (13:1—23:18); the so-called "Isaiah Apocalypse" (24:1—27:13); oracles related to the Sennacherib crisis of 701 b.c. (28:1—32:20); a collection of eschatological oracles (33:1—35:10); and an historical appendix (36:1—39:8).

I. Oracles Concerning Judah and Israel (1:1—12:6)

These chapters cover the earliest period in Isaiah's ministry, extending through the reigns of Jotham (742–735 b.c.) and Ahaz (735–715). Because of the large amount of biographical and autobiographical material found here, the section has sometimes been referred to as "the memoirs of Isaiah." The highlight of the early period in the prophet's ministry was his clash with Ahaz during the Syro-Ephraimitic crisis of 735–733 b.c. Ahaz's rejection of Isaiah's counsel to trust in God resulted in the prophet's temporary withdrawal from public ministry (cf. 8:16–20).

1. God's Case Against His People (1:1–31)

The first chapter consists of a collection of brief oracles gathered from different periods of Isaiah's ministry. It forms a representative cross section of his teaching and has been placed here to serve as an introduction to the entire book. The separate oracles appear to have been brought together on the basis of a common theme and, in some cases, on the basis of certain key words or catchwords, such as "sons" in vv. 2 and 4, and "Sodom" and "Gomorrah" in vv. 9 and 10. The theme that runs throughout the chapter is God's controversy with his apostate people. Minor themes also appear, such as the worthlessness of religion without morality, the demand for repentance, the threat of judgment, and the promise of redemption.

(1) Favor Without Gratitude (1:1–3)

¹ The vision of Isaiah the son of Amoz, which he saw concerning Judah and Jerusalem in the days of Uzziah, Jotham, Ahaz, and Hezekiah, kings of Judah.
² Hear, O heavens, and give ear, O earth;
    for the Lord has spoken:
"Sons have I reared and brought up,
    but they have rebelled against me.
³ The ox knows its owner,
    and the ass its master's crib;
but Israel does not know,
    my people does not understand."

As it now stands, the editorial heading in v. 1 introduces the entire book of Isaiah. It perhaps stood originally at the head of a shorter collection of oracles concerned primarily, if not exclusively, with **Judah and Jerusalem.** The fact that similar headings are found in 2:1 and 13:1 suggests that several collections of Isaianic materials probably circulated independently before being incorporated into the present book. When this process had been completed, the title verse of the initial collection, perhaps with slight alterations, was allowed to stand as the heading for the entire book. The title was already known to the author of 2 Chronicles 32:32, who refers to the deeds of Hezekiah as having been recorded in "the vision of Isaiah the prophet the son of Amoz."

The title calls attention to the **vision** of Isaiah which he *saw.* Other prophets whose messages are designated visions are Obadiah (Obad. 1) and Nahum (Nah. 1:1). The meaning of **vision** is clarified when 1:1 is compared with 2:1, for the latter makes reference to the "word" which Isaiah "saw." Here "word" and *vision* seem to be synonymous, and both are designations of the message which was revealed to the prophet. Together they suggest that God's revelation to Isaiah was both visual and auditory, although the verb used in both instances is translated "he saw." In this context to see clearly means to perceive or to understand.

Isaiah may mean either "the Lord will save" or "the Lord is salvation." His father *Amoz* should not be confused with the prophet Amos, since their names were written quite differently in Hebrew. They were confused by some early Christian writers, but this was due to the fact that the Septuagint made no distinction between them.

According to the Babylonian Talmud, Amoz was the brother of King Amaziah (2 Kings 14:1), the father of Uzziah. There is, however, no biblical support for such a claim, and it seems to have been based solely upon the fact that the two names Amoz and Amaziah were derived from the same verbal root. Therefore, the theory that Isaiah was of royal blood rests upon very tenuous evidence.

The title verse not only identifies the prophet and locates him geographically, but also provides a relative chronology for his ministry, which is dated according to the Judean kings who ruled during the latter half of the eighth century B.C. The inclusion of Uzziah in the list has sometimes been interpreted to mean that Isaiah had already begun to prophesy before the king's death.

This interpretation raises an interesting question concerning the vision recorded in chapter 6. Since it is dated in the year that King Uzziah died (6:1), was it the prophet's *inaugural* vision, or had he already begun to prophesy prior to this? Even though the available evidence does not provide a definitive answer to these questions, the prevailing view is that chapter 6 describes Isaiah's initial call to the prophetic ministry and that the call came shortly after the death of King Uzziah.

Hear, O heavens, and give ear, O earth is the introductory formula for an Old Testament literary form known as the covenant lawsuit.[42] This is a device designed to restore a breach of covenant and is, therefore, to be distinguished from the covenant renewal ceremony (cf. Josh. 24). Examples of the covenant lawsuit occur in almost all of the preexilic prophets (cf. 3:13 ff.; 5:1–7; Jer. 2:1 ff.; Hos. 2:2 ff.; 4:1 ff.; Amos 3:1 ff.; 4:1 ff.; Mic. 6:1 ff.).

The covenant lawsuits differ from each other in minor details, but they have certain characteristics in common. Depending upon their completeness, they will include some or all of the following elements: a call to the witnesses to give ear; an introductory statement by the divine Judge or his prophet; a recital of the gracious acts of God on behalf of his people; the specific indictment; and the sentence.

The role of the prophets in these lawsuits was highly significant. They literally believed that they were officers of the heavenly court sent to announce that God's covenant had been breached and that radical judgment was forthcoming. After announcing the divine sentence, which was usually very brief, they sometimes expounded on it, categorizing the sins of the people in greater detail. At other times they engaged in lamentation and intercession for the accused, thus demonstrating the fact that in the Old Testament the office of intercessor belongs not so much to the priest as to the prophet.

The accusation made against the people of Judah was that they had *rebelled* against God, even though he had cared for them as *sons*. God speaks here as a compassionate father who has been deeply hurt by the obstinacy and ingratitude of his children. The popular notion that the concept of the fatherhood of God did not originate until New Testament times is

[42] Cf. G. E. Wright, "The Lawsuit of God: A Form-Critical Study of Deuteronomy 32," *Israel's Prophetic Heritage*, ed. B. W. Anderson and Walter Harrelson (New York: Harper and Row, 1962), pp. 26–67.

totally disproved by passages such as this. God is the same, whether in the Old Testament or the New Testament, and when he addresses his people he speaks as their father.

This ox knows its owner . . . but Israel does not know. The thought expressed here is similar to that of Jeremiah 8:7: "Even the stork in the heavens / knows her times; / and the turtledove, swallow, and crane / keep the time of their coming; / but my people know not / the ordinance of the Lord." Each of these passages emphasizes the unnaturalness of Israel's rebellion. The birds of the heavens know when to migrate, and the ox and the ass, when led astray, instinctively find their way back to their master's crib. It is not so with the people of Israel, for they leave God and never return. They are neither as grateful nor as intelligent as the ox or the ass.

The truth of this verse is vividly illustrated in a news story that originated in Haifa, Israel. A policeman, while reading this passage from Isaiah, conceived a way to discover the owners of a caravan of asses loaded with contraband, the owners having fled. The asses were kept without food for several days, then released and followed; they went straight to the den of their owners, who were apprehended for their crime.[43]

(2) *Punishment Without Repentance* (1: 4–9)

4 Ah, sinful nation,
      a people laden with iniquity,
    offspring of evildoers,
      sons who deal corruptly!
    They have forsaken the Lord,
      they have despised the Holy One of
        Israel,
      they are utterly estranged.
5 Why will you still be smitten,
      that you continue to rebel?
    The whole head is sick,
      and the whole heart faint.
6 From the sole of the foot even to the head,
      there is no soundness in it,
    but bruises and sores

43 *The Courier-Journal* (Louisville), April 22, 1951.

and bleeding wounds;
    they are not pressed out, or bound up,
      or softened with oil.
7 Your country lies desolate,
      your cities are burned with fire;
    in your very presence
      aliens devour your land;
    it is desolate, as overthrown by aliens.
8 And the daughter of Zion is left
      like a booth in a vineyard,
    like a lodge in a cucumber field,
      like a besieged city.
9 If the Lord of hosts
      had not left us a few survivors,
    we should have been like Sodom,
      and become like Gomorrah.

Though some would group vv. 2–3 with 4–9, it seems best to treat the latter passage as a separate and self-contained oracle. Whereas the Lord was the speaker in the preceding section, here it is the prophet. The initial exclamation, *Ah* (Heb., *hoy*, perhaps better translated "Woe!" or "Alas!"), also marks the beginning of a new oracle. Furthermore, the oracle in vv. 4–9 presupposes a thoroughgoing devastation of the land of Judah. It therefore reflects a concrete historical situation, whereas the preceding verses are set in a more general and inclusive context.

Two dates have been proposed for the oracle. One possibility is that it belongs to the time of the devastation of the land of Judah during the Syro-Ephraimitic invasion of 735 B.C. (cf. 7:1–2; 2 Kings 16:5–9). More likely it refers to the Assyrian invasion of 701 (cf. 36:1—37:38; 2 Kings 18:13—19:37), carried out by Sennacherib, who in an inscription boasts that under his command the Assyrian army destroyed 46 walled cities of Judah, deported over 200,000 of her citizens, and shut King Hezekiah up in Jerusalem "like a bird in a cage" (ANET, p. 288).

The fourfold address in v. 4—*nation, people, offspring, sons*—is a progressively personal way of showing God's relationship to Judah, and of emphasizing the enormity of the sins of the people. They had *forsaken the Lord* and *despised the Holy One of Israel.*

Isaiah is generally credited with having

coined the phrase *the Holy One of Israel* as a designation for God. It occurs some 26 times in his book alone (cf. 5:19,24; 10:20; 12:6; etc.) but only six times in the remainder of the Old Testament (2 Kings 19:22; Psalms 71:22; 78:41; 89: 18; Jer. 50:29; 51:5). His comprehension of the holiness of God was rooted in his call experience (ch. 6). Through that experience he learned the meaning of divine holiness and of human sin. He also learned that the gulf standing between sinful man and the holy God could be bridged only by an act of divine mercy.

The result of Israel's wicked behavior was that she had become *utterly estranged* from God. To understand the full force of this statement one must observe how the verb *zur* is used elsewhere in the Old Testament. Its basic meaning is to be a stranger or to become alienated from another. Thus the participle *zar* is commonly used to designate strangers or foreigners (cf. 1:7; Ex. 29:33; Lev. 22:10; Job 19:15; Lam. 5:2). The verb itself is used to describe the process of becoming alienated, separated, or estranged (cf. Job 19:13; Psalms 58:3; 69:8; Ezek. 14:5). To say that the people of Israel had become *utterly estranged* meant that they had violated the covenant that bound them to God and in so doing had virtually become aliens and strangers.

The opening words of v. 5 have been interpreted in various ways. The question is whether they should be rendered, "Why will you still be smitten?" or "Where, i.e., on what part of the body, will you still be smitten?" According to the latter rendering, the nation is represented as an individual so bruised and battered from head to foot that there is no sound spot where a new wound might be inflicted. Both of these interpretations are possible from the standpoint of the Hebrew. In either case the meaning is essentially the same. The words express God's consternation and bewilderment in the face of Judah's persistent rebellion. What more could he do to bring his people to their senses?

The metaphor of the bruised and beaten body is continued in v. 6 and then applied specifically to Judah and Jerusalem in vv. 7–9. Their chastisement had taken the form of an invasion. The severity of the onslaught against the land is described with staccato effect by a series of short phrases. Their land lay waste; their cities were burned with fire. They had become *alienated* from God, and now *aliens* were overthrowing and devouring their land.

The punishment of Jerusalem is vividly described in a series of metaphors drawn from everyday life in ancient Israel. The city is personified as a maiden and referred to as *the daughter of Zion*. This is an instance where the construct relationship in Hebrew would be more accurately translated as "daughter Zion." The city, once fair and lovely, has now been left like a booth in a vineyard or like a lodge in a cucumber field. The practice referred to here is one which is still known in the Middle East: temporary lodges or booths are constructed in the vineyards and cucumber fields during the harvest season and then abandoned when the harvest is over. This figure of speech describes the utter loneliness and isolation of Jerusalem as alien armies surround her, cutting her off from the rest of Judah.

The Lord of hosts is an abbreviated form of the longer title "the Lord God of hosts." It is an ancient designation for God that emphasizes his power and majesty. The majestic nature of the title is clearly reflected in the Septuagint where it is customarily rendered as *kurios pantokrator,* "the Lord [God] Almighty," a title which reappears in certain New Testament passages (cf. 2 Cor. 6:18; Rev. 4:8; 11:17; 15:3; 19:6).[44]

The Hebrew word for *hosts* may refer to the congregation of Israel (cf. Ex. 7:4; 12: 41,51; Num. 31:48), to the fighting men

---

[44] In a few Old Testament passages the LXX translators simply transliterated the Hebrew word for "hosts" as *sabaoth*. This accounts for the unusual form *kurios sabaoth*, which is found in two New Testament passages, i.e., Rom. 9:29 and James 5:4, and which is translated in the KJV as "the Lord of Sabaoth."

within the congregation (cf. Josh. 5:14,15; 2 Sam. 2:8; 3:23), to the sun, moon, and stars (cf. 34:4; Gen. 2:1; Deut. 4:19), or to the angelic hosts of heaven (cf. 1 Kings 22:19; Psalm 103:21). It is first used in combination with Yahweh (Lord) in 1 Samuel 1:3.[45] Its appearance at this juncture in history suggests that its original function was to designate Yahweh as the God of the armies of Israel. Later its meaning was enlarged to include the hosts of heaven—astral as well as angelic. It is a title that emphasizes God's sovereign lordship over all created things, both in heaven and on earth.

Had it not been for God's mercy, Jerusalem would have utterly perished—like *Sodom* and *Gomorrah* (cf. Gen. 19:24 f.). As it was, she had been left with only *a few survivors.* Isaiah's prophecies contain numerous references to the survival of a remnant (4:2; 6:13; 10:20 f.; 17:6; 28:5), and his first son bore the symbolic name Shear-jashub, translated "a remnant shall return" (7:3). However, the word used here is not *shear,* the normal word for remnant, but *sarid,* which occurs nowhere else in Isaiah. This suggests that the prophet did not regard the survivors of the catastrophe of 701 B.C. as the purified remnant of Israel but as a decimated remnant hardly worthy of the name. Nevertheless, the very fact that a few survivors had been spared was a demonstration of the grace of God toward a city that deserved complete destruction.

(3) Religion Without Ethics (1:10–17)

10 Hear the word of the LORD,
     you rulers of Sodom!
   Give ear to the teaching of our God,
     you people of Gomorrah!
11 "What to me is the multitude of your sacrifices?
     says the LORD;

45 This title never occurs in the Pentateuch, Joshua, Judges, Proverbs, Ecclesiastes, or Daniel. It is found 11 times in 1 and 2 Samuel, three times in 1 and 2 Kings, three times in 1 and 2 Chronicles, 14 times in Psalms, 61 times in Isaiah, 78 times in Jeremiah, 15 times in the minor prophets from Hosea through Zephaniah, 14 times in Haggai, 48 times in Zechariah, and 24 times in Malachi.

I have had enough of burnt offerings of rams
     and the fat of fed beasts;
   I do not delight in the blood of bulls,
     or of lambs, or of he-goats.
12 "When you come to appear before me,
     who requires of you
     this trampling of my courts?
13 Bring no more vain offerings;
     incense is an abomination to me.
   New moon and sabbath and the calling of assemblies—
     I cannot endure iniquity and solemn assembly.
14 Your new moons and your appointed feasts
     my soul hates;
   they have become a burden to me,
     I am weary of bearing them.
15 When you spread forth your hands,
     I will hide my eyes from you;
   even though you make many prayers,
     I will not listen;
   your hands are full of blood.
16 Wash yourselves; make yourselves clean;
     remove the evil of your doings
     from before my eyes;
   cease to do evil,
17   learn to do good;
   seek justice,
     correct oppression;
   defend the fatherless,
     plead for the widow.

This oracle is clearly set off from that which precedes it by its different historical setting. Jerusalem is described not as a city under siege but as a peaceful city to which religious pilgrimages could be made. Isaiah probably delivered this message during one of the great religious festivals, when the Temple was crowded with worshipers and the altars were piled high with sacrifices. The context suggests a date early in his ministry, perhaps as early as the reign of Jotham. The oracle was evidently joined to the preceding on the basis of the catchword principle. The link between the two is the reference to Sodom and Gomorrah in both vv. 9 and 10.

It has been said that few things determine men's attitudes on religion more clearly than the statement of what they count essential to a right relationship to God. The men of Judah were confident that they fully comprehended the nature of God's demands upon them. They believed that in order to remain in his favor they must appear regularly at his Temple, offer the prescribed sacrifices, and repeat the appropriate prayers. This was as far as their comprehension went, however, and they saw no need for a practical application of the principles of righteousness and justice in their daily lives.

Isaiah's position was diametrically opposed to theirs. He did not attack religion as such, but rather the dichotomy of creed and conduct that he witnessed in the lives of his contemporaries. He declared that under such circumstances the sacrifices, prayers, and solemn assemblies of his people were worse than useless; they were an insult to God. Worship that did not penetrate into the hard realities of everyday life was regarded by him as nothing more than a pious fraud. His position with regard to these matters was similar to that taken by other preexilic prophets (cf. Jer. 7:21–22; Hos. 6:6; Amos 5:21–27; Mic. 6:6–8).[46]

The oracle is addressed to the *rulers of Sodom* and to the *people of Gomorrah*, figurative terms for the kings and common people of Judah and Jerusalem. The prophet could not have chosen more slanderous terms with which to address his audience. The wickedness of Sodom and Gomorrah had become proverbial. The word rendered *rulers* occurs only five times in the prophets (1:10; 3:6 f.; Mic. 3:1,9) and in each instance is used in a derogatory sense.

The parallelism in v. 10 indicates that *the law* is to be equated with *the word of the Lord*. Torah, the Hebrew word for law, is derived from a verb meaning to shoot. In ancient times one frequently shot an arrow to indicate direction (cf. 1 Sam. 20:20–22,35–40). The verb to shoot, therefore, came to be used in a figurative sense meaning to point out, to show the way,

to instruct, or to teach. *Torah,* derived from this verb root, has a much richer meaning than the translation *law* would seem to indicate. It would be more adequately rendered as teaching, instruction, direction, or revelation. In this context it refers to the religious and ethical teaching given to the people through the prophets.

The opening question in v. 11 could be translated: "Of what use to me is the abundance of your sacrifices?" *Burnt offerings* were those in which the whole sacrifice was consumed upon the altar (cf. Lev. 1: 3 ff.). In other types of sacrifices, such as the peace offering (cf. Lev. 3:1 ff.), those making the sacrifices, together with the officiating priests, were permitted to eat certain portions of the sacrificial animals, provided, of course, that the *fat* and the *blood* were reserved for God.

It is implied that the men of Judah and Jerusalem were piling the altars high with burnt offerings and with the fat and blood of their peace offerings. Their generosity exceeded the demands of the law. They naturally assumed that God was gratified by the prodigality of their giving. It must have been shocking to them, therefore, to hear the prophet announcing that God was offended by their sacrifices, that he had had enough and wanted no more.

The question propounded in v. 12, "Who requires of you this trampling of my courts?" has been interpreted by some as a thoroughgoing repudiation of the entire Jerusalem cult. Such an interpretation postulates an almost immeasurable gulf between the prophet and his listeners. It is more likely that his words were directed not against the Temple itself but against those who frequented the Temple when all the while their lives were filled with iniquity. He rejected the religion he found in Jerusalem because it had become divorced from righteous living and ethical conduct and, therefore, constituted a barrier to, rather than a means of, communion with God. There is always the danger that organized religion will become nothing more than the organized effort of unre-

---

46 For a more detailed discussion of the prophetic attitude toward the cult, see C. F. Whitley, *The Prophetic Achievement* (Leiden: E. J. Brill, 1963), pp. 63–92; R. E. Clements, "Prophecy and Covenant," *Studies in Biblical Theology*, No. 43 (Naperville: Alec R. Allenson, Inc., 1965), pp. 86–102.

generate men to manipulate God and to secure for themselves the rewards of temporal prosperity and spiritual security.

The offerings of the people are described as *vain*, i.e., empty, worthless, and without purpose. Their *incense*, perhaps a reference to the acrid smoke rising from their altars, was an *abomination* to God. The word *abomination* was used in the Old Testament to describe that which was grotesquely out of harmony with the revealed will and character of Israel's God.

The religious festivals that came under condemnation included *new moon, sabbath*, and the called *assemblies*. *New moon* is referred to twice (vv. 13 f.). This festival marked the beginning of each new month and was, like the sabbath, a day of rest (cf. Num. 28:11-15). The final statement in v. 13 means that God regarded *iniquity* and *solemn assembly* as disparate entities. Let none imagine, therefore, that they could practice iniquity and still participate meaningfully in the solemn assembly. The two were utterly incompatible. God looked upon the combination of such opposites as intolerable and unbearable. Their *new moons* and *appointed feasts* were no longer a source of joy to him, but rather a weary burden that he was obliged to bear.

Prayer was also included in the list of cultic acts that had lost their significance because of sin. God indicated his rejection of Israel's prayers by hiding his eyes and stopping his ears. He refused even to look upon hands outstretched in prayer, for these same hands were *full of blood*. This does not mean that they were simply stained with blood, for to be *full of blood* means to be *dripping with blood* (cf. 34:6). The accusation is made even more forceful by the use of the plural for *blood* (lit., *bloods*), a form that usually suggests blood that was shed violently, as in war (cf. 1 Chron. 22:8; 28:3) or in murder (cf. Gen. 4:10; 2 Kings 9:26). It is interesting to note that the Dead Sea Scroll of Isaiah (1QIs^a) completes v. 15 by adding the parallel phrase, "and your fin-

gers with iniquity," an ending that was obviously borrowed from 59:3.

Accusation is followed by exhortation. Nine imperatives in vv. 16–17 prescribe a course of action for the men of Judah. The first instructs them to *wash* themselves. The verb *rachats* occurs 72 times in the Old Testament and in all instances except one refers to the washing of the flesh, either of men (cf. Gen. 24:32; Ex. 2:5; 40:12; 2 Sam. 12:20; 2 Kings 5:10) or of sacrificial animals (cf. Ex. 29:17; Lev. 8:21; 9:14). Its only other occurrence in Isaiah is in 4:4, where it tells of a day "when the Lord shall have washed away the filth of the daughters of Zion and cleansed the bloodstains of Jerusalem."

It is absurd to argue, as some have done, that the men of Judah were murderers, and therefore incapable of washing themselves. It is inconceivable that God would have commanded them to do that which they were unable to do. The washing demanded of them was a symbolic act signifying a spirit of true repentance. Furthermore, as 4:4 clearly indicates, it was in reality God himself who effected the cleansing. What he demanded, that he also gave.

The negative command "cease to do evil" is balanced by the positive "learn to do good." Here, as elsewhere in the prophets, goodness has a social orientation. One demonstrates his goodness when he seeks justice, corrects oppression, and defends the fatherless and the widow. The good man, therefore, is not merely the religious man, or the temperate man, or the moral man; he must be also the man who befriends the poor and the needy; who will not take advantage of another's misfortune, but raises his voice in protest when others do so; who does everything in his power to correct oppression and to build a just and lasting society. Isaiah was saying, "This is what God demands of you. Do this, and you shall live; ignore this, and the result will be chaos and ruin."

The KJV apparently follows the Septuagint rather than the Hebrew text in v.

17, thereby incorrectly translating the third injunction to read: "relieve the oppressed." Even the RSV weakens the force of the original with its rendering: "correct oppression." A more accurate reading would be: "set right the oppressor" or "straighten out the oppressor." The injunction directs the men of Judah to deal with the causes of oppression rather than merely to treat the symptoms. An example of the application of this principle in a modern setting is that provided by the German theologian and martyr, Dietrich Bonhoeffer, who in justification of his opposition to Nazism declared, "It is not only my task to look after the victims of madmen who drive a motorcar in a crowded street, but to do all in my power to stop their driving at all." [47]

(4) A Call to Decision (1:18-20)

18 "Come now, let us reason together,
    says the LORD:
  though your sins are like scarlet,
    they shall be as white as snow;
  though they are red like crimson,
    they shall become like wool.
19 If you are willing and obedient,
    you shall eat the good of the land;
20 But if you refuse and rebel,
    you shall be devoured by the sword;
  for the mouth of the LORD has spoken."

God's summons to sinners to come before him in order that they might *reason together* should perhaps be understood in the sense of settling a case in court. The verb *to reason* belongs to the legal vocabulary of the Old Testament and is used elsewhere to mean to rebuke (cf. 29:21; 37:4; Gen. 31:42), to lodge a complaint (cf. Gen. 21:25; Mic. 6:2), to argue one's case (cf. Job 13:3; 23:7), to render a decision (cf. 11:3,4; Gen. 31:37), and to be vindicated (cf. Gen. 20:16). This verse therefore calls upon sinners not to enter into debate with God but to stand at attention before him while he sums up his case against them and explains the alternative open to them.

This interpretation calls into question the

47 Dietrich Bonhoeffer, *The Cost of Discipleship*, trans. R. H. Fuller (New York: Macmillan Company, 1959), p. 22.

translation of the latter half of v. 18 as it appears in both the KJV and the RSV. To regard the words of the prophet as an unconditional promise of forgiveness—one commentator has described it as "that tender, that incredible evangel"—is to ignore both the context in which it stands and the general tenor of Isaiah's preaching.

Since the particle *'im*, translated *though*, sometimes serves to introduce an interrogative sentence (cf. 10:15; 29:16; 1 Kings 1:27; Job 6:12; 39:13), some have translated the clauses in v. 18b as indignant questions: "If your sins are like scarlet, can they also be as white as snow? If they are red like crimson, can they be as wool?" According to this interpretation, Isaiah regarded such a possibility as unthinkable. He intended these rhetorical questions, therefore, to serve as a rebuke to those who looked upon the sacrificial system as an easy solution to the sin problem.

Others have suggested that the phrases should be treated as conditional sentences and that the verbs in the main clauses should be translated as jussives, i.e., as expressing a wish or command. The latter half of v. 18, therefore, would constitute God's challenge to the sinners in Judah: "Though your sins are like scarlet, *let them be made* as white as snow; though they are red like crimson, *let them become* as wool."

This interpretation does not preclude the possibility of forgiveness, but neither does it suggest that forgiveness will be given automatically or unconditionally. "Let them become as wool" is based upon the prior assumption that "they may become as wool," but this open possibility of divine forgiveness will be translated into reality only by the willing response of the people.

A clear statement of the alternatives open to the men of Judah is given in vv. 19-20. Isaiah was convinced that a dreadful reckoning awaited those who persisted in sin. On the other hand, forgiveness and prosperity would be the reward of those who were willingly obedient to the word of the Lord. A striking play on words is found in these verses, although it is obscured in English translations. In order to sharpen the contrast between the alternatives facing the nation, the prophet declares, "If you are willing and obedient, *you shall eat* . . . but if you refuse and rebel, *you shall be devoured* . . ." The forms translated "you shall eat" and "you shall be devoured" are derived from the same Hebrew verbal root. The prophet was saying in effect "If you obey, you shall eat; if you disobey, you shall be eaten."

(5) The Moral Decay of Jerusalem (1:21–23)

21 How the faithful city
   has become a harlot,
   she that was full of justice!
Righteousness lodged in her,
   but now murderers.
22 Your silver has become dross,
   your wine mixed with water.
23 Your princes are rebels
   and companions of thieves.
Every one loves a bribe
   and runs after gifts.
They do not defend the fatherless,
   and the widow's cause does not come to
   them.

These verses constitute a lament over the rise and fall of Jerusalem. The first verse is written in the *Qinah* meter, a literary device used to express sorrow and lamentation. It produces an unbalanced rhythm, sometimes referred to as a "limping" rhythm, by means of a succession of accented syllables in a 3 plus 2 pattern. This lament, like many others in the Old Testament, begins with the plaintive "How!" (cf. 2 Sam. 1:19; Psalm 137:4; Lam. 1:1; 2:1; 4:1; Hos. 11:8).

Jerusalem's past faithfulness stands in sharp contrast to her present infidelity. The prophet describes the city as it once was and as it is now. He was not so much attempting to idealize the past as to show the difference between the past and the present. The past which he had in mind was perhaps the period of David's reign.

In the past Jerusalem had been a *faith-*

ful city, the lodging place of *justice* and *righteousness.* Since words are known not only by their origins but also by the company they keep, it is instructive to note that *justice* and *righteousness* are often linked together in Old Testament usage (cf. 5:7,16; 9:7; 16:5; 28:17; 32:1,16; 33:5; 1 Kings 10:9; Psalms 72:1,2; 89:14; Prov. 21:3; Amos 5:24). In Hebrew thought *righteousness* stood for the principle of rectitude as reflected in the person of God himself. *Justice* was the practical expression of the principle of righteousness in one's dealings with others.

The city where righteousness used to lodge had now become the lodging place of *murderers.* She who once was *faithful* had now become a *harlot.* The context shows that the accusation was brought against her not because she was idolatrous but because she tolerated social injustice. The charge, therefore, was a serious one, for it meant not merely that she had ceased to love God but more importantly that she had ceased to be concerned with the welfare of men.

It has been suggested that Jerusalem's adultery resulted in her adulteration. Her moral deterioration is described under two metaphors, that of *silver* that has become slag, and of *wine* that has been weakened with water. The following verse indicates that these metaphors referred especially to the rulers of the people.

Princes refers not to members of the royal family but to the various classes of government officials and leaders, notably the judges, who had become contaminated through their lust for material gain. The verse opens with a pun that is difficult to reproduce in translation. The text transliterated would read: *sarayik sor*rim. In an effort to reproduce the meaning of the original as well as to preserve the play on words, some have rendered the phrase to read, "Your princes are unprincipled," while others have preferred the rendering, "Your rulers are unruly." One might also suggest that it be translated, "Your rulers have become rascals." The occurrence of a similar saying in Hosea 9:15 suggests that it may have been a proverbial expression.

Isaiah pictures the plight of the defenseless members of society whose only claim for consideration was their misfortune. Because the officials loved bribes and ran after gifts, they refused the petitions of any who could not afford to pay them. Justice was dispensed for a price, and the complaints of widows and orphans were not even considered.

(6) God's Purifying Judgment (1:24–26)

24 Therefore the Lord says,
     the LORD of hosts,
     the Mighty One of Israel:
   "Ah, I will vent my wrath on my enemies,
     and avenge myself on my foes.
25 I will turn my hand against you
     and will smelt away your dross as with
       lye
     and remove all your alloy.
26 And I will restore your judges as at the first,
     and your counselors as at the beginning.
   Afterward you shall be called the city of
       righteousness,
     the faithful city."

The preceding oracle treats of Jerusalem's past and present; this one focuses upon her future. Her deep defilement calls for drastic action; superficial cleansing will not avail in her case. God will have to deal with her harshly before he can deal with her kindly.

God addresses her in the first person, announcing his intention to visit her with his purifying and redemptive judgment. As a result, she will be refined like precious metal, and her dross and alloy will be taken away. God will remove the rebels who have been ruling over her, replacing them with righteous men. When the refining process is finished, she will again be called "the city of righteousness, the faithful city" (cf. v. 21).

If v. 24 were taken alone, it would suggest that the judgment was designed to be entirely punitive in nature, rather than re-demptive. Commentators have called attention to the unusual accumulation of divine names at the beginning of the

verse. The one judging Jerusalem is called "The Lord, Yahweh of hosts, the Mighty One of Israel." Whenever the title "Lord" ('adhon) occurs in Isaiah with the definite article (ha'adhon), it always introduces a threat or a warning (cf. 3:1; 10:16,33; 19:4). The generally accepted meaning of 'abhir, translated "Mighty One," is bull, or steer. "The Bull of Jacob (Israel)," therefore, is a metaphorical title describing God's great power and might (cf. 49:26; 60:16; Gen. 49:24; Psalm 132:2,5). The Mighty One of Israel is ready to vent his wrath on his enemies, who in this case are not the foreign nations, but Israel itself (cf. 63:10; Lam. 2:5).

In vv. 25–26 the thought emerges that only the wicked will perish in the fires of judgment. The good and bad alike must suffer; but in the end the good will come forth as pure silver, while the bad will be cast away as worthless dross. The passage therefore embodies Isaiah's concept of the remnant, although the actual word for remnant does not occur until later.

The reference to the use of *lye* in the refining process has been variously interpreted. Some have suggested that lye, an alkali obtained from a species of plant that grew in the salt marshes surrounding the Dead Sea, was used as a cleansing agent in the smelting process. Such a usage is unknown, however, and elsewhere in the Old Testament lye is associated with soap and mentioned as a cleansing agent in washing (cf. Jer. 2:22; Mal. 3:2). The KJV interprets the word as an adjective used adverbially and renders it "purely." The consonants in the Hebrew word translated "as with lye" are *kbr*. Some scholars have advocated rearranging these to read *bkr*, a word meaning "in the furnace." Thus Goodspeed translates, "And [I] will smelt out your dross in the furnace." While this slight emendation produces an attractive reading, it lacks the support of any of the early manuscripts or versions.

This passage is significant for the light it sheds upon Isaiah's eschatology. The prophet apparently expected the purification and restoration of Jerusalem to take place in the near future. He described the age of restoration in general terms, apart from any reference to a king. He envisioned a restored city that would be ruled over by righteous judges and wise counselors. In recognition of its new character it would be given a new name, *the city of righteousness.*

(7) The Righteous and the Wicked (1: 27-31)

27 Zion shall be redeemed by justice,
   and those in her who repent, by right-
      eousness.
28 But rebels and sinners shall be destroyed
      together,
   and those who forsake the LORD shall be
      consumed.
29 For you shall be ashamed of the oaks
      in which you delighted;
   and you shall blush for the gardens
      which you have chosen.
30 For you shall be like an oak
      whose leaf withers,
   and like a garden without water.
31 And the strong shall become tow,
      and his work a spark,
   and both of them shall burn together,
      with none to quench them.

A change from the third to the second person occurs between vv. 27-28 and 29-31 of the Hebrew text, although the Septuagint has the third person throughout. Because of the change of persons in the Hebrew text, some have concluded that the verses contain the remnants of two originally distinct compositions; however, such a change of persons is not uncommon in the prophetical books of the Old Testament.

The theme of the passage is the fate of the righteous and the wicked. The former are identified as those who *repent* in *Zion.* They will be *redeemed by justice* and *by righteousness.* This must not be interpreted to mean that they will qualify for salvation because of their justice and righteousness but rather that they will be saved by means of the Lord's righteous judgments.

Redeem (padah) is a rare word in Isaiah, occurring only here and in 29:22; 35:10; and 51:11. The original meaning of the word was to ransom a person or animal from death by means of a substitute or a money payment (cf. Ex. 13:13). The Septuagint, therefore, almost always rendered it by some form of the verb *lutroomai,* a technical term derived from commercial law. As used in the present context it means simply to save, or to deliver (cf. Psalms 25:22; 119:134; 130:8).

The specific charge brought against the wicked was that of idolatry, which had taken the form of tree worship. The most likely meaning of v. 29 is that the people were engaging in idolatrous rites beneath oaks or terebinths; some commentators, however, interpret the verse as an allusion to the rich and their country estates. If the reference is to some form of tree worship, it may have involved participation in the Canaanite fertility cult, which was generally practiced on the hilltops and under great trees (cf. 2 Kings 16:4; Jer. 2:20; Hos. 4:13). The *gardens* were probably groves of such sacred trees.

There is a play on words in vv. 29-30. The worshipers had chosen oaks and gardens; therefore they would perish like oaks —with withered leaves!—and like gardens —without water! In other words, their fate and that of the objects they worshiped would be the same.

The sin of idolatry brings its own punishment, according to v. 31. The *strong* is a rare term which occurs only here and in Amos 2:9, where it also stands in relationship to trees. It is a term used to designate the sinners in Zion. They shall become like tow, the fiber of flax and other similar plants which was used to start fires. Their work, that is, their idolatrous acts, will provide the spark that ignites the tow. It will be as if they were covered with inflammable materials and were playing with fire; suddenly they burst into a blazing flame which no man can quench. This is Isaiah's way of saying that sin brings its own punishment.

2. Jerusalem, Present and Future (2:1— 4:6)

The three chapters included under this heading consist of a combination of oracles of judgment and of redemption, all of which are addressed to Judah and Jerusalem. The section opens and closes with eschatological passages predicting the future glorification of Jerusalem (cf. 2:1–5; 4:2–6). Sandwiched in between these oracles of hope are oracles of judgment dealing with the city's sinful present. Those who attribute the oracles of hope to Isaiah usually date them in the latter part of his ministry. The judgment oracles, on the other hand, are generally regarded as among the earliest examples of his prophetic preaching.

(1) A Vision of Universal Peace (2:1–5)

1 The word which Isaiah the son of Amoz saw concerning Judah and Jerusalem.
2 It shall come to pass in the latter days
    that the mountain of the house of the Lord
  shall be established as the highest of the
      mountains,
  and shall be raised above the hills;
 and all the nations shall flow to it,
3   and many peoples shall come, and say:
"Come, let us go up to the mountain of the
     Lord,
  to the house of the God of Jacob;
  that he may teach us his ways
    and that we may walk in his paths."
For out of Zion shall go forth the law,
  and the word of the Lord from Jerusalem.
4 He shall judge between the nations,
  and shall decide for many peoples;
 and they shall beat their swords into plow-
    shares,
  and their spears into pruning hooks;
 nation shall not lift up sword against nation,
  neither shall they learn war any more.
5 O house of Jacob,
  come, let us walk
  in the light of the Lord.

The opening verse does not belong to the vision, but is the title of a larger collection of prophetic materials. Some believe that the larger collection may include chapters 2—12, with the possible exception of those oracles not addressed to Judah and Jerusalem. Others would limit the collection to chapters 2—4, to which chapter 5 was perhaps later appended. As a matter of fact, it is no longer possible to discover the limits of the collection to which this title was originally affixed.

Isaiah's prophecy of universal peace is repeated in a slightly longer form in Micah 4:1–4. It is also referred to in an inverted fashion in Joel 3:10. These factors all serve to complicate the question of authorship. Are these words to be attributed to Isaiah, or to Micah? Or are they to be attributed to neither, but rather regarded as an anonymous prophecy, a type of "floating oracle," that was introduced into both Isaiah and Micah either by the prophets themselves or by later editors? Each of these alternatives has had its advocates.

The position taken here is that Isaiah was the originator of this oracle and that Micah borrowed it from him. The objection that such a vision of universal peace was too advanced for the eighth century B.C. is invalidated by an examination of 9:2–7 and 11:1–9, where the concept of an eternal reign of peace is also to be found. The slightly longer form of the oracle in Micah can be explained on the basis of the expression "for the mouth of the Lord of hosts has spoken" (Mic. 4:4). This marks the only occurrence of the expression outside the book of Isaiah. Since it appears in three passages in Isaiah (1:20; 40:5; 58:14), it may be regarded as genuinely Isaianic in origin. The conclusion to be drawn from this evidence is that Micah 4:4 preserved the ending of what was originally an Isaianic oracle, but that for some unknown reason the ending has been lost from the book of Isaiah itself. It is also missing from the Dead Sea Scroll of Isaiah.

A distinction has sometimes been made between the messianic and the theocentric eschatology of the Old Testament. The former is represented by passages that envisage a future in which the king is the bearer or executor of Yahweh's salvation (cf. 9:2–7; 11:1–9; Mic. 5:2–4; Zech. 9: 9–10). The latter is related to passages in which Yahweh works alone without human assistance in the achieving of his purpose. Isaiah's vision of universal peace belongs to the second category, since it contains no reference to a messianic ruler.

Much theocentric eschatology is also apocalyptic, but this is not the case with

2:1-5. It does not point to a cataclysmic end to world history nor to the in-breaking of a new world order, but rather to a time within history when all nations will come to Zion to learn the ways of God and to walk in his paths. The vision is set *in the latter days,* an expression meaning simply in the future or in days to come. It is altogether likely that the prophet expected the actualization of his vision within his own lifetime.

The temple of the Lord, here designated as *the house of the Lord,* stands at the center of the vision. It serves a different function, however, from that of the Temple of Jerusalem in Isaiah's time. The nations are depicted as streaming to it not to place sacrifices upon its altar but to receive the *law (torah)* and the *word (dabhar)* of the Lord. The central purpose of the temple, therefore is prophetic rather than priestly.

The mountain upon which the house of the Lord stands is to be raised up so that it will tower above all other mountains. This is, of course, poetic hyperbole and must not be interpreted literally. In actuality, the hill upon which the Temple stood was not even the highest hill in the vicinity of Jerusalem, much less in all the world. To say that the mountain of the Lord's house will be exalted above all other mountains means simply that the glory and majesty of the Lord will be clearly revealed to all men everywhere. When this occurs all nations will converge on Jerusalem as if drawn by a magnetic force.

The stated purpose of their pilgrimage to Zion is that they might learn the ways of God and walk in his paths. It is significant that the law of the Lord goes forth from Zion and not from Sinai. Isaiah had virtually nothing to say about Sinai or the Exodus, but he showed himself to be especially interested in Zion. The name itself occurs 29 times in chapters 1—39, and 17 times in chapters 40—66. Isaiah's interest in Zion as the place of Yahweh's revelation is paralleled by a concern with the promises of Yahweh to the Davidic dynasty. Both of these emphases were perhaps associated with the ancient pre-Israelite Jerusalemite traditions of the Jebusites.

If this vision is to be dated in the latter part of Isaiah's ministry, as many scholars believe to be true, it should be interpreted as reflecting his disillusionment with foreign affairs through 40 years of crises. Prolonged strife and bloodshed had caused him to long for the day when the nations of the earth would renounce armed conflict and submit their differences to Yahweh for his arbitration. He did not envision a world in which there would be no tensions or conflicting interests, but rather a world in which men would resolve their tensions and conflicts without resort to arms.

Of special interest in this poem is the concept that war is "learned." The basic meaning of this of course is that the soldier has to be taught the skills of warfare. Thus the Old Testament expression "expert in war" (cf. 1 Chron. 5:18; Song of Sol. 3:8) means literally "learned in war." In an earlier passage in Judges 3:1 f. it is stated that Yahweh spared certain of the Canaanite nations in order that he might "teach war" to the generations of Israelites who had not known it before. In like manner Israel's kings attributed their success in battle to the fact that Yahweh "taught their hands to war" (cf. 2 Sam. 22:35; Psalms 18:34; 144:1). All of these passages reflect the Old Testament concept of holy war.

Isaiah's words constitute a challenge to the modern concept that it is the nature of things to be at war. He would have rejected the notion that eternal conflict between nations and classes is inevitable, if not indeed desirable. He also would have challenged the view that violent revolution is the only road to social and political justice. He saw a better solution to the world's problems. His view is that war is not an inevitable factor in human affairs but one that has developed from a body of acquired habits which could be replaced by another set of habits better serving the interests of mankind. The words of this tremendous vision have appropriately been inscribed on the walls of the United Nations Plaza in New York: "The nations shall beat their swords into plowshares, and their spears into pruning hooks: nation shall not lift up sword against nation, neither shall they learn war any more."

The conclusion to the oracle, which is missing from Isaiah but has been preserved in Micah 4:4, asserts that the disarming of the nations will result in the elimination of poverty and fear: ". . . they shall sit every man under his vine and under his fig tree, and none shall make them afraid; . . ." This is the Old Testament's way of saying that the only *truly effective war on poverty is a war on war.* Only when men have converted their swords into plowshares and their spears into pruning hooks will they be able to dwell in security amidst their own vineyards and orchards.

Translated into the idiom of a technological society, the oracle means that we should beware lest we devote our technological skills to destructive ends. Our own swords and spears are our guided missiles with their atomic warheads. The world will never know peace and security until these weapons of destruction have been converted into projects beneficial to mankind. If this is ever to occur, it must be preceded by a worldwide turning to the Lord such as that envisioned by the prophet.

Isaiah clearly understood the difficulty of translating vision into reality, and he therefore exhorted the house of Jacob to come and walk in the light of the Lord (v. 5). Light may be a symbol either of the law of the Lord (cf. Psalm 119:105; Prov. 6:23) or of the salvation of the Lord (cf. Psalm 27:1). In either case this verse exhorts Israel to begin to live in the present as if the age of peace had already arrived (cf. v. 3).

(2) The Day of the Lord (2:6–22)

6 For thou hast rejected thy people,
    the house of Jacob,
because they are full of diviners from the east
and of soothsayers like the Philistines,
    and they strike hands with foreigners.
7 Their land is filled with silver and gold,
    and there is no end to their treasures;
their land is filled with horses,
    and there is no end to their chariots.
8 Their land is filled with idols;
    they bow down to the work of their hands,
    to what their own fingers have made.
9 So man is humbled,
    and men are brought low—
    forgive them not!
10 Enter into the rock,
    and hide in the dust
from before the terror of the LORD,
    and from the glory of his majesty.
11 The haughty looks of man shall be brought low,
    and the pride of men shall be humbled;
and the LORD alone will be exalted
    in that day.
12 For the LORD of hosts has a day
    against all that is proud and lofty,
    against all that is lifted up and high;
13 against all the cedars of Lebanon,
    lofty and lifted up;
    and against all the oaks of Bashan;
14 against all the high mountains,
    and against all the lofty hills;
15 against every high tower,
    and against every fortified wall;
16 against all the ships of Tarshish,
    and against all the beautiful craft.
17 And the haughtiness of man shall be humbled,
    and the pride of men shall be brought low;
and the LORD alone will be exalted in that day.
18 And the idols shall utterly pass away.
19 And men shall enter the caves of the rocks
    and the holes of the ground,
from before the terror of the LORD,
    and from the glory of his majesty,
    when he rises to terrify the earth.
20 In that day men will cast forth
    their idols of silver and their idols of gold,
which they made for themselves to worship,
    to the moles and to the bats,
21 to enter the caverns of the rocks
    and the clefts of the cliffs,
from before the terror of the LORD,
    and from the glory of his majesty,
    when he rises to terrify the earth.
22 Turn away from man
    in whose nostrils is breath,
    for of what account is he?

The theme of the passage is the approaching day of judgment against human pride and idolatry. The "day of the Lord" is a term that occurs often in the Old Testament, especially in the prophetic books. It is sometimes abbreviated as "the day" (cf. Ezek. 7:12; 30:2 f.) or "that day" (cf. 2:11,17,20; 4:1; 11:10). Its primary reference is to the day of the Lord's triumph over his foes, and it probably has its roots in the holy war tradition. It designates those times and seasons in history when God intervenes to judge the wicked and to deliver the righteous. When all the references to the day of the Lord are placed together, however, the aspect of judgment outweighs that of salvation and deliverance (cf. Zeph. 1:15).

An interesting feature of this passage is the repetition, with slight variations, of two refrains, one in vv. 10,19,21, and another in vv. 9,11,17. More textual problems are found here than in perhaps any other passage in Isaiah. Verse 22 is missing from the Septuagint, and vv. 9b–10 are lacking in the Dead Sea Scroll of Isaiah.

The passage begins with a charge against the house of Jacob, a designation either of the Northern Kingdom or, as is more likely, of the whole family of Israel. The Israelites are condemned first of all for having filled their land with corrupting customs borrowed from their pagan neighbors. Chief among these is the art of soothsaying (v. 6), one of the superstitious means whereby the ancients sought to discover secret knowledge, especially concerning the future. Soothsaying and all other similar practices were regarded as totally inappropriate for God's people (cf. Deut. 18: 9–14). If God wished to impart knowledge concerning the future, he would do so through his servants the prophets.

The second charge brought against the people of Israel is that they have filled their land with wealth and with instruments of war (v. 7). The implication is that they have placed their trust in material possessions rather than in God. The reference to a land filled with silver and gold suggests that the oracle belongs to the earliest part of Isaiah's ministry, when the nation was still benefiting from the prosperous years of Uzziah's reign. They had let the splendor of his reign blind them to the impending judgment.

Israel is also charged with having filled her land with idols so that she bows down and worships that which her own fingers have fashioned (v. 8). In so doing she has violated the first of the Ten Commandments that God gave her. Her punishment, therefore, is inevitable. Verses 9–11 furnish a vivid description of inescapable judgment brought upon the people because of their own sins.

Verse 9 presents the interpreter with a number of problems. Do the verbs refer to the present or to the future? Are they to be understood in a reflexive or in a passive sense? According to one interpretation, they refer to the time of the prophet and their meaning is that everyone, both great and small, bows himself down before manmade gods. Because of the enormity of the sins of the people, therefore, the prophet asks God to withhold forgiveness from them. Others interpret the verbs as describing the future humiliation of the people because of their idolatry. The meaning according to this view is that when God arises to judge the earth arrogant and sinful men will be humbled and brought low. The weight of the evidence seems to favor the first interpretation.

The severity of the judgment is reflected in v. 10. Sinners are warned to enter into the caves and to hide in the dust in order to escape the terror of the Lord. Palestine was filled with limestone caves which afforded natural hiding places in times of danger (cf. 1 Sam. 13:6; 14:11; 22:1; 1 Kings 18:4; Hos. 10:8). Though the nature of the judgment is not otherwise indicated, the reference to hiding in caves would suggest a foreign invasion. It may well be that the prophet was thinking in terms of the Assyrian invasion.

The Hebrew prophets' concept of sin was rich and varied. Amos viewed it as social injustice, the callous exploitation of the weak by the strong. To Hosea it was infidelity, or spiritual harlotry. Isaiah saw the root of all evil in man's pride and rebellion, his inveterate tendency to live as though Yahweh were not king. He, therefore, announced a day when the pride and haughtiness of men would be brought low, and the Lord alone would be exalted (v. 10).

The scene of Yahweh's action is broadened in the latter part of the passage to include not only Israel but all mankind. Among the prophets Isaiah was the first to proclaim a universal judgment. He subscribed to the view that Yahweh was the sovereign ruler of all nations and that his law could not be disregarded with impunity. The law of the harvest applied to nations as well as to individuals; whatsoever a nation sowed that would it also reap.

The chief targets of Yahweh's wrath are human pride (vv. 12–17) and idolatry (vv. 18–22). Pride is depicted by a series of metaphors drawn from nature (vv. 13–14) and from the realm of human endeavor (vv. 15–16). The passage bears a striking resemblance to the story of the tower of Babel in Genesis 11:1–9, for both treat of man's overweening pride and self-adulation.

The metaphors from nature include the cedars of Lebanon, the oaks of Bashan, the high mountains, and the lofty hills. Because of the strength and loftiness of these natural phenomena, they served as fitting symbols of man's pride and vainglory. The high towers, fortified walls, Tarshish ships, and beautiful craft represented man's own works in which he took pride. Tarshish ships are included in the list because they were heavy ore-carrying vessels such as those that operated out of the Red Sea port of Ezion-geber (cf. 1 Kings 9:26–28; 2 Chron. 20:36).

Isaiah's message is that the Lord of hosts has a day on which he will judge all of the symbols of man's pride. The Lord alone will be exalted on that day. The emphasis is upon the word *alone* (v. 17). Men often make the mistake of conferring upon the works of their own hands a greatness that belongs to God alone. They forget that man's works—even his highest works— are not eternal but transitory and perishable. In a world of change and decay only God is eternal.

Verses 18–22 describe the coming destruction of all idols and the utter consternation of all idolaters. Their cry will be, "Back to the caves!" In vain will they attempt to find a hiding place from the fury of the Lord. Verse 18 states emphatically that their idols will utterly vanish. The play on words at the end of v. 19 is difficult to reproduce in translation. The two Hebrew words translated *to terrify the earth* are la'arots ha'arets. If we could borrow a foreign word, we might translate this to read "when he rises to terrify the terrestrial regions below." The same play on words is repeated in v. 21, and the Septuagint gives evidence that this verse was once joined to v. 10.

The prophets object to idolatry not only on theological but also on moral grounds, for idol worship inevitably leads to a lowering of moral and ethical standards (cf. Hos. 9:10). It is easy for us to condemn idolatry in ancient Israel and yet be unaware of our own forms of idolatry. An idol has been defined as any philosophical concept or material object that becomes a substitute for God. The essence of idolatry, therefore, is the setting of something less than God in the place of God. It is the denial of God's claim to absolute lordship over one's life. Let us not delude ourselves into thinking that we can hold on to God with one hand and to some cherished idol with the other. At the very heart of the Scriptures stands the injunction: "Choose you this day whom you will serve."

The utter futility of idolatry is set forth in vv. 20–21. It is in the day of calamity, when man most desperately needs help, that the impotence of idols is most clearly revealed. They offer no assistance and no protection, but must themselves be deposited in caves inhabited by moles and bats.

The concluding verse in chapter 2 is

missing from the Septuagint, which may
indicate that it represents a later scribe's
comment on the human situation. The author sees the frailty of man as symbolized
by the breath in his nostrils. The Old
Testament concept of man is that he is but
a creature of dust animated by the breath
of God (cf. Gen. 2:7; Psalms 104:29;
146:4; Eccl. 12:7). The question at the
end of v. 22 is rhetorical, and signifies
that man is to be regarded as of no account. The question must be understood,
of course, against the background of Isaiah's pessimistic view of the men of his
day (cf. Jer. 17:5).

(3) *The Disintegration of Judean Society*
   (3:1–15)

1 For, behold, the Lord, the Lord of hosts,
   is taking away from Jerusalem and from
       Judah
   stay and staff,
       the whole stay of bread,
       and the whole stay of water;
2 the mighty man and the soldier,
       the judge and the prophet,
       the diviner and the elder,
3 the captain of fifty
       and the man of rank,
   the counselor and the skilful magician
       and the expert in charms.
4 And I will make boys their princes,
       and babes shall rule over them.
5 And the people will oppress one another,
       every man his fellow
       and every man his neighbor;
   the youth will be insolent to the elder,
       and the base fellow to the honorable.
6 When a man takes hold of his brother
       in the house of his father, saying:
   "You have a mantle;
       you shall be our leader,
   and this heap of ruins
       shall be under your rule";
7 in that day he will speak out, saying:
   "I will not be a healer;
       in my house there is neither bread nor
           mantle;
   you shall not make me
       leader of the people."
8 For Jerusalem has stumbled,
       and Judah has fallen;
   because their speech and their deeds are
       against the Lord,
       defying his glorious presence.
9 Their partiality witnesses against them;
   they proclaim their sin like Sodom,

they do not hide it.
Woe to them!
   For they have brought evil upon them-
       selves.
10 Tell the righteous that it shall be well with
       them,
   for they shall eat the fruit of their deeds.
11 Woe to the wicked! It shall be ill with him,
   for what his hands have done shall be
       done to him.
12 My people—children are their oppressors,
       and women rule over them.
   O my people, your leaders mislead you,
       and confuse the course of your paths.
13 The Lord has taken his place to contend,
       he stands to judge his people.
14 The Lord enters into judgment
       with the elders and princes of his people:
   "It is you who have devoured the vineyard,
       the spoil of the poor is in your houses.
15 What do you mean by crushing my people,
       by grinding the face of the poor?" says
       the Lord God of hosts.

The section falls naturally into three divisions: (a) vv. 1–7, social chaos and
anarchy; (b) vv. 8–12, a ruined people;
(c) vv. 13–15, God's judgment against
Judah's rulers. The passage depicts a time
when Judah will experience a crisis in leadership, and the administration of the country will fall into the hands of incompetent
weaklings. Many have interpreted the crisis
as that which occurred at the anointing
of Ahaz, who succeeded to the throne
when he was only 20 years of age (2 Kings
16:2). The internal evidence, however, is
too vague and general for the passage to
be dated with any certainty.

The prophet attributes the removal of
all competent leaders of society and government to Judah's Lord, whose sovereign
power is emphasized by the formal title in
v. 1: *"the* Lord, Yahweh of hosts." He
removes from the structure of Judean society both "stay and staff." The alliteration,
"stay and staff," approximates that of the
the Hebrew text, where the same word is
repeated in its masculine and feminine
forms. Included in the phrase are all those
who serve as supports or pillars of Judah's
social and political structure. Their removal
will result in the total collapse of law and
order.

A representative list of those who are to be removed from their positions of responsibility is given in vv. 2 and 3. The fact that king and priests are omitted from the list indicates that it was not meant to be exhaustive. Since there are no definite articles in the Hebrew text, the translation should read: "mighty man, man of war, judge, prophet, diviner, elder," etc. The military leaders are listed first because they were the country's first line of defense in the troubled days in which Isaiah lived. The civil leaders are represented by judge, elder, and counselor; prophet, diviner, skilful magician, and expert in charms typify the religious leaders. The fact that Isaiah included in his list of religious leaders the diviner, the magician, and the expert in charms did not mean that he condoned the activities of these; he simply recognized that they were regarded as leaders of the popular religion of his day.

When the pillars of society have been removed, their place will be taken by mere *boys* and *babes,* young in years and lacking in wisdom and experience. With the restraints removed, violence and oppression will become the order of the day (v. 5). Youths will be insolent toward their elders, and base fellows toward the honorable. This is an appalling picture of a broken-down and leaderless society.

Verses 6 and 7 describe the desperate but futile efforts of men to find a leader in such a time of chaos. They lay hold of one whose only apparent qualification is that he possesses an outer garment. They try to persuade him to take the responsibility of restoring order. He declines, however, pleading that he is just as poor as all the others.

The ruin of Jerusalem and Judah is further elaborated in vv. 8 and 9. That the ruin will inevitably come to pass is shown by the prophet's use of the perfect form of the verb throughout these verses. As set forth in vv. 1–7, Judah's destruction will come as the result of her rejection of God's rule in her life. In both her speech and her deeds she has manifested a re-

bellious spirit.

The opening clause in v. 9 admits of two interpretations, as reflected in the translations of the RSV and the KJV. The former reads, *Their partiality witnesses against them.* Those who prefer this translation see in it a reference to Judah's inconsistency in the administration of justice (cf. Deut. 1:17; 16:19). The implication is that her judges have shown favor toward the rich but have robbed the poor of the justice due them. The rendering of the KJV, "The show of their countenance both witness against them," may be interpreted to mean that their guilt is written upon their very faces. Since this is the only occurrence of this particular expression in the Old Testament, it is difficult to determine which of these translations more closely approximates its original meaning.

Verses 10 and 11 provide a contrast between the fate of the righteous and the wicked similar to that found in Psalm 1. Since these verses stand apart from their context, many regard them as a later addition to Isaiah's prophecies.

Yahweh speaks in v. 12, twice referring to the inhabitants of Judah as *my people.* The repetition of the phrase reminds the people of their priviledged position as God's convenanted community. Because they have despised their spiritual heritage, confusion has overtaken them. The first part of the verse has an entirely different meaning in the Septuagint. Based upon a change of the vowels of *nashim* (women) to *noshim* (creditors), it reads, "O my people, your tax collectors are stripping you, and creditors [loan-sharks!] lord it over you." In this instance the Septuagint reading seems preferable to that of the Hebrew since it preserves the parallelism.

In vv. 13–15 Yahweh takes his stand to serve both as judge and accuser in the trial of Judah's leaders. The charge brought against them is that they have run roughshod over the weaker members of society. Instead of caring for the Lord's vineyard, they have destroyed it. The Old Testament lays great stress upon the duty of public officials to care for the poor and the oppressed. Judah's officials have failed to do this. Verse 15 is a scathing indictment addressed to them in the form of a question. Their only response is a guilty silence, for their crime is too obvious to be denied and too serious to be excused.

(4) The Haughty Women of Jerusalem (3:16—4:1)

16 The LORD said:
Because the daughters of Zion are haughty
and walk with outstretched necks,
glancing wantonly with their eyes,
mincing along as they go,
tinkling with their feet;
17 the Lord will smite with a scab
the heads of the daughters of Zion,
and the LORD will lay bare their secret
parts.
18 In that day the Lord will take away the finery of the anklets, the headbands, and the crescents; 19 the pendants, the bracelets, and the scarfs; 20 the headdresses, the armlets, the sashes, the perfume boxes, and the amulets; 21 the signet rings and nose rings; 22 the festal robes, the mantles, the cloaks, and the handbags; 23 the garments of gauze, the linen garments, the turbans, and the veils.
24 Instead of perfume there will be rottenness;
and instead of a girdle, a rope;
and instead of well-set hair, baldness;
and instead of a rich robe, a girding of
sackcloth;
instead of beauty, shame.
25 Your men shall fall by the sword
and your mighty men in battle.
26 And her gates shall lament and mourn;
ravaged, she shall sit upon the ground.
1 And seven women shall take hold of one man in that day, saying, "We will eat our own bread and wear our own clothes, only let us be called by your name; take away our reproach."

It must have been early in his ministry that Isaiah decided to take to task the proud women of Zion. Zion was the official designation for the Jerusalem acropolis, the upper fortified part of the city situated just south of the Temple area. Here lived the rich and the aristocratic, and it was to the women of these households that Isaiah directed his words. He used bold language in censuring them for their immodest and scandalous behavior. This was a subject about which he apparently had very strong

views.

Isaiah was not the only prophet who inveighed against the sensuality of women. Amos delivered a similar message to the women of Samaria (4:1–3). These prophets felt that a nation's destiny was largely determined by the quality of its womanhood. Its well-being was threatened when they became vulgar and self-indulgent. The women of Jerusalem shared the responsibility for their nation's moral collapse and were to be punished accordingly.

The fate of these fine women is graphically set forth by the prophet. They will soon be stripped of their soft clothing, their cosmetics, and their jewelry. The passage gives the most extensive catalogue of feminine finery to be found in the Old Testament. It mentions no less than 24 items of dress worn by the women of Zion. The antiquity of the list makes it virtually impossible to identify all the items, though many have been identified by archaeologists, and some are still in use today in the Near East.

Isaiah takes a certain savage satisfaction in describing the ostentatious vulgarity of these women. They go about the streets of Zion with head held high and with roving eye, jangling their bangles in order to attract the attention of men.

The form of their humiliation will be designed to fit their crime. The objects that feed their vanity will be turned to their shame. Heads now held high will be covered with scabs and smitten with baldness (v. 17). The final phrase in v. 17 appears in the RSV as *their secret parts*, although it could also be translated as "their foreheads." According to those who prefer the latter rendering, the reference is not to rape but to the loss of hair, which was to the ancient Hebrews a sign of deep shame (cf. 7:20).

Instead of a sweet odor, there will be the stench of decay; instead of the fashionable girdle, the captive's rope; instead of braided hair, baldness; and instead of the rich robe, a wrapping of sackcloth (v. 24). The latter part of v. 24 puzzled interpreters until the discovery of the Dead Sea Scroll of Isaiah. There is an obvious gap in the Masoretic Text, which reads: "For (*ki*) instead of beauty . . ." Translators tried to solve the problem by taking the conjunction *ki* (for) to be a rare noun meaning "branding," or "burning." Thus the KJV reads: "and burning instead of beauty." When the Dead Sea Scroll of Isaiah appeared, however, scholars noted that it supplied the word missing from the Masoretic Text. That word was *bosheth* (shame), and the resultant translation reads: "For instead of beauty there will be shame."

The worst fate in store for the women of Jerusalem was that the men of the city would fall by the sword. Verses 25–26 describe a city bereft of its male citizens. These verses are addressed not to the *daughters of Zion,* as are the preceding verses, but to the daughter of Zion, that is, to Jerusalem. The city sits as a solitary widow weeping over her slain. The passage presupposes an invasion of the land, although the invader is not named.

The desperate desire of the women of Jerusalem to find husbands is described in 4:1. The number *seven* is not to be taken literally but implies a large number of women. In the ancient world marriage arrangements were usually made by parents or legal guardians. In their distress, however, the women of Jerusalem abandon all reserve and adherence to custom and take the initiative in approaching the few remaining men with a proposition of marriage They plead with men to take them as wives and to let them bear children, thereby removing the disgrace of their childlessness. So desperate are they that they are even willing to be self-supporting, forgoing their legal right to be sustained by their husbands (cf. Ex. 21:10). On this somber note the oracles of judgment in this section come to a close.

(5) The Restoration of Jerusalem (4: 2–6)

2 In that day the branch of the LORD shall be beautiful and glorious, and the fruit of the land shall be the pride and glory of the survivors of Israel. **3 And he who is left in Zion and remains in Jerusalem will be called holy, every one who has been recorded for life in Jerusalem, 4 when the Lord shall have washed away the filth of the daughters of Zion and cleansed the bloodstains of Jerusalem from its midst by a spirit of judgment and by a spirit of burning. 5 Then the LORD will create over the whole site of Mount Zion and over her assemblies a cloud by day, and smoke and the shining of a flaming fire by night; for over all the glory there will be a canopy and a pavilion. 6 It will be for a shade by day from the heat, and for a refuge and a shelter from the storm and rain.**

This is the concluding oracle in the section comprising 2:1—4:6. Like the initial oracle (2:1–5) its theme is the future glorification of Jerusalem. It describes the eschatological age and the happy state of those who survive the judgments that are to sweep over Jerusalem. Those who remain in Jerusalem after the judgments have passed will be called holy and will experience the presence of the Lord like a mighty canopy protecting them from all harm and danger. This is one of the finest eschatological passages in the Old Testament, and its brevity enhances its beauty. Here Isaiah gives classic expression to his doctrine of a purified remnant, a doctrine that appears often throughout his writings (cf. 6:13; 10:20–21; 11:11; 28:5).

Many would assign this passage to the postexilic period. They cite its prosy style, its vocabulary, and its theological ideas, which they affirm to be later than the time of Isaiah. It may be argued, however, that while one cannot prove that Isaiah wrote the passage, neither is it possible simply on the basis of the arguments cited above to prove that he did not do so. It has been observed that the passage closely resembles 37:30–32, which scholars generally recognize to be Isaianic in character. It is possible, therefore, that both oracles are to be assigned to the latter part of Isaiah's ministry.

The word *branch* has been interpreted in at least three ways. In the light of its usage elsewhere in the Old Testament to describe the messianic king who comes forth from the stock of David (cf. Jer. 23:5; 33:15; Zech. 3:8; 6:12), some would interpret it as a reference to the Messiah. A second suggestion is that it refers to the righteous remnant that will emerge from the impending judgment. A third possibility is that this word (*tsemach*), whose literal meaning is "that which sprouts," should be rendered "the growth of the Lord." According to those who favor a literal interpretation of the term, therefore, it refers neither to the Messiah nor to a righteous remnant, but to the fertility of the land in the eschatological age. This would make it parallel to *the fruit of the land* in the latter half of the verse. Those who advocate this view point out that one of the recurring themes in Old Testament eschatology is the miraculous transformation of nature, resulting in the return of the earth to a paradisiacal state (cf. 11:6–9; Hos. 2:21–23; Amos 9:13–15).

The word *survivors* occurs in four other verses in Isaiah (10:20; 15:9; 37:31,32), and in all cases it refers to those who barely escape some threatening disaster. Though the precise nature of the disaster is not explained in the passage, its severity is nevertheless indicated by the reference to *a spirit of judgment* and *a spirit of burning*.

The fiery judgment will destroy sinners but purify saints. Three things are said about the latter. First, they are given a new name. They are called *holy*, a name which elsewhere in Isaiah is given to God alone. Second, their names are recorded in God's census book. In the clause *every one who has been recorded for life in Jerusalem* there is an allusion to the book of life in which God records the names of those who are his (cf. Ex. 32:32 f.; Dan. 12:1; Mal. 3:16; Rev. 20:12,15). The third distinction of those who survive the judgment is that their *filth* is washed away and their blood-stains cleansed. Thus the prophet forcefully declares that the qualifications for citizenship in the eschatological kingdom are moral and ethical.

The many obscurities in vv. 5–6 can easily be seen when one compares the Hebrew text with other ancient versions. The Septuagint, for example, reads: "And he shall come, and it shall be with regard to every place of Mount Zion, yea, all the region round about it shall a cloud overshadow by day, and there shall be as it were the smoke and light of fire burning by night: and upon all the glory shall be a defense. And it shall be for a shadow from the heat, and as a shelter and a hiding-place from inclemency of weather and from rain."

In spite of the differences between the versions, however, the meaning of the passage is fairly clear. In the eschatological age the whole site of Mount Zion will become a kind of holy of holies, and the glory of the Lord will protectively overshadow the people here as in the days of the wilderness wanderings (cf. Ex. 13:21 f.; 40:34–38). The words translated "canopy" and "pavilion" mean "bridal tent" (cf. Psalm 19:5; Joel 2:16) and "booth," respectively. The meaning is that God's protective presence will be extended over the inhabitants of Jerusalem like a bridal tent or like a booth set up to afford shelter for the harvest workers. God's people will be protected from all imaginable harm, symbolized here by the heat of the sun and the fury of the storm.

3. Sin and Judgment (5:1–30)

A parable opens this section (vv. 1–7), which is then continued with a series of six oracles against the wicked (vv. 8–25), and concluded with a threat of invasion (vv. 26–30). While the parable and the doom oracles probably belong to the early years of Isaiah's ministry, it must not be supposed that they were all delivered on the same occasion. It is more likely that they were first spoken on separate occasions and only later gathered together by the prophet's disciples. They seem to have been grouped together because of their common theme of sin and judgment. The threat of foreign invasion (vv. 26–30) is thought by many to be the misplaced conclusion to the oracle complex which stands in 9:8—10:4.

(1) The Parable of the Vineyard (5:1–7)

1 Let me sing for my beloved
  a love song concerning his vineyard:
My beloved had a vineyard
  on a very fertile hill.
2 He digged it and cleared it of stones,
    and planted it with choice vines;
he built a watchtower in the midst of it,
    and hewed out a wine vat in it;
and he looked for it to yield grapes,
    but it yielded wild grapes.
3 And now, O inhabitants of Jerusalem
    and men of Judah,
judge, I pray you, between me
    and my vineyard.
4 What more was there to do for my vineyard,
    that I have not done in it?
When I looked for it to yield grapes,
    why did it yield wild grapes?
5 And now I will tell you
    what I will do to my vineyard.
I will remove its hedge,
    and it shall be devoured;
I will break down its wall,
    and it shall be trampled down.
6 I will make it a waste;
    it shall not be pruned or hoed,
    and briers and thorns shall grow up;
I will also command the clouds
    that they rain no rain upon it.
7 For the vineyard of the LORD of hosts
    is the house of Israel,
and the men of Judah
    are his pleasant planting;
and he looked for justice,
    but behold, bloodshed;
for righteousness,
    but behold, a cry!

This beautiful vineyard song is actually a parable, one of the most striking examples of this literary genre to be found in the Old Testament. It belongs to a class aptly described as "Trojan horse" parables, in which the speaker disguises his intent until the very end, leading his unsuspecting listeners to pass judgment upon themselves. The same technique was used most effectively by Nathan in his rebuke of David (2 Sam. 12:1–12).

The parable of the vineyard, cast in the form of a love song, was probably sung by the prophet at one of the harvest festivals in Jerusalem. He may have appeared in the guise of a minstrel introducing a new song, a most effective way to capture the attention of the crowds milling about the Temple. He proposed to sing a song concerning his *beloved* and his *vineyard*. "Beloved" in this context simply means friend. The song immediately develops into a story of his friend's solicitous care for his vineyard and of the disappointing results. Only in the surprise ending is the friend identified as the Lord of hosts and the vineyard as the house of Israel.

It has been said that five things are essential to successful farming: the choice of good soil, careful cultivation of the soil, the selection of good seed, protection of the crop while it is in the field, and adequate preparation for harvesting and storing the crop. The prophet describes his friend as having attended to all these requirements.

A very fertile hill was chosen as the site of the vineyard. The Hebrew language, which is almost completely devoid of adjectives, expresses the idea of fertility through the use of a phrase which, if translated literally, is "a horn, the son of oil." This indicates that the field was located on the summit of a very fertile hill.

The second step taken by the farmer involved the preparation of the field for planting. The soil had to be digged and cleared of stones. The latter point was particularly important in Palestine, where the fields were profusely littered with stones of all sizes. Even today, after centuries of intensive cultivation, the soil there is still filled with stones. Their superabundance gave rise to an ancient rabbinical legend that at creation God dispatched an angel with a bag of stones to be scattered over all the earth; but when he passed over Palestine a terrible thing happened: the bag burst and all the stones spilled out!

After the soil had been prepared, the vineyard was planted with the choicest of vines. Their choice nature is indicated by the prophet's use of the word *soreq* instead of the ordinary word for vine, *gephen*. Deriving their name from a root meaning "to be red," the *soreq* vines produced a wine that was famous for its rich color and pleasant taste. For centuries these choice vines flourished in a valley resting in the foothills west of Jerusalem that came to be known as the Valley of Sorek (cf. Judg. 16:4). The selection of this species of vine revealed the farmer's solicitous care for his vineyard.

Adequate preparation was also made for the protection of the vineyard against thieves and marauders. A hedge and a wall were built around it, and a watchtower was constructed in its midst. The watchtower was a mound of stones upon which a guard was stationed when the grapes began to ripen. The guard's task was to protect the crop until it had been harvested.

Confident that he would reap a rich harvest, the farmer hewed out a wine vat in the midst of his vineyard. Such a vat usually consisted of two square pits cut into the surface of an outcropping of limestone rock. The upper pit, where the grapes were trodden out, was large and shallow. A trench led from this to a lower and deeper pit where the pressed-out juice accumulated until it could be stored in jars and wineskins. The preparation of such a wine vat was a major undertaking.

Having completed all these tasks, the farmer expectantly waited for a harvest of fine grapes. He was disappointed, however, for instead of grapes, the vineyard produced bitter, stinking fruit.

At this juncture in the telling of his parable, Isaiah paused and turning to his audience asked them to judge between him and his vineyard. He inquired of them, "What more was there to do for my vineyard, that I have not done in it?" Although their response is not recorded, they probably shouted their support of the prophet while loudly condemning the treacherous vineyard. They, too, were owners and cultivators of vineyards, and so could identify with him in his disappointment.

Having thus set the stage for the later application of his parable, Isaiah proceeds to tell the men of Judah and Jerusalem what Yahweh intends to do to his vineyard. At first sight the measures he proposes to take against it seem relatively mild. He could chop down the vines and grub out their roots, but instead he merely ceases to care for it. The hedge is taken away from the vineyard; its wall is broken down; the vines are no longer pruned or hoed; the clouds are commanded to withhold their rain. In the nature of the case, however, these were drastic measures, for, as every farmer knows, the most effective way to destroy a vineyard is to abandon it.

This says something about the biblical doctrine of the wrath of God. While it is sometimes depicted as active and virulent, as when God smites the wicked with his mighty outstretched arm, it often falls upon the sinner in a seemingly milder form. Nothing drastic happens to him; God simply leaves him alone. In the end, however, this proves to be the worst punishment of all. When all divine restraints are removed, the sinner is certain to wreck his own life. One writer has observed that the saddest day in any man's life is the day when God says to him, "Thy will be done!" How dreadful it was when God withdrew his presence from Israel! When this occurred, her name again became "Ichabod" (cf. 1 Sam. 4:21).

The conclusion to Isaiah's parable must have burst upon the people like a thunderclap. He identified the vineyard of the Lord of hosts as the house of Israel. Upon the nation God had bestowed years of loving care, hoping that his labors would produce a harvest of justice and righteousness. Instead there had been bloodshed and a cry of distress from the victims of Israelite oppression.

Here the prophet expresses his thought through a play on words that defies translation. Instead of justice (*mishpat*), there has been bloodshed (*mispach*); instead of righteousness (*tsedhaqah*), a cry (*tse'aquah*). The word *tse'aqah* is a technical legal term describing the crying out of those who have suffered some grave injustice (cf. Gen. 27:34; Ex. 3:7,9; 1 Sam. 9:16; Job 34:28). It was with such a cry for help that the injured appealed to the authorities for redress of the wrongs done to them. Where justice and righteousness prevailed, the cries of the afflicted were attended. Whenever they were ignored by the authorities, they ascended to the ears of the Lord of hosts, the champion of all earth's defenseless poor.

(2) *Six Woes Against the Wicked* (5:8–25)

8 Woe to those who join house to house,
who add field to field,
until there is no more room,
and you are made to dwell alone
in the midst of the land.
9 The LORD of hosts has sworn in my hearing:
"Surely many houses shall be desolate,
large and beautiful houses, without inhabitant.
10 For ten acres of vineyard shall yield but one bath,
and a homer of seed shall yield but an ephah."
11 Woe to those who rise early in the morning,
that they may run after strong drink,
who tarry late into the evening
till wine inflames them!
12 They have lyre and harp,
timbrel and flute and wine at their feasts;
but they do not regard the deeds of the LORD,
or see the work of his hands.
13 Therefore my people go into exile
for want of knowledge;
their honored men are dying of hunger,
and their multitude is parched with thirst.
14 Therefore Sheol has enlarged its appetite
and opened its mouth beyond measure,
and the nobility of Jerusalem and her multitude go down,
her throng and he who exults in her.
15 Man is bowed down, and men are brought low,
and the eyes of the haughty are humbled.
16 But the LORD of hosts is exalted in justice,
and the Holy God shows himself holy in righteousness.
17 Then shall the lambs graze as in their pasture,
fatlings and kids shall feed among the ruins.
18 Woe to those who draw iniquity with cords of falsehood,
who draw sin as with cart ropes,
19 who say: "Let him make haste,
let him speed his work
that we may see it;
let the purpose of the Holy One of Israel draw near,
and let it come, that we may know it!"
20 Woe to those who call evil good

and good evil,
who put darkness for light
and light for darkness,
who put bitter for sweet
and sweet for bitter!
21 Woe to those who are wise in their own eyes,
and shrewd in their own sight!
22 Woe to those who are heroes at drinking wine,
and valiant men in mixing strong drink,
23 who acquit the guilty for a bribe,
and deprive the innocent of his right!
24 Therefore, as the tongue of fire devours the stubble,
and as dry grass sinks down in the flame,
so their root will be as rottenness,
and their blossom go up like dust;
for they have rejected the law of the LORD of hosts,
and have despised the word of the Holy One of Israel.
25 Therefore the anger of the LORD was kindled against his people,
and he stretched out his hand against them and smote them,
and the mountains quaked;
and their corpses were as refuse
in the midst of the streets.
For all this his anger is not turned away
and his hand is stretched out still.

The introductory word *hoy* is found six times in this passage (vv. 8,11,18,20,21, 22). It has been variously interpreted as a curse (woe), a reproach (for shame) and a lament (alas). The latter view has been forcefully defended by G. Ernest Wright,[48] who believes that the prophet was uttering a funeral lament for the people of Judah. Wright thinks that the prophet was genuinely sorry for them since the judgment of God would soon fall upon them.

The unequal length of the six woes has led to speculation about their original form. Many regard vv. 14–17 as material that was later added to the second woe oracle. It is impossible, however, to determine the context in which these verses originally stood. They may simply represent a redactional expansion of the original text. Attention has also been called to the fact that drunkenness is the subject of both the second and the sixth woe, although the

---

48 Cf. "The Nations in Hebrew Prophecy," *Encounter*, Vol. 26, No. 2, pp. 231–233.

accompanying vices are not the same.

The first woe is addressed to the greedy land-grabbers. These were they who acquired house after house and field after field until they were left neighborless on their large estates. Prior to the eighth century Palestinian society had been predominantly agricultural and the landholdings small. Now, however, property was being concentrated in the hands of a few, and the uprooted masses were being reduced to poverty. While Isaiah does not specifically charge that the wealthy were acquiring lands through dishonest means, his contemporary Micah, nevertheless, indicates that such was the case (cf. Mic. 2:1-2,8-9).

A similar problem exists even today. In some sections of our country, for instance, the acquisition of large tracts of land by wealthy individuals, institutions, and corporations has reached serious proportions. Many rural communities have sharply declined as the local population has been largely displaced. The government has sometimes encouraged absentee ownership of the land through loopholes in its tax laws.

The landless masses of Latin America are rallying around the slogan of "Agrarian Reform." Disappointed with the government's failure to find a solution to their problems, they have organized to demand a fair share of their nation's wealth and resources. Their agitation is directed mainly against the *latifundiários*, the wealthy owners of large country estates, who live in luxury while their laborers are kept in a state of virtual bondage. It was situations such as this that caused the prophets to raise their voices in righteous indignation. North America and other parts of the world have like situations—at least in principle—of similar injustice.

In vv. 9-10 Isaiah pronounces a "futility curse" on the land-grabbers. They may build mansions but these will stand empty and desolate, and their fields will lose their productivity. Ten acres of vineyard will produce only one bath (approximately five

or six gallons of wine), and a homer of seed (ten bushels) will yield only an ephah (one bushel). No farmer could long survive a disaster such as this.

The second woe is addressed to Judah's heavy drinkers. While the Bible nowhere specifically prescribes total abstinence, it does, nevertheless, condemn those who drink until they are intoxicated. The prophets frequently warn against the vice of drunkenness (cf. Hos. 4:11; 7:5; Amos 4:1; 6:6). The wise men also condemn excessive drinking, because it leads to poverty (Prov. 21:17; 23:20 f.), to anger and brawls (Prov. 20:1), to the loss of decency (Prov. 23:29-35), and to the neglect of one's duties toward others (Prov. 31:4 f.).

The men of Judah are condemned for their insatiable desire for wine and strong drink. They are described as rising early and staying up late in order to put in a full day of drinking. Their parties are nothing but occasions for getting drunk to music. In the end their minds are inflamed and their judgment impaired.

In their drunken stupor they are totally unaware that God is at work in their day. They do not regard the deeds of the Lord, or see the work of his hands. The deeds of the Lord may refer either to his judgment upon individual sins or to his destruction of the nation as a result of their corporate guilt. In any event, the work of God is a work of judgment and destruction. How could it be otherwise when they are so bent upon satisfying their own appetites and desires?

Verse 13 contains a prediction of the exile, the coming of which is described in Hebrew by a prophetic perfect. The prophet is so certain of its coming that he describes it as if it had already arrived. The immediate cause of the coming exile is the people's *want of knowledge* (cf. Hos. 4:1,6). This does not mean that they are ignorant in the general sense of the term but that they lack knowledge of God and of his ways, like the drunkards described in v. 12. When the exile comes, honorable men will die of hunger and great multitudes of thirst.

Sheol, the shadowy abode of the dead, is pictured in v. 14 as a voracious monster opening wide its throat to receive the slain of earth. To this nether world of no return march noblemen and commoners alike. Their noisy exultation will soon be heard no more. Verse 17, which is like a postscript to vv. 13–16, states that after Jerusalem has been judged flocks will graze among her ruins. This signifies the return of the country to a pastoral state (cf. 7:23–25).

Verses 15–16, which seem to intrude upon this passage, are parallel in language and in thought to 2:6–22, to which they may originally have been joined. They emphasize the contrast between the abasement and humiliation of man and the exaltation of God. He is exalted and his holiness is revealed through *justice* and *righteousness*, the very qualities that are lacking in Israel (cf. v. 7). Here, as elsewhere in the Old Testament, justice and righteousness refer not so much to what God *is* as to what he *does*. He is the God who acts, who in the vicissitudes of history reveals who he is through what he does.

The third woe (vv. 18–19) is addressed to those who toil at sin and mock at God. On the basis of a Canaanite text from the ancient city of Ras Shamra (49:2:28–30), scholars have proposed that v. 18 should be translated: "Woe to those who drag iniquity with ewe-ropes, and sin with a calf-halter." This is a description of those who are harnessed to their sin, hauling it around behind them like a cart. At the same time they defiantly challenge God to prove himself by his mighty acts, so that they may be convinced that he is really God. They do not believe that he either can or will. This is practical atheism, the denial that God is at work in his world. Other prophets besides Isaiah had to face the same problem (cf. Jer. 17:15; Zeph. 1:12; Mal. 2:17; 3:13–15).

The fourth woe (v. 20) is aimed at those who have lost the power of moral discretion. How forcefully this word speaks to our generation, with its moral relativity and its situational ethic! Pity the person who, when shown a door, will say, "No, that's a wall!" but, when shown a wall, will respond, "No, that's a door!" The moral guidelines that have served others are no longer valid for him. His friends are regarded as enemies, and his enemies as friends. Thoroughly confused, he can no longer distinguish between good and evil, between light and darkness, between bitter and sweet. He is afflicted with a conscience that no longer accuses and a will that no longer responds. Surely, this is the last stage of moral depravity.

The last two woes are very brief. The first (v. 21) is addressed to Israel's self-appointed wise men. These are men who in their self-conceit feel no need for God. They are unaware of the fact that they are cut off from the source of true wisdom, which according to the Scriptures is found in God alone. In the final analysis, therefore, the self-appointed wise man is the world's greatest fool.

The final woe, like the second, deals with the problem of drunkenness. It is addressed to those who are skilled at mixing drinks and perverting justice. These were Israel's "men of distinction," her "heroes of the wine cup." They not only knew how to mix strong drinks, but they also knew how to gain favorable verdicts from unscrupulous judges. This resulted in such a miscarriage of justice that the innocent were usually condemned while the guilty went free. Such practices were undermining the social structure in Isaiah's day.

In the present arrangement of the text vv. 24–25 seem to apply to all those mentioned in the preceding woe oracles. These verses, therefore, constitute a conclusion to the entire section. Here sinners are likened to plants whose roots and blossoms are rotten and decayed. In the coming judgment they will be burned like dry grass and stubble. They are also charged with having rejected the law of the Lord and having despised the word of the Holy One of Israel (cf. Amos 2:4). Here as elsewhere in Isaiah the law refers not to Mosaic legislation but to the revelation of the will of God communicated through the prophets. Because of the seriousness of these offenses, the wrath of God falls upon Judah in a fearsome way. Her mountains quake before his outstretched hand, and the corpses of the slain lie like garbage in the streets of her cities.

The concluding refrain in v. 25 is repeated four times in the rather lengthy poem in 9:8—10:4. This has led to the suggestion that vv. 24–25 may have stood originally after 9:21, thus constituting a stanza of that poem. The textual problem is further complicated by the fact that 10:1–4 is also a "woe oracle," which suggests that it may have once stood in relationship to 5:23, thus providing a list of seven woes. Such speculation is interesting, but as redactional critics have recently reminded us, it does not alter the fact that we must deal responsibly with the text as we now have it.

(3) The Invader from Afar (5:26–30)

26 He will raise a signal for a nation afar off,
　　and whistle for it from the ends of the
　　　earth;
　and lo, swiftly, speedily it comes!
27 None is weary, none stumbles,
　　none slumbers or sleeps,
　　not a waistcloth is loose,
　　not a sandal-thong broken;
28 their arrows are sharp,
　　all their bows bent,
　their horses' hoofs seem like flint,
　　and their wheels like the whirlwind.
29 Their roaring is like a lion,
　　like young lions they roar;
　they growl and seize their prey,
　　they carry it off, and none can rescue.
30 They will growl over it on that day,
　　like the roaring of the sea.
And if one look to the land,
　　behold, darkness and distress;
and the light is darkened by its clouds.

The prediction of foreign invasion is thought by many to be the misplaced conclusion to the oracle complex appearing in 9:8—10:4. It has been described as "one of the most vivid pieces of descriptive verse in the Old Testament." The staccato effect of its short phrases, suggests the lightning speed of the invading armies. Though the foe is not named, it is evident that the prophet is thinking of the Assyrians.

The Lord whistles for a nation from afar, and it comes speedily at his command. The prophet regards Assyria's invasion of Judah, therefore, not as a fortuitous event in history, but as an occurrence ordained of God. His views on this subject are further developed in chapter 10, where he refers to Assyria as "the rod of God's anger."

Verses 27–30 vividly describe the terror caused by the swift advance of the invincible foe. His roar is like the roaring of the lion as he leaps upon his prey, or like the raging of the sea on a stormy day. Darkness and distress cover the earth, and the sun is obscured by the clouds. Mauchline comments that in the prophet's description of the day of judgment it is "as if the heavens themselves had put on mourning garb."

4. The Call of Isaiah (6:1–13)

When one surveys the book of Isaiah certain chapters stand out like tall mountain peaks. Surely the Matterhorn of the first half of the book is chapter 6, which tells of the call and commission of the prophet.

(1) Vision and Response (6:1–5)

1 In the year that King Uzziah died I saw the Lord sitting upon a throne, high and lifted up; and his train filled the temple. 2 Above him stood the seraphim; each had six wings: with two he covered his face, and with two he covered his feet, and with two he flew. 3 And one called to another and said:
"Holy, holy, holy is the LORD of hosts;
　the whole earth is full of his glory."
4 And the foundations of the thresholds shook at the voice of him who called, and the house was filled with smoke. 5 And I said: "Woe is me! For I am lost; for I am a man of unclean lips, and I dwell in the midst of a people of unclean lips; for my eyes have seen the King, the LORD of hosts!"

It is significant that Isaiah's call to the prophetic ministry is dated *in the year that King Uzziah died.* Uzziah had ruled Judah for approximately 40 years. Isaiah was born and grew to manhood during the years of his reign; he had, in fact, never known another king. The splendor of Uzziah's reign is described in detail in 1 Kings 15: 1–7 and 2 Chronicles 27. These accounts tell how he modernized the army, conquered the territory of Philistia, extended his commercial activities into Arabia, reconstructed the copper and iron works at Elath, and took an enlightened interest in agriculture. His reign brought peace and prosperity such as the nation had not known since the days of Solomon.

Since kingship is more or less alien to our experience, it is difficult for us to comprehend the significance of the king in ancient society. He was to the nation what the patriarch was to the clan. His presence inspired the people with a sense of strength and security. But his death filled them with consternation, for they were as sheep without a shepherd. The situation was aggravated by the weakness of his son Jotham and the menacing shadow of Assyria.

In the year that King Uzziah died, Isaiah saw another *King* seated upon a throne. Judah's throne was empty, but heaven's throne was occupied by the King of Glory. Judah's kings might come and go in an endless procession, but this King would reign for ever and ever. He was *the* King (*hammelekh*, v. 5), and his throne was exalted above all earthly thrones.

We must not minimize the significance of what Isaiah saw. While the vision may have come to him in the Jerusalem Temple, he saw far more than one could see in the Jerusalem Temple. For a brief moment the veil was drawn back and he was permitted to look into the heavenly temple, the spiritual reality of which the earthly temple was but a symbol.

Isaiah saw the Lord seated upon a throne, attended by the hosts of heaven. This was no ordinary occasion in the heavenly court, for the case of Judah was to be tried. God had summoned the heavenly council to sit in judgment upon the sinful nation.

Evidence that the biblical writers believed that such a council existed is found in numerous Old Testament passages (cf. Gen. 1:26; 3:22; 11:7; 1 Kings 22:19–22; Job 1:6–12; 2:1–6; Psalms 82:1; 89:5; Jer. 23:18,22). Thus while the Old Testament is strictly monotheistic, it never presents God as a solitary being but as one who is constantly attended by his heavenly messengers and ministers. For further information on the heavenly council, see James F. Ross, "The Prophet as Yahweh's Messenger," *Israel's Prophetic Heritage*, ed. Bernhard W. Anderson and Walter Harrelson (New York: Harper and Brothers, 1962), pp. 102–105. Isaiah actually witnessed only the final moments of this solemn assembly. When he was permitted to look in upon the proceedings, a verdict had already been handed down, and the nation had been pronounced guilty. However, God had not yet appointed a messenger to report the verdict to the nation and to pronounce sentence upon it. The most surprising development was the choice of Isaiah to be this messenger.

Around the Lord's throne stood an unspecified number of seraphim. The term designating these celestial beings is derived from a root which means "to burn." Elsewhere in the Old Testament it is used to describe snakes or fiery serpents, perhaps so described because of the burning sensation caused by their bites (cf. 14:29; 30: 6; Num. 21:4–9; Deut. 8:15). The derivation of the term, therefore, has led to the speculation that the *seraphim* in Isaiah's vision may have had the form of "standing serpents," similar to those found carved upon the thrones of the pharaohs.[49] The least that can be said is that they were strange composite beings, combining the characteristics of snakes, birds, and human beings. In later Jewish and Christian angelology the seraphim and the cherubim were ranked as the highest "choirs" of angels. In Isaiah's vision each of the seraphim had *six wings*, two with which to cover his

[49] Cf. Karen R. Joines, "Winged Serpents in Isaiah's Inaugural Vision," *Journal of Biblical Literature*, LXXXVI (1967), 410–415.

face in token of his reverence, two with
which to cover his feet (a euphemism for
the genital organs) in token of his modesty,
and two with which to fly, a symbol of his
readiness to serve. As they stood about the
heavenly throne the seraphim sang in an-
tiphony to the praise of God's glory. Their
threefold repetition of *holy* (*qadhosh*)
served to emphasize the uniqueness of
Israel's God. The latter part of their song
translated literally means: "the fullness of
all the earth is his glory." In other words,
the prophet was experiencing a "total
awareness" of God. Everything in the
created order spoke to him of God's glory.
He was completely surrounded by the divine presence, so that he could not escape
it no matter where he turned (cf. Psalm
139:1–18).

Holy is derived from a root which means
to separate, to cut off. To say that God is
holy means first of all that he is God and
not man. He is utterly separate from all
that is creaturely or sinful. In the words of
Rudolf Otto, he is "the Wholly Other One."
This does not mean, of course, that he is
remote from his creation; he is *different*
from man, but not *distant* from him. Hosea
expressed this better than any other: "For
I am God and not man, the Holy One in
your midst" (Hos. 11:9).

As a result of this experience the holiness
of God became one of the dominant themes
in Isaiah's preaching. His favorite term for
God was "the Holy One of Israel," a term
which appears about 30 times in his book.
He knew that Judah's very existence depended upon her attitude toward the holiness of God.

Having met God as the Holy One, Isaiah
was at once smitten with the consciousness
of his own sin and defilement. His experience represented a new dimension in man's
understanding of the concept of holiness.
Heretofore, someone brought into an
awareness of the holiness of God had been
smitten with a sense of his own creatureliness; Isaiah was aware only of his sinfulness. He feared God not because he was a
man, but because he was a sinful man.

Holiness, therefore, had taken on a moral
quality that it did not possess prior to this.

Isaiah's response to the vision of God was
that of a man brought face to face with
death. From his lips burst forth an agonizing cry of despair, *Woe is me! For I am
Lost!* The word translated "lost" means to
be cut off, cut down, or destroyed. Isaiah
thought that for one such as he to look
into the face of God meant certain death.
However, he had failed to make allowance
for the mercy of God.

Isaiah had never realized the depth of
his sin and depravity until he stood in the
revealing light of God's holiness. He was at
once aware of the defilement of his lips
and of the lips of his people. His lips were
unclean, like the flesh of a leper (cf. Lev.
13:45). Why his consciousness of defilement was focused here rather than elsewhere is not clear. Perhaps the best explanation is that he may already have sensed
that God wanted him to become a prophet,
a messenger of the heavenly court. Somewhat like Moses, though for different reasons, he felt himself unworthy to undertake
such a task. It has been noted that Acca-
dian and Egyptian prophets had to submit
to certain mouth purification rites before
they were permitted to speak the oracles
of the gods.[50] In like manner, Isaiah's commission was delayed until his lips had been
cleansed.

(2) Purification and Commission (6:6–13)

6 Then flew one of the seraphim to me, having in his hand a burning coal which he had
taken with tongs from the altar. 7 And he
touched my mouth, and said: "Behold, this has
touched your lips; your guilt is taken away,
and your sin forgiven." 8 And I heard the voice
of the Lord saying, "Whom shall I send, and
who will go for us?" Then I said, "Here am I!
Send me." 9 And he said, "Go, and say to this
people:
'Hear and hear, but do not understand;
see and see, but do not perceive.'
10 Make the heart of this people fat,
and their ears heavy,
and shut their eyes;

[50] Cf. Ivan Engnell, *The Call of Isaiah, An Exegetical and Comparative Study* (Uppsala: Universitets
Arsskrift, 1949), pp. 40 f.

lest they see with their eyes,
    and hear with their ears,
and understand with their hearts,
    and turn and be healed."
[11] Then I said, "How long, O Lord?" And he
    said:
"Until cities lie waste
    without inhabitant,
and houses without men,
    and the land is utterly desolate,
[12] and the Lord removes men far away,
    and the forsaken places are many in the
      midst of the land.
[13] And though a tenth remain in it,
    it will be burned again,
like a terebinth or an oak,
    whose stump remains standing
      when it is felled."
The holy seed is its stump.

The manner in which the prophet's lips were cleansed is highly significant. One of the seraphim flew to him with a burning coal which he had taken from the altar with a pair of tongs. He pressed this to Isaiah's lips, thus symbolizing the removal of his guilt. This part of the vision suggests that there is no painless cure for sin. Forgiveness has always been secured at the price of suffering and death.

When the seraph had touched Isaiah's lips, he pronounced his guilt removed and his sin forgiven. Rowley has vividly described the change that came over the prophet in that instant. He writes, "He who a moment before felt that in the presence of the Holy God sin could not exist, and that therefore he must perish with his sin, now felt that he was separated from his sin so that it alone might perish, and he might live." [51]

The climax to Isaiah's vision comes in v. 8. The touch of the burning coal had made him a new man. To his vision of God, of himself, and of redeeming grace, there was now added a further vision, the vision of world in need of his ministry. The consequence of his being cleansed and forgiven was something unique in the experience of the prophets. Instead of pleading his inadequacy, as Moses and Jeremiah did, he volunteered to be sent, even before he knew

the nature of his mission. He was so overwhelmed with a sense of gratitude that he was willing to place himself completely in God's hands. God had taken care of his past; he could have his future.

The words *Here am I! Send me.* appear as only two words in Hebrew. They were Isaiah's response to God's inquiry, *Whom shall I send, and who will go for us?* The question appears to have been directed not to the prophet but to the members of the heavenly council, which would account for the use of the first person plural pronoun *us.* God had assembled the council to pass judgment on Judah. A messenger was now needed to deliver the council's verdict to the sinful and rebellious nation. Isaiah, who had already injected himself into the proceedings of the council with his cry of confession, now did so again, with a cry no less urgent. He pleaded that he might be sent as the council's spokesman. The urgency of his response suggests that he was concerned lest someone else be chosen instead of him.

Since he did not know the nature of his mission, he was simply making himself available. He would go wherever God sent him. Only after he had volunteered for service did God commission him. Only after he had said "Send me!" did God say "Go!" Claus Westermann expressed it well when he said, "*Isaiah is sent,* for this is not an event 'between God and the soul,' but between God and his people and therefore between God and the world. The holiness of God is not there just for God, and the purification of man is not just for the bliss of man, but in order that, as a result of this encounter, something might go forth into the world. There is no genuine encounter with God without his third aspect, without this sending to others." [52]

From a human standpoint Isaiah's mission must have seemed impossible. He was commanded to make the heart of his people fat, to make their ears heavy, and to shut their eyes, lest they see with their eys, hear with their ears, understand with their heart,

[51] H. H. Rowley, *The Unity of the Bible* (London: Carey Kingsgate Press, 1953), p. 57.

[52] Claus Westermann, *op. cit.*, p. 217.

and turn and be healed. This must not be interpreted as the *intended* result of his preaching. Rather, in view of the rebellious nature of his listeners, this was the *inevitable* result. The meaning of the verse is that the prophetic word would serve to crystallize the character and seal the destiny of those who heard it (cf. 2 Cor. 2:15–16).

Isaiah was so startled by the disclosure of the nature of his mission that he cried out, *How long, O Lord?* This cry, familiar in psalms of lament (cf. Psalms 13:2; 74:10; 79:5; 89:46), was the anguished expression of a troubled soul. Isaiah was distressed because he had no sooner been relieved of his burden of sin than he was given an equally grievous burden of concern for a rebellious people.

God's response to Isaiah's lament was not encouraging. No time limit was set upon his ministry; he was simply told that he must continue until the existing Israel had been annihilated. Verse 13 has been interpreted in various ways. Traditionally, it has been regarded as setting forth the prophet's doctrine of a saved remnant that would spring into existence as if by a divine miracle. He believed that even after the nation had been destroyed, it would still contain a spark of life. As a felled tree retains life in its stump and begins to grow again, even so the fallen nation would give birth to a purified remnant through whom the eternal purposes of God would be realized.

If one asks upon what grounds the remnant would be prepared to fulfill, the purposes of God, the answer is suggested by the reference to burning in v. 13. As Ward [53] has pointed out, a direct correlation between vv. 6–7 and 11–13 is provided by the motif of burning. Just as Isaiah's guilt was symbolically burned away by the coal taken from the altar, so also must the people of Judah be subjected to a purification by fire. Nothing short of this would suffice. Only through such a process would they be made sufficiently humble and penitent to experience the forgiveness

[53] James M. Ward, *Amos and Isaiah* (Nashville: Abingdon Press, 1969), pp. 158–161.

and reconciliation of God. The symbol of their future as the people of God, therefore, would be a sapling growing from a burned stump. By this they would be constantly reminded of the cost and condition of their reconciliation.

5. A National Crisis (7:1—9:7)

The historical context of this section is that of 735–732 B.C., when the small Near Eastern states were under severe pressure from the Assyrians, led by Tiglath-pileser III (745–727). The oracles collected here probably represent only a cross section of Isaiah's preaching during this time of crisis.

Ably led by Tiglath-pileser III, Assyria had reached the zenith of her power by 735 B.C. Her armies constituted the most efficient fighting force the world had ever seen. Isaiah 5:27–30 probably contains a vivid description of the precision with which they marched and fought. Because of their ruthlessness in dealing with conquered peoples, they have been called "the Nazis of the eighth century B.C." They had made war their national industry. During the period covered by this passage they succeeded in bringing both Israel and Judah under their control.

(1) The Sign of Immanuel (7:1–17)

[1] In the days of Ahaz the son of Jotham, son of Uzziah, king of Judah, Rezin the king of Syria and Pekah the son of Remaliah the king of Israel came up to Jerusalem to wage war against it, but they could not conquer it. [2] When the house of David was told, "Syria is in league with Ephraim," his heart and the heart of his people shook as the trees of the forest shake before the wind. [3] And the LORD said to Isaiah, "Go forth to meet Ahaz, you and Shearjashub your son, at the end of the conduit of the upper pool on the highway to the Fuller's Field, [4] and say to him, 'Take heed, be quiet, do not fear, and do not let your heart be faint because of these two smoldering stumps of firebrands, at the fierce anger of Rezin and Syria and the son of Remaliah. [5] Because Syria, with Ephraim and the son of Remaliah, has devised evil against you, saying, [6] "Let us go up against Judah and terrify it, and let us conquer it for ourselves, and set up the son of Tabeel as king in the midst of it," [7] thus says the Lord GOD:

It shall not stand,
   and it shall not come to pass.
⁸ For the head of Syria is Damascus,
   and the head of Damascus is Rezin.
(Within sixty-five years Ephraim will be
broken to pieces so that it will no longer be a
people.)
⁹ And the head of Ephraim is Samaria,
   and the head of Samaria is the son of
     Remaliah.
If you will not believe,
   surely you shall not be established.' " ˉ
¹⁰ Again the LORD spoke to Ahaz, ¹¹ "Ask a
sign of the LORD your God; let it be deep as
Sheol or high as heaven." ¹² But Ahaz said,
"I will not ask, and I will not put the LORD to
the test." ¹³ And he said, "Hear then, O house
of David! Is it too little for you to weary men,
that you weary my God also? ¹⁴ Therefore the
Lord himself will give you a sign. Behold, a
young woman shall conceive and bear a son,
and shall call his name Immanuel. ¹⁵ He shall
eat curds and honey when he knows how to
refuse the evil and choose the good. ¹⁶ For before the child knows how to refuse the evil
and choose the good, the land before whose
two kings you are in dread will be deserted.
¹⁷ The LORD will bring upon you and upon
your people and upon your father's house such
days as have not come since the day that
Ephraim departed from Judah—the king of
Assyria."

In order to protect themselves against
the threat of Assyria, certain small nations
formed a coalition just prior to 735 B.C.
The leaders in the movement were Rezin of
Damascus and Pekah of Samaria. Pressure
was exerted to force King Ahaz of Judah to
join the coalition, but when he refused to
do so he was attacked by Pekah and Rezin.
Their objective apparently was to replace
him with a puppet king who would cooperate with them. Because of his youth and
inexperience, Ahaz was terrified at the
presence of invading troops on his soil. It
was perhaps at this time that he resorted
to the extreme measure of sacrificing one of
his own sons (2 Kings 16:3), hoping to
avert the wrath of God.

In the midst of these momentous events
Ahaz had his first recorded encounter with
Isaiah. The king had gone out to inspect
Jerusalem's water supply, perhaps just be-
fore the city came under seige. Isaiah went
out to meet him, accompanied by his young

son, *Shear-jashub.* The encounter took
place *at the end of the conduit of the upper
pool on the highway to the Fuller's Field.*

Jerusalem's main supply of water came
from the Gihon spring, a strong, intermit-
tent spring located on the eastern slope of
the hill on which the city was built. It is
better known today as the Virgin's Spring.
The Jebusites and later Judean kings constructed various conduits for bringing the
water of Gihon into the city. The water in
one of these conduits is referred to in 8:6
as "the waters of Shiloah that flow gently."
Shortly before 700 B.C. King Hezekiah had
a tunnel dug through the hill of Jerusalem
for bringing the water of Gihon more securely into the city (2 Kings 20:20). He
then closed up the upper pool which Ahaz
had gone out to inspect, since the water
from Gihon could be more safely stored in
the western, or "lower" pool, later known
as the pool of Siloam (2 Chron. 32:30).

Since Gihon seems to have been associated with the coronation of kings (cf. 1
Kings 1:33,38,45), Isaiah's appearance
there would have carried added significance. This was a crucial moment in the
history of Judah. God had indeed promised that David would never lack a son to
sit upon his throne, but now the very existence of the house of David was being
threatened. Pekah and Rezin intended to
dethrone Ahaz and to replace him with
Ben Tabeel, who is otherwise unknown,
and whose name probably means "good-
for-nothing."

The name of Isaiah's son, Shearjashub,
meant "a remnant shall return." His presence on this occasion was perhaps intended
as a warning to Ahaz that if he did not rely
upon God in this crisis his nation would be
severely judged so that only a remnant of
its people would escape.

Isaiah attempted to persuade Ahaz to
trust God to deliver him. The prophet's
advice was good religion and good politics.
It was good religion because the appropriate response to the crisis was faith, not
feverish activity and anxiety over the defenses of Jerusalem. It was good politics be-

cause it was based upon a sound appraisal of the political situation. The prophet knew the weakness of Pekah and Rezin, and called their threat a bluff. He referred to them disdainfully as *these two smoldering stumps of firebrands*, which meant that they were all smoke and no fire.

Isaiah buttressed his appeal to Ahaz with a play on words that is likely to be lost on the English reader. He said, *If you will not believe (ta'aminu), surely you shall not be established (te'amenu).*" To believe and to be established are derived from the same Hebrew verb. One translator has attempted to preserve the prophet's play on words with a paraphrase: "If your faith is not sure, your throne will not be secure." Another has suggested this rendering: "If you do not hold fast, surely you shall not stand fast."

Ahaz apparently listened to Isaiah's counsel in stony silence, since no response is recorded. Elsewhere we learn that he had already settled on a course of action. He had resolved to strengthen his own defenses and to send to Assyria for additional help (2 Kings 16). Isaiah was bitterly opposed to this plan. He regarded Ahaz's appeal to Tiglath-pileser as synonymous with arrogant pride and unbelief; it was setting the power of man above the power of God. Isaiah believed that God could deal with Pekah and Rezin without any assistance from Judah or Assyria. He also feared that acceptance of Assyrian aid would cost Judah her political independence and her spiritual integrity, fears that subsequent events proved to be well-founded (cf. 2 Kings 16:10–18).

There is every indication that vv. 10–17 describe a later encounter between Isaiah and King Ahaz. A literal translation of verse 10 would read, "And the Lord added to speak to Ahaz." How much time elapsed between this encounter and the first is a matter of speculation.

To the recalcitrant king the prophet now offers a sign. In fact, the king is challenged to request a sign anywhere from the heights of *heaven* to the depths of *Sheol,* and God

would perform it. The word sign is used 79 times in the Old Testament, of which 25 relate to the plagues of Egypt. A sign has been defined as "something ordinary or extraordinary, as the case may be, regarded as significant of a truth beyond itself, or impressed with a divine purpose." [54]

In the Old Testament, signs never stand alone, but are always closely linked with a word from God. Their purpose is to confirm the truth and power of the spoken word. Commenting on Deuteronomy 18:19, with its promise of a continuing succession of prophets, the Talmud states: "If a prophet who begins to prophesy gives a sign and a miracle, he is to be listened to, otherwise he is not to be heeded." When Moses employed signs of Egypt, it was in order to make the presentation of his message more effective, so that Pharaoh might be thoroughly convinced that the word he had spoken was true. Signs, therefore, were given to impress the skeptical and to make believers out of scoffers.

Ahaz piously refused to ask for a sign. To do so would have implied his acceptance of Isaiah's assessment of the situation. If he had requested a sign and the sign had been granted, he would have been obligated to alter his plans and policies. This was the last thing he wanted to do. Because he refused to ask for a sign, he was accused of wearying both God and man. His defiant attitude was an affront both to the prophet and to his Lord.

This sets the stage for the birth announcement in v. 14. Before entering into the interpretation of the verse, it would be advisable to inquire into the birth announcement as a literary form. Fortunately, there are other similar birth announcements in both biblical and nonbiblical sources. Genesis 16:11, for example, tells how Hagar is to conceive by Abraham and is to call her son Ishmael. Judges 13:5,7 tells of the announcement of the birth of Samson, and once again it is the mother who names the

[54] H. Wheeler Robinson, *Inspiration and Revelation in the Old Testament* (Oxford: The Clarendon Press, 1946), p. 37.

child (v. 24). In 1 Samuel 1:20 it is recorded that Hannah conceived and bore a son and called his name Samuel. An even closer parallel to 7:14 has been noted in a Ugaritic text from Ras Shamra. In a story entitled "The Wedding of Nikkal and the Moon God" there is a birth announcement which begins: "Behold, the young woman (*glmt*, the Ugaritic equivalent of the Hebrew *'almah*) shall bear (has borne?) a son. . . ." [55] It is evident from these examples that the basic form of the birth announcement in 7:14 has been borrowed from traditional sources.

Most discussion of this verse has centered around its use of *ha'almah* to designate the mother of the child who was to serve as a sign to Ahaz. The Hebrew word has been translated "a virgin" in the KJV and *a young woman* in the RSV.[56] This noun is derived from a verbal root meaning "to be ripe." Therefore it denotes a young girl who has passed the age of puberty and is presumably capable of bearing children.

The word *'almah* neither affirms nor denies virginity on the part of the one to whom it refers. The technical Hebrew term for virgin is *bethulah*, a term which is used elsewhere in Isaiah, but not in this passage (cf. 23:4,12; 37:22; 47:1; 62:5). The equivocal nature of *'almah* can be clearly seen when one examines its other occurrences in the Old Testament. In Genesis 24:43, for example, Rebecca is called an *'almah*, but it is in v. 16 that one is unequivocally informed that she is also a virgin (*bethulah*). Regarding Moses' sister in Exodus 2:8, there is only the argument from silence; presumably she is a virgin, but this is not a stated fact. In Song of Solomon 1:3 and 6:8, on the other hand, the context seems to imply that the young women in question are virgins, since they

belong to the king's harem, but are neither queens nor concubines. The only other occurrence of this term is in Proverbs 30:19, which is just as ambiguous as Isaiah 7:14.

The suggestion, therefore, that the young woman referred to by Isaiah was a virgin arose not from the Hebrew Bible, but from the Greek. In all but two places the Septuagint translators rendered *'almah* by the noncommittal *neanis* (young woman). The two exceptions were Genesis 24:43 and Isaiah 7:14, where *parthenos* (virgin) was used. The translators' decision to call Rebecca a *parthenos* was doubtless due to the very explicit statement regarding her virginity in Genesis 24:16. Why the mother in Isaiah 7:14 also was described as a *parthenos* has never been satisfactorily explained. It was, of course, the Greek version of this verse which was quoted by Matthew (Matt. 1:23).[57]

A particularly important rule to remember in exegesis is that no verse of Scripture can be properly understood apart from its context. In this case the context unquestionably demands that the promised child serve as a sign to King Ahaz, thus ruling out the possibility that Isaiah was looking into the far distant future. The birth and early childhood of Immanuel were related to events that transpired in the latter half of the eighth century B.C. The specific events in question were the defeat of Israel and Syria (vv. 15–16) and the invasion of Judah by the Assyrians (vv. 17–25). To overlook these facts is to miss the whole point of the passage.

Isaiah predicted that the young woman who was already pregnant would give birth to a son whom she would call Immanuel. Since Immanuel means "God is with us," it has often been inferred that the prophet was predicting the birth of a divine child. Two arguments, however, militate against

[55] Cf. Albrecht Goetze, "The Nikkal Poem from Ras Shamra," *Journal of Biblical Literature*, LX (1941), 353–374; Bruce Vawter, "The Ugaritic Use of Glmt," *The Catholic Biblical Quarterly*, XIV (1952), 319–322.

[56] Other modern translations read: "a young woman" (Goodspeed); "the young woman" (Jewish Publication Society of America); "the maiden" (Jerusalem Bible); "A young woman" (NEB).

[57] For a further discussion of Matthew's use of this prophecy, see Dale Moody, "Isaiah 7:14 in the Revised Standard Version," *Review and Expositor*, L (1953), 61–68; ————, "On the Virgin Birth of Jesus Christ," *Review and Expositor*, L (1953), 458–460; Robert G. Bratcher, "A Study of Isaiah 7:14," *The Bible Translator*, IX (July, 1958), 97–126.

such an inference. In the first place, as was shown above, the prophet expected that Immanuel would be born during the reign of Ahaz in the eighth century B.C. It seems highly unlikely, therefore, that he expected him to be divine. Furthermore, the simple fact that an Old Testament name was compounded with the name of God ('El) in no sense ascribed deity to the one who bore it. Actually, in the Old Testament 113 personal names are compounded with 'El—e.g., Elijah, Elimelech, Elnathan—and over 150 are compounded with Yahweh (Lord) —e.g., Jehoram, Joel, Jehoahaz, Obadiah. It has never occurred to anyone to suggest that those who bore these names were in any sense divine.

Having said this, one must hasten to add that the symbolic name of the child was a significant part of the sign to Ahaz. The name was a symbol of God's abiding presence with his people, even in the dark days of the Syro-Ephraimitic crisis. Attention has been called to the close parallel between this verse and Exodus 3:12. Moses also asked for a sign, and God's answer to him was almost identical to that given to Ahaz: "But I will be with you; and this shall be a sign for you, that I have sent you." A period should follow this statement. The sign to Moses was embodied in the promise "I will be with you." The prophet Isaiah offers the same sign to Ahaz, the sign of God's abiding presence. This is really the only promise that God ever gives to his followers. They are not promised success, riches, fame, or an easy road. The only assurance they have is that if they are obedient to the divine call they will never walk alone (cf. Matt. 28:19-20).

The sign of Immanuel was to be to Ahaz a sign both of promise and of threat. It was a promise because it signalled the downfall of the two kings who were threatening him. Ahaz was told specifically that before the child knew *how to refuse the evil and choose the good,* that is, before he reached the age of moral responsibility—perhaps to be understood as 12 years of age—the kings of Syria and Israel would be put to

flight. The prophecy was fulfilled in a most remarkable way, for in 732 B.C. Tiglath-pileser III not only destroyed Damascus but also compelled Samaria to surrender to him.

The threatening aspect of the sign consisted of a warning to Ahaz that Assyria would also invade the land of Judah (v. 17). The threat was probably added after Ahaz stubbornly refused to ask for the sign or to believe in it once it had been given.

Verse 8b seems to infer that the destruction of Ephraim will be delayed for 65 years. Because v. 8b breaks the sequence between v. 8a and v. 9a, it is treated as a parenthetical statement in the RSV. *The Jerusalem Bible,* following the earlier suggestion of Kissane,[58] places v. 8b after v. 9a and emends it to read: "Six or five years more and a shattered Ephraim shall no longer be a people." As the statement now stands it defies interpretation.

Ahaz was further informed that the child about to be born would eat *curds and honey* when he reached the age of moral responsibility. The statement has baffled interpreters, who have been unable to determine whether it describes a diet of plenty or of poverty. This depends upon whether it belongs to the threat or to the promise aspect of the sign. The equally obscure reference to the eating of curds and honey in vv. 21–22 does little to clarify the issue, although it seems to suggest a diet of plenty.

Since the birth of Immanuel was to be a sign to Ahaz of the imminent defeat of the two kings who were attacking him, we are left with the thorny problem of deciding who *Immanuel* was. Here scholarly opinion is sharply divided, but two views have commanded the widest support.

According to one view, *Immanuel* was Isaiah's own son. This view has been defended most recently by James M. Ward, who wrote, "According to the narrative, Isaiah was certain the sign would be given, that a child would be born, would be

---

58 Cf. Edward J. Kissane, *The Book of Isaiah,* Vol. 1 (Dublin: Brown and Nolan, 1941), pp. 78–79.

named a particular name, out of an infinite number of possibilities, and would be fed a particular diet during the first months (or years) of his life, this from a limited but still considerable number of possibilities. How could he be so sure that this name would be given and this diet maintained? He was sure because the pregnant woman was his wife, and because he himself would choose the name and the food." [59]

The other view regards Immanuel as a royal child promised to Ahaz and his queen. According to this view the definite article attached to the word 'almah (the young woman) is proof that the mother of the child was well-known to Ahaz and, therefore, most likely his wife. Since Ahaz had sacrificed his son (2 Kings 16:3), and since Israel and Syria had determined to remove Ahaz from his throne, the very existence of his dynasty was being threatened. The prophet, therefore, sought to reassure him with the promise of the birth of a royal heir. Jewish scholars have traditionally identified the child with Hezekiah, although it is difficult to harmonize this view with the chronology of 2 Kings 18:2.

If 7:14 is a prediction of the birth of a crown prince and therefore, in the strict sense of the word, a messianic prophecy, then it must be linked with other similar prophecies in 9:1–7 and 11:1–9 (cf. Mic. 5:2–6; Zech. 9:9–10). These three passages together constitute a trilogy of messianic prophecies dealing with Messiah's birth, his accession to the throne, and his righteous reign.

In recognition of the faithlessness of Ahaz, Isaiah pointed to the coming crisis as a time when God would raise up a worthy heir to the throne of David. The fact that he expected this to occur during his own lifetime should occasion no surprise—did not the apostle Paul also believe that Christ would return while he was still living? Isaiah had no way of knowing that the ultimate fulfillment of his hope would

be delayed for several centuries. In the fullness of time, therefore, this ancient prophecy was transposed to a higher key, and the messianic reign was inaugurated at the birth of Jesus Christ. The promise of God's presence with his people (Immanuel) was uniquely fulfilled in the advent of his Son.

(2) The Consequences of Unbelief (7:18–25)

18 In that day the LORD will whistle for the fly which is at the sources of the streams of Egypt, and for the bee which is in the land of Assyria. 19 And they will all come and settle in the steep ravines, and in the clefts of the rocks, and on all the thornbushes, and on all the pastures.
20 In that day the Lord will shave with a razor which is hired beyond the River—with the king of Assyria—the head and the hair of the feet, and it will sweep away the beard also.
21 In that day a man will keep alive a young cow and two sheep; 22 and because of the abundance of milk which they give, he will eat curds; for every one that is left in the land will eat curds and honey.
23 In that day every place where there used to be a thousand vines, worth a thousand shekels of silver, will become briers and thorns. 24 With bow and arrows men will come there, for all the land will be briers and thorns; 25 and as for all the hills which used to be hoed with a hoe, you will not come there for fear of briers and thorns; but they will become a place where cattle are let loose and where sheep tread.

This passage gives a vivid description of the tribulation in store for the land of Judah in consequence of Ahaz's headstrong policy. In a series of four oracles, each introduced by the phrase "In that day," the prophet describes the devastation of the land at the hand of Assyrians.

The first two oracles are strikingly metaphorical. The Lord is pictured as whistling for flies from Egypt and for bees from Assyria (cf. 5:26). *Sources of the streams of Egypt* refers to the various arms of the Nile in the delta region. The stinging insects completely cover the land of Judah, settling in the steep ravines, in the clefts of the rocks, on thornbushes, and on all the pastures. Anyone who has ever seen bees

---

[59] James M. Ward, *op. cit.*, p. 196; cf. Norman K. Gottwald, "Immanuel as the Prophet's Son," *Vetus Testamentum*, VIII (1958), 36–47.

swarming can appreciate the vividness of the metaphor.

The second oracle employs the metaphor of a hired razor used by the Lord to shave his people. A hired razor means one that is contracted for a specified period of time. The razor comes from beyond the *River*, that is, the Euphrates (cf. Gen. 31:21; Ex. 23:31; Jer. 2:18), and is none other than *the king of Assyria*. With such a hired razor the Lord will completely shave the land, removing the hair of the head, the hair of the feet, and even the beard. *The hair of the feet* is a euphemism for the hair of the genital organs (cf. 6:2; Judg. 3:24, Heb.; 1 Sam. 24:3, Heb.).

The last two oracles are less metaphorical and more literal. It is difficult to determine whether the first of these describes a condition of poverty or of luxury. At first sight it would seem that a man with only a young cow and two sheep would barely be able to subsist. *Abundance* may simply mean quantity or amount. The oracle may signify therefore that Judah is to be reduced to a pastoral state and that her citizens will be forced to subsist on a meager diet of curds and wild honey.

On the other hand, this oracle has been interpreted by many to mean that the land is to return to a paradisiacal state, where only a young cow and two sheep would provide a man with all the food he and his family could eat. If this is the correct interpretation, then the oracle is the only one in this section having an optimistic outlook.

The fourth oracle unquestionably describes the devastating effects of the Assyrian invasion upon the land and its people. Those who survive the invasion will be reduced to a life of utter simplicity, living like desert nomads. Their prized vineyards and cultivated fields will revert to thickets of briars and thorns, fit only as a place to hunt or as the grazing ground for stray cattle and sheep.

(3) The Sign of Maher-shalal-hash-baz (8:1–4)

[1] Then the LORD said to me, "Take a large tablet and write upon it in common characters, 'Belonging to Mahershalalhashbaz.' " [2] And I got reliable witnesses, Uriah the priest and Zechariah the son of Jeberechiah, to attest for me. [3] And I went to the prophetess, and she conceived and bore a son. Then the LORD said to me, "Call his name Mahershalalhashbaz; [4] for before the child knows how to cry 'My father' or 'My mother,' the wealth of Damascus and the spoil of Samaria will be carried away before the king of Assyria."

This oracle also belongs to the period of the Syro-Ephraimitic crisis. The prophet again predicts the destruction of Syria and Israel at the hands of the Assyrians. The prediction is given in two stages, represented by the prophet's performance of two symbolic acts.

The first act consisted of writing on a cylindrical clay seal the cryptic expression, *Belonging to Maher-shalal-hash-baz.* "Clay seal" is a better translation than *tablet.* Such cylindrical seals were used by the Assyrians and Babylonians to stamp clay jars with their owner's name. Maher-shalal-hash-baz means "the spoil speeds, the prey hastes."

There is no indication that Isaiah knew when he recorded the ominous name that he would later be commanded to give it to one of his sons. The fact that he secured reliable witnesses to attest the recording of the name may signify that he simply regarded it as a symbolic act stealing the doom of Syria and Israel. They were the victims who would be spoiled and plundered, and Assyria would be the plunderer. When these things came to pass, he wanted witnesses to verify that he had indeed predicted them beforehand. He seems to have been concerned, therefore, with establishing his reliability as a prophet.

Not long after the inscribing of the seal, Isaiah's wife became pregnant and gave birth to a son. Then the Lord commanded him to perform a second symbolic act; he was told to name the child Maher-shalal-hash-baz. He was also told that before the child was old enough to pronounce even the simplest words—words like "Daddy" and "Mamma"—both Syria and Israel would lie in ruins. This, therefore, was a message of doom for Syria and Israel, but a message of hope for Judah.

The similarities between this passage and the Immanuel passage (7:10–17) are remarkable. In each passage a message is addressed to the people of Judah, and particularly to the house of David. In each the birth of a child and his unusual name serve as a sign of God's favor toward his people and of his overthrow of their enemies. Both passages were designed to inspire Ahaz and his people to trust God in the hour of crisis, rather than to rely upon their own wisdom and strength. In both instances, however, the exhortation to faith fell upon deaf ears. No matter how earnestly the prophet pleaded with his people, they seemed determined to follow their own counsel.

(4) The Oracle of the Two Rivers (8:5–8)

5 The LORD spoke to me again: 6 "Because this people have refused the waters of Shiloah that flow gently, and melt in fear before Rezin and the son of Remaliah; 7 therefore, behold, the Lord is bringing up against them the waters of the River, mighty and many, the king of Assyria and all his glory; and it will rise over all its channels and go over all its banks; 8 and it will sweep on into Judah, it will overflow and pass on, reaching even to the neck; and its outspread wings will fill the breadth of your land, O Immanuel."

This oracle is in the form of a parable. In it the prophet contrasts the quiet waters of a Jerusalem stream with the turbulent waters of the Euphrates at flood tide. The Jerusalem stream is identified as *the waters of Shiloah that flow gently*. Shiloah is never mentioned again in the Old Testament, but it was probably the name of a small open channel leading from the Gihon spring to a reservoir inside the city. Some have identified it with "the conduit of the upper pool" mentioned earlier in 7:3.

The parable of the two rivers has been interpreted in a variety of ways. The principal problem connected with its interpretation concerns the identification of those to whom it is addressed and the determination of the exact nature of their offense.

According to the usual interpretation, the parable is addressed to Ahaz and to the people of Judah. It is they who have refused the waters of Shiloah that flow gently, and who melt in fear before the kings of Syria and Israel (cf. 7:1–9). The waters of Shiloah are seen as a symbol of God's protective presence within Jerusalem. The sin of Ahaz and his people was that they had refused God's proffered assistance and had instead appealed to Assyria for aid (cf. 2 Kings 16:7). The outcome would be something for which they had not bargained. The Assyrians would not only despoil Syria and Israel but would also sweep across the land of Judah like a mighty river on a rampage. The floodwaters would reach even to the necks of the unfortunate people. The alliance that they had hoped would bring relief would instead bring misery and ruin.

A significant variation of this interpretation has been suggested by Ward.[60] He interprets the people's refusal of the waters of Shiloah not as their failure to trust in God but as their refusal "to abide the threat of Aram and Israel," resulting in Ahaz's request for Assyrian intervention against Damascus and Samaria. The waters of Shiloah, in Ward's opinion, do not symbolize the quiet power of God, in which Judah was supposed to trust, but the harmless power of Rezin and Pekah, which she was not to fear.

The interpretations given above are all based upon an emendation of the text of v. 6. However, the second half of the verse should be read, "and *rejoice* in Rezin and the son of Remaliah." Most modern translations, including the RSV, emend this to read, "and *melt in fear* (i.e., tremble) before Rezin and the son of Remaliah." There is no support whatsoever for the proposed emendation, either in the Dead Sea Scrolls or in the Septuagint. The latter renders the text, "and [this people] wills to have Rezin and the son of Remaliah to be king over you."

In the light of the support the Hebrew text receives from other ancient versions, therefore, there seems to be no justification for emending the text. Isaiah's words make good sense when understood against the

60 *Ibid.*, pp. 218–221.

background of the conspiracy of Pekah and Rezin, whose stated purpose was to dethrone Ahaz and replace him with Tabeel (7:1–6). Evidently, there was a group within Jerusalem itself that lent its support to the conspiracy. It was primarily to this group that the prophet was addressing himself in the parable of the two rivers.

It was they who refused the waters of Shiloah and who desired to have Rezin and Pekah to rule over them. Following the suggestion of Slotki,[61] the waters of Shiloah should, therefore, be interpreted as a symbol for the house of David. Since Gihon seems to have been associated with the coronation of Judean kings (cf. 1 Kings 1: 33,38,45), this was an entirely appropriate symbol.

Isaiah predicted that as a consequence of the plot to oust Ahaz, the land of Judah would be overrun by the armies of Assyria. Two metaphors describe the frightful onslaught of the enemy: that of a raging river at flood tide and of a bird of prey descending upon the land with outstretched wings. The common symbol for Assyrian kings was the figure of the head of a man flanked on either side by eagles' wings.

The latter part of v. 8 seems to indicate that the prophet expected the Assyrian invasion to take place during the reign of Immanuel. This would support the view that Immanuel was a royal child and thus heir to the throne of Judah.

Some would dissociate the latter part of v. 8 from the preceding passage and attach it instead to vv. 9–10. Two reasons are given for this transposition. First, the imagery of outstretched wings suggests the idea of protection (cf. Psalms 17:8; 91:4), and therefore, vv. 8b–10 belong together as constituting a short liturgical poem celebrating Yahweh's power to save. The second reason is that "Immanuel" (God with us) appears twice in the Hebrew text, in vv. 8b–10. It is assumed, therefore, that these verses originally stood together. In

spite of the force of these arguments, however, it seems best to retain v. 8b as the conclusion to the oracle of the two rivers, and to regard vv. 9–10 as a separate oracle.

(5) Fearing God and Not Man (8:9–15)

9 Be broken, you peoples, and be dismayed;
  give ear, all you far countries;
gird yourselves and be dismayed;
  gird yourselves and be dismayed.
10 Take counsel together, but it will come to nought;
  speak a word, but it will not stand,
  for God is with us.
11 For the LORD spoke thus to me with his strong hand upon me, and warned me not to walk in the way of this people, saying: 12 "Do not call conspiracy all that this people call conspiracy, and do not fear what they fear, nor be in dread. 13 But the LORD of hosts, him you shall regard as holy; let him be your fear, and let him be your dread. 14 And he will become a sanctuary, and a stone of offence, and a rock of stumbling to both houses of Israel, a trap and a snare to the inhabitants of Jerusalem. 15 And many shall stumble thereon; they shall fall and be broken; they shall be snared and taken."

Verses 9–10 are written in poetic form and thus have all of the characteristics of a liturgical poem or hymn. They celebrate Israel's faith in the protective presence of her God and in his abundant power to deliver. Psalm 46, with its recurring refrain, "The Lord of hosts is with us," is a good commentary on these verses.

The hymn is addressed to *peoples* and *far countries*. They presumably include Syria and Israel, who are near at hand, and Assyria, who is far away. All who dare to conspire against God's chosen people will be dismayed and broken. In the end their cleverly devised plots will backfire, and they themselves will be the victims.

The closing words of the hymn have a significance that is often obscured in translation. The Hebrew reads, "speak a word, but it will not stand because of Immanuel." This passage closely parallels the Immanuel passage in 7:10–17. In both, the sign of Immanuel is the sign of hope and the assurance of ultimate victory. Isaiah believed that God was firmly in charge of history. Even when he judged his people, he did

---

61 I. W. Slotki, "Isaiah," *Soncino Books of the Bible* (London and Bournemouth: The Soncino Press, 1949), p. 39.

not relinquish his control over them.

The prose verses which follow the hymn (vv. 11–15) are peculiar in that they contain admonitions addressed to the prophet himself. In the panic-filled days of the Syro-Ephraimitic crisis, even he needed to have his faith strengthened. He is admonished to forget the fears of men and to be filled with the fear of God.

God spoke to the prophet *with his strong hand,* that is, he admonished him sharply. He warned him to stand against the tide of fear and dread sweeping over the nation. He must not join other men in their conspiracies nor fear what they feared. If he feared God, he would have no cause to fear man.

God is described in v. 14 both as a *sanctuary, and as a stone of offense* (cf. Luke 20:17 f.). To those who fear him he will become a sanctuary; but to those who succumb to the fears of men he will become *a rock of stumbling . . . a trap and a snare.* The point emphasized here is man's responsibility to make the right response to the revelation of God's presence and his power.

(6) A Time of Withdrawal (8:16–22)

16 Bind up the testimony, seal the teaching among my disciples. 17 I will wait for the LORD, who is hiding his face from the house of Jacob, and I will hope in him. 18 Behold, I and the children whom the LORD has given me are signs and portents in Israel from the LORD of hosts, who dwells on Mount Zion. 19 And when they say to you, "Consult the mediums and the wizards who chirp and mutter," should not a people consult their God? Should they consult the dead on behalf of the living? 20 To the teaching and to the testimony! Surely for this word which they speak there is no dawn. 21 They will pass through the land, greatly distressed and hungry; and when they are hungry, they will be enraged and will curse their king and their God, and turn their faces upward; 22 and they will look to the earth, but behold, distress and darkness, the gloom of anguish; and they will be thrust into thick darkness.

The primary importance of this passage is that it informs us about the relationship between Isaiah and his disciples, and it throws light upon the role and function of the disciples. The fact that Isaiah had gathered about him such a band of disciples need occasion no surprise, for in the ancient world this was the time-honored method whereby teachers passed on their instruction. The surprising fact is that so little is told in the Old Testament about the activities of the prophets' disciples.

Verse 16 should perhaps be translated, "I will bind up . . . and seal, etc." It is generally agreed that the passage is to be dated about 734–733 B.C., that is, during the Syro-Ephraimitic crisis. Because Isaiah's words had fallen upon deaf ears, and perhaps because he had encountered persecution, he resolved to withdraw temporarily from public ministry. He probably made a public announcement of his intentions. Upon this occasion the prophet performed a highly significant symbolic act: he delivered to his disciples a written scroll, tied with a cord and sealed with wax. Such a scroll, of course, could not be read until the command was given for it to be opened (cf. Dan. 12:9; Rev. 5:1–5).

It is beside the point to speculate about the nature of the contents of the sealed scroll. The import of the prophet's action was that there would be no open word from the Lord so long as Judah continued on her rebellious course. She would experience a "famine" of the word of the Lord similar to that which Amos had predicted in Israel (Amos 8:11–12).

This interpretation helps to clarify Isaiah's statement that in the meantime he would *wait for the Lord, who is hiding his face from the house of Jacob.* The same verb is repeated in Habakkuk 2:3, where it refers to the prophet's waiting for a vision. In both instances, therefore, it describes a prophet's patient waiting for a vision, when the vision has been temporarily delayed.

While the word of the Lord remains sealed, Isaiah and his children will serve as "living epistles" to the people of Judah (v. 18). The latter will receive little comfort from this, however, for Isaiah's children bear ominous names (cf. 7:3; 8:3). Their very presence among the people is a sign of judgment and a portent of evil to come. Some regard *children* not as a reference to Isaiah's sons but to his disciples. However, the word surely must refer to his sons, although it may also include his disciples.

The situation described in vv. 16–18 posed a threat to the people of Judah. They were accustomed to seeking the word of the Lord with regard to both their personal and their corporate decisions (cf. 1 Sam. 23:2; 28:6; 1 Kings 22:5 f.). So long as the prophet remained silent, therefore, there was no channel of communication open between them and their God. In their extremity they appealed to the prophet's disciples to seek the word of the Lord for them through divination and necromancy (v. 19). The prophet sternly warned his disciples to ignore such requests, since they involved illicit means of approaching God (cf. Lev. 19:31; Deut. 18:9–15).

If the people wished to hear the word of the Lord, let the disciples direct them *to the teaching and to the testimony.* Otherwise, darkness and distress would overtake them. The final verses of the chapter apparently are a description of the total despair of the Judeans as they wandered through their devastated land.

(7) The Messianic King (9:1–7)

¹ But there will be no gloom for her that was in anguish. In the former time he brought into contempt the land of Zebulun and the land of Naphtali, but in the latter time he will make glorious the way of the sea, the land beyond the Jordan, Galilee of the nations.
² The people who walked in darkness
  have seen a great light;
  those who dwelt in a land of deep darkness,
  on them has light shined.
³ Thou hast multiplied the nation,
  thou hast increased its joy;
  they rejoice before thee
  as with joy at the harvest,
  as men rejoice when they divide the spoil.
⁴ For the yoke of his burden,
  and the staff for his shoulder,
  the rod of his oppressor,
  thou hast broken as on the day of Midian.
⁵ For every boot of the tramping warrior in battle tumult

and every garment rolled in blood
  will be burned as fuel for the fire.
⁶ For to us a child is born,
  to us a son is given;
  and the government will be upon his shoulder,
  and his name will be called
"Wonderful Counselor, Mighty God,
  Everlasting Father, Prince of Peace."
⁷ Of the increase of his government and of peace
  there will be no end,
  upon the throne of David, and over his kingdom,
  to establish it, and to uphold it
  with justice and with righteousness
  from this time forth and for evermore.
The zeal of the LORD of hosts will do this.

It is well to begin the study of this passage by noting that v. 1 is written in prose and vv. 2–7 in poetry. It is important to determine what relationship, if any, exists between these two sections. Is v. 1 the conclusion to the oracle which precedes it?[62] Is it merely an editorial link between vv. 2–7 and the preceding oracle? Or is it the beginning of the messianic poem in vv. 2–7?[63] The latter view is supported by Matthew 4:15–16 and has the advantage of enabling one to set the poem in its historical context.

Verse 1 informs us that a dire calamity had overtaken Zebulun and Naphtali. These two northernmost tribes of Israel had borne the brunt of Tiglath-pileser's campaigns against northern Israel in 734–732 B.C. (cf. 2 Kings 15:29). This is what is meant by the statement that "in the former time" God had "brought into contempt the land of Zebulun and the land of Naphtali."

The prophet expected a reversal of the situation to be effected in *the latter time,* a reference to the messianic age, which was apparently viewed as near at hand. The term *Galilee of the nations* should perhaps be rendered "circle of the nations," in which case it would stand for the entire area ly-

62 Cf. Norman K. Gottwald, *All The Kingdoms of the Earth* (New York: Harper and Row, 1964), pp. 158–159.
63 Cf. Joh. Lindblom, *A Study of the Immanuel Section in Isaiah* (Lund: CWK Gleerup, 1958), pp. 33–41.

ing to the west, north, and east of Ephraim.

Alt has argued that the oracle was not originally intended for public recitation in Judah but was sent by a herald to be proclaimed in the occupied territories of Zebulun and Naphtali.[64] God's purpose in sending the herald was to assure the beleaguered peoples that the Assyrians would soon be driven from their lands, and that coincident with the departure of Assyria a new Davidic king would come to the throne in Judah. His rule would extend even to the territory of Israel. According to Alt, therefore, the prophet expected the reunion of the tribes of Israel under a Davidic king whose reign would endure for ever.

A crucial question facing the interpreter of the hymn in vv. 2–7 is whether it is the birth of the new Davidic king that is celebrated or his accession to the throne. The first alternative has been defended by Lindblom,[65] who maintains that the prophet composed the hymn immediately after the birth of the royal child referred to in 7:14. Scott (p. 231) on the other hand, regards this as a dynastic oracle uttered on the occasion of the anointing of a new king.

The weight of the evidence seems to support the latter view. In the throne names given the newly crowned king (v. 6), there is nothing that cannot be explained against the background of Nathan's oracle to David in 2 Samuel 7:11b–16. There is also a parallel between the exuberant language of this coronation hymn and the royal psalms, especially Psalms 2, 72, and 110. In highly metaphorical language prophets and psalmists depicted the king as having been begotten by Yahweh on the day of his anointing (cf. 2 Sam. 7:14; 1 Chron. 28:6; Psalms 2:7; 89:26–27; Isa. 9:6). It is altogether likely, therefore, that Isaiah's oracle was composed to celebrate the accession of an actual Judean king. While it is impossible to establish the positive identity of the king, Jewish interpreters have traditionally identified him with Hezekiah.

The verbs throughout the hymn are almost all in the perfect tense, indicating that the actions described had already taken place. This increases the likelihood that the prophet was referring to a contemporary king rather than to an ideal king of the future.

The hymn opens with an announcement that those who walk in darkness have seen a great light. The light breaking upon the darkness is like the first light of creation. With the coming of light the former anguish of the people is transformed into pure joy. There is a contradiction in the KJV translation of v. 3, which reads, "Thou hast multiplied the nation, and not increased the joy." "Not" (lo') should either be changed to "his" (lo) or be combined with the Hebrew letters of the nation to form a new word, "rejoicing" (haggailah). The latter alternative is to be preferred since it gives a smoother translation and restores the parallelism: "Thou hast multiplied the rejoicing, thou hast increased the joy."

Two metaphors are used to describe the job of the Israelites; they rejoice as those who reap a bountiful harvest and as those who divide the spoil on the field of battle (v. 3). The first cause for their rejoicing is that the rod of their oppressor has been broken and they no longer must bear the yoke of servitude. The figure here is that of an animal yoked to a grievous burden and urged on by the merciless rod of the oppressor. God has destroyed the power of the oppressor, as he did on the day of Midian. This refers to Gideon's slaying of the Midianites in the days of the judges (Judg. 6—8). Just as that ancient deliverance was wrought by God without regard to the number of men serving under Gideon, so now God will bring a mighty victory to Israel, in spite of her weakness and helplessness.

The second cause for Israel's rejoicing is that her warfare has ended and the battle gear has been gathered together to be burned as fuel. Verse 5 anticipates what is said about the reign of peace in the latter

64 A. Alt, "Jesaja 8:23–9:6. Befreiungsnacht und Kroenungstag," Kleine Schriften zur Geschichte des Volkes Israel, II (München: C. H. Beck, 1953), 206–225.

65 Joh. Lindblom, op. cit., pp. 37–39.

part of the hymn.

The climax of the hymn comes in v. 6, for all these mighty acts are predicated upon the anointing of a new king. That the verse refers not to the actual birth of the king but to the beginning of his reign is evident from the context. It should be recalled that Israelite kings could be described as divinely begotten on the day of their accession (cf. Psalm 2:7). The emphasis in Hebrew is upon the words "child" and "son" rather than upon the phrase "to us."

Just as ancient kings and pharaohs were given exalted titles when they took office, so this new king is given a series of throne names. The names which God bestows upon him reflect the uniqueness of his person and of his office. There are four names, as indicated in the RSV. The first, *Wonderful Counselor* (lit., wonder of a counselor) means "wonder-counselor" or "wonder-planner" and emphasizes his administrative ability. The second, *Mighty God* (lit., god of a warrior, i.e., a mighty warrior) stresses his supremacy over his enemies. The third, *Everlasting Father* (lit., father of eternity, i.e., father forever) points to his constant care for his people. The fourth and final name, *Prince of Peace,* stresses the rich, harmonious life that his subjects will enjoy. Moriarty has aptly observed that to this ideal king are ascribed "the wisdom of Solomon, the courage of David, and the religious virtues of the patriarchs and Moses." [66] It should be added that he possesses these qualities to a greater degree than any who ever lived before him.

The final verse in the hymn stresses the just and righteous rule of the coming king. Perhaps the most significant word in the entire verse is the word *peace* (*shalom*). Derived from a verb meaning "to be whole," or "to be complete," it describes a state of well-being, of wholeness, of prosperity. The word peace conveyed to the

[66] Frederick L. Moriarty, "Isaiah 1–39," *The Jerome Bible Commentary* (Englewood Cliffs: Prentice-Hall, Inc., 1968), p. 272.

ancient Hebrew that which the word success in its broadest sense conveys to modern man. It is related in meaning to the English word "health," which is derived from the old Anglo-Saxon "wholth." Peace in this context, therefore, means the rich, harmonious, joyful life of those privileged to live in Messiah's kingdom.

From this time forth and forevermore suggests that the prophet expected the ideal king to be the last representative of David's line, not merely one in a continuing succession of kings. His reign would inaugurate the eschatological age, an age of justice and righteousness. Further attention is given to this ideal age in the messianic oracle in 11:1–9.

Who was this king so divinely endowed? Certainly no historical king of Judah ever adequately realized the hopes attached to him. While some may have hoped that Hezekiah would be a wonderful counselor and a prince of peace, he was this in only a very limited sense. The messianic hopes of Israel were fully realized in Jesus, who was proclaimed both "Messiah" and "King of the Jews." Isaiah's prophecy, therefore, was fulfilled far beyond his highest expectations.

6. The Outstretched Hand of God (9:8—10:4)

This section has been called "the refrain song" (Lindblom), since it is divided into four sections, each of which ends with the refrain, "For all this his anger is not turned away and his hand is stretched out still" (cf. 9:12,17,21; 10:4). Some would add 5:25–30 to the end of chapter 9, making it a fifth stanza of the refrain song.

The first three stanzas (9:8–21) are addressed to the Northern Kingdom, called Israel and Jacob. They are condemnatory in nature and describe the progressively severe blows that God had rained upon the wicked and rebellious nation. The fourth stanza (10:1–4) is addressed to Judah, who should have been forewarned by the judgments visited upon Israel. It is difficult to determine the precise date for this passage; scholars agree only that it belongs to the period between the death of Pekahiah (737 B.C.) and the fall of Samaria (722).

(1) God's Fruitless Chastisement of Israel (9:8–17)

8 The Lord has sent a word against Jacob,
    and it will light upon Israel;
9 and all the people will know,
    Ephraim and the inhabitants of Samaria,
    who say in pride and in arrogance of heart:
10 "The bricks have fallen,
    but we will build with dressed stones;
    the sycamores have been cut down,
    but we will put cedars in their place."
11 So the LORD raises adversaries against them,
    and stirs up their enemies.
12 The Syrians on the east and the Philistines on the west
    devour Israel with open mouth.
For all this his anger is not turned away
    and his hand is stretched out still.
13 The people did not turn to him who smote them,
    nor seek the LORD of hosts.
14 So the LORD cut off from Israel head and tail,
    palm branch and reed in one day—
15 the elder and honored man is the head,
    and the prophet who teaches lies is the tail;
16 for those who lead this people lead them astray,
    and those who are led by them are swallowed up.
17 Therefore the Lord does not rejoice over their young men,
    and has no compassion on their fatherless and widows;
for every one is godless and an evildoer,
    and every mouth speaks folly.
For all this his anger is not turned away
    and his hand is stretched out still.

These first two stanzas are set against the background of a series of calamities that had befallen the Northern Kingdom (v. 10). The precise nature of the disasters is not spelled out, but they had not been severe enough to destroy the pride or to shake the confidence of the people. They may have been related to the events that accompanied the revolt against Pekahiah in 737 B.C., led by Pekah, perhaps aided and abetted by the Syrians and Philistines

(cf. vv. 11–12). This is the only known instance when it could be said that Syria and Philistia were devouring Israel "with open mouth."

Because of Israel's obstinacy the divine word of judgment has come crashing down upon her (v. 8). The prophets conceive of the word of the Lord as laden with power and able to produce both blessing and judgment (cf. Jer. 1:9–10; Zech. 5:1–4).

God's chastisement of Israel, however, has been in vain. She is still proud and self-sufficient. Her cocksure attitude is reflected in the response she has made to disasters already suffered (v. 10). The words of Israel may have been borrowed from a common proverb. Sunbaked bricks and sycamore trees, i.e., fig trees, were common building materials. Israel makes her boast that she will rebuild her ruins with dressed stones and cedar wood.

The meaning of the refrain in v. 12b is that God will visit the nation with even greater destruction. The parallelism between the two parts of the refrain indicates that the outstretched hand is a symbol of wrath and judgment and not of mercy (cf. 14:26 f.; 23:11; Ex. 6:6; Jer. 21:5).

Verses 13–17 show the utter confusion of those who refused to be corrected by the Lord's chastisements. *Head and tail, palm branch and reed* are figures of speech for the political and religious leaders of the community who will all be cut off in one day. The accusation brought against them is that they have taught the people lies and have led them astray. The whole nation, therefore, has become so godless and corrupt that God will no longer have compassion upon it. Even *widows* and *orphans,* who are so often commended to mercy in the Old Testament, will no longer be spared.

(2) The Fire of God's Wrath (9:18–21)

18 For wickedness burns like a fire,
    it consumes briers and thorns;
    it kindles the thickets of the forest,
    and they roll upward in a column of smoke.
19 Through the wrath of the LORD of hosts

the land is burned,
and the people are like fuel for the fire;
no man spares his brother.
20 They snatch on the right, but are still hungry,
and they devour on the left, but are not satisfied;
each devours his neighbor's flesh,
21 Manasseh Ephraim, and Ephraim Manasseh,
and together they are against Judah.
For all this his anger is not turned away
and his hand is stretched out still.

These verses reflect the social chaos and political anarchy that characterized life within the Northern Kingdom during the last few years of its existence. From the death of Jeroboam II in 746 B.C. until the fall of Samaria in 722, Israel had no fewer than six kings, only one of whom died a natural death. The years have been described as a time "when one nobody after another seized the throne without even the pretense of legitimacy." [66a]

The nation was being devoured by a double conflagration. On one hand, her own wickedness was burning like a forest fire out of control (v. 18). She was learning that sin inevitably brings its own judgment. On the other hand, the fire of God's wrath was kindled against her, devouring both land and people.

The destructive power of evil is nowhere more vividly described than in vv. 19b–21. The prophet speaks of brother turning upon brother and of men who in their awful hunger tear at one another like cannibals (cf. 2 Kings 6:24–31). Fratricide and cannibalism are accompanied by tribal strife and sectional warfare; the tribes of Ephraim and Manasseh fight one another and are united only in their mutual hatred of Judah. The reference is to the civil wars that racked Israel between 745 and 737 B.C. (cf. 2 Kings 15:8–26), as well as to Israel's hostility against Judah during the Syro-Ephraimitic crisis (735–734 B.C.).

Israel's sin, therefore, has provoked stroke after stroke, but the worst is yet to come. This is the inference to be drawn from the refrain at the close of v. 21. Many

66a Cf. John Bright, op. cit., p. 255.

scholars believe that 5:25–30 originally stood as the conclusion to this oracle against Israel, since it repeats the ominous words of the refrain and describes the relentless advance of an invading army. Though the invader is not named, he is usually identified as Assyria, whose troops destroyed Samaria in 722 B.C.

(3) Legalized Robbery (10:1–4)

1 Woe to those who decree iniquitous decrees,
and the writers who keep writing oppression,
2 to turn aside the needy from justice
and to rob the poor of my people of their right,
that widows may be their spoil,
and that they may make the fatherless their prey!
3 What will you do on the day of punishment,
in the storm which will come from afar?
To whom will you flee for help,
and where will you leave your wealth?
4 Nothing remains but to crouch among the prisoners
or fall among the slain.
For all this his anger is not turned away
and his hand is stretched out still.

This final stanza of the refrain song begins with Woe (cf. 5:8–25) and ends with the same refrain as the three stanzas in the preceding chapter.[67] Unlike the other stanzas, however, it is addressed to Judah rather than to Israel, as indicated by the prophet's reference to the oppressed as my people.

God's chastisement of Israel has produced no reformation in Judah. Instead, judges and scribes are busy formulating laws that will give an aura of legality to their iniquitous deeds. Those who bear the brunt of this legal chicanery are the needy, the poor, the widows, and the fatherless (v. 2). Isaiah directs three probing questions at those who have become rich through the exploitation of the poor (v. 3). Then without waiting for a reply, he answers his own questions (v. 4). The only option they will have on the day of

67 For a proposed solution to the question of the relationship between 5:8–25 and 9:7–10:4, see J. Lindblom, Prophecy in Ancient Israel (Oxford: Basil Blackwell, 1962), pp. 225 f.

punishment will be to crouch among the prisoners or fall among the slain.

7. Oracles Against Assyria (10:5–34)

Most scholars believe that this passage should be interpreted against the background of events that transpired near the end of the eighth century B.C. When Sargon died in 705 and was succeeded by his son Sennacherib (705–681), a wave of revolt spread throughout the vast Assyrian Empire. This was the signal for Hezekiah (715–687) to raise the standard of sevolt in Judah. Isaiah counseled against this move, but to no avail.

Sennacherib's retaliation came swiftly and decisively. He invaded Judah and, according to his own records, destroyed 46 fortified cities. He claims to have shut Hezekiah up in Jerusalem like a bird in a cage. The record of these events is found in 2 Kings 18—19, as well as in the parallel accounts in Isaiah 36—37 and 2 Chronicles 32.

Out of the turmoil of the Sennacherib crisis, Isaiah developed a remarkable philosophy of history. He came to believe that a nation could be both a rebel against God and an instrument of his purpose. Even though Assyria had reached the apex of her power and seemed to be invincible, the prophet saw her as a mere pawn in the band of God. God's overruling power and wisdom were such that he could control her brutal lust for blood and plunder, making it serve his righteous purpose in the chastening of his people. Assyria's will to power, therefore, was under his control, and her rise to power was but a minor episode in the ongoing history of his dealings with his chosen people.

The basis of Isaiah's position was the belief that power—the kind of power represented by Assyria—was not the key to life. The key lay rather in service to God. Long after the proud Assyrians had disappeared from history, God's servants—chatened and restored—would still abide. Nothing in the outward circumstances of the times would have led Isaiah to such a

philosophy of history. His belief in God as the Lord of history was not a logical deduction drawn from available evidence. It was rather a leap of faith, an inspired concept, a word from God.

(1) Assyria the Rod of God's Anger (10:5–11)

5 Ah, Assyria, the rod of my anger,
   the staff of my fury!
6 Against a godless nation I send him,
   and against the people of my wrath I command him,
to take spoil and seize plunder,
   and to tread them down like the mire of the streets.
7 But he does not so intend,
   and his mind does not so think;
but it is in his mind to destroy,
   and to cut off nations not a few;
8 for he says:
"Are not my commanders all kings?
9 Is not Calno like Carchemish?
   Is not Hamath like Arpad?
   Is not Samaria like Damascus?
10 As my hand has reached to the kingdoms of the idols
   whose graven images were greater than those of Jerusalem and Samaria,
11 shall I not do to Jerusalem and her idols
   as I have done to Samaria and her images?"

In the ancient world men supposed that conflicts between nations were really conflicts between their respective gods. When one nation conquered another, it was taken as an indication that the victor's gods were superior to those of the vanquished.

A logical conclusion, therefore, was that Assyria's conquest of Judah had proved the superiority of her gods over the God of the Hebrews. The Assyrians had, in fact, used this very argument in their challenge to the defenders of Jerusalem (cf. 36:18–20).

Isaiah, however, regarded such a notion as patently false. He saw Assyria as nothing more than *the rod of God's anger and the staff of his fury.* The rod and the staff are tools of the shepherd, and are used elsewhere in the Old Testament to suggest God's protective care over his people (cf. Psalm 23:4). That they are referred to in the present context as instruments of discipline and correction must not be interpreted to mean that God had momentarily ceased to care for Israel. The same love that blessed her when she was faithful also punished her when she was disobedient. It would have been something other than love if it had acted otherwise.

Godless means to be alienated from God. The same word appears in 9:17 and in 33:14, applying in each case to the inhabitants of Judah and Jerusalem. The name of Isaiah's son, Maher-shalal-hash-baz, is echoed in the phrase translated "to take spoil and to seize plunder" (Heb. *lishlol shalal w°laboz baz*).

While Isaiah saw the Assyrians as instruments in God's hands for the punishment of Judah, he was well aware that they did not accept this as their mission (v. 7). They were bent on conquest simply for the sake of wealth and self-glory. They would have scoffed at the idea that they were in any way under God's control.

To the Assyrians, therefore, all nations were alike. A partial list of those whom they had already conquered is given in v. 9. *Carchemish* was a city on the upper part of the Euphrates river. *Calno* and *Arpad* lay about 50 miles to the southwest of Carchemish. *Hamath* was on the Orontes river another hundred miles further south. Since *Samaria* is also listed here, the passage has to be dated after 722 B.C. The Assyrians were confident that Jerusalem would soon be added to this list.

(2) Punishment of the Pride of Assyria (10:12–19)

¹² When the Lord has finished all his work on Mount Zion and on Jerusalem he will punish the arrogant boasting of the king of Assyria and his haughty pride. ¹³ For he says:
"By the strength of my hand I have done it,
  and by my wisdom, for I have understanding;
I have removed the boundaries of peoples,
  and have plundered their treasures;
  like a bull I have brought down those who sat on thrones.
¹⁴ My hand has found like a nest
  the wealth of the peoples;
and as men gather eggs that have been forsaken
  so I have gathered all the earth;

and there was none that moved a wing,
  or opened the mouth, or chirped."
¹⁵ Shall the ax vaunt itself over him who hews with it,
  or the saw magnify itself against him who wields it?
As if a rod should wield him who lifts it,
  or as if a staff should lift him who is not wood!
¹⁶ Therefore the Lord, the LORD of hosts,
  will send wasting sickness among his stout warriors,
and under his glory a burning will be kindled,
  like the burning of fire.
¹⁷ The light of Israel will become a fire,
  and his Holy One a flame;
and it will burn and devour
  his thorns and briers in one day.
¹⁸ The glory of his forest and of his fruitful land
  the LORD will destroy, both soul and body,
  and it will be as when a sick man wastes away.
¹⁹ The remnant of the trees of his forest will be so few
  that a child can write them down.

Verse 12 shows that the Lord also was keeping a list. On his list Jerusalem's name stood first; but next to it stood that of Assyria. As he had punished the godlessness of the one, so would he punish the arrogance and pride of the other.

Assyria's boasting is illustrated in the verses that follow. This is a classic example of the essential idolatry of those who live by military might. One writer has described such an attitude of arrogant self-sufficiency as "the atheism of force." The king of Assyria boasted that by his own strength and wisdom he had removed boundaries and gathered the wealth of nations. To illustrate the ease with which he had accomplished this, he used the metaphor of one gathering eggs from an abandoned bird's nest. Pursuing the metaphor still further, he boasted that none of the plundered peoples had "moved a wing, or opened the mouth, or chirped."

To Isaiah the boasting of the conquering king was utter nonsense; it was as if a tool should boast that it controlled the one who used it (v. 15). God's punishment of the pride of Assyria is described in vv. 16–19 with the figures of a raging forest fire and a wasting sickness. The fire would be kindled by the *light of Israel,* which, as the parallelism of v. 17 shows, was another designation for God. It would sweep through the land, destroying not only thorns and briers but also forests and cultivated land. The surviving trees would be so few in number that even a child could count them. Assyria's "remnant," therefore, would be scant indeed!

(3) *Encouragement to the Remnant of Israel* (*10:20–27b*)

20 In that day the remnant of Israel and the survivors of the house of Jacob will no more lean upon him that smote them, but will lean upon the LORD, the Holy One of Israel, in truth. 21 A remnant will return, the remnant of Jacob, to the mighty God. 22 For though your people Israel be as the sand of the sea, only a remnant of them will return. Destruction is decreed, overflowing with righteousness. 23 For the Lord, the LORD of hosts, will make a full end, as decreed, in the midst of all the earth. 24 Therefore thus says the Lord, the LORD of hosts: "O my people, who dwell in Zion, be not afraid of the Assyrians when they smite with the rod and lift up their staff against you as the Egyptians did. 25 For in a very little while my indignation will come to an end, and my anger will be directed to their destruction. 26 And the LORD of hosts will wield against them a scourge, as when he smote Midian at the rock of Oreb; and his rod will be over the sea, and he will lift it as he did in Egypt. 27 And in that day his burden will depart from your shoulder, and his yoke will be destroyed from your neck."

The eschatological nature of the passage is clearly shown by the opening phrase *in that day.* The prophet sets forth the view that a repentant remnant will survive the judgment and in days to come will lean upon the Lord, rather than upon *him that smote them.* The latter phrase probably refers to Assyria, who first lent assistance to Judah but later viciously attacked her.

It is further stated that the remnant of Jacob (i.e., Israel) will return to *the mighty God.* The Hebrew reads to *'el gibbor,* the same name that appears in 9:6 as one of the titles given to the messianic king. Perhaps, as Bright has suggested,

there are messianic overtones in the passage. Perhaps the prophet was designating the ideal Davidic king as the ruler of the remnant.

A remnant will return is the translation of two Hebrew words, *shear jashub,* which, as noted above, is also the name that Isaiah gave to one of his sons (cf. 7:3). The name could be interpreted as either promise or threat, which explains the twofold sense in which it is used here. In v. 21 it stands as a message of hope ("a remnant will return"); in v. 22 it constitutes a threat ("*only* a remnant will return"). This double usage has led some to conclude that vv. 22–23 belong to an early stage in Isaiah's ministry, before the doctrine of the remnant became prominent, whereas vv. 20–21 represent a later stage in his reflection upon this subject.

The theme of vv. 24–27b is the sure deliverance of God's people from the Assyrians. Their deliverance will be like that of the Israelites who escaped from Egypt. Throughout the Old Testament the Exodus is regarded as the prototype of all subsequent acts of deliverance. The Lord will drive out the Assyrians as he once drove out the Midianites before Gideon (Judg. 6—8). Let Israel take heart for she will soon be free from her burden and her yoke of oppression.

Isaiah's hope was vindicated when the Assyrians withdrew from Jerusalem as abruptly as they had come. According to 2 Kings 19:35, their army was decimated in one night. The Greek historian Herodotus records that they were overrun by a plague of rats. Their sudden departure from Jerusalem, therefore, may have been caused by an outbreak of the bubonic plague.

(4) *The Assyrian Invasion* (*10:27c–34*)

He has gone up from Rimmon,
28   he has come to Aiath;
he has passed through Migron,
      at Michmash he stores his baggage;
29 they have crossed over the pass,
      at Geba they lodge for the night;
Ramah trembles,
      Gibeah of Saul has fled.

30 Cry aloud, O daughter of Gallim!
　　Hearken, O Laishah!
　　Answer her, O Anathoth!
31 Madmenah is in flight,
　　the inhabitants of Gebim flee for safety.
32 This very day he will halt at Nob,
　　he will shake his fist
　　at the mount of the daughter of Zion,
　　the hill of Jerusalem.
33 Behold, the Lord, the LORD of hosts
　　will lop the boughs with terrifying power;
　　the great in height will be hewn down,
　　and the lofty will be brought low.
34 He will cut down the thickets of the forest
　　with an ax,
　　and Lebanon with its majestic trees will
　　fall.

In one sense this passage is a recapitulation of the earlier oracles in the chapter. It reiterates the threat that Assyria will pose to Jerusalem, and predicts the ultimate deliverance of the latter through divine intervention. The passage is usually dated just prior to Sennacherib's invasion of Judah in 701 B.C.

The prophet gives a vivid description of the swift advance of the enemy, who occupy village after village on the northern approaches to Jerusalem until they arrive at the very outskirts of the city itself. Some have objected that Sennacherib did not in fact follow this route when he invaded Judah, but that he first marched down the coastal road into Philistia and then turned inland toward Jerusalem. The passage, therefore, has been interpreted by some as a description of the invasion of Judah by the combined forces of Syria and Israel in 734 B.C.

In reply to these objections, it should be noted that the editor of the materials obviously identified the invader with Assyria, else he would not have placed the passage in its present context. Furthermore, too little is known about Sennacherib's invasion for one to be dogmatic about the route he followed. Since Samaria was already an Assyrian province in 701 B.C., he may have mounted a two-pronged attack upon Jerusalem, sending one force down the central mountain range that ran from Samaria to Jerusalem while he himself led another force against the city from the southwest.

Most of the place-names mentioned in the passage have been identified; they were Israelite villages stretching along a line from north to south. Rimmon—if the RSV's emendation is accepted—was situated some five miles east of Bethel (cf. Judg. 20:45). Aiath, perhaps another name for Ai (cf. Josh 7:8), modern et-Tell, lay slightly to the east of Bethel. The site of Migron has not been identified, although 1 Samuel 14:2 gives the impression that it lay south and not north of the pass of Michmash. Michmash, modern Mukhmas, was two and a half miles south of Bethel (cf. 1 Sam. 14:1-5). Near Michmash to the south lay a narrow pass, where the Assyrians were forced to store their baggage in order to pass through unencumbered. Geba (cf. 1 Sam. 14:5) lay south of the pass, some six miles northeast of Jerusalem. Ramah, modern er-Ram, lay just north of Gibeah (cf. Judg. 19:13-14), near the frontier between Israel and Judah. Gibeah of Saul, modern Tell el-Ful, formerly the capital of Saul's kingdom, was only three miles north of Jerusalem. Between it and Jerusalem lay the other villages—Gallim, Laishah, Anathoth, Madmenah, Gebim, and Nob. It is thought that Nob was situated on the slopes of Mount Scopus, overlooking the city of Jerusalem from the northeast. From there the Assyrian could shake his fist at the besieged city.

Assyria's success will be short-lived, however, for the Lord will cut her down, as a mighty woodsman fells the trees of a forest. Some regard vv. 33-34 as a separate oracle directed not against Assyria but against either Israel or Judah. It seems best, however, to retain the verses as an integral part of the preceding oracle. They not only form an appropriate conclusion to the oracle but also prepare the way for the reference to the stump of Jesse at the beginning of the next oracle.[68]

---

[68] For the view that vv. 33-34 are the introduction to the oracle in 11:1-9, and that this oracle belongs to the period of the Syro-Ephraimitic crisis, see Brevard S. Childs, op. cit., p. 62.

8. The Messianic Age (11:1-16)

(1) The Messianic King (11:1-9)

1 There shall come forth a shoot from the
    stump of Jesse,
  and a branch shall grow out of his roots.
2 And the Spirit of the LORD shall rest upon
    him,
  the spirit of wisdom and understanding,
  the spirit of counsel and might,
  the spirit of knowledge and the fear of the
    LORD.
3 And his delight shall be in the fear of the
    LORD.
  He shall not judge by what his eyes see,
    or decide by what his ears hear;
4 but with righteousness he shall judge the
    poor,
  and decide with equity for the meek of
    the earth;
  and he shall smite the earth with the rod of
    his mouth,
  and with the breath of his lips he shall
    slay the wicked.
5 Righteousness shall be the girdle of his waist,
  and faithfulness the girdle of his loins.
6 The wolf shall dwell with the lamb,
  and the leopard shall lie down with the
    kid,
  and the calf and the lion and the fatling to-
    gether,
  and a little child shall lead them.
7 The cow and the bear shall feed;
  their young shall lie down together;
  and the lion shall eat straw like the ox.
8 The sucking child shall play over the hole
    of the asp,
  and the weaned child shall put his hand
    on the adder's den.
9 They shall not hurt or destroy
  in all my holy mountain;
  for the earth shall be full of the knowledge
    of the LORD
  as the waters cover the sea.

The passage contains the most complete
delineation of the personal characteristics
of the messianic king to be found in the
Old Testament. Isaiah prophesies that he
will come forth as "a shoot from the stump
of Jesse," that is, he will be of the house
and lineage of David the son of Jesse.

The word rendered *stump* is derived
from a root meaning to cut off. The same
word appears in Job 14:8, where it describes the stump that remains after a tree
has been cut down. Some, therefore, would
date the passage after the catastrophe of

587 B.C. when the house of David was cut
off. Others would place it in the time of the
Sennacherib crisis when the existence of
the house of David was merely threatened.
Bright has suggested that the oracle may
mean only "that a new twig will grow from
the house of David," in which case an
eighth-century date would be possible.

More important than the origin of the
king is his endowment with *the Spirit of
the Lord.* Whenever in the Old Testament
the Spirit of the Lord is given to men it is
in order that they may be divinely
equipped for some demanding task. Basically, the Spirit of the Lord connotes power,
and those upon whom the Spirit rests act
with superhuman wisdom and strength, as
they perform a variety of tasks (cf. Gen.
41:38; Ex. 31:3; Num. 11:25; Judg. 6:34;
Isa. 61:1; Joel 2:28 f.).

The king is endowed with the Spirit in
order that he might know how to rule his
subjects in the fear of the Lord. It should
be emphasized that it is *one* Spirit that
rests upon him. The remainder of v. 2
merely describes the outworking of the
Spirit in his life.

The virtues imparted to him are arranged in three pairs, which stress first his
wisdom, then his administrative ability,
and finally his piety. The juxtaposition of
Wisdom and understanding and *counsel
and might* means that he has not only the
insight to see what is right but also the
ability to bring it to pass. The "spirit of
counsel and might" parallels the first two
names given to the messianic king in 9:6.

The most important feature in the equip-
ment of the king is his knowledge and fear
of the Lord. *Knowledge* as the Hebrews
understood it meant more than possessing
certain information about someone; it
meant understanding that could be gained
only on the basis of a close personal relationship. To *fear* the Lord meant to be
reverent before his majesty and holiness.
To know and to fear the Lord, therefore,
expressed the essence of Old Testament
faith. Mowinckel has aptly described this
virtue as "the true crown of the future

king." [69]

Verses 3b–4a give a description of the manner in which the king will apply the spirit of wisdom and understanding in his judging of the people. His ability to see below the surface will enable him to judge with equity the poor and meek of the earth. His power to effect decisions, that is, "the spirit of counsel and might," is illustrated in his smiting the ruthless (reading *'arits*, ruthless, for *'erets*, earth) with the rod of his mouth and in his slaying the wicked with the breath of his lips. Both the judging (i.e., the delivering) of the poor (the innocent) and the slaying of the wicked (the guilty) should be understood as judicial acts, acts performed by the king in the administration of justice.

The Messiah, therefore, will be a just and righteous judge, delivering the innocent and punishing the wicked. Significantly, the main emphasis is laid upon the social and ethical aspects of his reign, not only here but elsewhere in the prophets (cf. 9:7; 16:5; 32:1; Jer. 23:5 f.). This is brought out most clearly in v. 5, where *righteousness* is said to be "the girdle of his waist" and faithfulness "the girdle of his loins."

Verses 6–9 give a highly symbolic and poetic description of the complete harmony and peace which is to prevail with the coming of the messianic age. The paradise motif, which figures prominently in the Old Testament (cf. 32:15; 41:17–19; Ezek. 34:25–28; 47:1–12; Joel 3:18; Amos 9:13–15; Zech. 14:4–11) and in other ancient Near Eastern literature,[70] reappears here. The righteous rule of the messianic king will result in the restoration of harmony to the natural order. The Old Testament looked upon sin as the cause of the disharmony that existed in the natural order (cf. 24:4–7; Gen. 3:14–19; Jer. 4:23–26; 12:4). Nature, therefore, was destined to share in the redemption of

[69] S. Mowinckel, *op. cit.*, p. 180.
[70] Cf. Brevard S. Childs, *Myth and Reality in the Old Testament*, "Studies in Biblical Theology, No. 27" (Naperville: Alec R. Allenson, Inc., 1960), 63–67.

God's people. With the coming of the messianic age, men and animals would live together in a paradise-like relationship, and no living creature would hurt or destroy another.

The climax of the oracle is reached in the affirmation that the knowledge of the Lord will fill the earth as the waters cover the sea. The emphasis is upon the universal and permeating influence of this knowledge. In this passage, therefore, the knowledge of the Lord begins as an attribute of the Messiah (v. 2) and ends as an attribute of all his subjects (v. 9).

(2) Reunion in the Messianic Kingdom (11:10–16)

[10] In that day the root of Jesse shall stand as an ensign to the peoples; him shall the nations seek, and his dwellings shall be glorious.
[11] In that day the Lord will extend his hand yet a second time to recover the remnant which is left of his people, from Assyria, from Egypt, from Pathros, from Ethiopia, from Elam, from Shinar, from Hamath, and from the coastlands of the sea.
[12] He will raise an ensign for the nations,
    and will assemble the outcasts of Israel,
and gather the dispersed of Judah
    from the four corners of the earth.
[13] The jealousy of Ephraim shall depart,
    and those who harass Judah shall be cut off;
Ephraim shall not be jealous of Judah,
    and Judah shall not harass Ephraim.
[14] But they shall swoop down upon the shoulder of the Philistines in the west,
    and together they shall plunder the people of the east.
They shall put forth their hand against Edom and Moab,
    and the Ammonites shall obey them.
[15] And the LORD will utterly destroy
    the tongue of the sea of Egypt;
and will wave his hand over the River
    with his scorching wind,
and smite it into seven channels
    that men may cross dryshod.
[16] And there will be a highway from Assyria
    for the remnant which is left of his people,
as there was for Israel
    when they came up from the land of Egypt.

The section consists of two oracles, each introduced by the phrase *in that day* (vv. 10 and 11). Most scholars assign the oracles to the postexilic period, mainly on the basis of the later historical situation which they reflect. Here the word *remnant* (vv. 11, 16) stands not for the Jews who survive the judgment in their own native land (cf. 10:20–21) but for those who have been exiled to foreign lands. The dispersion of the Jews as described here is far greater than one would expect it to be by the eighth century B.C. All indications therefore point toward a postexilic date for the passage, although, as Bright concedes, an earlier date is not inconceivable.

The word *root* (v. 10) appears in its plural form in v. 1, where it refers not to the messianic king but to the Davidic dynasty. By the time the oracle in v. 10 was written it had perhaps become a technical term for the Messiah. The same word is used in 53:2—"a root out of dry ground"—to describe the Servant of the Lord (cf. Rev. 22:16). Here the root of Jesse stands as a flagstaff or ensign around which the nations of the earth rally. The worldwide dominion of the Messiah is a concept that appears frequently in the Old Testament (cf. Psalms 18:43–45; 72:8–11; Mic. 5:4; Zech. 9:10).

The Exodus motif is particularly strong in vv. 11–16. The reference to the Lord's rescuing his people *a second time* presupposes the first deliverance at the Red Sea. Furthermore, the nations referred to in v. 14 are the same ones who tried to block Israel's entry into Canaan in the days of Moses and Joshua. Verses 15–16 describe the highway that the Lord will prepare for the return of the dispersed remnant of his people. He will dry up *the tongue of the sea of Egypt,* perhaps the gulf of Suez, and smite the River, that is, the Euphrates, into seven shallow brooks, so that men may cross it dryshod.

9. *Two Songs of Praise (12:1–6)*

When Israel had safely crossed the Red Sea on her way out of Egypt, she paused to sing a song praising God for his great salvation (Ex. 15:1–18). The prospect of an even greater deliverance calls for the singing of new songs of praise. The two brief hymns in chapter 12, therefore, form an appropriate conclusion to the first division of Isaiah's prophecies (chs. 1—12).

(1) A Song of Deliverance (12:1–2)

1 You will say in that day:
"I will give thanks to thee, O LORD,
   for though thou wast angry with me,
thy anger turned away,
   and thou didst comfort me.
2 "Behold, God is my salvation;
   I will trust, and will not be afraid;
for the LORD GOD is my strength and my
   song,
and he has become my salvation."

There are two brief hymns in chapter 12, each of which is introduced by the phrase "you will say in that day" (vv. 1, 4). It is probable, therefore, that v. 3 belongs to the first song, contrary to the division indicated in the RSV.

The verb to *say* is singular in form in v. 1 and plural in v. 4. This suggests that the first song is a song of individual thanksgiving and the second a song of community thanksgiving. The structure of the first song resembles the songs of individual thanksgiving in the Psalter (e.g., Psalm 116). The Exodus motif is prominent in this song, as evidenced by the fact that v. 2b is a repetition of Ex. 15:2.

The first song celebrates the singer's deliverance from great distress. He gives thanks to Yahweh because (*ki*) his anger, once directed toward him, has now been turned away from him. God has now become his *salvation,* which is the first time this important word is used in Isaiah (cf. 25:9; 26:1, 18; 33:2,6; 49:6,8; 51:6, 8; 52:7, 10; 56:1; 59:11,17; 60:18; 62:1). Because salvation is derived from a verbal root meaning "to be wide, spacious," it connotes the idea of deliverance from all that would thwart or hinder one's peace and prosperity. There is, of course, veiled reference to Isaiah's name in the threefold repetition of this word in vv. 2 and 3, since Isaiah means "the Lord is salvation."

The first hymn ends with the metaphor of the congregation of Israel joyfully drawing water from the wells of salvation. The metaphor had special significance for those whose lives were dependent upon wells and fountains. *To draw water from the wells of salvation* means to continue to share in the good life that Yahweh has provided for his people (cf. John 4:7–14).

(2) A Song of Thanksgiving (12:3–6)

3 With joy you will draw water from the wells of salvation. 4 And you will say in that day:
"Give thanks to the LORD,
    call upon his name;
make known his deeds among the nations,
    proclaim that his name is exalted.
5 "Sing praises to the LORD, for he has done gloriously;
    let this be known in all the earth.
6 Shout, and sing for joy, O inhabitant of Zion,
    for great in your midst is the Holy One of Israel."

Following the paragraph divisions of the RSV, v. 3 is printed here but has been interpreted as belonging with vv. 1–2, for reasons given above.

In this song Israel makes known among the nations the wondrous deeds of Yahweh. The phraseology of the song is largely borrowed from the Psalms (e.g., Psalms 66:2; 67:2; 105:1; 148:13). Yahweh is praised not only for his mighty acts on behalf of Zion but also for his abiding presence in her midst. The conclusion to the song shows that there is no conflict between Yahweh's holiness and his nearness to his people (cf. Hos. 11:9).

II. Oracles Addressed to Foreign Nations (13:1—23:18)

One of the most neglected areas of Old Testament studies is that of the prophetical oracles against the nations.[71] Examples of such oracles are found in almost all of the prophetic books, Hosea being a notable exception. Some are directed against the nations in general, but most are addressed to specific nations. These include Egypt

[71] Cf. John H. Hayes, "The Usage of Oracles Against Foreign Nations in Ancient Israel," *Journal of Biblical Literature*, LXXXVII (March, 1968), pp. 81–92.

(19:1–15; Jer. 46; Ethiopia (18), Elam (Jer. 49:34–39), Babylon (13; 21:1–10; Jer. 50:1—51:58), Kedar (Jer. 49:28–33), Philistia (14:28–32; Ezek. 25:15–17), Edom (34; Ezek. 25:12–14), Moab (15—16; Jer. 48), Ammon (Jer. 49:1–6; Ezek. 25:1–7), Tyre (Ezek. 26:1—28:19), Sidon (Ezek. 28:20–26), and Nineveh (Nah.).

In all of the foreign oracles the nations are regarded as the enemies of Israel. The oracles are directed *against* the nations. For this reason they are frequently introduced by the word *massā'*, meaning burden or load. When used to introduce a prophetic oracle, this word emphasizes its condemnatory and threatening nature. Like some dark cloud heavy with pent-up fury, these prophecies hang ready to pour their dreadful contents on those against whom they are directed. Ten of the foreign oracles in Isaiah are introduced by this term (13:1; 14:28; 15:1; 17:1; 19:1; 21:1, 11, 13; 22:1; 23:1). Scott has aptly described these as "doom oracles."

Gottwald is of the opinion that the oracle against the foreign nation "was one of the earliest, if not the earliest, form of Hebrew prophecy."[72] The origin of this type of oracle is probably to be sought in the ancient ritual of holy war. It was customary for a king or military commander, before going to do battle, to seek out a prophet to pronounce a curse upon his enemies. Such a curse was regarded as a potent secret weapon, insuring the foe's downfall. A classic example of a king attempting to place a prophetic curse upon his enemies is found in Numbers 23—24 in the story of Balak and Balaam.

The fact that foreign oracles are found in so many of the prophetical books raises some interesting questions. Was it customary for the canonical prophets to employ these oracles as ritual curses against their nation's enemies? If so, what were the occasions upon which they would utter such curses? Unfortunately, most of the foreign oracles now appear in collections com-

[72] *All the Kingdoms of the Earth*, p. 49.

pletely cut off from any specific historical context. It is impossible, therefore, to be certain about their original setting or about their function in Hebrew life and cult.

Some of Isaiah's oracles against foreign nations are preserved in larger contexts which reveal the historical setting. This is true, for example, of the oracles against Syria and Israel delivered in 735–734 B.C. (7:3–9,10–16; 8:1–4), and of those spoken against Assyria in 701 (ch. 37). The oracles grouped in chapters 13—23, however, give no data regarding the dates or circumstances of their delivery. These data must be determined solely on the basis of internal evidence, which is often inconclusive.

This is the only collection of foreign oracles in the book of Isaiah. Hence these oracles cover the entire time span of the book. Some belong to the eighth century B.C., and may with confidence be assigned to Isaiah of Jerusalem; others, however, arose during the Exile, or shortly thereafter, and must be assigned to later editors. This does not mean that the earlier passages are more important than the later, but rather that the understanding of the importance of both early and late passages depends to a great degree upon their being placed in their proper historical setting. All of the foreign oracles are extremely important and merit greater attention than has usually been given to them.

1. The Doom of Babylon (13:1—14:23)

No power in ancient times affected the fortunes of Israel in a more catastrophic way than did Babylon. It is understandable, therefore, that many Jews came to regard her as the very arch-foe of the people of God. The name "Babylon" became synonymous with tyranny and oppression, so much so that in the New Testament it was used symbolically for Rome (cf. 1 Peter 5:13; Rev. 14:8; 16:19; 17:5).

This is one of the sections in the oracles against the nations that must be dated later than the prophet Isaiah. The historical situation reflected here is not that of the

eighth century but of the sixth century B.C. The world ruler is not Assyria, as in the days of Isaiah, but Babylon. The turning point in Babylon's fortunes came in 626 B.C. when Nabopolassar defeated the Assyrians; prior to that, Babylon, like all the countries of the west, had been a vassal of Assyria. After she gained her independence she ruled the world with an iron hand, until she in turn was conquered by Cyrus the Persian in 539. The present passage belongs to the period of Babylon's ascendancy, for she is described as "the glory of kingdoms, the splendor and pride of the Chaldeans" (13:19).

(1) The Day of the Lord Against Babylon (13:1–22)

1 The oracle concerning Babylon which Isaiah
  the son of Amoz saw.
2 On a bare hill raise a signal,
  cry aloud to them;
 wave the hand for them to enter
  the gates of the nobles.
3 I myself have commanded my consecrated
  ones,
  have summoned my mighty men to execute my anger,
  my proudly exulting ones.
4 Hark, a tumult on the mountains
  as of a great multitude!
 Hark, an uproar of kingdoms,
  of nations gathering together!
 The LORD of hosts is mustering
  a host for battle.
5 They come from a distant land,
  from the end of the heavens,
 the LORD and the weapons of his indignation,
  to destroy the whole earth.
6 Wail, for the day of the LORD is near;
  as destruction from the Almighty it will
  come!
7 Therefore all hands will be feeble,
  and every man's heart will melt,
  and they will be dismayed.
 Pangs and agony will seize them;
  they will be in anguish like a woman in
  travail.
 They will look aghast at one another;
  their faces will be aflame.
9 Behold, the day of the LORD comes,
  cruel, with wrath and fierce anger,
 to make the earth a desolation
  and to destroy its sinners from it.
10 For the stars of the heavens and their constellations

will not give their light;
the sun will be dark at its rising
and the moon will not shed its light.
11 I will punish the world for its evil,
and the wicked for their iniquity;
I will put an end to the pride of the arrogant,
and lay low the haughtiness of the ruthless.
12 I will make men more rare than fine gold,
and mankind than the gold of Ophir.
13 Therefore I will make the heavens tremble,
and the earth will be shaken out of its place,
at the wrath of the Lord of hosts
in the day of his fierce anger.
14 And like a hunted gazelle,
or like sheep with none to gather them,
every man will turn to his own people,
and every man will flee to his own land.
15 Whoever is found will be thrust through,
and whoever is caught will fall by the sword.
16 Their infants will be dashed in pieces
before their eyes;
their houses will be plundered
and their wives ravished.
17 Behold, I am stirring up the Medes against them,
who have no regard for silver
and do not delight in gold.
18 Their bows will slaughter the young men;
they will have no mercy on the fruit of the womb;
their eyes will not pity children.
19 And Babylon, the glory of kingdoms,
the splendor and pride of the Chaldeans,
will be like Sodom and Gomorrah
when God overthrew them.
20 It will never be inhabited
or dwelt in for all generations;
no Arab will pitch his tent there,
no shepherds will make their flocks lie down there.
21 But wild beasts will lie down there,
and its houses will be full of howling creatures;
there ostriches will dwell,
and there satyrs will dance.
22 Hyenas will cry in its towers,
and jackals in the pleasant palaces;
its time is close at hand
and its days will not be prolonged.

This passage consists of an editorial heading (v. 1), an oracle describing the day of the Lord in apocalyptic imagery (vv. 2–16), and a concluding oracle describing the defeat of Babylon by the Medes (vv. 17–22). The oracle on the

day of the Lord may originally have stood as an independent oracle having no direct connection with the fall of Babylon, although in the present context it has been brought into conjunction with this event.

As seen above, the word translated "oracle" means burden or load and refers to a doom oracle (cf. Jer. 23:34–40). Verse 1 is probably to be understood as the editorial heading for all of the oracles included in 13:2—14:23.

The oracle on the day of the Lord (vv. 2–16) opens with a description of the mustering of the army of the Lord (vv. 2–5). The signal calling the troops together is given from the top of a *bare hill,* so that all might see it. They are summoned in order that they might *enter the gates of the nobles,* possibly a veiled reference to Babylon, since the Akkadian name for the city, *Bab-ili,* meant "the gate of God."

Verse 3 is reminiscent of the institution of holy war. Those being mustered by the Lord are called his *consecrated ones.* Soldiers who marched out to do battle in ancient Israel were regarded as holy and were required to keep themselves ritually clean (cf. Deut. 23:9–14; 1 Sam. 21:4; 2 Sam. 11:11).

Emphasis is placed upon the unusual size of the army being assembled by the Lord. It includes kingdoms and nations from distant lands and from the ends of the heavens, i.e., from horizon to horizon. Their sound is like that of a mighty tumult on the mountains. These are the "nations in commotion, prepared for Zion's war."

The terrors of the day of the Lord are vividly described in vv. 6–16. The day comes *as destruction from the Almighty* (v. 6), a translation of a phrase which in Hebrew reads *k^eshod mishshaddai.* Courage fails and men are in agony, like that of a woman in travail. Their faces are aflame, either with shame or with dismay (v. 8).

The prophet employs apocalyptic imagery to describe how that day will affect the whole cosmos. The earth becomes a desolation (v. 9), and is shaken out of its place (v. 13). There are cataclysms in the heavens, also, as the sun, moon, and stars are darkened (v. 10) and the heavens tremble (v. 13).

The effects of that day upon sinners will be even more devastating. It is a day designed to destroy the wicked, the arrogant, and the ruthless (vv. 9,11). Destruction will be so widespread that *men* will become *more rare than fine gold* (v. 12). They will flee from the avenger like hunted animals, and be scattered like sheep without a shepherd (v. 14). The horrors of warfare to be visited upon them are vividly described in vv. 15–16.

In vv. 17–22 the preceding oracle on the day of the Lord is applied specifically to Babylon. The agent of the Lord's vengeance against her is identified as the Medes, an Indo-Aryan people who early in the seventh century established a powerful kingdom in the northwestern part of what is now Iran. This kingdom, with its capital at Ecbatana, continued to exercise a strong influence in the ancient Near East until it fell to Cyrus the Persian about 550 B.C.

Babylon was conquered in 539 B.C. not by the Medes, as anticipated in this oracle but by Cyrus. Furthermore, its capture did not result in the slaughter and destruction pictured here. It was actually a very peaceful capitulation, with Cyrus received more as a liberator than as a conqueror. He dealt leniently with the city, and it continued to exist as an important cultural center throughout the Persian period. It began to decline during the Hellenistic period, and was finally captured and destroyed by the Parthians in 127. By the beginning of the Christian era it was inhabited only by a small group of astronomers and mathematicians.

This oracle predicts that Babylon will be destroyed with a fury that defies description. Her conquerors will be impervious to bribes (v. 17). They will spare none of the city's inhabitants (v. 18). The city itself will share the fate of the ancient cities of Sodom and Gomorrah (v. 19).

The picture in vv. 20–22 is one of utter desolation. After the destruction of the city its ruins become the habitat of wild beasts and satyrs. The word satyr (lit., a hairy one) refers to a demon with the form of a he-goat. Such demons were thought to frequent the ruins of deserted cities (cf. 34:14).

(2) The Return of the Exiles (14:1–2)

1 The Lord will have compassion on Jacob and will again choose Israel, and will set them in their own land, and aliens will join them and will cleave to the house of Jacob. 2 And the peoples will take them and bring them to their place, and the house of Israel will possess them in the Lord's land as male and female slaves; they will take captive those who were their captors, and rule over those who oppressed them.

These verses, together with vv. 3–4a, constitute a prose introduction to the taunt song which follows. When Babylon has fallen, Yahweh will again elect Israel as his own people and bring her back to her land. Many foreigners will also join her ranks in order to share in her benefits. Those who formerly oppressed her will find their respective roles reversed, with Israel now ruling over them. When these things have come to pass and Israel has been given rest from her hard service (cf. Ex. 1:14), she will then take up a taunt song against the king of Babylon. Hebrew lexicons define *mashal* (taunt) as "a mocking comparison, a proverb, or a parable."

(3) A Taunt Song Against the King of Babylon (14:3–21)

3 When the Lord has given you rest from your pain and turmoil and the hard service with which you were made to serve, 4 you will take up this taunt against the king of Babylon:
"How the oppressor has ceased,
 the insolent fury ceased!
5 The Lord has broken the staff of the wicked,
 the scepter of rulers,
6 that smote the peoples in wrath
 with unceasing blows,
that ruled the nations in anger
 with unrelenting persecution.
7 The whole earth is at rest and quiet;
 they break forth into singing.

8 The cypresses rejoice at you,
　　the cedars of Lebanon, saying,
　'Since you were laid low,
　　no hewer comes up against us.'
9 Sheol beneath is stirred up
　　to meet you when you come,
　it rouses the shades to greet you,
　　all who were leaders of the earth;
　it raises from their thrones
　　all who were kings of the nations.
10 All of them will speak
　　and say to you:
　'You too have become as weak as we!
　　You have become like us!'
11 Your pomp is brought down to Sheol,
　　the sound of your harps;
　maggots are the bed beneath you,
　　and worms are your covering.
12 "How you are fallen from heaven,
　　O Day Star, son of Dawn!
　How you are cut down to the ground,
　　you who laid the nations low!
13 You said in your heart,
　　'I will ascend to heaven;
　above the stars of God
　　I will set my throne on high;
　I will sit on the mount of assembly
　　in the far north;
14 I will ascend above the heights of the
　　clouds,
　　I will make myself like the Most High.'
15 But you are brought down to Sheol,
　　to the depths of the Pit.
16 Those who see you will stare at you,
　　and ponder over you:
　'Is this the man who made the earth trem-
　　ble,
　who shook kingdoms,
17 who made the world like a desert
　　and overthrew its cities,
　who did not let his prisoners go home?'
18 All the kings of the nations lie in glory,
　　each in his own tomb;
19 but you are cast out, away from your
　　sepulchre,
　like a loathed untimely birth,
　clothed with the slain, those pierced by the
　　sword,
　who go down to the stones of the Pit,
　　like a dead body trodden under foot.
20 You will not be joined with them in burial,
　　because you have destroyed your land,
　　you have slain your people.
　"May the descendants of evildoers
　　nevermore be named!
21 Prepare slaughter for his sons
　　because of the guilt of their fathers,
　lest they rise and possess the earth,
　　and fill the face of the world with cities."

According to the prose introduction (v. 4a), this remarkable poem celebrates the

death of a Babylonian king. There is nothing within the poem itself, however, to identify the person about whom it was originally written, beyond the statement that during his lifetime he was a mighty ruler. Consequently, many scholars are convinced that the poem was originally composed to celebrate the death of an Assyrian king, perhaps Sargon II (d. 705 B.C.),[73] and that a later editor borrowed the original poem, supplied it with a prose introduction, and made it apply to the king of Babylon. It has also been suggested that the original author of the poem did not have any particular king in mind, was giving a description that could be applied to all despotic rulers.

Scott's division of the poem into five strophes has been accepted by most modern scholars. The first strophe (vv. 4b–8), written in the limping meter of the dirge, the Qinah meter, describes the joy and relief that fills the earth at the news of the tyrant's death. The whole earth enters upon a state of quiet and rest, interrupted only by the sound of singing. Even the trees of the forest join in the celebration of his death, since he will no longer come to hew them down.

In the second strophe (vv. 9–11) the scene shifts to Sheol, the eternal abode of the ghostly dead. The word Sheol occurs 65 times in the Old Testament, and in 61 instances is translated into Greek as "Hades." The KJV renders it 31 times as "hell," 31 times as "the grave," and 3 times as "the pit." The RSV reads "the grave" in 1 Kings 2:9 and "Sheol" elsewhere.

The description of the king of Babylon entering Sheol reflects the early Hebrew concept of the afterlife, a concept that was simple but depressing. It was thought that upon death all men, irrespective of their station and rank in life, descended to the shadowy regions of Sheol. There they continued to exist only as "shades" (cf. v. 9), i.e., as spectral images of their former selves (cf. Job 3:17–19; 21:23–26; Psalm 6:5; Eccl. 9:3–6). In this democracy of the dead all former glory was laid aside.

[73] *Ibid.*, pp. 175–176.

Although ghostly kings still sat upon ghostly thrones, all power was taken from them. Maggots became their beds, and worms their covering (cf. v. 11).

One of the most unforgettable scenes in the Old Testament is this description of Sheol's royal welcoming committee feebly rising up to greet another king as he entered the netherworld. In contrast to the stagnant afterlife reflected here, the New Testament sets before us a living hope, which is anchored in Jesus Christ, who through his death and resurrection "abolished death and brought life and immortality to light through the gospel" (2 Tim. 1:10). We have been delivered from the fear of death and from the frightful prospect of an eternity in Sheol.

The third strophe (vv. 12–15) specifies pride as the chief cause of the tyrant's downfall. Pride is condemned in the Old Testament as the most odious of all sins (cf. 2:6–22; Gen. 11:1–9; Ezek. 16:48–50; 28:1–10; 31:1–14). In the traditional list of the seven deadly sins, pride stands first. In his overweening pride the king of Babylon sought to ascend to heaven, to set his throne above the heights of the clouds, and to make himself like the Most High. Suddenly, however, he was brought down to Sheol, to the depths of the Pit.

Scholars are convinced that the prophet has made use of a mythological story from Canaanite religion to illustrate the fall of the king of Babylon.[74] The story, preserved in fragmentary form in the Ugaritic literature from Ras Shamra, tells how a minor Canaanite deity, *Helal ben Shahar* (*Day Star, son of Dawn*), sought to ascend to the heavens, to sit on the mount of the assembly of the gods in the far north (Mount *Zaphon*), and to make himself like *'Elyon* (*Most High*), the chief god in the Canaanite pantheon. The pride of *Helal ben Shahar* was thwarted, however, and he

was cast down from the heavens to the depths of Sheol.

The original inspiration for this story came from nature itself. The Canaanites watched as each morning the planet Venus rose bravely in the east, only to be extinguished later in the brilliant rays of the rising sun. They saw in this natural phenomenon a daily reenactment of the cosmic struggle between *Helal* and *'Elyon*.

The prophetic writer has taken this ancient story and reworked it into his taunt song. The king of Babylon is still referred to as "the Morning Star, son of Dawn," and God is referred to as "The Most High." Like the mythical *Helal*, the king of Babylon sought to ascend to heaven, to achieve the status of a divine being, and even to make himself like the Most High. But now he has been brought down to Sheol, to the depths of the Pit.

As Childs has pointed out, the framework into which the ancient Canaanite story was placed had the effect of historicizing or "demythologizing" it. The story of *Helal* became only an illustration of the fall of an earthly tyrant. However, when the Vulgate translated *Helal* as "Lucifer," a whole new concept was introduced into the passage. Certain early Christian commentators (e.g., Tertullian, Gregory the Great, etc.) interpreted the passage in the light of Luke 10:18 as applying to the prehistory and fall of Satan, the prince of demons. This interpretation received additional support from Dante's *Inferno* and Milton's *Paradise Lost*. Not a few modern Christians accept this interpretation, despite its lack of biblical basis. As Childs has argued, to do this is to revive a mythology already overcome in the Old Testament. While the Old Testament takes sin seriously and comes to grips with the existential problem of evil, it is singularly free of any attempt to account for the origin of sin and evil, except perhaps in the story of Adam and Eve. To use this passage to pinpoint the origin of sin, therefore, is to misuse the Scriptures.

In the fourth strophe (vv. 16–19c) the scene again shifts to earth, where curious

---

[74] Cf. William Foxwell Albright, *Archaeology and the Religion of Israel* (Baltimore: The Johns Hopkins Press, 1953), pp. 84–86; Brevard S. Childs, *op. cit.*, pp. 67–71; R. E. Clements, *God and Temple* (Philadelphia: Fortress Press, 1965), pp. 6–9; Aubrey R. Johnson, *Sacral Kingship in Ancient Israel* (Cardiff; University of Wales Press, 1955), pp. 84–85n.

onlookers gaze at the body of the fallen tyrant and ponder his fate. They find it utterly incredible that one who exercised such power in the earth should come to so ignominious an end. Normally when kings died they were buried with pomp and ceremony; however, burial was denied to this one, and his body was left to rot where it had fallen. The phrase *who go down to the stones of the Pit* (v. 19) probably refers to the practice of giving hasty burial to those slain on the field of battle by casting stones over their dead bodies. This is not the treatment that should be accorded a king.

The final strophe (vv. 19d–21) describes the legacy of hatred which the fallen tyrant leaves behind him. Men place a curse upon his sons lest they should follow in their father's footsteps. What a terrible legacy for a father to bequeath to his children! He achieved outward success, but at what cost! Is it any wonder that the world celebrated his death with thanksgiving?

(4) God's Broom of Destruction (14:22–23)

22 "I will rise up against them," says the Lord of hosts, "and will cut off from Babylon name and remnant, offspring and posterity, says the Lord. 23 And I will make it a possession of the hedgehog, and pools of water, and I will sweep it with the broom of destruction, says the Lord of hosts."

This prose conclusion probably belongs with the prose introduction of the chapter, both having been designed to show that the intervening poem is to be applied to Babylon. The conclusion reiterates the threats made in the poem and applies them specifically to Babylon. God will utterly destroy the proud city, causing it to revert to a swampland inhabited only by hedgehogs, or as some have rendered it, "a haunt of hoot owls." The Lord himself will sweep the city with the broom of destruction.

2. The Destruction of Assyria (14:24–27)

This brief oracle belongs to the eighth century B.C., and may with confidence be assigned to Isaiah himself. It is so closely related in style and content to the anti-Assyrian oracle in chapter 10 that many are convinced that the two were originally joined, with 14:24–27 standing as the conclusion to the earlier oracle.

The oracle begins with the Lord taking an oath to destroy the Assyrians in the land of Judah. The probable occasion for the oracle was Sennacherib's invasion of Judah in 701 B.C. (cf. Isa. 36—37).

The destruction of Assyria will provide relief not only for Judah but also for all the nations of the earth (v. 26). The burden of the oracle is that history is under the control of Yahweh, not of Assyria. This truth is emphasized by the repetition of the verb *ya'ats*, "to purpose," and its noun derivative *'etsah*, "purpose" or "counsel" (cf. vv. 24,26,27). As Yahweh has planned and purposed, so shall it be.

3. Warning to Philistia (14:28–32)

24 The Lord of hosts has sworn:
"As I have planned,
  so shall it be,
and as I have purposed,
  so shall it stand,
25 that I will break the Assyrian in my land,
  and upon my mountains trample him under foot;
and his yoke shall depart from them,
  and his burden from their shoulder."
26 This is the purpose that is purposed
  concerning the whole earth;
and this is the hand that is stretched out
  over all the nations.
27 For the Lord of hosts has purposed,
  and who will annul it?
His hand is stretched out,
  and who will turn it back?
28 In the year that King Ahaz died came this oracle:
29 "Rejoice not, O Philistia, all of you,
  that the rod which smote you is broken,
for from the serpent's root will come forth an adder,
  and its fruit will be a flying serpent.
30 And the first-born of the poor will feed,
  and the needy lie down in safety;
but I will kill your root with famine,
  and your remnant I will slay.
31 Wail, O gate; cry, O city;
  melt in fear, O Philistia, all of you!
For smoke comes out of the north,
  and there is no straggler in his ranks."
32 What will one answer the messengers of the

nation?
"The LORD has founded Zion,
   and in her the afflicted of his people find
      refuge."

The editorial note at the beginning of the oracle places it in the year that King Ahaz died. The date traditionally assigned to his death is 715 B.C., although some have argued that it occurred as early as 727.[75] The latter date happens to coincide with the death of Tiglath-pileser III of Assyria. Since v. 29 seems to imply that an Assyrian king has recently died but that his successor has not yet asserted his authority, the earlier chronology becomes more attractive. The only other time during this period when the Assyrian throne changed hands was when Sargon II succeeded Shalmaneser V in 722 B.C.

Gottwald[76] has proposed another solution to the complicated problem of date. He suggests that the oracle may have been written either during Shalmaneser's reign or shortly after his death and then used again by the prophet during the Philistine revolt against Assyria in 715 B.C., at which time it was supplied with the note regarding the death of Ahaz.

The Philistine revolt was led by the ruler of Ashdod, aided by the Egyptians. Shortly after Hezekiah came to the throne in Judah, an attempt was made to persuade him also to join the revolt. The prophet Isaiah was bitterly opposed to this course of action, and pointedly expressed his opposition by walking barefoot and naked through the streets of Jerusalem for three years (20:1–6). His opposition is also the subject of this oracle. He not only predicts that the revolt will fail (vv. 29–31), but he also advises Hezekiah to tell the messengers sent to enlist his aid that Yahweh has founded Zion and will be her sure defense (v. 32). The clear implication of the passage is that Judah has no need to depend for security upon foreign alliances.

4. The Doom of Moab (15:1—16:14)

This passage is difficult to interpret. The major portion of it (15:1—16:12) describes an invasion of Moab by an unnamed enemy. The description of the land's devastation is followed by an epilogue (16:13–14) in which the preceding oracle is defined as an earlier prophecy against Moab which is to be fulfilled within the space of three years.

The task of the interpreter is to determine the setting, date, and authorship of both the earlier oracle and the epilogue, and to ascertain the relationship between the two. Because so little is known about the history of Moab,[77] this becomes an almost insuperable task. The situation is further complicated by the fact that much of 15:1—16:12 reappears in Jeremiah 48: 28–39, which suggests that these may be two recensions of the same oracle.

It is possible to attribute the epilogue to Isaiah and to regard 15:1—16:12 as an earlier prophecy spoken either by him or by some other prophet. Some regard this passage as an anonymous prophecy written about 770 B.C. and dealing with the defeat of Moab by Jeroboam of Israel (2 Kings 14:25). In this case the Moabites' appeal for refuge (16:1–5) would have been directed to King Uzziah of Judah. It is thought that Isaiah subsequently adopted this anonymous prophecy, added a postscript to it, and made it apply to the destruction of Moab by the Assyrians. The predicted destruction, according to this view, was that which took place under Sargon in 715.

An alternate theory has been proposed by Albright,[78] who connects 15:1—16:12 with the incursion of Arabian tribes into the territory of Moab between 652 and 648 B.C. According to Albright, therefore, the oracle was composed after the time of Isaiah but prior to that of Jeremiah. Because of its anonymous character and because of

75 Cf. H. H. Rowley, "Hezekiah's Reform and Rebellion," *Bulletin of the John Rylands Library*, XLIV (1961–1962), 395–431.

76 Norman K. Gottwald, *op. cit.*, p. 164.

77 Cf. A. H. van Zyl, *The Moabites* (Leiden: E. J. Brill, 1960).

78 Albright's position is set forth in his review of R. H. Pfeiffer's *An Introduction to the Old Testament*, which appears in *Journal of Biblical Literature* Vol. 61 (1942), 119.

the continuing hostility of the Jews toward the Moabites, it was subsequently included among the oracles of both Isaiah and Jeremiah.

Another alternative proposal merits consideration. It is possible that Isaiah himself composed the major part of 15:1—16:12 shortly after 715 B.C., after Moab had been overrun by Sargon of Assyria. His purpose would have been to express his deep and genuine grief over the devastation of the land and the plight of its people (cf. 15:1–9; 16:8–11). It is even possible, as Gottwald [79] has suggested, that the prophet urged Hezekiah to grant asylum to the hapless refugees of the Assyrian attack (cf. 16:1–5). The epilogue (16:13–14) should perhaps be understood as a scribal note added just prior to the destruction of Moab by the Nabataeans in 650 B.C. It is also possible that at a later date certain portions of Isaiah's oracle were incorporated into the book of Jeremiah (cf. Jer. 48:28–39).

(1) Distress in Moab (15:1–9)

1 An oracle concerning Moab.
  Because Ar is laid waste in a night
    Moab is undone;
  because Kir is laid waste in a night
    Moab is undone.
2 The daughter of Dibon has gone up
    to the high places to weep;
  over Nebo and over Medeba
    Moab wails.
  On every head is baldness,
    every beard is shorn;
3 in the streets they gird on sackcloth;
    on the housetops and in the squares
  every one wails and melts in tears.
4 Heshbon and Elealeh cry out,
    their voice is heard as far as Jahaz;
  therefore the armed men of Moab cry aloud;
    his soul trembles.
5 My heart cries out for Moab;
    his fugitives flee to Zoar,
    to Eglath-shelishiyah.
  For at the ascent of Luhith
    they go up weeping;
  on the road to Horonaim
    they raise a cry of destruction;
6 the waters of Nimrim
    are a desolation;
  the grass is withered, the new growth fails,

[79] Norman K. Gottwald, *op. cit.*, pp. 174–175.

    the verdure is no more.
7 Therefore the abundance they have gained
    and what they have laid up
  they carry away
    over the Brook of the Willows.
8 For a cry has gone
    round the land of Moab;
  the wailing reaches to Eglaim,
    the wailing reaches to Beer-elim.
9 For the waters of Dibon are full of blood;
    yet I will bring upon Dibon even more,
  a lion for those of Moab who escape,
    for the remnant of the land.

This brief chapter consists of a dirge over the downfall of Moab. A noteworthy feature of the dirge is the extraordinary number of place names which it contains, making it an invaluable summation of Moabite geography. It is impossible to locate all of the places mentioned, although many of them are known from other sources.

Ar was a fortified city lying south of the Arnon river (Num. 21:15). *Kir,* also called Kir-hareseth (16:7) and Kir-heres (16:11), and known today as el-Kerak, lay in the extreme south of Moab (cf. 2 Kings 3:25). The news of the destruction of these two cities spread northward across the Arnon River to *Dibon,* modern Dhiban, where the Moabite Stone was discovered in A.D. 1868; to *Nebo,* the traditional site of Moses' death (Deut. 32:49); to *Madeba,* modern Medabah, about 15 miles northeast of Dibon (Num. 21:30); to *Heshbon,* the ancient capital of King Sihon (Nuc. 21:21–30), and the site of modern Hesban, which lies five miles northeast of Nebo; to *Elealeh,* modern El'al, about two miles north of Heshbon; and to *Jahaz,* of unknown location but perhaps near Dibon (Num. 21:23). As the tidings spread from city to city the people expressed their grief in typical oriental fashion by going up to the high places (v. 2) and housetops (v. 3) to weep, by shaving their heads and their beards, and by putting on sackcloth. Even the armed men of Moab took part in the lamentation (v. 4).

The concluding portion of the dirge (vv. 5–9) tells of the hurried flight of the fugitives to *Zoar,* a city situated near the southern end of the Dead Sea. Most of the places mentioned here—*Eglath-shelishiyah, Luhith, Horonaim, Nimrim, Eglaim,* and *Beer-elim*—cannot be located with certainty. The *Brook of the Willows* (v. 7) has been identified as the Brook Zered, the modern Wadi el-Hesa, which formed the ancient boundary between Moab and Edom. Most scholars believe that 16:2 has been misplaced, and that it rightly belongs after 15:9. It describes the helplessness of the daughters of Moab at the fords of the Arnon; they are compared to timid fledglings suddenly scattered from their nests and forced to fly prematurely.

(2) A Request for Refuge (16:1–5)

1 They have sent lambs
      to the ruler of the land,
   from Sela, by way of the desert,
      to the mount of the daughter of Zion.
2 Like fluttering birds,
      like scattered nestlings,
   so are the daughters of Moab
      at the fords of the Arnon.
3 "Give counsel,
      grant justice;
   make your shade like night
      at the height of noon;
   hide the outcasts,
      betray not the fugitive;
4 let the outcasts of Moab
      sojourn among you;
   be a refuge to them
      from the destroyer.
   When the oppressor is no more,
      and destruction has ceased,
   and he who tramples under foot
      has vanished from the land,
5 then a throne will be established in stead-
      fast love
   and on it will sit in faithfulness
      in the tent of David
   one who judges and seeks justice
      and is swift to do righteousness."

Pausing at *Sela,* an Edomite stronghold otherwise known as Petra (cf. 2 Kings 14:7), the Moabite refugees dispatched messengers to the ruler of Judah in Jerusalem requesting asylum in his land. The messengers carried with them the customary gift of lambs (v. 1; cf. 2 Kings 3:4).

Most scholars agree with the translators of the RSV that vv. 3–5 contain the spoken appeal of the Moabite messengers to the king of Judah. Verse 5, with its strong messianic overtones, is generally regarded as an attempt on their part to ingratiate themselves with the king by predicting the permanence of the Davidic dynasty. Others regard the verse as being completely alien to this context. Gottwald's position is unique in that he regards vv. 3–5 as Isaiah's demand for Judah to receive the Moabite refugees. He views v. 5 as a quotation from an enthronement hymn, which the prophet used in order to remind Hezekiah that it was through the performance of such acts of mercy as the granting of asylum to political refugees that the Davidic dynasty would be established.

(3) Denial of the Request (16:6–7)

6 We have heard of the pride of Moab,
      how proud he was;
   of his arrogance, his pride, and his inso-
      lence—
   his boasts are false.
7 Therefore let Moab wail,
      let every one wail for Moab.
   Mourn, utterly stricken,
      for the raisin-cakes of Kirhareseth.

These verses suggest that the request of the Moabites to be granted refuge in the land of Judah was rejected because of their notorious pride and arrogance. The raisin-cakes referred to in v. 7 were made of pressed grapes and were used in religious festivals (cf. Hos. 3:1). The implication is that the gods of Moab have been powerless to deliver the land from oppression.

(4) Lamentation over Moab's Misfortune (16:8–14)

8 For the fields of Heshbon languish,
      and the vine of Sibmah;
   the lords of the nations
      have struck down its branches,
   which reached to Jazer
      and strayed to the desert;
   its shoots spread abroad
      and passed over the sea.
9 Therefore I weep with the weeping of
      Jazer
   for the vine of Sibmah;
   I drench you with my tears,

O Heshbon and Elealeh;
for upon your fruit and your harvest
the battle shout has fallen.
¹⁰ And joy and gladness are taken away
from the fruitful field;
and in the vineyards no songs are sung,
no shouts are raised;
no treader treads out wine in the presses;
the vintage shout is hushed.
¹¹ Therefore my soul moans like a lyre for
Moab,
and my heart for Kirheres.
¹² And when Moab presents himself, when
he wearies himself upon the high place, when
he comes to his sanctuary to pray, he will not
prevail.
¹³ This is the word which the LORD spoke
concerning Moab in the past. ¹⁴ But now the
LORD says, "In three years, like the years of a
hireling, the glory of Moab will be brought
into contempt, in spite of all his great multitude, and those who survive will be very few
and feeble."

Verses 8–11, like 15:1–9, constitute a
dirge over the desolation of Moab. The
poet expresses genuine sorrow over the
spoiling of Moab's vineyards. His heart
responds to her anguish like the strings of
the lyre to the musician's touch (v. 11).
Moab was famous for its viticulture, and
the vine of Sibmah had apparently become a proverbial symbol of excellence.
By the use of hyperbole the prophet describes the vine of Sibmah as covering the
entire land with its roots and branches and
spilling over into neighboring territories
(v. 8). Then suddenly it is smitten down
(v. 9), and the joy and gladness of harvest disappears from the land (v. 10). The
pathos of the passage is unsurpassed in all
the poetry of the Old Testament.

Verse 12 is a somber footnote to the
prophetic dirge. It declares that Moab will
spend its strength upon the high places in
unavailing prayer (cf. 15:2).

The passage concludes with a prose epilogue (vv. 13–14), referring to the previous lament as a past revelation from the
Lord and making a fresh prediction of
destruction against Moab. As stated above,
the epilogue is perhaps to be dated just
prior to the destruction of Moab by the
Nabataeans in 650 B.C. The reference to
three years, like the years of a hireling,

is to be understood in the light of the custom of contracting hired labor for a specified period of time (cf. Deut. 15:18;
Isa. 21:16). This is a pointed way of saying that Moab will be reduced to a feeble
remnant within precisely three years.

5. Oracles of Threat and Promise (17:1–14)

Chapter 17 is made up of fragmentary
oracles having little apparent relationship
to one another. It is difficult to discover a
unifying theme in the chapter, unless it
be the theme of judgment.

(1) The Doom of Damascus and Ephraim (17:1–6)

¹ An oracle concerning Damascus.
Behold, Damascus will cease to be a city,
and will become a heap of ruins.
² Her cities will be deserted for ever;
they will be for flocks,
which will lie down, and none will make
them afraid.
³ The fortress will disappear from Ephraim,
and the kingdom from Damascus;
and the remnant of Syria will be
like the glory of the children of Israel,
says the LORD of hosts.
⁴ And in that day
the glory of Jacob will be brought low,
and the fat of his flesh will grow lean.
⁵ And it shall be as when the reaper gathers
standing grain
and his arm harvests the ears,
and as when one gleans the ears of grain
in the Valley of Rephaim.
⁶ Gleanings will be left in it,
as when an olive tree is beaten—
two or three berries
in the top of the highest bough,
four or five
on the branches of a fruit tree,
says the LORD God of Israel.

The passage is addressed to *Damascus*
alone, but it is also concerned with the
fate of Israel, here referred to as *Ephraim*
(v. 3) and *Jacob* (v. 4). Most scholars are
agreed that the passage is genuinely Isaianic and that it has as its background the
Syro-Ephraimitic alliance against Judah
in 735–734 B.C. (cf. 7:1–8:4; 9:8–21). As
these two kingdoms had been partners in
crime, so also would they be partners in

punishment.

The prophet declares that Damascus will cease to exist (vv. 1–2) and that the fortress will disappear from Ephraim (v. 3). The latter reference apparently is to the fortress city of Samaria, the capital of the Northern Kingdom. The translation of v. 2 in the RSV, which follows the Septuagint, is to be preferred over that of the KJV, since no city named Aroer is known to have existed either in Syria or in Israel.

The statement that the *remnant of Syria* will be like the glory of the children of Israel is explained in v. 4, which speaks of the *glory of Jacob* (i.e., Israel) being brought low. The demise of Jacob is described by three figures of speech. It will be like a debilitating sickness (v. 4); like the harvesting of grain in the Valley of Rephaim, a valley just to the southwest of Jerusalem (v. 5); and like the gleanings of the olive harvest, when only a few berries are left on the topmost boughs (v. 6). The emphasis throughout the section is upon the near totality of the judgment against Syria and Israel.

(2) *The Restoration of True Worship* (17:7–8)

7 In that day men will regard their Maker, and their eyes will look to the Holy One of Israel; 8 they will not have regard for the altars, the work of their hands, and they will not look to what their own fingers have made, either the Asherim or the altars of incense.

Perhaps the purpose of these verses is to show the cleansing and purifying effects of judgment. It is declared that in days to come men will abandon the worship of that which their own fingers *have made* and will look instead to *their Maker,* the Holy One of Israel.

Of particular interest is the declaration that men will no longer look to the *Asherim* (v. 8). The word Asherim is the plural form of the name of an Amorite or Canaanite goddess worshiped in various parts of the ancient Near East. Many details concerning her place in the pantheon have been supplied from the Ras Shamra Texts, where she figures prominently as the mother-goddess, mistress of El, and mother of seventy gods, including Baal.

Counting both singular and plural forms, this word occurs a total of 40 times in the Old Testament. The KJV consistently renders it as "grove" or "groves," whereas the RSV transliterates it as "Asherah," "Asherahs," "Asheroth," and "Asherim." It is not always possible to distinguish between references to the Asherah as a goddess and as a cultic object. As cultic objects the Asherim consisted of wooden posts erected beside an altar (cf. Deut. 16:21; Judg. 6:25–26). They seem to have represented the female deity, whereas the *masseboth,* the stone pillars, represented the male deity. The prevalence of this type of idolatry is abundantly evident in the Old Testament (cf. 1 Kings 14:23; 2 Kings 17:10; 23:4,15).

(3) *The Futility of Idolatry* (17:9–11)

9 In that day their strong cities will be like the deserted places of the Hivites and the Amorites, which they deserted because of the children of Israel, and there will be desolation.
10 For you have forgotten the God of your salvation,
  and have not remembered the Rock of your refuge;
therefore, though you plant pleasant plants
  and set out slips of an alien god,
11 though you make them grow on the day that you plant them,
  and make them blossom in the morning that you sow;
yet the harvest will flee away
  in a day of grief and incurable pain.

The wide difference between the rendering of v. 9 in the KJV and in the RSV is due to the fact that the latter follows the Septuagint rather than the Hebrew. The *Hivites* and the *Amorites* were among the pre-Israelite inhabitants of the land of Canaan (Ex. 3:8). According to v. 9, the cities of Judah will become as desolate as those of the pagan peoples whom they have displaced. Since Judah has become like Canaan in its religion, it will also become like Canaan in its fate.

The meaning of vv. 10–11 is that the people of Judah are participating in the

worship of the Babylonian god Tammuz
(cf. Ezek. 8:14), also known as Adonis,
the god of vegetation. The worship of this
dying and rising god included the planting
of ceremonial gardens, sometimes referred
to as "Adonis gardens." In preparation for
the feast of Tammuz, held in the spring of
the year, women would plant fast-growing
seeds in pots or baskets. They believed
that through sympathetic magic the spring-
ing up of the seeds would bring to life the
dead god of vegetation. The fact that the
plants withered as soon as they had sprung
up is used as a reminder to Judah that her
hopes will likewise wither. The only harvest she will reap will be a harvest of
grief and incurable pain.

(4) The Raging of the Nations (17: 12-14)

12 Ah, the thunder of many peoples,
    they thunder like the thundering of the
        sea!
Ah, the roar of nations,
    they roar like the roaring of mighty
        waters!
13 The nations roar like the roaring of many
        waters,
    but he will rebuke them, and they will
        flee far away,
chased like chaff on the mountains before
        the wind
    and whirling dust before the storm.
14 At evening time, behold, terror!
    Before morning, they are no more!
This is the portion of those who despoil us,
    and the lot of those who plunder us.

The theme of the passage is the marvelous deliverance of God's people from an
attack by hostile foes. Some would date
the passage just prior to 734 B.C., thereby
identifying the attacking nations as Syria
and Israel (cf. 7:1-2). Most scholars,
however, prefer to place the passage just
after 701 and to identify the foe as the
Assyrian army, together with contingents
of troops from vassal nations (cf. 10:24-
34; 14:24-27; 37:21-36).

Though the assembled nations roar like
the thundering of the sea, they are utterly
subdued at the rebuke of Israel's God.
They are chased away like chaff before
the wind and scattered like dust before the

storm. In the evening their presence in-
spires terror, but in the morning they are
seen no more. The passage closes with an
affirmation of the prophet's faith that it
will always be thus with those who seek to
despoil and plunder the people of God (cf.
Psalm 46).

6. Oracles Concerning Ethiopia and Egypt (18:1—20:6)

The book of Isaiah refers to Ethiopia
and Egypt almost as if they were synonymous terms. This was because Egypt was
ruled by an Ethiopian dynasty (the
Twenty-fifth Dynasty) from 715 until 663
B.C. Under Ethiopian leadership Egypt experienced a resurgence of power and apparently entertained hopes of being able to
wrest control of the Middle East from the
Assyrians. All efforts to fulfill these hopes
ended in failure, however, and the
Twenty-fifth Dynasty came to an end
when the Assyrians overran Egypt and destroyed the capital city of Thebes in 663
(cf. Nah. 3:8-10).

(1) Oracle Addressed to the Envoys of Ethiopia (18:1-7)

1   Ah, land of whirring wings
        which is beyond the rivers of Ethiopia;
2   which sends ambassadors by the Nile,
        in vessels of papyrus upon the waters!
    Go, you swift messengers,
        to a nation, tall and smooth.
    to a people feared near and far,
        a nation mighty and conquering,
        whose land the rivers divide.
3   All you inhabitants of the world,
        you who dwell on the earth,
    when a signal is raised on the mountains,
        look!
    When a trumpet is blown, hear!
4   For thus the LORD said to me:
    "I will quietly look from my dwelling
        like clear heat in sunshine,
        like a cloud of dew in the heat of har-
            vest."
5   For before the harvest, when the blossom is
        over,
        and the flower becomes a ripening grape,
    he will cut off the shoots with pruning
        hooks,
        and the spreading branches he will hew
            away.
6   They shall all of them be left

to the birds of prey of the mountains
and to the beasts of the earth.
And the birds of prey will summer upon
them,
and all the beasts of the earth will winter
upon them.
7 At that time gifts will be brought to the
Lord of hosts
from a people tall and smooth,
from a people feared near and far,
a nation mighty and conquering,
whose land the rivers divide,
to Mount Zion, the place of the name of the
Lord of hosts.

The setting for this oracle was the arrival in Jerusalem of a group of Ethiopian ambassadors sent to enlist the aid of the Judean king in a coalition against Assyria. Various dates have been suggested for the oracle. Gottwald would place it as early as 720 B.C., on the assumption that only at that time "did Egypt actively lobby for revolt, whereas in the later uprisings under Sargon and Sennacherib it was the Syro-Palestinian states that implored Egypt for help." [80] This view seems to overlook the fact that the Ethiopians did not seize power in Egypt until 715. Bright's view, therefore, seems much more defensible. He dates the oracle at 714, "soon after the Ethiopian conquest of Egypt and before their reverses at the hands of Assyria." A less likely date would be the period between 705 and 701, when Hezekiah was encouraged by Egyptian intrigue to revolt against Sennacherib.

A notable feature of the oracle is the deference with which Isaiah addressed the Ethiopian envoys. In the polite language of diplomacy, he lauded them for their fast-sailing vessels of papyrus, their striking physical appearance, and their military prowess (v. 2). At the same time, he firmly informed them that they should leave Jerusalem and return to the land from whence they had come. He was clearly opposed to Judah's participation in the coalition that they were proposing.

He gives the basis of his opposition in vv. 3–6, a section addressed not to the Ethiopians alone but to all the inhabitants

of the earth. Men everywhere are exhorted to pay attention *when a signal is raised on the mountains,* and to listen *when a trumpet is blown.* When these things have come to pass, Yahweh will arise to inflict sudden and inexorable judgment upon his foes (v. 5–6). Although it is unclear whether the foe referred to is Ethiopia or Assyria, the latter seems more probable.[81]

The heart of the prophet's message is found in v. 4. In highly symbolic language he paints a picture of the serenity and self-restraint of Israel's God. In contrast to the Ethiopians, who set out to bring about at once and at whatever cost the downfall of Assyria, he calmly bides his time—"unresting, unhasting, and silent as light." Two similes are used to describe his imperturbable calm. He is *like clear heat in sunshine,* a reference to the intolerable glare of the summer sun at midday; and he is like *a cloud of dew in the heat of harvest,* a description of the towering white clouds that fill Palestinian skies in the summertime, conveying the impression of infinite height. There is no more vivid description of the transcendence of God in all the literature of the Old Testament.

Verse 7 has sometimes been regarded as a later addition to the oracle, although the reasons cited in support of this view are highly subjective. The verse repeats the description of the Ethiopians given in v. 2, and predicts that after the time of judgment has passed they will come to Mount Zion to render homage to the Lord of hosts. There is some indication that the verse may have influenced later Jewish efforts at proselytizing (cf. Acts 8:27 f.).

(2) The Doom of Egypt (19:1–15)

1 An oracle concerning Egypt.
Behold, the Lord is riding on a swift cloud
and comes to Egypt;
and the idols of Egypt will tremble at his
presence,
and the heart of the Egyptians will melt
within them.

---

80 *Ibid.,* pp. 162–163.

81 Cf. Lindblom's view that the allusion here is to a universal judgment: J. Lindblom, *op. cit.,* p. 366.

2 And I will stir up Egyptians against Egyptians,
and they will fight, every man against his brother
and every man against his neighbor,
city against city, kingdom against kingdom;
3 and the spirit of the Egyptians within them will be emptied out,
and I will confound their plans;
and they will consult the idols and the sorcerers,
and the mediums and the wizards;
4 and I will give over the Egyptians
into the hand of a hard master;
and a fierce king will rule over them,
says the Lord, the Lord of hosts.
5 And the waters of the Nile will be dried up,
and the river will be parched and dry;
6 and its canals will become foul,
and the branches of Egypt's Nile will diminish and dry up,
reeds and rushes will rot away.
7 There will be bare places by the Nile,
on the brink of the Nile,
and all that is sown by the Nile will dry up,
be driven away, and be no more.
8 The fishermen will mourn and lament,
all who cast hook in the Nile;
and they will languish
who spread nets upon the water.
9 The workers in combed flax will be in despair,
and the weavers of white cotton.
10 Those who are the pillars of the land will be crushed,
and all who work for hire will be grieved.
11 The princes of Zoan are utterly foolish;
the wise counselors of Pharaoh give stupid counsel.
How can you say to Pharaoh,
"I am a son of the wise,
a son of ancient kings"?
12 Where then are your wise men?
Let them tell you and make known
what the Lord of hosts has purposed against Egypt.
13 The princes of Zoan have become fools,
and the princes of Memphis are deluded;
those who are the cornerstones of her tribes
have led Egypt astray.
14 The Lord has mingled within her
a spirit of confusion;
and they have made Egypt stagger in all her doings
as a drunken man staggers in his vomit.
15 And there will be nothing for Egypt
which head or tail, palm branch or reed, may do.

This poetic oracle with its scathing condemnation of Egypt may with confidence be assigned to Isaiah himself. One of the recurring themes in his preaching was the folly of relying upon Egypt's help (cf. 20:1–6; 30:1–7; 31:1–3).

In three brief strophies the prophet describes the complete dissolution of the treacherous nation. The first strophe (vv. 1–4) begins with a description of the Lord riding upon a swift cloud as he comes to judge Egypt (cf. Psalms 18:10–11; 68:4; 104:3). At his approach consternation seizes both the idols of the land and those that worship them (v. 1). Verse 2 refers to the civil wars that racked the land just prior to the establishment of the Twenty-fifth (Ethiopian) Dynasty in 714 B.C. The Egyptians' response to the national crisis consisted of a frantic but futile effort to obtain help by consulting the idols, the sorcerers; the mediums, and the wizards (v. 3). In the end, however, the Egyptians were given over into *the hand of a hard master*. This may refer either to the Ethiopian Piankhi, who conquered Egypt in 714 B.C., or to the Assyrian Esarhaddon, who invaded Egypt and occupied Memphis in 671. On the other hand, Isaiah may not have had any particular person in mind when he spoke these words.

The second stanza (vv. 5–10) describes the most dreadful disaster that could possibly overtake the land of Egypt, namely, the drying up of the River Nile. Except for the waters of the Nile, Egypt would be nothing more than an eastward extension of the great Sahara Desert. The prophet pictures the complete collapse of the economy of the land with the drying up of the river. A noxious odor fills the air as reeds and rushes rot away (v. 6). Plants sown by the margin of the river dry up and are blown away (v. 7). The fishing and textile industries are brought to a standstill (vv. 8–9). The text of v. 10 has suffered greatly in transmission and is not easily translated. It seems, however, to refer to widespread unemployment with its attendant miseries.

The third strophe (vv. 11–15) depicts the failure of Egypt's vaunted wise men to steer the nation on a straight course.

Instead they give *stupid counsel*, so that the rulers are deluded and the land is led astray. Under such circumstances, the nation reels and staggers like a drunken man (v. 14). The situation is so hopelessly confused that neither high nor low are able to remedy it (v. 15).

The prophet designates two Egyptian cities as being under the rule of singularly stupid princes. The first, Zoan, also known as Tanis and as Raamses (Ex. 1:11), was located in the delta region near the eastern border (cf. Num. 13:22; Ezek. 30:14). The second, Memphis, otherwise known as Noph (cf. Jer. 2:16; Ezek. 30:13; Hos. 9:6), was situated on the left bank of the Nile near the site of modern Cairo. Its necropolis included the famous pyramids of Gizeh. Both of these cities had had the honor of serving as Egypt's capital.

(3) The Conversion of Egypt and Assyria (19:16-25)

16 In that day the Egyptians will be like women, and tremble with fear before the hand which the LORD of hosts shakes over them. 17 And the land of Judah will become a terror to the Egyptians; every one to whom it is mentioned will fear because of the purpose which the LORD of hosts has purposed against them.
18 In that day there will be five cities in the land of Egypt which speak the language of Canaan and swear allegiance to the LORD of hosts. One of these will be called the City of the Sun.
19 In that day there will be an altar to the LORD in the midst of the land of Egypt, and a pillar to the LORD at its border. 20 It will be a sign and a witness to the LORD of hosts in the land of Egypt; when they cry to the LORD because of oppressors he will send them a savior, and will defend and deliver them.
21 And the LORD will make himself known to the Egyptians; and the Egyptians will know the LORD in that day and worship with sacrifice and burnt offering, and they will make vows to the LORD and perform them. 22 And the LORD will smite Egypt, smiting and healing, and they will return to the LORD, and he will heed their supplications and heal them.
23 In that day there will be a highway from Egypt to Assyria, and the Assyrian will come into Egypt, and the Egyptian into Assyria, and the Egyptians will worship with the Assyrians.
24 In that day Israel will be the third with Egypt and Assyria, a blessing in the midst of the earth, 25 whom the LORD of hosts has blessed, saying, "Blessed be Egypt my people, and Assyria the work of my hands, and Israel my heritage."

This section is comprised of five brief oracles, each of which begins with the formula *in that day*. Most scholars are of the opinion that these oracles originated in the postexilic period, perhaps as late as 300 B.C. This opinion is based upon the prose form in which the oracles are cast, together with the differences in style, language, and subject matter between them and their context. This view has not gone unchallenged, however, and Gottwald [82] has argued that it would be difficult to imagine their having been written later than the destruction of the Assyrian Empire in 609 B.C. Gottwald proposes that the names Egypt and Assyria should be taken in their literal historical sense and not as apocalyptic code words for later powers.

The first oracle (vv. 16-17) is condemnatory in nature, describing the abject fear that will seize the Egyptians when the Lord shakes his hand over them (cf. 11:15; Zech. 2:9). The very mention of the land of Judah will strike terror in their hearts, because of the purpose which the lord of hosts has projected against Egypt (v. 17; cf. v. 12).

Verse 18 predicts that *in that day* there will be five cities in Egypt which speak the language of Canaan (i.e., Heb.) and swear allegiance to Yahweh. One of the cities is called the *City of the Sun*. Instead of "sun" (*cheres*), the Masoretic Text reads "destruction" (*heres*). Most scholars believe that "sun" was the original reading, indicating perhaps Heliopolis, one of the oldest cities of Egypt, situated near the southern end of the Nile Delta, and that this was deliberately altered to read "destruction" by Palestinian scribes who were opposed to the recognition of any cultic worship of Yahweh beyond the borders of Israel. The Septuagint reads City of Righteousness.

82 *Op. cit.*, pp. 224-225; cf. Robert Martin-Achard, *A Light to the Nations*, pp. 46-49.

The crucial problem in the interpretation of v. 18 is whether it refers to Egyptians who turn to the language and religion of the Jews or to Jews who, while living in Egypt, continue to speak their native tongue and to worship the God of their fathers. The position taken here is that the first alternative is to be preferred. This oracle, therefore, reflects the missionary spirit of the Old Testament at its best. In boldly universalistic tones it announces the day when there will be a significant turning to Yahweh in the land of Egypt.

The third oracle (vv. 19–22) states unequivocally that Yahweh will be worshiped in Egypt by the Egyptians. It even anticipates the setting up of an altar to Yahweh and full Egyptian participation in the worship of Yahweh.

This oracle is steeped in covenant terminology, although the word covenant itself does not appear. A pillar set up at the border of Egypt becomes a *sign and a witness* to the Lord (vv. 19 f.), suggesting the signs that ordinarily accompanied the formal establishment of a covenant (cf. Gen. 9:12 f.; 17:11; 31:44). The promise that when the Egyptians are oppressed and cry to the Lord he will send a savior to deliver them reminds one of Israel's deliverance at the Exodus and in the days of the judges (cf. Ex. 3:7–10; Judg. 2:16–19). The imparting of the knowledge of the Lord, such as is promised to Egypt (v. 21), also generally takes place within a covenant relationship (cf. Jer. 31:34; Hos. 2:20). The very way in which Yahweh proposes to deal with Egypt, smiting her and healing her (v. 22), is reminiscent of the way in which he dealt with wayward Israel. For all practical purposes, therefore, the prophet is describing a covenant relationship between Egypt and Yahweh.

The most startling feature of the passage is its proposal that there should be *an altar to the Lord* in the midst of the land of Egypt (v. 19). The theory that the prophet had in mind the establishment of a sanctuary where Jews living in Egypt might worship Yahweh is contradicted by v. 21, which specifies that the worshipers are Egyptians. Furthermore, it is doubtful that the prophet would have advocated the establishment of a sanctuary where Jews might worship outside the land of Canaan.

The fact that a garrison of Jewish mercenaries at Elephantine in Upper Egypt had erected a temple to Yahweh as early as 525 B.C. seems to be unrelated to the interpretation of the present passage, for their temple was intended for Jews only, and not for Egyptians. Josephus [83] informs us that a second temple also was built at Leontopolis in 160 by the exiled high priest Onias IV, who sought to justify his action by appealing to the prediction in 19:19. This temple also was intended for Jews only.

The fourth oracle (v. 23) mentions a highway extending from Egypt to Assyria, thus enabling Israel's two most powerful neighbors to have friendly intercourse with each other and to join in the worship of Yahweh. This intercontinental highway would of necessity pass through the land of Israel, as highways between Asia and Africa have always done. Those who refuse to recognize any missionary emphasis in this series of oracles interpret this verse to mean that a highway will be built to enable the Jews living in Egypt and Assyria to make religious pilgrimages to Jerusalem.

The final oracle (vv. 24 f.) has been described as "the most universal word in prophecy." Sublimely it is said that Egypt and Assyria will take their place alongside Israel as the peoples of God. When that day comes, Israel will be a blessing in the midst of the earth, or, as the NEB reads, "in the centre of the world." This must not be interpreted to mean that Israel will be regarded as superior to Egypt or Assyria. Rather it means that God's ancient promise that in Abraham and his seed all the families of the earth would be blessed (cf. Gen. 12:1–3) will now be fulfilled.

[83] *Antiq.*, XIII.3.1.

The theme of blessing is continued in v. 25. Yahweh blesses each member of the new confederation of nations by bestowing a special name upon it. Egypt is called *my people,* Assyria *the work of his hands,* and Israel *my heritage.* There is no indication that these titles are listed "in an ascending order of Divine affection," as one Jewish commentator has claimed. Actually, all of the titles are elsewhere applied exclusively to Israel (cf. Ex. 3:10; 5:1; Psalm 74:2; Isa. 1:3; 10:1; 60:21; 64:8; Joel 3:2). The revolutionary character of the oracle becomes even more apparent when it is remembered that Egypt and Assyria were the two nations most feared and hated by the ancient Israelites.

(4) A Sign Against Egypt and Ethiopia (20:1-6)

[1] In the year that the commander in chief, who was sent by Sargon the king of Assyria, came to Ashdod and fought against it and took it,— [2] at that time the LORD had spoken by Isaiah the son of Amoz, saying, "Go, and loose the sackcloth from your loins and take off your shoes from your feet," and he had done so, walking naked and barefoot— [3] the LORD said, "As my servant Isaiah has walked naked and barefoot for three years as a sign and a portent against Egypt and Ethiopia, [4] so shall the king of Assyria lead away the Egyptians captives and the Ethiopians exiles, both the young and the old, naked and barefoot, with buttocks uncovered, to the shame of Egypt. [5] Then they shall be dismayed and confounded because of Ethiopia their hope and of Egypt their boast. [6] And the inhabitants of this coastland will say in that day, 'Behold, this is what has happened to those in whom we hoped and to whom we fled for help to be delivered from the king of Assyria! And we, how shall we escape?'"

The word of the Lord in the Old Testament is communicated not only through the spoken words of the prophets but also through their symbolic acts.[84] The prophets sometimes felt themselves constrained to perform some rather strange deeds, the

[84] Cf. H. Wheeler Robinson, "Prophetic Symbolism," *Old Testament Essays,* ed. D. C. Simpson (London: Charles Griffin and Company, Limited, 1927), pp. 1–17; J. Pedersen, *Israel,* I–II (London: Oxford University Press, 1926), 168 ff.

doing of which constituted a category of enacted prophecy standing alongside and serving to reinforce spoken prophecy.

One of the most striking examples of this type of enacted prophecy was Isaiah's walking about the streets of Jerusalem *naked and barefoot* for the space of three years (v. 2). The prophet did this in order to dramatize the fate that awaited Egypt and Ethiopia at the hands of the Assyrians (vv. 3–4), and also to convince Hezekiah and the people of Judah of the futility of trusting in Egypt (vv. 5–6).

By a fortunate combination of circumstances, it is possible to date the passage very precisely. Verse 1 makes mention of the fact that the prophet's symbolic act was interpreted to the people of Judah in the year that Ashdod fell into the hands of the commander in chief of Sargon the king of Assyria. This event is known to have occurred in 711 B.C., as evidenced by Sargon's own inscriptions (ANET, p. 286 f.).

Sargon's record tells how the Philistine city of Ashdod engaged in a long series of rebellious acts that finally led to its capture and the deportation of its citizens. It was encouraged in its revolt by the promise of support from Egypt, which was then under the rule of the pharaohs of the Twenty-fifth (Ethiopian) Dynasty (cf. 19:1–15). The beginning of the revolt is usually dated in 714 B.C. Assuming that Isaiah began his strange "walking sermon" about the same time, he would have been able to complete his three years before Ashdod fell. The purpose behind his symbolic action was to prevent or discourage Judah's becoming involved in the revolt. His efforts apparently met with success, for Sargon makes no mention of punitive measures having been taken against Jerusalem. The destruction that Isaiah predicted for Egypt did not take place until 663, long after the prophet's death.

7. The Fall of Babylon (21:1-10)

[1] The oracle concerning the wilderness of the sea.

As whirlwinds in the Negeb sweep on,
    it comes from the desert,
    from a terrible land.
2   A stern vision is told to me;
    the plunderer plunders,
    and the destroyer destroys.
    Go up, O Elam,
    lay siege, O Media;
    all the sighing she has caused
    I bring to an end.
3   Therefore my loins are filled with anguish;
    pangs have seized me,
    like the pangs of a woman in travail;
    I am bowed down so that I cannot hear,
    I am dismayed so that I cannot see.
4   My mind reels, horror has appalled me;
    the twilight I longed for
    has been turned for me into trembling.
5   They prepare the table,
    they spread the rugs,
    they eat, they drink.
    Arise, O princes,
    oil the shield!
6   For thus the Lord said to me:
    "Go, set a watchman,
    let him announce what he sees.
7   When he sees riders, horsemen in pairs,
    riders on asses, riders on camels,
    let him listen diligently,
    very diligently."
8   Then he who saw cried:
    "Upon a watchtower I stand, O Lord,
    continually by day,
    and at my post I am stationed
    whole nights.
9   And, behold, here come riders,
    horsemen in pairs!"
    And he answered,
    "Fallen, fallen is Babylon;
    and all the images of her gods
    he has shattered to the ground."
10 O my threshed and winnowed one,
    what I have heard from the LORD of
        hosts,
    the God of Israel, I announce to you.

The passage is cast in the form of a dramatic vision announcing the downfall of Babylon (v. 9) before the combined forces of Elam and Media (v. 2). It is usually interpreted as postexilic in origin and as referring to the capture of Babylon by Cyrus in 539 B.C.

The fact that the prophet is apparently filled with anguish over the announcement of Babylon's fall (vv. 3–4) has led some to seek an alternate date for the vision. Crucial to the interpretation of the vision is the question of whether or not an

Israelite prophet of the exilic period would have expressed grief over the expected downfall of this ancient foe. Those who deny that he would have done so seek to date the vision in the preexilic period, at a time when the defeat of Babylon would have placed the Jewish nation in serious jeopardy.

Bright has suggested that such a situation existed in 689 B.C., at which time Sennacherib took Babylon, ravaged it, and carried the statue of Marduk to Assyria. According to Bright's view, the destroyer should be identified as Assyria, against whom Babylon and her allies, the Elamites and Medes, are in revolt (v. 2). Judah's rulers, therefore, are hopeful that Babylon will emerge the victor and that the power of Assyria will be broken, but the prophet knows that their hopes are doomed to disappointment. To him it has been revealed that the destroyer (Assyria) will go on destroying (v. 2). Therefore he regards any celebration of Babylon's victory is premature (v. 5). When traveling caravaneers finally bring the tragic news of Babylon's fall (v. 9), he is filled with anguish (vv. 3–4). It becomes his lot to advise the beleaguered people of Judah that their ally has been crushed and that there is no relief in sight for them (v. 10).

While this interpretation makes it possible to assign the oracle to Isaiah, rather than to an anonymous prophet of the exilic period, it, nevertheless, raises a number of problems. It identifies the destroyer of v. 2 as Assyria, and ignores the latter part of the verse, which apparently promises that the sighing caused by the destroyer will soon be brought to an end. Furthermore, as Wright[85] has recently demonstrated, it is conceivable that a prophet could pronounce a sentence of judment upon a foreign nation while at the same time showing "real depth of feeling, even of compassion," toward it. The weight of the evidence, therefore, supports the

[85] G. Ernest Wright, "The Nations in Hebrew Prophecy," *Encounter*, Vol. 26, No. 2 (1965), 231–234.

view that the vision presupposes the rise of Babylon as a world power, the subjugation of the Jewish people by the Babylonians, and the imminent downfall of Babylon before the combined forces of Elam and Media. This would indicate a date about 539 B.C.

Lindblom [86] has classified the oracle as a *dramatic* vision, i.e., one in which various persons appear and act out their parts, as in a drama. As the vision begins the prophet hears a noise, like the noise of *whirlwinds* sweeping through the desert (v. 1). A vision is then *made known* to him, a *stern vision* (v. 2; cf. Ex. 1:14; 6:9; 18:26; 1 Kings 12:4; Isa. 14:3; 19:4; 27:1; 8; 48:4). It was perhaps the manner in which the vision was given rather than the message which it conveyed, that filled the prophet with fear and trembling (vv. 3–4).

The prophet sees the continuing havoc wrought by one who is identified only as the *plunderer* and the *destroyer* (v. 2). He then hears a voice commanding Elam and Media to go on the attack. As the scene changes, he sees a royal banquet hall, perhaps in Babylon, where the feasting is suddenly interrupted by a call to arms (v. 5; cf. Dan. 5).

At this point one encounters a secondary vision within the main vision. The secondary vision is apparently set in Jerusalem. The prophet is told to post a *watchman* to await an important announcement (vv. 6–7). It is evident from the context that the watchman is none other than the prophet himself, who in his state of ecstasy can speak of himself as if he were another person. The sign which he is to await is the arrival of traveling caravaneers (v. 7). He watches for them day and night (v. 8), and when they finally appear, he proclaims to the beleaguered people of Judah the good news that Babylon has fallen (vv. 9–10; cf. Rev. 14:8; 18:2). The oracle ends with the prophet's solemn affirmation that the word he has spoken is an authentic word from the Lord.

[86] J. Lindblom, *op. cit.*, pp. 124–130.

8. *Edom's Uncertain Future* (21:11–12)

11 The oracle concerning Dumah.
One is calling to me from Seir,
    "Watchman, what of the night?
    Watchman, what of the night?"
12 The watchman says:
    "Morning comes, and also the night.
    If you will inquire, inquire;
    come back again."

This brief oracle is addressed to **Dumah**, a name used elsewhere in the Old Testament to designate an Arabian tribe descended from Ishmael (cf. Gen. 25:14; 1 Chron. 1:30). Instead of Dumah, the Septuagint reads "Edom." This identification is doubtlessly correct, since it is supported by the additional reference to Seir, which is another designation for the Edomite nation (cf. Gen. 32:3; Josh. 24:4).

There is nothing within the oracle itself to indicate its precise date, although it is generally assigned to the same period as the preceding oracle, i.e., just prior to the fall of Babylon. Edom's fortunes had been closely linked with those of Babylon since preexilic days. She had supported the troops of Nebuchadnezzar in their attack upon Jerusalem in 587 B.C. (cf. Obad. 10–14). In return for her support she had been granted part of the territory that had formerly belonged to Judah and Israel (cf. Ezek. 35:10–12,15; 36:5). She would naturally have been apprehensive about her own future as reports of Babylon's imminent downfall became more widespread.

It is assumed that the present oracle was delivered against the background of the threatened defeat of Babylon. The prophet, who is described as if he were a lookout stationed upon a city wall, receives an urgent request from Edom for a report on the current state of world affairs. How did matters appear from his vantage point? *Watchman, what of the night?*

The response of the prophet was obscure and ambivalent. He reported signs of the morning, but also of the night. This suggests that he had received no clear word from the Lord with regard to what the future might hold for Edom. All that he could do was to suggest that they come back later and inquire again.

9. The Doom of Dedan and Kedar (21: 13–17)

¹³ The oracle concerning Arabia.
In the thickets in Arabia you will lodge,
O caravans of Dedanites.
¹⁴ To the thirsty bring water,
meet the fugitive with bread,
O inhabitants of the land of Tema.
¹⁵ For they have fled from the swords,
from the drawn sword,
from the bent bow,
and from the press of battle.
¹⁶ For thus the Lord said to me, "Within a year, according to the years of a hireling, all the glory of Kedar will come to an end; ¹⁷ and the remainder of the archers of the mighty men of the sons of Kedar will be few; for the LORD, the God of Israel, has spoken."

There is no way to determine the precise date of this oracle or to identify the events to which it alludes. Some have suggested that it belongs to the period of the Assyrian invasions of the Middle East in the latter part of the eighth century. Others would relate it to the Arab invasions that took place about 650 B.C. Others cite Jeremiah 49:28–30 as evidence that it pertains to the period of Nebuchadnezzar's incursions into the area.

The **Dedanites** were an important nomadic tribe of traders who roamed the Arabian desert some 250 miles southeast of the Dead Sea (cf. Gen. 10:7; 25:3; Jer. 25:23; Ezek. 25:13; 27:20; 38:13). In this oracle they are described as having been forced to flee from their oasis settlement and to take refuge in the desert because of an invasion of their territory (vv. 13,15). The inhabitants of **Tema**, an important caravan station located about 50 miles northeast of Dedan on the road to Damascus (cf. Gen. 25:15; Job 6:19; Jer. 25:23),[87] are bidden to go to the aid of

the fugitive Dedanites with bread and water (v. 14).

The prose conclusion to the passage (vv. 16–17) tells of the coming destruction of **Kedar,** another desert tribe closely associated with Dedan and Tema (cf. Gen. 25: 13; Isa. 42:11; 60:7; Jer. 49:28–33; Ezek. 27:20–21). The time of the destruction is set as one year from the time of the giving of the oracle, "according to the years of a hireling" (cf. 16:14). This sets the time limit at precisely one year, since a hireling would not work any longer than his contract demanded. No reason is given for the word of judgment against Kedar. It has been suggested that she was perhaps responsible for the plight of the Dedanites. The Kedarites were defeated first by the Assyrians and later by the Babylonians.[88] It is not clear to which of these destructions the passage has reference.

10. Revelry on the Eve of Disaster (22: 1–14)

The background of the passage is to be sought in the Assyrian crisis of 701 B.C. (cf. 1:5–9; 36:1—37:38). This section perhaps represents the last recorded message of Isaiah prior to his death. In it is expressed the disillusionment that he felt as he approached the close of his ministry (cf. 6:9–12). Because of the expressed conviction that the inhabitants of Jerusalem have at last sinned beyond all possibility of pardon (v. 14), the passage has been termed "the most pessimistic of all Isaiah's prophecies."

(1) A Tumultuous City (22:1–4)

¹ The oracle concerning the valley of vision.
What do you mean that you have gone up,
all of you, to the housetops,
² you who are full of shoutings,
tumultuous city, exultant town?
Your slain are not slain with the sword
or dead in battle.
³ All your rulers have fled together,
without the bow they were captured.
All of you who were found were captured,
though they had fled far away.

---

[87] Nabonidus, the last king of Babylon, undertook an expedition against Tema in 552 B.C., at which time he slaughtered its inhabitants, and then completely rebuilt and repopulated the city. He made it his royal residence for perhaps ten years, leaving his son Belshazzar as his deputy ruler in Babylon. The exact reason for Nabonidus' long stay at Tema has never been determined.

[88] Cf. J. A. Thompson, "Kedar," IDB, Vol. III (Nashville: Abingdon Press, 1962), 3–4.

4 Therefore I said:
"Look away from me,
    let me weep bitter tears;
    do not labor to comfort me
        for the destruction of the daughter of
            my people."

These verses describe the prophet's reaction to the boisterous celebration that
took place in Jerusalem just after Sennacherib lifted the siege of the city in 701
B.C. The men of Jerusalem went up to the
housetops, *full of shoutings.* Isaiah witnessed their wild abandon with a heavy
heart. He reminded them that their conduct during the siege had been somewhat
less than commendable. Their slain had not
fallen in battle but had been captured and
executed as they attempted to escape.

The prophet was disappointed that the
withdrawal of the Assyrians had failed to
impress upon the people of Jerusalem the
need for repentance and righteous living.
In spite of the hardships they had suffered, they were still insensitive to the
true demands of God. In the midst of
their lighthearted festivities, therefore, he
asked to be left alone that he might weep
bitter tears over their destruction.

(2) A Besieged City (22:5-11)

5 For the Lord God of hosts has a day
    of tumult and trampling and confusion
    in the valley of vision,
    a battering down of walls
    and a shouting to the mountains.
6 And Elam bore the quiver
    with chariots and horsemen,
    and Kir uncovered the shield.
7 Your choicest valleys were full of chariots,
    and the horsemen took their stand at the
        gates.
8 He has taken away the covering of Judah.

In that day you looked to the weapons of the
House of the Forest, 9 and you saw that the
breaches of the city of David were many, and
you collected the waters of the lower pool,
10 and you counted the houses of Jerusalem,
and you broke down the houses to fortify the
wall. 11 You made a reservoir between the two
walls for the water of the old pool. But you
did not look to him who did it, or have regard
for him who planned it long ago.

These verses were apparently spoken in
retrospect. In them the prophet reviews

the events that had trasnpired during the
siege of Jerusalem. The siege is described
by a series of similar Hebrew sounds as a
day of *tumult* (*mᵉhumah*) and *trampling*
(*mᵉbusah*) and *confusion* (*mᵉbukah*). *The
valley of vision* may refer either to Jerusalem or to one of the valleys that lay
round about it, perhaps the valley of Hinnom, since the words Hinnom and vision
are quite similar in Hebrew. Elam and Kir
(cf. 2 Kings 16:9; Amos 1:5; 9:7) are
mentioned because their troops fought
beside the Assyrians during the siege of
Jerusalem. The attacking armies encircled
the city and thus exposed its defenseless-
ness (vv. 7–8a). The prophet reprimands
the inhabitants of Jerusalem and their king
for having responded to the crisis by working feverishly to strengthen the city's defenses but without taking counsel of God
(vv. 8b–11).

In preparation for the siege, the people
stockpiled weapons, repaired and fortified
the city wall, and took measures to safeguard their water supply. The *House of
the Forest* was an armory built in Jerusalem by Solomon, its name being derived
from the fact that its roof was supported
by rows of cedar pillars (cf. 1 Kings 7:2;
10:17). This storehouse was apparently
replenished with arms. In order to
strengthen the walls of the city, the people
broke down a number of houses and re-
used their stones for this purpose. The
water supply was secured by the construction of a reservoir between the two walls
to receive the water of the old pool, an
apparent reference to the tunnel that Hezekiah caused to be cut through the solid
rock of Ophel for almost a third of a mile
in order to bring the waters of Gihon to a
reservoir within the city (cf. 2 Kings
20:20).

The prophet seems not to have condemned military preparedness as such, but
rather the spirit in which it had been
undertaken. The men of Jerusalem had
acted as if the outcome of the struggle
depended solely upon their own plans and
maneuvers. To the prophet such an attitude

was but another example of the atheism of force, the substituting of the power of man for the power of God (cf. 37:23–29).

(3) An Unheeded Call to Repentance (22:12–14)

12 In that day the Lord God of hosts
    called to weeping and mourning,
    to baldness and girding with sackcloth;
13 and behold, joy and gladness,
    slaying oxen and killing sheep,
    eating flesh and drinking wine.
"Let us eat and drink,
    for tomorrow we die."
14 The Lord of hosts has revealed himself in
    my ears:
"Surely this iniquity will not be forgiven you
    till you die,"
    says the Lord God of hosts.

Whatever hopes Isaiah had entertained that Jerusalem's deliverance might lead to its repentance had been dashed to pieces. Instead of heeding God's call to mourning and contrition, its inhabitants had engaged in an orgy of feasting and merrymaking. With a hedonism rivaling that of their pagan neighbors they had cast aside all restraint, shouting, "Let us eat and drink, for tomorrow we die." The Lord's message to the prophet was that they would indeed die, and that their iniquity would never be forgiven.

11. Denunciation of an Ambitious Politician (22:15–25)

15 Thus says the Lord God of hosts, "Come, go to this steward, to Shebna, who is over the household, and say to him: 16 What have you to do here and whom have you here, that you have hewn here a tomb for yourself, you who hew a tomb on the height, and carve a habitation for yourself in the rock? 17 Behold, the Lord will hurl you away violently, O you strong man. He will seize firm hold on you, 18 and whirl you round and round, and throw you like a ball into a wide land; there you shall die, and there shall be your splendid chariots, you shame of your master's house. 19 I will thrust you from your office, and you will be cast down from your station. 20 In that day I will call my servant Eliakim the son of Hilkiah, 21 and I will clothe him with your robe, and will bind your girdle on him, and will commit your authority to his hand; and he shall be a father to the inhabitants of Jerusalem and to the house of Judah. 22 And I will

place on his shoulder the key of the house of David; he shall open, and none shall shut; and he shall shut, and none shall open. 23 And I will fasten him like a peg in a sure place, and he will become a throne of honor to his father's house. 24 And they will hang on him the whole weight of his father's house, the off-spring and issue, every small vessel, from the cups to all the flagons. 25 In that day, says the Lord of hosts, the peg that was fastened in a sure place will give way; and it will be cut down and fall, and the burden that was upon it will be cut off, for the Lord has spoken."

In this passage Isaiah vehemently denounces a public official named *Shebna*. When the denunciation was delivered, Shebna was serving as steward over the household of the king, a position that gave him considerable power and prestige (cf. Gen. 45:8). Since the Old Testament never mentions his father (cf. 2 Kings 18:37; 19:2; Isa. 36:3,11,22; 37:2), and since the form of his name suggests an Aramaic influence, some have surmised that he was an Aramaen serving under King Hezekiah, and that his primary responsibility was that of handling foreign diplomatic correspondence.[89]

More recent evidence, consisting of seal impressions from Lachish and other Palestinian sites, indicates that his name was thoroughly Jewish and that he probably belonged to a family of officials that extended over several generations. To suggest as some have done, that Isaiah was hostile toward him primarily because he was a foreigner is to ascribe to the prophet motives that were unworthy of him. A more likely interpretation is that the prophet's opposition to him was based not only upon his spirit of arrogance and vainglory but also upon his support of the pro-Egyptian party in Jerusalem and upon his efforts to persuade Hezekiah to revolt against Assyria, policies that would have brought him into sharp conflict with the prophet. If

---

[89] Cf. William McKane, "Prophets and Wise Men," *Studies in Biblical Theology*, No. 44 (Naperville: Alec R. Allenson, Inc., 1965), pp. 27–28; J. M. Ward, "Shebna," IDB, Vol. 4 (Nashville: Abingdon Press, 1962), 312; Norman K. Gottwald, *op. cit.*, pp. 169–173.

there is any truth in this interpretation, it may explain why an oracle against a political opportunist in Hezekiah's court came to be included among the oracles against the nations.

The prophet must have surprised Shebna when he appeared unannounced at the site of the rock *tomb* which the latter was having hewn out for himself on a prominent height overlooking Jerusalem. Isaiah upbraided him for his pride and presumption and predicted that the Lord would forcibly remove him from his office and replace him by *Eliakim*, a man more worthy of his position. Verse 22 is important to the Christian interpreter for the light it throws upon the background of the saying of Jesus recorded in Matthew 16: 19 (cf. Matt. 18:18; John 20:23), suggesting that Jesus was appointing Peter to be steward over the household of God in the messianic kingdom.

Both Shebna and Eliakim are mentioned later in Isaiah (36:3,22; 37:2) and in the parallel passages in 2 Kings (18:18,37; 19:2). All of these references are to be dated during the Assyrian crisis of 701 B.C. By that time a part of Isaiah's earlier prediction had been fulfilled, for Eliakim had succeeded Shebna as the chief steward of the royal household. On the other hand, Shebna had acquired a new title, that of secretary (36:3), which, while it may have represented a demotion, was, nevertheless, a title of honor. It is possible that his punishment came later, although there is no record that this occurred.

The conclusion to the passage (vv. 24–25) describes the subsequent downfall of Eliakim. He fell from his place like a peg upon which too much weight had been placed. The weight in this case resulted from his having given employment to too many members of his own family (v. 24). He was probably not the first and certainly not the last politician to practice nepotism. Most commentators are agreed that the prophecy of Eliakim's rejection was added to the passage after 701 B.C., either by Isaiah or by one of his disciples.

12. Oracles Concerning Tyre and Sidon (23:1–18)

This chapter consists of a lament over the destruction of Tyre (vv. 1–12), followed by a prediction of its ultimate restoration (vv. 13–18). The lament must be assigned to a time when the city was being besieged by a foreign invader. If it was composed by Isaiah, as seems likely, then the most appropriate date for its composition would be 701 B.C., at which time Sennacherib advanced against the city, causing its king to flee to Cyprus (cf. v. 12) and replacing him with another ruler. The city later survived a siege of 13 years (585–572 B.C.) at the hands of the Babylonians (cf. v. 13; Ezek. 29:18–20). It was finally destroyed by Alexander the Great in 332, after a siege of seven months. There is no reason to assign the lament to one of these later invasions, even though an editor has obviously tried to do this in v. 13. The prediction of the city's restoration, on the other hand, most likely belongs to a period later than the time of Isaiah.

(1) The Downfall of Tyre and Sidon (23: 1–12)

1 The oracle concerning Tyre.
Wail, O ships of Tarshish,
  for Tyre is laid waste, without house or haven!
From the land of Cyprus
  it is revealed to them.
2 Be still, O inhabitants of the coast,
  O merchants of Sidon;
your messengers passed over the sea
3   and were on many waters;
your revenue was the grain of Shihor,
  the harvest of the Nile;
  you were the merchant of the nations.
4 Be ashamed, O Sidon, for the sea has spoken,
  the stronghold of the sea, saying:
"I have neither travailed nor given birth,
  I have neither reared young men
  nor brought up virgins."
5 When the report comes to Egypt,
  they will be in anguish over the report about Tyre.
6 Pass over to Tarshish,
  wail, O inhabitants of the coast!

7 Is this your exultant city
    whose origin is from days of old,
    whose feet carried her
        to settle afar?
8 Who has purposed this
    against Tyre, the bestower of crowns,
    whose merchants were princes,
        whose traders were the honored of the
           earth?
9 The LORD of hosts has purposed it,
    to defile the pride of all glory,
    to dishonor all the honored of the earth.
10 Overflow your land like the Nile,
    O daughter of Tarshish;
    there is no restraint any more.
11 He has stretched out his hand over the sea,
    he has shaken the kingdoms;
    the LORD has given command concerning
        Canaan
    to destroy its strongholds.
12 And he said:
"You will no more exult,
    O oppressed virgin daughter of Sidon;
arise, pass over to Cyprus,
    even there you will have no rest."

The people of Tyre and Sidon and their environs were called Phoenicians by the Greeks and Canaanites by the Hebrews (cf. v. 11; Mark 7:25; Matt. 15:22). Actually, the Greek term for Phoenicia and the Hebrew term for Canaan mean exactly the same thing, i.e., purple or purple dye. The dye was obtained from mollusks from the Mediterranean and was used primarily for coloring wool and other woven materials. Purple garments were considered by ancient peoples to be a sign of distinction and of royalty. The Phoenicians monopolized the manufacture and sale of purple cloth during a considerable part of the Old Testament period.

Although both Tyre and Sidon are mentioned in the passage, primary attention is given to the former. This reflects the fact that most of Israel's previous contacts had been with Tyre rather than with Sidon (cf. 2 Sam. 5:11; 1 Kings 5:1–18; 9:26–28; 16:31). Furthermore, when the present oracle was composed, Tyre had become the leading city of Phoenicia, so much so that its name was often used to designate the whole of Phoenicia.

After the Canaanites had been cut off from their ancient hinterland by the in-

vading Hebrews, they were forced to turn to the sea to seek their livelihood. They became the world's first great maritime power, and by the beginning of the first millennium B.C. had established trading colonies in Sicily, Sardinia, North Africa, and Spain. Apparently several of these distant colonies were named Tarshish, meaning a smelting plant or refinery.[90] Accordingly, "Tarshish ships" were ships specially designed for the transport of smelted metal.

The oracle opens with a call to the *ships of Tarshish* to mourn the destruction of Tyre. News of its destruction had reached them when they stopped at Cyprus on their homeward journey. The news had apparently been brought to Cyprus by Phoenician fugitives who had escaped by sea (cf. v. 12).

In vv. 2–4 the author turns his attention to the inhabitants of *Sidon*. In early Phoenician history Sidon had overshadowed Tyre in importance, so that the inhabitants of the region were often known simply as "Sidonians" (cf. Deut. 3:9; Josh. 13:4; 6; Judg. 3:3; 10:12; 1 Kings 5:6; etc.). Verses 2–3 reflect the far-flung commercial enterprises of the Sidonians. Their ships were on many waters, bringing revenues from such distant places as the grain fields of the Nile. The city had come to be known as "the merchant of the nations." In v. 4 the sea is personified as the mother of the Sidonians, who now disowns her children, speaking of them as if they had never been born.

The last part of the lament (vv. 5–12) describes the consternation that seized the nations when they heard of Tyre's downfall. The effects were especially felt in those lands that had trade relations with her, such as Egypt (v. 5), Tarshish (vv. 6,10), and Cyprus (v. 12). Isaiah saw the cause of Tyre's downfall in her inordinate pride (vv. 8–9), a vice which

90 Cf. W. F. Albright, "The Role of the Canaanites in the History of Civilization," *The Bible and the Ancient Near East*, ed. G. Ernest Wright (Garden City: Doubleday and Company, Inc., 1961), pp. 328–362.

he frequently condemned in his preaching (cf. 2:11–17; 9:8–12; 10:12–15; 14:12–15).

(2) Tyre's Future Restoration (23:13–18)

13 Behold the land of the Chaldeans! This is the people; it was not Assyria. They destined Tyre for wild beasts. They erected their siege-towers, they razed her palaces, they made her a ruin.
14 Wail, O ships of Tarshish,
    for your stronghold is laid waste.
15 In that day Tyre will be forgotten for seventy years, like the days of one king. At the end of seventy years, it will happen to Tyre as in the song of the harlot:
16 "Take a harp,
    go about the city,
    O forgotten harlot!
Make sweet melody,
    sing many songs,
    that you may be remembered."
17 At the end of seventy years, the LORD will visit Tyre, and she will return to her hire, and will play the harlot with all the kingdoms of the world upon the face of the earth. 18 Her merchandise and her hire will be dedicated to the LORD; it will not be stored or hoarded, but her merchandise will supply abundant food and fine clothing for those who dwell before the LORD.

Verse 13 presents many translation problems. The best way to make sense of the strange verse, which seems to break the connection between vv. 12 and 14, is to regard it as a note inserted in the original prophecy in order to make it apply to a much later situation. It transfers the responsibility for the execution of Isaiah's threat against Tyre from the Assyrians to the Chaldeans. It was probably written as a postscript to the original prophecy around 585 B.C.

Verse 14 was perhaps the original conclusion to the lament in vv. 1–12. According to v. 15, the desolation of Tyre would last only 70 years, *like the days of one king.* The last phrase probably has reference to the normal span of a man's life (cf. Psalm 90:10). After 70 years had passed, Tyre would return to her trade like a forgotten harlot trying to regain her old customers by singing songs they would recognize. The *song of the harlot* in verse

16 is a classic model of Hebrew poetic composition, with its triads in 2'2' metre.

The metaphor of the harlot is continued in vv. 17–18. The use of the metaphor does not mean that the men of Tyre are guilty of immorality; the emphasis is rather upon their mercenary character. They return to their commercial ventures as a harlot might return to her trade. The prophet goes out of his way to say that it is the Lord who visits Tyre and permits her to "return to her hire" and to "play the harlot with all the kingdoms of the world" (v. 17). He even affirms that the profits from her "harlotry" will be dedicated to the Lord for the benefit of his people (cf. 45:14; 60:4–14; Hag. 2:6–9). He may have expected that the city itself would be converted to the Lord, although he does not say so. The prophecy of Tyre's restoration probably belongs to the sixth century B.C.

III. Prophecies of Judgment and Redemption (24:1—27:13)

These oracles have been the focal point of a long and inconclusive debate among Old Testament scholars. The debate has centered around the problems of unity, date, authorship, and literary form. Concerning each of these problems many proposals have been put forward, but no consensus has been reached.

Most scholars regard chapters 24—27 as a collection of originally independent oracles of a diverse nature which have been brought together by an unknown author to form a unified whole. Bernhard Duhm [91] has argued that the basic framework of the collection consists of an apocalypse foretelling the end of the world and the establishment of the divine rule on Mount Zion (24:1–23; 25:6–8; 26:20–21; 27:1,12–13). Into the framework has been inserted a series of songs celebrating the downfall of a hostile city (25:1–5,9–12;

91 Bernhard Duhm, *Das Buch Jesaia* (Göttingen: Vandenhoeck und Ruprecht, 1902). See also Otto Ludwig, *Die Stadt in der Jesaja-Apokalypse* (Köln: Walter Kleikamp, 1961), pp. 59–60.

26:1–19), besides a collection of secondary materials (27:2–11). Duhm assigned the apocalypse to the period of the Maccabeans (134–104 B.C.) but placed the songs in a slightly later period.

Was Duhm correct in designating certain portions of chapters 24—27 as an apocalypse? Those who answer in the affirmative do so on the basis of the presence in the chapters of certain prominent features of apocalyptic, including universal judgment, the eschatological banquet, the imprisonment of members of the heavenly host, and the resurrection of the dead.[92]

Other scholars maintain that the chapters cannot properly be called an apocalypse, at least not in the sense in which the term is applied to books like Daniel. They point out that the author omits many of the major motifs of apocalyptic, such as, for example, pseudonymity, the use of visions and cryptic numbers, world powers symbolized as fearsome beasts, the reinterpretation of earlier prophecies, and theological dualism. Because of the strong eschatological emphasis of the chapters, and because of their close affinity with other prophetic passages, many prefer to classify them as "eschatological prophecy."[93] One author has observed that while they may not be apocalyptic in the strictest sense of the word they nevertheless contain the "stuff" from which apocalyptic is made.[94]

Most scholars have rejected the date that Duhm assigned to the composition of the oracles, although there is little agreement with regard to an alternate date. Kaufmann[95] is representative of those who would advocate an eighth-century date

and Isaianic authorship for these oracles. Lindblom,[96] on the other hand, has adopted the position that chapters 24—27 should not be called an apocalypse but a "cantata." He believes an anonymous cult prophet of Jerusalem composed the "cantata" to be performed in the Temple in celebration of the overthrow of Babylon by Xerxes in 485 B.C. The tendency among those who have recently dealt with this problem, e.g., Bright and Scott, has been to accept a post-exilic date for the passage but to resist any attempt to relate it to particular historical circumstances.[97]

1. An Announcement of Judgment (24: 1–20)

The theme of this section is the coming world judgment. The key word in the passage is "earth," which occurs a total of 16 times.

March[98] has suggested that the literary form of the passage is based on a familiar cultic model known as the communal lament, which involved announcement, lamentation, and assurance (cf. Psalm 12:5; Jer. 14:1–10; Hos. 14:1–7). In this instance, however, the announcement (vv. 1–3) and the lamentation (vv. 4–15) are followed not by a word of assurance but by a further word of judgment (vv. 16–20). This significant alteration of the familiar form added an element of surprise to the prophet's preaching. He used the form to assure a hearing, but instead of giving the expected word of grace he delivered a word of doom.

---

[92] Cf. Stanley B. Frost, Old Testament Apocalyptic (London: The Epworth Press, 1952), pp. 1–31; Sheldon H. Blank, op. cit., pp. 164–170.

[93] Cf. Otto Eissfeldt, The Old Testament, An Introduction, trans. Peter R. Ackroyd (New York: Harper and Row, 1965), pp. 323–327.

[94] Cf. D. S. Russell, The Method and Message of Jewish Apocalyptic (Philadelphia: The Westminster Press, 1964), p. 91.

[95] Cf. Yehezkel Kaufmann, The Religion of Israel, translated and abridged by Moshe Greenberg (Chicago: The University of Chicago Press, 1960), p. 384.

[96] Cf. J. Lindblom, op. cit., pp. 155, 286. A fuller explanation of Lindblom's position is found in his earlier work: Die Jesaja-Apokalypse. Jes. 24—27 (Lund: Hakan Ohlssons Buchdruckerei, 1938).

[97] A notable exception is William Eugene March, "A Study of Two Prophetic Compositions in Isaiah 24:1—27:1," Unpublished Th.D. Dissertation, Union Theological Seminary, New York, 1966. After close analysis, March isolates two prophetic compositions, 24:1–20 and 24:21—27:1, which, on the basis of historical circumstances, theology, language, and various other factors, he would date in the exilic period, ca. 575 and 560 B.C. respectively. March's dissertation is an invaluable aid to the study of these chapters, not only because of the fresh insights it provides but also because of its comprehensive bibliography.

[98] Ibid., pp. 61 f.

(1) The Impending Doom (24:1–3)

1 Behold, the LORD will lay waste the earth
    and make it desolate,
    and he will twist its surface and scatter its
      inhabitants.
2 And it shall be, as with the people, so with
    the priest;
    as with the slave, so with his master;
    as with the maid, so with her mistress;
  as with the buyer, so with the seller;
    as with the lender, so with the borrower;
    as with the creditor, so with the debtor.
3 The earth shall be utterly laid waste and
    utterly despoiled;
    for the LORD has spoken this word.

These verses paint a picture of total devastation on a worldwide scale. The upheaval extends both to the physical order (v. 1) and to the social order (v. 2). Neither high nor low are exempt from its tragic consequences. The summary announcement of judgment is concluded on the same somber note with which it began. The entire announcement is reinforced by the affirmation that "the Lord has spoken this word," an affirmation that stresses the importance and reliability of the prophetic word.

(2) The Broken Covenant (24:4–13)

4 The earth mourns and withers,
    the world languishes and withers;
    the heavens languish together with the
    earth.
5 The earth lies polluted
    under its inhabitants;
  for they have transgressed the laws,
    violated the statutes,
    broken the everlasting covenant.
6 Therefore a curse devours the earth,
    and its inhabitants suffer for their guilt;
  therefore the inhabitants of the earth are
    scorched,
    and few men are left.
7 The wine mourns,
    the vine languishes,
    all the merry-hearted sigh.
8 The mirth of the timbrels is stilled,
    the noise of the jubilant has ceased,
    the mirth of the lyre is stilled.
9 No more do they drink wine with singing;
    strong drink is bitter to those who drink it.
10 The city of chaos is broken down,
    every house is shut up so that none can
    enter.
11 There is an outcry in the streets for lack of
    wine;

    all joy has reached its eventide;
    the gladness of the earth is banished.
12 Desolation is left in the city,
    the gates are battered into ruins.
13 For thus it shall be in the midst of the earth
    among the nations,
  as when an olive tree is beaten,
    as at the gleaning when the vintage is
    done.

This section describes the lamentation and weeping of those who witness the wholesale desolation of their land. The prophet poignantly describes the situation as a time when "all joy has reached its eventide" (v. 11). The earth itself mourns and languishes, and its grief is shared by the heavens above (v. 4). The severity of the judgment is such that few men are left (vv. 6,13), and even the few that remain face a bleak and desolate future (vv. 7–12).

The central problem in the interpretation of the passage is whether it describes the judgment of the Lord upon the land of Israel alone or upon the whole earth. Those who see it as referring to Israel alone interpret the reference to the *everlasting covenant* (v. 5) as applying to the Sinai covenant. Others refer the phrase to the Noachic covenant made between God and the entire human race after the flood (cf. Gen. 9:16). Under the Noachic covenant all men were subject to certain moral laws, one of which was the prohibition of murder (cf. Gen. 9:5–6). Because this law had been violated, the earth had become polluted, as in the days of Noah (v. 5; cf. Num. 35:33–34). The prominence of the flood motif throughout these chapters (cf. 24:18; 26:20) lends weight to the view that the prophet was thinking in terms of a universal judgment.

The reference to the destruction of the *city of chaos* (v. 10) has been variously interpreted. Duhm identifies the city as Samaria, Lindblom as Babylon, Eissfeldt as the capital of Moab, and March as Jerusalem. Bright shares the view that the passage is speaking of a hostile alien city rather than of Jerusalem, but he notes that it is idle to speculate about the city's

identity. This and the other references to
the downfall of a hostile city (cf. v. 12;
25:2; 26:5; 27:10), should perhaps be
interpreted as signifying the certain destruction of all world powers who defy
God and oppress his people.

(3) Premature Rejoicing (24:14–16)

¹⁴ They lift up their voices, they sing for joy;
   over the majesty of the Lord they shout
   from the west.
¹⁵ Therefore in the east give glory to the Lord;
   in the coastlands of the sea, to the name
   of the Lord, the God of Israel.
¹⁶ From the ends of the earth we hear songs
   of praise,
   of glory to the Righteous One.
   But I say, "I pine away,
   I pine away. Woe is me!
   For the treacherous deal treacherously,
   the treacherous deal very treacherously."

The exact relationship between these
verses and the preceding passage is
difficult to determine. The emphatic pronoun *they*, with which v. 14 begins, suggests that the songs of praise are sung by
the few survivors who have escaped the
judgment (vv. 6,13). This still leaves unanswered the question of their identity.
Are they Jews who have been dispersed
among the nations, or are they Gentiles?
It seems best in the light of the larger context to regard them as Jews of the diaspora.
These sing to the Lord in anticipation of
their coming deliverance from world tyranny.

However, their optimism is not shared
by the prophet. As he views the world
situation, he is sickened by the sight of
treacherous men still wielding power (v.
16b). Others may lift their voices in song,
but he can only lift his in lament.

(4) Inescapable Judgment (24:17–20)

¹⁷ Terror, and the pit, and the snare
   are upon you, O inhabitant of the earth!
¹⁹ He who flees at the sound of the terror
   shall fall into the pit;
   and he who climbs out of the pit
   shall be caught in the snare.
   For the windows of heaven are opened,
   and the foundations of the earth tremble.
¹⁹ The earth is utterly broken,

the earth is rent asunder,
   the earth is violently shaken.
²⁰ The earth staggers like a drunken man,
   it sways like a hut;
   its transgression lies heavy upon it,
   and it falls, and will not rise again.

This oracle is couched in eschatological
imagery. The prophet forecasts drastic
changes throughout the cosmic order. The
oracle opens with a curse which is perhaps
proverbial, especially since it is used elsewhere with regard to Moab (vv. 17–18;
cf. Jer. 48:43–44).

The *windows of heaven* are opened and
the foundations of the earth tremble (v.
18b). The reference to the opening of the
windows of heaven, if interpreted apart
from its context, might signify either
blessing (cf. 2 Kings 7:2,19; Mal. 3:10)
or cursing (cf. Gen. 7:11; 8:2). In the
present context, however, it can only signify cursing. The prophet apparently means
to say that God will again judge the world
as he did in the days of Noah. Before the
onslaught of his wrath the earth will be
broken and rent asunder. It will stagger
like a drunken man and sway like a straw
hut in an open field. It will collapse under
the weight of its transgression, never to
rise again.

2. A Liturgy of Praise and Promise (24:
21—27:1)

March has shown that the principal
motif teveloped throughout this section is
the motif of the kingship of Yahweh. The
materials that make up the section have
been arranged in a definite pattern designed to honor Yahweh and to offer the
promise of his universal rule to Israel and
to all peoples.

(1) The Lord's Enthronement on Mount
Zion (24:21–23)

²¹ On that day the Lord will punish
   the host of heaven, in heaven,
   and the kings of the earth, on the earth.
²² They will be gathered together
   as prisoners in a pit;
   they will be shut up in a prison,
   and after many days they will be punished.
²³ Then the moon will be confounded,

and the sun ashamed;
for the LORD of hosts will reign
  on Mount Zion and in Jerusalem
and before his elders he will manifest his
  glory.

The note of judgment is sounded here as in the preceding passage, but with an important difference; whereas in the preceding passage it was directed against the inhabitants of the earth, here it is expanded to include the host of heaven. The *host of heaven* has been variously identified as the stars, the angels, or other heavenly beings. Because the sun and moon are specifically mentioned in v. 23, the host of heaven probably has reference to the stars. Astral worship was commonplace in the ancient world, although Israel was strictly forbidden to participate in such worship (cf. Deut. 4:19; 2 Kings 17:16; Jer. 19:13).

The passage is concluded on a note of triumph. After the Lord has finished judging the rulers of the earth and the host of heaven, he will be enthroned as king on Mount Zion, and before his elders he will manifest his glory. Here as elsewhere in the Old Testament the revelation of the glory of the Lord is the sign and seal of his real and lasting presence with his people (cf. Ex. 40:34-35; 1 Kings 8:10; Ezek. 43:1-5).

(2) A Song of Thanksgiving (25:1-5)

1 O LORD, thou art my God;
  I will exalt thee, I will praise thy name;
for thou hast done wonderful things,
  plans formed of old, faithful and sure.
2 For thou hast made the city a heap,
  the fortified city a ruin;
the palace of aliens is a city no more,
  it will never be rebuilt.
3 Therefore strong peoples will glorify thee;
  cities of ruthless nations will fear thee.
4 For thou hast been a stronghold to the poor,
  a stronghold to the needy in his distress,
  a shelter from the storm and a shade from
    the heat;
for the blast of the ruthless is like a storm
    against a wall,
5   like heat in a dry place.
Thou dost subdue the noise of the aliens;
  as heat by the shade of a cloud,
  so the song of the ruthless is stilled.

This section is clearly set off from its context by its structure and contents. In form it belongs to the category of community songs of thanksgiving. It extols Yahweh for his mighty acts performed against the ruthless and on behalf of the *poor* and *needy*. In the end, even the ruthless are made to fear him (v. 3).

Verse 2 mentions the downfall of a fortified alien city. Some have argued that this song was originally written to celebrate the destruction of a particular city that was hostile toward Israel. While this may be true, the identity of the city is no longer apparent. It seems best, therefore, to interpret the song in its present context as the celebration of Yahweh's victory over all his enemies, whose ruthless power was symbolized by their cities (cf. 2:15; Gen. 11:4).

The song also stresses the care that Yahweh has extended to his people. To the poor and needy he has become a stronghold in time of distress, a shelter from the storm, and a shade from the heat (v. 4). The storm and the heat are but symbols of the ruthless and of their vain attempts to subdue the poor and needy. In the end they themselves will be subdued and their song will be stilled. In that day only the song of the Lord's people will be heard, celebrating his mighty deeds.

(3) The Lord's Enthronement Feast (25: 6-9)

6 On this mountain the LORD of hosts will make for all peoples a feast of fat things, a feast of wine on the lees, of fat things full of marrow, of wine on the lees well refined. 7 And he will destroy on this mountain the covering that is cast over all peoples, the veil that is spread over all nations. 8 He will swallow up death for ever, and the Lord GOD will wipe away tears from all faces, and the reproach of his people he will take away from all the earth; for the LORD has spoken.

9 It will be said on that day, "Lo, this is our God; we have waited for him, that he might save us. This is the LORD; we have waited for him; let us be glad and rejoice in his salvation."

The pivotal expression in this and the following section is the expression *on this mountain* (cf. vv. 6,7,10), an obvious reference to Mount Zion (cf. 24:23). The Lord prepares a banquet on Mount Zion in celebration of his enthronement as king. This is one of the earliest known references to an eschatological banquet, a concept that may have originated in connection with the annual celebration of the New Year festival. This was subsequently developed into the concept of a messianic banquet, to which reference is made in the apcryphal writings (cf. 2 Baruch 29:4; 4 Esdras 6:49–52), in the Qumran texts (cf. *Manual of Discipline* 2:18–22), and in the New Testament (cf. Luke 22:28–30; Rev. 19:9).

Verse 6 speaks not only of the sumptuous nature of the banquet which the Lord provides but also of the ecumenical character of his invitation, which is extended to *all peoples.* The prophet believed that Jews and Gentiles alike would share in the blessings of the eschatological kingdom. This passage, therefore, is to be identified with the stream of tradition which stresses the place of all peoples within the positive plan of God (cf. 19:19–25; 56:3–8; 66:18–21; Zech. 2:11; 8:20–23; 14:16).

Verses 7–8 mention three of the mighty acts that the Lord will perform when he has been installed as king on Mount Zion. In the first place, he will destroy *the covering . . . cast over all peoples.* Some have interpreted this as signifying the removal of all symbols of mourning (cf. 2 Sam. 15:30; 19:4; Esther 6:12; Jer. 14:3–4). Others hold that the removal of the veil symbolizes the imparting of God's revelation to the Gentiles. It seems more likely, however, that *covering* and *veil* stand for the tyranny and oppression to which Israel and other small nations were periodically subjected. The fact that the destruction of the veil is to take place "on this mountain" suggests that the prophet expected the decisive victory over tyranny to take place at Jerusalem.

The second great act of the Lord involves his victory over death, after which there will be no more cause for weeping (cf. 1 Cor. 15:26, 54; Rev. 21:4). Exactly

what is meant by the statement that he will *swallow up death for ever* is not clear. Lindblom has interpreted it not as a categorical denial that death will be present in the age to come but as a promise that no one will die before he has lived out his full span of years (cf. 65:20). This interpretation appears to be far too restrictive, however, especially in the light of 26:19. The prophet is apparently referring to the final removal of death as a threat to the Lord's people. This is perhaps one of those instances in which he uttered an inspired truth greater than even he was able to comprehend.

The third accomplishment of the Lord will be the removal of the reproach of his people. The reproach the prophet had in mind was probably Israel's humiliation at being subjected to foreign domination. When the Lord has become king in Jerusalem, no other king will ever again rule over his people.

All of this means that for Israel the time of waiting will have ended and the time of fulfillment will have begun. On that day, the day of the great enthronement festival, she will proclaim the Lord as her God and exult in his salvation. It is at least implied that her joy will be shared by other peoples and nations who have joined themselves to the Lord.

(4) *The Doom of Moab (25:10–12)*

10 For the hand of the LORD will rest on this mountain, and Moab shall be trodden down in his place, as straw is trodden down in a dung-pit. 11 And he will spread out his hands in the midst of it as a swimmer spreads his hands out to swim; but the LORD will lay low his pride together with the skill of his hands. 12 And the high fortifications of his walls he will bring down, lay low, and cast to the ground, even to the dust.

Most scholars regard the brief oracle against Moab as later material deriving from the period following the destruction of Jerusalem in 587 B.C., when the Moabites joined forces with the Babylonians in robbing and looting the city (cf. 15:1—16:14). Those who date the passage at this time point out that the mention of one specific enemy by name occurs nowhere else in chapters 24—27. Furthermore, the whole tenor of the oracle against Moab reverses the benevolent spirit of the preceding passage. Why should the prophet turn from his noble vision of the universal reign of God to describe in such inelegant language the miserable fate of Moab?

March, however, argues that vv. 10–12 are an integral part of the larger context, as evidenced by the recurrence within them of the expression *on this mountain.* To say that the hand of the Lord will rest "on this mountain" means that Zion will remain under his protective care. Moab's destruction is admittedly described in language that is more forceful than elegant. Her fate will be like that of one who is thrown into the foul waters of a dung-pit. All her efforts to swim out will be unsuccessful. Her high walls will be cast down to the ground, making her utterly defenseless.

(5) The Security of the Righteous (26: 1–6)

¹ In that day this song will be sung in the land of Judah:
"We have a strong city;
    he sets up salvation
    as walls and bulwarks.
² Open the gates,
    that the righteous nation which keeps faith
    may enter in.
³ Thou dost keep him in perfect peace,
    whose mind is stayed on thee,
    because he trusts in thee.
⁴ Trust in the LORD for ever,
    for the LORD GOD
    is an everlasting rock.
⁵ For he has brought low
    the inhabitants of the height,
    the lofty city.
He lays it low, lays it low to the ground,
    casts it to the dust.
⁶ The foot tramples it,
    the feet of the poor,
    the steps of the needy."

This hymn of praise is composed of two three-line strophes (vv. 1–3, 4–6), the first praising Yahweh for the protection and security he provides for the righteous and the second declaring his humbling of the arrogant wicked and his exaltation of the poor and needy. The "city" motif, so promi-

nent throughout chapters 24—27, is present in both of these strophes, although used in a different sense in each. It is entirely possible that an enthronement festival provided the background for the hymn. The first strophe perhaps includes portions of an older "entrance song" (cf. Psalms 15; 24). The primary purpose of the hymn is to celebrate the triumph of Yahweh and the security of those who trust in him.

According to March, the first line should be rendered "Our strength is a city," a translation which can be justified on the basis of the punctuation of the Hebrew text. The statement as thus interpreted would refer not to the impregnability of Jerusalem but to the dependability of Yahweh. *City* would be understood in a metaphorical sense, as if the singers were saying, "Yahweh protects us like a fortified city."

Two things are said to describe those who belong to the Lord: they are a *righteous nation* that keeps faith (v. 2); their minds are stayed on the Lord because they trust in him (v. 3). Here as elsewhere in Isaiah faith and faithfulness are shown to be inseparable. The righterous are rewarded by receiving the Lord's protection (v. 1), by being permitted to enter into his presence (v. 2), by being kept in perfect peace (v. 3; Heb. *shalom shalom,* peace, peace), and by sharing in his triumph over the wicked (v. 6).

Because of the reference to Moab in 25:10 ff., some have attempted to identify the *lofty city* in 26:5 as Dibon, the capital of Moab. Lindblom's view, however, is that it refers to Babylon. It seems unlikely that the words of the hymn should be limited to one particular city. The probability is that it describes the downfall of all cities that exalt themselves against the Lord. The traditional nature of v. 5 can be clearly seen when it is compared with 25:12.

(6) A Prayer for Vindication (26:7–19)

⁷ The way of the righteous is level;
    thou dost make smooth the path of the righteous.
⁸ In the path of thy judgments,
    O LORD, we wait for thee;

thy memorial name
is the desire of our soul.
9 My soul yearns for thee in the night,
my spirit within me earnestly seeks thee.
For when thy judgments are in the earth,
the inhabitants of the world learn righteousness.
10 If favor is shown to the wicked,
he does not learn righteousness;
in the land of uprightness he deals perversely
and does not see the majesty of the LORD.
11 O LORD, thy hands is lifted up,
but they see it not.
Let them see thy zeal for thy people, and be
ashamed.
Let the fire for thy adversaries consume
them.
12 O LORD, thou wilt ordain peace for us,
thou hast wrought for us all our works.
13 O LORD our God,
other lords besides thee have ruled over
us,
but thy name alone we acknowledge.
14 They are dead, they will not live;
they are shades, they will not arise;
to that end thou hast visited them with destruction
and wiped out all remembrance of them.
15 But thou hast increased the nation, O LORD,
thou hast increased the nation; thou art
glorified;
thou hast enlarged all the borders of the
land.
16 O LORD, in distress they sought thee,
they poured out a prayer
when thy chastening was upon them.
17 Like a woman with child,
who writhes and cries out in her pangs,
when she is near her time,
so were we because of thee, O LORD;
18 we were with child, we writhed,
we have as it were brought forth wind.
We have wrought no deliverance in the
earth,
and the inhabitants of the world have not
fallen.
19 Thy dead shall live, their bodies shall rise.
O dwellers in the dust, awake and sing for
joy!
For thy dew is a dew of light,
and on the land of the shades thou wilt
let it fall.

The prayer is set against the background
of a time of national distress and anguish.
It is cast in the form of a community
lament, of which there are many examples
in the Old Testament (cf. Psalms 44; 60;
74). As the worshipers pray and meditate
on the enigma of God's acts in history, they

are filled with alternating moods of hope
and of despair.

The first strophe of the prayer-lament
(vv. 7–10) draws a contrast between *the
righteous* and *the wicked.* The central truth
in this strophe is that God's judgments are
sent into the world in order to accomplish
a didactic or tutorial purpose (cf. Psalm
119:67,71). The righterous know this, and
eagerly wait for the Lord to reveal himself out of the midst of his acts of judgment
(vv. 7–9a). Of special significance is the
idea that righteousness is learned only
when God's judgments are abroad in the
earth (v. 9b). When favor is shown to the
wicked, they learn nothing but continue to
deal perversely and to disregard the majesty of the Lord (v. 10).

The second strophe (vv. 11–15) expresses the worshipers' confidence that the
Lord will preserve the righteous and destroy the wicked. It was inconceivable to
them that the wicked should finally gain
the upper hand in God's world. The Lord's
hand is already raised against the wicked,
but they see it not. The worshipers pray
that the wicked may see and be ashamed.
Let fire come upon them, but peace upon
Israel. The petition is followed by a remarkable confession that every significant
deed in Israel's history has been performed
by the Lord (v. 12b). Other masters
have ruled over them, but they own allegiance to the Lord alone.

The meaning of v. 14 is that the death
of the wicked will be final and irrevocable.
They are *shades,* and they will never rise
again. The word shades occurs only eight
times in the Old Testament, and it always
refers to those who have gone down to
Sheol, the common abode of all the dead
(cf. 14:9; 26:14,19; Job 26:5; Psalm
88:10; Prov. 2:18; 9:18; 21:16).

The strophe ends with an announcement
that Israel's borders have been enlarged
(v. 15). Some have interpreted this as a
reference to a recent event in Israel's
history. Even if this interpretation is correct, the uncertainty regarding the dating
of these chapters makes it impossible to

identify the event.

The final strophe in the lament (vv. 16–19) contains Israel's cry of distress and the Lord's response. Israel calls for the Lord to intervene on her behalf (vv. 16–18), and he responds to her call (v. 19). Israel's pain and weakness are expressed under the figure of a woman in childbirth. She has labored hard but has brought forth only wind, a vivid symbol of utter futility. Deliverance is far from her, and her oppressors have not fallen (v. 18).

The climax to the passage comes in God's response to Israel's lament. In contrast to the wicked dead, who will never live again (v. 14), the righteous *dead* shall *arise* from the dust and sing for joy (v. 19). By a wonderful act of the Lord, they will come forth from the grave and repopulate the land of Israel.

The revolutionary character of this statement must not be overlooked. It is the earliest reference in the Bible to the resurrection, and the only such reference in prophetic literature, since Daniel 12:2 must be classified as apocalyptic. It represents a great leap forward, a veritable mutation in Israel's theological understanding, for prior to this her future hope had been expressed in terms of national rather than individual destiny.

Commenting on this significant advance in Israel's understanding, David S. Russell has written: "At last the biblical writers had found that mould, as it were, into which they could pour their hopes and longings and which alone could give real shape to the belief that man's fellowship with God would not be broken by death." [99]

The latter part of v. 19 suggests that the dead are raised to life when the dew of heaven falls upon them. The *dew of light* may be interpreted either as the early morning dew or as the dew from the heavenly regions of light (cf. Hos. 14:5; Zech. 8:12). In either case, it comes from God and gives life to those upon whom it falls.

[99] *Op. cit.,* pp. 356 f.

(7) The Sword of the Lord (26:20—27:1)

20 Come, my people, enter your chambers,
  and shut your doors behind you;
 hide yourselves for a little while
  until the wrath is past.
21 For behold, the LORD is coming forth out of his place
  to punish the inhabitants of the earth for their iniquity,
 and the earth will disclose the blood shed upon her,
  and will no more cover her slain.

1 In that day the LORD with his hard and great and strong sword will punish Leviathan the fleeing serpent, Leviathan the twisting serpent, and he will slay the dragon that is in the sea.

The theme of world judgment is brought to a climax in this passage. As the Lord marches forth to do battle against the forces of evil, he admonishes his people to enter their houses and shut the doors until the wrath is past (v. 20). The shutting of the doors has been interpreted either as a reference to the flood (cf. Gen. 7:16) or to the Passover (cf. Ex. 12:21–23). When the Lord comes forth he will punish the inhabitants of the earth for their iniquities, and no murder that they have committed will escape his attention (v. 21).

Three adjectives are used in 27:1 to describe the Lord's *sword*—it is hard (cruel), great (mighty), and strong (powerful). With this sword he will attack and slay *Leviathan,* otherwise known as the serpent and the dragon. Leviathan, a mythical sea monster, also appears in Canaanite folklore from Ugarit, where he is described as "the fleeing serpent." According to the Canaanite myth, this primeval monster was slain by Baal at the creation of the world. Old Testament writers later attributed his slaying to Yahweh (cf. 51:9; Job 26:12; Psalm 74:13–14; 89:10). This is the only instance in the Old Testament where his slaying is projected into the future. The prophet uses this ancient symbol of chaos and evil to emphasize the decisive nature of God's victory over all his foes. His defeat of

Leviathan means that henceforth he will reign without a rival.

3. The Lord's Plans for His People (27: 2-13)

March regards this section as consisting of secondary materials which were appended to the preceding eschatological prophecies at a later date, perhaps near the end of the Babylonian captivity. It is difficult to determine whether or not this is a correct judgment, although these oracles are admittedly fragmentary and seem to bear little relationship to one another or to the oracles in the preceding chapters.

(1) The New Song of the Vineyard (27: 2-6)

2 In that day:
"A pleasant vineyard, sing of it!
3   I, the LORD, am its keeper;
   every moment I water it.
Lest anyone harm it,
   I guard it night and day;
4   I have no wrath.
Would that I had thorns and briers to battle!
   I would set out against them,
   I would burn them up together.
5 Or let them lay hold of my protection,
   let them make peace with me,
   let them make peace with me."
6 In days to come Jacob shall take root,
   Israel shall blossom and put forth shoots,
   and fill the whole world with fruit.

This song was obviously written to counter-balance the earlier song in 5:1-7. There Israel was described as a worthless vineyard; here she is called a *pleasant vineyard* (v. 2). There she bore no fruit; here she fills the whole world with her fruit (v. 6). There the Lord announced his intention to abandon her to destruction; here he speaks of her as his jealously guarded possession (v. 3). The purpose of the song, therefore, is to show that since the judgment proclaimed in chapter 5 has been executed the Lord's favor will return to his people.

The *thorns and briars* mentioned in v. 4 are figurative of the Lord's enemies. The prophet indulges in hyperbole as he de-

scribes the Lord as wishing that some enemy would attack Israel so that he might defend her. If this should occur, the attacker would either have to sue for terms of peace or else be utterly destroyed.[100]

(2) A People Without Discernment (27: 7-11)

7 Has he smitten them as he smote those who smote them?
   Or have they been slain as their slayers were slain?
8 Measure by measure, by exile thou didst contend with them;
   he removed them with his fierce blast in the day of the east wind.
9 Therefore by this the guilt of Jacob will be expiated,
   and this will be the full fruit of the removal of his sin:
when he makes all the stones of the altars like chalkstones crushed to pieces,
   no Asherim or incense altars will remain standing.
10 For the fortified city is solitary,
   a habitation deserted and forsaken, like the wilderness;
there the calf grazes,
   there he lies down, and strips its branches.
11 When its boughs are dry, they are broken;
   women come and make a fire of them.
For this is a people without discernment;
   therefore he who made them will not have compassion on them,
   he that formed them will show them no favor.

This is one of the most obscure passages in the book of Isaiah. Scholarly opinion differs widely both with regard to its translation and to its interpretation. It is generally regarded as a reflection on the meaning of Israel's past suffering. Although there is little indication of precise date, most would assign it to the postexilic period.

The oracle begins by asking if Israel had been punished as severely as her oppressors. The implication is that she had fared better than they. Assyria, for example, was blotted out in 605 B.C., and Babylon in 539 B.C. Israel, to be sure, had had to endure the Lord's punishment (v. 8), but

---

100 There are many textual problems in this pericope. The text of the Septuagint differs so greatly from that of the Hebrew that the two hardly resemble one another. No satisfactory explanation for these differences has been found.

there was hope for her future. If she would but destroy the pagan altars in her land, her punishment would be suspended and her relationship to the Lord restored (v. 9).

The most crucial problem related to the interpretation of the passage is the identification of the *fortified city* whose desolation is described in v. 10. Does it refer to Jerusalem or to an unspecified pagan city (cf. 24:10; 25:2; 26:5)? In view of the fact that the following verse seems to describe in traditional terms the continuing disobedience and apostasy of the Jewish people (cf. Hos. 2:4; 4:1,6), the city may cautiously be identified as Jerusalem. In this case the purpose of the passage would be to explain why the restoration of Jerusalem has been delayed. The prophet's explanation is that it is because her people are still idolatrous and without understanding. The latter part of v. 11 suggests that new chastisements are about to fall upon them.

(3) The Ingathering of Israel (27:12 –13)

¹² In that day from the river Euphrates to the Brook of Egypt the LORD will thresh out the grain, and you will be gathered one by one, O people of Israel. ¹³ And in that day a great trumpet will be blown, and those who were lost in the land of Assyria and those who were driven out to the land of Egypt will come and worship the LORD on the holy mountain of Jerusalem.

These verses provide a happy ending to chapters 24—27. They describe the ingathering of the dispersed of Israel under the twofold figure of the harvest (v. 12) and the trumpet call (v. 13). As good grain is separated from the chaff, so will the Lord thresh them and gather them in one by one. At the sound of the trumpet those lost in the land of Assyria and in the land of Egypt will assemble at Jerusalem to worship the Lord on his holy mountain. This is the first reference in the Bible to the blowing of the trumpet in connection with the beginning of the eschatological age (cf. Matt. 24:31; 1 Cor. 15:52; 1 Thess. 4:16; Rev. 8:2 ff.).

IV. Divine Wisdom and Human Folly (28:1—32:20)

Because these chapters are made up largely of messages which Isaiah addressed to Israel and Judah during the Assyrian crisis, they have sometimes been referred to as "the Assyrian cycle of prophecies." The arrangement of the material in a series of complexes, each introduced by the word "woe" (cf. 28:1; 29:1,15; 30:1; 31:1; 33:1), has resulted in their being known also as "the book of woes." As far as content is concerned, they consist of a mixture of messages of judgment and redemption, of threat and consolation.

1. Oracles Concerning Ephraim and Judah (28:1–29)

(1) Drunken Leaders of the Lord's People (28:1–13)

1   Woe to the proud crown of the drunkards of Ephraim,
    and to the fading flower of its glorious beauty,
    which is on the head of the rich valley of those overcome with wine!
2   Behold, the Lord has one who is mighty and strong;
    like a storm of hail, a destroying tempest,
    like a storm of mighty, overflowing waters,
    he will cast down to the earth with violence.
3   The proud crown of the drunkards of Ephraim
    will be trodden under foot;
4   and the fading flower of its glorious beauty,
    which is on the head of the rich valley,
    will be like a first-ripe fig before the summer:
    when a man sees it, he eats it up
    as soon as it is in his hand.
5   In that day the LORD of hosts will be a crown of glory,
    and a diadem of beauty, to the remnant of his people;
6   and a spirit of justice to him who sits in judgment,
    and strength to those who turn back the battle at the gate.
7   These also reel with wine
    and stagger with strong drink;
    the priest and the prophet reel with strong drink,
    they are confused with wine,
    they stagger with strong drink;

they err in vision,
    they stumble in giving judgment.
8 For all tables are full of vomit,
    no place is without filthiness.
9 "Whom will he teach knowledge,
    and to whom will he explain the mes-
        sage?
    Those who are weaned from the milk,
        those taken from the breast?
10 For it is precept upon precept, precept upon
        precept,
    line upon line, line upon line,
        here a little, there a little."
11 Nay, but by men of strange lips
    and with an alien tongue
        the LORD will speak to his people,
12   to whom he has said,
"This is rest;
    give rest to the weary;
        and this is repose";
    yet they would not hear.
13 Therefore the word of the LORD will be to
        them
    precept upon precept, precept upon pre-
        cept,
    line upon line, line upon line,
        here a little, there a little;
    that they may go, and fall backward,
        and be broken, and snared, and taken.

The opening oracle (vv. 1–4) is addressed to *Ephraim*, i.e., Israel, and should
perhaps be dated just prior to the fall of
Samaria in 722 B.C. The men of Ephraim
are described as living in a carnival atmosphere, blissfully ignorant of the judgment which is about to overtake them.

Judgment will come by the hand of **one
who is mighty and strong,** an obvious
reference to the king of Assyria. He will
trample under foot the "proud crown of
the drunkards of Ephraim." This is usually
interpreted as meaning the city of Samaria,
a seemingly impregnable fortress-city overlooking a broad and fertile valley. When
the king of Assyria sees it, he will devour
it as eagerly as one would devour first-ripe
fruit (v. 4).

Verses 5–6 interrupt the message of
judgment and treat of the glories of the
eschatological age which will follow the
Assyrian invasion. The present position of
the brief oracle of hope is probably due to
its description of the Lord as a crown. Unlike the fading crown on the head of
Ephraim (vv. 1,4), however, he will be

an everlasting crown of glory and a diadem
of beauty to the remnant of his people
(v. 5). In the glorious age to come he will
grant wisdom to Israel's judges and
strength to her defenders (v. 6). The implication is that the eschatological age will
be an age of justice and of peace (cf. 2:4;
9:6–7; 11:1–9).

Verses 7–13 describe an encounter between Isaiah and the drunken prophets
and reveling priests of Judah. Isaiah
charges that the prophets are too drunk to
receive a vision and the priests too confused to render a judgment (v. 7). Their
tables are full of vomit, and filthiness is
everywhere (v. 8). Judah's sodden and
befuddled religious leaders immediately
turn upon the prophet in anger. Their
sullen retort to his accusation is recorded
in vv. 9–10. *Whom will he teach knowledge?* They sarcastically inquire. "Does he
think that we are children in kindergarten
and that it is his responsibility to teach
us our ABC's?"

The quotation in v. 10 is probably taken
from an early Hebrew abecedary, a drill
book designed to teach the letters of the
alphabet to children. This particular quotation deals with *tsadhe* and *qoph,* the
eighteenth and nineteenth letters of the
Hebrew alphabet, transliterated as *ts* and
q. The prophet's opponents pretend to
mimic him as they say, "For it is *tsab la-
tsab, tsab la-tsab; qab la-qab, qab la-qab;*
here a little, there a little." The concluding
expression may mean "a little at a time," or
it may refer to the order in which the
teacher calls upon his pupils to recite—"the
little one here, the little one there."

Isaiah's reply is a classic example of the
use of irony. Because Judah's leaders have
refused instruction given in their own
language they will be taught in the
language of Assyria (v. 11). In that day
the word of the Lord will be to them
"*tsab la-tsab, tsab la-tsab; qab la-qab,
qab la-qab;* here a little, there a little" (v.
13). The concluding threat in v. 13 is
parallel to 8:15.

Verse 12 is fraught with rich meaning. It

defines God's intention for his people as that they might find rest and repose. It further declares that the way to the realization of this intention is the way of sacrificial self-giving, i.e., one *finds* rest only by *giving* rest to the weary. There is a close parallel between this verse and 30:15. In both instances God's good intentions for his people are frustrated because of their obstinate disobedience (cf. Luke 19:41–42).

(2) True and False Security (28:14–22)

14 Therefore hear the word of the LORD, you scoffers,
    who rule this people in Jerusalem!
15 Because you have said, "We have made a covenant with death,
    and with Sheol we have an agreement;
    when the overwhelming scourge passes through
    it will not come to us;
    for we have made lies our refuge,
    and in falsehood we have taken shelter";
16 therefore thus says the Lord GOD,
    "Behold, I am laying in Zion for a foundation
    a stone, a tested stone,
    a precious cornerstone, of a sure foundation:
    'He who believes will not be in haste.'
17 And I will make justice the line,
    and righteousness the plummet;
    and hail will sweep away the refuge of lies,
    and waters will overwhelm the shelter."
18 Then your covenant with death will be annulled,
    and your agreement with Sheol will not stand;
    when the overwhelming scourge passes through
    you will be beaten down by it.
19 As often as it passes through it will take you;
    for morning by morning it will pass through,
    by day and by night;
    and it will be sheer terror to understand the message.
20 For the bed is too short to stretch oneself on it,
    and the covering too narrow to wrap oneself in it.
21 For the LORD will rise up as on Mount Perazim,
    he will be wroth as in the valley of Gibeon;
    to do his deed—strange is his deed!
    and to work his work—alien is his work!

22 Now therefore do not scoff,
    lest your bonds be made strong;
    for I have heard a decree of destruction
    from the Lord GOD of hosts upon the whole land.

The Assyrian king Sargon II died in 705 B.C. and was succeeded by his son Sennacherib (705–681). This change of rulers triggered a wave of rebellion that spread throughout the Assyrian Empire. Judah was drawn into the rebellion when Hezekiah (715–687) attempted to throw off the Assyrian yoke (cf. 2 Kings 18:7). In taking this course of action he was influenced by a strong pro-Egyptian party in Jerusalem, a group of influential leaders who believed that Egypt could be counted on to aid their country in its bid for independence.

Isaiah reserved some of his strongest ridicule for this group. He regarded their reliance on Egypt as an act of blasphemy, for it placed the power of men above the power of God. He also saw it as an exercise in futility, for how could Egypt lend aid to others when she was too weak to defend herself?

This oracle is addressed to the political leaders of Jerusalem who had engineered the alliance with Egypt. They boasted that their *covenant with death and with Sheol* (i.e., their alliance with Egypt) would afford them protection when the overwhelming scourge (i.e., the Assyrian army) passed through. Their false optimism led them to say, "It can't happen here."

In contrast to the bogus security of which Judah's politicians boast, Isaiah points the way to true security and to true greatness (vv. 16–17a). These verses are full of metaphors drawn from the building trades, as the prophet speaks of "foundation," "cornerstone," "line," and "plummet." God announces that he is *laying in Zion for a foundation a stone.* This stone is *tested* and *precious*, and provides a *sure* foundation.

According to Koehler-Baumgartner, the word translated "tested" (*bochan*), which occurs only here in the Old Testament, is an Egyptian loanword descriptive of a special type of fine-grained stone used for carving statues, inscriptions, etc. Its appearance here suggests that Isaiah may have been thinking of a foundation stone upon which would be inscribed a special message, perhaps even the very words that stand at the close of v. 16: "He who believes will not be in haste."

This terse statement is the nucleus around which the rest of the passage revolves. It embodies Isaiah's conviction that there can be no enduring covenant community without a solid foundation of faith in Yahweh and in the reliability of his word (cf. 7:9; 30:15). The various translations that have been given to this crucial statement serve to amplify its meaning: "He who has faith shall not waver" (NEB); "He who believes shall not be worried" (Goodspeed); "He who has faith will not be in a frenzy" (J. A. Sanders); "A people that keeps faith has no cause for panic" (E. A. Leslie).

The demand for faith, however, does not exhaust God's requirements. It is not enough for a nation to lay its foundations in trust in God; it must also raise its walls in *justice* and in *righteousness*. As a good builder always tests his work with the line and the plummet, so God measures the lives of his people with the line of justice and with the plummet of righteousness (v. 17a). These verses contain the two most essential elements in Isaiah's preaching, for throughout his ministry he exhorted the people both to trust God and to practice justice and righteousness.

Verses 17b–22 describe the bankruptcy of Judah's foreign policy and forecast the judgment that is to overtake her. Judgment will come as a hailstorm and as a flood, sweeping away her refuge of lies and demolishing her shelter of falsehood (vv. 15b, 17b). Her covenant with death and her agreement with Sheol will not save her from the overwhelming scourge when it passes through. The Assyrians will harass the land by day and by night, and the mere reports of their activities will strike terror in the hearts of men (v. 19).

The prophet makes use of a proverb to describe the miserable condition into which Judah's foreign policy has led her. Her *bed is too short* for one to stretch himself upon it, and her *covering too narrow* for one to wrap himself in it (v. 20). In order to appreciate the proverb one must remember that Palestinian nights, even in summer, are cold and damp. Imagine the predicament of one who tries to sleep under the circumstances described here! If he stretches himself out, he extends beyond the foot of the bed; if he draws himself up, he has difficulty covering himself. There is simply no way for him to sleep in comfort. Isaiah is saying, in effect, that Judah has made her bed, and now she must lie in it.

Verse 21 contains an allusion to David's deeat of the Philistines, first at Mount Perazim (cf. 2 Sam. 5:17–21; 1 Chron. 14:8–12) and later at Gibeon (cf. 2 Sam. 5:22–25; 1 Chron. 14:13–17). In those days the Lord fought on the side of his people; now he is forced to fight against them! This latter course of action, however, is so contrary to his basic nature that it can only be described as his "strange deed" and his "alien work." The Lord delights in mercy; judgment is indeed his strange work.

The passage closes with a warning to scoffers that unless they cease their scoffing their bonds will be made stronger. The warning is based upon the decree of destruction which the prophet has heard from the Lord of hosts against the whole land. One may assume that this decree had been heard in the heavenly council (cf. Jer. 23:18). This would have made the prophet's message doubly authoritative.

(3) The Parable of the Farmer (28: 23–29)

23 Give ear, and hear my voice;
hearken, and hear my speech.
24 Does he who plows for sowing plow continually?
does he continually open and harrow his ground?
25 When he has leveled its surface,

does he not scatter dill, sow cummin,
and put in wheat in rows
    and barley in its proper place,
    and spelt as the border?
26 For he is instructed aright;
    his God teaches him.
27 Dill is not threshed with a threshing sledge,
    nor is a cart wheel rolled over cummin;
but dill is beaten out with a stick,
    and cummin with a rod.
28 Does one crush bread grain?
    No, he does not thresh it for ever;
when he drives his cart wheel over it
    with his horses, he does not crush it.
29 This also comes from the LORD of hosts;
    he is wonderful in counsel,
    and excellent in wisdom.

The parable of the farmer is told in the style of the wisdom teacher (v. 23; cf. Prov. 1:8; 3:1; 4:1–2, 10). In it the prophet expresses his admiration for the wisdom and skill exemplified by the farmer. As he had observed the latter at work during the successive seasons of the year, he had been struck by the degree of knowledge and skill demanded of him. He must know how to prepare the soil (v. 24), how to plant the seeds (v. 25), and how to harvest the crops (vv. 27–28). The fact that he was able to do these things successfully meant that he had been taught by God, who was both wonderful in counsel and excellent in wisdom (vv. 26,29).

What were the practical expressions of divine wisdom in the farmer's life? In the first place, he did not plow his field continually (v. 24), nor thresh his grain for ever (v. 28), otherwise both field and grain would have been destroyed. This means that he did everything in season and in moderation. In the second place, he treated each crop differently and in a manner suited to its individual characteristics, both at the time of planting (v. 25), and at the time of harvest (vv. 27–28).

Many different attempts have been made to explain the significance of the parable. It is proposed here that the key to its understanding lies in the prominence given in it to the ideas of plowing and of threshing. Both the word for plowing (*charash*) and the word for threshing (*dush*) are sometimes used in the Old Testament to describe acts of judgment or of vindictiveness (cf. 41:15; Psalm 129:3; Jer. 26:18; Amos 1:3). The context in which the parable is placed (cf. vv. 21–22) and the manner in which it is told suggest that there were scoffers in Judah who were complaining that the Lord's judgments upon them had been too severe and that he did not seem to know when to stop punishing them. In fact, they thought that he seemed to be bent upon destroying them altogether.

The response of the prophet to their complaint was that God's activity in history was infused with a wisdom at least commensurate with that of the farmer. If the latter knew when to stop plowing and when to start sowing, and if he knew when to stop threshing the grain lest it be crushed, then surely the Lord knew when to stop punishing his people. His purpose, like that of the farmer, was not to crush the grain, but only to separate it from the chaff. According to this interpretation, the parable of the farmer was designed to express Isaiah's conviction that judgment was a necessary but temporary activity of God; his ultimate purpose was the redemption of his people.

2. Oracles of Judgment and Redemption (29:1–24)

(1) The Distress and Deliverance of Jerusalem (29:1–8)

1 Ho Ariel, Ariel,
    the city where David encamped!
Add year to year;
    let the feasts run their round.
2 Yet I will distress Ariel,
    and there shall be moaning and lamentation,
    and she shall be to me like an Ariel.
3 And I will encamp against you round about,
    and will besiege you with towers
    and I will raise siegeworks against you.
4 Then deep from the earth you shall speak,
    from low in the dust your words shall come;
your voice shall come from the ground like the voice of a ghost,
    and your speech shall whisper out of the dust.
5 But the multitude of your foes shall be like

small dust,
and the multitude of the ruthless like passing chaff.
And in an instant, suddenly,
6 you will be visited by the LORD of hosts
with thunder and with earthquake and great
noise,
with whirlwind and tempest, and the flame
of a devouring fire.
7 And the multitude of all the nations that
fight against Ariel,
all that fight against her and her stronghold and distress her,
shall be like a dream, a vision of the night.
8 As when a hungry man dreams he is eating
and awakes with his hunger not satisfied,
or as when a thirsty man dreams he is drinking
and awakes faint, with his thirst not
quenched,
so shall the multitude of all the nations be
that fight against Mount Zion.

This oracle probably belongs to the period between 705 and 701 B.C. It gives evidence of having been delivered during one of the religious festivals in Jerusalem. It falls naturally into two divisions, the first (vv. 1-4) describing the city's distress under seige, and the second (vv. 5-8) the sudden discomfiture of her foes. In the first division Yahweh appears as Jerusalem's enemy, but through a complete turnabout in events he appears in the second as her defender. This probably reflects the abrupt transition through which the city passed during the Sennacherib crisis of 701.

The city is referred to not by its usual name, but as *Ariel* (vv. 1,2,7). This strange name comes from the Akkadian *arallu*, meaning "underworld," "ghost," or "mountain of the gods." The Hebrew word *ariel* occurs also in Ezekiel 43:15-16, where it is translated "altar hearth." Ariel is probably to be interpreted, therefore, as "altar of God," a name especially appropriate for Jerusalem because of the presence in it of Solomon's Temple.

The fact that the city has a temple and a well-organized cult, however, will not save it from the impending doom. No matter how faithful the people might be in attendance upon their religious festivals, judgment is still inevitable (cf. v. 1b).

There is a play on the different meanings of the term *Ariel* in v. 2. Ariel (altar of God) will be subjected to such deep distress that it will become like an Ariel (ghost). The Lord himself will lay seige to the city (v. 3), and it will be brought so low that its voice will sound as if it were coming from Sheol itself, that dusty land of the dead (v. 4).

At this point there is a sudden and inexplicable transition from words of threat to words of comfort. The Lord speaks to reassure Ariel, promising her that those who fight against her will soon crumble into dust and be blown away like chaff (v. 5). She will no longer remember them, except perhaps as one would remember a bad dream or a nightmare (v. 7). Her foe, who comes against her with visions of conquering and looting her, will go away as empty as a hungry man who dreams that he is eating and drinking, and then awakes to find that it was only a dream (v. 8).

(2) Spiritual Blindness and Hypocrisy (29:9-14)

9 Stupefy yourselves and be in a stupor,
blind yourselves and be blind!
Be drunk, but not with wine;
stagger, but not with strong drink!
10 For the LORD has poured out upon you
a spirit of deep sleep,
and has closed your eyes, the prophets,
and covered your heads, the seers.
11 And the vision of all this has become to
you like the words of a book that is sealed.
When men give it to one who can read, saying,
"Read this," he says, "I cannot, for it is sealed."
12 And when they give the book to one who
cannot read, saying, "Read this," he says, "I
cannot read."
13 And the Lord said:
"Because this people draw near with their
mouth
and honor me with their lips,
while their hearts are far from me,
and their fear of me is a commandment of
men learned by rote;
14 therefore, behold, I will again
do marvelous things with this people,
wonderful and marvelous;
and the wisdom of their wise men shall perish,
and the discernment of their discerning
men shall be hid."

This passage describes the spiritual condition of the people of Jerusalem just prior to 701 B.C. They were a blind people (vv. 9–12), whose only service to God was lip service (vv. 13–14). The description of their blindness reminds one of the words that were spoken to the prophet at the time of his call (cf. 6:9–10).

The fact that in both instances the blindness of the people is attributed either directly or indirectly to God is a testimony to the thoroughgoing monotheism of Old Testament writers, who, with only rare exception, regarded God as the ultimate cause of everything that happened in the world (cf. 45:7; Ex. 10:20; 1 Sam. 16:14; 2 Sam. 24:1). These writers also believed in the freedom and responsibility of man, and they apparently saw no contradiction between these two views. Israel, therefore, was held responsible for her blindness, even though God had permitted it to happen.

The condition of the people is like that of a man who is dazed, blind, and intoxicated—all at the same time! Their moral lethargy is compared to a *deep sleep*, a kind of hypnotic sleep like that of Adam (Gen. 2:21), of Abram (Gen. 15:12), of Saul (1 Sam. 26:12), or of Jonah (Jonah 1:5).

The latter part of v. 10 refers to the *prophets* and *seers* as the eyes and heads of the community. This reading speaks at once of a great responsibility and of a great failure. In a real sense the prophets were the eyes of Israel, for upon them rested the responsibility of seeing and declaring the word of the Lord. The closing of the eyes and the covering of the heads would, therefore, result in a dearth of prophetic vision, producing a famine of the word of the Lord such as that forecast earlier by Amos (cf. Amos 8:11–12).

All prophetic vision had become to the men of Jerusalem like a scroll that was rolled up and sealed with wax (v. 11; cf. Dan. 5:12,15; Rev. 5:1–9). The inability to understand the word of the Lord affected the educated as well as the uneducated (vv. 11b–12).

Verse 13 describes Jerusalem's worship as a display of lip service and empty ritual. The NEB renders the final clause in the verse to read, "and their religion is but a precept of men, learnt by rote." Their religion had become a mere formality, a meaningless echo from the past (cf. Matt. 15:8–9; Mark 7:6–7).

The "because" of v. 13 is followed by the "therefore" of v. 14. God announces that he will again intervene in Judah's history, performing works too marvelous for her wise men to comprehend or to explain (cf. 1 Cor. 1:19).

(3) Judah's Crafty Counselors (29:15–16)

15 Woe to those who hide deep from the LORD
    their counsel,
    whose deeds are in the dark,
    and who say, "Who sees us? Who knows
    us?"
16 You turn things upside down!
    Shall the potter be regarded as the clay;
  that the thing made should say of its maker,
    "He did not make me";
  or the thing formed say of him who formed
    it,
    "He has no understanding"?

This brief oracle condemns the leaders of Judah who were attempting to form a secret alliance with Egypt (cf. 28:7–22; 30:1–7; 31:1–3). They boasted that their plans had been devised and executed with such secrecy that not even the Lord himself knew what they had done. They thought that for once they had outwitted and outmaneuvered him and his meddling prophet. Isaiah reminded them that by giving expression to such arrogant thoughts they were denying their own creatureliness and casting aspersions on the intelligence of their Creator (cf. 45:9; Rom. 9:20).

(4) The Transformation of Nature and Society (29:17–24)

17 Is it not yet a very little while
    until Lebanon shall be turned into a fruitful field,
    and the fruitful field shall be regarded as
    a forest?

¹⁸ In that day the deaf shall hear
      the words of a book,
  and out of their gloom and darkness
      the eyes of the blind shall see.
¹⁹ The meek shall obtain fresh joy in the Lord,
      and the poor among men shall exult in
          the Holy One of Israel.
²⁰ For the ruthless shall come to nought and
          the scoffer cease,
      and all who watch to do evil shall be cut
          off,
²¹ who by a word make a man out to be an
          offender,
      and lay a snare for him who reproves in
          the gate,
      and with an empty plea turn aside him
          who is in the right.
²² Therefore thus says the Lord, who redeemed Abraham, concerning the house of
Jacob:
  "Jacob shall no more be ashamed,
      no more shall his face grow pale.
²³ For when he sees his children,
      the work of my hands, in his midst,
      they will sanctify my name;
  they will sanctify the Holy One of Jacob,
      and will stand in awe of the God of Israel.
²⁴ And those who err in spirit will come to un-
          derstanding,
      and those who murmur will accept in-
          struction."

Some scholars regard v. 17 as belonging
to the preceding oracle of judgment, and
interpret it as referring not to the restoration of the land but to its devastation. The
NEB, for example, adopts this interpretation and renders the verse: "The time is
but short before Lebanon goes back to
grassland and the grassland is no better
than scrub." The translators of the RSV, on
the other hand, understand the verse as a
promise of the restoration of the land, with
the forests of Lebanon becoming a fertile
field and the fertile fields a forest.

Most modern scholars regard this passage
as having been written during the same
period as chapters 40—66. This opinion is
based upon the similarities in thought and
language that exist between the two
sections. Others note that the evidence
cited in support of this position is highly
ambiguous, and might just as well be used
to prove that Isaiah himself wrote the
passage. It is unquestionably true that
hope was an essential ingredient in his

preaching.

Verse 18 promises that in the golden age
to come there will be a reversal of the
situation previously described in vv. 9–12.
The Lord's people, referred to as the meek
and poor of the earth, will find new joy in
him (v. 19). The ruthless and arrogant, on
the other hand, will cease to be, together
with all those who pervert justice (vv.
20–21).

Verses 22–24 describe the inner transformation that will take place among the
people of Israel in the age to come. Jacob's
shame and dismay will end when he sees
his children, the work of God's hands,
gathered around him. In that day they will
all sanctify the Holy One of Jacob and
stand in awe of the God of Israel. Even the
confused in mind and the rebellious among
them will come to an understanding of the
meaning of true religion.

3. The Rejection of Faith's Security (30:1—31:9)

(1) The Futility of Depending on Egypt (30:1-7)

¹ "Woe to the rebellious children," says the
      Lord,
  "who carry out a plan, but not mine;
  and who make a league, but not of my
      spirit,
      that they may add sin to sin;
² who set out to go down to Egypt,
      without asking for my counsel,
  to take refuge in the protection of Pharaoh,
      and to seek shelter in the shadow of
          Egypt!
³ Therefore shall the protection of Pharaoh
          turn to your shame,
      and the shelter in the shadow of Egypt
          to your humiliation.
⁴ For though his officials are at Zoan
      and his envoys reach Hanes,
⁵ every one comes to shame
      through a people that cannot profit them,
  that brings neither help nor profit,
      but shame and disgrace."
⁶ An oracle on the beasts of the Negeb.
  Through a land of trouble and anguish,
      from where come the lioness and the
          lion,
      the viper and the flying serpent,
  they carry their riches on the backs of
      asses,
      and their treasures on the humps of

camels,
to a people that cannot profit them.
7 For Egypt's help is worthless and empty,
therefore I have called her
"Rahab who sits still."

There are two oracles in this section
(vv. 1–5,6–7), both of which stress the
futility of depending upon Egypt for protection. The circumstance that called forth
these oracles was the sending of an embassy
from Judah to Egypt for the purpose of
arranging a treaty between the two countries. Judah had apparently taken the
initiative in this venture, for her envoys
bore expensive gifts with which to entice
the Egyptians to join forces with them. At
this particular juncture in history, Egypt
was under the rule of a very able king
named Shabako (710–696 B.C.), which
inspired the men of Judah to believe that
they would be safe if they had Egypt on
their side.

Isaiah gave two reasons for his opposition to the attempt to enlist Egypt's aid.
In the first place, the men of Judah had
made their plans without consulting the
Lord or seeking his counsel (vv. 1–2).
There was an established tradition in
Israel that all such high-level decisions
would be delayed until the word of the
Lord had been sought through one of the
prophets (cf. 1 Kings 22). The pro-
Egyptian party, however, had ignored this
tradition and had acted on their own
authority. The prophet regarded this not
as a personal affront but as an affront to
God himself.

The second reason for Isaiah's opposition
to the proposed alliance was his conviction
that Egypt's help would prove to be absolutely worthless (vv. 3–5). This is also
the subject of the second oracle (vv. 6–7),
which describes the dangerous and tortuous
journey that the envoys had to make as
they crossed the Sinai Desert on their way
to Egypt. The tragedy of it all was that it
was an exercise in futility, for Egypt's *help*
was *worthless and empty* (v. 7). The
prophet scornfully nicknamed her "Rahab
who sits still." Rahab was but another

name for the primeval dragon, also known
as Leviathan (cf. 27:1). However much
Egypt may have resembled a dragon, all
she ever did was sit still!

(2) A Written Testimony (30:8–17)

8 And now, go, write it before them on a
tablet,
and inscribe it in a book,
that it may be for the time to come
as a witness for ever.
9 For they are a rebellious people,
lying sons,
sons who will not hear
the instruction of the LORD;
10 who say to the seers, "See not";
and to the prophets, "Prophesy not to us
what is right;
speak to us smooth things,
prophesy illusions,
11 leave the way, turn aside from the path,
let us hear no more of the Holy One of
Israel."
12 Therefore thus says the Holy One of Israel,
"Because you despise this word,
and trust in oppression and perverseness,
and rely on them;
13 therefore this iniquity shall be to you
like a break in a high wall, bulging out,
and about to collapse,
whose crash comes suddenly, in an instant;
14 and its breaking is like that of a potter's
vessel
which is smashed so ruthlessly
that among its fragments not a sherd is
found
with which to take fire from the hearth,
or to dip up water out of the cistern."
15 For thus said the Lord GOD, the Holy One
of Israel,
"In returning and rest you shall be saved;
in quietness and in trust shall be your
strength."
And you would not, 16 but you said,
"No! We will speed upon horses,"
therefore you shall speed away;
and, "We will ride upon swift steeds,"
therefore your pursuers shall be swift.
17 A thousand shall flee at the threat of one,
at the threat of five you shall flee,
till you are left
like a flagstaff on the top of a mountain,
like a signal on a hill.

In the face of the stubborn refusal of
the people to heed the spoken word of
God, Isaiah was told to commit his message
to writing (v. 8; cf. 8:16–18). The written

record was to serve as a testimony for all time to come that the people had been rebellious and disloyal (v. 9), and that they had tried to silence their prophets and seers through intimidation and coercion (vv. 9–11). These architects of Israel's foreign policy wanted support from the prophets, not criticism. They were particularly tired of hearing Isaiah refer to God as the Holy One of Israel, for every such reference reminded them of their own unholiness.

Isaiah, however, refused to be coerced into silence. Speaking in the very name of the Holy One of Israel, he announced the coming judgment under two figures familiar to his listeners. Their downfall would be like the sudden collapse of a high, bulging wall (v. 13). The walls around ancient cities served not only as lines of defense but also as retaining walls. They were usually filled in to a considerable depth on the upper side with dirt and debris. Since they were built of unhewn stones held together by mud, they could easily be undermined by floods or weakened by landslides. Bulging walls had to be repaired immediately, or else they would carry to destruction the houses built above them (cf. Matt. 7:26–27).

The second figure used by the prophet was that of a potter's vessel so ruthlessly smashed that among its fragments no sherd could be found large enough to be used to take a coal of fire from the hearth or to dip up water from the cistern (v. 14). Normally, potsherds were used for these and for a variety of other similar purposes (cf. Job 2:8). The prophet's use of the figures of the bulging wall and the smashed potter's vessel stressed both the certainty and the thoroughness of the coming destruction.

The concluding oracle in the section (vv. 15–17) presents the true and the false way to national security. Verse 15, one of the best-known and best-loved texts in the book of Isaiah, declares that Judah's true security lies in returning to God in penitence, in calmly trusting in his promised

help, and in resting from her feverish efforts to secure her own safety. If she had chosen this path, she would have found true security and true stability.

Judah's leaders were not willing, however, to follow the path of faith, but chose instead the path of militarism. They were confident that an army supplied with horses, perhaps acquired from Egypt (cf. 31:3), would be invincible on the field of battle. The prophet scornfully replied that their horses would serve no useful purpose, other than that of enabling them to flee more swiftly from their pursuers (v. 16). He also affirmed that one enemy soldier would be able to chase a thousand of Judah's troops, and that at the threat of five the entire nation would be put to flight. When the dust of battle had settled, she would be left like a flagpole on a mountaintop or like a signpost on a hill (v. 17). The picture drawn by the prophet is one of utter isolation and loneliness. The situation described here corresponds to the events of 701 b.c., when Jerusalem was the only Judean city to escape destruction at the hands of the Assyrians (cf. 1:7–9).

(3) The Patience and Mercy of God (30:18–26)

18 Therefore the LORD waits to be gracious to you;
    therefore he exalts himself to show mercy to you.
For the LORD is a God of justice;
    blessed are all those who wait for him.
19 Yea, O people in Zion who dwell at Jerusalem; you shall weep no more. He will surely be gracious to you at the sound of your cry; when he hears it, he will answer you. 20 And though the Lord give you the bread of adversity and the water of affliction, yet your Teacher will not hide himself any more, but your eyes shall see your Teacher. 21 And your ears shall hear a word behind you, saying, "This is the way, walk in it," when you turn to the right or when you turn to the left. 22 Then you will defile your silver-covered graven images and your gold-plated molten images. You will scatter them as unclean things; you will say to them, "Begone!"
23 And he will give rain for the seed with which you sow the ground, and grain, the produce of the ground, which will be rich and

plenteous. In that day your cattle will graze in large pastures; 24 and the oxen and the asses that till the ground will eat salted provender, which has been winnowed with shovel and fork. 25 And upon every lofty mountain and every high hill there will be brooks running with water, in the day of the great slaughter, when the towers fall. 26 Moreover the light of the moon will be as the light of the sun, and the light of the sun will be sevenfold, as the light of seven days, in the day when the LORD binds up the hurt of his people, and heals the wounds inflicted by his blow.

This passage is generally regarded as an inspired addition to the book of Isaiah, made either in the exilic or postexilic period. It was written to inspire hope in the hearts of the people of Jerusalem at a time when they were experiencing great adversity (cf. vv. 19–20).

The delay in the deliverance of the people did not indicate a reluctance on the part of God to bless them. On the contrary, he *waits to be gracious* to them; let them also *wait* for him, and his blessing would return to them (v. 18). The verb translated "he exalts himself" may also be rendered "he desires, or yearns," as in Arabic; hence the translation of the NEB: "yet he yearns to have pity on you."

The people of Zion are comforted with the assurance that their weeping will soon end, for the Lord will hear the sound of their tortured cry and be gracious to them (v. 19). For a brief time it has been necessary for him to give them *the bread of adversity and the water of affliction* (v. 20; cf. 1 Kings 22:27), but the situation will soon be remedied.

Scholarly opinion is sharply divided with regard to the correct translation and interpretation of the latter part of v. 20. The question is whether it refers to Israel's *Teacher,* i.e., God, or to her teachers, i.e., the prophets. The Masoretic Text has a plural subject (teachers) followed by a singular verb (hides himself). The Dead Sea Scroll of Isaiah, however, has both a plural subject and a plural verb. Since it is said that the Israelites will see their teachers (plural) with their own eyes—a statement hardly applicable to God (cf. Ex. 33:20;

Isa. 6:5; John 1:18)—the probability is that this refers not to an appearance of God but to the renewal of prophecy. Israel's prophets, now in hiding because of persecution, will soon reappear; and when this takes place, the famine of the prophetic word will come to an end. Whenever the people go astray, either to the right or to the left, they will hear a voice behind them, saying, *This is the way, walk in it* (v. 21). As a result of the prophetic guidance given to them, they will defile their graven images and cast them away as things to be loathed (v. 22).

The restoration of Zion will be accompanied by a transformation in the realm of nature (vv. 23–26). God will bless his people with plenteous rainfall and abundant harvests (v. 23), so that even the work animals will be fed with salted silage and winnowed grain, a diet usually reserved for animals being fattened for slaughter (v. 24). Even the normally dry mountains and hills will be watered by flowing brooks, making them as fertile as the plains and valleys (v. 25). The reference to *the day of the great slaughter, when the towers fall* should perhaps be interpreted in an eschatological sense as referring to the final judgment of all of the enemies of the Lord's people. The day of slaughter for the Gentiles will be a day of healing for Israel (v. 26). On that day the brightness of the sun and moon will be enhanced, so that the light of one day will be equal to seven.

(4) Divine Judgment on Assyria (30: 27–33)

27 Behold, the name of the LORD comes from far,
   burning with his anger, and in thick rising smoke;
   his lips are full of indignation,
   and his tongue is like a devouring fire;
28 his breath is like an overflowing stream
   that reaches up to the neck;
   to sift the nations with the sieve of destruction,
   and to place on the jaws of the peoples
   a bridle that leads astray.
29 You shall have a song as in the night

when a holy feast is kept; and gladness of
heart, as when one sets out to the sound of
the flute to go to the mountain of the LORD,
to the Rock of Israel. ³⁰ And the LORD will
cause his majestic voice to be heard and the
descending blow of his arm to be seen, in
furious anger and a flame of devouring fire,
with a cloudburst and tempest and hailstones.
³¹ The Assyrians will be terror-stricken at the
voice of the LORD, when he smites with his
rod. ³² And every stroke of the staff of punishment which the LORD lays upon them will be
to the sound of timbrels and lyres; battling
with brandished arm he will fight with them.
³³ For a burning place has long been prepared;
yea, for the king it is made ready, its pyre
made deep and wide, with fire and wood in
abundance; the breath of the LORD, like a
stream of brimstone, kindles it.

Scott is of the opinion that the passage
as it now stands represents the collation of
two originally independent compositions.
The first (vv. 27–28,30–32a,33) was an
oracle of judgment against Assyria; the
second (vv. 25de,29,32b) was a song to be
sung by the people of Judah in celebration
of their deliverance. Scott advances the
theory that at an early stage in the transmission of the text, vv. 25de,29,32b were
written in the margin of a manuscript and
were subsequently copied mechanically in
sequence with the verses opposite which
they were written. If this theory could be
verified, it would greatly simplify the interpretation of this difficult passage.

Yahweh's coming to judge Assyria takes
the form of a storm theophany (cf. vv. 27–
28,30–32a,33), of which there are many
examples in the Old Testament (cf. Judg.
5:4–5,20–21; Psalm 18:7–15; Hab. 3:3–
15). The name of Yahweh (v. 27) is a cir-
cumlocution for Yahweh himself (cf. Deut.
12:5,11; 1 Chron. 29:16; Psalm 8:1); it
represents both his presence and his power,
as he draws near to man in his "real yet
never fully revealed nature." The name of
Yahweh is said to have come *from afar*,
perhaps to be understood as a reference to
Mount Sinai (cf. Deut. 33:2). He comes
burning with anger against the nations, and
his anger issues from his lips, his tongue,
and his breath (vv. 27–28).

The following verses, as they now stand,

(29–33) describe the slaughter of the
Assyrians as if it were taking place at
Jerusalem during the actual celebration of
a religious festival, which some identify as
Passover and others as Tabernacles. As the
Lord smites the terror-stricken Assyrians,
the force of his fury is matched only by
the joyful exuberance of his people. It is
slaughter set to music, for every stroke of
his rod falls to the rhythm of the tambou-
rines and the harps (v. 32).

Verse 33 mentions a sacrificial altar, i.e.,
a burning place, prepared by the Lord.
The word translated "a burning place"
(*Topheth*, a hearth), appears elsewhere as
the name of a place just outside Jerusalem
in the Valley of Hinnom, where sacrifices
were commonly made to Molech (cf. 2
Kings 23:10; Jer. 7:31–32). Molech, the
name of a pagan deity, is but a derisive
way of writing the Hebrew word for king,
melek. By means of this rather ingenious
play on words, the prophet is stating that
the sacrifice to be made upon Yahweh's
Topheth will not be offered to Molech;
instead the great *melek* himself, i.e., the
king of Assyria, will be the sacrificial
victim. The breath of the Lord, like a
stream of brimstone, will come forth and
ignite his funeral pyre.[101]

(5) Misplaced Trust (31:1–3)

¹ Woe to those who go down to Egypt for
      help
    and rely on horses,
  who trust in chariots because they are many
    and in horsemen because they are very
      strong,
  but do not look to the Holy One of Israel
    or consult the LORD!
² And yet he is wise and brings disaster,
    he does not call back his words,
  but will arise against the house of the evil-
      doers,
    and against the helpers of those who work
      iniquity.
³ The Egyptians are men, and not God;
    and their horses are flesh, and not spirit.
  When the LORD stretches out his hand,

[101] There are many problems connected with this
passage, not the least of which is how to reconcile it
with 22:1–14. Many have wondered how Isaiah could
approve of Israel's jubilant rejoicing over Assyria's
defeat in one passage and condemn it in another?

the helper will stumble, and he who is
helped will fall,
and they will all perish together.

As events built up to the crisis of 701
B.C., the men of Judah increasingly looked
to Egypt for help. They were fascinated by
the size and efficiency of her army and
decided that an alliance with her offered
them their greatest hope for security.

Isaiah takes them to task for having em-
barked on this course of action without
looking to the Holy One of Israel or seeking
his counsel (cf. 30:1–2). He reminds them
that they have no monopoly on wisdom;
God also is wise (v. 2). Furthermore, his
words of judgment have already been pronounced against *the house of evildoers*
and *those who work iniquity* (Judah) and
against their *helpers* (Egypt), and it will
not be recalled (cf. 55:10–11). There will
be no way for them to escape the judgment
of the spoken word of God.

Verse 3 is one of the truly great texts of
the Old Testament. In it the prophet confronted the men of Judah with a choice.
They must choose between *men* and *God*,
between *flesh* and *spirit*. The Egyptians
and their horses of flesh represent material
power, the brute strength of men and of
war-horses. Set over against this is spiritual
power, the power that belongs exclusively
to God. To choose material rather than
spiritual power is to choose failure. When
the Lord stretches out his hand, both he
that offers help (Egypt) and he that receives help (Judah) will fall down together.
No nation or group of nations is strong
enough to resist his power.

(6) The Downfall of Assyria (31:4–9)

4 For thus the LORD said to me,
  As a lion or a young lion growls over his
    prey,
  and when a band of shepherds is called
    forth against him
  is not terrified by their shouting
    or daunted at their noise,
  so the LORD of hosts will come down
    to fight upon Mount Zion and upon its
    hill.
5 Like birds hovering, so the LORD of hosts
    will protect Jerusalem;

he will protect and deliver it,
  he will spare and rescue it.
6 Turn to him from whom you have deeply
revolted, O people of Israel. 7 For in that day
every one shall cast away his idols of silver
and his idols of gold, which your hands have
sinfully made for you.
8 "And the Assyrian shall fall by a sword, not
    of man;
  and a sword, not of man, shall devour
    him;
  and he shall flee from the sword,
    and his young men shall be put to forced
    labor.
9 His rock shall pass away in terror,
  and his officers desert the standard in
    panic,"
says the LORD, whose fire is in Zion,
  and whose furnace is in Jerusalem.

It is difficult to determine whether v. 4
was originally intended as a promise to
Jerusalem or as a threat.[102] Does it express
the Lord's determination to defend Jerusalem against the Assyrians? If so, it reverses the normal meaning of the simile of
the lion and the shepherds, for it pictures
the lion as protecting his prey and the
shepherds as seeking to destroy it!

The more natural interpretation is that
the verse is an expression of the Lord's
determination to hold Jerusalem firmly in
his grasp (perhaps through the Assyrians),
even as a lion would clutch its prey, no
matter how hard the shepherds (perhaps
to be identified as the Egyptians) might
try to frighten him away. The interpretation that the Lord will attack Zion is
supported by the fact that the rare verb
"to fight" (*tsaba'*), when followed by the
preposition *'al*, always means "to fight
against" (cf. 29:7,8; Num. 31:7; Zech.
14:12).

In v. 5 the figure changes to one of protection for Jerusalem, although some have
interpreted the metaphor of the Lord protecting (*ganan*, to surround) the city *like
birds hovering* (*'uph*, to fly) as signifying
that only a few of its inhabitants will be
snatched away to safety. The more probable interpretation is that reflected in the
translation of the NEB: "Thus the Lord of

102 Cf. Brevard S. Childs, *Isaiah and the Assyrian
Crisis*, pp. 57–59.

Hosts, like a bird hovering over its young, will be a shield to Jerusalem; he will shield her and deliver her, standing over her and delivering her." The promise of Zion's deliverance from her foes reflected in this translation is parallel to that given in 29:1–8.

Verse 6 contains the only direct summons to repentance to be found in Isaiah 1—39 (cf. 44:22; 55:7). This is in sharp contrast to the frequency with which the call occurs in other prophetic books. In giving the call, the prophet stresses the magnitude of Judah's sin in having so greviously revolted against God. One of the results of her returning to him will be the forsaking of her idols of silver and gold (v. 7; cf. 2:20; 30:22).

Verses 8–9 take up the theme of the defeat of Assyria, a familiar theme throughout Isaiah's preaching. The sword by which the Assyrians are slain is not the sword of man but the sword of the Lord. This prophecy should probably be read as a reflection of the actual events of 701 B.C., when the Assyrians were forced to withdraw from Jerusalem without having captured it (cf. 37:21–38). The latter part of v. 9 suggests that any nation that dares attack Jerusalem will perish in the Lord's fiery furnace.

4. Oracles of Admonition and Promise (32:1–20)

(1) A Kingdom of Justice (32:1–8)

1 Behold, a king will reign in righteousness,
  and princes will rule in justice.
2 Each will be like a hiding-place from the wind,
  a covert from the tempest,
  like streams of water in a dry place,
  like the shade of a great rock in a weary land.
3 Then the eyes of those who see will not be closed,
  and the ears of those who hear will hearken.
4 The mind of the rash will have good judgment,
  and the tongue of the stammerers will speak readily and distinctly.
5 The fool will no more be called noble,

  nor the knave said to be honorable.
6 For the fool speaks folly,
  and his mind plots iniquity:
  to practice ungodliness,
  to utter error concerning the LORD,
  to leave the craving of the hungry unsatisfied,
  and to deprive the thirsty of drink.
7 The knaveries of the knave are evil;
  he devises wicked devices
  to ruin the poor with lying words,
  even when the plea of the needy is right.
8 But he who is noble devises noble things,
  and by noble things he stands.

Some have suggested that the king mentioned in v. 1 is the future Messiah, but the evidence does not seem to warrant this interpretation. Scott has noted, for example, that the announcement of the joint rule of a king and his princes is without parallel in other messianic prophecies. Verse 2 indicates that the prophet is speaking not of one ruler but of many. The general theme of the passage, therefore, is that Judah's future rulers will be men of integrity.

The passage is a noble tribute to good government. It describes what life could be like if a nation's rulers were righteous men. Verse 2 employs four beautiful metaphors drawn from daily life in a desert setting in order to illustrate the way in which good rulers provide protection for their people. When the righteous bear rule, the eyes and ears of men are open to the truth (v. 3). *The rash* learn restraint; and *stammerers* learn to speak (v. 4). Finally, fools and knaves, instead of being mistaken for the wise and noble, are known for what they really are (v. 5).

Verses 6–8 are in the nature of a commentary on v. 5. They tell how *the fool* may be distinguished from one who is noble. The fool is known by the folly of his speech, by the iniquity of his thoughts, and by the ungodliness of his deeds. The most distinguishing mark of the fool, however, is his mistreatment of the poor and needy, depriving them not only of the bread and water they need (v. 6) but also of the justice they deserve (v. 7). In contrast to the fool, the one who is noble thinks noble thoughts and stands firm in his noble deeds (v. 8).

These verses are written in the style of wisdom literature, and some therefore would deny their Isaianic authorship. However, the wisdom movement originated long before the time of Isaiah, and there is considerable evidence in his prophecies to suggest that he may have come under its influence (cf. Prov. 25:1). The manner in which wisdom is wedded to justice here is eminently worthy of the great prophet.

(2) The Outpouring of God's Spirit (32: 9–20)

9 Rise up, you women who are at ease, hear
  my voice;
  you complacent daughters, give ear to my
  speech.
10 In little more than a year
  you will shudder, you complacent women;
  for the vintage will fail,
  the fruit harvest will not come.
11 Tremble, you women who are at ease,
  shudder, you complacent ones;
  strip, and make yourselves bare,
  and gird sackcloth upon your loins.
12 Beat upon your breasts for the pleasant
  fields,
  for the fruitful vine,
13 for the soil of my people
  growing up in thorns and briers;
  yea, for all the joyous houses
  in the joyful city.
14 For the palace will be forsaken,
  the populous city deserted;
  the hill and the watchtower
  will become dens for ever,
  a joy of wild asses,
  a pasture of flocks;
15 until the Spirit is poured upon us from on
  high,
  and the wilderness becomes a fruitful
  field,
  and the fruitful field is deemed a forest.
16 Then justice will dwell in the wilderness,
  and the righteousness abide in the fruitful
  field.
17 And the effect of righteousness will be peace,
  and the result of righteousness, quietness
  and trust for ever.
18 My people will abide in a peaceful habitation,
  in secure dwellings, and in quiet resting
  places.
19 And the forest will utterly go down,
  and the city will be utterly laid low.

20 Happy are you who sow beside all waters,
  who let the feet of the ox and the ass
  range free.

The RSV presents this passage as one continuous piece, although it consists of two oracles dealing with contrasting themes. The first (vv. 9–14; cf. 3:16—4:1) is a condemnation of the women of Jerusalem for their frivolity and complacency in the face of the imminent destruction of the city and its adjacent farmlands. Since the prediction is made that the destruction will take place shortly, i.e., in *little more than a year* (v. 10), the oracle should probably be dated during the cirsis of 705–701 B.C., contrary to the opinion of those who would place it earlier. The later date would more adequately explain its present position in the book of Isaiah. It is altogether possible, as some have proposed, that the prophet spoke this message at a vintage festival, which would have given added weight to his words of warning.

The second oracle (vv. 15–20) describes the reversal of the judgments predicted in vv. 9–14. Verse 19 seems to be out of its original order and should perhaps be read after v. 14, since both speak of the destruction of the city. The remaining verses speak in superlative terms of the transformation that will take place in the world when the Spirit of the Lord is poured out on his people (v. 15; cf. 44:3; Joel 2:28–29; Zech. 12:10; Acts 2:1–21). The outpouring of the Spirit will result in the increased fertility of the earth (v. 15), and in the establishment of justice and righteousness throughout the world (v. 16; cf. 61:11; Psalm 85:10–12). The widespread practice of righteousness will in turn produce peace and tranquility forevermore (v. 17; cf. 30:15; 54:14). An atmosphere of security and quiet restfulness will pervade the land (v. 18; cf. 33:20). Then men will sow their crops beside all streams, not fearing the failure or drying up of any (v. 20a). It will even be safe for them to let their stock range free (v. 20b). It is on this positive note that the Assyrian cycle of prophecies comes to a close.

V. Present Distress and Future Blessedness (33:1—35:10)

The inclusion of these three chapters under one heading is not meant to suggest that they necessarily arose during the same period or were written by the same author. They have simply been grouped together for convenience of handling. The questions of date and authorship will be examined in connection with the study of individual chapters and pericopes.

1. The Tribulations and Triumph of Jerusalem (33:1–24)

This is one of the truly great chapters in the book of Isaiah. Most scholars are convinced that it belongs to the postexilic period, and that it represents a later reflection on the Assyrian invasion of 701 B.C.[103] Its use of alternating literary forms, including the woe oracle (v. 1), the lament (vv. 2–4,7–9), the prophetic response to lament (vv. 3–5,10–12), the Torah liturgy (vv. 13–16), and the salvation oracle (vv. 17–24), suggests that it was designed for use in public worship.

The themes that appear here are well-known from other passages in Isaiah. They include: the lamentable state of the Lord's people, which has resulted from their being delivered into the hands of foreign oppressors (vv. 7–9; cf. 1:7–8; 5:26–30; 8:5–8,21–22; 10:5–6; 29:1–4); the promise of the Lord's sudden appearing to redeem his chastened and repentant people and to avenge their oppressors (vv. 1,10–12; cf. 10:12–19,24–27; 29:5–8; 30:18–22,29–33); and the glories of the eschatological kingdom soon to be inaugurated (vv. 17–24; cf. 2:2–4; 4:2–6; 9:1–7; 11:1–9; 25:6–9; 27:12–13; 28:5–6; 29:17–24; 30:23–26). The new feature that is introduced here is the setting forth of the moral and spiritual requirements for those who would participate in the messianic kingdom (vv. 13–16).

---

[103] Ibid., pp. 112–117. The material presented here is based largely upon Childs' excellent treatment of this chapter.

(1) Condemnation of a Ruthless Conqueror (33:1)

1 Woe to you, destroyer,
    who yourself have not been destroyed;
you treacherous one,
    with whom none has dealt treacherously!
When you have ceased to destroy,
    you will be destroyed;
and when you have made an end of dealing treacherously,
    you will be dealt with treacherously.

This is a curse oracle pronounced against a destroyer who has *dealt treacherously* with the Lord's people. The fact that he is not identified by name supports the view that the passage was designed for liturgical use. This means that it was suitable for recital in the Temple whenever Israel was suffering oppression at the hands of foreigners. The Assyrians, of course, came to be regarded as the prototype of all subsequent oppressors.

(2) Congregational Prayer of Entreaty (33:2–4)

2 O LORD, be gracious to us; we wait for thee.
    Be our arm every morning,
    our salvation in the time of trouble.
3 At the thunderous noise peoples flee,
    at the lifting up of thyself nations are scattered;
4 and spoil is gathered as the caterpillar gathers;
    as locusts leap, men leap upon it.

A prayer is offered by those who have passed through a time of great trouble. They voice their confidence that the Lord will lift himself up and by his thunderous noise scatter their enemies, causing them to leave behind great spoil. The prayer apparently anticipates a mighty storm theophany.

(3) The Prophet's Reassuring Response (33:5–6)

5 The LORD is exalted, for he dwells on high;
    he will fill Zion with justice and righteousness;
6 and he will be the stability of your times,
    abundance of salvation, wisdom, and knowledge;
    the fear of the LORD is his treasure.

Verse 5 declares the Lord's intention to establish Zion as a city of justice and righteousness (cf. 1:24–27). When this occurs, the Lord himself will become the mainstay of his people, giving them an abundance of wisdom, salvation, and knowledge. They in turn will regard their fear of him, i.e., their religion, as their true riches. Although the text of v. 6 is exceedingly difficult, this interpretation seems to approximate its meaning.

(4) A Lament over the Distressed Land (33:–7–9)

7 Behold the valiant ones cry without;
   the envoys of peace weep bitterly.
8 The highways lie waste,
   the wayfaring man ceases.
   Covenants are broken,
   witnesses are despised,
   there is no regard for man.
9 The land mourns and languishes;
   Lebanon is confounded and withers away;
   Sharon is like a desert;
   and Bashan and Carmel shake off their leaves.

Once again the people take up their lament, this time with an even greater sense of urgency. The text of v. 7 is hopelessly obscure. The Dead Sea Scroll divides the words differently, but even it is unintelligible. Scholars have, therefore, proposed a very slight modification in the text, on the basis of which the verse may be translated, "Behold, the men of Ariel (cf. 29:1) cry without; the messengers of Salem weep bitterly." Both Ariel and Salem are alternate names for Jerusalem.

The situation as described here is indeed lamentable. There has been a complete breakdown of law and order and of respect for the rights of others (v. 8; cf. Judg. 5:6–7). Even nature itself is pictured as weeping over the physical and spiritual desolation that envelopes the land (v. 9; cf. 24:4–7; Hos. 4:1–3).

(5) The Impending Doom of the Oppressors (33:10–12)

10 "Now I will arise," says the Lord,
   "now I will lift myself up;

now I will be exalted.
11 You conceive chaff, you bring forth stubble;
   your breath is a fire that will consume you.
12 And the peoples will be as if burned to lime,
   like thorns cut down, that are burned in the fire."

The Lord responds to the people's request that he lift himself up (33:3) by saying, "Now I will lift myself up" (v. 10), the Hebrew verb being the same in both instances. Verse 11 is addressed to the enemies of Israel, who by their actions bring about their own destruction. They will be so completely destroyed by fire that only lime will remain (cf. Amos 2:1).

(6) Who May Dwell with God? (33:13–16)

13 Hear, you who are far off, what I have done;
   and you who are near, acknowledge my might.
14 The sinners in Zion are afraid;
   trembling has seized the godless:
   "Who among us can dwell with the devouring fire?
   Who among us can dwell with everlasting burnings?"
15 He who walks righteously and speaks uprightly,
   who despises the gain of oppressions,
   who shakes his hands, lest they hold a bribe,
   who stops his ears from hearing of bloodshed
   and shuts his eyes from looking upon evil,
16 he will dwell on the heights;
   his place of defense will be the fortresses of rocks;
   his bread will be given him, his water will be sure.

God's coming in judgment affects both those who are far off, i.e., the Gentiles, and those who are near, i.e., the godless among his own people (v. 13). The latter cry out in terror, "Who among us can dwell with the devouring fire? Who among us can dwell with everlasting burnings?" The form in which this question and the answer to it are cast is known as the "Torah liturgy," of which there are several examples in the Old Testament (cf. Psalms 15; 24; Mic.

6:6–8). Each of these liturgies asks what
are God's demands upon those who would
serve him, and then responds by giving a
summary list of these demands (cf. v. 15).
The liturgies frequently end with a promise
of well-being to those who satisfy God's
demands (v. 16; cf. Psalms 15:5; 24:5).

(3) The King in His Beauty (33:17–24)

17 Your eyes will see the king in his beauty;
      they will behold a land that stretches
      afar.
18 Your mind will muse on the terror:
      "Where is he who counted, where is he
         who weighed the tribute?
      Where is he who counted the towers?"
19 You will see no more the insolent people,
      the people of an obscure speech which
         you cannot comprehend,
      stammering in a tongue which you can-
         not understand.
20 Look upon Zion, the city of our appointed
         feasts!
      Your eyes will see Jerusalem,
      a quiet habitation, an immovable tent,
      whose stakes will never be plucked up,
      nor will any of its cords be broken.
21 But there the LORD in majesty will be for
      us
      a place of broad rivers and streams,
      where no galley with oars can go,
      nor stately ship can pass.
22 For the LORD is our judge, the LORD is our
         ruler,
      the LORD is our king; he will save us.
23 Your tackle hangs loose;
      it cannot hold the mast firm in its place,
      or keep the sail spread out.
      Then prey and spoil in abundance will be
         divided;
      even the lame will take the prey.
24 And no inhabitant will say, "I am sick";
      the people who dwell there will be for-
         given their iniquity.

Note the prominence in this oracle of the
verbs see, look, and behold (vv. 17,19,20).
When the eschatological age is ushered in,
men will gaze in wide-eyed wonder at the
glorious scene that surrounds them. They
will see the beauty and majesty of the
Lord their king, the grandeur of a land
that stretches afar, and the glories of the
New Jerusalem set in its midst. They will
muse on the absence of the former tax collectors who counted and weighed Israel's
tribute and the enemy spies who counted

her defense towers while secretly planning
to lay seige to her cities. No longer will the
streets of Jerusalem ring with the strange
sound of foreign speech. Instead, the city
will be transformed into an inviolable and
immovable habitation of the righteous. Its
broad rivers and streams will be closed to
galleys with oars and stately ships, perhaps
to be interpreted as ships of war. Verse 23
apparently refers to the immobilizing of all
ships of war, a symbol of the total inca-
pacitation of Zion's enemies. The final verse
describes the happy lot of those who dwell
in Zion, whose sickness is healed and
whose sins are forgiven.

2. The Judgment of the Nations (34:1–17)

It is probable that chapters 34—35 belong with chapters 40—66. The affinity in
vocabulary, literary form, and theological
content between the two sections is unmistakable, although it is difficult to explain
how they became separated. The most
likely explanation is that an editor made
the separation when he inserted the sup-
plementary historical material in chapters
36—39 into the Isaianic corpus. The Dead
Sea Scroll of Isaiah (IQIs^a) has three
blank lines at the end of chapter 33, suggesting that chapter 34 was formerly regarded as the beginning of a new section.
The position adopted here, therefore, is
that chapters 34 and 35 belong together
and that they are to be assigned to the
same general period as chapters 40—
66.[104] Chapter 34 describes Yahweh's intervention to judge the wicked, while chapter
35 counterbalances this with a description
of his coming to save the righteous. This
same alternation of judgment and salvation
is seen elsewhere in the book of Isaiah,
especially in chapters 24—27.

[104] See especially the commentaries on Second Isaiah
by McKenzie and Smart. See also Julian Morgenstern,
*The Message of Deutero-Isaiah in its Sequential Un-
folding* (Cincinnati: Hebrew Union College Press,
1961); Marvin Pope, "Isaiah 34 in Relation to Isaiah
35, 40—66," *Journal of Biblical Literature*, LXXI
(1952), 235–243; R. B. Y. Scott, "The Relation of
Isaiah, Chapter 35, to Deutero-Isaiah," *The American
Journal of Semitic Languages*, LII (1935–36), 178–
191.

(1) The Lord's Fury Against the Nations (34:1-4)

1 Draw near, O nations, to hear,
    and hearken, O peoples!
  Let the earth listen, and all that fills it;
    the world, and all that comes from it.
2 For the LORD is enraged against all the nations,
    and furious against all their host,
    he has doomed them, has given them over
      for slaughter.
3 Their slain shall be cast out,
    and the stench of their corpses shall rise;
    the mountains shall flow with their blood.
4 All the host of heaven shall rot away,
    and the skies roll up like a scroll.
  All their host shall fall,
    as leaves fall from the vine,
    like leaves falling from the fig tree.

The call to the witness to give ear (v. 1), the introductory statement of the case at issue (v. 2), and the pronouncing of the sentence (vv. 3-4) are indications that this section is cast in the form of a covenant lawsuit (cf. Mic. 6:1 ff.). A significant deviation from the normal structure of this form, however, is the omission of an indictment. Although the nations are to be judged, they are charged with no specific wrongdoing.

The predominant feature of the passage is its description of the Lord's fury. Enraged and furious against the nations, he condemns them and delivers them all over to be slaughtered. The bodies of the slain are not even buried, but are cast out to befoul the air with their stench. Their blood causes the mountains to dissolve and to flow like liquid.

The apocalyptic nature of the judgment is indicated by v. 4. It is not merely one of a continuing series of judgments within history, but a worldwide catastrophe marking the end of history. The skies will be rolled up like a scroll, and the stars will fall like the withered leaves of a grapevine or a fig tree.

(2) The Terrible Doom Awaiting Edom (34:5-17)

5 For my sword has drunk its fill in the heavens;
    behold, it descends for judgment upon Edom,
    upon the people I have doomed.
6 The LORD has a sword; it is sated with blood,
    it is gorged with fat,
    with the blood of lambs and goats,
    with the fat of the kidneys of rams.
  For the LORD has a sacrifice in Bozrah,
    a great slaughter in the land of Edom.
7 Wild oxen shall fall with them,
    and young steers with the mighty bulls.
  Their land shall be soaked with blood,
    and their soil made rich with fat.
8 For the LORD has a day of vengeance,
    a year of recompense for the cause of Zion.
9 And the streams of Edom shall be turned into pitch,
    and her soil into brimstone;
    her land shall become burning pitch.
10 Night and day it shall not be quenched;
    its smoke shall go up for ever.
  From generation to generation it shall lie waste;
    none shall pass through it for ever and ever.
11 But the hawk and the porcupine shall possess it,
    the owl and the raven shall dwell in it.
  He shall stretch the line of confusion over it,
    and the plummet of chaos over its nobles.
12 They shall name it No Kingdom There,
    and all its princes shall be nothing.
13 Thorns shall grow over its strongholds,
    nettles and thistles in its fortresses.
  It shall be the haunt of jackals,
    an abode for ostriches.
14 And wild beasts shall meet with hyenas,
    the satyr shall cry to his fellow;
  yea, there shall the night hag alight,
    and find for herself a resting place.
15 There shall the owl nest and lay
    and hatch and gather her young in her shadow;
  yea, there shall the kites be gathered,
    each one with her mate.
16 Seek and read from the book of the LORD:
    Not one of these shall be missing;
    none shall be without her mate.
  For the mouth of the LORD has commanded,
    and his Spirit has gathered them.
17 He has cast the lot for them,
    his hand has portioned it out to them with the line;
  they shall possess it for ever,
    from generation to generation they shall dwell in it.

Verse 5 marks the transition from a general description of world judgment to a more detailed description of how one nation, i.e., Edom, will be affected by the judgment. The feud between the Edomites, who were descendants of Esau, and the Israelites covered the entire span of biblical history (cf. 63:1–6; Gen. 25:22–34; 27:1–45; 32:3—33:17; Num. 20:14–21; Psalm 137:7; 1 Enoch 89:11–12; Jubilees 37:22–23). The cruelest blow dealt to the Israelites by the Edomites was when the latter assisted the Babylonians in destroying Jerusalem in 587 B.C. (cf. Obad. 10–14). After this "stab in the back," it was easy for the Jews to believe that even Yahweh himself must hate the Edomites (cf. Mal. 1:2–4). It is possible that the author of Isaiah 34 is thinking of Edom not merely as a historical entity but as a symbol of all nations that are hostile to God.

The gruesome description of Edom's destruction leaves little to the imagination. Her inhabitants are referred to in v. 5 as *the people I have doomed,* i.e., "the people whom I have devoted to destruction" (*cherem*) (cf. 34:2). In a bold personification of the sword of the Lord, the prophet describes it as having drunk its fill (v. 5) and as having become sated with blood and gorged with fat (v. 6). The slaughter of the Edomites is pictured under the figure of a sacrifice which the Lord offers in Bozrah, one of the principal cities of Edom. Animals also perish in the slaughter, and the soil becomes saturated with their blood and fat (v. 7).

Verse 8 speaks of that day as the Lord's *day of vengeance.* Wright has noted that the Hebrew word rendered "vengeance" has both a positive (cf. 35:4; 61:2) and a negative connotation. It refers to the action of God toward those whose cases have been tried in his court. Those found guilty experience his vengeance in the form of judgment; those found innocent experience vengeance as salvation. But in the case of Edom, it can only mean judgment.

The remainder of the chapter describes the utter desolation of the land of Edom. Its streams become pitch and its soil brimstone, and there is no quenching of its fire

(vv. 9–10). Verses 11–15 are filled with a number of terms that are obscure in meaning. The general sense of the passage, however, is clear enough. The ruins of Edom's fortresses, overgrown by thorns and thistles, become the haunt of wild birds, wild beasts, and demons. The latter include the satyr, a demon with goat-like features (cf. 13:21), and Lilith, the night hag.

The *book of the Lord* (v. 16) has been variously identified as chapter 13 of Isaiah; the book of Isaiah, the whole prophetic canon, and the book of life (cf. Psalm 139:16; Dan. 7:10; Mal. 3:16; Rev. 20:12). It has also been proposed that the reference is to a treaty solemnly entered into by Judah and Edom, an inscribed copy of which would have been preserved in the sanctuary in Jerusalem.[105] Because Edom had violated the treaty, the prophet pronounced doom upon her in language borrowed directly from the list of curses attached to the treaty. As a rhetorical device, he then invited his hearers to confirm his words by consulting the text of the treaty itself. This interpretation, if correct, would help to explain the seemingly crude and vicious language used to describe Edom's destruction.

3. The Day of Redemption for Zion (35: 1–10)

The message of redemption found here is in sharp contrast to the message of judgment in the preceding poem.

Attention has often been called to the numerous parallels between chapter 35 and those found in chapters 40—66. The themes shared in common include the transformation of the desert into a lush oasis at the appearing of God (vv. 1–2,6b–7; cf. 41:17–20; 43:19–21; 51:3; 55:12–13); the proclamation of the coming of God as a source of comfort and strength to a despairing people (vv. 3–4; cf. 40:9–

---

[105] This view was presented by D. R. Hillers in an address entitled, "The Meaning of *Seper Yhwh* in Isaiah 34:16," and delivered before The Society of Biblical Literature, meeting in New York on January 2, 1964.

11; 52:7–10); the restoration to health of the weak and the infirm (vv. 5–6a; cf. 42: 16; 61:1); the preparation in the desert of a highway for the redeemed (vv. 8–9; cf. 40:3–5; 49:8–11); and the joy of the redeemed as they return to Zion (v. 10; cf. 43:5–7; 49:12–13; 51:11). The close similarities between the two sections argue for a common background and origin.

(1) The Transformation of Man and Nature (35:1–7)

1 The wilderness and the dry land shall be glad,
    the desert shall rejoice and blossom;
  like the crocus 2 it shall blossom abundantly,
    and rejoice with joy and singing.
  The glory of Lebanon shall be given to it,
    the majesty of Carmel and Sharon.
  They shall see the glory of the LORD,
    the majesty of our God.
3 Strengthen the weak hands,
    and make firm the feeble knees.
4 Say to those who are of a fearful heart,
  "Be strong, fear not!
  Behold, your God
    will come with vengeance,
  with the recompense of God.
  He will come and save you."
5 Then the eyes of the blind shall be opened,
    and the ears of the deaf unstopped;
6 then shall the lame man leap like a hart,
    and the tongue of the dumb sing for joy.
  For waters shall break forth in the wilderness,
    and streams in the desert;
7 the burning sand shall become a pool,
    and the thirsty ground springs of water;
  the haunt of jackals shall become a swamp,
    the grass shall become reeds and rushes.

The miraculous transformation of *the desert* into a land of streams and forests is described in vv. 1–2,6a–7. Smart has noted that for Second Isaiah the desert was not just a barren waste separating the exiles from their homeland. It served primarily as a symbol of the world without God. The withdrawal of God brought stagnation and death; the return of God brought new vitality and new life.

The statement in v. 7 that *the burning sand shall become a pool* is pregnant with meaning. "Burning sand" apparently refers to a mirage. When the returning exiles cross the desert, they will not be deceived by the optical phenomenon known as a mirage; what appears to be a pool will prove to be precisely that.

The exiles are weak and despondent, and need to hear an encouraging word. The command to speak such a word is given to unspecified persons—perhaps to be identified as the prophets—in vv. 3–4. A brief statement of the message itself is also given. It could be summed up in the proclamation *Behold your God*, a proclamation that is repeated in 40:9. This is the word that the exiles need to hear more than any other. Verses 5–6a describe the physical healing that will take place preparatory to the return from exile. The blind will see, the deaf hear, the lame walk, and the tongue of the dumb sing for joy (cf. Matt. 11:5; Luke 7:22).

(2) The Highway of the Redeemed (35: 8–10)

8 And a highway shall be there,
    and it shall be called the Holy Way;
  the unclean shall not pass over it,
    and fools shall not err therein.
9 No lion shall be there,
    nor shall any ravenous beast come up on it;
  they shall not be found there,
    but the redeemed shall walk there.
10 And the ransomed of the LORD shall return,
    and come to Zion with singing;
  everlasting joy shall be upon their heads;
    they shall obtain joy and gladness,
    and sorrow and sighing shall flee away.

A highway is laid across the desert so that the exiles may return to Zion. It is called the *Holy Way*, because the unclean and fools are not permitted to enter it. It is a safe way, for no lion or ravenous beast may come up on it. Only the redeemed of the Lord may travel this way. Verse 10, which is repeated in 51:11, tells how, when the jubilant pilgrims enter Zion, sorrow and sighing shall flee away.

VI. Historical Supplement (36:1—39:8)

Except for slight modifications, these chapters are a reproduction of 2 Kings 18: 13—20:19. The most significant differences between the two versions are the deletion following 36:1 of 2 Kings 18:14–16 and the insertion following 2 Kings 20:11 of Hezekiah's prayer of entreaty in 38:9–20. An editor apparently borrowed these chapters from Kings and placed them in the book of Isaiah because they supplied additional information concerning the activities of the prophet during the crisis of 701 B.C. In this position they serve as a bridge between chapters 1—35 and 40—66.

There is considerable uncertainty about how the events described in these chapters should be interpreted. The uncertainty grows out of a number of factors, including the following: (1) The present arrangement of the material in 2 Kings 18:13 ff. makes it appear that Sennacherib renewed his attack upon Jerusalem immediately after he had reached an agreement with the representatives of Hezekiah over the terms of a peace treaty; (2) the crucial passage in 2 Kings 18:14–16 has been omitted from Isaiah, even though its contents have been verified by the Annals of Sennacherib (ANET, pp. 287–288); (3) Tirhakah is cited as the king of Ethiopia (37:9), although he did not become king until 685 B.C., at which time he was only about 25 years of age; (4) the impression is given that Sennacherib was murdered soon after his return to Ninevah (cf. 37:7, 37–38), although his death did not come until 681 B.C., some twenty years later; (5) finally, there is the ambivalent attitude on the part of Isaiah, who sometimes condemns Judah for rebelling against Assyria (cf. 1: 2–9; 28:1–22; 30:1–7; 31:1–3), while at other times he severely condemns Assyria and predicts that Jerusalem will be spared (cf. 10:24–27; 14:24–27; 30:27–33; 37: 5–7,22–35).

Various attempts have been made to deal with these difficulties. John Bright,[106] for example, has proposed the theory that Sennacherib launched two separate campaigns against Hezekiah, the first in 701 B.C. and the second in 688 B.C. Bright, therefore, suggests that the editor of Kings,

followed by Isaiah, has inadvertently telescoped the accounts of these two campaigns, thus making it appear that there was only one. He finds the record of the first campaign in 2 Kings 18:13–16 (Isa. 36:1) and in the Annals of Sennacherib. This campaign is presumed to have ended with Hezekiah's surrender to Sennacherib and with his payment of the tribute imposed upon him. Bright believes that Isaiah's attitude during this campaign is reflected in those passages in which he condemns the rebellion and counsels surrender.

According to Bright, the record of the second campaign is found in 2 Kings 18: 17—19:37 (Isa. 36:2—37:38). This was the campaign that resulted in the marvelous deliverance of Jerusalem. Isaiah's attitude changed completely during this campaign and is reflected in those passages in which he condemns the Assyrians and urges Hezekiah to have no fear of them.

Childs [107] criticizes Bright's proposal on the grounds that it attempts to gloss over the complexities of the problem and that it suffers from "basic methodological errors." He argues that 2 Kings 18—19 contains three separate literary sources, which he designates as A(18:13–16), B¹(18:17—19:9a,36–37), and B²(19:9b–35).[108] Gottwald [109] ignores the proposals made by Bright, and takes the position that there was only one campaign of Sennacherib against Jerusalem. He acknowledges, however, that the differences between the biblical and non-biblical accounts of this campaign are so complex that it is impossible to reconstruct events in detail without resorting to questionable synchronization of the accounts or to selection of the details of one account at the expense of the other. He would attribute the ambivalence on the part of Isaiah during the Assyrian crisis to "a curiously thoroughgoing dialectic" in the prophet's thought, which enabled him to announce in one breath that Judah was to

106 John Bright, *op. cit.*, pp. 282–287.

107 Brevard S. Childs, *op. cit.*, p. 93.

108 Cf. Adolphe Lods, *The Prophets and the Rise of Judaism,* tr. S. H. Hooke (London: Routledge & Kegan Paul Ltd., 1937), p. 32.

109 Norman K. Gottwald, *op. cit.*, pp. 175–196.

be brought low and in the next that Assyria had exceeded her function as the rod of God's anger against his people (cf. 10:5–15). Gottwald recognizes that the dialectic in Isaiah's thought must have been "a source of amazement and bewilderment to Hezekiah and to the Judeans."

The approach taken by Gottwald has much to commend it, for while it does not minimize the seriousness of the problems involved, it nevertheless seeks to solve them in a way that does not involve a radical reconstruction of the biblical materials. The best solution to a hermeneutical problem is not necessarily the one with the least ambiguity.

Due to the fact that these chapters are borrowed from 2 Kings, the attention given to them here will necessarily be brief. For a fuller treatment of their contents, see the commentary on Kings.

1. Sennacherib's Invasion of Judah (36: 1—37:38)

(1) Sennacherib's Message to Hezekiah (36:1–20)

¹ In the fourteenth year of King Hezekiah, Sennacherib king of Assyria came up against all the fortified cities of Judah and took them. ² And the king of Assyria sent the Rabshakeh from Lachish to King Hezekiah at Jerusalem, with a great army. And he stood by the conduit of the upper pool on the highway to the Fuller's Field. ³ And there came out to him Eliakim the son of Hilkiah, who was over the household, and Shebna the secretary, and Joah the son of Asaph, the recorder.

⁴ And the Rabshakeh said to them, "Say to Hezekiah, 'Thus says the great king, the king of Assyria: On what do you rest this confidence of yours? ⁵ Do you think that mere words are strategy and power for war? On whom do you now rely, that you have rebelled against me? ⁶ Behold, you are relying on Egypt, that broken reed of a staff, which will pierce the hand of any man who leans on it. Such is Pharaoh king of Egypt to all who rely on him. ⁷ But if you say to me, "We rely on the Lord our God," is it not he whose high places and altars Hezekiah has removed, saying to Judah and to Jerusalem, "You shall worship before this altar"? ⁸ Come now, make a wager with my master the king of Assyria: I will give you two thousand horses, if you are able on your part to set riders upon them. ⁹ How then can you

repulse a single captain among the least of my master's servants, when you rely on Egypt for chariots and for horsemen? ¹⁰ Moreover, is it without the Lord that I have come up against this land to destroy it? The Lord said to me, Go up against this land, and destroy it.' "

¹¹ Then Eliakim, Shebna, and Joah said to the Rabshakeh, "Pray, speak to your servants in Aramaic, for we understand it; do not speak to us in the language of Judah within the hearing of the people who are on the wall." ¹² But the Rabshakeh said, "Has my master sent me to speak these words to your master and to you, and not to the men sitting on the wall, who are doomed with you to eat their own dung and drink their own urine?"

¹³ Then the Rabshakeh stood and called out in a loud voice in the language of Judah: "Hear the words of the great king, the king of Assyria! ¹⁴ Thus says the king: 'Do not let Hezekiah deceive you, for he will not be able to deliver you. ¹⁵ Do not let Hezekiah make you rely on the Lord by saying, "The Lord will surely deliver us; this city will not be given into the hand of the king of Assyria." ¹⁶ Do not listen to Hezekiah; for thus says the king of Assyria: Make your peace with me and come out to me; then every one of you will eat of his own vine, and every one of his own fig tree, and every one of you will drink the water of his own cistern; ¹⁷ until I come and take you away to a land like your own land, a land of grain and wine, a land of bread and vineyards. ¹⁸ Beware lest Hezekiah mislead you by saying, "The Lord will deliver us." Has any of the gods of the nations delivered his land out of the hand of the king of Assyria? ¹⁹ Where are the gods of Hamath and Arpad? Where are the gods of Sepharvaim? Have they delivered Samaria out of my hand? ²⁰ Who among all the gods of these countries have delivered their countries out of my hand, that the Lord should deliver Jerusalem out of my hand?' "

Rabshakeh (v. 2) is not a proper name but an Assyrian title meaning "chief officer." The Rabshakeh's speech was delivered at the very spot where Isaiah had earlier encountered Ahaz (v. 2; cf. 7:3). The speech, a masterpiece of political propaganda, was designed to undermine the morale of the people and to weaken the authority of the king. The Rabshakeh taunted the Judeans for relying on Egypt (vv. 5–6,9), and challenged their claim that Yahweh their God would deliver them (vv. 7,10,18–20). When asked to speak in

Aramaic, the diplomatic language of that day, he refused to do so, choosing instead to speak in Hebrew so that even the common people might understand him (vv. 11–13). He warned them not to listen to Hezekiah (vv. 14–15). The climax of his speech came when he tried to entice them to surrender, with the promise that those who did so would receive lenient treatment and would be taken to a land not unlike their own (vv. 16–17).

(2) Hezekiah's Appeal and Isaiah's response (36:21—37:7)

21 But they were silent and answered him not a word, for the king's command was, "Do not answer him." 22 Then Eliakim the son of Hilkiah, who was over the household, and Shebna the secretary, and Joah the son of Asaph, the recorder, came to Hezekiah with their clothes rent, and told him the words of the Rabshakeh.
1 When King Hezekiah heard it, he rent his clothes, and covered himself with sackcloth, and went into the house of the LORD. 2 And he sent Eliakim, who was over the household, and Shebna the secretary, and the senior priests, clothed with sackcloth, to the prophet Isaiah the son of Amoz. 3 They said to him, "Thus says Hezekiah, 'This day is a day of distress, of rebuke, and of disgrace; children have come to the birth, and there is no strength to bring them forth. 4 It may be that the LORD your God heard the words of the Rabshakeh, whom his master the king of Assyria has sent to mock the living God, and will rebuke the words which the LORD your God has heard; therefore lift up your prayer for the remnant that is left.' "
5 When the servants of King Hezekiah came to Isaiah, 6 Isaiah said to them, "Say to your master, 'Thus says the LORD: Do not be afraid because of the words that you have heard, with which the servants of the king of Assyria have reviled me. 7 Behold, I will put a spirit in him, so that he shall hear a rumor, and return to his own land; and I will make him fall by the sword in his own land.' "

Hezekiah responded to the Rabshakeh's speech by taking upon himself the signs of mourning and by dispatching a prestigious committee of political and religious leaders to implore the prophet Isaiah to intercede on behalf of the beleaguered city (vv. 1–4). The committee prefaced its request for prayer with a type of proverbial statement

illustrating their desperate need for divine help (v. 3). Their expectation that Yahweh might intervene on their behalf was based on the blasphemous words of the Rabshakeh, whom they accused of having been sent "to mock the living God" (v. 4).

Isaiah's response to Hezekiah's appeal was prompt and straightforward. The messengers were told to advise Hezekiah not to fear the words of the Rabshakeh, for the Assyrian king would soon hear a rumor, return to his own land, and there fall by the sword (vv. 5–7). The record of the fulfillment of this prophecy is found in 37: 37–38.

(3) A Second Message from Sennacherib (37:8–13)

8 The Rabshakeh returned, and found the king of Assyria fighting against Libnah; for he had heard that the king had left Lachish. 9 Now the king heard concerning Tirhakah king of Ethiopia, "He has set out to fight against you." And when he heard it, he sent messengers to Hezekiah, saying, 10 "Thus shall you speak to Hezekiah king of Judah: 'Do not let your God on whom you rely deceive you by promising that Jerusalem will not be given into the hand of the king of Assyria. 11 Behold, you have heard what the kings of Assyria have done to all the lands, destroying them utterly. And shall you be delivered? 12 Have the gods of the nations delivered them, the nations which my fathers destroyed, Gozan, Haran, Rezeph, and the people of Eden who were in Telassar? 13 Where is the king of Hamath, the king of Arpad, the king of the city of Sepharvaim, the king of Hena, or the king of Ivvah?' "

When the Rabshakeh returned to Lachish, he learned that Sennacherib had departed to lay siege to Libnah, a fortress-city situated some ten miles north of Lachish (v. 8). The reason given for Sennacherib's departure from Lachish is that he had been told that the king of Ethiopia (i.e., Egypt) was advancing to attack him. Therefore the impression is given that the Assyrians were on the retreat.

From his temporary headquarters at Libnah, Sennacherib sent a second group of messengers to Jerusalem. Their message to Hezekiah seems to have been delivered both orally (vv. 10–13) and in written form (v. 14). The gist of it was that Yahweh could not be trusted to fulfill his promise to protect Jerusalem. Why should he be expected to do for Hezekiah what the gods of other kings had been unable to do for them?

(4) Hezekiah's Prayer and Isaiah's Prophecy (37:14–35)

14 Hezekiah received the letter from the hand of the messengers, and read it; and Hezekiah went up to the house of the LORD, and spread it before the LORD. 15 And Hezekiah prayed to the LORD: 16 "O LORD of hosts, God of Israel, who art enthroned above the cherubim, thou art the God, thou alone, of all the kingdoms of the earth; thou hast made heaven and earth. 17 Incline thy ear, O LORD, and hear; open thy eyes, O LORD, and see; and hear all the words of Sennacherib, which he has sent to mock the living God. 18 Of a truth, O LORD, the kings of Assyria have laid waste all the nations and their lands, 19 and have cast their gods into the fire; for they were no gods, but the work of men's hands, wood and stone; therefore they were destroyed. 20 So now, O LORD our God, save us from his hand, that all the kingdoms of the earth may know that thou alone art the LORD."

21 Then Isaiah the son of Amoz sent to Hezekiah, saying, "Thus says the LORD, the God of Israel: Because you have prayed to me concerning Sennacherib king of Assyria, 22 this is the word that the LORD has spoken concerning him:

'She despises you, she scorns you—
    the virgin daughter of Zion;
she wags her head behind you—
    the daughter of Jerusalem.
23 'Whom have you mocked and reviled?
    Against whom have you raised your voice
and haughtily lifted your eyes?
    Against the Holy One of Israel!
24 By your servants you have mocked the Lord,
    and you have said, With my many chariots
I have gone up the heights of the mountains,
    to the far recesses of Lebanon;
I felled its tallest cedars,
    its choicest cypresses;
I came to its remotest height,
    its densest forest.
25 I dug wells
    and drank waters,
and I dried up with the sole of my foot
    all the streams of Egypt.
26 'Have you not heard
    that I determined it long ago?
I planned from days of old

what now I bring to pass,
that you should make fortified cities
    crash into heaps of ruins,
27 while their inhabitants, shorn of strength,
    are dismayed and confounded,
and have become like plants of the field
    and like tender grass,
like grass on the housetops,
    blighted before it is grown.
28 'I know your sitting down
    and your going out and coming in,
    and your raging against me.
29 Because you have raged against me
    and your arrogance has come to my ears,
I will put my hook in your nose
    and my bit in your mouth,
and I will turn you back on the way
    by which you came.'

30 "And this shall be the sign for you: this year eat what grows of itself, and in the second year what springs of the same; then in the third year sow and reap, and plant vineyards, and eat their fruit. 31 And the surviving remnant of the house of Judah shall again take root downward, and bear fruit upward; 32 for out of Jerusalem shall go forth a remnant, and out of Mount Zion a band of survivors. The zeal of the LORD of hosts will accomplish this.

33 "Therefore thus says the LORD concerning the king of Assyria: He shall not come into this city, or shoot an arrow there, or come before it with a shield, or cast up a siege mound against it. 34 By the way that he came, by the same he shall return, and he shall not come into this city, says the LORD. 35 For I will defend this city to save it, for my own sake and for the sake of my servant David."

In this instance Hezekiah went directly to God in prayer, without waiting to consult the prophet (vv. 14–15). Childs has noted that the basic structure of his prayer is that of the "complaint psalm," consisting of an invocation (v. 16), a complaint (vv. 17–19), and a plea (v. 20).

The answer to the king's prayer is given in vv. 21–35. The order of the verses within this section seems to have been disturbed during the period of the formation of the text. Verses 33–35 read as if they are the direct continuation of vv. 21–22a. The intervening verses contain a taunt song against Assyria (vv. 22b–29; cf. 10:5–19), and a sign oracle promising Hezekiah that agricultural conditions in Judah will return to normal within three years (vv. 30–32; cf. 7:10–14; 38:7–8,22). The sign oracle would fit very well after v. 35. The promise to Hezekiah regarding the threat of Assyria is stated first negatively, in terms of Assyria's inability to gain entrance into Jerusalem (vv. 33–34), and then positively, in terms of the Lord's firm commitment to defend the city (v. 35).

(5) The Fulfillment of Isaiah's Predictions (37:36–38)

36 And the angel of the Lord went forth, and slew a hundred and eighty-five thousand in the camp of the Assyrians; and when men arose early in the morning, behold, these were all dead bodies. 37 Then Sennacherib king of Assyria departed, and went home and dwelt at Nineveh. 38 And as he was worshiping in the house of Nisroch his god, Adrammelech and Sharezer, his sons, slew him with the sword, and escaped into the land of Ararat. And Esarhaddon his son reigned in his stead.

These verses record the fulfillment of the predictions made in v. 7 and in vv 33–35. As noted above, the death of Sennacherib did not come until 681 B.C., at which time he was slain by his own sons.

2. Hezekiah's Illness and Recovery (38:1–8)

1 In those days Hezekiah became sick and was at the point of death. And Isaiah the prophet the son of Amoz came to him, and said to him, "Thus says the Lord: Set your house in order; for you shall die, you shall not recover." 2 Then Hezekiah turned his face to the wall, and prayed to the Lord, 3 and said, "Remember now, O Lord, I beseech thee, how I have walked before thee in faithfulness and with a whole heart, and have done what is good in thy sight." And Hezekiah wept bitterly. 4 Then the word of the Lord came to Isaiah: 5 "Go and say to Hezekiah, Thus says the Lord, the God of David your father: I have heard your prayer, I have seen your tears; behold, I will add fifteen years to your life. 6 I will deliver you and this city out of the hand of the king of Assyria, and defend this city. 7 "This is the sign to you from the Lord, that the Lord will do this thing that he has promised: 8 Behold, I will make the shadow cast by the declining sun on the dial of Ahaz turn back ten steps." So the sun turned back on the dial the ten steps by which it had declined.

Some modern translations, including the NEB, place 38:21–22 between v. 6 and v.

7. This alteration is made on the basis of the parallel passage in 2 Kings 20:1–11, which makes it clear that this was where they stood originally. The editors of the book of Isaiah, apparently, have not only altered the original order of the verses but have also substantially abbreviated the account of Hezekiah's sickness and recovery, omitting many of the details given in the Kings account. One of the most glaring omissions is in v. 5, where in the longer account in 2 Kings 20:5 Hezekiah is promised that within three days he will be able to go up to the house of the Lord. The situation is further complicated by 38:22, which reads as if the omission had never been made!

It is difficult to determine the precise date of Hezekiah's sickness. According to v. 6, it came at a time when Jerusalem was being threatened by Assyria, which would suggest a date between 705 and 701 B.C. The additional evidence supplied by 39:1 suggests that it fell during the early part of this period. The envoys of Merodach-baladan visited Hezekiah soon after his recovery from sickness and for the ostensible purpose of congratulating him on his good fortune. It is generally agreed that their visit should be dated soon after 705 B.C. and that its real purpose was to enlist Hezekiah's support in a rebellion against Assyria. Hezekiah's sickness, therefore, must have occurred prior to the events related in chapters 36—37.

This passage provides a classic example of a conditional prophecy. The sick king was advised by the prophet to set his house in order, for he would not recover. However, when the king prayed to the Lord with bitter weeping, the prophecy of death was set aside and 15 years were added to his life. This may provide a key to the understanding of some of the other unfulfilled prophecies in the Old Testament (cf. 17:1–3; Jer. 18:7–10; Jonah 3:4).

The words of promise to the ailing king were accompanied by a sign (vv. 7–8). The sign involved the return of the sun's shadow ten "steps" from the point it had already reached as indicated on the "steps" constructed by Ahaz. This may have been a simple stairway where the sun's rays just happened to fall, or it may have been a stairway designed specifically to function as a sun-clock. In any event, the return of the shadow from the direction in which it was traveling was an impressive miracle. How this was done is not indicated.

3. Hezekiah's Hymn of Thanksgiving (38: 9–22)

9 A writing of Hezekiah king of Judah, after he had been sick and had recovered from his sickness:
10 I said, In the noontide of my days
      I must depart;
   I am consigned to the gates of Sheol
      for the rest of my years.
11 I said, I shall not see the LORD
      in the land of the living;
   I shall look upon man no more
      among the inhabitants of the world.
12 My dwelling is plucked up and removed
      from me
      like a shepherd's tent;
   like a weaver I have rolled up my life;
      he cuts me off from the loom;
   from day to night thou dost bring me to an
      end;
13   I cry for help until morning;
   like a lion he breaks all my bones;
      from day to night thou dost bring me to
      an end.
14 Like a swallow or a crane I clamor,
      I moan like a dove.
   My eyes are weary with looking upward.
      O Lord, I am oppressed; be thou my se-
      curity!
15 But what can I say? For he has spoken to
      me,
      and he himself has done it.
   All my sleep has fled
      because of the bitterness of my soul.
16 O Lord, by these things men live,
      and in all these is the life of my spirit.
   Oh, restore me to health and make me
      live!
17 Lo, it was for my welfare
      that I had great bitterness;
   but thou hast held back my life
      from the pit of destruction,
   for thou hast cast all my sins
      behind thy back.
18 For Sheol cannot thank thee,
      death cannot praise thee;
   those who go down to the pit cannot hope
      for thy faithfulness.

19 The living, the living, he thanks thee,
      as I do this day;
   the father makes known to the children
      thy faithfulness.
20 The LORD will save me,
      and we will sing to stringed instruments
   all the days of our life,
      at the house of the LORD.
21 Now Isaiah had said, "Let them take a cake of figs, and apply it to the boil, that he may recover." 22 Hezekiah also had said, "What is the sign that I shall go up to the house of the LORD?"

Hezekiah's hymn of thanksgiving is missing from the account in 2 Kings. Its inclusion in the book of Isaiah is perhaps related to the prediction of Hezekiah's visit to the Temple in 2 Kings 20:5,8 (cf. 38:22). There are many similar hymns in the Old Testament that were sung by worshipers as they went up to the Temple to present a thanksgiving offering and to express their gratitude to God for having delivered them out of great trouble (cf. 1 Sam. 2:1–10; Psalms 18; 30; 34; 66; 116; Jonah 2:2–9).

There are many obscurities in the text of the hymn, as a comparison of the various translations of it will reveal. It opens with the worshiper recalling the threat of his untimely death. He feared that he would go down to Sheol in the "noontide" of his days, ie., with his life only half-spent (v. 10). He thought of Sheol as a dark and foreboding place from which one could never emerge and where there would be no further opportunity to praise God (vv. 11,18; cf. Psalms 6:5; 115:17; Eccl. 9:3–6). It is in the study of passages like this that one comes to a fuller appreciation of the hope of immortality that has been brought to light through the gospel of Jesus Christ (2 Tim. 1:10).

The hymn moves from the thought of the finality of death to that of the fragility of life (v. 12). The king's life is brought to an end as easily as a shepherd's tent is taken down. God severs the thread of his life as a weaver severs the threads that link the cloth to the loom. The king views his situation as strangely anomalous, for while he cries out to God for deliverance, he is also forced to recognize that it is God who has brought him into this situation (vv. 13–15). Still he implores God to restore him to health and to let him live (v. 16).

Verses 17–20 describe the king's reflection upon his harrowing experience after it had passed and declare his strong resolve to render praise to God. He regards the healing of his sickness as evidence that God has also forgiven his sins (v. 17). He apparently believed that there was a causal relationship between sin and suffering, so that recovery from illness and forgiveness of sins were but two sides of the same experience. In order to express the fullness of divine forgiveness, he used the striking figure of God casting *all his sins behind his back.* The gifts of healing and forgiveness prompt him to resolve to spend the rest of his days praising God and telling others of his faithfulness. He has discovered that a redeemed life finds its highest meaning in praise and testimony.

4. The Embassy from Merodach-baladan (39:1–8)

¹ At that time Merodachbaladan the son of Baladan, king of Babylon, sent envoys with letters and a present to Hezekiah, for he heard that he had been sick and had recovered. ² And Hezekiah welcomed them; and he showed them his treasure house, the silver, the gold, the spices, the precious oil, his whole armory, all that was found in his storehouses. There was nothing in his house or in all his realm that Hezekiah did not show them. ³ Then Isaiah the prophet came to king Hezekiah, and said to him, "What did these men say? And whence did they come to you?" Hezekiah said, "They have come to me from a far country, from Babylon." ⁴ He said, "What have they seen in your house?" Hezekiah answered, "They have seen all that is in my house; there is nothing in my storehouses that I did not show them."

⁵ Then Isaiah said to Hezekiah, "Hear the word of the LORD of hosts: ⁶ Behold, the days are coming, when all that is in your house, and that which your fathers have stored up till this day, shall be carried to Babylon; nothing shall be left, says the LORD. ⁷ And some of your own sons, who are born to you, shall be taken away; and they shall be eunuchs in the palace of the king of Babylon." ⁸ Then said Hezekiah to Isaiah, "The word of the LORD which you have spoken is good." For he thought, "There will be peace and security in my days."

Merodach-baladan, whose name in its Mesopotamian form was *Marduk-apal-iddin,* meaning "Marduk has given a son," occupied the throne of Babylon from 721 until 710 B.C., and again for a brief period of time after 705. He was forced to vacate the throne by Sargon in 710 and by Sennacherib shortly after 705. In each instance he fled to the lower provinces of Babylonia to await another chance to harass the Assyrians.

The visit of Merodach-baladan's envoys to Hezekiah is usually dated around 704 B.C. They came under the pretext of congratulating the Judean king upon his recent recovery from sickness, although their real purpose was to draw him into an alliance against Assyria. This explains why Hezekiah was willing to show them the provisions in his storehouses and the weapons in his arsenal. His willingness to share his state secrets with a power known to be hostile toward Assyria was tantamount to rebellion.

Isaiah promptly appears and takes Hezekiah to task for his precipitate action. Nothing has happened to change the prophet's attitude toward Judah's involvement in foreign alliances (cf. 7:3–9; 30:1–5,15). There is a touch of poetic justice in his prediction that in days to come Judah will be punished by the very nation from whom she now seeks support. This prediction was fulfilled in the fall of Jerusalem to the Babylonians over a century later. It is to the prophetic oracles related to this later period that we now turn our attention.

Part Two: Chapters 40—55

The reasons for treating chapters 40–66 as a separate unit were discussed in the Introduction to this work. There it was pointed out that when the reader turns from chapter 39 to chapter 40 he covers a time span of over a century and a half. It is almost as if he had closed one book and opened another. There are profound differences in style, content, and historical background between the materials in chapters 1—39 and those in 40—66. The theory that most satisfactorily accounts for these differences is the theory of joint authorship, according to which chapters 40—66 were written not by the eighth-century Isaiah but by one or more of his disciples living in the late exilic and early postexilic period.

Chapters 40—55 are treated as a separate division within chapters 40—66 because they reflect a Babylonian setting and deal with events that transpired before 538 B.C., whereas chapters 56—66 are set in postexilic Palestine in the period after 538 B.C. Chapters 40—55 may be further divided into two sections (40—48 and 49—55) with Cyrus' conquest of Babylon in 539 B.C. serving as the approximate point of demarcation between the two.

Chapters 40—55 contain a rich variety of literary forms arranged in a pattern that is sometimes bewildering. Perhaps no other part of the Bible is as difficult to outline as this. There is no single theme that is logically and consistently developed throughout, but rather a medley of themes that appear, then disappear, only to reappear later. This has led some to compare these chapters to a symphony with its development of one motif through many variations, or to a great tapestry woven from the strands of many literary forms. If there is one form that stands out above all others, it is that of the eschatological hymn, sung in celebration of the glorious triumph of Israel's God (cf. 40:9–11; 42:10–13; 49:13; 52:9–10).

It was out of the deep gloom of the Exile when the Jews were a people without a country that these prophecies of comfort and encouragement were given. One of the titles which is frequently applied to chapters 40—66 is "the Book of Consolation." John R. Sampey preferred to call them "the heart of the Old Testament."

I. Deliverance from Babylon (40:1—48:22)

1. "Behold Your God!" (40:1–11)

(1) The Forgiveness of God (40:1–2)

¹ Comfort, comfort my people,
   says your God.

² Speak tenderly to Jerusalem,
   and cry to her
that her warfare is ended,
   that her iniquity is pardoned,
that she has received from the LORD's hand
   double for all her sins.

Many scholars regard vv. 1–11 as the record of the call and commission of the great prophet of the Exile. In vv. 1–2 he reports what he hears God saying to him, and perhaps to his fellow prophets. They are commanded to comfort God's disconsolate people. This is the only time in the Scriptures that the prophets are commanded to comfort (cf. 61:2); ordinarily they are sent not to comfort but to condemn (cf. 6:9–10; Jer. 28:8–9). Elsewhere in these chapters whenever Israel is comforted it is God himself who gives the comfort (cf. 49:13; 51:3,12; 52:9; 66:13).

The *comfort* offered to Israel is not the comfort of a cheap grace that simply glosses over the sins of the past. She is comforted rather with the assurance that her *iniquity* has been *pardoned* and that she has received from the Lord's hand double for all her sins. Her *warfare*, i.e., her term of bondage, is over, and she is free to return home. Her release from bondage would have been meaningless, however, if she had not first heard this spoken word of forgiveness.

Speak tenderly (v. 2) is the translation of a Hebrew idiom, which, if rendered literally, would read, "speak to the heart." Of its eight other occurrences in the Old Testament, four express the idea of encouragement, praise, and reassurance (cf. Gen. 50:21; 2 Sam. 19:7; 2 Chron. 30:22; 32:6); and the remaining four describe the expression of affection and tender concern of a lover for his beloved (cf. Gen. 34:3; Ruth 2:13; Hos. 2:14). Both aspects of the meaning of the idiom are combined in this passage (cf. 54:4–8).

(2) The Glory of God (40:3–5)

³ A voice cries:
"In the wilderness prepare the way of the
   LORD,
   make straight in the desert a highway for
   our God.

4 Every valley shall be lifted up,
    and every mountain and hill be made low;
the uneven ground shall become level,
    and the rough places a plain.
5 And the glory of the LORD shall be revealed,
    and all flesh shall see it together,
for the mouth of the LORD has spoken."

In these verses an unidentified speaker, acting in response to the command to give comfort to Israel, calls for the preparation in the wilderness of *a highway for our God*. The Septuagint apparently ignored the accentuation and parallelism of v. 3, with the result that it speaks of a voice "crying in the wilderness," rather than of a highway being "prepared in the wilderness" (cf. Matt. 3:3).

The *wilderness* is to be understood as encompassing far more than just the Syrian desert which separated Palestine from Babylon. Here as elsewhere in the Old Testament, the wilderness is a symbol of servitude, of discipline, and of punishment for sin (cf. Hos. 2:14). God's withdrawal from people always leaves their life barren and empty—like a wilderness. Only his return can restore its beauty and usefulness.

The command to prepare a highway is given in anticipation of a divine theophany. Upon the completion of the highway, *the glory of the Lord* will be revealed, and all flesh shall see it together (v. 3). This should perhaps be understood as the sequel to Ezekiel's earlier vision of the departure of the glory of the Lord from Jerusalem (cf. Ezek. 11:23). The new revelation of God's glory is given not just to Israel, however, but to *all flesh*, i.e., to all mankind. Already in the call experience of Second Isaiah, therefore, there is sounded the note of universality that will be heard again and again throughout his ministry (cf. 42:6–7; 45:22; 49:6).

(3) *The Word of God* (40:6–8)

6 A voice says, "Cry!"
    And I said, "What shall I cry?"
All flesh is grass,
    and all its beauty is like the flower of the field.
7 The grass withers, the flower fades,

when the breath of the LORD blows upon it;
    surely the people is grass.
8 The grass withers, the flower fades;
    but the word of our God will stand for ever.

The prophet's initial reaction to his call seems to have been one of despair. The voice that commanded him to *cry*, i.e., to proclaim or preach (cf. v. 2; 58:1; Jonah 3:2), was probably that of a heavenly messenger. The prophet's immediate response to such a compound is, *What shall I cry?* The ground and cause of his reluctance to prophesy is his pessimistic view of man. In his eyes all flesh is as transient as grass and all its steadfastness (*chesed*) like the flower of the field (cf. Hos. 6:4). These metaphors underscore his concept of the frailty and impermanence of human existence (cf. Job 14:1–2; Psalm 90: 5–6; Luke 12:28).

The heavenly messenger's response to the objections voiced by the prophet is given in v. 8. He bids him in effect to cease to be concerned about the unreliability of man and focus his attention instead upon the reliability of the word of God. Men soon pass away, like grass that withers and like flowers that fade; but *the word of God* endures forever. The permanence of the word of God, therefore, is to be the prophet's hope and the source of his strength. The word which he is to proclaim is not his own, but God's, and is even charged with power to effect its own fulfillment (cf. 55:10–11).

(4) *The Strength and Gentleness of God* (40:9–11)

9 Get you up to a high mountain,
    O Zion, herald of good tidings;
lift up your voice with strength,
    O Jerusalem, herald of good tidings,
lift it up, fear not;
say to the cities of Judah,
    "Behold your God!"
10 Behold, the Lord GOD comes with might,
    and his arm rules for him;
behold, his reward is with him,
    and his recompense before him.
11 He will feed his flock like a shepherd,
    he will gather the lambs in his arms,

he will carry them in his bosom,
and gently lead those that are with young.

As one continues through this chapter, he finds the scenes changing in kaleidoscopic fashion. In vv. 9–11 the scene shifts to Jerusalem/Zion, which is addressed as *herald of good tidings.* In chapters 40—55, emphasis is ordinarily placed upon the desolation and despair of Jerusalem. For 50 years it has lain in ruins, while its former inhabitants languish in captivity (cf. 42: 22; 49:19; 51:17–20). For this reason the city is usually represented as the recipient of comfort and as the one to whom the good news of salvation is proclaimed (cf. 40:1–2; 51:3; 52:2,7–9). Here, however, the comforted becomes the comforter, and the redeemed becomes the evangelist, as Zion proclaims good tidings to the other cities of Judah. The message entrusted to her is, of course, given in anticipation of the coming deliverance. For this reason it has been assigned to the literary category of the eschatological psalm of praise (Westermann).

An unidentified voice instructs Jerusalem (Zion) to ascend a high mountain and to announce to the other cities of Judah the glad tidings, *Behold your God!* The great Shepherd of Israel is now returning to his scattered flock. The words of the proclamation "Behold your God!" constitute the text for Second Isaiah's preaching; all the rest is commentary.

The Lord who returns to Zion is both strong and gentle. His strength is like that of a warrior-king (v. 10; cf. 42:13) and his gentleness like that of a shepherd (v. 11). These two qualities are displayed simultaneously, rather than in some alternating sequence. Furthermore, they are not to be regarded as contradictory, but complementary. The word *shepherd* is often used figuratively in the Old Testament, and in such instances may apply either to a king (cf. 2 Sam. 5:2; Psalm 78:70–71; Ezek. 34:23) or to the Lord himself (cf. Gen. 49:24; Psalms 23:1; 78:52; Jer. 31:10).

The Lord who returns to Zion brings with him his *recompense* and his *reward*

(v. 10). In this context recompense and reward should not be understood as that which the Lord distributes to others, but as that which he has earned for himself. It is his people, the gathered flock which he leads back to Jerusalem ever so gently, that constitutes his "recompense."

2. The Incomparable God (40:12–31)

(1) Creator and Lord of the Universe (40:12–26)

12 Who has measured the waters in the hollow of his hand
and marked off the heavens with a span,
enclosed the dust of the earth in a measure
and weighed the mountains in scales
and the hills in a balance?
13 Who has directed the Spirit of the LORD,
or as his counselor has instructed him?
14 Whom did he consult for his enlightenment,
and who taught him the path of justice,
and taught him knowledge,
and showed him the way of understanding?
15 Behold, the nations are like a drop from a bucket,
and are accounted as the dust on the scales;
behold, he takes up the isles like fine dust.
16 Lebanon would not suffice for fuel,
nor are its beasts enough for a burnt offering.
17 All the nations are as nothing before him,
they are accounted by him as less than nothing and emptiness.
18 To whom then will you liken God,
or what likeness compare with him?
19 The idol! a workman casts it,
and a goldsmith overlays it with gold,
and casts for it silver chains.
20 He who is impoverished chooses for an offering
wood that will not rot;
he seeks out a skilful craftsman
to set up an image that will not move.
21 Have you not known? Have you not heard?
Has it not been told you from the beginning?
Have you not understood from the foundations of the earth?
22 It is he who sits above the circle of the earth,
and its inhabitants are like grasshoppers;
who stretches out the heavens like a curtain,
and spreads them like a tent to dwell in;
23 who brings princes to nought,
and makes the rulers of the earth as nothing.
24 Scarcely are they planted, scarcely sown,

scarcely has their stem taken root in the
    earth,
when he blows upon them, and they wither,
    and the tempest carries them off like stub-
    ble.
25 To whom then will you compare me,
    that I should be like him? says the Holy
    One.
26 Lift up your eyes on high and see:
    who created these?
He who brings out their host by number,
    calling them all by name;
by the greatness of his might,
    and because he is strong in power
    not one is missing.

In order to understand these verses, one
must remember that in ancient times war
was regarded not only as a struggle between two nations but also as a test of
strength between their respective deities. A
nation's defeat, therefore, was interpreted
to mean that its gods had failed; its victory,
on the other hand, meant that its gods had
prevailed over their rivals.

Many of the Jewish exiles shared this
point of view. Accordingly, they looked
upon their defeat at the hands of Babylon
in 587 B.C. as proof that Bel and Marduk
were superior to Yahweh. Some were even
tempted during the subsequent period of
exile to abandon their former religion and
adopt that of their conquerors.

The prophet met this challenge in two
ways; first, by proclaiming the incomparable greatness of Israel's God; and second,
by heaping scorn and ridicule upon the
man-made gods of Babylon. His strong opposition to idolatry explains the argumenta-
tive style that characterizes so much of his
writing. He was addressing men who had
lost all confidence in Yahweh's ability and
willingness to help them. His task was to
convince them that Yahweh was still the
sovereign Lord of creation and history and
that they were still his chosen people.

In contrast to the frequent use of the
imperative in vv. 1–11, this section makes
wide use of the question, a favorite literary
device of this prophet. Most modern scholars agree that vv. 12–14 contain a series of
rhetorical questions, to which the only possible answer is "No one!" The point of the
prophet's argument is that Israel's incom-

parable God derives none of his power or
wisdom from men. Men are no more capable of directing his Spirit, i.e., mind (cf.
Rom. 11:34; 1 Cor. 2:16), or of instructing
him, than they are of measuring the seas
in the hollow of the hand, or of marking off
the heavens with a span.

The prophet sensed neither fear nor
fascination as he contemplated the mighty
power of Babylon. In comparison to the
majesty of his God, all the nations combined were as inconsequential as a drop
that fell from a bucket as it was being
drawn up from the well, or as the fine dust
that accumulated on scales in the market-
place. If all Lebanon were an altar, if all its
forests were cut for fuel, and if all its beasts
were slain for a burnt offering, even that
would not be a sufficient sacrifice to honor
Yahweh.

Verses 18–20 belong to a special literary
genre which apparently arose during the
Exile, and which has come to be known as
the "idol satire" (cf. 41:6–7; 44:9–20; 46:
1–7). This particular genre was designed
to demonstrate to the exiles the uniqueness
of their God and to convince them of the
absurdity of idol worship.

Verse 18 has been described as "the
culminating expression of Hebrew monotheism in the Old Testament." Its two
rhetorical questions suggest both the in-
comparability of Israel's God and the impossibility of representing him by an image
(cf. Ex. 20:2–6). The affirmation of Yahweh's uniqueness is followed by a brief
description of the process by which Babylonian idols were manufactured (vv. 19–
20; cf. 41:6–7; 44:9–20; 46:6–7). The rich
man's idol was cast of silver and gold (v.
19); the poor man's idol was carved from
a piece of wood (v. 20).

It has been suggested that the realism
and vividness with which the prophet described the process of idol-making must
have grown out of his own personal observation. The widespread manufacture of
images in Babylon must have made a profound impression on the Jewish exiles. A
similar description of idol-making has been
discovered in an ancient Babylonian New

Year Festival liturgy (ANET, pp. 331–2).

The urgent questions in v. 21 are designed to arouse the Israelites from their spiritual lethargy by reminding them of their rich religious heritage. The prophet next makes use of a series of bold anthropomorphisms to describe Yahweh's lordship over creation and history (vv. 21–24). It is *he who sits* enthroned (cf. Psalms 2:4; 9:7; 29:10) *above the circle of the earth,* i.e., at the pinnacle of the firmament that overarches the earth. From his vantage point the inhabitants of the earth appear as grasshoppers (cf. Num. 13:33). It is he who stretches out the skies in order to make a tent for himself. It is also he who *brings princes* of the earth *to nought,* even the mighty princes of Babylon. He has but to breathe upon them and they wither and blow away.

The questions of v. 18 are repeated in **v. 25,** with Yahweh as the speaker. He is identified simply as *Holy One* (*qadhosh,* without the article). *Holy* therefore, is treated almost as if it were a proper name.

Verse 26 reaffirms the power of Yahweh by pointing to his creation and control of the stars. The verb to create (*bara'*) occurs a total of twenty-one times in chapters 40—66, which is almost twice as often as it occurs in Genesis. While it does not in itself mean to create out of nothing, it, nevertheless, is used only with God as subject. It thus describes an activity which he alone can perform.

The mention of Yahweh as creator and ruler of the stars had special significance in this setting, for Babylon was the ancient home of astrology and star worship. The Babylonians not only regarded the stars as gods, but also believed that their movements governed the destinies of men. The prophet, however, strips them of their divinity, and reduces them to the rank of private in the Lord's army. He speaks as if the heavens are but a parade ground where the starry hosts are daily assembled for roll call. As the Lord calls their names, *not one is missing*—not one fails to report for duty! This orderly procession of the heavenly hosts is to the prophet irrefutable

proof of the Lord's power and might. Seen in its Babylonian setting, this is indeed a bold concept.

(2) *Sustainer of the Weary (40:27–31)*

27 Why do you say, O Jacob,
   and speak, O Israel,
"My way is hid from the LORD,
   and my right is disregarded by my God"?
28 Have you not known? Have you not heard?
   The LORD is the everlasting God,
      the Creator of the ends of the earth.
   He does not faint or grow weary,
      his understanding is unsearchable.
29 He gives power to the faint,
   and to him who has no might he increases
      strength.
30 Even youths shall faint and be weary,
   and young men shall fall exhausted;
31 but they who wait for the LORD shall renew
      their strength,
   they shall mount up with wings like eagles,
they shall run and not be weary,
   they shall walk and not faint.

The demoralizing effect of the Babylonian captivity upon the Jewish exiles is nowhere more apparent than here (cf. Psalm 137; Ezek. 18:2; 37:11–14). It afforded them little comfort to be told that Yahweh was enthroned somewhere above the firmament, or that he was the creator and ruler of the stars. What they desperately needed to know was whether he was able to help them and whether he cared to have anything more to do with them.

The long years of captivity and foreign rule have so embittered their spirits and filled them with self-pity that they accuse God of having ignored their plight (v. 27). The prophet counters their accusation with one of the sublimest confessions of faith to be found anywhere in the Scriptures (vv. 28–31). He begins by telling them that their concept of God is entirely too small; they have forgotten the true dimensions of his strength and understanding (v. 28).

The climax of the chapter comes in the declaration that God's unfailing strength is available to the faint and weary who wait for him. He not only *has* power (v. 28), but he also *gives* power (v. 29). Westermann has noted the paradox in vv. 30–31: the strong and stalwart fall exhausted; but the faint and weary receive strength to complete their journey.

The basic meaning of the verb to wait is to wind or twist. From this root come such nouns as rope and spider's web. To *wait for the Lord*, therefore, means to let him become your lifeline, your cord of escape.

The emphasis in this word is not upon waiting passively but eagerly. It is used, for example, in Psalms 56:6 and 119:95 to describe evildoers waiting in ambush to slay the righteous. It appears also in 5:4,7, where it describes the farmer's eagerness as he awaits the coming harvest. This series of pictures—the taut cord, the tense waiting in ambush, and the farmer's eager expectation—reveals the richness of the term.

To such as wait upon him, the Lord imparts new strength. They do not merely *renew their strength*, but they "exchange" (a more accurate rendering of the Heb.) their failing strength for God's unfailing strength. Thus they discover a new source of power for living. Although some have detected an anticlimax in v. 31—from flying, to running, and finally, to walking—this is, nevertheless, an accurate description of the life of faith. The man of faith may sometimes soar on eagles' wings or run without wearying, but most of the time he merely walks. And the real test of his faith comes, not when he flies or runs, but when he must plod along. It is in the monotony of everyday life that the man of faith reveals his true character.

To wait for the Lord, therefore, means to respond in faith to the proclamation of his coming (cf. vv. 9–11). Although his coming still lies in the future, the response of faith makes its benefits immediately available to the prophet's listeners. Faith is never merely the means by which victory is achieved; faith *is* the victory!

3. God Who Acts (41:1–29)

(1) The Conqueror from the East (41:1–4)

1 Listen to me in silence, O coastlands;
  let the peoples renew their strength;
 let them approach, then let them speak;
  let us together draw near for judgment.

2 Who stirred up one from the east
  whom victory meets at every step?
He gives up nations before him,
  so that he tramples kings under foot;
he makes them like dust with his sword,
  like driven stubble with his bow.
3 He pursues them and passes on safely,
  by paths his feet have not trod.
4 Who has performed and done this,
  calling the generations from the beginning?
I, the LORD, the first,
  and with the last; I am He.

In this section there is further development of the theme of God's sovereign control over history. The setting is that of a courtroom. The mighty nations, feared by Israel but regarded as inconsequential by God (cf. 40:15,23), are summoned to an encounter with the Lord of history. As they draw near, they are commanded to listen in silence and to *renew their strength*. The reference to the renewing of strength links the passage with 40:31. These words were probably spoken in derision, as if to warn the nations that they would need all the strength they could muster.

The question to be decided is stated in v. 2: *Who stirred up one from the east whom victory meets at every step?* Verses 2b–3 give a more detailed description of the irresistible march of the unnamed conqueror. The Lord repeats his initial question in v. 4, and then provides his own answer: "I, the Lord, the first, and with the last; I am He."

The passage does not identify the invincible conqueror from the east. Jewish interpreters have almost unanimously applied the passage to Abraham and his victory over the four kings (cf. Gen. 14:13–16). North has aptly observed, however, that it seems unrealistic to suppose that the nations should have been urgently summoned to debate who was responsible for calling Abraham more than a thousand years previously. Smart holds the view that the conqueror is to be identified as Israel (cf. vv. 14–16). This interpretation is based upon the rather dubious position that every reference to Cyrus in these chapters is a gloss. The most widely held view among Christian exegetes is that the conqueror is Cyrus, who is mentioned by name in 44:28 and 45:1. Few men have so profoundly influenced the course of world history as he. He became king of Anshan in 558 B.C., annexed Media in 550, seized Lydia in 546, and conquered mighty Babylon in 539. In this passage, which should perhaps be dated between 546 and 539, the astounding claim is made that this mighty conqueror has been raised up and launched on his meteoric career by Yahweh himself.

(2) *The Ridicule of Man-made Gods* (41:5–7)

5 The coastlands have seen and are afraid,
   the ends of the earth tremble;
   they have drawn near and come.
6 Every one helps his neighbor,
   and says to his brother, "Take courage!"
7 The craftsman encourages the goldsmith,
   and he who smooths with the hammer him
      who strikes the anvil,
   saying of the soldering, "It is good";
   and they fasten it with nails so that it
      cannot be moved.

This is the second of the prophet's idol satires (cf. 40:18–20; 44:9–20; 46:1–7). Verse 5 describes the panic that seizes the nations when they hear that Cyrus has been chosen as the instrument of Yahweh's purpose. They frantically set about trying to make more potent gods, in the hope that these may be able to nullify the successes of Cyrus. There is a touch of humor in the description of the workmen trying to encourage one another. The prophet knows that all their hammering and soldering is so much wasted effort, for nothing can stop Cyrus until he has conquered Babylon itself.

(3) *Reassurance for Israel* (41:8–20)

8 But you, Israel, my servant,
   Jacob, whom I have chosen,
   the offspring of Abraham, my friend;
9 you whom I took from the ends of the earth,
   and called from its farthest corners,
   saying to you, "You are my servant,
   I have chosen you and not cast you off";
10 fear not, for I am with you,
   be not dismayed, for I am your God;
   I will strengthen you, I will help you,

I will uphold you with my victorious right
      hand.
11 Behold, all who are incensed against you
   shall be put to shame and confounded;
   those who strive against you
   shall be as nothing and shall perish.
12 You shall seek those who contend with you,
   but you shall not find them;
   those who war against you
   shall be as nothing at all.
13 For I, the LORD your God,
   hold your right hand;
   it is I who say to you, "Fear not,
   I will help you."
14 Fear not, you worm Jacob,
   you men of Israel!
   I will help you, says the LORD;
   your Redeemer is the Holy One of Israel.
15 Behold, I will make of you a threshing
      sledge,
   new, sharp, and having teeth;
   you shall thresh the mountains and crush
      them,
   and you shall make the hills like chaff;
16 you shall winnow them and the wind shall
      carry them away,
   and the tempest shall scatter them.
   And you shall rejoice in the LORD;
   in the Holy One of Israel you shall glory.
17 When the poor and needy seek water,
   and there is none,
   and their tongue is parched with thirst,
   I the LORD will answer them,
   I the God of Israel will not forsake them.
18 I will open rivers on the bare heights,
   and fountains in the midst of the valleys;
   I will make the wilderness a pool of water,
   and the dry land springs of water.
19 I will put in the wilderness the cedar,
   the acacia, the myrtle, and the olive;
   I will set in the desert the cypress,
   the plane and the pine together;
20 that men may see and know,
   may consider and understand together,
   that the hand of the LORD has done this,
   the Holy One of Israel has created it.

This section consists of a series of messages designed to comfort and encourage Israel. The literary form in which it is cast is known as the oracle of salvation (cf. 43:1–7; 44:1–5; 54:4–10). These oracles were probably given in response to a lament, such as that expressed in 40:27.

The Lord addresses Israel directly in vv. 8–16. He speaks first to reassure her that her election still stands (vv. 8–10). This word needed to be spoken, for many of the Israelites supposed that the Exile signified the end of God's covenant with them.

One of the titles by which the Lord addresses his people is *my servant* (vv. 8–9). This is the first time in the book of Isaiah that the title is applied to *Israel* (cf. 42:1, 19; 43:10; 44:1,2,21,26; 45:4; 48:20; 49: 3,5,6; 50:10; 52:13; 53:11). Israel's servanthood means not only that she belongs to Yahweh and owes him her allegiance, but also that she is his trusted friend and enjoys the security of his care and protection. She has nothing to fear, therefore, for God is with her and victory is assured (v. 10).

She is further encouraged by being told that none of her enemies will prevail against her (vv. 11–16). The nations that fight against her will soon vanish and become as nothing at all (vv. 11–12). The Israelites must have understood this promise as referring primarily to Babylon.

Three times in this section Israel is told not to fear (vv. 10,13,14; cf. 43:1,5; 44:2, 8; 51:7,12; 54:4,14). Westermann has noted that such a command from God to men is given in the Old Testament either in the context of a theophany (cf. Ex. 20: 18–20; Judg. 6:23; Dan. 10:8–12; Luke 2:8–12) or in the face of an imminent threat or danger (cf. Ex. 14:13–14; Num. 21:34; Deut. 1:21; Josh. 8:1; 10:8). In Second Isaiah the occasion of the command is Israel's fear of her conquerors.

In the oracle beginning with v. 14, Israel is addressed as a *worm*. This should not be regarded as a term of abuse or of insult. It likely reflects the low estimate that Israel placed upon herself (cf. Psalm 22:6). The amazing announcement made in this oracle is that the feeble worm will be transformed into a mighty *threshing sledge* (v. 15). Such a sledge, with iron spikes driven into its runners, was dragged about over the threshing floor in order to separate the grain from the chaff (cf. Amos 1:3). Israel will *thresh the mountains* and *the hills,* and the wind will take them away (vv. 15–16). The mountains and hills may refer either to the obstacles that block God's return to his people (cf. 40:4) or to the na-

tions that are their oppressors (cf. Zech. 4:7). In either case, the end result will be the resurrection of joy and praise in Israel.

The oracle in vv. 14–16 begins and ends with a reference to the Holy One of Israel. There are eleven other occurrences of this title in chapters 40—55 (41:20; 43:3,14, 15; 45:11; 47:4; 48:17; 49:7a, 7b; 54:5; 55:5). This title emphasizes both the majesty (the *Holy One*) and the condescension (the Holy One *of Israel*) of Yahweh (cf. Hos. 11:9).

Yahweh is also designated as Israel's *Redeemer* (*go'el*). While this term never appears in chapters 1—39, it is found thirteen times in 40—66 (41:14; 43:14; 44:6,24; 47:4; 48:17; 49:7,26; 54:5,8; 59:20; 60:16; 63:16). The only other prophet who applies this title to God is Jeremiah, and he does so only once (Jer. 50:34).

"Redeemer" is a technical term borrowed from the realm of family and tribal law. A man's *go'el* was his next of kin, who in certain emergencies was expected to come to his assistance. For example, if a man was forced by poverty to sell himself into slavery, his "redeemer" was under obligation to purchase his freedom (cf. Lev. 25:47–54). The *go'el* was also expected to avenge the blood of a murdered kinsman (cf. Num. 35:16–21; Josh. 20:1–6). A particular function of the *go'el* was to marry the childless widow of his deceased brother in order to beget children who would preserve his brother's name (cf. Gen. 38:7–8; Deut. 25:5–10; Ruth 2:20; 3:12; 4:1–12).

It seems likely that Second Isaiah borrowed the concept of the Lord acting as the redeemer of his people from Exodus 6:6, especially in view of the fact that the Exodus motif is so prominent in chapters 40—55. To say that Yahweh is related to Israel as redeemer means that he is willing to act as her kinsman and to champion her cause even though she has no other helper. It also means that no price is too great for him to pay for her release from bondage (cf. 43:3–4; 54:5–8).

In vv. 17–20 the Lord speaks a further

word of consolation to the exiles, who are here referred to as *the poor and needy.* They apparently are frightened at the prospect of having to cross the inhospitable Syrian desert (cf. Ezra 8:21–23,31). The Lord promises that for their sakes he will open rivers and fountains in the desert (cf. 35:6–7), thus transforming the latter into a fertile oasis. All men will witness this mighty act, and acknowledge it to be the handiwork of Yahweh, the Holy One of Israel (v. 20).

(4) A Challenge to the Nations (41:21–29)

21 Set forth your case, says the LORD;
    bring your proofs, says the King of Jacob.
22 Let them bring them, and tell us
    what is to happen.
Tell us the former things, what they are,
    that we may consider them,
that we may know their outcome;
    or declare to us the things to come.
23 Tell us what is to come hereafter,
    that we may know that you are gods;
do good, or do harm,
    that we may be dismayed and terrified.
24 Behold, you are nothing,
    and your work is nought;
an abomination is he who chooses you.
25 I stirred up one from the north, and he has come,
    from the rising of the sun, and he shall call on my name;
he shall trample on rulers as on mortar,
    as the potter treads clay.
26 Who declared it from the beginning, that we might know,
    and beforetime, that we might say, "He is right"?
There was none who declared it, none who proclaimed,
    none who heard your words.
27 I first have declared it to Zion,
    and I give to Jerusalem a herald of good tidings.
28 But when I look there is no one;
    among these there is no counselor
who, when I ask, gives an answer.
29 Behold, they are all a delusion;
    their works are nothing;
their molten images are empty wind.

This passage is a continuation of the trial speech of 41:1–7. The gods of the nations are summoned to appear before Yahweh and to prove that they are truly divine.

They are called upon to submit to three tests. First, let them demonstrate their capacity to interpret past events so as to reveal their underlying significance (v. 22). Second, let them show their ability to make future predictions (v. 23a). Third, let them prove that they can actively intervene in history, either to do good or to do harm (v. 23b).

The challenge goes forth from Yahweh, but there is no response from the gods. Their silence proves that they are nothing, and can do nothing (v. 24; cf. v. 29). Yahweh, on the other hand, has actively intervened on behalf of his people by raising up a deliverer from the east (v. 25) and by declaring this beforehand by the mouth of his prophet (v. 26). By this action he has demonstrated that he alone is God.

4. The Servant of the Lord (42:1—43:7)

(1) The Mission of the Servant (42:1–9)

1 Behold my servant, whom I uphold,
    my chosen, in whom my soul delights;
I have put my Spirit upon him,
    he will bring forth justice to the nations.
2 He will not cry or lift up his voice,
    or make it heard in the street;
3 a bruised reed he will not break,
    and a dimly burning wick he will not quench;
he will faithfully bring forth justice.
4 He will not fail or be discouraged
    till he has established justice in the earth;
and the coastlands wait for his law.
5 Thus says God, the LORD,
    who created the heavens and stretched them out,
who spread forth the earth and what comes from it,
who gives breath to the people upon it
    and spirit to those who walk in it:
6 "I am the LORD, I have called you in righteousness,
    I have taken you by the hand and kept you;
I have given you as a covenant to the people,
    a light to the nations,
7 to open the eyes that are blind,
to bring out the prisoners from the dungeon,
    from the prison those who sit in darkness.
8 I am the LORD, that is my name;
    my glory I give to no other,
nor my praise to graven images.

⁹ Behold, the former things have come to pass,
　　and new things I now declare;
　before they spring forth
　　I tell you of them."

In his famous commentary on Isaiah, published in 1892, Bernhard Duhm isolated four poems (42:1–4; 49:1–6; 50:4–9; 52:13–53:12) from the rest of Second Isaiah and designated them as "Servant Songs." He argued that they were written not by Second Isaiah but by a later prophet who placed them among the oracles of Second Isaiah. His theory was based upon the alleged differences between the portrait of the servant within the four songs and that of the servant Israel outside the songs. Most modern scholars subscribe to Duhm's view that these four poems are unique in their presentation of the servant of the Lord, but are less inclined to agree with him that they are unrelated to their context or are to be attributed to someone other than Second Isaiah himself.

The first word *Behold* occurs also in 41:24,29. It thus serves to connect the two passages and to emphasize the contrast between the idols chosen by the nations and the servant chosen by the Lord.

Verse 1 bears many striking similarities to 41:8–10: both are direct quotations of the words of the Lord; both are concerned with the Lord's servant; both describe the *servant* as having been *chosen* by the Lord; both state that the Lord will uphold his servant. The latter point takes on added significance when it is noted that *uphold* (*tamakh*) is used by Second Isaiah in only these two instances.

The main difference between the two passages is that the servant in 41:8–10 is identified as Israel, whereas in 42:1–4 he remains anonymous. The weight of the evidence seems to indicate, however, that he is the same in both places. The prophet probably assumed that his readers would make the identification without his having to do so.

The *Spirit* of the Lord is placed upon the servant in order to equip him for his ministry. The Spirit (*ruach*) is given to certain men in the Old Testament in order that they may fulfill assigned responsibilities. Through the gift of the Spirit, for example, artisans become more proficient (cf. Ex. 31:1–5), prophets are inspired (cf. Num. 11:29; 24:2; 2 Chron. 24:20; Ezek. 11:5; Mic. 3:8), leaders are equipped for office (cf. Num. 11:17; Judg. 3:10; 6:34), kings are prepared to rule (cf. 1 Sam. 11:6; 16:13; Isa. 11:2), and the Lord's servant is prepared to minister (cf. Isa. 42:1; 61:1). In a number of Old Testament passages the hope is expressed that in the eschatological age God's Spirit will be poured out upon all his people (cf. 32:15; 44:3; Ezek. 36:26–27; Joel 2:28–29).

The mission of the servant is to *bring forth justice to the nations*. Lindblom [110] has interpreted this to mean that the servant is a conqueror-king, a type of vassal-king in the service of Yahweh the heavenly King, who by peaceful means will conquer the world and subdue the nations, bringing them into subjection to the laws and will of his Lord and Sovereign. Westermann, likewise, thinks of the servant as a royal figure, and compares the first Servant Song to the public presentation of Saul as king in 1 Samuel 9:15–17. He understands the mission of the servant as being to challenge the claim of the Gentiles' gods to divinity and to affirm the sole divinity of Yahweh. Mowinckel,[111] on the other hand, identifies the servant as the prophet, and defines his task as that of establishing "right religion" among the nations. He finds the closest parallel to the servant's call in the account of Jeremiah's call (Jer. 1:5).

According to v. 2, the servant does not *cry or lift up his voice, or make it heard in the street*. The usual interpretation placed upon these words is that the servant is not loud and condemnatory, like earlier prophets, or tyrannical and fierce, like earlier conquerors, but works peaceably and gently to accomplish his mission. However, this interpretation demands that the

110 Joh. Lindblom, *The Servant Songs in Deutero-Isaiah*, pp. 15–18.
111 S. Mowinckel, *op. cit.*, p. 190.

verb "cry out" (*tsa'aq*) be assigned a meaning unlike that which it has in other Old Testament passages. Elsewhere it is most often used of the weak crying to the strong for help. In most instances it describes the oppressed crying out to God for relief (cf. Gen. 4:10; Ex. 3:7; 14:10; Judg. 4:3; Psalm 107:6; Isa. 19:20; Lam. 2:18). In the light of this usage, therefore, it becomes clear that the prophet is describing not the manner in which the servant will accomplish his mission, but, rather, the wonderful relief that the Lord will provide for him, thus forever banishing from his lips the cry of distress. A remarkable parallel to this verse is found in 65:14, where the glorious future of the righteous is contrasted to the miserable fate of the wicked: the wicked "cry out (*tsa'aq*) for pain of heart," but the Lord's servants "sing for gladness of heart."

Verses 3–4 complete the prophet's description of the servant's mission. He will not destroy or discourage those who are striving after righteousness, however feeble they may be. Neither will he *fail or be discouraged* until he has succeeded in establishing justice in the earth.

Verses 5–9 are thought by some to be an extension of the first Servant Song, or at least an editorial response to it. Some have even been willing to accord to these verses the status of an independent Servant Song. Mowinckel thinks that they were written to aid Israel in the interpretation of vv. 1–4, so that she might recognize herself in the portrait of the servant.

God is presented in v. 5 as the one who created the earth and who gives life to those who dwell upon it (cf. Gen. 2:7; Job 34:14–15; Psalm 104:29–30; Eccl. 12:7). Second Isaiah's emphasis on the creation motif was designed to strengthen Israel's faith. If God by his power had *created the heavens* and the earth, then surely he could be trusted to sustain his people in every crisis.

Israel is described in vv. 6–7 as the servant and benefactor of the nations. God has appointed her to be "a covenant to the people" (cf. 49:8) and "a light to the nations" (cf. 49:6). *People* and *nations* are to be regarded as parallel expressions. Israel will be instrumental in bringing sight to the blind and liberty to the prisoners. Verse 8 suggests that those to whom she ministers are Gentiles who still worship and serve graven images. By means of her witness, however, they will turn from idolatry to the worship of Yahweh, thus experiencing true vision and true liberty.

Verse 8 declares God's unwillingness to share his glory and praise with graven images. He is absolutely intolerable of all rivals. One indication of his superiority over idols is his ability to make predictions, to declare *new things* before they *spring forth* (v. 9). New is one of the key words in chapters 40—66 (cf. 41:15; 42:9–10; 43:19; 48:6; 62:2; 65:17; 66:22), although it never occurs in chapters 1—39. Its meaning includes more than a simple renewal of the old and the familiar; it describes the emergence of that which was previously unknown and totally unexpected. The "new things" anticipated by the prophet included Cyrus' conquest of Babylon, Israel's release from bondage, and the inauguration of the eschatological age.

(2) A New Song of Redemption (42:10–17)

10 Sing to the LORD a new song,
    his praise from the end of the earth!
Let the sea roar and all that fills it,
    the coastlands and their inhabitants.
11 Let the desert and its cities lift up their voice,
    the villages that Kedar inhabits;
let the inhabitants of Sela sing for joy,
    let them shout from the top of the mountains.
12 Let them give glory to the LORD,
    and declare his praise in the coastlands.
13 The LORD goes forth like a mighty man,
    like a man of war he stirs up his fury;
he cries out, he shouts aloud,
    he shows himself mighty against his foes.
14 For a long time I have held my peace,
    I have kept still and restrained myself;
now I will cry out like a woman in travail,
    I will gasp and pant.

15 I will lay waste mountains and hills,
    and dry up all their herbage;
I will turn the rivers into islands,
    and dry up the pools.
16 And I will lead the blind
    in a way that they know not,
in paths that they have not known
    I will guide them.
I will turn the darkness before them into
    light,
    the rough places into level ground.
These are the things I will do,
    and I will not forsake them.
17 They shall be turned back and utterly put
    to shame,
    who trust in graven images,
who say to molten images,
    "You are our gods."

This is another of the eschatological
hymns of praise that burst upon the scene
so frequently in Second Isaiah (cf. 40:9–
11; 44:23; 45:8; 48:20–21; 49:13; 52:7–
10; 54:1–3; 55:12–13). The exiles are
called upon to sing in anticipation of their
coming deliverance from Babylon. The
close similarity between this hymn and that
which was sung at the Red Sea (cf. Ex.
15:1–18) is further proof that the liberation of the exiles was looked upon as a
second exodus. A new exodus called for a
new song (cf. Psalms 96:1; 98:1).

Because God's saving act toward his
people has as its ultimate goal the blessing
of all mankind, the call is sent out for his
praise to be proclaimed from one end of the
earth to the other. The sea is to contribute
its mighty roar as nature's part in this
miscellany of praise. Songs are to arise
from the western *coastlands,* i.e., islands,
and from the villages of the eastern *desert.*
Even the Edomites in Sela, traditionally
regarded as enemies of Israel, are encouraged to sing for joy.

Two figures are used to describe the
setting in motion of God's saving activity:
he *goes forth like a mighty man* of war to
subdue his foes (vv. 13,17; cf. Ex. 15:3;
Psalms 24:8; 46:8–9; Isa. 63:1–6; Zeph.
3:17); and he interrupts his period of
silence and self-imposed restraint to cry out
like a woman in travail (v. 14; cf. 62:1;
64:12). The use of these bold metaphors
shows that the prophet thought that a new

world was about to be born and that it
would come through divine travail.

God's intervention on behalf of his people will result in the transformation of
fertile lands into a desert (v. 15), which is
the exact opposite of the effects described
in 41:18. The *mountains* and *hills* that are
to be laid waste and the *rivers* and *pools*
that are to be dried up are obviously those
belonging to Israel's foes. In both contexts
the transformation wrought by God prepares the way for the exiles to return home.
Though they are presently blind (v. 16; cf.
vv. 18–19), God will lead them safely
along unfamiliar paths, changing the darkness into light and making the rough places
smooth (cf. 40:4; 43:2). The reason why
the prophet refers to the exiles as blind is
that they see no hope in their future, but
regard themselves as forsaken by God.

(3) Israel the Blind Servant (42:18–25)

18 Hear, you deaf;
    and look, you blind, that you may see!
19 Who is blind but my servant,
    or deaf as my messenger whom I send?
Who is blind as my dedicated one,
    or blind as the servant of the LORD?
20 He sees many things, but does not observe
    them;
    his ears are open, but he does not hear.
21 The LORD was pleased, for his righteous-
    ness' sake,
    to magnify his law and make it glorious.
22 But this is a people robbed and plundered,
    they are all of them trapped in holes
    and hidden in prisons;
they have become a prey with none to res-
    cue,
    a spoil with none to say, "Restore!"
23 Who among you will give ear to this,
    will attend and listen for the time to
    come?
24 Who gave up Jacob to the spoiler,
    and Israel to the robbers?
Was it not the LORD, against whom we
    have sinned,
    in whose ways they would not walk,
    and whose law they would not obey?
25 So he poured upon him the heat of his
    anger
    and the might of battle;
it set him on fire round about, but he did
    not understand;
    it burned him, but he did not take it to
    heart.

This passage contains more than the usual number of textual problems, thus prompting North's comment that "it reads more like a poet's notes than a finished poem." Disputed readings are found in verses 19,20,22, and 25.

Here the tone changes from one of comfort to one of censure, as the prophet upbraids the exiles for their spiritual lethargy. Westermann has proposed that the background to the passage may have been a complaint voiced by the exiles that God was deaf to their cry and blind to their predicament. The complaint is taken up by the prophet and hurled back at the people: *they* are blind and deaf, and hence unable to function as the Lord's servant and messenger (vv. 18–20; cf. 6:9–10; Deut. 29:2–4).[112] Thus, in spite of his enthusiasm for God, Second Isaiah has no illusions about the spiritual state of his people nor about the difficulties of the task facing him.

It has been God's purpose to work through his servant Israel *to magnify his law and make it glorious* (v. 21). Smart is apparently following a correct impulse when he relates this verse to v. 4 and, on the basis of the similarity between the two, defines the magnifying of God's law as the establishing of his rule over all mankind.

God's purpose has not been realized, however, for Israel has proved unfaithful and has been sent into exile. The hopelessness of her present situation is described in v. 22. The language of this verse is perhaps drawn from the psalms of community lament and not intended, therefore, to be taken literally. The evidence suggests that the actual plight of the Babylonian captives was not so serious as this.

The heart of the passage is found in the probing questions that the prophet directs to his countrymen in vv. 23–24. His questions underscore their lack of spiritual perception, for they have been unable to fathom the meaning of their recent misfortunes. The prophet, therefore, insists

[112] In v. 19 Israel is referred to as "the servant of the Lord," which is the only time this title in its full form is used in chapters 40—66.

that these have come about as a result of their disobedience rather than because of the superior strength of their foes (cf. Neh. 9:6–38; Psalm 106; Dan. 9:4–19). The prophet's use of the first person plural, *we have sinned*, shows his sense of solidarity with his people. In v. 25 he returns to the thought of the spiritual passivity of the exilic community, whom he likens to a man standing in the midst of a blazing fire, yet insensitive to its heat.

(4) Promise of Redemption (43:1–7)

1 But now thus says the Lord,
    he who created you, O Jacob,
    he who formed you, O Israel:
  "Fear not, for I have redeemed you;
    I have called you by name, you are mine.
2 When you pass through the waters I will
    be with you;
  and through the rivers, they shall not
    overwhelm you;
  when you walk through fire you shall not
    be burned,
  and the flame shall not consume you.
3 For I am the Lord your God,
    the Holy One of Israel, your Savior.
  I give Egypt as your ransom,
    Ethiopia and Seba in exchange for you.
4 Because you are precious in my eyes,
    and honored, and I love you,
  I give men in return for you,
    peoples in exchange for your life.
5 Fear not, for I am with you;
    I will bring your offspring from the east,
    and from the west I will gather you;
6 I will say to the north, Give up,
    and to the south, Do not withhold;
  bring my sons from afar
    and my daughters from the end of the
    earth,
7 every one who is called by my name,
    whom I created for my glory,
    whom I formed and made."

These verses belong to the literary category of the oracle of salvation. The words *But now* (v. 1) mark the abrupt transition that takes place between this oracle and that which precedes it, the tone changing from one of accusation to one of encouragement. The note of encouragement is accented by the repetition throughout these verses of the personal pronouns "I-you."

The Creator of the heavens and the earth (cf. 40:26; 42:5) is also Israel's

Creator (cf. vv. 15,21; 44:2,21,24). Therefore, she should have no fear, for he has
redeemed her (cf. 41:14) and taken her
for his very own (v. 1). The perfect form
of the verb speaks of her redemption as if
it has already occurred.

When Israel passes *through the waters,*
they will not overwhelm her; and when she
walks *through fire,* it will not burn her (v.
2; cf. 42:25). Fire and water represent all
the obstacles she will encounter on her
homeward journey (cf. Psalm 66:12). She
will be able to overcome these, because
God will be with her.

Savior (v. 3) is derived from a verb
meaning to be wide or spacious and hence,
in the causative stem, "to set in a wide
place, to liberate." Not once in chapters
1—39 is God called "Savior," but this title
is frequently used in chapters 40—66 (cf.
45:15,21; 49:26; 60:16; 63:8), which also
contain examples of the use of the verb
save with God as its subject (cf. 43:12;
46:4; 49:25; 63:1). The predominant idea
of the verb is that of providing deliverance
for someone in distress.

Verses 3–4 are usually interpreted to
mean that Yahweh will give the African
territories of Egypt, Ethiopia, and Seba to
Cyrus in return for the liberation of the
exiles. The Persians did not actually invade
Egypt until the reign of Cambyses (530–
522 B.C.). Smart has aptly observed that
the language used here "must not be
pressed too closely as though it were a
careful theological statement." The general
tenor of the passage is that Israel has a
Savior who will pay any price, even the
whole of Africa, to secure her freedom.

The divine statement recorded in v. 4a
inspired Westermann to write: "Here we
also have one of the most beautiful and
profound statements of what the Bible
means by 'election.' A tiny, miserable and
insignificant band of uprooted men and
women are assured that they—precisely
they—are the people to whom God has
turned in love; they, just as they are, are
dear and precious in his sight. And think
who says this—the lord of all powers and

authorities, of the whole of history and of
all creation!" [113]

Verses 5–7 speak of the return of the
Jews not only from Babylon but also from
all other places where they have been
driven (cf. 49:22). Verse 7 echoes the
words of v. 1, although they are applied
here to individual Israelites rather than to
the nation as a whole. This is an indication
of the increased significance that began to
be attached to the individual during the
exilic period.

5. Israel's Witness to Her Redeemer (43: 8–13)

8 Bring forth the people who are blind, yet
　　have eyes,
　　who are deaf, yet have ears!
9 Let all the nations gather together,
　　and let the peoples assemble.
　Who among them can declare this,
　　and show us the former things?
　Let them bring their witnesses to justify
　　them,
　　and let them hear and say, It is true.
10 "You are my witnesses," says the LORD,
　　"and my servant whom I have chosen,
　that you may know and believe me
　　and understand that I am He.
　Before me no god was formed,
　　nor shall there be any after me.
11 I, I am the LORD,
　　and besides me there is no savior.
12 I declared and saved and proclaimed,
　　when there was no strange god among
　　you;
　　and you are my witnesses," says the
　　LORD.
13 "I am God, and also henceforth I am He;
　　there is none who can deliver from my
　　hand;
　　I work and who can hinder it?"

The setting here, as in 41:1–4 and
41:21–29, is that of a courtroom. The
nations are summoned to appear before
Yahweh and to produce witnesses who
can validate the claim that their gods are
truly divine (v. 9). As in the previous
passages, the proofs of their divinity are to
be based upon their ability to disclose the
meaning and relationship of past, present,

[113] Claus Westermann, *Isaiah 40—66,* trans. by
David M. G. Stalker (Philadelphia: The Westminster
Press, 1969), p. 118.

and future events in history. Because the nations are unable to find witnesses who can testify to their gods' involvement in history, they remain silent throughout this encounter.

Yahweh also commands that a people who are *blind* and *deaf* be brought into court (v. 8). The context clearly indicates that these are the Jewish exiles (cf. 42:18–20) who, in spite of their spiritual infirmities, are summoned to serve as living witnesses to Yahweh's sole divinity and to his absolute lordship over history (vv. 10–13). One of the amazing things that emerges from this passage is that a task so momentous as this should have been entrusted to a people so unfit as Israel (cf. 2 Cor. 4:7).

McKenzie favors emending the text of verse 10*b* to read: "that they [rather than *you*] may know and believe me, and may understand that it is I." However, this proposed emendation obscures the fact that the Lord is addressing Israel, and that it is she, rather than the nations, who needs to have her eyes opened and her faith strengthened. Furthermore, it is as she is engaged in witnessing to the sole deity and lordship of Yahweh that she grows in knowledge, faith, and understanding. A universal truth is involved here, for spiritual growth always results from active service, and not from idle contemplation.

6. Redemption by Grace (43:14—44:5)

(1) The New Exodus (43:14–21)

14 Thus says the Lord,
  your Redeemer, the Holy One of Israel:
"For your sake I will send to Babylon
  and break down all the bars,
    and the shouting of the Chaldeans will
    be turned to lamentations.
15 I am the Lord, your Holy One,
  the Creator of Israel, your King."
16 Thus says the Lord,
  who makes a way in the sea,
  a path in the mighty waters,
17 who brings forth chariot and horse,
  army and warrior;
  they lie down, they cannot rise,
    they are extinguished, quenched like a
    wick:

18 "Remember not the former things,
  nor consider the things of old.
19 Behold, I am doing a new thing;
  now it springs forth, do you not perceive
    it?
I will make a way in the wilderness
  and rivers in the desert.
20 The wild beasts will honor me,
  the jackals and the ostriches;
for I give water in the wilderness,
  rivers in the desert,
to give drink to my chosen people,
21   the people whom I formed for myself
that they might declare my praise.

There are difficulties in the text of v. 14 for which no adequate explanation has yet been found. Many attempts have been made to remove the difficulties by emending the text, but none of the proposed emendations has gained wide support. In spite of Muilenburg's comment that the rendering of the RSV is "perhaps the best that can be made of a difficult text," it seems advisable to reject the emendations upon which it is based and to attempt to reproduce the Hebrew in a more literal translation. It is proposed, therefore, that the last part of the verse be read as follows: "For your sake I will send to Babylon, and I will put all of them to flight, even the Chaldeans, in their festive ships (i.e., the ships of their rejoicing)."

In spite of the textual obscurities, the general sense of the passage is quite clear: The Chaldeans will be subdued and put to flight, perhaps by Cyrus, although he is not specifically named until 44:28; they will take to flight in their festive ships, perhaps referring to the ships which they used to transport their idols along the Euphrates during the New Year Festival.

Israel's liberation from exile is presented in vv. 16–21 as a new exodus. The exodus themes that recur here include the making of a path through the sea (v. 16), the overthrow of the chariot and horse (v. 17), the opening of a highway in the wilderness (v. 19), and the providing of water in the wilderness (v. 20). The parallelism of v. 19 is greatly improved in the Dead Sea Scroll of Isaiah (1QIs[a]), which substitutes "paths" for "rivers" (cf. vv. 16,20).

The prophet admonishes Israel to forget the *former things* (v. 18), and to turn her attention instead to the *new thing* which is about to spring forth (v. 19). The former things refer to the events surrounding the first exodus; the new thing is the imminent liberation of Israel from exile and the transformation of the wilderness into a paradise. The meaning of the prophet's admonition is that the wonders of the new exodus will be such as to cause the first exodus by comparison to pale into insignificance.

The new exodus, like the first, will issue in the joyous praise of the Redeemer by the redeemed (v. 21; cf. 41:16; Ex. 15:1–18). This must not be interpreted to mean that Yahweh needed to be praised by men, and that he, therefore, created Israel to perform this function. Such an interpretation would lower him to the level of the Babylonian gods, who, according to tradition, created man in order to be served by him. In contrast to this, the prophet states that Yahweh formed Israel that she might belong to him and that she might recount his praiseworthy deeds. It is by maintaining this relationship and performing this ministry that she fully realizes the purpose of her creation.

(2) Justly Punished but Freely Forgiven (43:22–28)

22 "Yet you did not call upon me, O Jacob;
    but you have been weary of me, O Israel!
23 You have not brought me your sheep for
    burnt offerings,
    or honored me with your sacrifices.
I have not burdened you with offerings,
    or wearied you with frankincense.
24 You have not bought me sweet cane with
    money,
    or satisfied me with the fat of your sac-
    rifices.
But you have burdened me with your sins,
    you have wearied me with your iniquities.
25 "I, I am He
    who blots out your transgressions for my
    own sake,
    and I will not remember your sins.
26 Put me in remembrance, let us argue to-
    gether;
    set forth your case, that you may be
    proved right.

27 Your first father sinned,
    and your mediators transgressed against
    me.
28 Therefore I profaned the princes of the
    sanctuary,
    I delivered Jacob to utter destruction
    and Israel to reviling.

Here the prophet denounces the sins of Israel in what Westermann has described as a "trial speech," similar in form to that found in 50:1–3. The burden of the speech is that the whole sweep of Israelite history has been a failure from beginning to end (vv. 22–24,27–28; cf. Hos. 12:3–5). Seldom in the prophets does one encounter such a negative judgment on the nation's past. For a brief moment Second Isaiah sounds more like the preexilic prophets of judgment than the exilic prophet of consolation.

Westermann has suggested that the basis of the "trial speech" was a charge brought against God by Israel. Her complaint was that he had ignored the faithful service she had rendered to him through her sacrifices and had unjustly delivered her over to destruction and reviling (v. 28).

The speech opens with a denial of the efficacy of Israel's sacrifices (vv. 22–24; cf. 1:10–17; 66:3; Jer. 7:21–23; Amos 5:21–25; Mic. 6:6–8). Each new line in vv. 22–24a begins with the forceful negative *lo', not*. The verbs in this section are all perfects and are, therefore, descriptive of completed actions. The pronoun *me* is emphatic by position in v. 22 and, by implication, in vv. 23a and 24a.

There is irony in Yahweh's charge that Israel has not brought him *sheep for burnt offerings,* nor honored him with her *sacrifices* (v. 23). To interpret this simply as a reference to the suspension of sacrifices during the exilic period is to miss the point of the argument. Yahweh seems, rather, to be expressing his disappointment with Israel's worship throughout her entire history. He does not deny that she has ostensibly offered many sacrifices to him; but he does deny that he has imposed this burdensome service upon her or that the performance of it has resulted in his honor and pleasure (v. 23).

The situation was, in fact, quite the reverse. During all her previous history, Israel had never really called upon *him,* nor with her sacrifices truly honored *him.* Instead, she had grown weary of him (v. 22), had burdened him with her sins (v. 24), and had wearied him with her iniquities (v. 24).

Commenting on the second half of verse 24, Stuhlmueller has written: "Nowhere in the Old Testament is God weighted with such pitiable weariness as here. We sense the shadow of the Cross falling upon the Word of God!" [114]

The verb *burdened* (vv. 23–24) is the causative form of *abhadh* (to serve). This is the same root from which the noun *ebhedh* (servant) is derived. The causative form occurs eight times in the Old Testament, and always means to enslave, to reduce to slavery, or to cause to serve (cf. Ex. 1:13; 6:5; 2 Chron. 2:18; Jer. 17:4; Ezek. 29:18).

God has not caused Israel to serve (v. 23), but Israel has caused him to serve with her sins (v. 24). Westermann has noted that this action on the part of Israel signified a reversal of the normal relationship between God and man, for a necessary corollary to his divinity was a recognition of his lordship. One is reminded by this passage of the paradox of Christ, who was both Lord of all and servant of all (cf. Phil. 2:5–11).

Israel is appropriately referred to as Jacob (v. 22) and is reminded that he, the father of the nation, was a sinner from the beginning (v. 27). Furthermore, her mediators, identified by Smart as "the succession of prophets, priests, and kings who have stood between God and Israel through the centuries," are accused as transgressors. This means that even the best among the people have sinned.

The purpose of the prophet's devastating indictment was to prove to the exiles that they had been justly punished. Because of their burden of guilt the Lord had *profaned the princes of the sanctuary* (holy princes) and had delivered them over to destruction (the ban, *cherem*) and reviling. "Holy princes" is a more adequate rendering of the Hebrew than "princes of the sanctuary." North is probably correct in his judgment that the reference "is almost certainly to 'sacral' kings."

At the very center of Yahweh's accusation against Israel stands a gracious proclamation of divine forgiveness (v. 25; cf. 40:2). The contrast between this verse and its context is both deliberate and impressive. The truth expressed here is that Yahweh's forgiveness does not depend upon Israel's worthiness. He forgives *for my own sake,* i.e., because it is his nature to do so (cf. Psalms 23:3; 25:11; 31:3). Rignell has described these words as "truly evangelical in tone." [115]

(3) Israel Renewed by God's Spirit (44: 1–5)

1 "But now hear, O Jacob my servant,
    Israel whom I have chosen!
2 Thus says the LORD who made you,
    who formed you from the womb and will help you:
Fear not, O Jacob my servant,
    Jeshurun whom I have chosen.
3 For I will pour water on the thirsty land,
    and streams on the dry ground;
I will pour my Spirit upon your descendants,
    and my blessing on your offspring.
4 They shall spring up like grass amid waters,
    like willows by flowing streams.
5 This one will say, 'I am the LORD's,'
    another will call himself by the name of Jacob,
and another will write on his hand, 'The LORD's,'
    and surname himself by the name of Israel."

This oracle is attached to the preceding by the words, *But now.* Having previously stated that *Jacob* was a sinner from the beginning (cf. 43:27), the prophet now declares that he was also God's *chosen* servant from the beginning, having been

114 Carroll Stuhlmueller, "The Book of Isaiah, Chapters 40—66, *Old Testament Reading Guide* (Collegeville, Minnesota: The Liturgical Press, 1965), p. 47.

115 L. G. Rignell, *A Study of Isaiah Ch. 40—55* (Lund: C. W. K. Gleerup, 1956), p. 40.

formed in the womb to be the instrument of his purpose (vv. 1–2; cf. 49:1; Jer. 1:5; Gal. 1:15). God's gracious forgiveness of his past sins (cf. 43:25; 40:1; 44:22) had created for him the prospect of a glorious future.

As Jacob's name was once changed to Israel (cf. Gen. 32:27–28), so now it is changed to Jeshurun, usually interpreted to mean "the upright one" (v. 2; cf. Deut. 32:15; 33:5,26). This is a title of honor, and is perhaps intended to describe the transformed character of Israel in the eschatological age.

Israel is admonished *fear not* (v. 2), for a new era of salvation is about to dawn (vv. 3–5). Commentators are generally agreed that the *dry ground* in v. 3 refers to the exiles in their present circumstances. Soon, however, they will receive an outpouring of water and of the Spirit of God, both symbols of life-giving power. The descendants of the exiles, upon whom this blessing will come, will multiply like blades of grass in a well-watered meadow and flourish like trees beside flowing streams (v. 4; cf. 54:1–3; Psalm 1:3).

Verse 5 is the first explicit reference in Second Isaiah to the future expansion of Israel through the assimilation of proselytes from among the nations (cf. 45:14). The coming of each proselyte is described as based upon a personal decision involving a profession of faith (*I am the Lord's*) and an outward sign of commitment (the writing on the hand). Those who take the name of the Lord take also the name of Israel, which, as Westermann has observed, suggests that it is impossible to be committed to the Lord without at the same time becoming involved with his people.

7. God and the Gods (44:6–23)

(1) No God but the Lord! (44:6–8)

6 Thus says the LORD, the King of Israel
   and his Redeemer, the LORD of hosts:
"I am the first and I am the last;
   besides me there is no god.
7 Who is like me? Let him proclaim it,
   let him declare and set it forth before me.

Who has announced from of old the things
   to come?
Let them tell us what is yet to be.
8 Fear not, nor be afraid;
   have I not told you from of old and declared it?
And you are my witnesses!
Is there a God besides me?
There is no Rock; I know not any."

This brief oracle, which may have originally stood with vv. 21–22, is a forceful defense of Yahweh's claim to be the sole God of the universe. Many of the themes already encountered in Second Isaiah reappear here: (1) the presentation of Yahweh as Israel's King (v. 6; cf. 41:21; 43:15), Redeemer (v. 6; cf. 41:14; 43:14), the first and the last (v. 6; cf. 41:4; 48:12), besides whom there is no other god (vv. 6,8; cf. 43:10–11); (2) the challenge to the gods of the nations to demonstrate their claim to lordship over history (v. 7; cf. 41:22–23,26,28–29; 43:9); (3) the divine admonition to Israel to stop fearing (v. 8; cf. 41:10,13–14; 43:1,5; 44:2); (4) Yahweh's lordship over history as evidenced by the reliability of his word (v. 8; cf. 40:8, 21,28; 41:27; 42:9); and (5) Israel's responsibility to witness to the uniqueness of Yahweh (v. 8; cf. 43:10–12).

The new feature that appears in the passage is the designation of Yahweh as *Lord of hosts* (cf. 45:13; 47:4; 48:2; 51:15; 54:5) and *Rock* (cf. 17:10; 26:4; 30:29). The latter title, which was perhaps borrowed from the psalms, emphasizes the trustworthiness of Yahweh as Israel's shield and defense.

(2) The Stupidity of Idolatry (44:9–20)

9 All who make idols are nothing, and the things they delight in do not profit; their witnesses neither see nor know, that they may be put to shame. 10 Who fashions a god or casts an image, that is profitable for nothing? 11 Behold, all his fellows shall be put to shame, and the craftsmen are but men; let them all assemble, let them stand forth, they shall be terrified, they shall be put to shame together.
12 The ironsmith fashions it and works it over the coals; he shapes it with hammers, and forges it with his strong arm; he becomes hungry and his strength fails, he drinks no water

and is faint. [13] The carpenter stretches a line, he marks it out with a pencil; he fashions it with planes, and marks it with a compass; he shapes it into the figure of a man, with the beauty of a man, to dwell in a house. [14] He cuts down cedars; or he chooses a holm tree or an oak and lets it grow strong among the trees of the forest; he plants a cedar and the rain nourishes it. [15] Then it becomes fuel for a man; he takes a part of it and warms himself, he kindles a fire and bakes bread; also he makes a god and worships it, he makes it a graven image and falls down before it. [16] Half of it he burns in the fire; over the half he eats flesh, he roasts meat and is satisfied; also he warms himself and says, "Aha, I am warm, I have seen the fire!" [17] And the rest of it he makes into a god, his idol; and falls down to it and worships it; he prays to it and says, "Deliver me, for thou art my god!"
[18] They know not, nor do they discern; for he has shut their eyes, so that they cannot see, and their minds, so that they cannot understand. [19] No one considers, nor is there knowledge or discernment to say, "Half of it I burned in the fire, I also baked bread on its coals, I roasted flesh and have eaten; and shall I make the residue of it an abomination? Shall I fall down before a block of wood?" [20] He feeds on ashes; a deluded mind has led him astray, and he cannot deliver himself or say, "Is there not a lie in my right hand?"

Many commentators adopt the position that this prose satire against the manufacture and worship of idols—the only prose passage in chapters 40—55—represents the work of a later disciple of Second Isaiah. This position is open to question, however, for the passage fits naturally into the context (cf. vv. 6–8). Furthermore, it is similar to other idol satires that are generally attributed to Second Isaiah (cf. 40:19–20; 41:6–7; 42:17; 45:16–17,20; 46:1–2,5–7). The probability, therefore, is that the passage originated with him, and that it reflects his reaction to what he had observed firsthand in Babylon.

His attack upon idolatry is designed, however, not to convince Babylonians of the error of their ways, but to bolster the determination of Israelites who are being tempted to adopt these ways. This temptation must have been especially strong during the seemingly hopeless years of the Exile.

The people of God are forever faced with the same temptation. Tillich has defined idolatry as man's attempt to make an absolute out of that which is relative. It is setting something less than God in the place of God, thereby denying his claim to absolute lordship over life. At the fountainhead of biblical faith stands the divine imperative, "You shall have no other gods before me."

One of Second Isaiah's favorite words is *tohu*, meaning emptiness, nothing, or chaos (cf. 40:17,23; 41:29; 45:18,19; 49:4; 59:4). He employs it in v. 9 to express his estimation of anyone who would be foolish enough to make an idol. The *witnesses* (v. 9; cf. 44:8; 43:10,12) are the worshipers of idols, of whom it is said that they are blind and ignorant, and destined to be *put to shame* (vv. 9,11).

Babylonian idols consisted of a carved wooden core overlaid with metal. In vv. 12–17 the prophet gives a brief description of the process by which such idols were made. Commentators have noted that the description is in fact stated in reverse order: in v. 12, the ironsmith forges a covering for the idol; in v. 13, the carpenter shapes the wooden core; in v. 14a, he cuts down a tree; in v. 14b, he chooses a tree; and in v. 14c, he plants a tree!

McKenzie has observed that v. 13 seems deliberately to reverse the process of creation as it is described in Genesis 1:26–27: there God makes man in his image and likeness, but here deluded man shapes a god in his own likeness. The final statement in the verse is a further expression of the prophet's disdain for idols. They are made to dwell in houses; whereas no house would be sufficient to contain the God of Israel, whose throne is heaven and whose footstool is the earth (cf. 57:15; 66:1).

The prophet's scorn for the maker of idols reaches its climax in vv. 15–20, where he contrasts the two uses to which the carpenter puts the wood in his workshop. With part of it he kindles a fire to provide warmth and to cook his food; and with the remainder he makes a god and falls down before it—a mere block of wood!—and prays, "Deliver me, for thou art my God!" A deluded mind has thus led him astray, and he is unable to see the obvious absurdity of his actions (vv. 18–20). This entire passage has been characterized as "a masterpiece of satirical writing" (Westermann).

(3) The Redeemer of Israel (44:21–23)

21 Remember these things, O Jacob,
  and Israel, for you are my servant;
 I formed you, you are my servant;
  O Israel, you will not be forgotten by me.
22 I have swept away your transgressions like a cloud,
  and your sins like mist;
  return to me, for I have redeemed you.
23 Sing, O heavens, for the LORD has done it;
  shout, O depths of the earth;
 break forth into singng, O mountains,
  O forest, and every tree in it!
 For the LORD has redeemed Jacob,
  and will be glorified in Israel.

This section consists of words of assurance and exhortation spoken by Yahweh to his servant Israel (vv. 21–22), followed by a hymn of praise to Yahweh for his mighty act of redemption (v. 23). Some scholars believe that these verses once stood as the conclusion to the oracle in 44:6–8. The question of their original position, however, has little effect upon the interpretation.

The Septuagint and the Dead Sea Scroll (1QIs[a]) exhibit a slightly different text in the final clause of v. 21; where the Masoretic Text reads "you will not be forgotten by me," they read "do not forget me." The latter reading has much to commend it, especially when it is placed beside the two other exhortations found here—"Remember these things" (v. 21), and "return to me" (v. 22; cf. 55:7; 59:20).

Yahweh's assurance to Israel is given in five affirmations: *you are my servant* (v. 21; cf. 41:9; 43:10; 49:3); *I formed you* (v. 21; cf. 43:1,7,21; 44:2,24; 49:5); *you will not be forgotten by me* (v. 21; cf. 49:14–16); *I have swept away your transgressions* (v. 22; cf. 40:2; 43:25); *I have*

redeemed you (v. 22; cf. 43:1; 44:23; 48:20; 52:9).

Everything in the created universe—from the distant heavens to the trees near at hand—is called upon to praise Yahweh for what he has done for Israel (v. 23). Because he has forgiven her transgressions and redeemed her from bondage, a bright future awaits her. The verbs in this verse are perfects, indicating that the prophet regarded the future as though it had already come, and the victory of Israel as though it had already been achieved. It should be noted, however, that the eschatological age is described not as a time when *Israel* will be glorified, but, rather, as a time when *Yahweh* will be glorified in her.

8. Cyrus and the Salvation of the World (44:24—45:25)

(1) The Sovereign Purpose of God (44:24–28)

24 Thus says the LORD, your Redeemer,
  who formed you from the womb:
 "I am the LORD, who made all things,
  who stretched out the heavens alone,
  who spread out the earth—Who was with me?—
25 who frustrates the omens of liars,
  and makes fools of diviners;
 who turns wise men back,
  and makes their knowledge foolish;
26 who confirms the word of his servant,
  and performs the counsel of his messengers;
 who says of Jerusalem, 'It shall be inhabited,'
  and of the cities of Judah, 'They shall be built,
  and I will raise up their ruins';
27 who says to the deep, 'Be dry,
  I will dry up your rivers';
28 who says of Cyrus, 'He is my shepherd,
  and he shall fulfil all my purpose';
 saying of Jerusalem, 'She shall be built,'
  and of the temple, 'Your foundation shall be laid.' "

This passage is composed of a series of participial clauses describing the mighty acts of God leading up to the advent of Cyrus. In this respect its literary form resembles that of the hymns of praise found in the Psalter. God is praised both as

Creator (v. 24) and as Lord of history (vv. 25–28).

The new thing that is said concerning God's activity in creation is that when he stretched out the heavens and spread out the earth he was alone. This should remind us that God's mightiest works have always been those which he performed alone. He was alone not only when he created the world, but also, in a real sense, when he redeemed it through Jesus Christ.

Verse 25 suggests that the nations hastily consulted their diviners and wise men when they began to feel threatened by Cyrus. Herodotus, the Greek historian, tells how Croesus of Lydia became alarmed when Cyrus annexed Media in 550 B.C., whereupon he decided to seek counsel from the renowned oracle of Apollo at Delphi. The oracle returned an enigmatic reply, warning Croesus to be prepared to defend himself when a mule ruled over Media. Since Cyrus was the son of a Persian father and a Median mother, Croesus interpreted the words of the oracle as applying to him. He, therefore, asked the oracle a second question: Should he take the initiative by crossing the River Halys to attack Cyrus? The oracle again gave an obscure reply. "By crossing the Halys," it said, "Croesus will destroy a great empire." Interpreting this as a favorable response, Croesus proceeded to cross the Halys, only to discover to his sorrow that the empire in question was his own.[116]

While the Lord frustrates the omens of diviners and makes foolish the knowledge of wise men (v. 25), he, nevertheless, confirms the word of his servant and the counsel of his messengers (v. 26; cf. 40:8; 55:10–11). The word that is confirmed has to do with the rebuilding of Jerusalem and of the cities of Judah (v. 26b).

The climax to the passage comes in the Lord's announcement that he has designated *Cyrus* as his *shepherd* and the one through whom all his purpose is to be fulfilled (v. 28). This includes not only the rebuilding of Jerusalem and its Temple

116 Cf. F. F. Bruce, *op. cit.*, pp. 97–98.

but also the return of the exiles to their homeland and the initiation of the glorious future which the Lord has in store for them. The amazing thing is that the prophet should have expected all this to be accomplished through the instrumentality of a pagan ruler.

(2) The Commission of Cyrus (45:1–8)

1 Thus says the LORD to his anointed, to Cyrus,
   whose right hand I have grasped,
  to subdue nations before him
   and ungird the loins of kings,
  to open doors before him
   that gates may not be closed:
2 "I will go before you
   and level the mountains,
  I will break in pieces the doors of bronze
   and cut asunder the bars of iron,
3 I will give you the treasures of darkness
   and the hoards in secret places,
  that you may know that it is I, the LORD,
   the God of Israel, who call you by your name.
4 For the sake of my servant Jacob,
   and Israel my chosen,
  I call you by your name,
   I surname you, though you do not know me,
5 I am the LORD, and there is no other,
   besides me there is no God;
  I gird you, though you do not know me,
6 that men may know, from the rising of the sun
   and from the west, that there is none besides me;
  I am the LORD, and there is no other.
7 I form light and create darkness,
   I make weal and create woe,
  I am the LORD, who do all these things.
8 "Shower, O heavens, from above,
   and let the skies rain down righteousness;
  let the earth open, that salvation may sprout forth,
   and let it cause righteousness to spring up also;
  I the LORD have created it.

The words of the oracle are addressed to Cyrus, in what has been variously designated as an "epistolary form" (North) and a "royal oracle" (Westermann). No hint is given as to how the prophet expected that his words should reach the Persian king— if, indeed, such was his expectation. It is probable that the oracle was intended for an Israelite audience, even though it was ostensibly directed to Cyrus.

The prophet refers to **Cyrus** as the Lord's *anointed* (Heb., *mashiᵃh;* Gk., *christos*), a title which elsewhere in the Old Testament is applied only to an Israelite. It is used to designate priests (cf. Lev. 4:3,5,16; 6:15), reigning kings (cf. 1 Sam. 24:6,10; Psalm 2:2), and, in a metaphorical sense, the patriarchs (cf. Psalm 105:15). Oddly enough, it is never used in the Old Testament as a title for the future messianic king. It had not yet acquired sufficient eschatological content for such use.

The origin of the term is to be found in the Israelite custom of anoinitng with oil those who were to assume positions of responsibility and leadership in the community. The ceremony of anointing symbolized the consecration of the person to his office and the bestowal upon him of divine grace and strength. Cyrus, therefore, was called by the title because the Lord had installed him as ruler over the nations and had endowed him with strength to fulfill all his purpose.

The oracle addressed to Cyrus contains both commission and promise, although the latter is predominant. More emphasis is placed upon what the Lord will do for him than upon what he is expected to do for the Lord. It is the Lord who has grasped his right hand to subdue nations before him. His invincibility is vividly expressed in the contrasting statements in vv. 1 and 5: the Lord ungirds the loins of hostile kings (v. 1), but he girds Cyrus to do battle against them (v. 5; cf. Ex. 12:11; Deut. 1:41; 1 Kings 18:46; 20:11; Luke 12:35; Eph. 6:14). The conventional language used throughout the oracle makes it unnecessary to try to relate the promises to specific events in the career of Cyrus.

The passage clearly states that the Lord's use of Cyrus did not mean that the latter knew him or was willing to acknowledge his sovereignty (cf. vv. 4–5). It is, of course, possible that the prophet may have entertained the hope that Cyrus would eventually become a worshiper of Yahweh

(cf. v. 3), but, if so, this hope was never realized. Evidence to the contrary is found in the Cyrus Cylinder, an inscribed clay cylinder dating from about 538 B.C. and containing Cyrus' own account of his conquest of Babylon (ANET, pp. 315–316). In recounting his history, he attributes his successes not to Yahweh, but to Marduk, the god of Babylon, whom he addresses as "my lord."

The implication to be drawn from this passage is that the prophet believed that Yahweh could call and equip worshipers of foreign gods to fulfill his purposes, even without their knowledge or concurrence. Earlier prophets had spoken of the Lord's use of foreign rulers to punish Israel (cf. 10:5–6; Jer. 25:9; 27:6–8), but Second Isaiah was the first to speak of one who was raised up to serve as a deliverer.

Cyrus' commission is given for the twofold purpose of liberating Israel (v. 4) and of causing men of all nations to acknowledge the majesty and uniqueness of Yahweh (v. 6). Yahweh's claim to be the one and only God is repeated in these chapters almost to the point of monotony, which indicates the supreme importance that the prophet attached to the truth.

Second Isaiah's monotheism was so thoroughgoing that it left no room for a dualistic view of reality. He, therefore, did not hesitate to attribute to Yahweh the creation of both *light* and *darkness,* of both weal (*shalom;* however, 1QIsᵃ reads *tobh*) and woe (*ra'*). This meant that Yahweh was regarded as the supreme and only cause in the entire universe, the Creator of all things. One is inclined to agree with Westermann that these words have such far-reaching implications "that we can only tremble and fall silent as we contemplate them."

The Cyrus oracle is appropriately concluded with a brief hymn (v. 8). North has described the hymn as "a perfect miniature in verse. The skies are bidden to *rain victory.* The fecund earth is to *open her womb.* The issue of this 'marriage' of heaven and earth is to be *prosperity* and *salvation*." [117]

(3) The Potter and the Clay (45:9–13)

9 "Woe to him who strives with his Maker,
    an earthen vessel with the potter!
Does the clay say to him who fashions it,
    'What are you making'?
    or 'Your work has no handles'?
10 Woe to him who says to a father, 'What
    are you begetting?'
    or to a woman, 'With what are you in
    travail?' "
11 Thus says the LORD,
    the Holy One of Israel, and his Maker:
"Will you question me about my children,
    or command me concerning the work of
    my hands?
12 I made the earth,
    and created man upon it;
it was my hands that stretched out the
    heavens,
    and I commanded all their host.
13 I have aroused him in righteousness,
    and I will make straight all his ways;
he shall build my city
    and set my exiles free,
not for price or reward,"
    says the LORD of hosts.

Yahweh's choice of Cyrus as his "shepherd" (cf. 44:28) and "anointed" one (45:1) became a dramatic issue with some of the exiles, who felt that their own uniqueness as the people of God was being threatened. The prophet answers their objections by reaffirming the absolute sovereignty of Yahweh over nature and history. His relationship to all created things is compared to that of the *potter* to the *clay* (v. 9; cf. 29:16; Jer. 18:1–11; Rom. 9:20–24) and of the parent to the child (vv. 10–12). It is as preposterous, therefore, to think that men should find fault with him as to suppose that the clay should challenge the potter, or the child the parent. The degree of seriousness with which the prophet views this matter is indicated by the fact that this is the only time in chapters 40—66 that he addresses Israel through a "woe" oracle (cf. 5:8–23; 10:1; 30:1; 31:1).

117 Christopher R. North, *The Second Isaiah* (Oxford: The Clarendon Press, 1964), p. 152.

The most surprising feature about this passage is its ending (v. 13). In spite of the murmuring and complaining of the exiles, Yahweh still is determined to set them free through one whom he has raised up for this purpose. This was accomplished in 538 B.C., when Cyrus issued his famous decree permitting Jews to return to their homeland and to rebuild their ruined capital (cf. Ezra 1:1–4). He not only did this without *price or reward*, but he even assisted in the restoration of the land through a grant from the royal treasury.

(4) The Conversion of the Nations (45:14–25)

14 Thus says the LORD:
"The wealth of Egypt and the merchandise
    of Ethiopia,
    and the Sabeans, men of stature,
shall come over to you and be yours,
    they shall follow you;
    they shall come over in chains and bow
    down to you.
They will make supplication to you, saying:
'God is with you only, and there is no
    other,
    no god besides him.' "
15 Truly, thou art a God who hidest thyself,
    O God of Israel, the Savior.
16 All of them are put to shame and confounded,
    the makers of idols go in confusion together.
17 But Israel is saved by the LORD
    with everlasting salvation;
you shall not be put to shame or confounded
    to all eternity.
18 For thus says the LORD,
who created the heavens
    (he is God!),
who formed the earth and made it
    (he established it;
he did not create it a chaos,
    he formed it to be inhabited!):
"I am the LORD, and there is no other.
19 I did not speak in secret,
    in a land of darkness;
I did not say to the offspring of Jacob,
    'Seek me in chaos.'
I the LORD speak the truth,
    I declare what is right.
20 "Assemble yourselves and come,
    draw near together,
    you survivors of the nations!
They have no knowledge

who carry about their wooden idols,
and keep on praying to a god
that cannot save.
21 Declare and present your case;
let them take counsel together!
Who told this long ago?
Who declared it of old?
Was it not I, the LORD?
And there is no other god besides me,
a righteous God and a Savior;
there is none besides me.
22 "Turn to me and be saved,
all the ends of the earth!
For I am God, and there is no other.
23 By myself I have sworn,
from my mouth has gone forth in righteousness
a word that shall not return:
'To me every knee shall bow,
every tongue shall swear.'
24 "Only in the LORD, it shall be said of me.
are righteousness and strength;
to him shall come and be ashamed,
all who were incensed against him.
25 In the LORD all the offspring of Israel
shall triumph and glory."

The fact that the personal pronoun "you"
—which appears six times as a suffix in v.
14—is feminine in form suggests that the
one being addressed is Jerusalem. The
prophet envisions a time when the leading
nations of Africa (cf. 43:3), perhaps representative of all nations of the earth, will
come bringing tribute and making supplication to Jerusalem because of the presence
of God within her (cf. 2:2-4; 49:23;
60:8-16; 66:18-23; Zech. 6:15; 14:16-19;
Rev. 21:22-26). The fact that the nations
are pictured as coming over in chains is
indicative of the strong tension between
nationalism and universalism that one encounters throughout chapters 40—66.
The speaker in vv. 15-17 is most likely
the prophet. Concerning v. 15, North has
written: "Nowhere in the OT is the thought
of the 'hidden' God, the deus absconditus
of theology, so plainly stated as here."
Smart has noted that in the present generation the mere suggestion that God is
hidden, i.e., that he can not be comprehended by reason alone, is considered "almost an insult to human nature." Actually,
the hiddenness of God is but one side of a
paradox, for he who hides himself is also

he who reveals himself as Savior. The
makers of idols, therefore, are put to shame
(v. 16), but Israel is saved by the Lord
with an everlasting salvation (v. 17).
Verses 18-19 declare that there has been
a consistency in God's actions from the
time of creation until the present moment
in history. Just as he did not create the
earth to be a chaos but to be inhabited
(v. 18), even so his words of revelation to
Israel have not been designed to lead her
into chaos but into a life of peace and
stability (v. 19). If, therefore, she is experiencing chaos in her present situation,
it is because she has ignored God's revelation and walked in her own ways.
Verses 20-25 are cast in the form of a
trial speech (cf. 41:1-5,21-29; 43:8-13;
44:6-8). The survivors of the nations are
commanded to assemble themselves and to
justify their worship of idols in the face of
Yahweh's claim to be the one true God.
The Hebrew word for "survivor" is always
used of one who has escaped from the
destruction of his own city or nation (cf.
Gen. 14:13; Judg. 12:4-5; Ezek. 24:26-
27; 33:21-22; Obad. 14). Here it presumably refers to those who have survived the
judgments predicted in the preceding
chapters (41:11-16; 42:10-17; 45:1-6).
In v. 20b, which has the appearance of
a parenthetical aside, the prophet attributes
the worship of idols to men's ignorance and
stupidity. As in earlier trial speeches, the
nations are challenged to prove the authen-
ticity of their gods by producing evidence
that these have spoken beforehand of the
coming of Cyrus (v. 21a). In the absence
of such proof, the Lord again enters his
claim to be the only true God and Savior,
besides whom there is no other (v. 21b).
What follows in this passage is totally
unexpected. Instead of pronouncing judgment on those whose idolatrous worship
has been so thoroughly discredited, the
Lord invites them to look to him and be
saved (v. 22). His purpose in raising up
Cyrus, therefore, is not to destroy the
nations, but to enable them to participate
in his salvation. The world-encompassing

nature of divine love is nowhere more adequately expressed than here (cf. Gen. 12:1–3).

The verb save appears 27 times in Isaiah, 20 of which are in chapters 40—66. Its basic meaning is "to give room or space," hence to liberate, to deliver, to rescue, or to lead out (cf. Judg. 2:16,18; 3:15; 1 Sam. 9:16; Isa. 37:20; Jer. 14:8). To *be saved*, therefore, means to be liberated from all confining circumstances, to be set in a broad place, to be given room to breathe freely (cf. Gen. 26:22; Ex. 3:8; 2 Sam. 22:20; Job 36:16; Psalms 4:1; 18:19).

Davidson has referred to v. 23 as "the death-knell of all idolatry."[118] Yahweh swears by himself, i.e., by "the integrity of his own being" (Smart), and by the immutability of his word (cf. 40:8; 55:10–11) that every knee shall bow to him (cf. 1 Kings 8:54; 19:18; 2 Chron. 7:3; 29:29; Psalm 95:6) and every tongue swear allegiance (cf. 48:1; 65:16; Rom. 14:11; Phil. 2:9–11). Thus those who once were his enemies now humbly acknowledge his sovereignty (v. 24; cf. 41:11–12) and participate with Israel in his salvation (v. 25; cf. 41:16*b*). According to these verses, therefore, membership in the people of God is based not upon race or nationality but upon the individual's willingness to confess that Yahweh alone is God.

9. Impotence and Omnipotence (46:1–13)

(1) The Burdensome Gods of Babylon (46:1–2)

1 Bel bows down, Nebo stoops,
   their idols are on beasts and cattle;
 these things you carry are loaded
   as burdens on weary beasts.
2 They stoop, they bow down together,
   they cannot save the burden,
 but themselves go into captivity.

In George Adam Smith's classic exposition of this chapter, which is entitled "Bearing or Borne," he makes the observation that "it makes all the difference to a man how he conceives his religion—

whether as something that he has to carry, or as something that will carry him."[119] In other words, it may be a load or a lift.

The prophet clearly conceives of the religion of Babylon as being all load and no lift. Verses 1–2 apparently refer to the frantic efforts of the men of Babylon to save their two chief gods, Bel and Nebo, from falling into the hands of Cyrus. Their efforts are pronounced a failure, however, for although the idols are loaded on the backs of weary beasts, they are soon captured and taken away into captivity.

(2) God's Unfailing Support of Israel (46:3–4)

3 "Hearken to me, O house of Jacob,
   all the remnant of the house of Israel,
 who have been borne by me from your birth,
   carried from the womb;
4 even to your old age I am He,
   and to gray hairs I will carry you,
 I have made, and I will bear;
 I will carry and will save.

The gods of Babylon have to be borne about by men (vv. 1–2), but the God of Israel has borne and carried his people since their birth, and will continue to do so until they reach old age. This is a figurative way of saying that there has been no lapse in his caring for them in the past, nor shall there ever be in the future.

The full significance of these words becomes apparent only when they are seen against the background of the Exile. Many of the Jews who had been taken to Babylon are convinced that God has ceased to be concerned about them (cf. 40:27; 49:14). The prophet's reassuring words are addressed to this discouraged **remnant of the house of Israel**. They are told that he who made them in the beginning will bear them to old age and will save them. The latter promise doubtlessly refers to their deliverance from exile.

(3) The Absurdity of Idolatry (46:5–7)

5 "To whom will you liken me and make me equal,

---

118 A. B. Davidson, *The Theology of the Old Testament* (New York: Charles Scribner's Sons, 1904), p. 102.

119 George Adam Smith, *The Book of Isaiah*, II, Rev. Ed. (New York: Harper and Brothers, 1927), 198.

and compare me, that we may be alike?
6 Those who lavish gold from the purse,
  and weigh out silver in the scales,
  hire a goldsmith, and he makes it into a
    god;
  then they fall down and worship!
7 They lift it upon their shoulders, they carry
    it,
  they set it in its place, and it stands there;
  it cannot move from its place.
  If one cries to it, it does not answer
  or save him from his trouble.

The religion of the Babylonians apparently held a strange fascination for many of the Jewish exiles. This is borne out by the fact that the prophet wages such a relentless battle against idolatry (cf. 40:18–20; 41:5–7; 44:9–20; 46:1–2). He realizes that in this struggle the stakes are high and that upon its outcome depends the whole future of the faith of Israel.

Verse 5 is almost identical to 40:18. It reiterates the impossibility of representing Yahweh by means of an image. There follows in vv. 6–7 a list of the liabilities that one encounters when he practices idolatry: (1) even though idols may consist of such costly items as silver and gold, they are still nothing more than man-made gods; (2) therefore, they must be carried about from place to place; (3) when they are set down, they can not move; (4) when one prays to them, they do not respond; (5) they can not save a man out of his troubles. It would be difficult to imagine a more scathing indictment of idolatry than this.

(4) Exhortation to Unbelievers (46:8–13)

8 "Remember this and consider,
  recall it to mind, you transgressors,
9 remember the former things of old;
  for I am God, and there is no other;
  I am God, and there is none like me,
10 declaring the end from the beginning
  and from ancient times things not yet
    done,
  saying, 'My counsel shall stand,
  and I will accomplish all my purpose,'
11 calling a bird of prey from the east,
  the man of my counsel from a far country.
  I have spoken, and I will bring it to pass;
  I have purposed, and I will do it.

12 "Hearken to me, you stubborn of heart,
  you who are far from deliverance:
13 I bring near my deliverance, it is not far off,
  and my salvation will not tarry;
  I will put salvation in Zion,
  for Israel my glory."

This passage is marked by the reappearance of themes from the preceding chapters. These include: the present stubbornness and rebelliousness of the exiles (vv. 8,12; cf. 42:18–20; 43:27; 48:8); the uniqueness of Israel's God (v. 9; cf. 43:11); an exhortation to faith based on the appeal to prophecy (v. 10a; cf. 42:9; 43:18–19; 48:3); the certainty of the fulfillment of the Lord's purpose (vv. 10b,13; cf. 44:26–28; 55:11); and the emergence of Cyrus as the agent of the Lord's deliverance (v. 11; cf. 41:2–4,25; 44:28; 45:1–6; 48:14–15). The fact that deliverance is proclaimed as being near at hand (v. 13) suggests a date for the passage just prior to Cyrus' conquest of Babylon.

10. Babylon's Day of Reckoning (47:1–15)

Chapter 47 predicts the downfall of Babylon and should, therefore, be dated before 539 B.C. It is the only passage in Second Isaiah that belongs to the literary category of "the oracles against the nations," of which there are many examples elsewhere in the prophets (cf. chs. 13—23; Jer. 46–51; Ezek. 25–32; Amos 1–2).

Other oracles against Babylon occur in Isaiah 13—14 and Jeremiah 50—51. All of these reflect the deep hatred that the Jews felt toward this ancient enemy (cf. Psalm 137:8–9). Even in New Testament times, Jewish Christians continued to refer to Babylon as a symbol of all that was ruthless and evil (cf. Rev. 17—18).

Westermann has commented on the sheer audacity of the prophetic word which is recorded here: ". . . the vanquished God of a petty, vanquished nation takes vengeance on the mighty colossus Babylon!" If anyone other than a prophet of Israel had uttered such words, he would have been laughed to scorn.

(1) *The Fallen Daughter of Babylon* (47:1–4)

1 Come down and sit in the dust,
     O virgin daughter of Babylon;
  sit on the ground without a throne,
     O daughter of the Chaldeans!
  For you shall no more be called
     tender and delicate.
2 Take the millstones and grind meal,
     put off your veil,
  strip off your robe, uncover your legs,
     pass through the rivers.
3 Your nakedness shall be uncovered,
     and your shame shall be seen.
  I will take vengeance,
     and I will spare no man.
4 Our Redeemer—the LORD of hosts is his
     name—
  is the Holy One of Israel.

Babylon is addressed as *virgin daughter,* which means that she is still unconquered and unravished. The prophet warns, however, that like some virgin queen she will soon be removed from her throne and made to sit in the dust. She will have to take the millstones and grind meal like a common slave girl. Her royal attire will be stripped from her, and her nakedness will be uncovered. This latter expression apparently means that she will be raped by her conquerors (cf. Lev. 18:6–19).

The prophet's confidence in the ultimate downfall of the tyrant nation is grounded in his concept of Yahweh and of Yahweh's relationship to Israel. This is expressed in v. 4, which many mistakenly regard as an interpolation. This verse expresses both the condescension ("Our Redeemer") and the majesty ("the Holy One of Israel") of Yahweh. The parenthetical statement, *the Lord of hosts is his name,* is perhaps intended as a polemic against the Babylonian worship of the hosts of heaven, which, according to the prophet, are all under the suzerainty of Yahweh.

(2) *A City Without Compassion* (47:5–7)

5 Sit in silence, and go into darkness,
     O daughter of the Chaldeans;
  for you shall no more be called
     the mistress of kingdoms.
6 I was angry with my people,
     I profaned my heritage;

I gave them into your hand,
     you showed them no mercy;
  on the aged you made your yoke
     exceedingly heavy.
7 You said, "I shall be mistress for ever,"
     so that you did not lay these things to
        heart
  or remember their end.

The first charge brought against Babylon is that she has dealt harshly with Israelite prisoners of war, especially the aged, on whom her yoke has been *exceedingly heavy* (v. 6; cf. Lam. 1:19; 2:21). Yahweh's anger is directed toward her, therefore, not because she destroyed Judah and Jerusalem but because she mistreated defenseless men and women. Human values are thus placed above property values, and mighty Babylon is judged on the basis of her violation of the former. Smart has shown the relevance of this ancient word to our day through his warning that power can be "the most dangerous poison to the soul of a nation, exalting its ego in such a fashion that it ceases even to be aware of what is happening when it is walking over the little people of the world." [120]

Babylon has refused to recognize that she is but an instrument in Yahweh's hands for the chastisement of Israel (v. 6; cf. 10:5–6). Instead, she has boasted in her arrogant self-sufficiency that she will be mistress over the nations forever (v. 7; cf. 10:7–15). In his response to her, the prophet appropriates her own words as he announces the end of her dominion (v. 5).

(3) *Pride and Self-idolatry* (47:8–9)

8 Now therefore hear this, you lover of pleas-
        ures,
     who sit securely,
  who say in your heart,
     "I am, and there is no one besides me;
  I shall not sit as a widow
     or know the loss of children":
9 These two things shall come to you
     in a moment, in one day;
  the loss of children and widowhood
     shall come upon you in full measure,
  in spite of your many sorceries
     and the great power of your enchantments.

120 James D. Smart, *op. cit.,* pp. 140–141.

The second charge is that Babylon has arrogated to herself divinity by saying in her heart, *I am, and there is no one besides me* (v. 8; cf. Zeph. 2:15). These are words that may be spoken only by Yahweh, else they become the ultimate blasphemy (cf. Ex. 3:14; Isa. 43:11; 45:5–6,21).

Because of her pride and self-adulation, Babylon will suffer both the loss of children and widowhood in a single day. Even her elaborate system of sorceries and enchantments will be inadequate to prevent these disasters (v. 9).

(4) A False Sense of Security (47:19–11)

10 You felt secure in your wickedness,
  you said, "No one sees me";
your wisdom and your knowledge
  led you astray,
and you said in your heart,
  "I am, and there is no one besides me."
11 But evil shall come upon you,
  for which you cannot atone;
disaster shall fall upon you,
  which you will not be able to expiate;
and ruin shall come on you suddenly,
  of which you know nothing.

Verse 10 repeats the blasphemous words of Babylon found in v. 8. The prophet adds the further charge that she has imagined that she could practice wickedness with impunity, as though she were accountable to no one besides herself (cf. 29:15). She is unaware that her own wisdom and knowledge have led her astray.

Neither the intellectual resources at her disposal nor the atoning sacrifices that she might offer will be sufficient to avert the disaster that threatens. When it strikes, it will be unlike anything that she has ever experienced before (v. 11).

(5) Salvation by Divination and Magic (47:12–13)

12 Stand fast in your enchantments
  and your many sorceries,
    with which you have labored from your youth;
perhaps you may be able to succeed,
  perhaps you may inspire terror.
13 You are wearied with your many counsels;
  let them stand forth and save you,

those who divide the heavens,
  who gaze at the stars,
who at the new moons predict
  what shall befall you.

The prophet sarcastically advises Babylon to turn to her magicians and diviners for help in the present crisis. She has devoted her entire lifetime to the practice of their occult arts, so perhaps now they can help her (v. 12).

For *those who divide the heavens* (v. 13), the Septuagint reads *astrologoi* (astrologers). Astrology, or divination by the stars, originated in Mesopotamia perhaps as early as the third millennium B.C. Astrologers believed that the heavens were divided into twelve sections, indicated by the twelve signs of the zodiac, and that the movement and geometrical relationship of the heavenly bodies within these sections determined the destiny and welfare of men and nations. Basic to the entire system was the belief that the heavenly bodies were in reality gods with varying degrees of power. This pseudo science is, of course, as alien to biblical faith today as it was in the sixth century B.C.

(6) Judgment by Fire (47:14–15)

14 Behold, they are like stubble,
  the fire consumes them;
they cannot deliver themselves
  from the power of the flame.
No coal for warming oneself is this,
  no fire to sit before!
15 Such to you are those with whom you have labored,
  who have trafficked with you from your youth;
they wander about each in his own direction;
  there is no one to save you.

Fire will destroy Babylon's astrologers like stubble. The prophet notes with a touch of grim humor that this will be no fire for one to sit beside and warm himself! Since the astrologers are unable to deliver themselves from the flames, how could they possibly render assistance to others? The answer is obvious. Though Babylon has labored with them from her youth, they now leave her, and wander about as helpless and confused as she. There is no one to save her. It is on this note of finality that the oracle comes to a close.

11. Exhortations to the Exiles in Babylon (48:1–22)

This is a chapter of extremes, for it contains not only the threat of judgment and condemnation but also the promise of forgiveness and deliverance. The key words that give it unity are "hear" (vv. 1,6, 12,14,16,18); "call" (vv. 1,2,12,13,15), "name" (vv. 1,2,9,11,19), and "Jacob" (vv. 1,12,20).

Westermann, following Duhm and Volz, takes the position that Second Isaiah preached a message of "salvation and nothing but salvation" and that, therefore, the passages of condemnation found here were inserted by a later hand (cf. Moffatt's translation). North and Smart, however, reject the notion that Second Isaiah was solely a prophet of salvation and note that there is a close parallel between these condemnatory words and those found elsewhere in his writings (cf. 42:18–25; 43:22–28; 45:9–11; 46:8,12). It seems preferable, therefore, to regard the chapter as a unity and to attribute it to Second Isaiah.

The chapter ends with a stirring summons to the exiles to depart from Babylon, thus indicating that it is to be dated after Cyrus had conquered the city and had issued a decree permitting them to leave. Neither Cyrus nor Babylon is referred to again in the remaining chapters.

(1) Israel's Moral and Spiritual Failure (48:1–8)

1 Hear this, O house of Jacob,
     who are called by the name of Israel,
     and who came forth from the loins of Judah;
     who swear by the name of the LORD,
     and confess the God of Israel,
     but not in truth or right.
2 For they call themselves after the holy city,
     and stay themselves on the God of Israel;
     the LORD of hosts is his name.
3 "The former things I declared of old,
     they went forth from my mouth and I made them known;
     then suddenly I did them and they came to pass.
4 Because I know that you are obstinate,
     and your neck is an iron sinew
     and your forehead brass,
5 I declared them to you from of old,
     before they came to pass I announced them to you,
     lest you should say, 'My idol did them,
     my graven image and my molten image commanded them.'
6 "You have heard; now see all this;
     and will you not declare it?
     From this time forth I make you hear new things,
     hidden things which you have not known.
7 They are created now, not long ago;
     before today you have never heard of them,
     lest you should say, 'Behold, I knew them.'
8 You have never heard, you have never known,
     from of old your ear has not been opened.
     For I knew that you would deal very treacherously,
     and that from birth you were called a rebel.

The continuing apostasy of the Lord's people becomes the focus of attention here. Even on the eve of their departure from Babylon, they are described as obstinate, stiff-necked, hardheaded, idolatrous, deaf, treacherous, and rebellious (vv. 4,5,8).

Where does the root of their problem lie? Is it not in their stubborn refusal to give heed to the word of the Lord (v. 8; cf. v. 18; 6:9–10; 42–19–20)? The prophet's fourfold repetition of the command to *hear* (vv. 1,12,14,16) indicates the apathy with which even his own words were received.

To be sure, the people of Israel still maintain a semblance of loyalty: they *swear* by the name of Yahweh, *confess* the God of Israel, and *call* themselves after the holy city (cf. Psalm 137:5–6). All this however, they do without truth and without righteousness (cf. 29:13; Hos. 6:4–6).

The prophet draws a contrast between God's revealing activity in the past (vv. 3–6a) and in the present (vv. 6b–7). In the past he announced beforehand the important events in Israel's history—here

designated as *the former things* (v. 3)—
lest she attribute these to her idols (v. 5;
cf. Amos 3:7). In the present, however, he
is preparing to do *new things* or hidden
(lit., guarded) things of which she knows
nothing (v. 6). The reason she has not
been informed of the coming events is in
order that she might not say, *Behold, I
knew them* (v. 7). To know, as used here,
probably means to choose or to ordain (cf.
Gen. 18:19; Jer. 1:4; Amos 3:2). In other
words, Israel is prone to boast that she is
the architect of her own future.

One must not overlook the revolutionary
character of the *new things* envisioned
here. They are sometimes interpreted as
having reference to the mission of the
servant (cf. 49:1–6), but it is more likely
that they describe Cyrus' conquest of
Babylon, the liberation of the exiles, the
second exodus, and the establishment of
God's universal kingdom. Smart correctly
states the significance of the passage when
he writes: "What God is about to bring
forth is nothing less than a new creation, a
new beginning for Israel and for the world.
It is unbelievable, unheard of, and yet
true." [121]

Israel's responsibility before the revelation of God—both past and present—is described as being twofold: she must *hear*
the word spoken to her by the prophets,
and she must *declare* that which she has
heard (v. 6b). In other words, she must be
Yahweh's witness before the nations, as she
receives his word and bears witness to its
fulfillment in her history (cf. 43:10,12;
44:8).

The sad truth, however, is that she has
failed in her responsibility. According to
v. 8, she has never heard, has never known,
and her ear has never been opened. The
verse suggests that there is opposition even
to Second Isaiah's message and that he is
having difficulty persuading the exiles to
receive God's word of salvation and to act
upon it.

[121] James D. Smart, *op. cit.*, p. 146.

**(2) Tried in the Furnace of Affliction
(48:9–11)**

9 "For my name's sake I defer my anger,
  for the sake of my praise I restrain it for
    you,
  that I may not cut you off.
10 Behold, I have refined you, but not like
    silver;
  I have tried you in the furnace of afflic-
    tion.
11 For my own sake, for my own sake, I do it,
  for how should my name be profaned?
  My glory I will not give to another.

The theme of this section is the failure
of the exile to purge Israel of her dross.
Even though she has been *refined* and
tried in the furnace of affliction, she has not
come forth like silver (v. 10; cf. Deut.
4:20; 1 Kings 8:51; Jer. 11:4). If God,
therefore, were to treat her as she deserves,
he would cut her off completely (v. 9). It
is for his own *name's sake,* rather than because of any merit on her part, that he has
deferred and restrained his anger (vv.
9,11). For him to act for his name's sake
means to act in accord with his own nature
and purpose as these have been revealed
to Israel (cf. 30:27; 42:8; Ezek. 20:9;
36:22–23; 39:7,25).

**(3) The Sovereign Creator and Redeemer
(48:12–16)**

12 "Hearken to me, O Jacob,
  and Israel, whom I called!
  I am He, I am the first,
  and I am the last.
13 My hand laid the foundation of the earth,
  and my right hand spread out the heav-
    ens;
  when I call to them,
  they stand forth together.
14 "Assemble, all of you, and hear!
  Who among them has declared these
    things?
  The LORD loves him;
  he shall perform his purpose on Babylon,
  and his arm shall be against the Chalde-
    ans.
15 I, even I, have spoken and called him,
  I have brought him, and he will prosper
    in his way.
16 Draw near to me, hear this:
  from the beginning I have not spoken in
    secret,

from the time it came to be I have been there."
And now the Lord GOD has sent me and his Spirit.

In a renewed appeal, based upon Yahweh's lordship over creation (vv. 12–13) and history (vv. 14–16), Israel is exhorted to draw near and to hear the word of the Lord (vv. 12,14,16). The everlasting God (v. 12), who by his hand *laid the foundation of the earth* and *spread out the heavens* (v. 13), has now chosen Cyrus to perform his purpose on Babylon (vv. 14–15).

Verse 16 presents problems for which there are no easy solutions. The first part is a continuation of the divine exhortation to Israel to hear. Yahweh tells her that from the beginning he has not spoken to her in secret, which implies that he has spoken openly and in language easy to be understood (cf. 45:19; Deut. 30:11–14). Furthermore, whenever his word has come to pass, he has been there, i.e., he has been responsible for its fulfillment.

The problems arise in the latter part of v. 16 and have to do primarily with the identity of the speaker and with his relationship to the *Spirit*. The speaker identifies himself simply as one whom God has sent. Scholarly opinion is divided as to whether this refers to Cyrus, to the servant, or to the prophet. The last suggestion is probably correct, since in the Old Testament those who are sent by God are almost always messengers or prophets (cf. 6:8; 42:19; 61:1; Jer. 1:7; 7:25; Hag. 1:12).

The relationship of the anonymous speaker to the Spirit is also unclear. From the position of the word Spirit in the sentence, it is impossible to tell whether it is intended as subject or as object. In other words, one is unable to determine if the speaker has been sent *by* the Spirit, or *with* the Spirit (cf. 42:1; 61:1). The position adopted here is that the prophet is making the claim that he has been sent by God and also endowed with his Spirit (Mic. 3:8; Zech. 7:12). The apparent

reason for his making this claim is to establish his credentials as a true prophet of Yahweh and to reinforce his appeal to the exiles to heed his words.

(4) The High Cost of Rebellion (48:17–19)

17 Thus says the LORD,
    your Redeemer, the Holy One of Israel:
"I am the LORD your God,
    who teaches you to profit,
    who leads you in the way you should go.
18 O that you had hearkened to my commandments!
    Then your peace would have been like a river,
    and your righteousness like the waves of the sea;
19 your offspring would have been like the sand,
    and your descendants like its grains;
their name would never be cut off
    or destroyed from before me."

"O that you had hearkened to my commandments!" With these words the prophet reminds Israel that her past history has been "a tragedy of wasted opportunities" (North). It is a tragedy that could easily have been avoided, for her teacher and guide has been none other than the Lord himself, her *Redeemer, the Holy One of Israel* (v. 17). Even the best teacher fails, however, when his pupils are unwilling to learn.

Verses 18–19 remind Israel of what she has lost by refusing to be taught (cf. Psalm 81:13–16; Luke 13:34–35; 19:41–44). What are the benefits that would have accrued to her if she had chosen a different course? First, her peace would have been like a river, and her righteousness like the waves of the sea. *Peace*, which translates a word derived from the verb to be whole, is comparable in meaning to the English word health, which in its old Anglo-Saxon form was written "wholth." It, therefore, signifies wholeness of being, happiness, success, prosperity. It is no accident that the prophet associates peace with righteousness, for it is inconceivable that the former could exist apart from the latter (cf. v. 22).

The peace that Israel has forfeited is very fittingly compared to a river. At the time these words were spoken the exiles were living in the fertile Mesopotamian valley, bounded on the north by the Tigris and on the south by the Euphrates. These two rivers, whose waters were extensively used for irrigation purposes, brought life to a land that otherwise would have been barren desert. The prophet's symbolism, therefore, is especially meaningful in a setting such as this.

The second of Israel's lost benefits is the fulfillment of God's ancient promise to make her sons as numerous as the grains of sand beside the sea (v. 19; cf. Gen. 13:16; 22:17–18; 32:12; Hos. 1:10). Had she but listened to the Lord's commands, her name would have been established so that it could never be cut off (cf. 56:5).

(5) Summons to Leave Babylon (48:20–22)

20 Go forth from Babylon, flee from Chaldea,
   declare this with a shout of joy, proclaim it,
   send it forth to the end of the earth;
   say, "The LORD has redeemed his servant Jacob!"
21 They thirsted not when he led them through the deserts;
   he made water flow for them from the rock;
   he cleft the rock and the water gushed out.
22 "There is no peace," says the LORD, "for the wicked."

The long-awaited call for the exiles to depart from Babylon is finally given in v. 20. One can sense the joy and excitement with which the prophet shouts out the tidings that Israel is free at last. He calls upon others to join him in spreading the good news to the ends of the earth. *The Lord has redeemed his servant Jacob*, even in spite of the fact that the Exile has wrought no great change in his character or conduct (cf. vv. 4,8,10).

Some of the exiles are apparently reluctant to undertake the difficult journey across the desert. They are fearful that they might not survive its rigors. The prophet

seeks to allay their fears by reminding them of the provisions that the Lord made for their forefathers when they came out of Egypt. He caused water to flow from the rock, so that they suffered no thirst when they were led through the desert (v. 21; cf. Ex. 17:6; 1 Cor. 10:4). Will he not, therefore, show a similar concern for the welfare of the exiles as they return to Jerusalem?

The chapter ends on a somber note: *No peace . . . for the wicked!* These words are not misplaced, as some have suggested, but form a natural conclusion to the preceding passage. They are addressed to those among the exiles who are reluctant to leave Babylon and to participate in the redemption that the Lord has provided for them. Josephus (*Antiq.*, XI.1,3) reports that many of the Jews chose to remain in Babylon, "being unwilling to leave their possessions." For such as these, the prophet declares, there is no peace.

II. Israel's Glorious Future (49:1—55:13)

Chapters 49—55 contain no further references to Cyrus or Babylon, no attacks upon idolatry, and no appeals to the fulfillment of former prophecies. It is possible, therefore, that they belong to a later period than chapters 40—48, i.e., to the period after Cyrus' conquest of Babylon, but prior to the return of the Jews to Palestine (cf. 55:12–13). One should be careful, however, not to exaggerate the differences between chapters 40—48 and 49—55, for both sections portray a unity of style and thought that bespeaks a common authorship.

1. From Present Despair to Future Glory (49:1–26)

(1) The Servant's Address to the Nations (49:1–6)

1 Listen to me, O coastlands,
   and hearken, you peoples from afar.
   The LORD called me from the womb,
   from the body of my mother he named my name.
2 He made my mouth like a sharp sword,

in the shadow of his hand he hid me;
he made me a polished arrow,
   in his quiver he hid me away.
3 And he said to me, "You are my servant,
   Israel, in whom I will be glorified."
4 But I said, "I have labored in vain,
   I have spent my strength for nothing and
     vanity;
yet surely my right is with the LORD,
   and my recompense with my God."
5 And now the LORD says,
   who formed me from the womb to be
     his servant,
to bring Jacob back to him,
   and that Israel might be gathered to him,
for I am honored in the eyes of the LORD,
   and my God has become my strength—
6 he says:
"It is too light a thing that you should be
   my servant
to raise up the tribes of Jacob
   and to restore the preserved of Israel;
I will give you as a light to the nations,
   that my salvation may reach to the end
     of the earth."

The elusiveness of the servant's identity is nowhere more apparent than in this second Servant Song (cf. 42:1–4; 50:4–9; 52:13—53:12). On the one hand, he is unequivocally identified as Israel (v. 3), and many of the things said of him here are said elsewhere of Israel: The Lord called him from the womb (vv. 1,5; cf. 44:2,24); he was entrusted with the word of the Lord (v. 2; cf. 44:26; 50:4; 51:16; 59:21); he was hidden in the shadow of the Lord's hand (v. 2; cf. 51:16); the Lord appointed him as his servant (v. 3; cf. 41:9; 43:10; 44:21); the purpose of his ministry was to glorify God (v. 3; cf. 43:7; 44:23; 46:13; 60:2); his initial ministry seemingly ended in failure (v. 4; cf. 40:27; 42:19; 49:14); and he was charged with the responsibility of being a light to the nations (v. 6; cf. 42:6).

In spite of the support that the collective view receives from the passage, however, there are serious objections to it in vv. 5–6. These verses describe the servant's mission as being initially that of raising up the tribes of Jacob and restoring the preserved of Israel. If, therefore, the *servant* is interpreted collectively, then one is confronted with the strange anomaly of the

nation effecting its own spiritual renewal. Even Muilenburg, who believes that every reference to the servant in Second Isaiah applies to Israel, is forced to admit that vv. 5–6 constitute "the most serious obstacle to the collective view."

One way out of the impasse would be to delete the word "Israel" from v. 3.[122] This suggestion, however, lacks support among the ancient versions. The wiser course, therefore, would be to accept the text as it now stands, rather than attempting to alter it to suit a particular theory.

An objective view recognizes that there is no easy solution to the problem of the servant's identity, and acknowledges that the tension between the individual and collective interpretations is inherent in the text itself. For while the servant coexists with Israel, and may even be addressed as Israel, he is, nevertheless, distinct from Israel, and has a ministry to perform to Israel. The paradox involved here must have been just as obvious to the prophet as it is to us, and, therefore, fully intentional. Furthermore, the figure of the servant retains its paradoxical character across the centuries, for when the time of its fulfillment comes, is it fulfilled in Jesus Christ *and* his church.

The *servant* himself speaks in the second Servant Song and bids those in distant lands to give heed to his words (cf. 42:1, 4). He tells how the Lord called him (v. 1) and prepared him for his mission (v. 2). The statement that his *mouth* has been made *like a sharp sword* suggests that the weapon with which he will do battle is the word of the Lord (50:4; Deut. 18:18; Jer. 1:9; 5:14; 23:29; Eph. 6:17; Heb. 4:12; Rev. 1:16). Verse 2, with its reference to sharp sword and polished arrow, sounds surprisingly warlike and aggressive, especially when compared with the portrait of the servant found elsewhere (cf. 42:3; 50:6; 53:7). This is but another

---

122 A proposal supported by Westermann, who argues that the term "Israel" is "the earliest witness to the collective interpretation of the Servant, one gloss among the many that seek to interpret the text."

indication of the paradoxical nature of the servant.

Twice it is said that the Lord hides the servant (v. 2). To be hidden by the Lord means to be under his care and protection (cf. Psalms 17:8; 27:5; 31:20; 64:2; Jer. 36:26). To interpret this to mean that the Lord keeps his servant hidden for a while and afterwards reveals him to the world (cf. North), or to see in the hiding of the servant a parallel to the hiddenness of God (cf. 45:15), as if the true nature of the servant were hidden from the eyes of men (cf. Smart), is to ignore the plain meaning of the text. This is the servant's way of expressing his assurance that the Lord will always watch over him (cf. vv. 4b,5b).

The task initially assigned to the servant is that of restoring Jacob/Israel to the Lord (v. 5a). It soon becomes apparent, however, that this is no easy assignment. On the contrary, the difficulties are so great that the servant becomes discouraged and cries out in despair, *I have labored in vain, I have spent my strength for nothing and vanity* (v. 4a). His uttering of such a cry calls to mind Jeremiah's reaction to a similar situation (cf. Jer. 15:10,18; 20: 14–18).

The similarity between the servant's experience and that of Jeremiah can also be seen in the manner in which God responds to their laments. In each instance he answers discouragement with a call to greater responsibility (v. 6b; cf. Jer. 12:5; 15:19–21). The servant's field of operations, therefore, is extended beyond the borders of Israel to include all the nations of the earth. God often responds to our discouragements by enlarging our field of responsibility (cf. 1 Kings 19:9–16). The second Servant Song thus ends on the same note of universalism with which it begins.

(2) God's Encouragement to Captive Israel (49:7–13)

7 Thus says the LORD,
　　the Redeemer of Israel and his Holy One,
　to one deeply despised, abhorred by the nations,

　　the servant of rulers:
　"Kings shall see and arise;
　　princes, and they shall **prostrate themselves**;
　because of the LORD, who is faithful,
　　the Holy One of Israel, who has chosen you."
8 Thus says the LORD:
　"In a time of favor I have answered you,
　　in a day of salvation I have helped you;
　I have kept you and given you
　　as a covenant to the people,
　to establish the land,
　　to apportion the desolate heritages;
9 saying to the prisoners, 'Come forth,'
　　to those who are in darkness, 'Appear.'
　They shall feed along the ways,
　　on all bare heights shall be their pasture;
10 they shall not hunger or thirst,
　　neither scorching wind nor sun shall smite them,
　for he who has pity on them will lead them,
　　and by springs of water will guide them.
11 And I will make all my mountains a way,
　　and my highways shall be raised up.
12 Lo, these shall come from afar,
　　and lo, these from the north and from the west,
　　and these from the land of Syene."
13 Sing for joy, O heavens, and exult, O earth;
　　break forth, O mountains, into singing!
　For the LORD has comforted his people,
　　and will have compassion on his afflicted.

These verses clearly show that Israel is still in exile. Her present status is that of one *deeply despised, abhorred by the nations, the servant of rulers.* Her land lies desolate (v. 8b); she languishes in prison (v. 9a); and her lot has been to suffer affliction (v. 13b).

Her suffering and humiliation will, however, soon come to an end. When she has been restored to her land, kings and princes shall come to prostrate themselves before her *because of the Lord* (v. 7b). Their obeisance, it should be noted, is directed not so much toward Israel as toward "the Holy One of Israel" (cf. 49: 22–23). The prophet recognizes that the true glory of Israel lies not in herself but in her God.

The nation's release from captivity is described in greater detail in vv. 8–12. The exodus motif is especially strong throughout this section. God rescues his people from prison and leads them across the wilderness, as if he were a second Moses. He tends them as a shepherd would tend his flock, providing pasture for them along the way (v. 9), and leading them by springs of water (v. 10). He prepares a highway in the wilderness for their greater comfort (v. 11; cf. 35:8–10; 40:3–4). Zion's children will return not only from Babylon but also from all the far-flung places of the earth where they have been scattered (v. 12).

The wonder of it all causes the prophet to burst forth into a hymn of praise (v. 13; cf. 42:10–13; 52:9). He is filled with joy at the prospect of what God is about to do. The hymn he sings is one of the many literary gems that adorn this prophecy. One is reminded by it of the earlier hymn that the Israelites sang after their deliverance at the Red Sea (cf. Ex. 15:1–18).

(3) The Repopulation of Zion (49:14–21)

14 But Zion said, "The Lord has forsaken me,
    my Lord has forgotten me."
15 "Can a woman forget her sucking child,
    that she should have no compassion on
        the son of her womb?"
Even these may forget,
    yet I will not forget you.
16 Behold, I have graven you on the palms of
        my hands;
    your walls are continually before me.
17 Your builders outstrip your destroyers,
    and those who laid you waste go forth
        from you.
18 Lift up your eyes round about and see;
    they all gather, they come to you.
As I live, says the Lord,
    you shall put them all on as an ornament,
    you shall bind them on as a bride does.
19 "Surely your waste and your desolate places
    and your devastated land—
surely now you will be too narrow for your
        inhabitants,
    and those who swallowed you up will be
        far away.
20 The children born in the time of your be-
        reavement
    will yet say in your ears:
'The place is too narrow for me;
    make room for me to dwell in.'
21 Then you will say in your heart:
'Who has borne me these?
I was bereaved and barren,
    exiled and put away,

but who has brought up these?
Behold, I was left alone;
    whence then have these come?' "

The city of Zion, here personified as a forlorn woman (cf. 50:1; 51:17–23; 54: 1–8), laments that the Lord has forsaken and forgotten her (cf. 40:27; Psalm 137; Ezek. 37:11–14). Her cry of despair calls forth one of the tenderest expressions of divine love to be found anywhere in the Scriptures. God's love for his people is said to be infinitely greater than the strongest form of human love, that is, greater than a mother's love for her infant child. There is more likelihood, therefore, that a mother would forget to have compassion on her child than that God would forget Zion (v. 15). How can he forget her, when he has her engraved (perhaps tattooed) on the palms of his hands, and when her walls are never out of his mind (v. 16)?

In the light of passages such as this, it is strange that some still speak of God in the Old Testament as a God of strict justice, as over against a God of love in the New Testament, as if there were actually two separate beings radically different in nature. The concept of an unloving God is, in fact, as foreign to the Old Testament as it is to the New. His unfailing love, even in the face of human indifference and disobedience, is the cord that binds both Testaments together.

The remainder of the section describes the miraculous rebuilding and repopulation of Zion. Instead of *banayik* (*your builders*) (v. 17), the Dead Sea Scroll of Isaiah IQIsᵃ) and other ancient versions read *bonayik* ("your sons"). This is perhaps one of those rare instances where both readings express the original intention of the author: Zion's sons will return from exile and will also rebuild her ruins.

The Lord bids the desolate city *lift up* her *eyes* and see her children coming to her from every direction. She is to adorn herself with these, as a bride might adorn herself with her ornaments (v. 18). In hyperbolic language the prophet describes the land as being entirely too small to contain the vast hosts of returning exiles (vv. 19–20). Zion, so long bereft of her children, can only cry out in amazement and joy, "Where have all these come from?"

(4) The Rescue and Return of the Exiles (49:22–26)

22 Thus says the Lord GOD:
"Behold, I will lift up my hand to the nations,
    and raise my signal to the peoples;
and they shall bring your sons in their bosom,
    and your daughters shall be carried on their shoulders.
23 Kings shall be your foster fathers,
    and their queens your nursing mothers.
With their faces to the ground they shall bow down to you,
    and lick the dust of your feet.
Then you will know that I am the LORD;
    those who wait for me shall not be put to shame."
24 Can the prey be taken from the mighty,
    or the captives of a tyrant be rescued?
25 Surely, thus says the LORD:
"Even the captives of the mighty shall be taken,
    and the prey of the tyrant be rescued,
for I will contend with those who contend with you,
    and I will save your children.
26 I will make your oppressors eat their own flesh,
    and they shall be drunk with their own blood as with wine.
Then all flesh shall know
    that I am the LORD your Savior,
    and your Redeemer, the Mighty One of Jacob."

The decidedly nationalistic spirit of this passage stands in sharp contrast to the universalistic spirit which is usually found in chapters 40—66 (cf. 40:5; 44:5; 45: 22–23; 49:5–6; 56:3–8). Some scholars have concluded on the basis of this passage and others like it that Second Isaiah was exclusively nationalistic in outlook and that, therefore, the universalistic passages were written by a later prophet (cf. Snaith and Orlinsky).

However, to take such a position is to demand of the prophet a uniformity of thought on the subject that was not characteristic of biblical writers in general. Other prophets were rarely consistent in their statements concerning the relative importance of Israel and the nations in the plan of God. The tension between universalism and nationalism, therefore, is not limited to these chapters, but appears in all parts of the Scriptures, even in the sayings of Jesus (cf. Matt. 10:5–6; 15:24; 28:18–20).

When Yahweh lifts his hand as a signal to the nations, they will bring Zion's children to her with all haste (v. 22). Kings and queens will accompany them to serve as their caretakers. Dramatic proof will be given that the tables have now been turned as kings and queens bow down and kiss the feet of their former slaves (v. 23). The nationalistic spirit of the passage is tempered somewhat by the absence of any suggestion of coercion: the homage rendered to Israel by kings and queens is a free and spontaneous act on their part (cf. 45:14).

In v. 24 the prophet raises a question that must have been uppermost in the minds of his listeners: Was God able to take *the prey* (the exiles) from *the mighty* (Babylon)? Earlier the Israelites had expressed doubt that God loved them (49: 14); now they were questioning whether or not he was able to deliver them. In these two questions—Is God able? Does he care? —are expressed the hopes and fears of troubled men across the centuries. They are the questions that clamor for an answer whenever the silence of God in the face of human suffering and evil seems to indicate that he is either unwilling or else unable to intervene.

The question of v. 24 is given an affirmative reply in v. 25. The mighty (Babylon) will indeed have his prey (the exiles) snatched from him. Afterwards he will be forced to eat his own flesh and drink his own blood (v. 26a). This does not mean that the Babylonians will literally resort to cannibalism but that they will destroy themselves through civil war and internal strife.

The ultimate purpose of God in the rescue of his people from Babylon is that all flesh might come to understand his true nature and divinity (v. 26b). The statement of this purpose saves the passage from an exclusive nationalism. God's redemption of Israel is thereby shown to be but an initial step in the realization of a larger plan, a plan that encompasses all the nations of the earth.

2. Faithless Israel and the Faithful Servant (50:1–11)

(1) Israel's Responsibility for Her Predicament (50:1–3)

1 Thus says the LORD:
"Where is your mother's bill of divorce,
　　with which I put her away?
Or which of my creditors is it
　　to whom I have sold you?
Behold, for your iniquities you were sold,
　　and for your transgressions your mother
　　　was put away.
2 Why, when I came, was there no man?
　　When I called, was there no one to answer?
Is my hand shortened, that it cannot redeem?
　　Or have I no power to deliver?
Behold, by my rebuke I dry up the sea,
　　I make the rivers a desert;
their fish stink for lack of water,
　　and die of thirst.
3 I clothe the heavens with blackness,
　　and make sackcloth their covering."

These verses are designed to refute Israel's allegation that the responsibility for her predicament rests upon Yahweh. She had apparently complained that he had arbitrarily divorced her and sent her away into captivity. If he had taken such action, however, he would have been required by the law to give her a bill of divorce (cf. Deut. 24:1–4). The prophet challenges her, therefore, to substantiate her charge against God by producing the document with which she has been divorced. The fact that she is unable to do this—the questions in v. 1 are obviously rhetorical—proves that her complaint is totally unfounded.

This does not mean, however, that no *divorce* has occurred. Israel has indeed been sent away into exile (cf. Mal. 2:16); she has indeed been sold into captivity (v. 1b). Nevertheless, this has not resulted from Yahweh's arbitrary rejection of her, but from her own corruption and disloyalty. She has remained deaf to his call in the past and is still deaf even in the present (v. 2a).

The second complaint of Israel is that the prolongation of her exile has resulted from Yahweh's inability to intervene on her behalf. The rhetorical questions in v. 2b constitute the Lord's response to this complaint: his hand is not *shortened* so *that it cannot redeem*, nor does he lack *power to deliver*. The implication is that any delay that may have occurred in Israel's redemption has been caused by her own disobedience (cf. 59:1–2).

The affirmation of Yahweh's power to save is followed by an illustration of his power to destroy (vv. 2c–3). The destruction envisioned here is that which will be visited upon Yahweh's foes (cf. 42:15). The words, therefore, are intended as a further rebuke to Israel for her lack of faith.

(2) The Servant's Assurance of Vindication (50:4–9)

4 The Lord GOD has given me
　　the tongue of those who are taught,
that I may know how to sustain with a word
　　him that is weary.
Morning by morning he wakens,
　　he wakens my ear
　　to hear as those who are taught.
5 The Lord GOD has opened my ear,
　　and I was not rebellious,
　　I turned not backward.
6 I gave my back to the smiters,
　　and my cheeks to those who pulled out
　　　the beard;
I hid not my face
　　from shame and spitting.
7 For the Lord GOD helps me;
　　therefore I have not been confounded;
therefore I have set my face like a flint,
　　and I know that I shall not be put to
　　　shame;
8 he who vindicates me is near.
Who will contend with me?
　　Let us stand up together.
Who is my adversary?
　　Let him come near to me.
9 Behold, the Lord GOD helps me;
　　who will declare me guilty?

Behold, all of them will wear out like a
   garment;
   the moth will eat them up.

This passage is generally regarded as
the third Servant Song (cf. 42:1–4; 49:
1–6; 52:13—53:12), although the term
"servant" is not found in it. The first two
songs emphasize the servant's mission; the
third one, however, treats of his obedience
and of his steadfast endurance under persecution. Because of the song's description
of the growing hostility toward the servant,
North has entitled it: "The Gethsemane of
the Servant."

Verses 4–5 describe the teachableness
of the servant: he is sensitive to every
divine impulse and word. He, therefore,
has both the tongue and the ear of a true
disciple. His teachableness has not been
acquired automatically, however, for it has
been necessary for the Lord to waken his
ear morning by morning that he might
learn. Though the discipline of the Lord
has been rigorous, the servant has not
turned away from his task or displayed a
rebellious spirit. He is, indeed, the ideal
learner.

What, then, is the purpose of his learning? Why has the Lord taught him so
assiduously? It is that he might know how
to console the weary with a word (v. 4;
cf. 49:2). He whom the Lord has taught,
therefore, must himself become the teacher
of others; and the word which has been
spoken in his ear must be spread abroad.
The word in question is perhaps the word
of consolation that was sent to the weary
exiles (cf. 40:1–2,9,27–31).

Speaking the word of the Lord—even
such a consoling word—soon brings the
servant into serious difficulty (cf. Jer. 20:
8). He becomes the object of physical
violence and insult (v. 6). Persecution
does not cause him to waver, however, as
he willingly endures the grievous assaults
that are made upon him. North has observed that v. 6 is "a startling anticipation
of the maltreatment of Christ on the morning of the crucifixion."

Verses 7–9 are an expression of the

servant's assurance of vindication. The language used here is clearly that of the law-
court. The servant does not fear the trials
that may come in the future, for he is sure
that the Lord God will help him (vv. 7a,
9a; cf. 41:10,13,14; 44:2; 49:8). In any
confrontation with his accusers, therefore,
he will be vindicated, but they will perish
like a moth-eaten garment. This sublime
affirmation of faith reminds one of the
later words of the apostle Paul, "If God be
for us, who can be against us?" (Rom.
8:31, KJV).

(3) The Consequences of Belief and Un-belief (50:10–11)

10 Who among you fears the LORD
      and obeys the voice of his servant,
   who walks in darkness
      and has no light,
   yet trusts in the name of the LORD
      and relies upon his God?
11 Behold, all you who kindle a fire,
      who set brands alight!
   Walk by the light of your fire,
      and by the brands which you have kin-
         dled!
   This shall you have from my hand:
      you shall lie down in torment.

Verse 10 begins with the interrogative
pronoun mi, translated "Who?" The RSV
regards the entire verse as a question. According to this interpretation, the conduct
of the servant is held up as the model for
others to emulate. Although he walks in
darkness without any light, he, nevertheless, trusts in the name of the Lord and
leans upon his God. It is fitting, therefore,
that the faithful in Israel should follow
his example, obeying his voice and fearing
the Lord whom he serves.

An alternate interpretation results from
placing the question mark after the word
"servant," which in the Hebrew bears a
heavy disjunctive accent, and regarding
the last two verbs in the verse as jussives.
The resultant translation reads: "Who
among you fears the Lord, obeying the
voice of his servant? Whoever walks in
darkness and has no light, let him trust in
the name of the Lord and lean upon his
God." According to this rendering, it is not

the servant but the prophet's listeners who talk in darkness without any light. These are the persecuted saints who suffer because of their fear of the Lord and their obedience to the voice of his servant. As they grope in the shadows, they are exhorted by the prophet to trust in the name of the Lord, "name" being used here as a synonym for the Lord himself (cf. Ex. 33:19; Lev. 24:11,16; Isa. 52:6). This interpretation seems to be preferable to that reflected in the RSV.

Verse 11 describes the present conduct and future destiny of those who rebel against the Lord. It is not clear whether these are Israelites or foreigners, although a comparison with v. 9 would suggest the latter. These are described as kindling fires to their idols, perhaps by means of friction or flint, only to be engulfed by the flames they have kindled. They suddenly find themselves trapped by their own flames with no means of escape. The path they have followed, therefore, leads ultimately and inevitably to torment and destruction. This is vividly stated in the phrase *you shall lie down in torment,* where to "lie down" means to die (cf. 14:18; Job 20:11; Ezek. 32:21). In these verses, therefore, the prophet confronts his listeners with two alternatives: they must either walk in the light of faith, or else perish in the fires of destruction.

3. The Consolation of Zion (51:1—52:12)

(1) Encouragement for Fainthearted Believers (51:1-8)

1 "Hearken to me, you who pursue deliverance,
    you who seek the LORD;
look to the rock from which you were hewn,
    and to the quarry from which you were digged.
2 Look to Abraham your father
    and to Sarah who bore you;
for when he was but one I called him,
    and I blessed him and made him many.
3 For the LORD will comfort Zion;
    he will comfort all her waste places,
and will make her wilderness like Eden,
    her desert like the garden of the LORD;
    joy and gladness will be found in her,

thanksgiving and the voice of song.
4 "Listen to me, my people,
    and give ear to me, my nation;
for a law will go forth from me,
    and my justice for a light to the peoples.
5 My deliverance draws near speedily,
    my salvation has gone forth,
    and my arms will rule the peoples;
the coastlands wait for me,
    and for my arm they hope.
6 Lift up your eyes to the heavens,
    and look at the earth beneath;
for the heavens will vanish like smoke,
    the earth will wear out like a garment,
    and they who dwell in it will die like gnats;
but my salvation will be for ever,
    and my deliverance will never be ended.
7 "Hearken to me, you who know righteousness,
    the people in whose heart is my law;
fear not the reproach of men,
    and be not dismayed at their revilings.
8 For the moth will eat them up like a garment,
    and the worm will eat them like wool;
but my deliverance will be for ever,
    and my salvation to all generations."

There are three strophes in this passage each of which begins with the command to *hearken* or to *listen* (vv. 1–3,4–6,7–8). The first task of the interpreter is to determine the identity of those to whom the commands are given. Unless one denies the unity of the passage and, like Westermann, resorts to a radical construction of the text, it becomes clear that those who are being addressed are the faithful—but fearful—Israelites. For example, it is said of them that they pursue righteousness and *seek the Lord* (v. 1), that they are the offspring of Abraham and Sarah (v. 2), that they are the Lord's people and his nation (v. 4), that they *know righteousness,* and that they are the people in whose heart is the law of the Lord (v. 7).

The prophet writes, therefore, to convince his fellow exiles of the certainty and permanence of the coming deliverance. In the first strophe he bids them look to the past and remember the miracle with which their history began. When *Abraham* was but *one,* God called him and blessed him and made him *many.* Now he is ready to perform a himilar miracle with the fainthearted exiles: though they be little in their own sight (cf. 40:27; 41:14; 49:14), they will soon be transformed into a great and mighty nation (cf. 41:15–16; 49:7, 17–21). The fact that the prophet addresses these words to them in the very land in which Abraham and Sarah first received their call gives added meaning to what he says.

The appeal to the past is followed by a promise for the future (v. 3). To say that *the Lord will comfort Zion* means that he will effectively intervene to put an end to her troubles (cf. 40:1; 49:13). Her devastated lands will be transformed into Eden, the garden of the Lord. *Joy and gladness* —two words that often appear together in the Old Testament (cf. v. 11; 35:10; Psalms 45:15; 51:8; Zech. 8:19)—*will be found in her*. The Dead Sea Scroll of Isaiah (IQIsᵃ) adds an additional line to the end of v. 3: "sorrow and sighing shall flee away" (cf. v. 11; 35:10).

The second strophe (vv. 4–6) describes God's salvation as comprehending all mankind and as outlasting the heavens and the earth. In spite of all its majesty and apparent permanence, the universe is subject to change and decay, and will ultimately *vanish like smoke* (v. 6). In such a transitory world, only God remains constant (cf. 40:6–8; Psalm 90:1–6). Verse 6 sets the stage for the announcement of the new heavens and the new earth, although this is delayed until 65:17 (cf. 66:22).

The third strophe (vv. 7–8) describes the people of God as presently having to endure persecution. While their oppressors are not named, they are probably to be understood as the Babylonians. The Israelites are exhorted not to fear the reproach of men and not to be dismayed at their revilings (cf. Zeph. 2:8). Tyrants will soon vanish like moth-eaten garments (cf. 50:9), but the deliverance wrought by the Lord will never end (v. 8). The victorious refrain that closes the second strophe (v. 6b) reappears in a slightly modified form at the close of the third (v. 8b). The meaning in both instances is

that the salvation of God is the only enduring reality in a world that is destined to perish (cf. 2 Peter 3:8–13).

(2) The Prophet's Plea and God's Response (51:9–16)

9 Awake, awake, put on strength,
  O arm of the Lord;
awake, as in days of old,
  the generations of long ago.
Was it not thou that didst cut Rahab in pieces,
  that didst pierce the dragon?
10 Was it not thou that didst dry up the sea,
  the waters of the great deep;
that didst make the depths of the sea a way
  for the redeemed to pass over?
11 And the ransomed of the Lord shall return,
  and come to Zion with singing;
everlasting joy shall be upon their heads;
  they shall obtain joy and gladness,
  and sorrow and sighing shall flee away.
12 "I, I am he that comforts you;
  who are you that you are afraid of man who dies,
of the son of man who is made like grass,
13 and have forgotten the Lord, your Maker,
  who stretched out the heavens
  and laid the foundations of the earth,
and fear continually all the day
  because of the fury of the oppressor,
when he sets himself to destroy?
  And where is the fury of the oppressor?
14 He who is bowed down shall speedily be released;
  he shall not die and go down to the Pit,
  neither shall his bread fail.
15 For I am the Lord your God,
  who stirs up the sea so that its waves roar—
  the Lord of hosts is his name.
16 And I have put my words in your mouth,
  and hid you in the shadow of my hand,
stretching out the heavens
  and laying the foundations of the earth,
  and saying to Zion, 'You are my people.' "

In vv. 9–11 the prophet assumes the role of intercessor (cf. 63:7–64:12) and pleads with the Lord to manifest his power on behalf of Israel, even as he did in days of old. A characteristic feature of this and succeeding sections is the emphatic repetition of key words at the beginning of new stanzas (cf. 51:9,12,17; 52:1,11).

The prophet addresses his plea to the *arm of the Lord,* which is an example of the objectifying of the Lord's power to save (cf. v. 5; 40:10; 52:10; 53:1; 59:16; 62:8; 63:5,12). *Put on* is sometimes used of a warrior putting on his armor (cf. 1 Sam. 17:5,38; Isa. 59:17; Jer. 46:4), so that the picture suggested by the arm of the Lord putting on strength is that of "a heavily gauntleted forearm brandishing a sword" (North).

From the viewpoint of the prophet, the two occasions in the past when God's power was most dramatically displayed were creation and the Exodus. The terminology with which he alludes to creation is borrowed from the ancient cosmological myth in which creation has its beginning with the deity's slaying of the monster of chaos. In the Babylonian version of the myth the god Marduk slays Tiamat the dragon and from the two severed parts of her body creates the heavens and the earth. The Old Testament counterpart to Tiamat is variously known as "the serpent" (cf. Job 26:13; Isa. 27:1), "the dragon" (cf. Isa. 27:1), "Leviathan" (cf. Psalm 74:14; Isa. 27:1), and "Rahab" (cf. Job 9:13; 26:12; Psalm 89:10). The latter name is also twice applied symbolically to Egypt (cf. Psalm 87:4; Isa. 30:7).

Second Isaiah's use of terminology drawn from an ancient myth does not mean that he endorses it. He is, rather, appropriating its language for polemical reasons. To say that Yahweh *cut Rahab to pieces* and pierced the dragon (v. 9b) means that he, and not Marduk, is the creator of the heavens and the earth.

The first half of v. 10 could apply equally well to the creation (cf. Gen. 1:2; Psalm 104:6-9; Prov. 8:27-29) or to the Exodus (cf. Ex. 14:21); the second half, on the other hand, refers exclusively to the Exodus. The themes of creation and redemption are thus brought together in a manner thoroughly characteristic of Second Isaiah, who often speaks of God as both Creator and Redeemer (cf. 43:1, 14-15; 44:2,24; 54:5). Not only does he see a relationship between creation and redemption in the past, but he also believes that Israel's future redemption will result in a new creation (cf. 41:17-20; 51:3; 55:12-13; 65:17-25). His concept of salvation-history, therefore, could be represented by the following diagram: Creation←Exodus out of Egypt←Exile→ Exodus out of Babylon→New Creation. From his vantage point in the exile, therefore, he looks backward to the first creation and the first exodus, and forward to the new exodus and the new creation.

Verse 11 is hymnic in character (cf. v. 3), and is almost a word for word repetition of 35:10. Hymns of this nature were often handed down in oral form, which perhaps explains why this one has been included twice among the oracles of Second Isaiah. In both its occurrences it is preceded by a reference to the *way* prepared by the Lord for his redeemed (cf. 35:8-9; 51:10).

There is a depth of tenderness in the Lord's response to the prophet's prayer of intercession. His repetition of the personal pronoun *I* (v. 12) has the effect of drawing Israel's attention away from the momentary threat posed by her oppressors and focusing it instead upon him and the salvation he is so generously providing for his people. Here, as elsewhere in Second Isaiah, to comfort means much more than merely to console another in his troubles: it denotes, rather, to deliver one out of his troubles.

Israel is told not to fear her oppressors, i.e., the Babylonians, who are, after all, mere men, *made like grass* and destined to die (v. 12b; cf. 40:6-8; Psalm 8:4). The warning is one she needs to hear, for her fear of men has caused her to forget the *Lord* her *Maker* (v. 13). In spite of her lack of faith, however, she is promised that her people will soon be saved from bondage, from death, and from hunger (v. 14; cf. v. 23). This promise is made on the authority of the Lord of hosts, the Creator of the universe and the covenant-God of Israel (vv. 15-16).

(3) The Cup of God's Wrath (51:17-23)

17 Rouse yourself, rouse yourself,
   stand up, O Jerusalem,
   you who have drunk at the hand of the
      LORD
      the cup of his wrath,
   who have drunk to the dregs
      the bowl of staggering.
18 There is none to guide her
      among all the sons she has borne;
   there is none to take her by the hand
      among all the sons she has brought up.
19 These two things have befallen you—
      who will condole with you?—
   devastation and destruction, famine and
      sword;
   who will comfort you?
20 Your sons have fainted,
      they lie at the head of every street
      like an antelope in a net;
   they are full of the wrath of the LORD,
      the rebuke of your God.
21 Therefore hear this, you who are afflicted,
      who are drunk, but not with wine:
22 Thus says your Lord, the LORD,
      your God who pleads the cause of his
         people:
   "Behold, I have taken from your hand
      the cup of staggering;
   the bowl of my wrath
      you shall drink no more;
23 and I will put it into the hand of your
      tormentors,
   who have said to you,
      'Bow down, that we may pass over';
   and you have made your back like the
      ground
      and like the street for them to pass
         over."

The previous section began with the prophet's urgent plea to the Lord to awaken and to manifest his power on behalf of Israel as in days of old (v. 9; cf. 64:1-4). In v. 17 the prophet turns to Jerusalem with an equally urgent appeal that she awaken herself (a reflexive imperative) in anticipation of her day of deliverance (cf. 52:1; Rom. 13:11).

The prophet's appeal is followed by the most plaintive description of the desolate state of Jerusalem to be found in Second Isaiah (cf. vv. 17-20). There is a close similarity between the thought of this section—especially of vv. 17-19—and that of 40:1-2. In both instances, Jerusalem's suffering is attributed not to blind chance or happenstance but to the hand of the Lord. Both passages also express the idea that the city has been punished in double measure for all her sins. Finally, both passages teach that Jerusalem's comfort will come only from the Lord.

The city is pictured as a woman's staggering about in a drunken stupor. In her hand she holds an empty cup, called the cup of his wrath and the bowl of staggering (v. 17b). It is empty because she has drained it "to the dregs." As she reels and staggers along, none of her sons takes her by the hand to steady her or to guide her (v. 18). The reason they do not do so is that they, too, are drunk with the wrath of the Lord; they have passed out and lie helpless in the streets, like wild antelopes caught in a net (v. 20). It would be difficult to imagine a more depressing scene than this.

The remainder of the passage, however, consists of a glorious salvation oracle (vv. 21-23). The Lord announces to the drunken city that he has taken from her hand the cup of staggering, and that she shall drink no more from the bowl of my wrath (note the reverse order of the two phrases). Instead, he will place the cup of his wrath in the hands of her tormentors, who have abused her and treated her with such contempt. As one reads v. 23, he can sense the Lord's indignation over the manner in which the haughty Babylonians have degraded his people (cf. 47:6). His indignation always manifests itself when the strong take unfair advantage of the weak. The truth in this passage is relevant to the "big powers" of our day.

(4) Redeemed Without Money (52:1-6)

1 Awake, awake,
   put on your strength, O Zion;
   put on your beautiful garments,
      O Jerusalem, the holy city;
   for there shall no more come into you
      the uncircumcised and the unclean.
2 Shake yourself from the dust, arise,
      O captive Jerusalem;
   loose the bonds from your neck,
      O captive daughter of Zion.
3 For thus says the LORD: "You were sold

for nothing, and you shall be redeemed without money. ⁴ For thus says the Lord God: My people went down at the first into Egypt to sojourn there, and the Assyrian oppressed them for nothing. ⁵ Now therefore what have I here, says the Lord, seeing that my people are taken away for nothing? Their rulers wail, says the Lord, and continually all the day my name is despised. ⁶ Therefore my people shall know my name; therefore in that day they shall know that it is I who speak; here am I."

Verses 1–2 contain a series of imperatives addressed to Zion: *Awake, awake* (cf. 51:9,17); *put on your strength* (cf. 51:9); *put on your beautiful garments* (cf. Rev. 21:2); *shake yourself from the dust* (cf. 51:23); *arise* (cf. 60:1); *loose the bonds from your neck.* Many interpreters have pointed out that these commands stand in sharp contrast to those spoken to Babylon in 47:1–2. The prophet thus foresees a time when the roles of the two cities will be completely reversed: Babylon will be abased, and Zion will be exalted.

Jerusalem is addressed in v. 1 as *the holy city,* a title which is only rarely used of her (cf. Neh. 11:1,18; Isa. 48:2; Dan. 9:24; Matt: 4:5; 27:53; Rev. 11:2; 21:2, 10; 22:19). Because she is holy, or at least destined to be so the uncircumcised and unclean will not be permitted to enter her gates (cf. Gen. 17:14; Ex. 12:48; Ezek. 44:9; Rev. 21:27). This apparently refers to the exclusion of uncircumcised foreigners from the worship of Yahweh, although it perhaps includes apostate Israelites as well.

Verses 3–6, which the RSV renders as prose, are regarded by many as a later addition to the oracles of Second Isaiah. The evidence does not seem to warrant such a conclusion, however, especially since many of the themes and expressions that are characteristic of the prophet are to be found here. These include the statement that Israel's redemption will be *without money* (cf. 45:13; 55:1), the comparison of the Babylonian exile to previous periods of captivity in Israel's history, the description of God as acting out of concern for his name (cf. 42:8; 48:11), and the

announcement of God's saving presence with his people (v. 6; cf. 40:9; 58:9; 65:1). There is no sound reason, therefore, to deny these verses to Second Isaiah.

In v. 5 God is described as exclaiming, *What have I here?* This is his reaction to the deplorable state in which he finds his people. It is a situation that demands his intervention, for in their continual humiliation his own name is despised. Soon this will be reversed, for in the glorious age to come, here referred to by the only occurrence in Second Isaiah of the phrase *in that day,* Yahweh's name will again be revealed to his people in all its majesty and holiness (v. 6; cf. Ex. 3:13–15). Smart has written (p. 190): "An Israel that knows God's name and responds to him when he says, 'Behold me,' is an Israel in covenant with God and assured of deliverance."

(5) The Good News of God's Reign (52:7–10)

7 How beautiful upon the mountains
  are the feet of him who brings good tidings,
who publishes peace, who brings good tidings of good,
  who publishes salvation,
  who says to Zion, "Your God reigns."
8 Hark, your watchmen lift up their voice,
  together they sing for joy;
for eye to eye they see
  the return of the Lord to Zion.
9 Break forth together into singing,
  you waste places of Jerusalem;
for the Lord has comforted his people,
  he has redeemed Jerusalem.
10 The Lord has bared his holy arm
  before the eyes of all the nations;
and all the ends of the earth shall see
  the salvation of our God.

The form of this oracle is that of the watchman's song (cf. 21:11–12; 62:6–7; Hab. 2:1–3). In unforgettable language it describes the joy that fills Jerusalem when she is told that Yahweh is returning to establish his rule over her. It is no accident that the words of these verses have so often been set to music. They constitute a grand finale that calls for full orchestration. Surely they were meant to be sung!

In his imagination the prophet sees a

runner speeding across the hills toward Jerusalem, loudly proclaiming the good news of peace and salvation (v. 7; cf. Rom. 10:15). As he comes near the city he cries out, *Your God reigns!* The watchmen stationed on the walls catch the sound of his words and lift up their voices in song. Before their very eyes they see the Lord returning to dwell in Zion (v. 8; cf. Ezek. 43:1–5).

As soon as the watchmen begin to sing, they are joined by the entire city, here designated as the *waste places of Jerusalem* (v. 9). At long last the Lord has comforted and redeemed his people. The prayer of 51:9 has now been answered, for *the Lord has bared his holy arm* before the eyes of all the nations, and all the ends of the earth will see the salvation that has been provided for Israel (v. 10). How beautiful, indeed, are the feet of those who bear such tidings as these!

When the prophet spoke these words, there was so much in the contemporary situation that seemed to contradict them. How could one believe that God reigned when Jerusalem still lay under the oppressor's heel? Men of every age have faced the same problem: how can one believe that God is king when evil seems to be enthroned on every hand? The prophet had discovered faith's answer to these questions: *Your God reigns!* He believed that God was firmly in control of history, regardless of how much the circumstances at any given moment might seem to contradict this. His song, therefore, was one of praise to the Lord of history, a song sung in anticipation of the glorious reality we know as the kingdom of God.

(6) Zion's Emancipation Proclamation (52:11–12)

11 Depart, depart, go out thence,
    touch no unclean thing;
  go out from the midst of her, purify your-
    selves,
    you who bear the vessels of the LORD.
12 For you shall not go out in haste,
    and you shall not go in flight,
  for the LORD will go before you,

and the God of Israel will be your rear guard.

The Jewish exiles are summoned to depart from Babylon (cf. 48:20–22; 55:12–13). The giving of the summons implies that the city has already fallen to Cyrus, or else is on the verge of doing so. The urgency with which the prophet speaks suggests that some of his listeners are less than enthusiastic about returning to Jerusalem. Having followed the earlier advice of Jeremiah (cf. Jer. 29:1–7), they have put down roots in the land of their captivity. They hesitate, therefore, to exchange their present security for an uncertain future (cf. Ex. 16:2–3; Num. 14:2–4).

Those who *bear the vessels of the Lord* are commanded to purify themselves in preparation for the homeward journey. Most interpreters assume that these are the priests who are to be entrusted with the responsibility of returning the Temple vessels to Jerusalem (cf. 2 Chron. 36:7, 10, 18–19; Dan. 1:2; 5:2–3; Ezra 1:7–11). They must be ritually clean so as not to defile the sacred vessels entrusted to them.

Those who participate in the exodus from Babylon will not go out in haste as their forefathers did from Egypt (v. 12; cf. Ex. 12:11,33,37–39). They will journey across the desert peacefully and securely, for God will go before them and will also be their rear guard. No harm, therefore, will befall them, but they will all be safely led to the fold of the holy city (cf. 40:10–11).

4. The Travail and Triumph of the Servant (52:13—53:12)

The fourth Servant Song has been variously described as "the most influential poem in any literature," "the highest peak of Old Testament revelation," and "the heart of the Old Testament." If for some reason the entire song were to disappear from the book of Isaiah, it could be almost completely reconstructed from the quotations borrowed from it by New Testament writers. Of the 12 verses in chapter 53, for example, there is only one which does not reappear, in whole or in part, somewhere in the New Testament. Quotations from the chapter are found in all four Gospels and in Acts, Romans, Philippians, Hebrews, and 1 Peter. The wide use of the passage by these New Testament writers shows that they considered it to be vital to the understanding of the gospel. Without it, as North has suggested, the problem of the crucified Messiah might have remained for them a baffling enigma (cf. Acts 8:26–35).

In the first three Servant Songs (42: 1–4; 49:1–6; 50:4–9), it is difficult to determine whether the servant is the nation itself or an individual within the nation. In the fourth song, however, he is unmistakably an individual, ministering to the nation but distinct from it. The strongest support for the individual interpretation is the statement that the servant suffers for no guilt of his own (cf. 53:8–9), a statement which the prophet could not have made concerning the nation without at the same time contradicting what he had so forcefully stated elsewhere, namely, that the exile was the merited punishment for Israel's sins (cf. 40:2; 42:22–25; 43: 22–24; 47:6; 48:8).

The basic character of the fourth Servant Song is often obscured by the titles given to it, the most frequent being the "Suffering Servant" and the "Man of Sorrows." The author's primary concern, however, is not with the servant's suffering, but with his amazing triumph over suffering. All references to his suffering, therefore, are to be translated in the past tense: "He *was* despised and rejected" (53:3); "he *was* wounded for our transgressions" (53:5); he *was* cut off out of the land of the living" (53:8). On the other hand, the verbs that speak of his triumph and glory are to be translated in the future tense: "Behold, my servant *shall* prosper" (52:13); "he *shall* see his offspring, he *shall* prolong his days" (53:10); "he *shall* divide the spoil with the strong" (53:12). A more fitting title for the song, therefore, would be "The Travail and Triumph of the Servant"

or "The Song of the Servant's Victory."

One of the song's lasting contributions is the light it throws upon the problem of suffering. Paterson [123] speaks of three discernible levels in the understanding of suffering during the period of the Old Testament. The first level is represented by the friends of Job, who assume that *all sufferers are sinners.* The next level is reached when the experiences of men like Jeremiah demonstrate that *some sufferers are saints.* Finally, in the fourth Servant Song, it is revealed that *some sufferers are saviors.* Beyond this level of understanding it was impossible to go until one came who was both Son of God and Suffering Servant.

(1) From Humiliation to Exaltation (52: 13–15)

13 Behold, my servant shall prosper,
    he shall be exalted and lifted up,
    and shall be very high.
14 As many were astonished at him—
    his appearance was so marred, beyond
      human semblance,
    and his form beyond that of the sons of
      men—
15 so shall he startle many nations;
    kings shall shut their mouths because of
      him;
    for that which has not been told them they
      shall see,
    and that which they have not heard they
      shall understand.

These verses give a summary statement of the servant's rise from humiliation to world renown. Westermann has called attention to the identical words that stand at the beginning of verse 13—*Behold my servant*—and at the beginning of the first Servant Song in 42:1–4, which he interprets as evidence that the two songs belong together, the first indicating the origin of the figure of the servant and the second the culmination of his work.

Verse 14, with its description of the servant's initial humiliation, corresponds to 53:1–9; whereas v. 15, which depicts a dramatic reversal in the servant's fortunes, finds its parallel in 53:10–12. Verses

123 Cf. John Paterson, *The Praises of Israel* (New York: Charles Scribner's Sons, 1950), pp. 225–227.

14–15 emphasize the contrast between the *many* and the *one,* a contrast which is continued throughout the song (cf. 53:4–6, 11–12).

Verse 14 suggests that the servant has become so disfigured through suffering that he scarcely appears to be human. For this reason men are astonished at him, which means that they regard him with a mixture of surprise, contempt, and aversion (cf. 53:2–3).

The KJV renders the initial clause in **v.** 15: "So shall he sprinkle many nations." The verb sprinkle is often used in the Old Testament to describe a purificatory rite performed by a priest (cf. Lev. 4:6; 8:11; 14:7; Num. 8:7; etc.). A possible interpretation of the clause, therefore, is that the servant will sprinkle many nations as a symbol of their purification from sin.

An alternate rendering of the clause appears in the RSV: "so shall he startle many nations." This reading has the support of the major Greek and Latin versions, and is preferred by most modern interpreters. The meaning according to this reading is that the nations will be startled when they behold the servant's sudden rise from ignominy to fame.

(2) The Servant's Unlikely Beginning (53: 1–3)

¹ Who has believed what we have heard?
  And to whom has the arm of the LORD
      been revealed?
² For he grew up before him like a young
      plant,
  and like a root out of dry ground;
he had no form or comeliness that we should
      look at him,
  and no beauty that we should desire him.
³ He was despised and rejected by men;
  a man of sorrows, and acquainted with
      grief;
and as one from whom men hide their faces
  he was despised, and we esteemed him
      not.

Those who identify the servant as Israel regard vv. 1–9, with their prominent use of first person pronouns, as a confession of the nations, articulated by their kings (cf. 52:15) and designed to express their as-

tonishment upon discovering the true meaning of the servant's suffering. Those who prefer an individual interpretation, on the other hand, consider the verses to be a confession of the prophet and his fellow-countrymen concerning the marvelous transformation they have witnessed in the life of one who has grown up in their midst.

Almost all possible misfortunes are attributed to the servant in these verses. He grows up in a hostile environment, like *a root out of dry ground.* He is so unimpressive and unattractive that men are repelled at the sight of him. He is exposed to scorn, rejection, sorrow, grief, and the bitterness of loneliness. In the words of Westermann, he is "a man without a blessing." How incredible that one who had such an unlikely beginning should accomplish such a glorious mission!

(3) The Servant's Vicarious Suffering (53: 4–6)

⁴ Surely he has borne our griefs
    and carried our sorrows;
  yet we esteemed him stricken,
    smitten by God, and afflicted.
⁵ But he was wounded for our transgressions,
    he was bruised for our iniquities;
  upon him was the chastisement that made us
      whole,
    and with his stripes we are healed.
⁶ All we like sheep have gone astray;
    we have turned every one to his own way;
  and the LORD has laid on him
      the iniquity of us all.

In v. 4 the speakers describe their initial reaction to the servant's suffering, a reaction they now acknowledge to be totally inaccurate. They supposed that he was being smitten by God for some unspeakable crime which he had committed. Their confession thus reveals that they shared the commonly held assumption that all suffering was the direct result of sin. What happened subsequent to this to change their minds is not stated, but it must have been a momentous experience. The outcome of it is that they now recognize that the servant's sufferings are not a consequence of his own sins but of theirs.

Verse 6 is most meaningful when read in the original Hebrew, where it begins and ends with the same word, *kullanu,* meaning "all of us." The verse contains a threefold description of sin: it is universal and inescapable; it separates and scatters; and it is essentially self-willed. The idea of substitution also comes to the fore in the speaker's confession that the Lord has caused their iniquity to be laid upon the servant.

(4) The Servant's Sacrificial Death (53: 7–9)

7 He was oppressed, and he was afflicted,
    yet he opened not his mouth;
like a lamb that is led to the slaughter,
    and like a sheep that before its shearers
    is dumb,
    so he opened not his mouth.
8 By oppression and judgment he was taken
    away;
and as for his generation, who considered
that he was cut off out of the land of the
    living,
    stricken for the transgression of my peo-
    ple?
9 And they made his grave with the wicked
    and with a rich man in his death,
although he had done no violence,
    and there was no deceit in his mouth.

The servant's suffering leads eventually to his death, which is described here in sacrificial terms. There is a profound difference, however, between this sacrifice and those mentioned in the priestly legislation. It is a sacrifice offered outside the Temple, and the victim is a blameless man rather than an unblemished animal. Furthermore, it is a sacrifice that makes all other sacrifices unnecessary.

Rowley has written that this chapter

brings together the Law and the Prophets. The death of the Servant is described in sacrificial terms. It is not merely the use of the word *'asham* that shows this. The whole thought of the chapter is sacrificial, and it is the most profound and far-reaching passage on sacrifice found in the Old Testament. This sacrifice is not offered by a priest in the Temple, and it is mentioned in the Prophets and not in the Law. It is the sacrifice of a blameless man whether thought of as an individual or as a symbol of the community instead of an unblemished an-

imal. It is a sacrifice of wider validity than any mentioned in the Law. There sacrifices offered for individuals or for Israel are mentioned; but here is a sacrifice which Gentiles are represented as acknowledging to have been for them. It is not therefore surprising that the Church which believed the concepts of the Servant to find its supreme fulfilment in Christ, who expressed its mission in Himself and carried it to a point no other should reach should feel no need of further sacrifice for Christians even before the Temple was destroyed. For here was a sacrifice which took up into itself Old Testament sacrifice at its highest point, and which fulfilled a promise and a hope which the Old Testament offered.[124]

This does not mean, however that the sacrifice of the servant works automatically to provide atonement. It accomplishes this only for those who make it the vehicle of their approach to God. Only those who through faith and repentance make his sacrifice their own and confess that he was wounded for their transgressions and bruised for their iniquities receive forgiveness.

A deliberate contrast is drawn between the one and the many in vv. 6 and 7: all we *like sheep* have gone astray, and he *like a sheep* has been sacrificed for us all. And unlike other victims led to the slaughter, *he opened not his mouth.* No word of accusation or of self-pity fell from his lips. In the familiar words of the spiritual, "He never said a mumblin' word." This statement alone is sufficient to exclude Israel from consideration as the servant, for in her time of suffering she complained both loudly and bitterly (cf. 40:27; 49:14).

The death and burial of the servant are described in vv. 8–9. To be *taken away* (cf. v. 8) means to be forcibly removed from one place to another, here from the land of the living to the place of the dead (cf. Gen. 5:24; 2 Kings 2:3; Prov. 24:11). The text does not make it clear whether he died of some dread disease, was slain by a mob, or was executed after a farcical trial. In any event, he died the death of a

---

[124] H. H. Rowley, *The Changing Pattern of Old Testament Studies* (London: The Epworth Press, 1959), pp. 29 f.

sinner and was buried with the wicked. The presence of sin in the situation, therefore, is indisputable; what has not been clear prior to this is that the one suffering is not himself the sinner, but is bearing the consequences of the sins of others. The parallelism of v. 9 suggests that the wicked are to be equated with the rich (cf. Prov. 11:16; Jer. 17:11; Mic. 6:12; Matt. 19: 23; Luke 6:24; 16:19–26). The verse ends with a ringing affirmation of the servant's innocency.

(5) The Servant's Ultimate Triumph (53: 10–12)

¹⁰ Yet it was the will of the Lord to bruise him;
 he has put him to grief;
when he makes himself an offering for sin,
 he shall see his offspring, he shall prolong his days;
the will of the Lord shall prosper in his hand;
¹¹ he shall see the fruit of the travail of his soul and be satisfied;
by his knowledge shall the righteous one, my servant,
make many to be accounted righteous;
 and he shall bear their iniquities.
¹² Therefore I will divide him a portion with the great,
and he shall divide the spoil with the strong;
because he poured out his soul to death,
 and was numbered with the transgressors;
yet he bore the sin of many,
 and made intercession for the transgressors.

The revolutionary truth announced in these verses is that the servant's vindication comes after his death. A great miracle takes place, therefore, for after his death and burial he is enabled to see his offspring, to prolong his days, and to witness the successful completion of his mission. Whether the passage implies his resurrection from the dead is not clear, but there can be no doubt that it portrays his ministry as coming to a climax beyond the grave. His death, therefore, is not his defeat, but his noblest achievement and the means by which many are reconciled to God.

To say that it was the will of the Lord

to bruise the servant (v. 10) means that the events leading up to his death were part of the divine plan to conquer sin. The Lord permitted him to suffer, therefore, not out of anger toward him, but out of love toward the sinner.

Verse 10, as rendered by the RSV, seems to teach that the servant's triumph will be contingent upon his offering of himself as a sacrifice of sin. The Jerusalem Bible reflects a similar interpretation: "If he offers his life in atonement," etc. These and other similar translations are based upon the Vulgate, whereas a literal rendering of the Hebrew would read: "When (or, if) you make his soul an offering for sin," etc. "His soul" obviously means the servant himself. According to the Hebrew, therefore, it is the worshiper who must appropriate the servant's sacrifice and make it the means of his own approach to God.

Once this has been done, certain results will follow. The servant will see his *offspring* (seed) and *prolong his days.* The "seed" should perhaps be understood not as his physical but as his spiritual descendants. Through these his power and influence will be extended after his death.

The will of the Lord, that is, his eternal purpose, will prosper, that is, come to fruition, in his hand. The theme of the will or purpose of the Lord is found throughout these chapters: it is his purpose to magnify the law and make it glorious (42:21); Cyrus is sent to fulfill his purpose (44:28); his purpose is accomplished through his word (55:11). Above all, however, it s through the servant that the divine purpose is ultimately fulfilled.

North has suggested that the first clause in v. 11 be rendered: "After his soul's travail he shall see light (and) be fully satisfied by his knowledge" (*The Second Isaiah,* p. 233). The insertion of the word "light" is supported by the Septuagint and by both of the Dead Sea Scrolls of Isaiah. This rendering not only has the support of ancient manuscripts but also suits the context better than that of the RSV.

The phrase *by his knowledge* must not

be interpreted as an objective genitive, "by the knowledge of him," as if sinners received justification by their knowledge of the servant. The meaning, rather, is that through the knowledge (experience) that he has gained the servant is able to make many to be accounted righteous. It is his knowledge that effects the change. North does not hesitate to speak of his redeeming activity as coming after his resurrection.

Verse 12 describes the distribution of the spoils of victory after the battle has been won. Muilenburg has suggested that the expression *with the great* (*barabbim*) should be interpreted as the direct object of the verb, thus making it possible to render the opening clause: "Therefore, I will apportion to him the great as a reward, etc." This avoids the connotation that the servant is only one among many who share the spoils of victory.

The fourth Servant Song comes to a climax on the note of the servant's continuing ministry of intercession on behalf of *transgressors*. What does it mean to intercede on behalf of another? The Septuagint reads: "and he was *handed over* because of their iniquities." The Hebrew verb is *paga'*, (to meet, to encounter) and the causative form, which is used here, means to interpose or to intervene. The same verb occurs in v. 6, where it is rendered: "and the Lord *has laid* on him the iniquity of us all." The Hebrew, therefore, does not mean simply to pray for transgressors—a concept which originated with the Vulgate, which reads *rogavit*—but, rather, to put oneself in the place of transgressors and to absorb the full impact of the punishment due them. To intercede, therefore, means to intervene between a man and the consequences of his sin (cf. 59:16). The mission of the servant provides the noblest example to be found in the Old Testament of one who performed such a ministry of intercession. It was superseded only when the Servant Songs were transposed to a higher key and found their fulfillment in Jesus of Nazareth.

Just as the servant was *numbered with* transgressors before he could make intercession for them, even so must our own intercessory prayer include more than a benevolent attitude toward those in need. True intercession is always more than prayer, although it includes prayer. It really involves a way of life, for one cannot offer intercessory prayer unless he is living an intercessory life. One cannot address God on behalf of the needy unless he is willing to become involved in their situation, sharing in their griefs and bearing their injuries. Otherwise such prayer becomes a sham and a mockery. Perhaps this explains why the church so rarely engages in intercessory prayer. This kind of prayer is terribly costly.

5. The Song of the Redeemed (54:1-17)

The note of suffering, so prominent in the preceding passage, is entirely absent from this chapter, which describes the magnificent splendor of the new age which is about to dawn. It is a pleasant piece of music, as if Israel had emerged from the darkness of despair into the dazzling light of a new day.

(1) The Enlargement of Zion (54:1-3)

1 "Sing, O barren one, who did not bear;
    break forth into singing and cry aloud,
    you who have not been in travail!
  For the children of the desolate one will be more
    than the children of her that is married,
    says the LORD.
2 Enlarge the place of your tent,
    and let the curtains of your habitations be stretched out;
  hold not back, lengthen your cords
    and strengthen your stakes.
3 For you will spread abroad to the right and to the left,
    and your descendants will possess the nations
  and will people the desolate cities.

The vivid description of the desolate city suddenly faced with the problem of overpopulation forms a close parallel to 49:14-21. Zion is bidden to burst forth into singing, for although she is presently a barren wife (v. 1; cf. vv. 5-6), she will soon become the mother of many children. In order that there may be room to house these, she is told to enlarge her tent and to *lengthen* the *cords* and *strengthen* the *stakes* that hold it upright.[125] Her overflowing population will spread to the right and to the left, taking possession of the nations and filling up their desolate cities.

(2) Zion's Reconciliation to God (54:4-8)

4 "Fear not, for you will not be ashamed;
  be not confounded, for you will not be put to shame;
for you will forget the shame of your youth,
  and the reproach of your widowhood you will remember no more.
5 For your Maker is your husband,
  the LORD of hosts is his name;
and the Holy One of Israel is your Redeemer,
  the God of the whole earth he is called.
6 For the LORD has called you
  like a wife forsaken and grieved in spirit,
like a wife of youth when she is cast off,
  says your God.
7 For a brief moment I forsook you,
  but with great compassion I will gather you.
8 In overflowing wrath for a moment
  I hid my face from you,
but with everlasting love I will have compassion on you,
  says the LORD, your Redeemer.

An appropriate title for this section would be "the return of the prodigal wife." In language strongly reminiscent of Hosea, the prophet describes the restoration of Israel to God's favor. No longer will she remember the shame and reproach of the past, but she will be reconciled to her husband, who is none other than her *Maker* and *Redeemer, the Lord of hosts, the Holy One of Israel, the God of the whole earth.*

God's momentary wrath is contrasted with his great compassion and everlasting

---

125 Baptists—and other evangelical groups as well— have a special affinity for v. 2, for it served as the text for William Carey's epoch-making sermon delivered May 31, 1792, before a group of Baptist ministers at Kettering, England. His two points were: (1) expect great things from God; (2) attempt great things for God. The enthusiasm kindled by the sermon led to the formation on October 2, 1792, of the Baptist Missionary Society, the precursor of the modern missionary movement.

---

love (vv. 7–8; cf. 28:21; Rom. 8:18; 2 Cor. 4:17). *Compassion* and *everlasting love* are two of the most important concepts in the Old Testament. The first describes God's pity for men in their frailty, misery, and weakness (cf. Psalm 103: 13–14). The second, "everlasting love" (Heb. *chesed*), conveys the basic idea of steadfastness, or reliability, and stands for the proper attitude that each party to a covenant should maintain toward the other. In the majority of cases the Septuagint renders it as *eleos* (mercy). The nature of *chesed* as mercy can perhaps best be illustrated by the example of the good Samaritan, who "showed mercy" on the man who fell among thieves (cf. Luke 10: 25–37). Everlasting love, therefore, involves the practical expression of helpfulness toward those whose only claim on another's assistance is their misfortune.

(3) An Everlasting Covenant (54:9-10)

9 "For this is like the days of Noah to me:
  as I swore that the waters of Noah should no more go over the earth,
  so I have sworn that I will not be angry with you
  and will not rebuke you.
10 For the mountains may depart
  and the hills be removed,
but my steadfast love shall not depart from you,
  and my covenant of peace shall not be removed,
  says the LORD, who has compassion on you.

The prophet thinks of the Exile as being like the flood in the days of Noah. North's translation of v. 9 brings this out very clearly: "This is to me like the days of Noah over again, when I declared on oath that the waters of the flood should never again sweep over the earth; so now I swear that never again will I be wroth with you or rebuke you." God's promise of everlasting goodwill toward Israel is like a rainbow etched upon the storm clouds of the Exile.

God's covenant with Noah after the flood (cf. Gen. 9:8–17) has its counterpart in the *covenant of peace* which he now proposes to establish with Israel (v.

10; cf. 55:3). The aspect of the covenant which receives the greatest emphasis is its everlastingness: mountains may disappear and hills be removed, but the covenant of peace will never be withdrawn (cf. 49: 15–16; Psalm 46:1–2).

(4) Zion's Heritage of Peace and Prosperity (54:11-17)

11 "O afflicted one, storm-tossed, and not comforted,
    behold, I will set your stones in antimony,
    and lay your foundations with sapphires.
12 I will make your pinnacles of agate,
    your gates of carbuncles,
    and all your wall of precious stones.
13 All your sons shall be taught by the LORD,
    and great shall be the prosperity of your sons.
14 In righteousness you shall be established;
    you shall be far from oppression, for you shall not fear;
    and from terror, for it shall not come near you.
15 If any one stirs up strife,
    it is not from me;
    whoever stirs up strife with you
    shall fall because of you.
16 Behold, I have created the smith
    who blows the fire of coals,
    and produces a weapon for its purpose.
    I have also created the ravager to destroy;
17 no weapon that is fashioned against you shall prosper,
    and you shall confute every tongue that rises against you in judgment.
This is the heritage of the servants of the LORD
    and their vindication from me, says the LORD."

The terms applied to Israel in v. 11 are a sharp reminder that her redemption still lies in the future. The purpose of the passage, therefore, is to give her a preview of what it will be like to live under a covenant of peace.

The passage begins with a description of the physical splendor of the New Jerusalem, whose builder and maker is God (vv. 11–12). Scholars have not determined the positive identification of all the stones mentioned here. The vision of a city whose foundations, walls, and gates are built of precious stones reappears in Revelation 21:9–27, reminding us that Second Isaiah exerted a formative influence upon the eschatological thought of the writer of Revelation. Both Old Testament prophet and New Testament apocalyptist alike envisioned the establishment of a city without a temple.

Verses 13–17 depict an idyllic situation in which Zion's sons are blessed with prosperity and freedom from all oppression and terror. The promise that no weapon fashioned against them shall prosper is reminiscent of Psalms 91 and 121. North has translated verse 14a to read: "You shall be built on a foundation of righteousness." Zion's future establishment as a city of *righteousness* is a theme that runs throughout the book of Isaiah (cf. 1:26; 28:16–17; 33:5; 60:17,21). The summary statement in v. 17b applies to all of chapter 54: "This is the heritage of the servants of the Lord and their vindication from me, says the Lord."

6. The Great Invitation (55:1-13)

Cyrus' conquest of Babylon in 539 B.C. presented the Jews with a momentous decision: Should they remain in Babylon, or should they take advantage of Cyrus' edict granting them permission to return to Jerusalem? It was not an easy choice, for they had formed ties and established relationships during the 50 years of their exile which they were reluctant to sever. On the whole, their captors had treated them with leniency, even to the point of allowing them to acquire property and to engage in business and commercial activities. It is not surprising, therefore, to learn from Josephus (*Antiq.* XI.1.3) that many of them chose to remain in Babylon, "as not willing to leave their possessions."

The widespread reluctance on the part of the exiles to undertake the arduous journey back to Jerusalem forms the background of chapter 55 (cf. 48:1–22; 52: 1–12). Like a recruiting sergeant in the army of the Lord, the prophet pleads with them to return without delay. He warns them that their recalcitrant spirit is threatening their very existence as the people of God. A glorious future awaits them, but only if they are obedient. In reaction to their feverish efforts to acquire wealth, he asks, "Does all this really satisfy you? Is this what you are laboring for?" In their concern for earthly riches, they are neglecting the true riches which God has provided for them.

(1) The Generosity of God (55:1-5)

1 "Ho, every one who thirsts,
      come to the waters;
   and he who has no money,
      come, buy and eat!
   Come, buy wine and milk
      without money and without price.
2 Why do you spend your money for that
         which is not bread,
      and your labor for that which does not
         satisfy?
   Hearken diligently to me, and eat what is
         good,
      and delight yourselves in fatness.
3 Incline your ear, and come to me;
      hear, that your soul may live;
   and I will make with you an everlasting
         covenant,
      my steadfast, sure love for David.
4 Behold, I made him a witness to the peoples,
      a leader and commander for the peoples.
5 Behold, you shall call nations that you know
         not,
      and nations that knew you not shall run
         to you,
   because of the LORD your God, and of the
         Holy One of Israel,
      for he has glorified you.

North compares this passage to Jesus' parable of the great supper (Luke 14: 15-24; cf. John 7:37-38; Rev. 22:17). He also reminds us that water is a precious commodity in the Near East, and that it is often sold in the streets. One wishing to show generosity, therefore, could buy up the stock of a water-carrier and order that it be distributed without charge to any who were thirsty. God's bounty far exceeds this, however, for he offers, besides *waters,* also *wine and milk.* That which he provides can be described as a feast of "fatness" (v. 2).

Smart (p. 221) has noted that throughout Second Isaiah "water is a symbol of God's presence in the world. . . . So also, we may infer, the bread, wine, and milk that alone can give man life are symbols of the God for whom man hungers and thirsts. . . . Man without God is an aching void for which the Easterner could find no closer likeness than the painful thirst of the body for water. . . . He does not thirst for 'something' from God; he thirsts for God, for the living God (cf. Psalm 42:2)."

A marked feature of this chapter is its accumulation of imperatives: the prophet commands the exiles to *come, buy, eat* (v. 1); *hearken, eat, delight yourselves* (v. 2); *incline your ear, come, hear* (v. 3); *seek, call* (v. 6); and *forsake, return* (v. 7). These imperatives prove that God's redemption does not operate independent of human response. While God's gifts cannot be purchased or earned, they still must be received through a spirit of faith and willingness to obey.

The central truth in vv. 1-3 is that God alone can satisfy the deep inner needs of the human spirit. Water, wine, and milk are but symbols of the spiritual sustenance afforded those who live in fellowship with him. All who do not seek him, therefore, are spending their substance for that which is not bread and wasting their energy in pursuit of that which does not satisfy. It is to forestall this happening among his own people that the prophet makes his earnest appeal.

God's future intention for Israel is forcefully described in v. 3: "Give heed and come to me, listen, that you may have life in its fulness; and I will make a lasting covenant with you, with the dependable manifestations of my love for David" (North's translation).

In the statement *I will make an everlasting covenant* with you, the suffix "you" is plural, indicating quite clearly that the promise is addressed to Israel. Some have interpreted the final clause in the verse, "my steadfast, sure love for David," as indicating that the prophet expected Israel's restoration to Palestine to be followed by a revival of the Davidic dynasty.

Most scholars, however, believe that the verse teaches that the promises once made to David (cf. 2 Sam. 7:8–16; 23:5; 1 Kings 8:23–26; Psalm 89) have now been transferred to the nation Israel. In other words, the messianic hope has been transferred from an individual king to the entire people of God. In the light of this interpretation, vv. 4–5 should be regarded as drawing a contrast between the mission of David and that of Israel: whereas David was appointed leader of the nations in a political and military sense, Israel is charged with the responsibility of summoning the nations to acknowledge the sovereignty of the Lord her God. Whether she succeeds or fails in accomplishing this mission will depend upon her response to the word of God spoken through the prophet.

(2) A Call to Repentance (55:6–9)

6 "Seek the Lord while he may be found,
  call upon him while he is near;
7 let the wicked forsake his way,
  and the unrighteous man his thoughts;
  let him return to the Lord, that he may
    have mercy on him,
  and to our God, for he will abundantly
    pardon.
8 For my thoughts are not your thoughts,
  neither are your ways my ways, says the
    Lord.
9 For as the heavens are higher than the
    earth,
  so are my ways higher than your ways
  and my thoughts than your thoughts.

Before the exiles can participate in the new age which is about to dawn, they must forsake their own evil thoughts and ways and turn to the Lord for mercy and pardon. Even the wicked and the unrighteous may participate in this homegoing if they will but abandon their apostasy and seek the Lord. *Seek the Lord* in the context of the exile means not to bring sacrifice to him but to approach him through prayer and repentance. Lest the exiles should protest their innocence or deny their need for repentance, the prophet reminds them of the great gulf that separates their thoughts and ways from those of God. This

reminder is needed in every age, for there is a perennial tendency among men—especially religious men—to confuse their own thoughts and ways with those of God, and to claim for themselves a moral and intellectual infallibility that belongs only to God.

The words of the prophet anticipate a further objection raised by his listeners, namely, that there is no need for haste in responding to the call to repentance. The prophet answers this objection with a declaration that the time for decision is *now*: Israel must *seek the Lord while he may be found* and *call upon him while he is near.* The opportunity for response has to be seized at once, or it may be lost forever. From a positive standpoint this declaration means that God is no longer alienated from his people but that he is near and can be found. The hour of redemption and salvation has arrived. This is the hour of theophany, the moment of God's appearing. Nowhere does the "gospel" in Second Isaiah shine more clearly than here.

(3) God's Unfailing Word (55:10–11)

10 "For as the rain and the snow come down
     from heaven,
   and return not thither but water the
     earth,
   making it bring forth and sprout,
     giving seed to the sower and bread to
       the eater,
11 so shall my word be that goes forth from
     my mouth;
   it shall not return to me empty,
   but it shall accomplish that which I purpose,
   and prosper in the thing for which I sent
     it.

The prophet buttresses his plea to the exiles to return to Jerusalem by assuring them that the word of God can be relied upon. The word he has in mind is primarily the promise of restoration which they have heard so often but have found so difficult to believe. Let them but receive this word and act upon it, and they will discover that the promised results will as surely come as new growth comes to fields that have been watered by the rains and snows from heaven. There is a similarity between this affirmation of the reliability of the word of God and that found in 40:8.

(4) Homeward Bound! (55:12-13)

12 "For you shall go out in joy,
  and be led forth in peace;
the mountains and the hills before you
  shall break forth into singing,
  and all the trees of the field shall clap
    their hands.
13 Instead of the thorn shall come up the cypress;
  instead of the brier shall come up the myrtle;
  and it shall be to the LORD for a memorial,
    for an everlasting sign which shall not
    be cut off."

In a final attempt to elicit a response from his listeners, the prophet describes a vivid poetic imagery their departure from Babylon and their journey across the desert. North has observed that there is "an expansiveness about these concluding verses such as we do not often find in Hebrew poetry. It is as if the river, as it finishes its course, broadens into an estuary open to the tides of comprehensive revelation" (*The Second Isaiah,* p. 260).

The departure from Babylon is described as a victory march. The exiles *go out in joy* and are *led forth in peace.* As they journey along, *the mountains and the hills . . . break forth into singing* and *the trees* of the field *clap their hands,* keeping time with the music. The desert through which they pass is transformed into a memorial garden commemorating the Lord's victory over his foes. Furthermore, it does not revert to its former condition once the exiles have completed their journey, but remains in its transformed state for all time to come.

We have chosen to speak of chapter 55 as "the great invitation." Here the people of God who are bowed down under the bondage of Babylon are offered a great redemption which includes spiritual sustenance (vv. 1-2), a renewal of the covenant (vv. 3-5), mercy and pardon (vv. 6-7), and a joyful return to their homeland (vv. 12-13). The prophet's appeal

to the Israelites to accept God's gracious invitation is based upon four vital truths: (1) God alone can satisfy the deep inner needs of the human spirit; (2) Israel's true destiny to be a witness to the nations can only be realized as she herself returns to God; (3) the day of redemption has drawn near and the time of response is now; (4) God is faithful to his promises and his word never fails. All the fitness he requires is to feel your need of him.

The second part of the book of Isaiah begins with chapter 40 and ends with chapter 55. Chapter 55 appears to have been written on the eve of the return of the exiles to Jerusalem under the leadership of Sheshbazzar in 538 B.C. (cf. Ezra 1:2-11). Westermann (p. 292) has observed that the final words in this section of the book "point away from the redemption to the redeemer. In the last analysis, whatever comes about comes about for God's honour, just as all creation exists in order to render him praise."

Part Three: Chapters 56—66

Chapters 56—66 constitute the final section in the book of Isaiah and are usually dated in the period between the return of the exiles in 538 B.C. and the completion of the Temple in 515 (cf. 60:13; 64:11; 66:1). Scholarly opinion is divided over the question of the authorship of these chapters: Some (e.g., Smart, Francisco) would assign them to Second Isaiah; others (e.g., Muilenburg, Westermann) would attribute them to an anonymous disciple of Second Isaiah, generally referred to as Third Isaiah; still others (e.g., Snaith, McKenzie) would divide the section into two main sources, assigning chapters 60—62 to Second Isaiah and the remaining chapters to one or more of his disciples. The inconclusive nature of the evidence makes it impossible to determine with certainty which of these views is the correct one.

The circumstances reflected in these chapters are those that prevailed in Jerusalem following the return of the exiles from Babylon in 538 B.C. These arrived in Jerusalem with the promises of Second Isaiah ringing in their ears. Had he not told them that the city and its temple would be restored (cf. 44:28), that Zion would be filled to overflow with inhabitants (cf. 49:19–21; 54:1–3), that the wealth of all nations would become theirs (cf. 45:14), and that kings would come from the ends of the earth to pay homage at their feet (cf. 49:22–23)?

It would be an understatement to say that the fulfillment of these promises fell far short of the Israelites' expectations. It soon became apparent, for example, that they lacked the resources to rebuild Jerusalem. Opposition from their neighbors also forced them to postpone the rebuilding of the Temple (cf. Ezra 4:1–5). Economic conditions went from bad to worse, as droughts, plagues, and hail storms resulted in crop failures (cf. Hag. 1:6,9–11; 2:16–17). In spite of their poverty, they were forced to pay a heavy annual tribute to Persia and to furnish provisions for the soldiers quartered in their land (cf. Neh. 5:15). Instead of seeing Zion become a crown of beauty and a bastion of freedom, they saw themselves completely dominated by their Persian overlords.

As the years lengthened into decades and nothing happened to improve the situation, expectations disappointed became doubts, and hopes long deferred made hearts sick. A dangerous reaction set in, and many of the Israelites began to doubt that the Lord loved them (cf. Mal. 1:2) or that there was any benefit to be derived from serving him (cf. Mal. 3:14).

It was against such a background of reaction and disillusionment that the prophet delivered the oracles recorded in these chapters. It fell his lot to proclaim the word of God in a time of transition and adjustment. Few prophets have ever faced a more difficult task. He needed to accomplish at least two things, i.e., furnish a satisfactory explanation for the delay in the fulfillment of Israel's expectations, and

rekindle the people's confidence in the Lord and in the ultimate fulfillment of his purpose for the world. That he accomplished his task is attested by the fact that the faith of Israel survived the crises of the succeeding years.

I. Oracles of Judgment and Redemption (56:1—59:21)

1. The Status of Foreigners and Eunuchs (56:1–8)

1 Thus says the LORD:
"Keep justice, and do righteousness,
for soon my salvation will come,
and my deliverance be revealed.
2 Blessed is the man who does this,
and the son of man who holds it fast,
who keeps the sabbath, not profaning it,
and keeps his hand from doing any evil."
3 Let not the foreigner who has joined himself to the LORD say,
"The LORD will surely separate me from his people";
and let not the eunuch say,
"Behold, I am a dry tree."
4 For thus says the LORD:
"To the eunuchs who keep my sabbaths,
who choose the things that please me
and hold fast my covenant,
5 I will give in my house and within my walls
a monument and a name
better than sons and daughters;
I will give them an everlasting name
which shall not be cut off.
6 "And the foreigners who join themselves to the LORD,
to minister to him, to love the name of the LORD,
and to be his servants,
every one who keeps the sabbath, and does not profane it,
and holds fast my covenant—
7 these I will bring to my holy mountain,
and make them joyful in my house of prayer;
their burnt offerings and their sacrifices
will be accepted on my altar;
for my house shall be called a house of prayer
for all peoples.
8 Thus says the Lord GOD,
who gathers the outcasts of Israel,
I will gather yet others to him
besides those already gathered."

The key word in vv. 1–2 is *keep*: the godly man must keep *justice*, keep *the sabbath*, and keep *his hand from doing any evil.* It is generally recognized that sabbath-keeping attained a significance during the Exile that it had not previously had; here it is placed on a par with practicing justice and righteousness and refraining from doing evil (cf. Neh. 13:15–22). Upon those who live by this threefold standard the prophet pronounces a blessing in the style of the ancient beautitudes (cf. Deut. 33:29; 1 Kings 10:8; Psalm 1:1). The Hebrew words for *man* and *son of man* are those which stress his humble origin (cf. 51:12; Psalm 8:4). God's salvation is not the property of a privileged few but belongs to those who act righteously, however poor and lowly they may be (cf. 57:15).

The question at issue in v. 3–8 is whether or not the *foreigner* and the *eunuch* are to be received into the community of Israel and allowed to participate in its worship. The eunuchs are probably to be understood as Jewish exiles who had been mutilated by their Babylonian overlords so that they could be trusted to work in the royal palaces. There were many Jews in the postexilic period who had adopted a policy of rigid exclusiveness and were, therefore, opposed to letting anyone not of their race or anyone who was physically deformed become a part of the worshiping community. These could even claim scriptural support for their position by citing passages such as Deuteronomy 23:1–8.

The separatists were opposed by another group, however, which favored a more open attitude toward non-Jews. The prophet doubtlessly was a leader among this group. He taught that the ancient Deuteronomic regulations has now been superseded and that, henceforth, no man was to be denied entrance to the Temple or membership in the community of Israel because of racial or physical considerations. The only requirements imposed upon these were that they hallow the sabbath and accept the obligations of the covenant (vv. 4,6).

Enunchs who met these requirements were promised that they would receive in God's house and within his walls a *monument* and a name *better than sons and daughters* (cf. 2 Sam. 18:18). Foreigners also who joined themselves to the Lord, i.e., became proselytes, were told that they would be brought to the Lord's house, and that their burnt offerings and sacrifices would be accepted upon his altar (v. 7). In one of the most universal statements to be found in the Old Testament, the Lord declares that his house shall henceforth be called *a house of prayer for all peoples* (cf. Mark 11:17). In the light of the context, v. 8 seems to mean that in addition to the outcasts of Israel who have been brought back from Babylon, the Lord will bring yet others, i.e., Gentiles, and will incorporate them into his covenant people (cf. 49:5–6; John 10:16).

The problem treated in this passage is one that is of perennial importance to the people of God. Upon what basis are men to be admitted to membership in a church or allowed to participate in its worship services? The church that rules that its members must be of one race or color or class is in danger of obscuring the essential universality of the gospel and of refusing to accept as brothers those whom God has accepted as sons.

2. Problems of the Restored Community (56:9—57:13)

(1) Blind Leaders (56:9–12)

9 All you beasts of the field, come to devour—
    all you beasts in the forest.
10 His watchmen are blind,
    they are all without knowledge;
they are all dumb dogs,
    they cannot bark;
dreaming, lying down,
    loving to slumber.
11 The dogs have a mighty appetite;
    they never have enough.
The shepherds also have no understanding;
    they have all turned to their own way,
    each to his own gain, one and all.
12 "Come," they say, "let us get wine,
    let us fill ourselves with strong drink;
and tomorrow will be like this day,
    great beyond measure."

The postexilic community of Israel is compared in these verses to a defenseless flock entrusted to blind *watchmen* and self-indulgent *shepherds*. The watchmen symbolize the prophets (cf. 21:6-10, 11-12; 62:6; Ezek. 3:16-21; 33:7-9), and the shepherds the political leaders of Israel (cf. Ezek. 34:1-10; Zech. 10:3).

Two different interpretations have been given to the opening verse in this section. Some regard it as a sarcastic invitation to wild beasts, perhaps to be identified as Israel's enemies, especially Edom (cf. 63:1-6), to take advantage of the unconcern of Israel's shepherds and to devour her like a defenseless flock. Others see in it a proclamation of the downfall of the watchmen and shepherds themselves, who are to suffer a grievous defeat and whose corpses will provide food for the beasts of the field. The latter interpretation seems to be the better of the two, since it describes the fate that the nation's religious and political leaders so richly deserve.

Israel's prophets are compared to blind watchmen, a vivid metaphor of their inability to warn the nation of approaching danger. They are all said to be *without knowledge*, thus unable to instruct the people in the will of the Lord (cf. 5:13; Hos. 4:6; Mal. 2:7). The most devastating accusation made against them is that they are all *dumb dogs* that *cannot bark*. The prophet is nothing unless he is a speaker, lifting up his voice in protest against sin and oppression (cf. 58:1; Amos 3:8; Mic. 3:8). Israel's prophets, however, are dumb dogs who love to sleep; even in their waking moments they do not proclaim the word of the Lord but spend their time indulging their own insatiable appetites. The latter charge is all the more serious because of the extreme poverty of the postexilic period; while the prophets gorge themselves with food and drink, many of their fellow Israelites face starvation. They present a sorry spectacle of religious leaders interested only in their own welfare. Their tribe, unfortunately, is not yet extinct.

The shepherds, Israel's political leaders, are no better, for they too are concerned only for their own gain. Whereas 53:6 states that the *sheep* have gone astray, v. 11 lays this same charge at the feet of the *shepherds*. The passage ends with a raucous drinking song reflecting the libertine attitude of these leaders (cf. 22:13; 1 Cor. 15:32).

(2) Corrupt Worship (57:1-13)

1 The righteous man perishes,
   and no one lays it to heart;
   devout men are taken away,
   while no one understands.
   For the righteous man is taken away from
      calamity,
2   he enters into peace;
   they rest in their beds
   who walk in their uprightness.
3 But you, draw near hither,
   sons of the sorceress,
   offspring of the adulterer and the harlot.
4 Of whom are you making sport?
   Against whom do you open your mouth
      wide
   and put out your tongue?
   Are you not children of transgression,
   the offspring of deceit,
5 you who burn with lust among the oaks,
   under every green tree;
   who slay your children in the valleys,
   under the clefts of the rocks?
6 Among the smooth stones of the valley is
      your portion;
   they, they, are your lot;
   to them you have poured out a drink offer-
      ing,
   you have brought a cereal offering.
   Shall I be appeased for these things?
7 Upon a high and lofty mountain
   you have set your bed,
   and thither you went up to offer sacrifice.
8 Behind the door and the doorpost
   you have set up your symbol;
   for, deserting me, you have uncovered your
      bed,
   you have gone up to it,
   you have made it wide;
   and you have made a bargain for yourself
      with them,
   you have loved their bed,
   you have looked on nakedness.
9 You journeyed to Molech with oil
   and multiplied your perfumes;
   you sent your envoys far off,
   and sent down even to Sheol.
10 You were wearied with the length of your

way,
　but you did not say, "It is hopeless";
　you found new life for your strength,
　　and so you were not faint.
11 Whom did you dread and fear,
　　so that you lied,
　and did not remember me,
　　did not give me a thought?
　Have I not held my peace, even for a long
　　time,
　and so you do not fear me?
12 I will tell of your righteousness and your
　　doings,
　but they will not help you.
13 When you cry out, let your collection of
　　idols deliver you!
　The wind will carry them off,
　　a breath will take them away.
　But he who takes refuge in me shall possess
　　the land,
　　and shall inherit my holy mountain.

Verses 1–2 are generally regarded as an independent unit, the subject of which is the unconcern of the wicked at the death of *the righteous*. The prophet reacts with alarm to a situation in which the removal of good men from society is regarded with indifference. Even in his death, however, the righteous is more blessed than the wicked, for he is taken away from calamity and enters into peace, whereas for the wicked there is no peace (cf. vv. 19–21).

The polemic against idolatry in verses 3–13 is so sharply worded that some would assign it to the preexilic period. However, there is no reason to suppose that idolatry disappeared from Israel after the Exile. Jones (p. 38) has suggested that after the fall of Jerusalem, when the foundations of society had been undermined and when there was no authorized place of worship, pagan practices which had long been dormant came to life again and wicked men began to practice the kind of abominations that are mentioned here (cf. 65:1–7). The present passage, therefore, is an illustration of the meaning and application of 56:9–12: this is what happens to a nation whose shepherds fail to provide leadership and whose prophets are dumb dogs that cannot bark. The people resort to superstition and magic, so that the battle against idolatry has to be fought all over again.

Verse 3 is a summons to idolaters to draw near in order to hear the indictment which the Lord is bringing against them. The list of crimes they have committed includes blasphemous mockery (v. 4; cf. Psalms 22:13; 35:21), cultic prostitution (vv. 5,7–8), child sacrifice (v. 5), and the offering of sacrifices and the paying of homage to idols (vv. 6,9).

Verse 10 seems to be a description of those who are caught in the clutches of idolatry, who are often weary of it, but who, nevertheless, are unable to break away from it. They suffer from what might be called atrophy of the will. Their false religion does not satisfy them, but it offers them just enough enticement to keep them from abandoning it. What a miserable state for one to be in!

Verse 11 contrasts the fear of the Lord with the fear of idols. Israel had ceased to fear the Lord apparently because she misunderstood his silence (cf. 42:14). The concluding verses in the passage stress the truth that the nation's security lies not in its righteous deeds (v. 12), nor in its accumulation of idols (v. 13a), but only in the Lord its God. He promises that those who take refuge in him will again possess the land and inherit his holy mountain (v. 13b).

(3) The Judgment and Mercy of God (57:14–21)

14 And it shall be said,
"Build up, build up, prepare the way,
　remove every obstruction from my peo-
　　ple's way."
15 For thus says the high and lofty One
　who inhabits eternity, whose name is
　　Holy:
"I dwell in the high and holy place,
　and also with him who is of a contrite
　　and humble spirit,
to revive the spirit of the humble,
　and to revive the heart of the contrite.
16 For I will not contend for ever,
　nor will I always be angry;
　for from me proceeds the spirit,
　　and I have made the breath of life.
17 Because of the iniquity of his covetousness
　　I was angry,
　I smote him, I hid my face and was angry;

but he went on backsliding in the way of
   his own heart.
18 I have seen his ways, but I will heal him;
   I will lead him and requite him with comfort,
   creating for his mourners the fruit of the
   lips.
19 Peace, peace, to the far and to the near,
   says the LORD;
   and I will heal him.
20 But the wicked are like the tossing sea;
   for it cannot rest,
   and its waters toss up mire and dirt.
21 There is no peace, says my God, for the
   wicked."

There are indications in this passage
that the Israelites experienced a decline in
spiritual vitality after their return from
Babylon in 538 B.C. In spite of the severe
judgments that had been visited upon
them, they continued to backslide (v. 17).
Their corporate life was like a highway
which had fallen into such disrepair and
had become so strewn with debris that it
was no longer usable (v. 14).

God's judgment upon the situation, however, was overshadowed by his mercy.
Verse 14 contains his command to the
prophet to prepare the way of the people
and to remove every obstacle that would
prevent their returning to him (cf. 40:3–
5; 62:10–12).

Lest the people should imagine that their
crushing defeat and national humiliation
have cut them off from fellowship with
God, they are reminded that the high and
lofty God *whose name is Holy* dwells not
only in the high and holy place but also
with those of *a contrite and humble spirit.*
The preposition *with* means literally "at
the side of," and indicates the intimate
nature of the fellowship that God establishes with the humble and contrite (cf.
Matt. 5:3–5; 11:28–29). His purpose is
not to be angry with them forever, but to
revive their spirits and to restore their
vitality (vv. 15–16).

Verse 17 explains why it has been necessary for God to hide his face from his
people (cf. 45:15). The last line in the
verse records the failure of the exile to
produce a spirit of true repentance on their

part (cf. 42:25). It is debatable whether
the punishment of evildoers ever results in
the transformation of their character.

The first line of v. 18 declares that God
has taken note of all of Israel's sinful ways.
The conclusion that one would normally
expect to follow such a statement would
be: "therefore I will bring upon him the
punishment that he so justly deserves."
God's grace shines through in all its brilliance, however, as he says, *but I will heal
him.*

God declares his purpose to lead his
people, to requite them with comfort, and
to provide for those who now mourn *the
fruit of the lips.* This perhaps means that
their mourning will be turned into praise
(cf. Hos. 14:2). Some, however, interpret
the phrase as a reference to the pronounce-
ment that follows: "Peace, peace, to the
far and to the near." The repetition of the
word *peace* occurs also in 26:3, where it
is rendered "perfect peace." Peace is promised to the *far,* i.e., the Jews still dispersed
among the nations, and to the *near,* i.e.,
those who have already returned to Palestine. This verse expresses the ultimate purpose of God to provide a bountiful life for
his ingathered people.

The fate of the wicked, however, will be
completely different. Like a mighty ocean
that never rests, but whose waves incessantly toss up mire and dirt upon the shore,
so shall *the wicked* be forever restless. The
dire warning in v. 21 appears also at the
end of chapter 48.

4. True Religion (58:1–14)

(1) True and False Fasting (58:1–12)

1 "Cry aloud, spare not,
   lift up your voice like a trumpet;
   declare to my people their transgression,
   to the house of Jacob their sins.
2 Yet they seek me daily,
   and delight to know my ways,
   as if they were a nation that did righteous-
     ness
     and did not forsake the ordinance of
     their God;
   they ask of me righteous judgments,
   they delight to draw near to God.
3 'Why have we fasted, and thou seest it not?

Why have we humbled ourselves, and
    thou takest no knowledge of it?'
Behold, in the day of your fast you seek
    your own pleasure,
    and oppress all your workers.
4 Behold, you fast only to quarrel and to
    fight
    and to hit with wicked fist.
Fasting like yours this day
    will not make your voice to be heard on
    high.
5 Is such the fast that I choose,
    a day for a man to humble himself?
Is it to bow down his head like a rush,
    and to spread sackcloth and ashes under
    him?
Will you call this a fast,
    and a day acceptable to the LORD?
6 "Is not this the fast that I choose:
    to loose the bonds of wickedness,
    to undo the thongs of the yoke,
    to let the oppressed go free,
    and to break every yoke?
7 Is it not to share your bread with the hun-
    gry,
    and bring the homeless poor into your
    house;
when you see the naked, to cover him,
    and not to hide yourself from your own
    flesh?
8 Then shall your light break forth like the
    dawn,
    and your healing shall spring up speed-
    ily;
your righteousness shall go before you,
    the glory of the LORD shall be your rear
    guard.
9 Then you shall call, and the LORD will an-
    swer;
    you shall cry, and he will say, Here I am.
"If you take away from the midst of you the
    yoke,
    the pointing of the finger, and speaking
    wickedness,
10 if you pour yourself out for the hungry
    and satisfy the desire of the afflicted,
then shall your light rise in the darkness
    and your gloom be as the noonday.
11 And the LORD will guide you continually,
    and satisfy your desire with good things,
    and make your bones strong;
and you shall be like a watered garden,
    like a spring of water,
    whose waters fail not.
12 And your ancient ruins shall be rebuilt;
    you shall raise up the foundations of
    many generations;
you shall be called the repairer of the
    breach,
    the restorer of streets to dwell in.

The prophet is commanded to *lift up* his
voice like a trumpet in order to make the
people of Israel aware of their transgressions (v. 1; cf. Hos. 8:1; Mic. 3:8). Although they appear to be a very religious
people—they seek the Lord daily, and perform their religious rites with enthusiasm—
all is not well with them (v. 2). They
bitterly complain that the fasts they have
observed have not resulted in any recip-
rocal action on the part of God (v. 3).
They seem to think that their fasting has
placed God in their debt and that he has
defaulted in his payments.

Fasting was a form of self-humiliation
involving abstention from food and drink.
Its purpose was to reinforce prayers offered
in times of distress (cf. 1 Sam. 7:6; 31:13;
Joel 1:14; 2:15). The only fast referred to
in the Pentateuch is that of the Day of
Atonement (cf. Lev. 16:29; Num. 29:7;
Acts 27:9), but four additional fast days
were added during the exile to commemo-
rate the fall of Jerusalem and its accompanying disasters (cf. Zech. 7:3,5; 8:19).
The prophet may well have delivered
his oracle on one of these days of national
fasting. The fact that a message dealing
with religious observances makes no mention of temple or of sacrifices suggests a
date between 538 and 520 B.C., i.e., after
the return from Babylon, but prior to the
rebuilding of the temple. According to
Zechariah 7 and 8, the observance of days
of fasting was a source of great perplexity
to the postexilic community. From the beginning there was a tendency for the
custom to get out of hand and to lead to
such pharisaical attitudes as are reflected
here (cf. Jer. 14:12; Joel 2:13; Matt.
6:16–18; 9:14; Luke 18:10–12).
While the prophet does not reject fasting
as such, he does redefine it as an act to be
directed not toward God but toward one's
fellowman. He begins by describing the
unacceptable features of Israel's present
method of fasting (vv. 3b–5). He condemns employers who derive pleasure from
their fasting, but who are callous and in-

different toward the needs of their workers. Fasting like theirs will not please God or make him more attentive to their prayers.

The *fast* in which God delights is something altogether different. It is so different, in fact, that Westermann has asked in what sense it may even be called a fast. It consists of seeking to eradicate all forms of human bondage (cf. 61:1), and of sharing one's substance with *the hungry, the homeless poor,* and *the naked* (cf. Matt. 25:31–46; 1 Cor. 13). The essential link that Westermann sees between these acts of mercy and the rite of fasting is the element of self-denial, doing without something for the sake of another. The revolutionary truth set forth in this passage, however, is that such acts of self-denial have religious value only when they are performed in order to alleviate human need. What would happen if all our religious practices were judged by this standard?

The benefits that will follow such a fast of liberation are enumerated in vv. 8–12. They include light, healing, divine guidance, answered prayer, strong bones, unfailing strength, and a continuing ministry of restoration. If the men of Israel *take away . . . the yoke* of the oppressed, refrain from *pointing . . . the finger* in scorn (cf. Prov. 6:13), avoid wicked speech, and pour out themselves for the hungry and afflicted, then all these blessings will be theirs. The author of this passage thus displays a passion for social justice as strong as that of any of the preexilic prophets. His words should challenge us to reexamine our own religious practices and the motives which underlie them.

(2) True Sabbath-keeping (58:13–14)

13 "If you turn back your foot from the sabbath,
    from doing your pleasure on my holy day,
and call the sabbath a delight
    and the holy day of the LORD honorable;
if you honor it, not going your own ways,
    or seeking your own pleasure, or talking idly;
14 then you shall take delight in the LORD,

and I will make you ride upon the heights of the earth;
I will feed you with the heritage of Jacob your father,
    for the mouth of the LORD has spoken."

In addition to participating in "fasts" designed to alleviate human need, the men of Israel are enjoined to honor the *sabbath* as a day holy unto the Lord. Although sabbath observance was of ancient origin, it came into special prominence during the exilic period. After the Jews had been cut off from temple and sacrifice, they maintained their religious distinctiveness by meticulously observing the sabbath and by practicing circumcision. Sabbath observance and circumcision, therefore, became the signs that most clearly distinguished them from their Gentile neighbors (cf. Neh. 13:15–22).

5. God's Return to a Penitent People (59: 1–21)

(1) Israel's Alienation from God (59:1–8)

1 Behold, the LORD's hand is not shortened, that it cannot save,
    or his ear dull, that it cannot hear;
2 but your iniquities have made a separation between you and your God,
    and your sins have hid his face from you so that he does not hear.
3 For your hands are defiled with blood and your fingers with iniquity;
    your lips have spoken lies, your tongue mutters wickedness.
4 No one enters suit justly, no one goes to law honestly;
    they rely on empty pleas, they speak lies, they conceive mischief and bring forth iniquity.
5 They hatch adders' eggs, they weave the spider's web;
    he who eats their eggs dies, and from one which is crushed a viper is hatched.
6 Their webs will not serve as clothing; men will not cover themselves with what they make.
    Their works are works of iniquity, and deeds of violence are in their hands.
7 Their feet run to evil, and they make haste to shed innocent blood;
    their thoughts are thoughts of iniquity, desolation and destruction are in their

highways.
8 The way of peace they know not,
 and there is no justice in their paths;
they have made their roads crooked,
 no one who goes in them knows peace.

This passage can be understood best when seen in its postexilic setting. The Israelites had returned from Babylon with the promises of Second Isaiah ringing in their ears. They had been told that upon their return to Jerusalem the city and its temple would be restored (cf. 44:28), the land would be filled to overflow with happy people (cf. 49:19–21; 54:1–3), the wealth of the nations would be brought to enrich them (cf. 45:14), and kings would come to render homage at their feet (cf. 49:22–23).

When these promises were not immediately fulfilled, the people lost heart and began to doubt both the goodness and the power of God. They openly complained that his hand was shortened, so that it could not save (v. 1; cf. 50:2; Num. 11:23), and his ear dull, so that it could not hear (cf. 6:10; Zech. 7:11).

The prophet challenges the premise upon which the people's complaint is based, namely, that the delay in the coming of the promised salvation is God's fault. He lays the blame squarely upon the people themselves, charging that their *iniquities have made a separation* between them and their God (cf. 56:3; Rom. 5:10–11; 2 Cor. 5:18–20; Eph. 2:12–13), and their *sins have hid his face* so that he does not hear their prayers (cf. 54:8; 64:7; Deut. 31:17–18; Psalms 13:1; 102:2; Mic. 3:4).

The prophet's indictment against the nation is expanded in vv. 3–8. The picture presented here is one of spiritual and moral bankruptcy almost beyond remedy (cf. Rom. 1:18–32). *Hands* are *defiled with blood* (cf. 1:15); justice is perverted; the lives of men are imperiled; and innocent blood is shed. The surprising thing is that such a serious list of crimes should be charged to those who make up the post-exilic community.

One of the underlying themes in this

passage is that the way of the transgressor is hard. Unscrupulous men may weave spiders' webs to catch the unsuspecting (v. 5), but their webs will not cover their own nakedness (v. 6). Those who live by violence (v. 7) will never know the way of peace (v. 8). Sin is indeed a hard task-master (cf. Gal. 6:7–8).

(2) Israel's Confession of Guilt (59:9–15a)

9 Therefore justice is far from us,
 and righteousness does not overtake us;
we look for light, and behold, darkness,
 and for brightness, but we walk in gloom.
10 We grope for the wall like the blind,
 we grope like those who have no eyes;
we stumble at noon as in the twilight,
 among those in full vigor we are like dead men.
11 We all growl like bears,
 we moan and moan like doves;
we look for justice, but there is none;
 for salvation, but it is far from us.
12 For our transgressions are multiplied before thee,
 and our sins testify against us;
for our transgressions are with us,
 and we know our iniquities:
13 transgressing, and denying the LORD,
 and turning away from following our God,
speaking oppression and revolt,
 conceiving and uttering from the heart lying words.
14 Justice is turned back,
 and righteousness stands afar off;
for truth has fallen in the public squares,
 and uprightness cannot enter.
15 Truth is lacking,
 and he who departs from evil makes himself a prey.

These verses constitute a prayer of confession offered by the prophet on behalf of the people. The fact that he includes himself in the confession means that he did not set himself apart from the people nor look down upon them from a position of moral superiority.

The primary emphasis of the prayer is upon the misery and disillusionment that have resulted from the people's disobedience. They wait in vain for righteousness, i.e., God's promised salvation, to overtake them (v. 9); they grope and stumble like blind men (v. 10); they groan in their despair like dumb animals (v. 11); their consciences are burdened with guilt (vv. 12–13); and injustice stalks their land (vv. 14–15a). Concerning the large accumulation of words for sin in these verses, Muilenburg has written, "Few chapters in the Bible are so rich and diverse in their vocabulary of sin (cf. Psalm 51)."

(3) God's Intervention to Save (59:15b–21)

The LORD saw it, and it displeased him
    that there was no justice.
16 He saw that there was no man,
    and wondered that there was no one to
      intervene;
    then his own arm brought him victory,
    and his righteousness upheld him.
17 He put on righteousness as a breastplate,
    and a helmet of salvation upon his head;
he put on garments of vengeance for clothing,
    and wrapped himself in fury as a mantle.
18 According to their deeds, so will he repay,
    wrath to his adversaries, requital to his
      enemies;
    to the coastlands he will render requital.
19 So they shall fear the name of the LORD
    from the west,
and his glory from the rising of the sun;
for he will come like a rushing stream,
    which the wind of the LORD drives.
20 "And he will come to Zion as Redeemer,
    to those in Jacob who turn from trans-
      gression, says the LORD.
21 "And as for me, this is my covenant with them, says the LORD: my spirit which is upon you, and my words which I have put in your mouth, shall not depart out of your mouth, or out of the mouth of your children, or out of the mouth of your children's children, says the LORD, from this time forth and for evermore."

The prophet responds to the people's prayer of confession with an oracle of salvation. The description of God that is given here is important for several reasons. First, it shows that he is not remote from his people or unconcerned about their problems: he sees their present state of affairs, is displeased by it, and resolves to correct it. Second, it is impossible that the failure of Israel should defeat the purposes

of God: when, therefore, he finds no human helper to intervene on behalf of the downtrodden (cf. Jer. 5:1; Ezek. 22:30), he enters the fray alone and wins the victory (cf. 63:3–5). Third, although God is portrayed as a warrior, his armor is unlike that of men: his *breastplate* is righteousness, his *helmet* salvation, and his *garments* vengeance and fury (cf. Eph. 6:14–16; 1 Thess. 5:8). Fourth, the intervention of God results in release for the devout in Israel (v. 20) but destruction for the transgressors (v. 18). Fifth, the advent of God to punish the wicked and to deliver the righteous takes place before the eyes of all the world: from west to east men see his glory and fear his name (v. 19).

The chapter closes with a note of assurance that God's covenant with his people will be maintained. Their special endowment with his spirit (cf. 42:1; 44:3; 61:1) and with the knowledge of his word (cf. 40: 8; 55:10–11) is to endure "from this time forth and for evermore."

II. The Proclamation of Salvation to Zion (60:1—66:24)

1. The Glorious Restoration of Zion (60:1–22)

The theme of chapters 60—62 is the proclamation of the nearness of the restoration of Jerusalem. Unlike chapters 56—59, they contain no reference to the city's sinfulness or to its need for repentance. Some interpreters (e.g., Snaith, McKenzie) believe that the close parallels between these chapters and chapters 40—55 indicate that both were written by Second Isaiah. Others (e.g., Westermann) maintain that chapters 60—62 "form the corpus of a self-contained message of salvation quite distinct from that of Deutero-Isaiah, yet having at the same time, in many ways, a clear connection with it." The inconclusive nature of the evidence makes it impossible to determine with certainty if either of these views is correct. The first, however, seems to be better supported by the evidence.

(1) The Coming of the Gentiles to the Light (60:1–14)

1 Arise, shine; for your light has come,
    and the glory of the Lord has risen upon
    you.
2 For behold, darkness shall cover the earth,
    and thick darkness the peoples;
    but the Lord will arise upon you,
    and his glory will be seen upon you.
3 And nations shall come to your light,
    and kings to the brightness of your rising.
4 Lift up your eyes round about, and see;
    they all gather together, they come to you;
    your sons shall come from far,
    and your daughters shall be carried in the
    arms.
5 Then you shall see and be radiant,
    your heart shall thrill and rejoice;
    because the abundance of the sea shall be
    turned to you,
    the wealth of the nations shall come to
    you.
6 A multitude of camels shall cover you,
    the young camels of Midian and Ephah;
    all those from Sheba shall come.
    They shall bring gold and frankincense,
    and shall proclaim the praise of the Lord.
7 All the flocks of Kedar shall be gathered to
    you,
    the rams of Nebaioth shall minister to you;
    they shall come up with acceptance on my
    altar,
    and I will glorify my glorious house.
8 Who are these that fly like a cloud,
    and like doves to their windows?
9 For the coastlands shall wait for me,
    the ships of Tarshish first,
    to bring your sons from far,
    their silver and gold with them,
    for the name of the Lord your God,
    and for the Holy One of Israel,
    because he has glorified you.
10 Foreigners shall build up your walls,
    and their kings shall minister to you;
    for in my wrath I smote you,
    but in my favor I have had mercy on you.
11 Your gates shall be open continually;
    day and night they shall not be shut;
    that men may bring to you the wealth of
    the nations,
    with their kings led in procession.
12 For the nation and kingdom
    that will not serve you shall perish;
    those nations shall be utterly laid waste.
13 The glory of Lebanon shall come to you,
    the cypress, the plane, and the pine,
    to beautify the place of my sanctuary;
    and I will make the place of my feet glo-
    rious.
14 The sons of those who oppressed you

shall come bending low to you;
    and all who despised you
    shall bow down at your feet;
    they shall call you the City of the Lord,
    the Zion of the Holy One of Israel.

The poem opens with a double imperative addressed to Zion: *Arise, shine*. The
summons is for her not only to accept joyfully the proclamation of her salvation but
also to reflect the light of the glory of the
Lord, which has risen upon her. The
glory of the Lord stands for the revelation
of his power and holiness (cf. Ex. 24:16;
40:34; 1 Kings 8:11; Psalms 19:1; John
1:14).

The author of these verses had the eye
of an artist, for he pictures Mount Zion as
an island of light in the midst of a sea of
darkness (v. 2). Out of the thick darkness
that covers the earth, nations and kings
come to Zion to share the brightness of her
rising (v. 3). The prophet thus emphasizes
the centripetal (as opposed to the centrifu-
gal) nature of Zion's mission to the nations:
her first task is not to go out and seek to
evangelize the nations, but rather to reflect
the light of the glory of God with such
clarity that they will be drawn to her (cf.
45:14–15; 49:7; Zech. 8:20–23).

A second double imperative—*lift up
your eyes . . . see*—bids Zion behold the
streams of people converging upon her.
Radiant with joy and excitement (v. 5),
she sees her sons and daughters being
borne from afar in the arms of strangers
(v. 4b). She also sees a multitude of
camels bringing gold and frankincense from
many lands (v. 6). The tribes of Arabia
also bring sacrificial offerings of flocks and
rams (v. 7).

The prophet's eye for beauty is again
evident in v. 8: as he sees the white sails
of fleets of ships approaching Palestine
from the west, he exclaims, "Who are these
that fly like a cloud, and like doves to their
windows?" The answer is that these are
ships of Tarshish, bearing Zion's sons from
afar, and laden also with cargoes of silver
and gold. Treasures are thus borne to her
from every direction.

Verses 10–14 describe the restoration of Zion to her former glory. *Foreigners* voluntarily assume the task of rebuilding her walls, and kings gladly serve her (cf. 61:5–6). Her *gates* remain *open continually* to receive the tribute of the nations. Timber from the forests of Lebanon is brought to adorn her Temple (cf. Ezra 3:7); and the sons of her former oppressors come bending low to her, and calling her by her new name, "the City of the Lord, the Zion of the Holy One of Israel." The glorious prophecy in these verses is interpreted in Revelation 21:24–27 as referring to the heavenly Jerusalem.

(2) The Reversal of Zion's Humiliation (60:15–22)

15 Whereas you have been forsaken and hated,
    with no one passing through,
I will make you majestic for ever,
    a joy from age to age.
16 You shall suck the milk of nations,
    you shall suck the breast of kings;
and you shall know that I, the LORD, am your Savior
    and your Redeemer, the Mighty One of Jacob.
17 Instead of bronze I will bring gold,
    and instead of iron I will bring silver;
instead of wood, bronze,
    instead of stones, iron.
I will make your overseers peace
    and your taskmasters righteousness.
18 Violence shall no more be heard in your land,
    devastation or destruction within your borders;
you shall call your walls Salvation,
    and your gates Praise.
19 The sun shall be no more
    your light by day,
nor for brightness shall the moon
    give light to you by night;
but the LORD will be your everlasting light,
    and your God will be your glory.
20 Your sun shall no more go down,
    nor your moon withdraw itself;
for the LORD will be your everlasting light,
    and your days of mourning shall be ended.
21 Your people shall all be righteous;
    they shall possess the land for ever,
the shoot of my planting, the work of my hands,
    that I might be glorified.
22 The least one shall become a clan,
    and the smallest one a mighty nation;

I am the LORD;
    in its time I will hasten it.

These verses present a contrast between Zion's former desolation and her future glory. She who was once forsaken and hated is soon to become the joy of all the ages. Once treated like a motherless child, she is now to be suckled at the *breast of kings* (cf. 49:23). Her bronze will be replaced by gold, her iron by silver, her wood by bronze, and her stones by iron. Her new *taskmasters* and *overseers* will be *peace* and *righteousness* (cf. 32:17). The results of the rule of peace and righteousness are explained in v. 18: violence is heard no more in the land, so that Zion's walls are called "Salvation" and her gates "Praise."

The theme of light, which is first introduced in vv. 1–3, reappears in vv. 19–20. Zion is told that in the time of her restoration she will have no need of sun or moon, for the Lord himself will be her everlasting light (cf. Rev. 21:23–25). Darkness will be banished from her forever, and with it all previous sorrow (cf. 25:8; 35:10; 65:18–19; Rev. 21:3–4).

Only the righteous, i.e., those who are *the shoot* of God's *planting* and *the work* of his *hands*, will participate in Zion's glorious future (cf. 35:8). It is said of these that they will possess the land forever, and that the least among them will become a clan, and the smallest a mighty nation. Through the gifts of land and offspring, the ancient promises made to the patriarchs will be fulfilled (cf. 51:1–2; Gen. 13:14–17). The last part of v. 22 emphasizes the trustworthiness of God and the reliability of his word: what he has promised, he will bring to pass in its appointed time.

2. Tidings of Great Joy (61:1–11)

(1) The Anointed Herald of Salvation (61:1–4)

1 The Spirit of the Lord GOD is upon me,
    because the LORD has anointed me
to bring good tidings to the afflicted;
    he has sent me to bind up the broken-

hearted,
to proclaim liberty to the captives,
and the opening of the prison to those
who are bound;
2 to proclaim the year of the LORD's favor,
and the day of vengeance of our God;
to comfort all who mourn;
3 to grant to those who mourn in Zion—
to give them a garland instead of ashes,
the oil of gladness instead of mourning,
the mantle of praise instead of a faint
spirit;
that they may be called oaks of righteousness,
the planting of the LORD, that he may be
glorified.
4 They shall build up the ancient ruins,
they shall raise up the former devastations;
they shall repair the ruined cities,
the devastations of many generations.

Some have interpreted these verses as a fifth Servant Song (cf. 42:1–4; 49:1–6; 50:4–9; 52:13—53:12). It seems more likely, however, that they represent the prophet's description of his own mission to the postexilic community. He has been called to minister to a people whose captivity has not yet ended (v. 1), and whose land has long lain in ruins (v. 4). His audience is specifically located in Zion (v. 3), and the distressing nature of their situation is indicated by the threefold reference to their mourning (vv. 2–3). They are further characterized as afflicted, brokenhearted, bound, and of a faint spirit. That they are the same persons whose restoration is promised in the preceding chapter is clearly indicated by a comparison of v. 3b with 60:21b; in both passages it is stated that the divine intention is to form a people that may be called *the planting of the Lord,* and in whom *he may be glorified.* The date suggested for the passage, therefore, would be shortly after the return of the first band of exiles to Jerusalem in 538 B.C.

The prophet begins his oracle with the announcement that he has been divinely appointed to his task and endowed with *the Spirit of the Lord God* (cf. 11:2; 42:1; Mic. 3:8). He has been sent to proclaim a message that will effect a wondrous change

in his disheartened listeners: the *poor* (marg.) will hear the good news, the *brokenhearted* will be healed, prisoners will be set free, the blind will receive their sight, and mourners will be comforted. These changes in the circumstances of the people will signal the dawning of the age of salvation, designated here as "the year of the Lord's favor, and the day of vengeance of our God."

"Today this scripture has been fulfilled in your hearing." Such was the declaration made by Jesus in the synagogue at Nazareth after he had read v. 1 and the first line of v. 2 (Luke 4:16–21; cf. 7:18–23). He saw in the description of the prophet's ministry an apt portrayal of his own, as he went about healing the sick and preaching the good news of the kingdom of God. There is also a sense in which the passage presents a blueprint for the type of ministry that God's servants are to perform in every age.

(2) A People Blessed of the Lord (61: 5–9)

5 Aliens shall stand and feed your flocks,
foreigners shall be your plowmen and
vine-dressers;
6 but you shall be called the priests of the
LORD,
men shall speak of you as the ministers
of our God;
you shall eat the wealth of the nations,
and in their riches you shall glory.
7 Instead of your shame you shall have a double portion,
instead of dishonor you shall rejoice in
your lot;
therefore in your land you shall possess a
double portion;
yours shall be everlasting joy.
8 For I the LORD love justice,
I hate robbery and wrong;
I will faithfully give them their recompense,
and I will make an everlasting covenant
with them.
9 Their descendants shall be known among
the nations,
and their offspring in the midst of the peoples;
all who see them shall acknowledge them,
that they are a people whom the LORD
has blessed.

Zion's restoration will result in a new mission for her people: they will all become *priests* and ministers of *the Lord* (cf. Ex. 19:5–6; 1 Peter 2:9). In order that they may devote themselves fully to such a spiritual ministry, aliens will voluntarily tend their flocks, cultivate their fields, and sustain them with their wealth. Just as the Levitical priests were supported by the tribes among whom they served, so will the Israelites enjoy the support of the nations among whom they minister as priests.

The reference to Israel's *double portion* in v. 7 echoes 40:2 (cf. Zech. 9:12). A second possibility is that Israel is to be treated as the firstborn among the nations, receiving a double portion of the Lord's inheritance (cf. Deut. 21:17).

Verses 8–9 complete the picture of the future blessedness of the people of Zion. Because the Lord hates robbery and wrong, he will recompense them for all the years they have suffered. He also promises that he will establish a new and *everlasting covenant* with them. Their descendants will then be known among the nations as the people whom the Lord has blessed.

(3) A Hymn of Rejoicing (61:10–11)

10 I will greatly rejoice in the LORD,
    my soul shall exult in my God;
  for he has clothed me with the garments of salvation,
    he has covered me with the robe of righteousness,
  as a bridegroom decks himself with a garland,
    and as a bride adorns herself with her jewels.
11 For as the earth brings forth its shoots,
    and as a garden causes what is sown in it to spring up,
  so the Lord GOD will cause righteousness and praise
    to spring forth before all the nations.

Zion responds to these promises with a hymn of thanksgiving. In preparation for the institution of the everlasting covenant, she is clothed with *garments of salvation* and with *the robe of righteousness* (cf.

Eph. 6:14–17). These are spoken of as wedding garments, and the metaphor of the bridegroom and the bride emphasizes the joy and delight shared mutually by God and his redeemed people (cf. 49:18; 62:5; Rev. 21:2).

In the closing verse the prophet repeats the promise that the word of God will surely come to fruition (cf. 40:8; 55:10–11). The Lord will cause Zion's redemption to spring forth in its proper season, just as a garden causes the seed sown in it to spring up and grow. The restoration of Zion's righteousness and praise, therefore, will be accomplished in the sight of all the nations.

3. Pleading the Promises of God (62:1–12)

(1) Beulah Land (62:1–5)

1 For Zion's sake I will not keep silent,
    and for Jerusalem's sake I will not rest,
  until her vindication goes forth as brightness,
    and her salvation as a burning torch.
2 The nations shall see your vindication,
    and all the kings your glory;
  and you shall be called by a new name
    which the mouth of the LORD will give.
3 You shall be a crown of beauty in the hand of the LORD,
    and a royal diadem in the hand of your God.
4 You shall no more be termed Forsaken,
    and your land shall no more be termed Desolate;
  but you shall be called My delight is in her,
    and your land Married;
  for the LORD delights in you,
    and your land shall be married.
5 For as a young man marries a virgin,
    so shall your sons marry you,
  and as the bridegroom rejoices over the bride,
    so shall your God rejoice over you.

The prophet solemnly declares to Zion that while the coming of her salvation is delayed he *will not keep silent* nor rest. Instead, he will intercede before God for her until *her vindication* goes forth as brightness and her salvation as a burning torch. The promise is repeated that her vindication will be manifested before all nations and her glory before their kings (cf. 61:11).

In the age to come Zion's name will be changed from *Forsaken* to *My delight is in her,* and that of the land of Judah from *Desolate* to *Married.* Here as elsewhere in the Scriptures the receiving of a new name signifies a radical change in one's character and status. Zion, therefore, can be referred to as a crown of beauty and a royal diadem, although the prophet is careful to say that these are held in the Lord's hand rather than being placed upon his head. The metaphor of marriage is carried over into v. 5 with the result that the sons of Zion are rather curiously described as married to their mother. The heart of the verse, however, is found in the statement that the Lord rejoices over Zion as a bridegroom rejoices over his bride. There is no finer statement of the Lord's personal concern for his people in all the Old Testament.

(2) The Prayer Vigil of Zion's Watchmen (62:6–9)

6 Upon your walls, O Jerusalem,
   I have set watchmen;
all the day and all the night
   they shall never be silent.
You who put the LORD in remembrance,
   take no rest,
7 and give him no rest
   until he establishes Jerusalem
   and makes it a praise in the earth.
8 The LORD has sworn by his right hand
   and by his mighty arm:
"I will not again give your grain
   to be food for your enemies,
and foreigners shall not drink your wine
   for which you have labored;
9 but those who garner it shall eat it
   and praise the LORD,
and those who gather it shall drink it
   in the courts of my sanctuary."

The prophet announces to Jerusalem that he has placed *watchmen* upon her *walls* to engage in perpetual prayer on her behalf. This is their only duty and responsibility, which sets them apart from ordinary watchmen. They therefore represent all those who join with the prophet in the ministry of intercession. They are addressed as those *who put the Lord in*

remembrance, and are charged to take no rest and to give God no rest until he has blessed Jerusalem with peace and prosperity.

Smart has noted that the passage raises anew the entire problem of intercessory prayer: why should God need to be reminded of his own promises? If he is both good and omnipotent, why must he be implored to right earth's wrongs and to heal its hurts? Without denying the seriousness of the problem, Smart concludes that our common humanity binds us together in such a way that we are able to reach out in prayer and draw others into the presence of God, whether they are aware of it or not. Intercession, therefore, is seen as "a sign of the inseparableness of our human lives in their relation with God."

The Lord has given his solemn oath that foreigners will no longer confiscate the harvests for which his people have labored (v. 8). On the contrary, those who reap the harvests shall eat and drink of them, and render praise to the Lord in the courts of his sanctuary (v. 9). The latter reference probably has to do with their joyful celebration of the feast of Tabernacles (cf. Zech. 14:16–19).

(3) The Highway of the Redeemed (62: 10–12)

10 Go through, go through the gates,
   prepare the way for the people;
build up, build up the highway,
   clear it of stones,
   lift up an ensign over the peoples.
11 Behold, the LORD has proclaimed
   to the end of the earth:
Say to the daughter of Zion,
   "Behold, your salvation comes;
behold, his reward is with him,
   and his recompense before him."
12 And they shall be called The holy people,
   The redeemed of the LORD;
and you shall be called Sought out,
   a city not forsaken.

The inhabitants of Jerusalem are urged to go out through the gates of the city and to prepare a highway for the return of the exiles who are still scattered among the nations (cf. 40:3–4). In v. 11*b*, which is a repetition of 40:10*b*, the prophet assures the daughter of Zion that now at last her long-awaited salvation will come. In token of her renewed state, her name will be changed to *Sought out, a city not forsaken,* and that of her people to *The holy people, The redeemed of the Lord* (cf. v. 4).

4. The Divine Avenger (63:1–6)

¹ Who is this that comes from Edom,
　　in crimsoned garments from Bozrah,
　he that is glorious in his apparel,
　　marching in the greatness of his strength?
　"It is I, announcing vindication,
　　mighty to save."
² Why is thy apparel red,
　　and thy garments like his that treads in the wine press?
³ "I have trodden the wine press alone,
　　and from the peoples no one was with me;
　I trod them in my anger
　　and trampled them in my wrath;
　their lifeblood is sprinkled upon my garments,
　　and I have stained all my raiment.
⁴ For the day of vengeance was in my heart,
　　and my year of redemption has come.
⁵ I looked, but there was no one to help;
　　I was appalled, but there was no one to uphold;
　so my own arm brought me victory,
　　and my wrath upheld me.
⁶ I trod down the peoples in my anger,
　　I made them drunk in my wrath,
　　and I poured out their lifeblood on the earth."

This passage is cast in the form of a dialogue between God and the prophet. In his mind's eye the prophet sees a lone figure approaching Jerusalem from the direction of Edom. When he asks who this is who comes from Edom with his garments stained red, marching in his mighty strength, the Lord answers him, "It is I, who announce that right has won the day, I, who am strong to save" (NEB).

When the prophet inquires of the Lord why his garments are stained red, like the garments of those who tread out grapes, the answer comes back, "I have trodden the winepress alone; no man, no nation was with me. I trod them down in my rage, I trampled them in my fury; and

their life-blood spurted over my garments and stained all my clothing" (NEB).

The theme of the passage is the Lord's readiness to act; he has not stood idly by, but has entered the struggle on the side of his oppressed people. The Edomites are perhaps to be understood as representative of all those who are hostile toward Israel (cf. 34:5–6,9; Psalm 137:7; Obad. 9–14; Mal. 1:4). The Lord, therefore, will deal harshly with all nations who try to prevent the realization of his purpose for his people.

The Lord is presented elsewhere in the Old Testament as a warlike figure (cf. Ex. 14:14,25; Psalm 24:8; Isa. 42:13) but never in such violent terms as here. Many Christians, therefore, find it difficult to reconcile the prophet's view of God with that found in the New Testament. How could the same God love his enemies enough to send his Son to be their Saviour, and also seek to destroy them?

North (*The Second Isaiah,* p. 116) has proposed a solution to the problem based upon a consideration of the two possible sequels to the Old Testament's anthropomorphic conception of the warrior-God: such a conception either could have been outgrown and replaced by an abstract monotheism, or it could have culminated in the incarnation of Christ. The latter possibility is what actually occurred. God did visit the earth, in the incarnation, and his coming did result in the shedding of blood. However, as North has indicated, "it was man, not God, who shed it, and the blood that was shed was not man's, but the blood of the incarnate Son of God."

5. A Psalm of Intercession (63:7—64:12)

In this passage the prophet speaks as intercessor for his people, identifying himself with them in their darkness and despair (cf. 62:1). The first part of his prayer (63:7–14) is a review of God's ancient redemptive acts; the second part (63:15—64:12) is a confession of national guilt and an earnest appeal to God to save Israel from her present distress. Most scholars date the prayer between the first return of the exiles in 538 B.C. and the completion of the Temple in 515 (cf. 63:17–19; 64:10–11).

(1) Remembrance of Past Mercies (63:7–14)

7 I will recount the steadfast love of the
     Lord,
         the praises of the Lord,
     according to all that the Lord has granted
       us,
         and the great goodness to the house of
           Israel
     which he has granted them according to
       his mercy,
         according to the abundance of his stead-
           fast love.
8 For he said, Surely they are my people,
       sons who will not deal falsely;
     and he became their Savior.
9 In all their affliction he was afflicted,
       and the angel of his presence saved
         them;
     in his love and in his pity he redeemed
       them;
       he lifted them up and carried them all
         the days of old.
10 But they rebelled
     and grieved his holy Spirit;
   therefore he turned to be their enemy,
     and himself fought against them.
11 Then he remembered the days of old,
     of Moses his servant.
   Where is he who brought up out of the sea
     the shepherds of his flock?
   Where is he who put in the midst of them
     his holy Spirit,
12 who caused his glorious arm
     to go at the right hand of Moses,
   who divided the waters before them
     to make for himself an everlasting name,
13   who led them through the depths?
   Like a horse in the desert,
     they did not stumble.
14 Like cattle that go down into the valley,
     the Spirit of the Lord gave them rest.
   So thou didst lead thy people,
     to make for thyself a glorious name.

In language reminiscent of the psalms (cf. Psalms 89:1–2; 106:1–2), the author recalls the past mercies of God on behalf of Israel. Verse 7 begins and ends with the Hebrew word *chesed* (*steadfast love*) a word so rich in meaning as almost to defy translation. It is a covenant word combining the two basic ideas of love and loyalty. The verse also uses three other

terms to designate the mighty acts of the Lord: *praises, great goodness,* and *mercy.*

Verse 8 describes the high expectations with which God chose the Israelites to be his sons. The verse has reference to the Exodus, and is parallel in meaning to Hosea 11:1: "When Israel was a child, I loved him, and out of Egypt I called my son."

The Exodus is also in view in v. 9, which boldly describes God as sharing the affliction of his people in Egypt (cf. Ex. 3:7–10; 6:2–5). Because of his compassion for them, he sent the angel of his presence to save them (cf. Ex. 14:19; Num. 20:14–16); in his love and pity he redeemed them (cf. Ex. 6:6–7; Psalm 74:2); and he lifted them up and carried them all the days of old (cf. Ex. 6:8; Deut. 32:11–12).

The first two words in v. 10 stand in an emphatic position in the Hebrew text: "*But they . . .*" In spite of all that the Lord had done for the sons of Israel, they had rebelled against him (Heb. *marah;* cf. Num. 20:24; Deut. 9:23; Psalm 106:7), and *grieved his holy Spirit* (cf. v. 11; Psalm 51:11). These words vividly express the grief and pain that man's rebellion always brings to God (cf. Acts 7:51; Eph. 4:30).

Most commentators regard the antecedent of "he" at the beginning of v. 11 as Israel. Remembering the miracles that God had performed in the past, Israel now cries out in plaintive tone, *Where is he?* This question was ordinarily spoken in derision by the nation's foes (cf. Psalms 42:3; 79:10; Joel 2:17). Here, however, it is asked by a deeply troubled Israel, which is itself unable to explain the apparent absence of God from its midst.

(2) A Plea for Present Help (63:15—64:12)

15 Look down from heaven and see,
     from thy holy and glorious habitation.
   Where are thy zeal and thy might?
     The yearning of thy heart and thy com-
       passion
     are withheld from me.
16 For thou art our Father,

though Abraham does not know us
  and Israel does not acknowledge us;
thou, O LORD, art our Father,
  our Redeemer from of old is thy name.

17 O LORD, why dost thou make us err from
    thy ways
  and harden our heart, so that we fear
    thee not?
Return for the sake of thy servants,
  the tribes of thy heritage.

18 Thy holy people possessed thy sanctuary a
    little while;
  our adversaries have trodden it down.

19 We have become like those over whom
    thou hast never ruled,
  like those who are not called by thy
    name.

1 O that thou wouldst rend the heavens and
    come down,
  that the mountains might quake at thy
    presence—

2 as when fire kindles brushwood
  and the fire causes water to boil—
to make thy name known to thy adversaries,
  and that the nations might tremble at thy
    presence!

3 When thou didst terrible things which we
    looked not for,
  thou camest down, the mountains quaked
    at thy presence.

4 From of old no one has heard
  or perceived by the ear,
no eye has seen a God besides thee,
  who works for those who wait for him.

5 Thou meetest him that joyfully works right-
    eousness,
  those that remember thee in thy ways.
Behold, thou wast angry, and we sinned;
  in our sins we have been a long time, and
    shall we be saved?

6 We have all become like one who is unclean,
  and all our righteous deeds are like a
    polluted garment.
We all fade like a leaf,
  and our iniquities, like the wind, take us
    away.

7 There is no one that calls upon thy name,
  that bestirs himself to take hold of thee;
for thou hast hid thy face from us,
  and hast delivered us into the hand of our
    iniquities.

8 Yet, O LORD, thou art our Father;
  we are the clay, and thou art our potter;
  we are all the work of thy hand.

9 Be not exceedingly angry, O LORD,
  and remember not iniquity for ever.
Behold, consider, we are all thy people.

10 Thy holy cities have become a wilderness,
  Zion has become a wilderness,
  Jerusalem a desolation.

11 Our holy and beautiful house,
  where our fathers praised thee,
has been burned by fire,
  and all our pleasant places have become
    ruins.

12 Wilt thou restrain thyself at these things, O
    LORD?
  Wilt thou keep silent, and afflict us sorely?

The prophet, speaking for the entire postexilic community, implores God first to *look down* 63:15 and then to *come down* (64:1) from heaven and rescue his people from their wretchedness and despair. What the prophet asks for is nothing less than a theophany, a self-revelation of God in all his power and majesty (64:1*b*–3; cf. Ex. 19:16–18; 2 Sam. 22:8–16; Psalm 18:7–15).

A unique feature of the prophet's prayer is its emphasis on the fatherhood of God (cf. 63:16; 64:8). The designation of God as father rarely occurs in the Old Testament, perhaps due to the danger of implying that men are physically descended from him. The more common designation for him, therefore, is creator. Even when he is spoken of as father, the usual implication is that men are his children by creation. Fatherhood and creatorship are combined in 64:8, where God is addressed as both father and potter (cf. 29:16; 45:9; Jer. 18:6).

Throughout the prayer there is an intermingling of words of confidence (63:16; 64:4–5*a*,8), of entreaty (63:15*a*,17*b*; 64: 1–3,9), of lament (63:15*b*,17*a*, 18–19; 64:10–12), and of confession (64:5*b*–7). The lament in v. 17*a* reflects the notion that God is without peer or rival in the universe, and that everything that happens is directly due to his will (cf. 6:9–10; 45:7). It was as easy for the Israelites to believe that he had hardened their hearts as that he had once hardened the heart of Pharaoh (cf. Ex. 7:3).

A similar thought occurs in 64:5: *Behold, thou wast angry, and we sinned.* The modern reader is shocked by this statement, for it seems to confuse cause with effect. Upon closer examination, however, it is seen to express a vital truth: the wrath of God sometimes manifests itself through the sinner's being delivered over to greater sinfulness (cf. Rom. 1:18–32). Sin is its own punishment, for it leads to uncleanness and pollution, and in the end carries the sinner away to destruction like leaves driven by the wind (64:6). Nothing, therefore, is more frightening than to be delivered into the hands of one's own iniquities (64:7).

The prophet expresses his agonizing concern over the present state of Jerusalem's Temple. His deep love for it is revealed in the terms he uses to describe it: *thy sanctuary* (63:18), and *"Our holy and beautiful house, where our fathers praised thee"* (64:11). Now it lies in ruins, trodden down by Israel's adversaries and burned by fire. The prophet is confident that God will not remain impassive in the face of these things, although his confidence takes the form of a question (64:12).

6. Prophecies of Judgment and Salvation (65:1—66:24)

(1) God's Warning to an Apostate People (65:1–16)

¹ I was ready to be sought by those who did
      not ask for me;
   I was ready to be found by those who did
      not seek me.
   I said, "Here am I, here am I,"
      to a nation that did not call on my name.
² I spread out my hands all the day
      to a rebellious people,
   who walk in a way that is not good,
      following their own devices;
³ a people who provoke me
      to my face continually,
   sacrificing in gardens
      and burning incense upon bricks;
⁴ who sit in tombs,
      and spend the night in secret places;
   who eat swine's flesh,
      and broth of abominable things is in their
         vessels;
⁵ who say, "Keep to yourself,
      do not come near me, for I am set apart
         from you."
   These are a smoke in my nostrils,
      a fire that burns all the day.
⁶ Behold, it is written before me:
   "I will not keep silent, but I will repay,
   yea, I will repay into their bosom
⁷   their iniquities and their fathers' iniqui-
         ties together,

says the LORD;
      because they burned incense upon the
         mountains
      and reviled me upon the hills,
   I will measure into their bosom
      payment for their former doings."
⁸ Thus says the LORD:
   "As the wine is found in the cluster,
      and they say, 'Do not destroy it,
      for there is a blessing in it,'
   so I will do for my servants' sake,
      and not destroy them all.
⁹ I will bring forth descendants from Jacob,
      and from Judah inheritors of my moun-
         tains;
   my chosen shall inherit it,
      and my servants shall dwell there.
¹⁰ Sharon shall become a pasture for flocks,
      and the Valley of Achor a place for herds
         to lie down,
      for my people who have sought me.
¹¹ But you who forsake the LORD,
      who forget my holy mountain,
   who set a table for Fortune
      and fill cups of mixed wine for Destiny;
¹² I will destine you to the sword,
      and all of you shall bow down to the
         slaughter;
   because, when I called, you did not answer,
      when I spoke, you did not listen,
   but you did what was evil in my eyes,
      and chose what I did not delight in."
¹³ Therefore thus says the Lord GOD:
   "Behold, my servants shall eat,
      but you shall be hungry;
   behold, my servants shall drink,
      but you shall be thirsty;
   behold, my servants shall rejoice,
      but you shall be put to shame;
¹⁴ behold, my servants shall sing for gladness
         of heart,
      but you shall cry out for pain of heart,
      and shall wail for anguish of spirit.
¹⁵ You shall leave your name to my chosen
         for a curse,
      and the Lord GOD will slay you;
      but his servants he will call by a different
         name.
¹⁶ So that he who blesses himself in the land
      shall bless himself by the God of truth,
   and he who takes an oath in the land
      shall swear by the God of truth;
   because the former troubles are forgotten
      and are hid from my eyes.

Verses 1–2 contrast God's eager readiness to be sought and found with Israel's total indifference to his overtures. All day long God has spread out his hands and called to his people, but they have turned away from him and followed their own devices (cf. 55:6–9; Rom. 10:20–21).

The people are accused of engaging in religious practices borrowed from their pagan neighbors (vv. 3b–5a,7). These include the offering of sacrifices in gardens (v. 3b) and upon the mountains (v. 7; cf. Jer. 3:23; Hos. 4:13); the burning of incense upon bricks; sitting in tombs, presumably for the purpose of consulting the spirits of the dead; spending the night in "secret places," perhaps a reference to the practice of sleeping in holy places in order to receive dream messages from the other world; the eating of swine's flesh (cf. Lev. 11:7); and the false notion that engaging in these practices impregnated one with such a degree of holiness that he became unapproachable (v. 5a).

The Lord labels those who engage in such abominable practices as *a people who provoke me to my face continually* and *a smoke in my nostrils, a fire that burns all the day.* The things they have done have been written down before him (v. 6a). They shall be repaid in full for all their iniquities (vv. 6b–7).

As the prophet considers the problem of Israel's continuing apostasy, he wonders about the severity of the coming judgment. What hope is there for a nation that has once again demonstrated its inability to repent? Has God's patience finally been exhausted, and will he now destroy the nation in his wrath?

The answer to these questions comes in the announcement of a momentous change in the manner in which God proposes to deal with the people of Israel in the future. The transition occurs in v. 8, which employs a vintage proverb to teach that the nation will be spared only because of the presence within it of a righteous remnant (cf. Gen. 18:22–32). The promises previously made to the nation as a whole will now be transferred to this remnant (cf. vv. 9–10). God will still judge the nation, but a distinction will be made between the two segments within it. His coming will bring ruin to the unrighteous, but salvation to

his servants (cf. Matt. 25:31–46; Rev. 20:11–15).

The unrighteous are addressed in vv. 11–12 and condemned for their idolatry. The two pagan gods whom they are accused of worshiping are *Fortune* (*God*) and *Destiny* (*Meni*). Through a play on words, the Lord announces that he will "destine" them to the sword. The latter part of v. 12 is repeated in 66:4 (cf. 50:2).

The contrast between the fate of God's servants and the unrighteous is sharply drawn in vv. 13–15 (cf. Luke 6:20–26). The latter have nothing to look forward to except hunger, thirst, shame, grief, and death. After their death their name (Israel?) will become a curse, whereas the faithful remnant will receive a new and different name (v. 15; cf. 62:2; Rev. 2:17; 3:12). The ancient promises made to Abraham will then be fulfilled in the lives of the faithful, as they "bless themselves" by the God of truth (cf. Gen. 12:2–3). *The God of truth* could also be rendered "the God of Amen," the Hebrew word *amen* meaning truth, faithfulness, or steadfastness. The prophet may perhaps be suggesting that in the age to come even God himself will be called by a new name. The "God of Amen" is the faithful God of a faithful people (cf. 2 Cor. 1:20; Rev. 3:14).

(2) New Heavens and a New Earth (65:17–25)

17 "For behold, I create new heavens
    and a new earth;
  and the former things shall not be remembered
    or come into mind.
18 But be glad and rejoice for ever
    in that which I create;
  for behold, I create Jerusalem a rejoicing,
    and her people a joy.
19 I will rejoice in Jerusalem,
    and be glad in my people;
  no more shall be heard in it the sound of weeping
    and the cry of distress.
20 No more shall there be in it
    an infant that lives but a few days,
  or an old man who does not fill out his days,

for the child shall die a hundred years old,
and the sinner a hundred years old shall
be accursed.
21 They shall build houses and inhabit them;
they shall plant vineyards and eat their
fruit.
22 They shall not build and another inhabit;
they shall not plant and another eat;
for like the days of a tree shall the days of
my people be,
and my chosen shall long enjoy the work
of their hands.
23 They shall not labor in vain,
or bear children for calamity;
for they shall be the offspring of the blessed
of the Lord,
and their children with them.
24 Before they call I will answer,
while they are yet speaking I will hear.
25 The wolf and the lamb shall feed together,
the lion shall eat straw like the ox;
and dust shall be the serpent's food.
They shall not hurt or destroy
in all my holy mountain,
says the Lord."

The subject of this oracle is the glorious
destiny awaiting the servants of God. For
their sakes the heavens and the earth will
be recreated, and former troubles will be
remembered no more (v. 17; cf. 2 Peter
3:10–13; Rev. 21:1–4). It should be
noted that the future envisaged by the
prophet is still very much this-worldly. It
is a future which is completely earth-cen-
tered, where, for example, women still give
birth to children (v. 23; cf. Gen. 3:16);
men still build houses, cultivate fields, and
harvest crops (vv. 21–22; cf. Gen. 3:
17–19); and serpents still eat the dust of
the earth (v. 25; cf. Gen. 3:14). Most
important of all, it is a future in which all
must still die (v. 20).

In what, then, does Israel's future hope
consist? *First,* it is found in the promise
that sorrow and distress will be eliminated
and their place be taken by joy and gladness (vv. 18–19). *Second,* it rests in the
assurance that the righteous will not die
prematurely but will live to a ripe old age
(v. 20). One who attains a mere hundred
years will still be considered a child, while
one who fails to attain a hundred years will
be regarded as under a curse. The participle *chote'*, which is usually rendered "sin-

ner," is derived from a verb root whose
basic meaning is to miss the mark or to
fall short. The final clause in v. 20, therefore, should be translated: "and whoever
falls short of a hundred years shall be
accursed."

Third, in the future the labor of the
righteous will not be in vain (vv. 21–23);
they will not build houses for others to
inhabit nor sow crops for others to consume; their wives will no longer bear children for calamity or misfortune. The righteous, therefore, will enjoy the fruits of
their labor, and their children will be
called *the offspring of the blessed of the
Lord. Fourth,* in the age to come God will
respond to the prayers of the righteous,
answering them before they call, and hearing them whenever they speak (v. 24).
Fifth, all hostility and animosity will be
removed from the earth, so that even
animals will live together in peace (v. 25;
cf. 11:6–9). The prophet thus clearly foresees a return to Paradise and an undoing
of all the results of the fall of man into sin.
With their rendering of v. 22b, the Septuagint and the Targum provide additional
support for relating this passage to the
early chapters of Genesis; their translation
reads: "for like the days of the tree of life
shall be the days of my people" (cf. Gen.
2:9; Ezek. 47:1–12; Rev. 22:1–2,14).

**(3) God's Disapproval of Corrupt Worship
(66:1–4)**

1   Thus says the Lord:
"Heaven is my throne
and the earth is my footstool;
what is the house which you would build
for me,
and what is the place of my rest?
2   All these things my hand has made,
and so all these things are mine,
says the Lord.
But this is the man to whom I will look,
he that is humble and contrite in spirit,
and trembles at my word.
3 "He who slaughters an ox is like him who
kills a man;
he who sacrifices a lamb, like him who
breaks a dog's neck;
he who presents a cereal offering, like him
who offers swine's blood;

he who makes a memorial offering of
frankincense, like him who blesses an
idol.
These have chosen their own ways,
and their soul delights in their abominations;
4   I also will choose affliction for them,
and bring their fears upon them;
because, when I called, no one answered,
when I spoke they did not listen;
but they did what was evil in my eyes,
and chose that in which I did not delight."

These verses are usually dated between
538 and 520 B.C. They seem to express
God's opposition to the rebuilding of the
Temple (vv. 1–2), and his disapproval of
the manner in which sacrificial worship is
being conducted by his people (vv. 3–4).
One should not interpret these words as
addressed to Jews who are contemplating
building a temple to Yahweh in Babylon,
nor to schismatic Samaritans who are
threatening to erect their own temple on
Mount Gerizim, but to the returning exiles
who feel that it is necessary to rebuild
Jerusalem's temple in order to provide a
dwelling place for Yahweh. It is not the
temple as such that is condemned, but an
inadequate view of Yahweh, combined
with a corrupt and pagan syncretism.

The question posed by v. 1 is whether
any man-made temple is adequate to house
him whose throne is heaven and whose
footstool is the earth (cf. 1 Kings 8:27;
Matt. 5:34–35; Acts 7:48–50). Where does
the Most High dwell? Not in houses made
with hands, but in the hearts of those who
are humble and contrite in spirit and who
tremble at his word (v. 2; cf. 57:15). The
prophet thus anticipates the matchless definition of true religion given later by Jesus:
"God is spirit, and those who worship him
must worship in spirit and truth" (John
4:24).

The correct interpretation of v. 3 depends upon the relationship between the
freestanding participles in the first four
lines. Since there are no connectives between the participles, a literal rendering
would read: "He who slaughters an ox, he
who kills a man; he who sacrifices a lamb,

he who breaks a dog's neck; he who offers
a cereal offering, [he who offers] swine's
blood; he who burns incense as a memorial
offering, he who worships an idol . . ."

The RSV sees the relationship between
the pairs of participles as one of comparison: "He who slaughters an ox *is like* him
who kills a man; he who sacrifices a lamb,
like him who breaks a dog's neck") etc.
According to this interpretation, the verse
constitutes one of the most violent rejec-
tions of the Temple cult to be found in the
Old Testament. It places the sacrifice of an
ox on a par with the murder of a man, and
the offering of a lamb with the breaking of
a dog's neck.

An alternate interpretation has been proposed by Westermann, who prefers to render the verse: "He who slaughters an ox *is
also* he who kills a man"; etc. A similar
reading appears in the NEB: "But to sacrifice an ox or to kill a man, slaughter a
sheep or break a dog's neck, offer grain or
offer pigs' blood, burn incense as a token
and worship an idol—all these are the
chosen practices of men who revel in their
own loathsome rites." According to this
interpretation and the translators of the
NEB, therefore, the verse is a polemic
against a crass form of postexilic syncretism,
which combines the traditional Old Testament sacrifices with loathsome practices
borrowed from pagan cults. This interpretation has much to commend it.

Because these have *chosen their own
ways* in preference to God's ways (cf.
53:6; 55:9; 65:2,12), he will also *choose*
affliction for them (v. 4). Smart has aptly
observed that *"their* choice is followed by
God's choice. They are free to choose their
own road, but it is God who determines
the outcome of their choice" (p. 288). The
divine threat comes to a climax in the
statement: "and I will bring their fears
upon them." Nothing is more dreadful than
for a person to find that his fears have
materialized. A comparison of the latter
half of v. 4 with 65:24 points up the contrast between faithless men and the faithful God.

(4) The Voice of Judgment (66:5-6)

5 Hear the word of the LORD,
    you who tremble at his word:
"Your brethren who hate you
    and cast you out for my name's sake
have said, 'Let the LORD be glorified,
    that we may see your joy';
    but it is they who shall be put to shame.
6 "Hark, an uproar from the city!
    A voice from the temple!
The voice of the LORD,
    rendering recompense to his enemies!

These verses presuppose a schism within
the Jewish community, with the faithful
believers being persecuted and cast out by
their own brethren. The faithful are characterized as those who tremble at the
Lord's word (cf. v. 2). The verb translated *cast . . . out* later came to mean
"to put out of the synagogue, to excom-
municate" (cf. John 9:34-35). It is generally assumed, therefore, that those whom
the prophet accuses of casting out the
righteous are the civil and religious authorities in the community. They suppose
that in so doing they are rendering a service to God, for they say, "Let the Lord be
glorified" (cf. John 16:2).

When the day of judgment comes the
wicked will themselves be put to shame
(cf. 41:11; 45:24; 65:13). The voice of
the avenging God is heard in v. 6, as he
arises to render recompense to his enemies.
Once again it is emphasized that those
being judged are Israelites, for the sound
of the Lord's voice comes from the Temple
itself (cf. 1 Peter 4:17).

(5) The Rebirth of Zion (66:7-14)

7 "Before she was in labor
    she gave birth;
before her pain came upon her
    she was delivered of a son.
8 Who has heard such a thing?
    Who has seen such things?
Shall a land be born in one day?
    Shall a nation be brought forth in one
        moment?
For as soon as Zion was in labor
    she brought forth her sons.
9 Shall I bring to the birth and not cause to
        bring forth?
    says the LORD;
shall I, who cause to bring forth, shut the

womb?
    says your God.
10 "Rejoice with Jerusalem, and be glad for her,
    all you who love her;
rejoice with her in joy,
    all you who mourn over her;
11 that you may suck and be satisfied
    with her consoling breasts;
that you may drink deeply with delight
    from the abundance of her glory."
12 For thus says the LORD:
"Behold, I will extend prosperity to her like
    a river,
    and the wealth of the nations like an
        overflowing stream;
and you shall suck, you shall be carried up-
    on her hip,
    and dandled upon her knees.
13 As one whom his mother comforts,
    so I will comfort you;
    you shall be comforted in Jerusalem.
14 You shall see, and your heart shall rejoice;
    your bones shall flourish like the grass;
    and it shall be known that the hand of the
        LORD is with his servants,
    and his indignation is against his ene-
        mies.

God's coming in judgment will bring
destruction to his enemies but vindication
to his servants (cf. v. 14b). Throughout
this section Zion is spoken of as the mother
of the faithful remnant that survives the
judgment. Suddenly, without even experiencing labor pains, she gives birth to a
new citizenry: a nation is born in a day
(vv. 7-8; cf. 49:19-21; 54:1-3). In response to those who express skepticism
that such an event will ever take place, the
Lord asks if he would allow a nation to
come to the moment of its birth and then
shut the womb upon it (v. 9). The rhetorical questions in this verse demand a
negative answer; what the Lord has begun,
he will bring to completion (cf. Phil. 1:6).

Those who love Jerusalem and who
mourn over her present despicable condition are enjoined to rejoice with her in
anticipation of her coming redemption (v.
10). In v. 11 the prophet again takes up
the metaphor of motherhood (cf. vv. 7-8)
as he promises the faithful that they will
be suckled at the breast of Jerusalem.
Jones has noted that in the light of recently
discovered evidence from Ugaritic litera-

ture the phrase "the abundance of her glory" should be altered to read "her bountiful breast." Those who nurse at Mother Jerusalem's ample bosom, therefore, will receive nourishment that satisfies, consoles, and brings delight.

Zion's prosperity (*shalom*, peace) will be like a river (v. 12*a*; cf. 48:18), and the wealth of the nations will flow to her like a stream at flood tide (cf. 60:5,11; 61:6). Her children will receive motherly care from her (v. 12*b*), and also from the Lord himself (v. 13). Kessler notes that this is "the first time in the Old Testament that the witness borne to Yahweh breaks through the reserve which elsewhere it observes so strictly and associates feminine predications with him." [126] It is fitting that the theme of comfort, which figures so prominently in chapters 40–66 (cf. 40:1; 49:13; 51:3,12,19; 52:9; 57:18; 61:2), should be brought to a climax in this manner.

(6) The Judgment of the Nations (66: 15–16)

15 "For behold, the LORD will come in fire,
 and his chariots like the stormwind,
to render his anger in fury,
 and his rebuke with flames of fire.
16 For by fire will the LORD execute judgment,
 and by his sword, upon all flesh;
 and those slain by the LORD shall be many.

These verses describe the Lord's coming to execute judgment upon all flesh (cf. vv. 23–24; 40:5–6; 49:26). His coming is accompanied by stormwind and flames of fire (cf. Ex. 19:18; 2 Kings 2:11; Psalms 18:7–15). The Septuagint preserves a slightly different reading in v. 16*a*: "For by the fire of the Lord shall all the earth be judged, and all flesh by his sword."

(7) Condemnation of Pagan Worship (66:17)

17 "Those who sanctify and purify themselves to go into the gardens, following one in the midst, eating swine's flesh and the abomination and mice, shall come to an end together, says the LORD.

126 Quoted by Claus Westermann, *op. cit.*, p. 420.

Those condemned here are Israelites who are participating in illegitimate cult practices (cf. v. 3; 3; 57:5–10; 65:3–5). Sacrificing in gardens is condemned in 65:3 (cf. 1:29). *Following one* [Heb. feminine] *in the midst* perhaps refers to marching in a procession behind a pagan goddess or priestess. The eating of swine's flesh or mice is strictly forbidden in the Levitical law (cf. Lev. 11:7,29). Those who practice these abominations shall all come to an end together.

(8) The Gathering of the Nations on Mount Zion (66:18–23)

18 "For I know their works and their thoughts, and I am coming to gather all nations and tongues; and they shall come and shall see my glory, 19 and I will set a sign among them. And from them I will send survivors to the nations, to Tarshish, Put, and Lud, who draw the bow, to Tubal and Javan, to the coastlands afar off, that have not heard my fame or seen my glory; and they shall declare my glory among the nations. 20 And they shall bring all your brethren from all the nations as an offering to the LORD, upon horses, and in chariots, and in litters, and upon mules, and upon dromedaries, to my holy mountain Jerusalem, says the LORD, just as the Israelites bring their cereal offering in a clean vessel to the house of the LORD. 21 And some of them also I will take for priests and for Levites, says the LORD.

22 "For as the new heavens and the new earth
 which I will make
 shall remain before me, says the LORD;
 so shall your descendants and your name remain.
23 From new moon to new moon,
 and from sabbath to sabbath,
all flesh shall come to worship before me,
says the LORD.

The textual obscurities found in these verses make their interpretation difficult. The passage opens with the Lord's announcement that he is ready to gather all nations and tongues in order that they may come and see his glory. Verse 18, therefore, brings to a climax the theme of *glory*, which runs like a golden thread throughout the book of Isaiah (cf. 6:3; 24:15,23; 35:2; 40:5; 58:8; 59:19; 60:1).

Those who see his glory will soon become evangelists, proclaiming his glory among the nations (v. 19). Some scholars have detected a dependence upon Ezekiel in the listing of the place-names in v. 19 (cf. Ezek. 27:10,13; 30:5). *Tarshish* is to be identified as a Phoenician colony in Spain, *Put* as a later name for the part of Lybia, *Lud* as another land in North Africa, *Tubal* as a land southeast of the Black Sea, and *Javan* as the home of the Ionians on the west coast of Asia Minor.

When the nations have heard God's fame and have seen his glory, they will gather together the Jews living in their midst and bring them back to Jerusalem as an offering to the Lord (cf. 11:11–12; 43:5–6; 49:6; 56:8). Every available means of transportation will be used to convey them—horses, chariots, litters, mules, and dromedaries. From those who return the Lord will take some to serve as priests and Levites (v. 21). It is not clear whether those admitted to the priesthood are Gentiles or non-Levitical Jews, although the latter seems more probable.

In v. 22 Zion is promised that her descendants and her name (cf. 62:2; 65:15) will be as enduring as the new heavens and the new earth (cf. 65:17). The Lord himself will abide in her, and month by month and sabbath by sabbath all flesh will come to worship him (v. 23; cf. Zech. 14:16).

(9) The Everlasting Punishment of the Rebels (66:24)

24 "And they shall go forth and look on the dead bodies of the men that have rebelled against me; for their worm shall not die, their fire shall not be quenched, and they shall be an abhorrence to all flesh."

As in Zechariah 14:17–19, severe punishment falls upon those who will not worship and serve the Lord. Verse 24 presents a terrifying scene of the *dead bodies* of the rebels lying just outside the city of Jerusalem, perhaps in the valley of Hinnom. This valley had come to be regarded as an accursed spot because of its associations with the worship of Molech (cf. 57:9; Jer. 7:31–33). It eventually became the refuse dump of Jerusalem, where worms abounded, and where fires burned incessantly to consume the city's rubbish and filth. The traditions associated with the valley profoundly influenced the later development of the concept of hell, a place "where the worm does not die, and the fire is not quenched" (cf. Mark 9:43–49; Rev. 11:9–10; 20:10,14–15). Even the term Gehenna itself is but a transliteration of the Hebrew words for "valley of Hinnom."

Scholars have called attention to the proximity of the resting place of the damned to the city of Jerusalem. Their dead bodies are left nearby so that those who come to Zion to worship may go out and look upon them and be reminded of the terrible consequences of rebellion against God.

In order to provide a happy ending to the book of Isaiah, ancient Jewish rabbis gave instructions that when this chapter was read in the synagogues v. 23 should be repeated after v. 24. Modern readers who are offended that the book should end on such a somber note would do well to ponder the concluding statement in Thexton's study of Isaiah: "And while we may regret that the vision of the New Jerusalem ends with the terrible words of verse 24, they are not out of place if they remind us that from the gate of Heaven there is a road to Hell, and that before every man there lies the choice—the power to make which is the hallmark of his humanity—between the way of life and the way of death." [127]

127 S. Clive Thexton, *Isaiah 40–66* (London: The Epworth Press, 1959), pp. 154—155.